MARRIAGE

AND

FAMILY

TRADITIONS
AND
TRANSITIONS

MARRIAGE
AND
FAMILY
TRADITIONS
AND
TRANSITIONS

JEFFREY S. TURNER
Mitchell College

DONALD B. HELMS
Mitchell College

HARCOURT BRACE JOVANOVICH, PUBLISHERS

San Diego   New York   Chicago   Austin   Washington, D.C.
London   Sydney   Tokyo   Toronto

Preface

■   Nothing more fully characterizes contemporary marriage and family life than the transitions that must be faced in moving from one way of life to another: courtship to marriage to parenting, even the adjustments that accompany divorce and the death of one's spouse. At each of these transitions, couples confront unique developmental challenges. We find this aspect of family life so compelling that we have organized *Marriage and Family* around the many themes that run through such transitions, progressing, after a brief look at the nature of research activity today and family life in past cultures, to a chronological study of the marriage process—from relationship-building to widowhood.

■   Our approach to the subject is twofold, both empirical and pragmatic. The book offers a comprehensive overview of the field, discussing both the classic studies and contemporary areas of concern. Boxed "Research Highlights" throughout the book detail some of the most important work being conducted by contemporary sociologists. At the same time, we strive to make the "facts" of the book interesting and relevant to the contemporary student by revealing how other societies deal with familiar family issues ("Cross-Cultural Focus") and by offering ways for students to apply the hard data of the text to their own lives ("Applications").

■   The current makeup of the typical college student body is as diverse and fluctuating as the contemporary family. As divorce rates have risen, as dual-career households have become the norm rather than the exception, and as single-parenthood has become a way of life for many, the population of our schools has changed to include individuals of all ages and from all walks of life. *Marriage and Family* speaks to the needs of all these students, surveying and responding to the transitions they have faced, or will face, as daughters and sons, wives and husbands, mothers and fathers, and even grandparents. We approach this task both scientifically and humanely; there are data to be conveyed and understanding to be sought.

■   We live in an age of near-overwhelming change, an age in which we must embrace our past in order to live through our present and prepare for the future. For, contrary to that most popular of adages, while ignorance may well be bliss, knowledge is survival—knowledge of oneself and of others. Toward this end, *Marriage and Family* seeks to encompass our current knowledge about that most central of human groups—the family—and stands as witness to the current alterations to its form.

■ The book is divided into six parts, each covering a different period in family life. At the beginning of each part and chapter is an outline of its major contents, followed by a series of preview questions we call "Contemplations," designed to prod students' thinking and arouse their curiosity. We end each chapter with a list of key terms (boldfaced within the text) and an annotated list of ten readings recommended for the serious student. A comprehensive glossary and reference section appear at the back of the book.

ACKNOWLEDGMENTS

Although authors bear the primary responsibility for the works they create, many other individuals play a part in a book's development, preparation, and eventual publication. We would like to thank those who reviewed the manuscript for *Marriage and Family* during its early stages:

Sandy Bucknell, Modesto Junior College

Lawrence A. Clarke, Shoreline Community College

Gail Cromack, Onondaga Community College

John Dykstra, Jersey City State College

Willie J. Edwards, Richland College

Robin Franck, University of California, San Diego

Glenn Hoffman, Butte College

Richard Jolliff, El Camino College

Jack Peterson, Mesa Community College

James D. Wemhaner, Tulsa Junior College (Metro)

Martha Wengert, Antelope Valley College

We would also like to thank those persons at Harcourt Brace Jovanovich who contributed their expertise to this project, especially Marcus Boggs, our editor, who saw the early promise of this book and oversaw its production from conception to publication. We appreciate the talents of Johanna Schmid, acquisitions editor; Kenneth Cherry, manuscript editor; Karen Denhams, production editor; Lynne Bush, production manager; Rebecca Lytle, art editor; and Merilyn Britt, designer.

A special note of thanks goes to Ruth Roohr and Molly Helms, who typed and proofread the manuscript. They always met their deadlines and constantly offered constructive criticism. Without them and their expertise in word processing, this project would have been much less enjoyable.

Finally, to our wives and families goes our heartfelt gratitude. Writing always requires a measure of personal and family sacrifice, but the patient understanding of our loved ones allowed us to devote long hours toward the completion of this project. Their empathy, support, and love were sources of inspiration from beginning to end.

Jeffrey S. Turner
Donald B. Helms

Contents

MARRIAGE

AND

FAMILY

TRADITIONS
AND
TRANSITIONS

Part One

INTRODUCTION TO MARRIAGE AND FAMILY TRANSITIONS

The Social Context of Marriage and Family

CONTENTS

CONTEMPLATIONS

■ The study of marriage and family is a relatively recent pursuit so it might, at first, appear that solid research data would be limited. However, our knowledge is steadily increasing as sociologists and others in related disciplines supply a steady stream of research findings. How do sociologists set about exploring topics in marriage and family, and designing the research they seek to undertake? Do they adhere to the same principles and methodologies prescribed for other sciences? And what problems, if any, do they encounter in their quest for scientific data? This opening chapter will supply some answers to these and related questions.

■ They pushed west from Illinois in 1846 and settled in the Great Salt Lake Valley in 1847. They called themselves Mormons and were led by Brigham Young, dubbed the "Lion of the Lord," bringing to Utah unique religious convictions as well as polygyny—a type of plural marriage allowing husbands to have more than one wife. Why was polygyny practiced by the Mormons? Do other people practice it? What was the public reaction toward it? And what were the circumstances behind its prohibition? Read on and you'll discover the answers.

■ Think about how often we're exposed to surveys. We hear reference to the Gallup and Harris polls on the evening news and read about them in our daily newspapers. Or, more directly, we're stopped in the aisle of a supermarket or on a busy street corner and asked our opinion on a variety of topics, from presidential candidates and product brands to television programming. In this opening chapter, we'll discover why the survey is one of the more widely used data collection techniques in marriage and family research. We'll also discuss what a survey does and look at the varieties that exist—in the process offering some hints to help you better design your own. By the time we're done, the question, "What's your opinion?" will take on a new meaning and relevancy.

Contemporary marriage and family life is one of sociology's most active areas of investigation. It is an exciting and fundamental field because, as you'll discover, marriage supplies the foundation for family life, and families are the basic building blocks of every society in the world. In fact, the family is the oldest human institution and in many respects, the most important. Exploring this importance, including the purposes and functions of marriage and family, is the focal point of this chapter. More specifically, we will introduce and clarify the important concepts and terminology of the field, thus establishing a vocabulary for understanding later chapters.

DIMENSIONS OF MARRIAGE AND FAMILY

Definitions and Functions

Marriage is an institutional act that unites a man and a woman. Marriage is intended to be a stable, enduring relationship and involves a legal agreement between husband and wife. This legal agreement exists in the form of a marriage contract, which stipulates reciprocal rights and obligations between spouses. These rights and obligations are expected to continue unless the marriage is dissolved by further legal action.

The social institution of marriage is the basis for the social institution of the family. A **family** is defined as a social arrangement consisting of two or more persons related by blood, marriage, or adoption. Typically, the family consists of parents and children. A family shares a common residence and represents a social system that operates with a set of norms and roles, although these vary from culture to culture.

What is universal in virtually all societies though are the functions the family performs. At least six such functions have been identified, all of which are essential in bringing order to society:

1. Regulates sexual behavior and reproduction.
2. Meets the biological needs of a society's members (such as food, shelter, and protection).

3. Provides status placement, bestowing status or rank on people by virtue of their birth and determining their relationship to one another.
4. Provides emotional maintenance, including a sense of security and being wanted.
5. Offers socialization by training children in appropriate skills and actions, as well as transmitting norms, values, and beliefs.
6. Is a form of social control, demanding certain behaviors and restricting others, which lessens the need for overt control (Christensen and Johnsen, 1985).

EXPLORING THE VARIETIES OF MARRIAGE AND FAMILY LIFE

Because marriage and family are shaped by culture, the form of each differs between societies. As James Henslin (1985a) observes, these variations provide unique contrasts. For example, in society A, a man or woman may have only one spouse at at time, while in society B they may have multiple partners. In society A, premarital sex is forbidden, tolerated in B, and even encouraged in C, D, and E. Or, consider that, in some societies, the male handles the disciplining of the children, the female in others, and, in still others, both husband and wife shoulder this responsibility. With such variations in mind, let's take a closer look at the marital customs and practices that exist as well as the many forms that family life can take in different societies.

Marital Customs and Practices

Monogamy vs. Polygamy **Monogamy** is the marriage of one man to one woman. This is the characteristic form of marriage in the United States, and the only type that is legal. However, because of escalating divorce rates, some observers feel that **serial monogamy** is the more accurate title for marriage in this country. Serial monogamy is a succession of partners through the process of marriage, divorce, remarriage, and so on.

One of the family's major functions is to provide trust and security to its members.

It might seem to you that all societies would regard monogamy as the preferable marital arrangement, but this is not the case. Rather, a significant number of societies practice what is called **polygamy**, or plural marriage. The word polygamy comes from two Greek words meaning "many marriages." There are two basic forms of polygamy: polygyny and polyandry.

Polygyny is the marriage of one man to two or more women. Of the two forms of polygamy, polygyny is the more prevalent. Many societies have practiced polygyny at one time or another and many still do, particularly in regions of Asia and Africa. However, while a given society may permit polygyny, a monogamous relationship is usually the preferred arrangement. Often, polygyny is a sign that a man is successful, rich, and even powerful. Some Kings and noblemen throughout history provide testimony to this, in some cases, in extreme ways. For example, the Bible discloses that King Solomon had as many as 700 wives, while Lukengu, a legendary chief of the Bakuba tribe in Zaire, kept 800! Imagine the complexities arising from such arrangements!

POLYGYNY AMONG THE MORMONS

The Mormons are members of the Church of Jesus Christ of Latter-day Saints, which was established during the early 1800's by Joseph Smith. The Mormons claim that the Church as established by Christ did not survive in its original form and was restored in modern times by divine means. Consequently, the Mormons

A polygamous Mormon family in the Great Salt Lake Valley in the mid-1860s. The husband, his wives, and his children all lived in this one-room cabin.

▶

maintain that their church is the true church of Jesus Christ. Although their first church was founded in New York, many of the Mormons travelled west and settled in Salt Lake City, Utah.

Between 1844 and 1890, polygyny was considered the marriage ideal among the Mormons. While condemned by most of the nation, Mormons defended the practice primarily on the grounds that God had chosen to introduce it in ancient Israel, and He had made His intentions known again to spokesmen on Earth. Thus, polygyny was most often viewed in religious terms, a restoration of the Old Testament practice. However, the Mormons also cited other reasons for practicing polygyny: it was a way of introducing marriage and parenthood to women who might otherwise remain single, and it offered women an alternative to a variety of social evils and temptations.

But even though polygyny was considered the ideal, it was not widely practiced. In fact, only about 5 percent of married Mormon men had more than one wife, and a significant majority of this figure had only two wives. The financial hardship of supporting additional wives and the fact that many of these women would not be legally recognized as wives in the United States, were the primary reasons for the limited enthusiasm among the congregation. There were, however, exceptions to

---

While the Mormon Church no longer advocates polygamy and it is prohibited in the United States, examples can still be found. For instance, policeman Royston Potter was fired from his Murray, Utah, job in 1985 when city officials learned that he was a polygamist.

▶

these low figures. Brigham Young, who led the Mormon's westward trek to Utah, was said to have had as many as 70 wives. He accepted his first plural wife in 1842 at the age of 41 and the last in the 1870's, shortly before his death.

In the wake of growing national disdain and condemnation toward this practice, the Mormon church prohibited polygyny in 1890. In 1895, the Utah state constitution promised that the practice would not be revived in the future. However, among some contemporary fundamentalist Mormons, polygyny still remains the ideal marital arrangement and is practiced despite its illegality. ■

Polyandry is the marriage of one woman to two or more men. Polyandry has been an extremely rare occurence throughout history. It is practiced, though, among some Buddhist Tibetans, some groups in Nigeria, and the Toda in Southern India. In the Himalayas, some polyandrous households involve a number of brothers who share a wife, thus preventing the dissolution of family wealth or property.

Patterns of Residency Where a couple chooses to reside may also be influenced by social norms. **Patrilocal** living arrangements mean that the couple lives with or near the husband's relatives. **Matrilocal** residency, on the other hand, places the couple with or near the wife's relatives. While these two patterns of residency can apply to some couples in the United States, another is more apparent: **neolocal** residency. Neolocal residency occurs when the couple established its own separate living arrangement. The geographical location is not based on ties originating from either the husband's or the wife's family.

Patterns of Descent An important feature of marriage and family life is **kinship**, how family members are related to one another. Patterns of descent, important for the tracing of one's lineage as well as for inheritance and other purposes, can be traced in three separate ways. **Patrilineal** descent traces lineage on the husband's side of the family. **Matrilineal** descent places the importance on the wife's side. As we'll see in the next chapter, the concepts of patrilineal and matrilineal descent have created some unique situations for families

throughout history. In the United States today, though, **bilateral descent** is the more prevalent pattern. Bilateral descent places equal importance on the families of both the husband and wife. Power, property, and the like are transferred from both the husband's and the wife's side of the family to their offspring.

Patterns of Authority Variation also exists in who dominates the household and is responsible for making decisions. **Patriarchal** households place the husband in this dominating position, while in **matriarchal** homes, the wife has the greater authority. To date, there have been no truly matriarchal societies. In contemporary times, though, an egalitarian (or equalitarian) pattern of authority is emerging in the United States and other industrialized nations. The **egalitarian** system emphasizes the sharing of marital power between husband and wife. Spouses are regarded as equals and decisions are reached mutually.

Types of Family Composition

There are several important types of family composition that we can identify. The **nuclear family** is the most preferred family form in the United States and consists of the mother, father, and children. Sometimes called the *conjugal family,* the nuclear family is two-generational; that is, it includes parents and offspring. Most individuals can expect to live in two nuclear families during their lives — the one into which they are born, called the **family of orientation**, and the one that is established

APPLICATIONS

STUDYING FAMILY DESCENT: HOW TO TRACE YOUR LINEAGE

The study of family descent develops a deep appreciation for those who have gone before us. Whether they are princes or paupers, prisoners or prima donnas, their life stories are treasures to those who patiently and persistently delve into their family history.

Researching your family tree is no easy chore, though. Records may be difficult to locate, and information is often unreliable. Over the years, names were changed on census and other forms to protect the innocent and the guilty, and records are filled with errors made by incompetent or indifferent clerks. In addition, informants who provided the "facts" were not above falsifying their ages, relationships, and places of origin. Compounding the problem are equally suspect marriage and death records and ever-changing spellings of family names.

In spite of such obstacles, a successful search for your ancestors can take place. The following guidelines will help you in your efforts:

- **Begin with Yourself**   Fill out a family chart (see end of box) to the best of your memory. Consult Bibles, letters and diaries. Don't overlook a fading photograph or other memorabilia that might yield information.
- **Interview Living Relatives**   If any are inveterate "savers" check with them first. They may already have done much of your work.
- **Check Local Records**   A first stop is the county repository of vital statistics — birth and marriage certificates, land and cemetary records. Most town libraries will also have a section devoted to genealogy and local history.
- **Tap Distant Resources**   Comprehensive genealogical collections include the New England Historic Genealogical Society (101 Newbury Street, Boston, MA 02110); the National Genealogical Society (4527 17th Street North, Arlington, VA 22207); the National Archives and Records Administration (Washington, DC 20540); the libraries of Los Angeles, New York City, Chicago (the Newberry Library) and Fort Wayne, Indiana; and the library operated by the Church of Jesus Christ of Latter-day Saints (Mormons) in Salt Lake City (LDS Genealogical Library, 35 North West Temple Street, Salt Lake City, UT 84150).
- **Read Books**   For do-it-yourselfers there is Ethel Williams' *Know Your Ancestors* (Rutland, VT: Charles E. Tuttle Co., 1976), or *Genealogy for Beginners* by Arthur Willis (London: Phillimore and Company, 1965). Another acclaimed source is *Family History* by Vincent Jones (Salt Lake City, UT: Publishers Press, 1972).
- **Hire a Professional Genealogist**   Lists of accredited researchers can be obtained through the LDS Genealogical Library or the Board of Certification of Genealogists (P.O. Box 19165, Washington, DC 20036). You should keep in mind, however, that this can be an expensive venture.

Adapted from Van Atta, 1986.   ▶

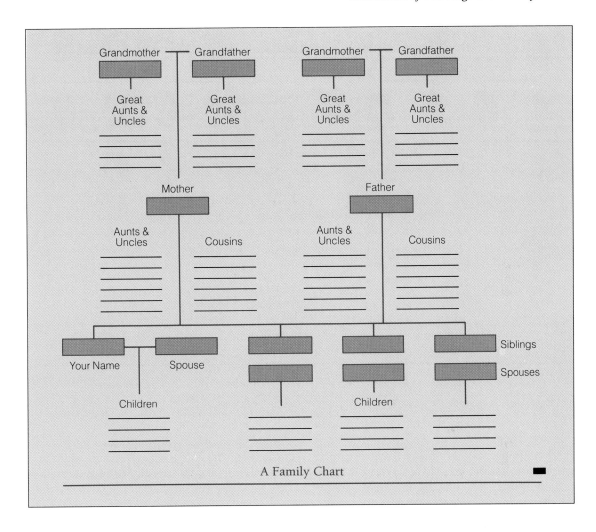

A Family Chart

through marriage and parenthood, known as the **family of procreation**.

The **extended family** consists of parents and offspring as well as other relatives such as grandparents, aunts, and uncles. Also called the *family of kinship,* the extended family is thus multi-generational. This is not a common living arrangement in the contemporary United States.

The **blended family** results when a divorced parent with custody of children remarries. Also called the *compound* or *reconstituted family,* this household consists of parent, children, and stepparent. However, more complex arrangements are possible. For example, both parents may have children from previous marriages, or choose to conceive their own offspring. The blended family, as well as **single-parent households,** in which one parent is absent, is rapidly growing today because of the increasing incidence of divorce. Figure 1-1 on page 12 displays the various family types.

TRANSITIONS OF MARRIAGE AND FAMILY

Monica McGoldrick and Elizabeth Carter (1982) propose that marriage and family life represents a series of stages, transitions that present

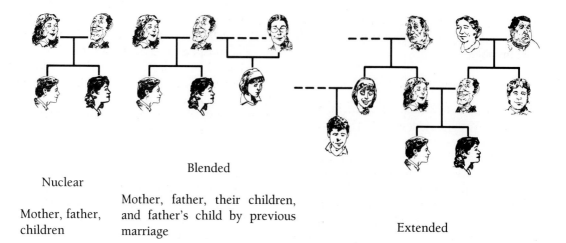

Nuclear

Mother, father, children

Blended

Mother, father, their children, and father's child by previous marriage

Extended

Mother, father, children, mother's widowed sister and child, mother's widowed father, father's unmarried brother and parents

Source: Johnson, A. *Human Arrangements*. San Diego, CA: Harcourt, 1986

FIGURE 1-1   Some Types of Families

couples with a number of developmental tasks. These tasks are unique for each transition and must be adequately dealt with before the next stage can be entered. While we will explore in detail the many transitions that characterize the marriage and family life cycle, the following is a brief description of McGoldrick and Carter's stages.

The Unattached Young Adult

Key tasks during young adulthood are accepting the separation from one's parents and developing intimate peer relationships. A cornerstone of the family life cycle, this stage also requires the person to formulate life goals and heighten self-awareness before joining with another to create a new family subsystem. This stage also provides the opportunity to separate emotionally what one will take from the family of origin and what will be changed. Problems arise at this time when parents continue to encourage the dependence of their young adult children. Or, young adults may choose to sacrifice

the independence necessary at this time and remain emotionally bound to the home. What is needed here is a mutually respectful form of relating and understanding between young adults and their parents. Parents need to be reconnected in new ways, and young adults need to redefine their status in relation to their parents for this stage to be successfully resolved.

The Newly Married Couple

Marriage is a complex and difficult transition. Among other tasks, a couple must renegotiate an assortment of personal issues that they had previously defined for themselves or that were decided by their parents — from where and how to live, to patterns of eating and sleeping. Relationships also need to be renegotiated, particularly those involving parents, siblings, friends, and other relatives. Also, marriage involves a shifting of family boundaries to some degree for members of both sides. A number of factors appear to make the adjustment to this life cycle transition more difficult, such as divergent cultural backgrounds or financial instability.

The Family with Young Children

During this stage, adults move up a generation and become caregivers to the young. Adjustments are numerous and conflict may result when parents struggle with each other about assuming new responsibilities or executing the myriad of new chores. Some parents may also have difficulty setting limits for their children or exerting necessary authority. Some find that they have to develop a new patience so that their children can express themselves as they develop.

The Family with Adolescents

This stage heralds a new era because it means new roles for the children and the parents in relation to each other. A major task here is establishing qualitatively different boundaries than when the children were younger. Boundaries need to be permeable and parents must realize that they can no longer control every aspect of their offspring's lives. Flexible boundaries that allow teenagers to

---

Parenthood presents couples with an assortment of challenges and adjustments.

be dependent when they cannot handle things, as well as increasing degrees of independency when the situation warrants it, are needed. This is also the time when adolescents start to establish their own, independent relationships with the extended family. This development may require adjustments between parents and grandparents to allow and foster new patterns of interaction.

Launching of Grown Children

This is the longest phase of the family life cycle and for many, the most problematic. Launching one's children from the nest and finding substitute activities for oneself can lead to feelings of emptiness and depression, particularly for women who have focused their entire lives and energies on their offspring. However, this stage can also be a liberating time, one characterized by a brighter financial picture and the freedom to engage in new and unexplored activities. The launching of grown children, though, is only one of numerous exits and entries of family members. In time, there will be the entry of the grown children's spouses and children, as well as the prospect of illness or death among one's aging parents. At the very least, aging parents will require numerous caretaking responsibilities. Beyond this, parents must deal with the change in their own status as they make room for the next generation and acquire the role of grandparents.

The Family in Later Life

Contrary to societal myths, the majority of the elderly are not rejected by their families, nor are they feeble and senile. This period can be a socially satisfying and healthy stage of the family life cycle, although it is not without its share of developmental tasks. Paramount among these is successfully adjusting to retirement. Retirement not only creates a vacuum for the retiree, but it may also place strain on a marriage that until now may have been balanced in different spheres. In addition, financial insecurity or dependency creates problems, particularly for family members who value

TABLE 1-1

The Stages of the Family Life Cycle

Family Life Cycle Stage	Emotional Process of Transition: Key Principles	Changes in Family Status Required to Proceed Developmentally
1. Between families: The unattached young adult	Accepting parent-offspring separation	a. Differentiation of self in relation to family of origin b. Development of intimate peer relationships c. Establishment of self in work
2. The joining of families through marriage: The newly married couple	Commitment to new system	a. Formation of marital system b. Realignment of relationships with extended families and friends to include spouse
3. The family with young children	Accepting new generation of members into the system	a. Adjusting marital system to make space for child(ren) b. Taking on parenting roles c. Realignment of relationships with extended family to include parenting and grandparenting roles
4. The family with adolescents	Increasing flexibility of family boundaries to include children's independence	a. Shifting of parent-child relationships to permit adolescents to move in and out of system b. Refocus on midlife marital and career issues c. Beginning shift toward concerns for older generation
5. Launching children and moving on	Accepting a multitude of exits from and entries into the family system	a. Renegotiation of marital system as a dyad b. Development of adult to adult relationships between grown children and their parents c. Realignment of relationships to include in-laws and grandchildren d. Dealing with disabilities and death of parents (grandparents)
6. The family in later life	Accepting the shifting of generational roles	a. Maintaining own and/or couple functioning and interests in face of physiological decline; exploration of new familial and social role options b. Support for a more central role for middle generation c. Making room in the system for the wisdom and experience of the elderly; supporting the older generation without overfunctioning for them d. Dealing with loss of spouse, siblings, and other peers, and preparation for own death. Life review and integration

Source: McGoldrick, M. and Carter, E. A., 1982. The stages of the family life cycle. In F. Walsh (Ed.), *Normal family processes.* Reprinted by permission of the Guilford Press, New York, NY.

autonomy. The death of friends and relatives and the eventual loss of one's spouse also requires considerable adjustment. Reorganizing one's entire life after many years as a couple and having fewer relationships to help replace that loss is a formidable task. Table 1-1 displays all of the stages of the marriage and family life cycle.

ALTERNATIVE APPROACHES TO THE STUDY OF MARRIAGE AND FAMILY

The examination of marriage and family from a developmental or life cycle perspective is not the only way to approach this discipline. Researchers employ several other methods to interpret data and analyze events. Theoretical frameworks emerge from all of these approaches, explanations that help us organize our knowledge systematically and see how concepts are related to one another. Let's briefly examine a few representative approaches.

The **social-exchange approach** proposes that interpersonal relationships are formed largely for the purpose of meeting each partner's needs, emphasizing that individuals desire the maximum positive outcomes or rewards in relationships along with the least amount of costs or trade-offs. The relationship thus resembles a bargaining situation; that is, each partner weighs the rewards gained (companionship, intimacy, enjoyment) against the costs incurred (time, money, unpleasant interactions). At the heart of this theory is the notion that individuals will seek rewarding relationships and avoid those that are too costly.

The **symbolic interaction approach** seeks to show how families interact through symbols — including social roles, words, and actions. Proponents of this approach explore how daily interaction is influenced by the meaning attached to these symbols. To cite an illustration, when the social roles of mother and father are assigned to a couple, attitudes and expectations regarding oneself as well as one another are affected. As other examples, a wedding ring, anniversary gift, and baby shower are symbols that prompt people to interact in certain ways. Unique gestures and expressions displayed within the realm of family life are other instances of symbols that influence the way we relate. Symbolic interactionists emphasize how we come to learn the meaning of symbols, how meanings are shared among family members, and how they can undergo transformation.

The **social conflict approach** seeks to expose how disequilibrium, disharmony, and conflict are inevitable features of human interaction. Because of its inevitability, conflict is not viewed as disruptive or as an "evil" force; rather, it is an expected feature of social systems. Consequently, the emphasis in this approach is on conflict management and other ways to reduce disharmony. The conflict that often exists in husband-wife or parent-child relationships, to cite but a few areas, provides fertile grounds for the exploration and application of conflict resolution strategies.

In many respects, the **structural-functional approach** is just the opposite of the conflict approach. Here, the emphasis is on how a society can operate in harmony and equilibrium because of its interdependent parts. In other words, subsystems within society (religious, political, economic) are in a relationship with one another and work to promote total cohesion and stability. Related to the family, its sum parts (husband, wife, offspring) are vital to one another and seek to maintain an ordered and functional existence.

THE SCIENTIFIC STUDY OF MARRIAGE AND FAMILY

In surveying the literature, one finds that some ideas regarding marriage and family life were developed without the support of much empirical evidence. That a theoretical preconception sounds right or makes sense is no guarantee that it is correct. In sociology and related disciplines, reliable data are needed. This is as true for research undertaken in the laboratory as it is for general theories related to marriage and family.

In addition to these theoretical preconceptions,

cultural and societal myths regarding marriage and family have been passed down from generation to generation. For example, many of the myths that surround marriage and parenthood tend to have a ring of perfectionism about them—adults are expected to get married, raise the "perfect" family, and "live happily ever after."

Other myths stress that at a certain age a person is supposedly qualified to do something. For example, by young adulthood one is expected to get married, and by middle adulthood couples supposedly attain financial security. At age 65, society paints a bleak picture of individuals and married couples alike: "Over the hill," abondoned by their families, and physically inept.

Still other myths portray all socioeconomic, ethnic, and racial groups as having the same needs or experiencing the same family conditions. This is hardly the case. Rather, to a large extent, the circumstances of a couple's present status and background shape their way of adjusting to family needs and demands.

All of this goes to show that myths are not based in fact and are contaminated with sweeping gener-

alities and unfair stereotypes. Sociologists within this investigative area seek to combat such misconceptions by presenting a realistic image of marriage and family. It is from their efforts that clearer and more accurate data has emerged.

The Goals of Science

The scientific study of marriage and family is a relatively recent development. While this field of investigation has carved out its own unique way of gathering data, all scientific research shares some similar goals and basic principles. Brent Miller (1986) summarizes these commonalities:

- *Description* **Description** is the most common tool of science. Researchers exploring marriage and family seek to describe the averages or central tendencies of such phenomena as the age of marriage or the number of children per household. Describing marriages and families is a largely empirical process that often relies on counting, frequencies, percentages, and descriptive statistics.

UNDERSTANDING THE TOOLS OF DEMOGRAPHY

Demography is the scientific study of populations and an important example of an empirical endeavor that provides sociologists with data. Throughout this book, we will be referring to those demographic trends relevant to marriage and family life, be it the number of marriages or divorces per year, the proportion of marriages that end in divorce, or remarriage rates. To understand such data and place it into a meaningful context, some important demographic terminology needs to be clarified:

- Count   This term refers to the absolute number of a population or any demographic event occurring in a specified area in a specified time period (for example, 3,614,000 live births in the United States in 1983). The raw quantities of demographic events are the basis of all other statistical refinements and analyses.
- Rates   Here we are analyzing the frequency of demographic events in a population in a specified time period (for example, birth rate: 15.5 live births per 1,000 population in the United States in 1983). Rates tell how frequently an event is occurring—how common it is. *Crude rates* are rates computed for an entire population. *Specific rates* are rates computed for a specific subgroup—   ▶

usually the population at risk of having the event occur (for example, general fertility rate: births per 1,000 women aged 15–44 years). Thus, rates can be age-specific, sex-specific, race-specific, occupation-specific, and so on.

- Ratio   Ratio refers to the relation of one population subgroup to another subgroup in the same population. Put another way, one subgroup is divided by another (for example, sex ratio: 95 males per 100 females in the United States in 1983).

- Proportion   When we speak of proportion, we are referring to the relation of a population subgroup to the entire population. In other words, a population subgroup is divided by the entire population (for example, the proportion married: 60 percent of the total U.S. population ages 15 and over were married in 1983).

- Constant   When the term constant is used, it means the use of an unchanging, arbitrary number (for example, 100 or 1,000 or 100,000) by which rates, ratios, or proportions can be multiplied to express these measures in a more understandable fashion. For example, 0.0155 live births per person occurred in the United States in 1983. Multiplying this rate by a constant (1,000) gives the same statistic in terms of 1,000 people, a clearer way of expressing the same thing. There were 15.5 births per 1,000 population. Most rates are expressed "per 1,000 population."

Adapted from the Population Reference Bureau, 1985. ■

- *Explanation*   **Explanations** attempt to provide reasons for *why* something happens or is the way it is. Marriage and family researchers seek to explain their discipline by identifying antecedents and consequences of the behaviors of interest. As an illustration, the antecedents of mate selection can be better fathomed through an assortment of explanations, including personal attributes, background similarity, compatible goals and role expectations.

- *Prediction*   Being able to tell in advance that something is going to occur is known as **prediction**. Many feel that prediction rests on the same empirical and theoretical underpinning as explanation. That is, the same ideas and relationships must be grasped in order to explain what has occurred and why, or to predict what is likely to happen; for example, knowing the extent of *partner congruence* in role expectations, values, and background might be modestly predictive of marital compatibility and stability.

- *Control*   When natural phenomena are understood so that they can be explained and

predicted, it is sometimes possible to exert **control** over them. For our purposes, control takes such forms as *intervention, therapy, or prevention*. For instance, a therapist might be

Research areas such as interpersonal attraction, dating, and relationship-building have fallen under the scrutiny of contemporary sociologists.

able to intervene and assist family members to reduce or eliminate (control) a negative aspect of domestic life.

The Role of Facts and Theories

As marriage and family investigators collect research findings, new data must be integrated with existing data—a difficult organizational chore, but a necessary one for any science that continually seeks to refine and heighten its knowledge.

Collected data are called **facts** and represent a *statement of observation*. Facts are extremely important to any scientist. They have been called the building blocks of a science; however, just as a pile of bricks does not make a house, a pile of facts does not make a science. A pile of facts is no good whatsoever unless you can give them meaning. Therefore, the task of the researcher is to collect data by making observations and then to relate them to one another, thus establishing relationships. However, when **conclusions** are drawn from any data, special attention must be directed toward the *validity* of the findings.

Two types of validity related to the clarity of research findings have been identified. A set of observations has **internal validity** if the observations are logically interrelated and fit the theoretical structure of which they are a part. **External validity** refers to the degree to which conclusions drawn from one set of observations can be generalized to other sets of observations.

If the facts are valid, we next come to the role of theory. A **theory** is an *explanation that unifies a set of facts or hypotheses*. A theory is never "proven"; it may be supported by additional data or not supported because of conflicting data. Theories help us grasp the meaning of a multiplicity of facts and thus gain an understanding of the topic at hand. They are *attempts to explain various phenomena*.

Frequently, however, different theories explain the same phenomenon. The many theories of mate selection all try to explain how and why individuals are attracted to one another. The various childrearing theories attempt to explain the best

possible way to raise one's offspring. In this text we will not only offer the "facts" but will also encase them in the most meaningful theory and explain their relevance to everyday life. Making the connection between theory and practice, however, is no easy task. Perhaps the most difficult obstacle sociologists (or other scientists) face is the search for the vital link between a theory and the way in which it can be successfully implemented.

The Scientific Method

Any scientific investigation must begin with a plan or structure, known more technically as the **scientific method**. Broadly defined, the scientific method is *an organized series of steps designed to promote maximum objectivity and consistency in gathering and interpreting observable evidence*. It is sociology's use of the scientific method and related activity that qualifies it as a science.

A number of research steps characterize the scientific method. But the degree to which each step (or stage) is emphasized varies according to purpose, size of the study, and whether the researcher wants to *describe, illustrate, predict,* or *test*. Also, action taken in one stage has a direct influence on other stages, making it essential that one understands the entire process. The research steps can be summarized as follows:

1. A statement of the problem is given.
2. A refinement of the problem takes place so that it is restated with a research orientation.
3. A research design is developed and mapped out for use.
4. Techniques to obtain relevant data are developed and tested for use.
5. The data are collected in accordance with research rules.
6. The data are analyzed and results are interpreted.
7. The findings are typically written in a medium so that they can be shared with others (Adams and Schvaneveldt, 1985).

Source: King Features Syndicate

The survey is one of many research methodologies available to marriage and family investigators.

METHODS OF GATHERING DATA

While the scientific method offers fairly uniform guiding principles, there are many different ways of gathering data. Among marriage and family researchers, surveys and observations are popular modes of data collection. In addition, experimental research as well as longitudinal and cross-sectional designs assist sociologists in their quest for scientific information.

Surveys

A **survey** (or poll) is a technique for gathering information from people and generally takes the form of a questionnaire or an interview that is directed toward a sample. A **sample** is a group of people deemed to be representative of a larger population.

Questionnaires require that respondents mark their own answers. Because of this, questionnaires are relatively simple, fast, and inexpensive. Also, questionnaires can be administered so that respondents remain anonymous—an important advantage in encouraging complete responses, particularly when what is being studied is socially sensitive. Another plus for questionnaires is that interviewers do not need to be recruited, trained, and sent out. Thus, questionnaires greatly reduce the personnel costs that accompany the interviewing technique (Miller, 1986).

Sociologists must take great care in the wording of instructions as well as the actual items on questionnaires. Wording must be clear and concise so that respondents do not get confused or frustrated. Confused or frustrated respondents often supply inaccurate information or, in some cases, give up completely. Surveys can supply sociologists with valuable information on how people think and act, but only if this assessment instrument is properly designed and worded.

Unlike questionnaires, interviews involve a face-to-face encounter. In the typical format, a

---

APPLICATIONS

SUGGESTIONS FOR WRITING SURVEY ITEMS

While some surveys employ an open-ended format of questions in which respondents answer the item in their own words, the majority of surveys rely on multiple choice or close-ended questions. This is because the latter are more efficient in terms of usage, scoring, and coding, not to mention overall assessment reliability. However, such items need to be carefully constructed so that accurate responses are gleaned. Arlene Fink and Jacqueline Kosecoff (1985) offer the follow- ▶

ing tips for writing close-ended survey items:

■ **Use Standard English**   In order to insure accuracy for each survey item, conventional spelling and grammar must be used. Specialized words, slang, and abbreviations should be avoided, as well as lengthy survey items.

■ **Use Meaningful Questions**   To avoid confusion, strive for relevancy throughout the survey. For example, in a survey of political views, questions should be about the political process, candidates, parties, and so forth. If other questions are introduced that have no readily obvious purpose, such as those about age or sex of the respondent, an explanation must be given as to why they're a part of the survey.

■ **Make Questions Concrete**   A deliberate effort should be made to make questions reflect the respondent's personal experience. For example, asking respondents if they enjoyed a particular book is more abstract than asking if they recommended it to others or have read more books by the same author. The more a question strays from a respondent's direct experience, the greater the risk associated with forgetting.

■ **Avoid Biased Words and Phrases**   Certain views, names, and places are likely to trigger an emotional reaction, and as a result unfairly influence a person's response. Examples include such words as *communist, drug addict,* or *racist.* To capture objectivity, such emotionally charged words need to be eliminated.

■ **Check Your Own Biases**   Some survey writers may be unaware of their own position toward a topic, which represents an additional source of bias. When questions are asked that may promote strong views on either side, it is helpful to have them reviewed. Wording of items must be unbiased and acceptable to persons holding contrary opinions.

■ **Don't Get Too Personal**   Another source of bias results from questions that may insult the respondent. For example, questions such as, "How much money do you earn each year?" or, "Are you single or divorced?" are personal and may offend some respondents. And they might then refuse to give an accurate response. When personal information is absolutely essential to the survey, the provision for "categories of response" is likely to elicit the least emotional reaction.

■ **Include Just One Idea per Question**   Questions in which a respondent's truthful answer could be both yes and no should not be used. So, too, for those questions where one can agree and disagree at the same time. Also, in some instances, asking for absolutely positive or negative views may prompt a refusal to answer.   ■

trained interviewer asks questions and then records the responses. While the interview technique is more expensive than questionnaires, it is generally recognized that the interview yields more accurate data and is more flexible.

Gerald Adams and Jay Schvaneveldt (1985)

concur with this and feel that when properly executed, the interview technique has the potential to be an extremely sensitive device for the acquisition of reliable data. This is because the interview has at least seven specific and particular advantages over the questionnaire:

1. The interviewer can explain the purpose of the study, discuss the interview, establish rapport, and respond to questions at any time. All of this tends to enhance the *cooperation* rate.
2. While the typical return rate of the mailed questionnaire is a limitation, one of the main strengths of the interview is its *participation* rate.
3. A skilled interviewer can "read" individuals; that is, a respondent's moods can be assessed and information can be sought accordingly. It is likely that the same information can be gathered in a different way at a later time in the same interview, thus enabling the interviewer to determine the truthfulness of responses.
4. Not only can the interviewer listen to the responses, but the respondent can also be observed. Body language, mood, and facial expressions are often valuable in understanding the totality of the interview.
5. Face-to-face interaction can be instrumental in building the needed rapport, which in turn often leads to a higher degree of respondent motivation. When motivation is heightened, the quality of data is likely to be superior to that obtained when respondents are participating out of obligation or pressure.
6. It is generally recognized that people enjoy talking — a definite plus for this data gathering device. Skilled interviewers can guide conversation so that a more thorough understanding of the subject can be attained.
7. The interview is especially valuable for gathering information about personal, sensitive, and perceived deviant data. Once trust has been established, respondents will usually disclose such information to skilled practitioners.

Interviews are not perfect, however. While items on questionnaires are uniform and consistent, a staff of interviewers can ask the same question in different ways. Also, interviewers may not record clear and concise responses. For that matter, some interviewers may be uncertain as to which responses to record. And, as mentioned earlier, interviews are much more expensive than questionnaires.

Observation

Another technique for gathering data is through observation, such as live action or through videotapes, audio tapes, and the like. While it is true that suppositions may emerge following the observation of a solitary incident, one must also recognize the danger of generalizing from a limited number of situations. Consequently, while a study of a single subject may be of assistance toward studying that one person, it does not necessarily mean that other subjects will exhibit identical behavior, or, if they do, that it will be for the same reasons.

Naturalistic observation is the examination of behavior under **unstructured** (natural) conditions. **Structured observation** represents a slight exten-

Reprinted with special permission of King Features Syndicate, Inc.

sion of naturalistic observation, enabling the researcher to administer simple tests. **Participant observation**, on the other hand, involves the researcher as a participant in the interaction being studied. In this way, one's direct involvement with subjects provides observational data. It should be noted that these forms of observation differ markedly from **controlled experiments**, which employ situations requiring that subjects be placed in contrived and perhaps unnatural environments.

Sometimes, the results obtained from controlled experiments are of little value since they have a tendency to create unnatural behavior. However, it is felt by some that the same could hold true for observational techniques in general. This is especially true when researchers become obtrusive and thrust themselves onto others without invitation. The more obtrusive the observer, the greater the chance of subjects behaving in atypical or guarded ways (Adams and Schvaneveldt, 1985).

All of the foregoing suggests that research designs involving observation must be carefully executed. For, while all forms of observation described can be extremely valuable in gathering significant information, we need to emphasize that naturalistic methods at least partially reduce the individual's awareness of being observed and thus often produce the most meaningful data.

Experimental Research

In **experimental research**, a series of steps are designed so that relationships between differing phenomena can be determined. This is done either to discover principles underlying behavior or to find cause-effect relationships.

Each experimental investigation must follow a procedure that is relevant to the phenomenon being investigated. Therefore, an experimental design for one experiment may differ completely from the design for an investigation of a completely different nature. For example, studying married couples and how they choose to discipline their children would involve methods totally different from those employed for investigating the

electrical activity of the brain after tranquilizers have been administered to an adult suffering from acute anxiety neurosis. However, the basic principles of experimental design remain the same regardless of specific experimental differences. Certain common terms, definitions, and formats are universal to those using the experimental method.

Let's look at some of the universal parts of this design. The experimental method typically begins with a **hypothesis**, an educated guess made by the researcher. Let's suppose our hypothesis is that students will know more about marriage and family after a semester is over than before they enrolled in a course focusing on this topic. Before this hypothesis is tested on a large group of people, say 1,000 undergraduate students, sociologists usually employ a **pilot study**. A pilot study is a small-scale research investigation designed to discover problems, errors, or other obstacles that might develop when the large-scale study is undertaken. Discovering procedural problems while testing 10 to 20 subjects will save much time, effort, and many headaches when we start testing 1,000 subjects.

When sociologists are ready to begin their research, two groups of subjects are chosen to prove or disprove the hypothesis. The **experimental group** is subjected to special treatment, and is carefully observed by the experimenter. The special treatment given to the experimental group is called the **independent variable**. In our example, the experimental group would be students enrolled in marriage and family classes who will receive formal instruction in this discipline (the instruction being the independent variable). The behavior affected by the independent variable (knowledge acquired in class from the professor) is termed the **dependent variable**.

Our other group of subjects, called the **control group**, is used primarily for comparison purposes. The control group does not receive the independent variable. This means that in our example this group of students will not benefit from the formal instruction that the experimental group receives. To determine whether or not our hypothesis is correct, usually a **pre-test** and **post-test** are ad-

APPLICATIONS

HOW TO SHARPEN YOUR OBSERVATION ABILITIES

Effective observation requires special skills and talent. Whether observers are stationed behind one-way windows or simply attempting to keep unobtrusively out of sight, certain points regarding effective observation should be kept in mind:

- Remain out of the way as much as possible. When subjects know that they are being watched, unnatural behavior often results.
- With paper and pencil, tape recorder, or camera, record such things as the physical setting, activities being undertaken, and so on.
- If you are observing a group of subjects, quickly scan the scene and then focus on one person or one couple for at least 10 to 15 minutes. Then, refocus on the group at large and pay attention to other interactions.
- Which other items to look for depends, of course, on your research topic. Possibilities include emotional expression, body language, physical appearances, power in relationships, decision-making strategies, patterns of interaction, childrearing techniques, and so on.

Immediately upon finishing your observation, write your report—while the various scenes are still fresh in your mind. Remember to maintain your objectivity by not making simultaneous interpretations of scenes you're recording. Judgements, inferences, and conclusions must be avoided. You might want to keep the following in mind to enhance your objective recording:

- Record only the facts.
- Record every detail without omitting anything.
- Do not interpret as you observe.
- Do not record anything you do not see.
- Use words that describe but do not judge or interpret.
- Record the facts in the order they occur.

It is important that subjects feel at ease—unaffected by the observation or measurement, in both actions and words. Thus, if testing is part of your research design and is to be effective, it must take place in a friendly, nonthreatening atmosphere. If possible, you should spend several sessions with a subject to avoid any unnecessary apprehensions or other behavior that might interfere with the situation. Rapport with subjects and building up their trust are especially important if accurate responses are to be elicited.

Adapted from Cartwright and Cartwright, 1984; Beaty, 1986.

ministered to both the experimental and control groups. The pre-test and post-test in our case would seek to measure the students' knowledge of marriage and family. Changes, if any, would appear in the experimental group, especially when contrasted with the control group.

In the final phase of the experimental method, sociologists seek to draw conclusions and interpretations. **Correlational methods** may be employed, such as the analysis of the experimental events and the comparison of any relationships that may exist. A well-executed experiment may provide insight into a hypothesis, but the results of an experiment may also raise many new questions and lead the researcher into still other avenues of experimentation.

Longitudinal and Cross-Sectional Research Designs

The dynamics of marriage and family life can also be studied by employing a longitudinal or cross-sectional research design. In a **longitudinal study** the sociologist collects data on the same group of individuals at intervals over a considerable period — years and sometimes even decades. Let's suppose someone wanted to collect data concerning various facets of early married life. The researcher employing the longitudinal method might begin studying a particular group of couples at age 20. Follow-up studies would be made at fairly regular intervals until the subjects reached a desired age. At each follow-up session, relevant data would be recorded, to be applied to the final research analysis.

In a **cross-sectional study**, sociologists obtain comparative data from different groups of subjects more or less simultaneously. In studying married life, then, the analyst would select a number of groups of married couples aged (for example) 20, 30, 40, 50, and 60 and record the differences among the various age groups. The differences would then be analyzed.

Each method has its own advantages and disadvantages. For example, the cross-sectional approach is relatively inexpensive, easier to execute, and not overly time-consuming, but it sometimes overlooks individual changes, and it is contaminated with generational differences. The longitudinal method probably provides a fairly accurate picture of developmental changes within an individual, but this approach takes a long time, is generally expensive, and frequently suffers from subject attrition.

A more recent addition to the methodologies is the *short-term longitudinal method*. Using this less complicated method, a study would last a maximum of five years and include investigations into fewer behavioral phenomena. Not only does this method take less time, there is also less attrition of subjects and a greater likelihood that the original staff of investigators will carry out the entire project. An extension of this method is the *cross-sectional short-term longitudinal method,* a combination of the above methods. If one wishes to study certain parenting traits developmentally, let's say from ages 30 to 40, a ten-year longitudinal study would be in order. By doing simultaneous cross-sectional studies of two groups however, one for ages 30–35 and the other for ages 35–40, the total study can be completed in five years — hence the term cross-sectional short-term longitudinal study.

It is obvious that each of these methods has its own strengths and weaknesses. Whichever methodological approach is used, the data will be only as good as the measurement techniques used to obtain them and the conception behind their collection. These factors operate in any methodological design.

To better comprehend the differences between the longitudinal methods, one must also understand such factors as age and cohorts. In either methodological approach, age is always a variable. A second variable is **cohort**, a reference to those people born at approximately the same time (the same year or within a year or two of each other). Because they are born about the same time, cohorts have experienced situations and events unique to their particular age group. For example, being married in 1930 was different from being married in 1986. Thus, the age factor distinguishes people by their chronological age, and the cohort factor places that age within a time frame.

With age and cohort factors in mind, let us reexamine the nature of cross-sectional and longitudinal studies. All of the subjects in a longitudinal study are members of the same cohort. If a study was started in 1950 with couples in their twenties, and these subjects were tested every five years, we would be gathering information about **age changes**. In a cross-sectional design we would be studying subjects who were, let's say, 25, 30, 35, and 40 years of age. Here we would be gathering information about *age differences*. In a cross-sectional study the results may be affected by age or cohort differences.

Cohort analysis is an effort among researchers to explore the experiences common to a particular age group. Whenever a research design is put into operation and data are collected, one must go a step further and examine cohort differences. This is especially true in cross-sectional studies, since we are dealing with subjects of varying ages at the same time. For example, let's say we discover in our data that retired couples are more financially cautious than young, newly married couples. Could that have been influenced by the retired couples having lived through the stock-market crash and the Great Depression? Or was it because the young, newly married couples were reared in a world of charge cards, layaways, and instant credit?

When such factors as age and cohort cannot be assessed separately, the data are **confounded**. Cross-sectional designs for the most part are inexpensive and can be quickly executed, but they contain confounded data in that the facts may be attributed to either age or cohort differences.

Longitudinal studies can also give us con-

Sociologists conducting research must take into account experiences unique to whatever age groups are being studied.

ETHICAL RESEARCH STANDARDS

The sociologist interested in studying marriage and family, just as with other research pursuits, must realize that certain ethical principles must be taken into consideration. To safeguard the rights of subjects, the American Sociological Association (1984) has proposed the following principles:

1. Research is to always maintain objectivity and integrity.
2. The subject's right to privacy and dignity must always be respected.
3. The researcher is to protect subjects from personal harm and danger.
4. Information obtained about the subjects during the study is confidential.
5. The researcher is to disclose all sources of financial support.

founded data. More specifically, longitudinal studies have a tendency to confound a person's age with time-of-measurement changes. As a result, we can't really tell whether changes in a person are the result of developmental processes or environmental influences.

One other weakness of the longitudinal design is that of *repeated measurement*. Here the subject is repeatedly given the same tests over time. The gathered results may therefore be due not to improvement, but rather to familiarity with the test itself. All of this discussion illustrates the many ways that sociologists are confronted with confounded data.

CHAPTER HIGHLIGHTS

The study of marriage and family is an active research pursuit. Definitively speaking, marriage is an institutional act that legally unites a man and a woman. Marriage is the basis for the family — broadly defined as a social arrangement consisting of two or more persons related by blood, marriage, or adoption. Typically, the family consists of parents and children. The family fulfills at least six basic functions: regulation of sexual behavior and reproduction, provision for biological needs of its members, the bestowing of status and rank, emotional maintenance, socialization of children, and the implementation of social control.

This chapter explored the numerous varieties of marriage and family that exist. As far as marital customs and practices are concerned, monogamy is the marriage of one man to one woman. Serial monogamy is a succession of marriage partners through the process of marriage, divorce, remarriage, and so on. Plural marriage, known as polygamy, consists of two main varieties: polygyny and polyandry. Polygyny is the marriage of one man to two or more women, while polyandry is the union of one woman to two or more men. Of the two, polygyny is more popular, particularly in regions of Asia and Africa.

Patterns of residency can be patrilocal — with or near the husband's relatives; matrilocal — with or near the wife's relatives; or neolocal — based on the couple's own separate living arrangement. Patterns of descent can be patrilineal — emphasizing the husband's lineage; matrilineal — stressing the wife's side of the family; or bilateral — emphasizing both the husband's and wife's lineage. As far as authority is concerned, the patriarchal power structure places the husband in the dominant position, the matriarchal household is dominated by the wife, and a sharing of authority characterizes the egalitarian home.

We also spent some time examining types of family composition. The nuclear family consists of parents and children, while the extended family is comprised of parents, offspring, and other relatives. The blended family results when a divorced parent with custody of children remarries, although this family form has even more complex possibilities.

As far as transitions of the marriage and family cycle are concerned, six stages are known to exist: the unattached young adult, the newly married couple, the family with young children, the family with adolescents, the launching of grown children, and the family in later life. Exploring marriage and family from such a developmental perspective is not the only way of studying this discipline. Rather, other perspectives have been advanced, including the social-exchange, symbolic interaction, social conflict, and structural-functional approaches.

The study of marriage and family represents a scientific field of exploration. Indeed, the scientific principles of description, explanation, prediction, and control can be applied to the research being gathered. Sociologists seek to collect facts, the building blocks of theories. And, when a relationship between facts can be established, researchers must examine the validity of their findings. Internal validity refers to the degree to which one's research allows for accurate identification and interpretation. External validity refers to the degree to which conclusions drawn in one set of relationships can be generalized to other situations.

Sociologists also adhere to the scientific method, an organized series of steps designed to promote maximum objectivity and consistency in gathering and interpreting observable evidence. Among the data gathering techniques are surveys (including questionnaires and interviews), observation, experimental research, and longitudinal and cross-sectional research designs. With all data gathering techniques, ethical research standards must be followed.

KEY TERMS

bilateral descent
blended family
cohort
cohort analysis
conclusion
confounded data
control
control group
controlled experiment
correlational methods
cross-sectional study
dependent variable
description
egalitarian
experimental group
experimental research
explanation
extended family
external validity
fact

family
family of orientation
family of procreation
hypothesis
independent variable
internal validity
kinship
longitudinal study
marriage
matriarchal
matrilineal
matrilocal
monogamy
naturalistic observation
neolocal
nuclear family
participant observation
patriarchal
patrilineal
patrilocal

pilot study
polyandry
polygamy
polygyny
post-test
prediction
pre-test
sample
scientific method
serial monogamy
single-parent household
social conflict approach
social exchange approach
structured observation
structural-functional approach
  survey
symbolic interaction approach
  theory
theory

RECOMMENDED READINGS

Askham, J. (1984). *Identity and stability in marriage.* New York: Cambridge University Press. A look at what couples seek in a marriage, including the search for identity, stability, and security.

Bohannan, P. (1985). *All the happy families: Exploring the varieties of family life.* New York: McGraw-Hill. An examination of how contemporary social trends are changing the nature of the family, with the child as the center of focus.

Filsinger, E. E. (1983). *Marriage and family assessment.* Beverly Hills, CA: Sage. This text focuses on tools and techniques for marriage assessment, including the accuracy and validity of the major measurement devices.

Fink, A., and **Kosecoff**, J. (1985). *How to conduct surveys.* Beverly Hills, CA: Sage. A readable, step-by-step account of how to organize a survey and evaluate the credibility of other ones.

Howard, G. (1985). *Basic research methods in the social sciences.* Glenview, IL: Scott, Foresman & Co. A broadly based perspective on methodology. Howard surveys the various research methods used in the social sciences and in the process, shows the logic, strength, and weakness of each.

Lein, L. (1984). *Families without villains: American families in an era of change.* Lexington, MA: D. C. Heath. Lein takes a look at contemporary families and explores their triumphs and concerns.

Lonner, W. J., and **Berry**, J. W. (1986). *Field methods in cross-cultural research.* Beverly Hills, CA: Sage. A handy and practical book containing guidelines on conducting cross-cultural research.

Miller, B. C. (1986). *Family research methods.* Beverly Hills, CA: Sage. This paperback nicely shows how fundamental research methods can be applied to the field of marriage and family.

Minuchin, S. (1984). *Family kaleidoscope.* Cambridge, MA: Harvard University Press. The author explores new ways of comprehending family disruption and what society must do to promote domestic harmony and stability.

Skolnick, A. S., and **Skolnick**, J. H. (1986). *Family in transition* (5th ed.). Boston: Little, Brown & Co. Chapters 1 and 2 of this collection of readings examines the changing American family.

2

Marriage and Family through the Ages

CONTENTS

CONTEMPLATIONS

■ This chapter presents marriage and family life as it existed in past eras and explains how it evolved into its present-day forms. We think you'll be fascinated by some of the historical practices. For example, did you know that in Rome during the third century, a wife committing adultery could be killed by her husband, all within the framework of Roman law? However, no such punishment existed if husbands committed the same adulterous act.

■ Among ancient Hebrews, Greeks, Romans, as well as many other civilizations, romance and courtship as we know it today had little to do with marriage. Rather, fathers usually chose wives for their sons and gave their daughters' hands in marriage with little regard for their offspring's wishes. Indeed, as we shall see, marital arrangements often resembled a crude business transaction between families rather than a romantic exchange of vows between bride and groom.

■ By the late A.D. 300s, Christianity had become the official religion of the Roman Empire. History reveals that Christianity sought to implement many changes, including a rather strict code on sexual behavior. For example, many Church Fathers felt that all sexual desires were evil and passionate love should be condemned. Some, such as Saint Augustine, actually encouraged celibacy, the abstention from any sexual activity. Why did the Church take such a position? Why was such a strict code encouraged? This chapter will explore some of the reasons.

■ It was called *bundling,* and it was a form of courtship practiced in colonial America during the late eighteenth century. Bundling was a custom in which two unmarried persons of the opposite sex shared the same bed while remaining fully clothed. The bed was usually in the home of the female, and the suitor was encouraged to spend the entire night. Sound too permissive for colonial America? Want to know the reasons prompting such a nocturnal invitation? Later on in your reading you'll know why.

To fully comprehend and appreciate the nature of contemporary marriage and family life, it is important to examine the various civilizations of the past. By so doing, we will be able to see the family in relation to historical, social, and cultural forces. This type of analysis will reveal that practices related to marriage and family life are a reflection of a society's place in time.

This historical narrative will also help us better appreciate how the family evolved and aid our efforts to understand modern day perspectives and theories. It might also enable us to avoid past mistakes, borrow what was "good" from them, and continually examine accepted modes of family functioning.

MARRIAGE AND FAMILY THROUGH THE AGES: RECURRENT HISTORICAL TRENDS

One of the more interesting and obvious features about marriage and family life as it existed in the past is that certain trends and practices appear to be recurrent. This is important, since marriage and family life is, at least in part, a practical extension of society's beliefs, customs, and viewpoints. Let's look at a few of these recurring trends:

Marriage Was Strongly Encouraged   Our historical narrative will reveal that marriage was strongly encouraged by most civilizations. In many instances, marriages were also prearranged by the parents, more often than not by the fathers. Remaining single earned disdain from many; indeed, unmarried adults were often viewed with suspicion and fear. In colonial America, for example, single men had to pay special taxes because of their unmarried status.

Individuals Entered the Institution of Marriage at Early Ages   Througout much of history, people married at surprisingly early ages. While much of this was due to a shorter life expectancy, prompting for early marriages by one's parents also took place. For example, while in Rome the legal age for marriage was 14 for boys and 12 for girls, it was not uncommon for fathers to betroth their children at even younger ages.

Marriages Were Patriarchal in Scope   The husband typically controlled the household and wives occupied a subordinate position. Husbands were responsible for family decision making and those factors affecting the family's welfare and operation. In some civilizations, such as ancient Greece, women were continually told of their lesser status. Plato, for instance, perceived women as being intellectually and biologically inferior to their male counterparts.

Household Activities Reflected Sex-role Stereotyping   Domestic chores usually mirrored clear-cut sex-role stereotyping; that is, chores were assigned on the basis of one's sex rather than on individual ability. While there were exceptions, household responsibilities followed a fairly predictable pattern. Husbands saw to the farming or other financial enterprise. Wives handled such domestic chores as cooking, weaving, and child-rearing. While women were relegated to a subordinate position in the home, it should be added that throughout much of history, they were respected for the work they did.

Families Were Self-sufficient Economic Units   The agrarian family of the past, complete with its sex-typed division of labor, was a self-sufficient economic unit. It produced and consumed as a unit. This was a trend that persisted from the earliest of time to the Industrial Revolution.

Children Were Regarded as Economic Commodities   Throughout history, children were expected to make meaningful contributions to the family enterprise. They were gradually taught the sex-typed chores just described at early ages, many by their seventh birthday. While youngsters today are more or less economic liabilities, children of yesteryear loomed as valuable economic commodities.

Provisions for Divorce Have Existed for Centuries   Contrary to the beliefs of many, provisions for divorce have been around for some time. For example, a divorce could have been obtained in Mesopotamia and ancient Egypt as well as in most

---

In order to maintain the farming enterprise in years gone by, all family members were expected to make meaningful contributions.

early civilizations. However, while provisions existed, the number of persons actually obtaining a divorce was relatively small. In many instances, those securing a divorce also met with social disapproval.

Each of these trends is but a segment of a central theme of this chapter—the influence a given civilization's beliefs, viewpoints, and needs have in shaping the course of marriage and family life. To add perspective to the trends presented and to gain further insight into the nature of marriage and family through the ages, let's look back through history and examine representative civilizations.

ANCIENT CIVILIZATIONS

Mesopotamia

Mesopotamia was a region settled before 3500 B.C. in the areas known as Iraq and Egypt. The people who settled it probably came from the highlands of present-day Turkey or Iran. The culture as a whole included the Sumerians, Persians, Assyrians, and Babylonians.

Mesopotamia grew from a small settlement into a number of powerful city states. The economy was largely based on farming, and Mesopotamia was noted for its intricate network of irrigation canals and waterways. Sumerians are also recognized for inventing cuneiform, a system of writing in evidence prior to 3,000 B.C. This wedge-form of writing became one of the most important systems of communication in the ancient world.

Sumerians practiced monogamy, and marriages were arranged by the elders of the families. As a **betrothal**—an agreement or promise for a future marriage—the bridegroom gave a money gift to his future father-in-law. This gift was forfeited if the bridegroom broke off the engagement, but it could be recovered twofold if the bride-to-be changed her mind.

In some instances, the wife received certain privileges. For example, once married, she assumed possession of the betrothal and added to it a **dowry**—gifts given by the bride's relatives. Combined, this was her inalienable property, which on her death she could bequeath to her children, if she so desired. If her husband died, she inherited the same share of his property as did each of his children. She could marry again when she desired, taking with her the original dowry but relinquishing her share of the late husband's estate to his children.

Other facets of married life were not characterized by such equality and fairness. On the contrary, Sumerian marriages were a clear reflection of male dominance and superiority. For example, a husband could under certain conditions sell his wife, and he could also hand her over as a slave for years at a time in payment of a debt. A husband could also divorce his wife on very slight grounds, while the reverse was much more difficult. **Adultery**—sexual intercourse with a person other than one's spouse—by the woman was regarded as an extremely serious offense. During certain points in the Sumerian civilization, it was punishable by death by drowning.

Because farming was the primary family enterprise, large numbers of children were encouraged by the Sumerians. Should a wife not be capable of bringing children into the world, she was often divorced. By Sumerian law, children were absolutely under the authority of their parents. They worked long hours doing farming and domestic chores and were expected to be subservient and cater to to their parents wishes. The parents at will could disinherit or disown them, sell them into slavery, or temporarily surrender them as slaves in payment of debt.

Egypt

The Egyptian civilization rose to power over 5,000 years ago and existed for nearly 2,500 years. Egypt, like Mesopotamia, relied chiefly on farming for food. Therefore, most Egyptians lived near the Nile, an area rich with fertile soil.

The Egyptians divided themselves into four social classes: the royalty and nobles; artisans, craftsmen, and merchants; workers; and slaves. In time, Egypt's professional army almost became a separate class. But at no point in their civilization

The ancient Egyptians practiced matrilineal descent, including the much-married Cleopatra.

did Egypt have a fixed caste system. This meant, among other things, that a person of the poorest class could rise to the highest.

Egyptian men and women married early — the average age for men was 15 and for women, 13. A husband could take more than one wife, and if he was wealthy enough, he could keep a harem. While the husband was clearly the dominant figure in the marital arrangement, Egyptian women were held in high regard. They were the recipients of much affection from their husbands, and some of their social and legal privileges reflected the respect accorded them. For example, Egyptian women could own property and level court suits.

Interestingly, although the husband ruled the family, Egyptians practiced matrilineal descent. That is, all property descended in the female line from mother to daughter. When a man married an heiress, he enjoyed her property only as long as his wife lived. On her death it passed to her daughter and her daughter's husband.

The practice of matrilineal descent helps to explain why Egyptians accepted marriage between brothers and sisters. Such marriages were very evident in royal families, with many pharaohs marrying their sisters or even their infant daughters. The marriages of Cleopatra serve as an excellent illustration of matrilineal descent. Cleopatra first married her eldest brother, whose right to the throne was thus established. When he died, Cleopatra married her younger brother, who ruled by right of this marriage. There were no children by either of these unions. When Caesar conquered Egypt, he in turn had to marry Cleopatra to make his accession legal in the eyes of the Egyptian people. Next came Marc Antony, who by marrying Cleopatra secured the throne. She had a son by Caesar, a son and daughter by Antony. When Antony fell and Octavius arrived, he too was ready to espouse the much-married Queen.

Children were very much a part of married life in Egypt and large families were encouraged. The

Egyptians held children in high esteem and parents were very protective towards them. This is suggested by the numerous depictions of children that adorn the tombs at Memphis, Amarna, and Thebes. The young were viewed as essential parts of a growing civilization and were reared with care and concern. Supportive of this is the fact that as early as 1500 B.C., treatment for childhood diseases was prescribed, different from that given adults.

The principle occupation of most Egyptian mothers was homemaking, a busy combination of activities. When children were reared, the infant was strapped to the mother virtually all of the time. Usually, babies were carried against the breast in a pouch suspended from the mother's neck. Children were raised to respect the devotion and dedication exhibited by Egyptian mothers. Egyptian youths were also advised to repay their parents for all the care they received. Usually this meant caring for them as they became older, making certain that all of their needs were met.

Divorces were fairly easy to obtain in ancient Egypt. However, a man had to make financial provisions for his divorced wife. Should a wife want to divorce her husband, she too had to make arrangements for some form of compensation.

Ancient Hebrews

The ancient Hebrews were a nomadic desert people initially led by Abraham, his son Isaac, and his grandson Jacob in 1900 B.C. Jacob, who was also called Israel, had 12 sons. These 12 sons headed 12 tribes that came to characterize the Jewish people. This is why the Jews came to be known as the children of Israel or Israelites.

Many of the ancient Hebrews traveled to Canaan, an area later called Palestine. Here they lived for many years tending their flocks of sheep or farming. The tribal life of the Jews had all but disappeared by the seventh century B.C. when they became a nation with a king, a capital, and a temple at Jerusalem. This also heralded a social class system, with aristocracy and military dignitaries occupying the upper division and the working class, landless, and debtors in the lowest position.

Similar to the Egyptians, the ancient Hebrews married at young ages. The wedding was a simple affair, arranged by the fathers of the bride and groom. During early centuries, there was a purchase price for the wife, most often in the form of goods and services. In later centuries, a dowry was required. The wedding was a domestic ceremony that did not require the participation of a priest or magistrate.

The Hebrew marriage was patriarchal in scope. Polygyny was also recognized by Hebrew law, and its practice extended into the Middle Ages. The husband wielded considerable influence within the family, evidenced by the power of life and death he had over his wife and children. He could sell his children or divorce his wife without much of a reason if he so desired. He could also have his wife put to death for adultery.

Obviously, this meant that the Hebrew wife played a subservient role, although she was respected by her husband. She was expected to obey her partner, bear his children, and perform the customary domestic chores. While the husband tended the flocks or tilled the soil, she typically saw to the cooking, weaving, and childrearing obligations.

The Bible of the Hebrews was the Old Testament, and within it were directives for their existence. Paramount among these was God's directive to "be fruitful and multiply." Procreation was extremely important so that family lineage could be maintained and the tribes of Israel could be perpetuated. Sons in particular were desired, not only to carry on the family line but for economic purposes as well. Nonreproductive sex was discouraged among the Hebrews since it was perceived as not fulfilling any useful purpose.

The Hebrew family produced as a unit and consumed as a unit. At an early age, children were expected to contribute to the household—boys typically helped their fathers tend the sheep while girls assisted with the preparation of food. Strict discipline was employed by both parents in an

Hebrew family customs and religious traditions have endured for centuries, including the Passover meal.

effort to discourage irresponsibility and foolishness. Obedience was demanded, and the duty and obligation that children had to their father was second only to their obligation to God.

Greece

The ancient Greeks of 2,000 years ago called themselves *Hellenes,* and their land *Hellas.* While they never formed a national government, the Greeks were united by a common culture, religion, and language. The classes in Greek society varied from one city-state to another. Athens, for example, had three classes: citizens, slaves, and *metics,* or resident aliens.

Marriage in ancient Greece was regarded as a means of producing legitimate children and perpetuating the civilization. Many of the marriages were arranged by the fathers with little regard for the inclinations of the parties involved. And, although Greek brides were expected to be virgins,

this expectation was not leveled against the bridegroom.

As far as structure was concerned, marriages were monogamous and, consistent with other civilizations, patriarchal. Greek women were viewed as inferior to men and were expected to be subservient. The perceived inferiority of women was a persistent theme in Greek literature. Plato, for example, wrote that there was not one branch of human industry in which the female sex was not inferior to the male. While they possessed similar capacities and powers, he felt that women were weaker and less competent overall.

The ancient Greeks practiced **infanticide,** the killing off of children born weak, deformed, or mutant. Good health and fitness were continually emphasized so that children could fill the needs of this civilization. In Sparta, for example, an ancestral need for military preparation and a strict social code prevailed. Children were brought up under rigid discipline and were viewed as a necessity for

Among the ancient Greeks, marriages were monogamous and patriarchal in structure.

the continued existence of Spartan civilization in the Hellenic world. Upon birth it was necessary for parents to have their child's health status determined by a council of elders. Babies pronounced in good health were automatically adopted by the State, but left in the home until seven years of age.

In most Spartan families, boys and girls grew up together under the supervision of the mother, but in wealthy families, an older house slave cared for the young. Attempts to discipline the mind and body began shortly after birth. Swaddling was not permitted by the State, since it was thought that physical growth might be hampered in the process. Children left alone in the dark were not permitted to scream or cry out, the belief being that self-control should be taught as early as possible. And, at the age of seven, Spartan boys were removed to the State's barracks to begin their training in the military while girls remained at home and learned domestic responsibilities.

The infant in Athens was examined at birth and was left exposed to the elements to die if judged unfit or deformed. During early childhood, the Athenians also emphasized the importance of physical fitness; however, this took the form of gymnastics, not military training. Unlike Sparta, however, Athens also sought to educate the child's mind as well as the body. Greater responsibility and authority was given to the parents in regard to the child's upbringing. For example, the father, not the State, decided whether an infant should live or die, and Athenian parents were not required to send their boys away for military training.

Rome

At its height in A.D. 117, the Roman Empire included about a fourth of Europe, much of the Middle East, and the entire northern coastal area of Africa. While its millions of people spoke many languages and worshipped different gods, Romans were united by the Empire's government and military power. The Roman Empire fell about 1,500 years ago.

Roman society had two main divisions — citizens and noncitizens. Cititzens included the ruling class of senatorial aristocracy; *equites,* a group of wealthy businessmen; and *plebians,* or lower-class citizens. Noncitizens included aliens and slaves.

As with earlier civilizations, romance often had little to do with the Roman approach to marriage. Roman fathers chose wives for their sons, and the marriage was viewed as a private arrangement made between families. Betrothals were common in Rome, usually consisting of a number of presents from the bridegroom to the bride. A wedding ring was also given to the bride, which she immediately slipped onto her finger. The ring usually consisted of a circle of iron set in gold or a plain circle of gold. (While there is some speculation that the ancient Egyptians made use of the wedding ring, it is known for certain that the Romans had this custom.)

As far as the wedding ceremony itself was concerned, a sacrifice to the gods was first made — sometimes a ewe, but most often a pig. Ten witnesses and a selected official observed the exchange of vows and affixed their seal to the marriage contract, if one was desired. Following hours of festivities, a procession led by flutists and torchbearers brought the newly married couple to the husband's home.

The Roman family was patriarchal, and should unhappiness prevail, a divorce was relatively easy for the husband to obtain. The success of a marriage was often judged by the number of children brought into the world, preferably boys. Large families were continually stressed, particularly during the rule of Augustus Caesar, who offered material rewards to parents who could conceive three healthy male children. If this goal was attained, the mother was given full legal independence while the father usually received some form of promotion in his career.

Like earlier civilizations, the Romans had no use

Family life was an integral part of the ancient Roman civilization.

for weak or deformed children since they could not be counted on for future civilian manpower or service in the Army. When these unfortunate children were born, the parents generally decided upon infanticide, usually after consultation with five neighbors, who had to agree with the parent's sentence if it was to be carried out. Until the fourth century A.D., neither public opinion nor law found infanticide to be morally wrong.

A child of Rome grew up chiefly under his mother's care. At six years, however, the boy was instructed by the father on how to become a respectful citizen, to till the ground, and to carry arms. Fathers also stressed physical fitness; they sought to teach their boys how to endure heat and cold, and to survive other physical hardships. Girls, on the other hand, were instructed by the mother in methods of preparing food and making clothing.

THE MIDDLE AGES

Historians chart the Middle Ages between the end of the Roman Empire in A.D. 400 to the 1500s. Also known as the medieval period, the Middle Ages were characterized by Germanic tribes moving in from Scandinavia and conquering land in central Europe previously occupied by Romans.

MARRIED LIFE AND EARLY CHRISTIANITY

While the Romans persecuted the Christians for many years, Christianity spread rapidly due to the work of Saint Paul and other apostles. In the Edict of Milan in A.D. 313, Emperor Constantine granted Christians the freedom of religion. By the late 300s Christianity had become the official religion of the Roman Empire.

The Church would come to affect many facets of life, including marriage and family functioning. For example, the Church in time adopted a formal liturgy for the wedding ceremony and imposed sanctions, including those related to allowable kinship between bride and groom. Also, the Church took a stand against interfaith marriages, carefully outlining stipulations and implications for violations. In addition, virginity was demanded at marriage, and the Church condemned divorce, although it would fluctuate on this latter edict for some time.

Sexual relationships and activity also came under the scrutiny of the Church. In time, the Church would develop a separate legal system known as **canon law** to handle issues related to sex and morality. In general, the Church was suspicious of

St. Augustine (A.D. 354–430).

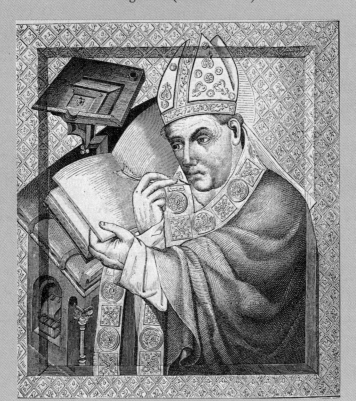

▶

sex and spoke out strongly against it. Among the more vociferous spokesmen was Saint Augustine (A.D. 354–430), who advocated strict sexual repression. He firmly believed that all mankind must learn to control sexual impulses. While sexual activity within a marriage to procreate was tolerated as a necessary evil, all other forms were condemned. Saint Augustine, along with others including Saint Paul, encouraged **celibacy**, the abstention from sexual activity. He regarded celibacy as the highest form of virtue and evidence that willpower can overcome lust and sin.

The Church's position on sex had numerous implications for other behaviors. For example, while masturbation, adultery, contraception, and abortion were condemned, so too was engaging in "suggestive" dances, wearing improper or revealing clothing, or singing "wanton" songs. Finally, while kisses were often a form of salutation among early Christians, townspeople were warned that kissing more than once for the purpose of pleasure was sinful and should be avoided. ▬

Here, the Germanic way of life integrated with the Roman lifestyle. However, the medieval civilization was also influenced by the Moslems in Spain and the Middle East, and by the Byzantine Empire in southeastern Europe.

It would be impossible in the confines of this chapter to explore all of the marriage and family customs throughout all of Europe during the Middle Ages. Therefore, our historical narrative will only expose a representative few. In medieval England, for example, the household was still regarded as an important economic unit and marriages were therefore encouraged. They were arranged by one's parents, typically the father. In

A MEDIEVAL WEDDING

The Bride being attyred in a gowne of sheepes russet and a kertle of fine woosted, her head attyred with a billiment of gold and her haire as yeallow as gold hanging downe behinde her, which was curiously combed and pleated, according to the manner in those days; shee was led to church betweene two sweete boyes, with Bridelaces and Rosemary tied about their silken sleeves.

Then was there a fair Bride-cup of silver and gilt carried before her, wherein was a goodly branch of Rosemary gilded very faire, hung about with silken Ribands of all colours; next was there a noyse of Musicians that played all the way before her; after her came all the chiefest maydens of the Country, some bearing great Bride Cakes and some Garlands of wheate finely gilded and so she past unto the Church.

It is needless for mee to make any mention here of the Bridegroome, who being a man so well beloued, wanted no company and those of the best sort, beside diuers Marchant strangers of the Stillyard that came from London to the wedding. The marriage being solemnized, home they came in order as before and to dinner they went where was no want of good cheare, no lack of melody. . . . The wedding endured ten dayes, to the great reliefe of the poore that dwelt all about.

Adapted from Power, 1965, p. 165.

many instances the arrangements made between the two families resembled a shrewd business transaction — concern was often expressed over the worth of the bridal partners, property ownership, and the size of the dowry.

The male was the undisputed head of the household and whatever property and possession a woman brought into a marriage, including the dowry, became his. Laws on inheritance also favored the male. Throughout the Middle Ages, though, wives were treated with respect.

To function adequately as an economic unit and reap productive harvests, families were large in size. However, infant mortality rates were frighteningly high due to poor medical care, disease, and unsanitary conditions. As far as childrearing techniques were concerned, two important developments transpired during the Middle Ages. The first was the belief that the child was **inherently sinful.** Because the Church felt that all children were born wicked and sinful, it was not only justifiable, but considered right and appropriate for parents to physically punish youngsters as often as possible. Parents were often told that children who behaved badly were expressing the results of this innate sin; consequently the Devil had to be literally driven from the body.

Those parents who were neglectful of their duty to punish their children faced the disapproval of their more Christian neighbors who conscientiously beat the Devil out of their offspring. This type of parental obligation to rid the child of the devil illustrates how both the child *and* the adult were affected by the religious teachings of the day. The alliance of children and grownups alike in the fear of Satan and the hope of salvation was thus a mirror of the social organization at the time.

A second development at this time in history was the relinquishment or, in some cases, the actual abandonment of the child by many parents. Documentation reveals that many children were sold as slaves, or abandoned to monasteries or nunneries. **Child relinquishment** in its most common form, though, consisted of sending the infant or young child away to live with a wet nurse (a woman who breast-feeds other women's children)

for two to four years. After this period of time, the child was returned to the family. Such practices were usually reserved for wealthier families and serve to illustrate the minimal amount of time many parents spent in raising their young. Education for all children was woefully lacking during the Middle Ages. In general, children were regarded as miniature adults and were expected to make meaningful contributions to the household at early ages.

THE RENAISSANCE AND REFORMATION (FOURTEENTH TO SEVENTEENTH CENTURIES)

Marriages created in northern Europe during the periods known as the Renaissance and the Reformation experienced a social milieu where both peoples and institutions were undergoing significant religious, moral, and social changes. Indeed, the Renaissance and the Reformation swept away customs and institutions that had dominated Europe for almost a thousand years. Among numerous developments, commerce and wealth vastly increased, intellectual advancements were made, and the Protestant faith was established.

The livelihood of most families during the Renaissance and the Reformation continued to be agricultural. Many hands were needed to cultivate the soil, and the institution of marriage remained an economic necessity. While there was an increase in clandestine marriages, those of a prearranged nature continued to dominate. For many, romance played little or no role in the overall path to marriage. Indeed, in some instances the bride and bridegroom had not even met prior to their wedding day.

Married life revolved around a simple but rugged farming existence. Work began at sunup for both husband and wife and continued through the day into the sundown hours. Husband and wife made a formidable and impressive economic pair — he handled primarily the outside farming chores, while she executed the domestic tasks nec-

Throughout history, children were often treated as miniature adults and clothed in grown-up attire.

essary for day-to-day survival. To say that each relied on the other would be an understatement.

As in other historical eras, children were needed to maintain maximum agricultural yield on the farm. Or, they were needed to provide the necessary manpower to continue a family trade or business. With skilled merchants being in ever-growing demand, many children were taught the practical aspects of a given trade. Many parents sent their children away to the home of a middle-class citizen willing to teach a particular trade. Bearing obvious similarities to child relinquishment, as practiced in the Middle Ages, the boy would live in his new home as he became a skilled apprentice. Girls would remain at home and learn domestic chores from their mothers.

COLONIAL AMERICA

The colonists who voyaged to America in search of a better life brought a number of European marriage and family customs to the New World. For example, early marriages were encouraged. Delaying marriage was viewed as impractical since it resulted in a loss of harvest and a failure to cultivate important farmland. Throughout colonial history, bachelors were viewed with suspicion and in some instances, fear. In several colonies, such as Plymouth, single men had to pay special taxes which were levied against them because of their unmarried status.

The struggle that existed between Church and State for the control of marriage also found its way to colonial America, although it was more evident in northern colonies than in southern ones. Divorces were also recognized in the New World, but divorce laws varied throughout the colonies and, in general, were not widespread. Consider that there were only 40 divorces granted in the entire state of Massachusetts between 1639 and 1692.

Unlike customs in the Old World, most marriages in colonial America were not prearranged. However, it was expected that the prospective bridegroom would secure the father's permission for the bride's hand in marriage. In general, the courtship period was short.

While marriages were created early, the physical hardships that abounded created many widows and widowers. Females, usually assuming the responsibilities of motherhood at immature ages, typically suffered ill health and often succumbed to an early death. The fatality rate for males was also high for a host of reasons including disease and famine, and the lack of proper sanitation. But while marriages were often short-lived, widows and widowers alike remarried, and for the most

DATING AND COURTSHIP IN COLONIAL AMERICA

When nights were cold and stormy in colonial America, some unique dating customs and practices emerged. While lovers could walk off into the woods or other locations during warm months to share intimate moments, cold nights forced them and everyone else inside to gather around the fireplace. Because there was no central heating, the fireplace became a crowded location in most colonial homes.

Under such conditions, carrying on a private conversation was nearly impossible. However, suitors sometimes resorted to the ingenious method of communica-

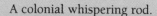

A colonial whispering rod.

▶

tion known as the *whispering rod*. This long, tube-like device allowed two people to talk in hushed tones without being overheard by others.

Bundling was another interesting Colonial practice. Bundling was a custom in which two unmarried persons of the opposite sex shared the same bed while remaining fully clothed. No one knows exactly where bundling originated, although the English and Dutch are often mentioned as the originators. Frigid weather, simple hospitality, and usually a parental desire to hasten the courtship process often brought an invitation for the suitor to stay and share the young woman's bed.

A centerboard was kept in many colonial homes for nights when bundling was practiced. This was a board placed between the male and female to discourage sexual intimacy. Whether or not the board remained in place was secondary to the fact that parents knew where their daughter was, and with whom.

Bundling was an accepted part of courtship in New England and the Middle Colonies by the late eighteenth century. It appears to have been most prevalent in Connecticut. But by the early 1800s it had been abandoned, although sporadic instances of it occurred as late as 1845.   ■

part, this was done rather quickly. Because of the cited reasons, three marriages by the same person was not at all uncommon during colonial times.

The colonial family was patriarchal, and the husband decided important matters affecting the household. His wife and children were expected to obey him without question. For children, respect for both parents was mandatory. This was very much in evidence in Puritan New England, where children had to stand up when addressing their parents, usually calling them "honored sir" or "honored madam." The physical abuse of children was no stranger to colonial America.

As in the Old World, children were viewed as economic commodities and needed hands on the farm. They were taught how to make contributions to the household at an early age and over time became vital components of the family enterprise. Boys were usually taught how to hoe, weed, plant, mend fences, and other farm-related chores. Girls were given domestic chores such as milking, tending the garden, or candlemaking.

Before leaving our brief narrative of marriage and family life during colonial times, we'd like to clear up several misconceptions regarding family life at this point in history. Often, the colonial family is portrayed as having large numbers of children and being extended in scope. While this might have been true within some families, it was more often the exception rather than the rule. The typical colonial family averaged about three children and was nuclear in its structure.

THE INDUSTRIAL REVOLUTION

America in the late nineteenth century was a nation at the beginning of a transformation. The **Industrial Revolution**, as it has come to be known, began to change the predominantly agrarian society of America into an urban and industrialized one. This change had many implications for marriage and family life. Paramount among the changes was a new economic alignment of the family. Instead of functioning as a productive agrarian unit, families now seldom physically worked together on the land as they once did. Rather, the husband went off to work in an industrial setting while the mother and children remained at home.

The Industrial Revolution thus brought about an important shift in role responsibilities within marriage and family life. Women, once partners in labor in colonial families, were exclusively assigned to the home and the hearth. Employment outside of the home and away from the family became the province of the male. It can be said then, that as the Industrial Revolution brought about significant technological change, it also introduced a new dimension to sex-role behaviors and expectations.

The Industrial Revolution did not produce a role realignment in all families, though. Many lower-class families continued to work together out of sheer necessity. Both parents and children trudged off to the factories and worked long hours, often leaving at dawn and returning home at sunset.

The manner in which children were perceived also changed at this time. Recall that they had been regarded as needed hands on the farm and were expected to make worthwhile and productive contributions. Now, children became economic liabilities as parents had more mouths to feed in their daily struggles to carve out an existence in this new stage of American history. Work and family life thus became separate enterprises; families began to consume as a unit but did not produce as a unit.

Other changes related to children and family life took place at this time. For one, children began remaining with the family beyond the customary ages of seven to ten. Also, they became the objects of a new type of sentimentality from their parents. Caring for children became a central concern, particularly for women. Many adults became committed to childrearing and the concept of parenting. And, as children became older, formal schooling began to exert more of an impact on their lives.

This latter point is part of a much larger theme that would have implications for children of the twentieth century; that is, parents saw fit to let other adults guide, instruct, nurture, stimulate, and protect their youngsters. Whereas the family was once the primary socialization agent, other

For many, the agrarian nature of family life was transformed by the Industrial Revolution. The plow was often replaced by the factory, such as this New York City sweatshop, circa 1900.

institutions now played a role in the child's development. In addition to school, churches had youth groups, the concept of Sunday School emerged, and there were organized places away from the home in which youngsters learned, socialized, and developed a sense of self and group identity.

CONTEMPORARY MARRIAGE AND FAMILY LIFE

The exploration of marriage and family life as it exists in contemporary society lies at the heart of this textbook. What we'd like to do here is bring our historical narrative into the present by briefly examining several key trends and changes of the past century. By so doing, we can make comparisons to other historical eras while, at the same time, developing a springboard for what lies ahead.

Let's begin with the institution of marriage itself and its choice as a lifestyle in contemporary society. As in other historical periods, marriage continues to be the choice for a truly significant portion of the population. An estimated 95 percent will opt to get married at one point or another in their lifetime (Glick, 1984a).

We need to acknowledge, however, that other lifestyles besides marriage are being chosen by growing numbers of persons. Two of these, single-hood and cohabitation, are especially popular today and have been met with increasing amounts of public acceptance. We might also add that some new wrinkles have come to characterize marriage in the 1980s. For example, couples are waiting longer to get married, an interesting comparison to the historical pattern of early marriages.

RESEARCH HIGHLIGHT

PERCEPTIONS OF SINGLEHOOD AS AN ALTERNATIVE TO MARRIAGE

Marriage continues to be valued by most Americans, but it is no longer perceived as necessarily better than remaining single. Research undertaken by Arland Thornton and Deborah Freedman (1985) indicates that most young people do not disapprove of singlehood; on the contrary, it is regarded as a legitimate and acceptable lifestyle. According to these researchers, such perceptions may be indirectly providing the basis for more stable marriages since young people may no longer feel pressured into marriage as a primary goal.

Thornton and Freedman gathered their data by conducting an 18-year intergenerational study of mothers and their children between 1962 and 1980. While viewing singlehood as a viable lifestyle, 90 percent of the 18-year-olds questioned in the study said that they expected to marry eventually. And despite the high divorce rates the respondents expect to stay married to the same person for life. In addition, the young people said that they expected to marry later in life than their counterparts did 20 years ago; only 20 percent of men and 25 percent of women expected to marry by age 21 or 22 in 1980, compared with 25 percent and 33 percent respectively in 1960. They also did not intend to permit marriage to interfere with education and work plans. Almost 60 percent of the men and 50 percent of the women questioned said they would be unwilling to reduce school attendance in order to marry, and 56 percent of men and 49 percent of women said they considered it very important to work for a year or two before marrying. If these plans are carried out, the researchers feel that a major positive impact on marriage can occur since marriages between more mature partners tend to have a better survival rate.

Only 25 percent of the 18-year-old respondents felt they would be "bothered a great deal" if they did not marry. Another 25 percent said it would bother them "only a little." More than 40 percent of the mothers in the intergenerational study said they would not be bothered at all if a son or daughter did not marry, and only 10 percent said that this situation would trouble them a great deal.

Interestingly, divorce did affect perceptions or marriage among both young and older respondents. Thirty-seven percent of both mothers and offspring agreed that "there are few good or happy marriages these days." Mothers who had experienced divorce were more likely to believe that singleness had more advantages ▶

than marriage. They were less inclined to agree that it was better for a person to marry than to remain single, and they preferred that their children marry at an older age.

The researchers also found among the older respondents some noticeable shifts in attitudes since 1962, when the study was launched. For example, in 1962, 43 percent of the respondents said that in families with children, parents should stay together even if they don't get along. By 1980, only 15 percent of the same respondents agreed with that statement. In 1962, 84 percent of those respondents agreed that "almost all married couples who can, ought to have children." By 1980, only 43 percent supported that view.   ■

Many of today's marriages are also characterized by changing activities within the household.

Balancing married life with vocational responsibilities challenges today's dual-career couples.

Many couples share domestic chores and choose to deemphasize traditional sex-role stereotyping, a concept known as **androgyny**. As a result, the operation of many homes is based on mutuality and reciprocity. We also find more dual-career households; that is, both husbands and wives are working outside of the home. This provides a unique comparison to the antiquated sex-oriented work roles we explored in this chapter.

Mothers, in particular, have joined the labor force in increasing numbers. Figures for women overall indicate that over half of all mothers with school-age children work outside the home. Mothers of preschool-age and younger children are currently the fastest-growing segment of the workforce (Zigler and Muenchow, 1983). Figure 2-1 shows the labor force participation rates of married women.

The issue of who is going to care for the children of working parents is an important one today. Whereas the Industrial Revolution virtually dictated that mothers would remain at home to care for their young, today's dual-career couples must turn to the outside for childcare assistance. The relinquishment of the youngster to childcare facilities offers a new twist to childrearing practices, and may place contemporary parents at odds with their historical counterparts. Many of the older generation cling to the notion that "a woman's place is in the home," and the modern woman's

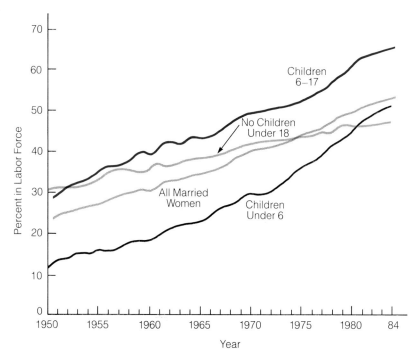

Source: Thornton, A., and Freedman, D. (1983). The changing American family. *Population Bulletin,* Vol. 38 (4). Washington DC: Population Reference Bureau.

FIGURE 2-1   Labor Force Participation Rates of Married Women

removal of these chains sometimes produces ambivalence and, in some cases, hostility. Yet, the trend toward finding childcare assistance must be understood in relation to the common thread of this chapter. That is, a society's customs and practices related to marriage and family life are usually a reflection of its needs, living conditions, and beliefs. Along with the growing acceptance of women entering the employment world will undoubtedly come increasing approval of childcare assistance.

Another contemporary trend is the shrinkage of family size. Today, there are just about two children per household. By 1990, it is projected that there will be approximately 60 million American homes without children under the age of 15 (U.S. Bureau of the Census, 1984; Masnick and Bane, 1980). Figure 2-2 displays the average number of

children per woman in the United States as well as in other nations.

There are several reasons for this decrease in family size. As we mentioned earlier, the economic value of children to families has changed. Once an economic commodity, children have become an economic liability. While many children were an asset to families living in preindustrial societies, this is not the case with families of the post-industrial age. Children today must be loved and wanted for reasons other than the work they can perform.

The total cost of housing, feeding, and clothing one child, as well as educating him or her through college, is between $80,000 and $150,000 (Price, 1982). Furthermore, as schooling has lengthened, the financial drain of maintaining children within the home may be prolonged to over 20 years. Other reasons for having fewer children include

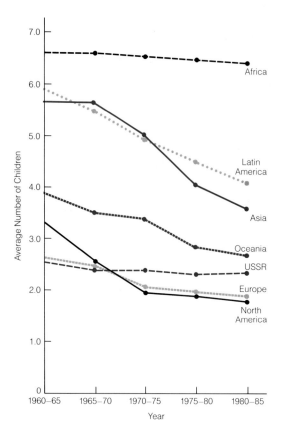

Source: United Nations, Population Division, *World Population Prospects: Estimates and Projections as Assessed in 1984* (United Nations publication, Sales No. E. 86. XIII.3), Table A-12, October 1985.

FIGURE 2-2   Average Number of Children per Woman, by Selected Nation

adult concern for overpopulation, greater numbers of women pursuing careers, the greater diversity of contraceptives that are now available, and the practice of abortion.

You should also recognize that there are many couples today who delay parenting, or even opt for childless marriages. As far as the latter is concerned, demographers predict that 25 to 30 percent of young married women will elect not to have children (U.S. Bureau of the Census, 1980). This is an interesting trend when compared to the high premium placed on having children during early historical periods. Compare this, too, to the

sentiment expressed today in certain countries, such as China, where only one child per family is *allowed*.

Yesterday's American family was a rather permanent, immobile unit. Of course, there were those who pushed West to explore the nation's territorial borders. Once settled, though, most new additions to the family were raised and died in pretty much the same geographical location. This physical permanence was due to a number of factors, among them the independent and self-sufficient nature of towns and villages, as well as the fact that many children were groomed to take over the family enterprise. If one did venture away, it was usually for only short distances to gain local employment.

The twin forces of industrialization and urbanization have created an increasingly mobile family unit. The contemporary family is likely to change its residency as often as career and economic needs dictate. This in itself is a striking contrast to employment and economic situations in early American history. At one time, machines and jobs followed the population as we expanded our nation. Now, the reverse appears to be the case. Our population usually follows the machines to gain employment. There are obvious implications here for all family members. Moving from location to location implies the repeated introduction of new career demands, living arrangements, financial adjustments, friends, and school systems. Adaptation and adjustment to such residential instability is an important challenge for all concerned.

In light of rising divorce rates, our discussion of modern day marriage and family life would be incomplete without some mention of marital dissolution. Marital disharmony and collapse did occur in the past, but as we mentioned, it was not widespread. In comparison, consider today's divorce statistics. Divorce rates hit an all-time peak in 1946 and then declined steadily until the late 1950's. Since then, however, the proportion of first marriages ending in divorce has sharply risen. The approximately one million divorces granted in 1974 marked the first time in American history that more marriages ended in divorce than through death. Between 1970 and 1980, the number of divorces in this country increased almost 70 percent. One source (Cherlin and Furstenberg, 1983) contends that at current rates, half of all American marriages begun in the 1980s will end in divorce. The United States has the rather dubious distinction of currently having a higher divorce rate than any other Western nation. Figure 2-3 charts marriages ended by divorce and death from 1860 through 1982.

Looking back at our historical narrative, why did so many of yesterday's couples remain together, even in the wake of disharmony? Most stayed together under the same roof for purely economic reasons. The family functioned as a working unit and a divorce would cripple the household's overall operation and finances. In this sense, it was simply economically unfeasible to divorce. Other reasons to remain together included a concern for one's standing in the community as well as the expense of the actual divorce, not to mention the rather tedious and time-consuming chore of obtaining one.

Although these reasons for remaining together still exist for some, we are living in a society that transmits a new orientation to the topic of divorce. As we know, households today rarely produce as a total working unit, and large numbers of women

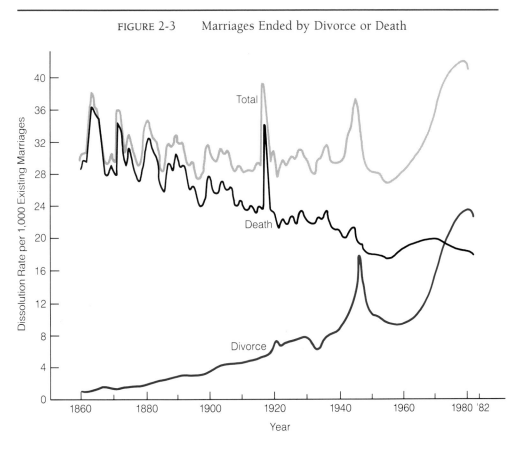

FIGURE 2-3   Marriages Ended by Divorce or Death

Source: Thornton, A., and Freedman, D. (1983). The changing American family. *Population Bulletin*, Vol. 38 (4). Washington DC: Population Reference Bureau.

are no longer economically dependent on their husbands. Divorces are now relatively easy to obtain, particularly in those states supporting a "no-fault" concept. And while divorced parties do experience role readjustment, the sheer numbers of divorced parties in this country has lessened negative community reaction.

Individuals are also receiving another unique type of value orientation as divorce rates continue to escalate. Our society is placing an increasingly high premium on individual choice and personal fulfillment. Divorce for many may reflect this attitude. Divorce is often not viewed as personal disorganization, but rather as a mechanism for individuals to improve their overall lives.

Of particular concern are the numbers of divorces involving children. It is estimated that over one million children each year will see their parents' marriage end in divorce. If current divorce rates continue, it is proposed that an individual faces a 50 percent probability of becoming a member of a blended family (step-family) as a child, parent, or step-parent. It is also projected that over 11 million children will live in a single-parent family if present rates continue (Furstenberg, 1980).

Single-parent families have also fallen under the scrutiny of sociologists. The single-parent family is the fastest growing family form today (see Figure 2-4). It is estimated that approximately 11.3 million children live in single-parent families. In the 1980s almost one out of every five families is of the single-parent variety (Furstenberg and Nord, 1982; Grossman, 1981).

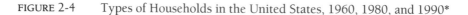

FIGURE 2-4   Types of Households in the United States, 1960, 1980, and 1990*

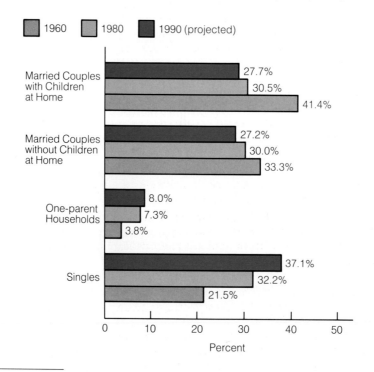

*The single-parent household is the fastest-growing family form.

Source: George Masnick and Mary Jo Bane. *The Nation's Families: 1960–1990*. Cambridge, MA: Joint Center for Urban Studies of MIT and Harvard University. 1980. Computed from Table 2.13.

Approximately 85 percent of all single-parent families are headed by women. Often single-parent families are also poor. Figures gathered in 1980 disclose that approximately 40 percent of female-headed single-parent homes were classified as living in poverty, while only 16 percent of male-headed single-parent families were (Payton, 1982; Johnson, 1980).

While we must not lose sight of the number of families remaining together, all of these conditions represent significant social problems of the 1980s. Disruptive family life creates considerable stress and poses numerous adjustment tasks for all concerned. More in-depth coverage on the topic of divorce and single-parent families will be presented in Chapter 14.

RESEARCH HIGHLIGHT

A DEMOGRAPHIC LOOK AT CONTEMPORARY BLACK FAMILIES

Demographer Paul Glick's (1981) examination of black marriage and family life in the United States shows some similarities as well as dissimilarities to the trends established by whites. In relation to this, consider the following:

- Eighty-six percent of black families in 1980 were maintained by a married couple or by one parent, typically the mother, and one or more of the parent's sons and/or daughters. As far as the latter is concerned, the number of one-parent families has increased at a faster rate among black families than other families. Despite this, 50 percent of the black population living in the United States reside in households maintained by a married couple.

- Black families are more likely than other families to have children. In 1980, for example, 62 percent of black families included one or more sons and/or daughters under 18 in the home. Historically, black families have had more children than other families as a whole, but this must be placed into a proper statistical perspective. For example, poorly educated black women tend to have high birth rates, while highly educated black females tend to have low birth rates.

- The rate of improvement in educational level for black parents under age 45 has been about twice that of other parents.

- More than one-half of black married couples have both husband and wife in the labor force. Young wives with no children constitute a relatively high proportion of black women in the labor force, but significant increases of black mothers with children under age 18 in the home are apparent.

- Rates of divorce are higher among blacks than other races. In 1980, there were 15 percent more black divorced men than black married men and 26 percent more black divorced women than black married women. For black men, the smallest proportion of divorces occurs among those in the middle income range. Women college graduates with no graduate training tend to have the most stable first marriages, regardless of race.

- The proportion of divorced persons who remarry is higher among whites than among blacks. Among divorced women, remarriage rates are higher for those with less than a full high school education than they are for those with more ▶

education, regardless of race. Remarriage is more likely to be followed by
redivorce among black women between the ages of 35 to 44 than among other
women of the same age.

■ In 1980, 3.5 percent of all black households included a male and a female not
related to each other, and no other adults. Blacks maintained 11 percent of all
households in 1980, but maintained 19 percent of all unmarried-couple households. Also, unmarried couples living together are more likely to be interracial
than married couples.

■ Most of the 2.4 million nonfamily households in 1980 consisted of black
persons living alone. Black persons living alone under 35 years of age were
almost twice as numerous in 1980 as they were in 1970.   ■

Putting History into Perspective

Combined, these structural and functional
changes offer a unique comparison to the historical marriage and family life patterns. These
changes, as well as others likely to take place in our
ever-changing society, represent areas needing
our continual monitoring and attention. This is
especially true for those changes threatening the
very foundation of marriage. At a time when the
individual family's instability and need for economic, social, and educational supports are intensified, our society must work together to prepare a
better future for all concerned.

As we shall see throughout this book, this latter
point demonstrates the need for effective *family policy*, government-sponsored legislation designed to assist the overall welfare and well-being
of the family. Marriage and family life in the 1980s
creates its share of stress and difficulties, and many
members need to turn to the outside for assistance
—from elderly and childcare needs to parenting
programs and domestic abuse intervention. It is
generally agreed that the national government
needs to have an adequate, ongoing, pro-family
policy for these and countless other needs arising
from the turbulence of contemporary times.

However, as James Henslin (1985a) asks, to
what end should family policy be aimed? Of
course, we want it to improve marriage and family
life and provide the best for all, but just what is
"best"? How does one go about getting the "best"?

Moreover, how do we guard ourselves against un-
anticipated, even perverse, consequences of well-
intentioned family policy programs? Obviously,
there are many unanswered questions regarding
the best way to provide government assistance to
today's families.

Few would argue that efforts have not been
made to better understand marriage and family
life. This is expressed today by the sheer number of
people, institutions, social service organizations,
publications, and government bodies that are involved in studying it. They have given us a better
understanding of married life and the needs of
modern day families. Never before have so many
attempted to gain insight and understanding,
whether it be through the work of sociologists or
related disciplinarians.

But while there has been progress made in understanding the family and meeting its needs, the
task is not finished. In some cases the needs of
families are overlooked, particularly among the
poor, minority, and neglected populations. This
void ranges from inadequacies in medical and
health care to social service support. We have yet
to provide all families in this country with equal
opportunities to live and grow to their fullest potential. Our attention needs to be directed towards preserving the rights of all family members and fulfilling their basic needs in life. How
successful will our efforts be? Since we are products of history ourselves, only future generations

By using the past as a guide, sociologists and related researchers are better able to understand the needs of modern-day families.

will beable to critically examine and objectively evaluate our contributions to marriage and family life.

CHAPTER HIGHLIGHTS

In order to better understand contemporary marriage and family life, we examined various past civilizations. In the process, a number of recurrent historical trends became evident: marriage was strongly encouraged, individuals married at early ages, marriages were patriarchal in scope, household activities reflected sex-role stereotyping, families were self-sufficient economic units, children were regarded as economic commodities, and provisions for divorce were almost always available.

These recurrent themes were particularly evident in the civilizations of Mesopotamia, Egypt, the ancient Hebrews, Greece, and Rome. Throughout the Middle Ages and the historical periods known as the Renaissance and the Reformation, the institution of marriage continued to be an economic necessity. The livelihood of most families centered around farming, and tradition as well as pure survival dictated the assignment of domestic roles and responsibilities. Colonial America was no exception to the customs and beliefs that had been practiced for centuries.

The Industrial Revolution would change the complexion of society, including the family unit. Most families experienced an economic realignment, and sex-role behaviors and expectations changed. Employment away from the family became the province of the male, while females remained behind at home. For the first time in history, work and family life became separate enterprises. Children were also viewed in a new light at this time. Rather than economic commodities, they now were regarded as liabilities.

Marriage and family life in contemporary society has many different dimensions. While marriage as a lifestyle is still the choice for a clearcut majority of the population, other lifestyles have emerged as alternatives. Many marriages today are dual-career in nature, more mobile, and smaller in size than yesteryear's households. Also, divorce rates are extremely high in today's society — another marked contrast to earlier times.

The complexity and changing quality of society dictates the importance of assisting today's families. This embodies economic, social, and educational support, as well as carefully planned family policy legislation. Moreover, such assistance needs to be monitored and evaluated on a regular basis.

KEY TERMS

adultery

androgyny

betrothal

bundling

canon law

celibacy

child relinquishment

dowry

dual-career household

industrial revolution

infanticide

inherent sin

RECOMMENDED READINGS

Albin, M., and Cavallo, D. (Eds.). (1981). *Family life in America, 1620–2000*. New York: Revisionary Press. A central theme in this book is the impact of social events on the family and how its members respond.

Fox, V. C., and Quitt, M. H. (1980). *Loving, parenting, and dying: The family cycle in England and America, past and present*. New York: Psychohistory Press. Part Two of this book consists of a historical narrative of family life between 1500 and 1800, including a comparison of development on both sides of the Atlantic.

Hareven, T. K. (1984). Themes in the historical development of the family. In R. D. Parke (Ed.), *The family: Review of child development research* (Vol. 7). Chicago: University of Chicago Press. The many complexities of the family as it evolved throughout history are systematically analyzed in a scholarly fashion.

Harris, C. C. (1983). The family and idustrial society. *Studies in Sociology* (No. 13). Winchester, MA: Allen and Unwin. Of special interest are discussions focusing on the English family prior to industrialization, the household and family under capitalism, and the mobility of the English family.

Herlihy, D. (1983). The making of the medieval family: Symmetry, structure, and sentiment. *Journal of Family History, 8*(2), 116–130. For those wanting more information on family life during the Middle Ages, much detail and insight is contained in this article.

McNall, S. G., and McNall, S. A. (1983). *Plains families*. New York: St. Martin's Press. The authors provide an interesting analysis of family life in the Great Plains region of the United States from the 1860s to the present.

Pollock, L. A. (1983). *Forgotten children: Parent-child relations from 1500 to 1900*. London: Cambridge University Press. Pollock shares with us the nature of childhood as it existed in past historical eras, including an emphasis on the relations that existed between parent and child.

Rosen, B. C. (1982). *The industrial connection: Achievement and the family in developing societies.* New York: Aldine. This book explores the changes that occur in the strength and meaning of kinship ties, husband-wife interaction, and childrearing practices when industrialization of a society takes place.

Scanzoni, J. (1983). *Shaping tomorrow's family: Theory and policy for the 21st century.* Beverly Hills, CA: Sage. A thought-provoking look at where the family has been in terms of structure and function, where it is now, and where it is going.

Weiner, L. Y. (1985). *From working girl to working mother: The female labor force in the United States, 1820–1980.* Chapel Hill: University of North Carolina Press. A highlight of this book is the interaction of work, family, and cultural patterns in the history of the working woman in America.

Part Two

RELATIONSHIP TRANSITIONS

3

The Developing Relationship

CONTENTS

CONTEMPLATIONS

■ Two people meet, fall in love, and marry. The dynamics surrounding courtship and mate selection have intrigued sociologists for years, and we're going to share some of their major findings in this chapter. We'll show the importance of establishing intimate relationships and the relationship transitions that exist. And for those of you who have ever suffered from a broken heart, we'll examine how some relationships are ticketed for destruction. Along the way, though, we'll supply you with some tips on how to emotionally survive the breakup of a relationship.

■ Yale psychologist Robert Sternberg maintains that love is one of the most important things in life. People have been known to lie, cheat, steal, and kill for it. Even in the most materialistic of societies, it remains one of the few things that cannot be bought. And it has puzzled poets, philosophers, writers, sociologists, psychologists, and practically everyone else who has tried to understand it. Love has been called a disease, a neurosis, a projection of competitiveness with a parent, and the enshrinement of suffering and death. But just what is love? What does it emcompass? In this chapter, we'll discover what researchers have learned about the complex and diverse nature of love.

■ What kind of lover are you? If you haven't really thought about it, this chapter is designed to stimulate your personal awareness. In particular, we're going to examine different types of loving, from playful and sexually permissive types to intense and obsessive forms. In fact, we'll even supply a chart so that you can graph your own style of loving. When you're done, we think that you'll appreciate the multifaceted nature of love and loving.

■ Is the traditional practice of dating becoming a violent and dangerous activity? One might not think so, but a relatively recent topic of investigation is proving otherwise. Increasing numbers of women between the ages of 15 to 25 are becoming victims of date rape — physical force used by a dating partner to have sexual intercourse. Read on to learn more about this growing problem, including how widespread it is, the trauma it inflicts on its victims, and how it can be prevented.

There are few of us who can thrive on loneliness or isolation. On the contrary, millions of men and women search for a partner for "meaningful" human interaction. The desired outcome of this quest is usually two-fold: to know and better understand oneself and to construct a worthwhile and satisfying relationship with another person (Pocs and Walsh, 1985).

The social vehicle for *pair bonding* is dating, which for the most part begins at an early age in America. This is largely due to our encouragement of early heterosexual interactions in the school system or at social functions, or through the individual's contact with the mass media. This exposure and prompting, coupled with the perceived importance of dating, exerts significant influences on the individual's personality and socialization.

By young adulthood, dating evolves as a conscious, deliberate process of mate selection. Because of heightened levels of maturity, dating now tends to be characterized by greater levels of mutuality and reciprocity. Young adults have typically declared their identities and have reached a point where they can share themselves intimately with others. To put this another way, people first have to learn who they are before they can give of themselves to another person.

INDIVIDUAL MATURITY AND INTIMATE RELATIONSHIPS

For intimate relationships to flourish, a considerable degree of adult maturity is needed. Generally speaking, **maturity** is *a state that promotes physical and psychological well-being.* The mature person possesses a well-developed value system, an accurate self-concept, stable emotional behavior, satisfying social relationships, and intellectual insight. A mature individual is also realistic in his or her assessment of future goals and ideals. In this respect, maturity gives us the ability to cope successfully with life's problems, increasing the effectiveness of our planning strategies, deepening our appreciation of our environment, and expanding our resources for happiness and satisfaction.

The Quest for Adult Maturity

We need to stress that maturity is not a unitary concept or an all-or-nothing phenomenon; it is a multifaceted characteristic which varies in degree and kind for all of us. For instance, some people may have attained moral maturity, but are not emotionally mature. Moreover, age is no guarantee of maturity. Reaching adult status does not automatically mean that maturity is reached. Maturity requires considerable conscious effort that depends on the individual, not a preset age.

Maturity has biological, psychological, sociological, and philosophical dimensions. These dimensions include the following qualities, although adults often attain them with varying degrees of success:

- Finding a sense of purpose and meaning in life.
- Maintaining intimate relationships and caring for oneself.

- Assuming responsibility for one's choices in life.
- Handling frustrations and disappointments.
- Balancing individual, career, and family roles on a regular basis. (Okun, 1984)

Throughout their quest for adult maturity, individuals must reexamine old values and attitudes as they experiment with new ones. For many, this may be anxiety producing, and, while anxiety is essential for growth, our society frequently regards this emotional reaction negatively. Thus, some members of the older generation may become poor guides for the young, unable to help them tolerate psychological growing pains.

There are many adults who do not attain a sense of maturity and as a result fall short of accurate identity achievement. Because of this, a type of personality foreclosure results, in which people identify with the values and goals of others without questioning whether or not they are right for them. When this occurs, the painful task of self-growth and the quest for adult maturity is abandoned for the easier alternative of letting oneself be socialized by others. The consequence of such identity foreclosure may be lifelong psychological immaturity, and when that immaturity is brought into relationships, the result is often shallow and superficial modes of interaction.

Dimensions of Maturity

One of the better descriptions of adult maturity has been developed by Gordon Allport (1961). Allport suggests that maturity is an ongoing process best characterized by a series of attainments on the part of the individual. Each period of life has its share of obstacles that must be overcome — roadblocks that require the development of goal-formulation and decision-making abilities. Methods for dealing with life's failures and frustrations — as well as accepting its triumphs and victories — have to be devised, if maturity is to be developed.

Allport identifies seven specific dimensions of adult maturity: extension of the self, relating warmly to others, emotional security, realistic perception, possession of skills and competencies, knowledge of the self, and establishing a unifying philosophy of life. Combined, these seven dimensions are characteristic of smoothly functioning, stable, and mature persons.

Extension of the Self   This dimension requires that people slowly extend themselves to multiple facets of their environment. The world of the young child is primarily limited to the family, but gradually the youngster becomes involved in various peer groups, school activities, and clubs. In time, strong bonds develop with members of the opposite sex as well as interest in career, moral, and civic responsibilities. All of this provides the opportunity to become involved in more meaningful personal relationships.

Allport cautions, however, that just being involved in something does not necessarily imply satisfaction. Maturity is measured by movement away from a state in which interests are casual. Mature self-extension is promoted when the activity undertaken has true significance to the self and is actively pursued.

Relating Warmly to Others   Allport's second criterion of maturity is the ability to relate the self warmly to others. By this, Allport means the capacity to be intimate with, as well as compassionate toward, others. (As we shall presently see, **intimacy** means becoming close with another person.) The mature person places a high premium on brotherly love and a sense of oneness with others. Relating warmly towards others also involves a tolerance of the weaknesses and shortcomings of others. Mature individuals are capable of seeing beyond limitations in others, perhaps because they have seen and accepted similar weaknesses in themselves.

While the focal point of this textbook is on marriage, we need to establish that other intimate relationships can exist. This is a central theme in the writings of Erik Erikson (1963, 1980, 1982). Erikson has posited eight specific *life stages* and describes the manner in which personality forces operate throughout the life cycle (see Chapter 12). During early adulthood, mature personality functioning is measured by the successful

Adult maturity and competency can be expressed in a myriad of ways.

resolution of a stage known as "Intimacy versus Isolation." Prior to early childhood, the individual was in the midst of an identity crisis, a struggle that often peaks during adolescence. Erikson stresses the idea that as a young adult, the individual is now motivated to fuse this newly established identity with that of others.

Beyond marriage, individuals may develop strong bonds of intimacy in friendships that offer mutuality and reciprocity. Intimate relationships can emerge from caring and seeking to understand others; thus, mature persons effectively communicate with others, are sensitive, and tolerant. The development of friendship, love, and devotion is much more evident among mature individuals than among the immature.

Emotional Security   Four qualities of maturity are important in this category: self-acceptance, emotional acceptance, frustration tolerance, and confidence in self-expression.

- *Self-acceptance* is the ability to acknowledge one's self fully, particularly in terms of one's imperfections. Mature people realize that they cannot be perfect in every way, yet they nevertheless seek to fulfill their own potential. Total self-acceptance requires exploring and accepting one's weaknesses and shortcomings.
- *Emotional acceptance* is the acknowledgement of emotions as part of the normal self. People acquiring this dimension of maturity do not allow emotions to rule their lives, but at the same time, they do not reject emotions as alien to their natures.
- *Frustration tolerance* is the capacity to continue functioning even during times of stress. To be able to handle life's frustrations and still manage to carry on is a formidable challenge. For maturity to develop, one must learn how to best deal with life's frustrations and still maintain a healthy existence.
- *Confidence in self-expression* implies spontaneity — one is aware of one's own emotions, is not afraid of them, and has control over their expression. Immaturity, conversely, can manifest itself in a number of different ways, including timidity and shyness, emotional underreaction, or emotional overreaction.

Realistic Perception   Maturity in this respect means being able to keep in touch with reality, without distorting the environment to meet individual needs and purposes. Sometimes the complexities of situations, coupled with the ego defenses of the individual, may produce an inaccurate interpretation of the environment. The mature mind is able to perceive the surroundings accurately. This does not mean that the mature person does not use any type of defense mechanism; it is the overuse or misuse of such mechanisms that usually distorts one's perceptions.

Possession of Skills and Competencies   Unless one possesses some basic skill, it is virtually impossible to develop the kind of security necessary for maturity to flourish. While the immature person may argue, "I'm no good at anything," mature individuals seek to nurture whatever skills they feel they have. Moreover, skilled individuals are driven by a need to express their competence through some type of activity. They identify with their work and display pride in the skills needed to produce a finished product. In this respect, task absorption and ego-relevant activities are important to physical and psychological harmony.

Knowledge of the Self   Most mature people possess a great deal of self-insight, while many immature individuals have little. Knowledge of the self involves three important elements: knowing what one can do, knowing what one cannot do, and knowing what one ought to do.

Knowledge of the self may be one of the most important growth trends of adulthood. In general, the stabilization process owes much to those enduring roles that are characteristic of adult life. In other words, as individuals modify their behavior in order to fulfill their roles as workers, marriage partners, and parents, their experience begins to accumulate more and more selectively. As such, the stored-up sources of stability and ego identity emerge increasingly out of behavior within roles.

Establishing a Unifying Philosophy of Life   The last dimension of maturity is the development of a unifying philosophy of life. Such a philosophy should embrace the concepts of a guiding purpose, ideals, needs, goals, and values. Since the mature human being is a goal-seeking person, such a synthesis enables him or her to develop an intelligent theory of life and to work toward implementing it. Mature people thus perceive goals from a balanced perspective and are able to cope with failure if these goals are not fulfilled.

In retrospect, each of these dimensions of maturity is important, but they can be expressed differently by different people. Also, these dimensions may not be possessed by everyone. Consequently, unfavorable conditions may hinder personality growth and prevent the attainment of maturity. There are those who will remain immature because they are trapped in a conflict between cultural expectations and personal requirements. Others may be prevented at the very beginning of life, by forces outside their control, from ever reaching personal fulfillment and satisfaction. As we shall see, such limited personality and social functioning has implications for individual behavior as well as for relationship-building.

Self-Actualization, Maturity, and Intimate Relationships

Attaining a *self-actualizing state* also has implications for mature personality functioning and the ability to share oneself with others in meaningful relationships. **Self-actualization** is a harmonious integration of the personality, enabling individuals to make full use of their potentialities, capabilities, and talents. When self-actualization is reached, a highly refined state of being is achieved, one that is characterized by *autonomy, individuation,* and *authenticity.* It should be noted, however, that attaining self-actualization requires considerable ego strength and few reach this level of functioning.

An extensive description of self-actualization has been provided by Abraham Maslow (1968, 1970). Maslow proposes that human needs (and consequently motivations) exist in a hierarchy, from the most basic to the most advanced. The higher one climbs on this motivational pyramid, the more distinctly ''human'' one becomes; basic motives and needs must be satisfied before higher ones are developed.

The first need theorized by Maslow is *physiological* in nature, embracing adequate nourishment, rest, and the like. At the second level is *safety,* or the attainment of a sense of security. Next is *belongingness* and *love.* Belongingness may be defined as the need to be involved in a meaningful relationship, or the need to be part of a group and experience sharing. *Esteem* is the fourth need — individuals must receive feedback from others (in the form of respect and assurance) in order to realize that they are worthwhile and competent. The fifth need, *self-actualization,* lies at the zenith of this hierarchy. To reach the fulfillment of one's

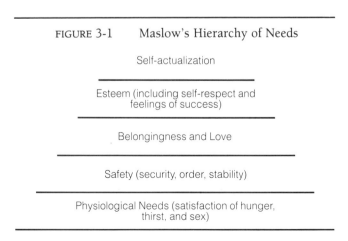

FIGURE 3-1   Maslow's Hierarchy of Needs

Self-actualization

Esteem (including self-respect and feelings of success)

Belongingness and Love

Safety (security, order, stability)

Physiological Needs (satisfaction of hunger, thirst, and sex)

potential, all previous needs have to be met adequately. And an essential component of self-actualization is freedom from cultural and self-imposed restraints. (Figure 3-1 displays the hierarchy of needs proposed by Maslow.)

Examples used to illustrate the self-actualizing personality are often of extraordinary individuals. However, let us point out that one need not be a great artist, statesman, or scientist to be in a self-actualizing state. Moreover, all people have a variety of talents and interests that can be deemed creative and special in their own way.

Those experiencing daily satisfaction and fulfillment may well be self-actualizing, provided they are making full use of their abilities. Career competency, success, and fulfillment in leisure activities, or giving and receiving in a meaningful relationship are potential examples of self-actualizing skills. So, individuals do not have to be a Pablo Picasso, Mahatma Gandhi, or Albert Einstein to be self-actualizing (McMahon and McMahon, 1982).

EXPLORING INTIMATE RELATIONSHIPS

Terms and Concepts

Most persons will be involved in one or more serious, intimate relationships over the course of their lives. While we mentioned earlier that there are many different types of intimate relationships, our purpose in this part of the chapter will be to examine the male-female love relationship.

An **intimate relationship** represents the process by which we come to know the innermost, subjective aspects of another person, and we are known in a like manner. Put another way, an intimate relationship involves the *mutual exchange of experiences in such a way that a further understanding of oneself and one's partner is achieved* (Chelune, Robison, and Kommor, 1984).

Intimacy embodies **self-disclosure**, the process by which individuals let themselves be known by others. Self-disclosure involves decisions about whether to reveal one's thoughts, feelings, or past experiences to another person, at what level of

intimacy to reveal personal information, and the appropriate time, place, and target person for disclosure. As a relationship progresses to more intimate levels, partners generally disclose more information about themselves and at a more personal level (Derlega, 1984).

Self-disclosure can be expressed through a number of different channels. Verbal self-disclosure is the use of words to let others know about you. Self-disclosure can also take place through body language or by one's tone of voice. The manner in which one gestures or chooses to emphasize words also says something about the person. Finally, persons disclose themselves through their actions (Corey, 1986).

Components of Intimate Relationships

Gordon Chelune and his associates (1984) emphasize that certain qualities are necessary for the development and existence of human relationships. These qualities include knowledge of the innermost being of one another, mutuality, interdependence, trust, commitment, and caring. These dimensions are interdependent, different from one another, but also overlapping. Chelune and colleagues offer the following description of each of these dimensions.

Knowledge As intimate relationships develop, mutual self-disclosure of increasingly personal information coincides with reports of increased appraisals of intimacy. It appears to be of central importance to people that they be able to share with others all aspects of themselves, and to feel understood and accepted as the people they are. Also, it is important to know, understand, and accept other people thoroughly at the same time. In an intimate relationship, these processes occur simultaneously and reciprocally. They appear to represent a single process characteristic of the relationship as a whole rather than descriptions of the needs and actions of two separate people.

Mutuality Earlier, we pointed out that at the foundation of an intimate relationship lies the assumption that both partners are engaged in a joint

APPLICATIONS

HOW INTIMATE ARE YOU?

Now that we've explored the concepts of intimacy and self-disclosure, let's get a little more personal. Are you an intimate person? To find out, ask yourself whether the following statements apply to you never (n), seldom (s), or often (o).

_____ 1. You spend time and energy cultivating and tending your friendships.

_____ 2. You maintain friendships with members of the opposite sex with whom you are not romantically involved.

_____ 3. You like to touch and be touched in affectionate ways.

_____ 4. Sexual intimacy for you is a way of expressing and sharing your feelings of closeness to another.

_____ 5. You enjoy solitude without being lonely and are comfortable with your different moods and feelings.

_____ 6. You feel naturally high either alone or in the company of others without ever needing the help of alcohol or drugs.

_____ 7. You feel accepted, cherished, valued and understood by your family and friends.

_____ 8. You express feelings of anger as well as of tenderness, and display grief as well as joy with those individuals closest to you.

_____ 9. You enjoy listening to other people's life stories and philosophies and try to figure out what makes them tick.

_____ 10. You share your secret shames and dreams, your self-doubts as well as your cherished hopes.

_____ 11. You can tell what other people are feeling and empathize with them.

_____ 12. Other people seem friendly and respond generously when you make an effort to show them you care.

To arrive at your total, do the following: give yourself a score of 1 for every never; a 2 for every seldom; a 3 for every often. Your intimacy quotient is low if you score 12; medium if you score 24, and high if you score in the neighborhood of 36. To get another perspective, ask the person with whom you are most intimate to score you, then compare the totals.

Adapted from Keen, 1985.

venture. As the relationship evolves, both come to know one another in great depth. Intimate relationships have at their core a mutual process of sharing. When considering the quality of intimate self- and other-knowledge, it is clear that the process of sharing this knowledge is as important as the knowledge itself.

It must be pointed out that while mutuality embodies shared interaction, it does not require highly similar or identical interaction patterns. Intimate relationships seem to involve both *reciprocal* interactions—with the partners showing similar behavior either simultaneously or alternately—and *complementary* interactions—in which the behavior of each partner differs from, but complements, that of the other. Reciprocal interactions revealing similarity between partners seem to be associated with such areas as facilitation of communication and positively shared belief systems. Similarity in needs, skills, expectations, and view of the world allow partners to interact as equals and to select life goals and directions satisfactory to both. Complementary interaction allows the partners to satisfy each other and provides opportunities for them to behave in a manner that they like to see in themselves.

One other facet of mutuality is the concept of "fairness" in rewards and costs resulting from interactions within the relationship. Intimate relationships are often characterized by a sense of fairness, shared by both partners, relating to their needs, input, and outcome. This concept of fairness is important to the mutuality of *relationship definition* and the mutuality of *relationship control* that characterize intimate relationships.

Interdependence   Within intimate relationships, partners learn in what ways they can depend upon one another for support, resources, understanding, and action. They also agree upon future dependency. Partners also share knowledge and goals, increase their interactions with one another while limiting interaction with others, pooling resources, and slowly intertwining their lives in a variety of ways. But, as intimate relationships escalate, there seems to be increasing room for interdependence with persons outside of the relationship also. Pathologically enmeshed marriages indicate extreme interdependence of the partners without the other qualities central to the existence of an intimate relationship. In this sense, an interdependence structure that allows for the delicate intertwining of two lives for the greater satisfaction of each, but with limits and some flexibility, characterizes mature intimate relationships.

It should also be added that interdependence carries with it considerable *mutual power*. To the

RESEARCH HIGHLIGHT

THE INTIMATE RELATIONSHIPS OF OLDER ADULTS

Traditionally, research on dating and intimate relationships has confined itself to high school- and college-aged samples. Unfortunately, little has been done to advance our understanding of the intimate relationships of middle-aged or older persons. While dating relationships among older adults are most frequently subsequent to divorce or widowhood, the meaning and context of dating relationships is of no less consequence on the lives of those involved. Indeed, in a world of reduced social roles, dating in later life may have elevated importance for the self-concept of the older person.

Kris and Richard Bulcroft (1985) sought to explore the dimensions of dating and intimate relationships among older populations, so they interviewed single men and women over the age of 60, the average age being 62.7. The amount of time the respondents considered themselves to be on the "dating scene" ranged from four months to 19 years.

Compared to their younger counterparts, older adults dated through more formal means, such as through singles club dances or other structured organizations or activities. Also, unlike younger generations, few reported having met their dating partner through friends. Interestingly, dating settings had more variety   ▶

among those surveyed, a factor perhaps due to greater financial stability and diversity of interests among older adults.

Sex-role stereotypes and expectations characterized the elderly's intimate dating arrangements. For example, men were expected to drive and pick up the women for the date, as well as absorb the expenses. In long-term relationships, though, couples tended to share expenses. While persons interviewed felt that it was becoming more acceptable for women to ask men out on dates, none of the women sampled chose to do so.

In contrast to the societal myth that portrays the elderly as asexual, the researchers found that sexuality played a very important part in the intimate relationship. Both men and women expected sexual intercourse to be part of the relationship. Moreover, those surveyed felt that the experience of sexual intercourse was better in later life. There was also evidence that new learning can and does take place in the sexual activities and behaviors of older adults.

Other differences characterized the intimate relationships of older generations. Most of the men and women reported being up front with motives and feelings early on in the relationship. Because of this, dating tended to accelerate at a faster pace than the arrangements of younger persons. Also, rather than emphasizing romanticism, older couples tended to stress the pragmatic side of the relationship, such as companionship and role compatibility.

Finally, most of the respondents acknowledged that the selection of a marital partner was of prime importance in their underlying reasons for dating. Secondary motives for dating included an exchange of intimacies, a desire to remain socially active, and relearning to interact with persons of the opposite sex. Prestige also appeared to be somewhat of a byproduct of the relationship, especially for women. ■

extent that interdependency is characteristic of a relationship, the partners will have mutual power to grant or withhold gratification of needs. We'll see that one thing that makes this interdependency possible is the quality of *trust.*

Trust As intimacy and increasing amounts of self-disclosure are shared, partners become psychologically vulnerable. Thus, the intimate relationship requires trust, a sense of confidence in the integrity, truthfulness, and fairness of the partner. In a general sense, trust ensures that no undue harm will be associated with the relationship. More specifically, partners trust one another to be accepting, to avoid purposeful hurt of the other, to have the best interests of the partner and of the relationship in mind, to feel warmth and caring for the partner, to need the partner and respond to the needs of the partner, to share, and to continue the relationship.

Commitment Earlier, we stressed the importance of commitment to an intimate relationship. Partners within an intimate relationship continually assess their own desires for commitment and also those of the other. The other qualities of intimate relationships seem to be influenced by the extent of this mutual commitment. For example, it has been found that people will disclose easily and at great depth if the relationship is expected to be short-term. On the other hand, commitment to the possibility of a long-term relationship instills caution, exemplified by slow, stepwise disclosures dependent upon reciprocal behavior in kind.

Intimacy is a multifaceted form of expression.

Partners may also be committed to the relationship in varying ways; for example, as friends who realize that eventually circumstances will separate them geographically and in time, but who are committed to the continuation of the relationship in an altered form. Or, we have couples who express their commitment to remain together emotionally and physically through engagement or the ceremony of marriage. The variations in the type of commitment are not as crucial as the mutuality of understanding and agreement to the terms of commitment.

Caring The final dimension of intimate relationships outlined by Chelune and colleagues is *caring*. Relationships are formed for many reasons, including companionship, money, status, or power. Intimate relationships may develop from

any or all of these reasons, but at least one reason will always be a strong sense of caring and affection between partners.

Benefits of Intimate Relationships

All of the foregoing suggest that there are many benefits attached to intimate relationships. An intimate relationship is a social vehicle that enables people to learn more about themselves and how they are perceived by others, their strengths as well as weaknesses. An intimate relationship also teaches the importance of sensitivity and reciprocity and makes it possible to experience love as well as sexuality within mutually acceptable boundaries. For many unmarried persons, an intimate relationship also represents a process through which one will ultimately select a marriage partner.

Intimate relationships offer other benefits as well. They provide partners with a sense of security and attachment. Partners typically provide one another with a reassurance of worth and competency. Also, an intimate relationship provides a commitment and a common purpose. As David Burns (1985) sees it, the satisfaction that a couple feels when each partner has made a commitment to the other and struggled to resolve their differences can lead to feelings of tenderness that are deeper and more gratifying than any feelings of romantic excitement.

A growing body of evidence also indicates that a link exists between intimacy and healthy adjustment (see Cunningham and Strassberg, 1981; Waring and associates, 1981; Waring and Russell, 1980). Some researchers (Berscheid and Peplau, 1983; Fisher and Stricker, 1982) go so far as to say that intimate relationships represent one of life's most rewarding and important activities. A review of the literature by Sadell Sloan and Luciano L'Abate (1985) indicates other positive features as well. For example, intimacy serves as a major source of comfort and defense in the presence of crises throughout the life cycle. Indeed, the inability to be intimate with others triggers depression in many people.

Barriers to Intimate Relationships

Despite the numerous advantages that intimate relationships offer, many choose to avoid them. Why is this so? According to Valerian Derlega (1984), disclosing personal information while investing in an intimate relationship makes oneself psychologically vulnerable. He points to five potential risks that individuals incur when they self-disclose.

Rejection of One's Self-Concept Individuals may find that others don't like them after they make a complete disclosure about certain matters. For example, disclosed information may be unacceptable or offensive to another, who in turn may terminate the relationship.

Discovery that One's Partner Is Not Interested in Having an Intimate Relationship Here a person may disclose intimate information with the hope of developing a serious relationship. But, one's partner may not be interested in developing the relationship and become indifferent to this motive.

Use of Information by One's Partner to Gain Control or Power in the Relationship The person listening to the disclosure may use the information to gain some advantage over the other. For example, sensitive and potentially embarrassing information may be disclosed by a partner but used against him or her when dominance in the relationship is sought.

Betrayal of Information to Others and Breaking Relationship Boundaries Similar to the previous situation, disclosed information is used against the person. This time, though, personal and sensitive information goes outside of the relationship and is given to others. In other words, confidentiality is broken. The leakage of information to uninvited third parties erodes or totally breaks down the boundaries that a couple has established.

Some individuals choose to avoid intimate relationships because of perceived barriers and obstacles.

Inequality Originating from a Lack of Equivalent Input into the Relationship   Should individuals perceive that they are on the giving end of an inequitable relationship, they may become resentful and hurt. If one party always reveals something personal and the second person never does, the high discloser may see this arrangement as unfair as well as unrewarding.

According to Elaine Hatfield (1984), risks such as these do exist in relationships, as does the psychological pain of disappointment and rejection.

However, the avoidance of intimate involvements is not the answer to these problems. Rather, what is needed is a reappraisal of oneself and relationships in general. Perhaps the first step is encouraging people to establish independence and accept themselves as they are. People are entitled to be just who they are—to think the way they think, feel the way they feel, and do the things that they can do. Accepting individuality and establishing tolerance in a relationship is important for all concerned. Still, at the same time, people need to

---

APPLICATIONS

RULES FOR AVOIDING INTIMACY

If you are not as intimate as you'd like to be, maybe it's time to begin focusing on behaviors you use to avoid getting close to others. Sam Keen (1985) notes that unfortunately many of the most popular rules for success in life today, if followed, will result in the construction of barriers to love. The following represent some of these regulations:

- Always be pleasant. If you can't say something nice, don't say anything at all. Think and speak positively. Above all, don't ever express your angry or critical feelings.
- If a conflict threatens, withdraw and wait for the negative feelings to pass over. Don't get angry, but make sure to get even.
- Always keep busy. Make work, accomplishments, efficiency and success more important than any other things in your life.
- Never lose control.
- Look out for Number 1. Be a winner. Get ahead of everybody.
- Schedule your time and stick to it. Limit lovemaking, conversation, or play to their allotted slots in the week. Remember that "time is money."
- Always stand firm. Don't back down or negotiate.
- When something goes wrong, find somebody to blame. Try to make others feel guilty and responsible for your dissatisfaction, wounds, failures or lack of happiness.
- Don't tell other people what you want and expect from them. If they really love you, they will guess what pleases you and do it without your having to ask them.
- When you find something you don't like in somebody, try to change it.
- Insist upon doing things the way your parents did.
- Assume that you know and understand others better than they understand themselves.

move away from the notion that they come into the world perfect.

People also need to accept their intimates for who they are. We are often hard on ourselves, but we are generally even harder on our partners. No one is entitled to a perfect partner, nor is there any guarantee that somewhere out there is someone better than the one currently available. To enjoy an intimate relationship, we must learn to take people as they come, without hoping to "fix them up."

Finally, persons need to learn to be more comfortable about self-disclosure. To be intimate, partners have to push toward a more honest, trusting, complete, and patient communication process. Such qualities can reduce many, if not all, of the risks within intimate relationships. Partners must also understand that a person's ideas and feelings are necessarily complex, with many nuances, shadows, and inconsistencies. In love relationships, though, there is plenty of time to clear things up.

RELATIONSHIP TRANSITIONS

How relationships begin, continue, intensify, or decline and terminate has attracted considerable research attention (see Murstein, 1986; Perlman and Fehr, 1986; Snyder and Simpson, 1986; Surra and Huston, 1986; Perlman and Duck, 1986). However, one of the most extensive and comprehensive models of relationship development has been proposed by George Levinger (1983). The strength of Levinger's theory is that it embraces the relatively broad, often diffuse, changes over time in *relationship properties* that emerge from a couple's personal, environmental, and *relational causal conditions*. The following discussion highlights the stages in Levinger's theory.

Acquaintance Stage

The *acquaintance* stage begins when one person "attends" to another, either directly or via indirect information supplied by mutual friends or other channels. Becoming acquainted with another person is influenced by physical, social, and psychological dimensions. For example, the physical environment (density and size of a community, urban or rural setting, and so on) affects whom the person encounters and continues to see. Socially, our culture defines rules of eligibility for friendship and mate selection. Psychologically, one's personality tends to initiate and maintain acquaintanceships, including the impressions we form about others.

Initial impressions often govern subsequent interaction. We'll soon see that a person's impressions are often affected by the potential partner's characteristics (for example, physical appearance or perceived competence) as well as by one's own values, goals, or moods. Should a potential partner be judged desirable and available, interaction begins.

Interaction offers individuals the opportunity to explore each other's enjoyability. Should initial interaction prove to be unrewarding to either party, little more may transpire between the two. Should it be enjoyable, on the other hand, the interaction will escalate.

It is interesting to note that early interaction may undergo transformations over time. For example, two college students first meet as members of the same theater class and only discuss drama. Over time, though, their interaction is transformed from that of classmates to that of dates, bringing with it new behaviors and standards of evaluation.

During the acquaintance stage, certain behaviors and dating strategies emerge. Traditionally, it is the male who takes the initiative to ask the female out, provides transportation, and absorbs the expenses incurred. Also along traditional lines, males usually initiate whatever sexual interaction is to take place. However, such sex-typed dating behaviors may be waning, at least according to Naomi McCormick and Clinton Jesser (1983). With more individuals today preferring an egalitarian orientation to relationships, the potential for transforming traditional behaviors and expectations exists.

DENNIS the MENACE

"THAT'S THE WORST THING ABOUT GETTIN' **OLD**, JOEY...
YA START GETTIN' INNERESTED IN **GIRLS**!"

The Buildup Stage

During the *buildup* stage, partners move from merely knowing each other to caring for each other. This transition is usually characterized by both partners' successful testing of their compatibility. Usually, each finds it easy to further the other's goals, and both come to anticipate mutually rewarding future interaction. The couple's interdependence expands not only with the increased frequency and diversity of these bonds, but also with increases in the affective strength of these connections.

Also in operation at this time are **filtering agents**, a sequence of decisions made by the couple about the quality of "fit" between their individual attributes. As two individuals become acquainted, they acquire information about each other through a series of "filters." Filtering agents, then, test the compatibility of partners and serve to narrow down the field of eligibles.

Types of Filtering Agents   What is it that attracts one person to another? How do filtering agents operate in the overall process of mate selection? These are difficult questions to answer since attraction and mate selection represent highly complex processes. However, sociologists have managed to isolate certain features of the overall filtering process.

To begin with, interaction is enhanced when individuals reside near one another, be it at home or at work. This nearness in place is referred to as **propinquity**. In its broadest sense, propinquity means that individuals need to have continual contact if the relationship is to endure.

Another early filtering agent is physical attraction. Richard Maier (1984) writes that in virtually all societies, physical appearance is important in attractiveness. However, there are wide variations in what is considered attractive. The physical traits considered attractive in one culture may be repulsive in others.

In support of this, one cross-cultural study measuring physical beauty (Gregersen, 1982) uncovered some interesting findings. Physical attractiveness included crossed eyes (Mayans), flattened heads (Kwakiutl), black gums and tongue (Maasai), black teeth (Yapese), joined eyebrows (Syrians), absence of eyebrows and eyelashes (Mongo), enormously protruding navels (Ila), pendulous breasts (Ganda), gigantic buttocks (Hottentot), and fat calves (Tiv).

Males, more so than females, are likely to be concerned about the physical appearance of their partners. Both males and females, though, respond more favorably to attractive dates than to unattractive ones. Interestingly, physically attractive persons tend to behave in more traditionally sex-typed ways. That is, physically attractive males tend to be assertive and socially active, and physically attractive females tend to be unassertive and socially passive (Brehm, 1985).

Perceived attractiveness can vary markedly from culture to culture. For example, the tattooed face of a Danakil female (left) and the many adornments worn by Transvaal-Ndebele women (right) are both deemed beautiful.

RESEARCH HIGHLIGHT

MEASURING A MAN BY THE COMPANY HE KEEPS

While many individuals consider both looks and personality in choosing a date, the emphasis placed on each varies. However, recent research undertaken by Mark Snyder and colleagues (1986) indicates that for men, the difference appears to be largely how concerned they are with the image they project to others.

In this study, the researchers told 39 college men that as part of an investigation on "social interaction" each of them could have a brief coffee date with a female student. Before the date, though, the subjects filled out a questionnaire measuring a trait called *self-monitoring*. Approximately half of the subjects scored high and half low on this trait.

High self-monitors, according to the researchers, are very conscious of the ways others react to them, and they tend to adjust their actions accordingly. Low self-monitors don't seem to know or care much about what others think and usually act in line with their own attitudes or dispositions. ▶

The researchers suggest that in real life, men might have to choose between a physically attractive woman and a woman with a "good" personality. To reproduce this choice, both high and low self-monitors were asked if they would meet a woman student for a date. The men had to choose between "Kristen" — physically unattractive but highly personable, or "Jennifer" — very attractive but not personable. After the students went on their dates, they rated each woman's personality and physical attractiveness.

It was discovered that the subjects did find Jennifer more attractive and Kristen's personality much more desirable. Interestingly, when it came to choosing one, 81 percent of the low self-monitors picked Kristen, while 69 percent of the high self-monitors selected Jennifer.

It was proposed by the investigators that since high self-monitors are more concerned with the self-image they project to others, they are similarly attentive to images conveyed by potential partners with whom they may be associated. In simple terms, they endorse the old adage, "A man is known by the company he keeps." Thus, they prefer externally attractive company as their dates. ▬

The buildup stage enables partners to get to know each other better. Usually, persons tend to associate with others with whom they have something in common (known as **homogamy**). More specifically, homogamy is the filtering agent based on such factors as similar socioeconomic status, race, education, religion, age, and physical appearance. Sociologists maintain that **endogamous** pressures (such as social approval or disapproval) encourage persons to marry within their own social group. In other words, a Catholic marries a Catholic, or a black marries a black. To marry outside of one's particular social group would be an **exogamous** choice; for example, a Catholic might marry a Protestant, or a black might marry a white.

While the foregoing filtering agents are sociological in scope, others are more psychological. A **complementary need**, for example, assumes that individuals seek out mates to complement their own personalities. This filtering agent operates on the premise that the need patterns of the partners will be complementary. A mate is chosen to fill the void of one's own personality. Complementary need also implies that individuals tend to complement personality traits that they lack, but still hold in high regard.

Another filtering agent known as **parental image theory** is Freudian in origin, implying that during childhood a person nurtured a deep affection for the parent of the opposite sex. When mate selection takes place, the individual sees the image of this childhood attachment. The popular cliches, "She's looking for someone with her father's qualities" or "He wants someone like his mother" are applicable in this case. This explanation places mate selection at a level below consciousness.

Two other filtering agents are exchange and role compatibility. **Exchange** means that persons are attracted to those who provide the greatest relational rewards and the fewest number of trade-offs or sacrifices. **Role compatibility** embodies the notion that between two persons there is stability and harmony in role "fit." That is, the set of roles one brings into a relationship, as well as the role expectations one has for the partner, are mutually agreeable.

Continuation Stage

The continuation stage follows a mutual commitment to a long-term relationship. Partners have removed themselves from the interpersonal marketplace and have agreed to restrict their closest intimacies to each other. This stage is characterized by the consolidation of the relationship in a relatively durable midstage, marked by marriage in many couples.

Earlier, the relationship was characterized by the couple's experience of *ambiguity, novelty,* and *arousal.* Here the relationship reflects *familiarity, predictability,* and *the reduction of emotional and cognitive tension.* The more stable a relationship is, the less will be the partners' ambivalence or their self-consciousness.

Theodore Isaac Rubin (1983) adds that trust and openness are essential to the continuation of a healthy relationship. He writes that trust embodies confidence in one's mate, including a realization that a partner will not hurt or manipulate within the relationship. Also characteristic of high levels of trust is the lack of concern about equality, about sharing material goods, services, or responsibilities. Partners simply take what they need spontaneously, knowing that they will not in any way be exploited by a greedy mate. It is characteristic of relationships of low trust that there is preoccupation with sharing equally. In fact, getting a "fair share" or equal share takes precedence over needs and desires.

One characteristic of trust is the presence of *loyalty.* However, it must be understood that loyalty does not in any way imply effacement of self. Indeed, in large part it springs from high self-esteem. Openness mainly involves discussion of the emotionally laden "private" areas of a person's life. This may be very threatening indeed. Openness precludes pretense and the constrictive, censoring effects of affectation and lack of communication. Thus, in openness all the relating selves are tapped, and this serves as a powerful antidote to stultification and boredom.

Beyond this, openness involves nonjudgmental receiving and giving of information, opinions, and the like. Open giving and receiving is perhaps the most potent and important form of human giving. Giving is also a crucial part of receiving, since the privilege of giving is so therapeutic to the person doing the extending. Openness also means being

Companionship and sharing often rest at the foundation of stable and enduring relationships.

in a condition to receive other people's messages, and to respond to them. These messages convey ideas, thoughts, opinions, values and, above all, moods and feelings without pride or prejudice of any kind. When this happens there is no pretense between partners.

Deterioration Stage

There are numerous indications and signs related to couple deterioration. For example, there may be an increase in interference or a reduction in the strength, diversity, and/or frequency of the couple's interconnections, especially those that involve mutual pleasure. Also, deterioration is often accompanied by one or both parties feeling that their relationship's outcome has become unsatisfying, either in regard to outcomes obtainable in alternative relationships or to their own absolute comparison standard.

In general, a series of repeated, incompatible events is necessary for a relationship to begin to deteriorate. For example, a partner's actions, or even his or her mere presence, may interfere with the other's plans to carry out personal plans or activities. Regardless of what triggers the conflict,

APPLICATIONS

HOW TO SURVIVE THE BREAKUP OF A RELATIONSHIP

Separation from an intimate relationship presents an assortment of adjustment problems. Anthony Grasha and David Kirschenbaum (1986) observe that bouts of loneliness, anger towards a former partner, and worrying about "what I did wrong" enter the lives of the separated. Many believe they have been failures as partners and some may even question their ability to engage in future relationships. Many also experience stress originating from the separation itself.

Forming new relationships or strengthening existing ones are important tasks in the aftermath of separation. This is initially difficult to do if the relationship extended itself over a considerable amount of time. Separated parties may not feel like spending time with others; compounding the problem may be the lack of single friends. In spite of such problems, Grasha and Kirschenbaum believe persons can bounce back. They offer the following ideas to help.

First of all, try to follow a role model who has gone through a similar situation. You may know someone you like and respect who has been faced with the task of adjustment. Talk to that person and borrow whatever ideas you find useful. This person may also help to lend objectivity and sensitive guidance to the situation.

Also, seek out a support group. Other people have had similar problems, and the chance to talk to such people is helpful. The lessons others have learned working through a separation may be just what is needed. In most cities, groups are organized to deal with specific problems. Also, many colleges and universities offer courses in interpersonal communications, personal adjustment, and coping skills for daily living. Such courses often give people a chance to share experiences, to work on the issues they face, and, not incidentally, to meet new people.

You also need to stop putting yourself down. When a separation occurs this is a common reaction. It is easy to think the worst about yourself. Many people become depressed, pity themselves, or blame themselves for what has happened. In the long run, however, being overly critical of yourself will get you nowhere.

According to the authors, there are ways to handle personal put-downs. In fact, there are even techniques to counter them, or at least balance the perspective of the situation. For instance, "Joyce broke off our relationship because of my anger" can be countered with "I did get angry but she did, too. Whenever I tried to smooth the waters, she wanted too many things her way." Such thinking may help to bring about a more balanced perspective on **the relationship** itself, rather than perpetuating self-critical thoughts.

a negative cycle of behaviors occur. During this transition, partners experience a loss of trust, enjoyment, and vitality in their relationship.

Termination Stage

The termination stage is marked by the ending of the relationship. At this time, ties to one's partner are severed and emotional and psychological wounds need to heal. In the aftermath of separation, new relationships will be needed to replace old ones.

The emotional impact of the termination stage is highly individual and subject to wide variation. However, an important determinant of the emotional impact of this stage is the degree to which a person's plans and behaviors involved the partner. The disruptiveness of the separation is often determined by the extent of such connections.

LOVE AND INTIMATE RELATIONSHIPS

Love is perhaps the most complex and diverse of all human emotions and the pivotal feature of the intimate relationship. As such, it can be expressed and received in a number of different ways. Love and love relationships are often the central theme of movies, plays, and popular songs. Descriptions, accounts, and narratives of it can be found in virtually all forms of the media, from movies and television to paperback books and supermarket tabloids. The study of love has also produced a flurry of research activity (see, for example, Rubenstein, 1983; Loudin, 1981; Branden, 1981; Money, 1980).

Jim Henslin (1985a) feels that from childhood on we learn the romantic ideal attached to love. From many different agents of socialization, we are taught to expect to "fall in love" at some point in our lives. Moreover, we are taught that that love is the eventual outcome of dating and the appropriate basis for establishing marriage and having children. Because of this programming, we come to expect the experience of love.

Taking a similar stance, Anne Kazak and Dicken

Reppucci (1980) remark that we strive for love, revel in its pleasures, and often lose love. Romantic love is also different from other, more stable forms of love, such as that between brothers and sisters or parents and offspring. The latter is more predictable, much like the climate in a particular area. Romantic love is different, more seasonal than climatic.

Components of Love

The research of Robert Sternberg (1985) indicates that love may feel, subjectively, like a single emotion. However, love consists of a set of feelings, cognitions, and motivations that contribute to communication, sharing, and support. Broken

---

Depictions and narratives of romantic love have abounded throughout history.

down even further, love includes the following components:

- Promoting the welfare of the loved one.
- Experiencing happiness with the loved one.
- Having high regard for the loved one.
- Being able to count on the loved one in times of need.
- Mutually understanding the loved one.
- Sharing oneself and one's things with the loved one.
- Receiving emotional support from the loved one.
- Giving emotional support to the loved one.
- Communicating intimately with the loved one.
- Valuing the loved one in one's own life.

Related to the above, Clifford Swensen (1985) writes that the main content of a love relationship between two adults is *communication,* and the main method for mutual reward is verbal. For a couple who are in love and who plan to marry, love is expressed through mutual statements of love and affection, self-disclosure, interest in each other's activities, encouragement and moral support, and toleration of the less-desirable characteristics of each other. The amount of self-disclosure that furthers the relationship depends upon the degree to which the couple accept themselves and each other.

Love vs. Infatuation

Harold Bessell (1984) maintains that true love and infatuation can feel identical in the early stages. For example, both initially produce strong feelings of pleasurable excitement as well as a strong desire to be with a particular person. However, there is one primary difference — with love, the feelings not only last but can deepen.

Theodore Isaac Rubin (1983) adds that the most significant aspect of infatuation is the lack of caring for the other person as a real person, rather than as an aberrated image. In loving relationships, there is "real" caring about a "real" person. In infatuations, persons project an idealized version of

themselves onto the other and then become infatuated with those idealizations. Individuals also become infatuated with a person on whom they can displace characteristics that impressed them from others in earlier times of their lives. Additionally, a crush may be formed on a person who seems to be a prototype of culturally accepted images, especially with regard to superficialities such as material possessions, notoriety, and looks.

Bessell believes that the more you are with someone and get to know that person, the better able you are to judge the difference between fantasy and reality. Should it be infatuation, time together usually brings fantasies to an end and romance to a halt. If such feelings do not weaken, love is most likely being experienced. The table on the right charts the differences between infatuation and love.

Friendship and Love Compared What differences exist between friendship and love? While we readily distinguish between friends and lovers in everyday life and value each differently, researchers have generally not provided a systematic answer regarding how these two types of relationships differ. Research undertaken by Keith Davis and Michael Todd (1985), though, suggests that certain distinctions can be made.

Let's begin with friendships. Beyond the fact that two people participate in a relationship as equals, friendships envelop the following characteristics:

- *Enjoyment* Friends enjoy each other's company most of the time, although there may be temporary states of anger, disappointment or mutual annoyance.
- *Acceptance* Friends accept one another as they are, without trying to change or make the other into a new or different person.
- *Trust* Friends share mutual trust in the sense that each assumes that the other will act in light of his or her friend's best interest.
- *Respect* Friends respect each other in the sense of assuming that each exercises good judgment in making life choices.
- *Mutual Assistance* Friends are inclined to assist and support one another, and, specifi-

Differences between Infatuation and Romantic Love

Infatuation	Romantic Love
Based on limited time and real association	Lasts more than three or four months, usually indefinitely
A fantasy trip based on your wishes	Reality—based on genuine attraction and long-continuing satisfaction with the companionship of this person
The sexual interest weakens	The sexual interest persists
Real and frequent contact breaks the spell	Real and frequent contact reinforces the "chemical" attraction whether you like, trust, and respect the person or not
When the relationship ends it is over forever, and you feel enlightened, relieved	The attraction of the other person's personality usually lasts indefinitely, whether or not you like, trust, or respect this person
The desire for association ends, a case of "mistaken identity"	The desire for association remains indefinitely
Strong emotion triggered by wish-fulfilling fantasy	Strong emotion as a normal positive biopsychological sense of excitement that is an intrinsic response not based upon or continued by fantasy
Almost always starts immediately, and ends soon	Though often starts immediately, sometimes it grows and blossoms with more frequent contact
Feelings die	Feelings persist

Adapted from Bessell, 1984.

cally, they can count on each other in times of need, trouble, and personal distress.

- **Confiding** Friends share experiences and feelings with each other. ("He tells me things that no one else knows about him.")

- **Understanding** Friends have a sense of what is important to each and why the friend does what he or she does. In such cases, friends are not routinely puzzled or mystified by each other's behavior.

- **Spontaneity** Each feels free to be himself or herself in the relationship rather than feeling required to play a role, wear a mask, or inhibit revealing personal traits.

All of these characteristics of friendships also apply to love relationships. However, the researchers found that two additional broad categories can be identified: *passion* and *caring* clusters. The passion cluster consists of the following:

- **Fascination** Lovers tend to pay attention to the other person even when they should be involved in other activities. They are preoccupied with the other person and tend to think about, look at, want to talk to, or merely be with the other. A person worthy of this kind of attention is worthy of devotion. In this regard, fascination provides one basis for idealizing the other, a phenomenon so often noted in romantic love.

- **Exclusiveness** Lovers have a special relationship that precludes having the same relationship with a third party. Thus, a romantic love relationship is given priority over other relationships in one's life.

- **Sexual Desire** Lovers want physical intimacy with the partner, wanting to touch and be touched and to engage in sexual intercourse. They may not always act on the desire, even when both members of the couple share it, since it may be overriden by moral, religious, or practical considerations.

The caring cluster, on the other hand, has two components: "giving the upmost" and "being a champion/advocate":

- **Giving the Utmost** Lovers care enough to give the utmost when the other is in need, sometimes to the point of extreme sacrifice.

- **Being a Champion/Advocate** The depth of lovers' caring shows up also in an active championing of each other's interests and in a positive attempt to make sure that the partner succeeds. Figure 3-2 shows the passion and caring cluster of love and how it can be compared to friendship.

Davis and Todd tested their models of love and friendship against the experiences and expectations of approximately 250 college students and community members, both single and married. They discovered, as expected, that the typical best friendship shared many characteristics with spouse/lover relationships. For example, levels of trust, respect, and acceptance were almost identical. Also, levels of understanding, mutual assistance, and spontaneity were very similar. And, as expected, the passion cluster differentiated lovers and spouses from best friends. Levels of fascination and exclusiveness were much higher among lovers and spouses (see Figure 3-3).

Three unexpected findings also appeared. First, it was expected that lovers and spouses would be more willing than best friends to give the utmost when needed and be an advocate of the other's interests. However, only the "giving to the utmost" scale showed the anticipated difference. Also, the difference between lovers/spouses and best friends was much smaller than in the case of the passion cluster.

The second unexpected finding came in the area of enjoying each other's company. Subjects were asked to respond to the statement, "I enjoy doing things with (name of lover or best friend) more than doing them with others." It was discovered that lovers were more likely than friends to endorse this statement. According to the researchers, this finding may reflect the greater range of human needs that can be satisfied in the typical love relationship.

The third unexpected finding was that best friendships were viewed as more stable than love relationships. The lower levels of stability may reflect a greater concern about the possibility of the relationship breaking up, especially among the unmarried lovers.

FIGURE 3-2   Love Is Friendship plus the "Passion Cluster" and the "Caring Cluster"

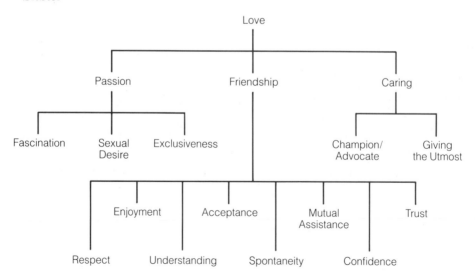

Source: Davis, K. E. (1985). Near and dear: Friendship and love compared. *Psychology Today,* (February), pp. 22–30.

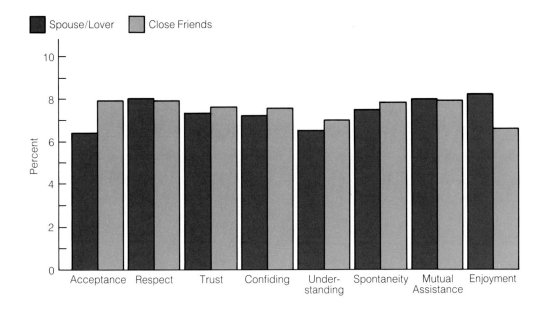

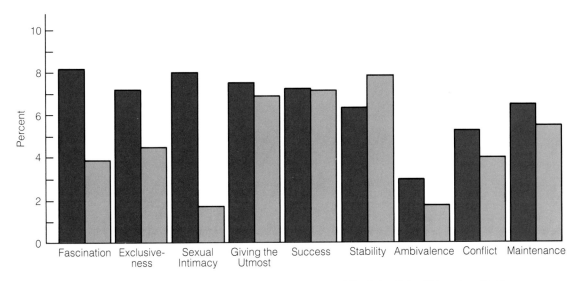

Source: Davis, K. E. (1985). Near and dear: Friendship and love compared. *Psychology Today*, (February), pp. 22–30.

FIGURE 3-3   Close Friends and Spouses/Lovers Compared for Various Traits and Behaviors

GRAPH YOUR OWN STYLE OF LOVING

Consider each characteristic as it applies to a current relationship that you define as love, or to a previous one if that is more applicable. For each, note whether the trait is *almost always* true (AA), *usually* true (U), *rarely* true (R), or *almost never* true (AN).

#	Characteristic	Eros	Ludus	Storge	Mania	Ludic Eros	Storgic Eros	Storgic Ludus	Pragma
1	You consider your childhood less happy than the average of peers	R		AN	U				
2	You were discontent with life (work, etc.) at time your encounter began	R		AN	U	R			
3	You have never been in love before this relationship					U	R	AN	R
4	You want to be in love or have love as security	R	AN		AA		AN	AN	U
5	You have a clearly defined ideal image of your desired partner	AA	AN	AN	AN	U	AN	R	AA
6	You felt a strong gut attraction to your beloved on the first encounter	AA	R	AN	R		AN		
7	You are preoccupied with thoughts about the beloved	AA	AN	AN	AA		R		
8	You believe your partner's interest is at least as great as yours		U	R	AN		R	U	
9	You are eager to see your beloved almost every day this was true from the beginning	AA	AN	R	AA		R	AN	R
10	You soon believed this could become a permanent relationship	AA	AN	R	AN	R	AA	AN	U
11	You see "warning signs" of trouble but ignore them	R	R		AA		AN	R	R
12	You deliberately restrain frequency of contact with partner	AN	AA	R	R	R	R	U	
13	You restrict discussion of your feelings with beloved	R	AA	U	U	R		U	U
14	You restrict display of your feelings with beloved	R	AA	R	U	R		U	U
15	You discuss future plans with beloved	AA	R	R				AN	AA
16	You discuss wide range of topics, experiences with partner	AA	R				U	R	AA
17	You try to control relationship but feel you've lost control	AN	AN	AN	AA	AN	AN		
18	You lose ability to be first to terminate relationship	AN	AN		AA	R	U	R	R

#	Characteristic	Eros	Ludus	Storge	Mania	Ludic Eros	Storgic Ludus	Storgic Eros	Pragma
19	You try to force beloved to show more feeling, commitment	AN	AN		AA			AN	R
20	You analyze the relationship; weigh it in your mind			AN	U		R	R	AA
21	You believe in the sincerity of your partner	AA				U	R	U	AA
22	You blame partner for difficulties of your relationship	R	U		R	U	R	AN	
23	You are jealous and possessive but not to the point of angry conflict	U	AN		R		R	AN	
24	You are jealous to the point of conflict, scenes, threats, etc.	AN	AN	AN	AA	R	AN	AN	AN
25	Tactile, sensual contact is very important to you	AA			AN		U	AN	R
26	Sexual intimacy was achieved early, rapidly in the relationship	AA			AN	AN	U	R	U
27	You take the quality of sexual rapport as a test of love	AA	U		AN	U	AN	U	R
28	You are willing to work out sex problems, improve technique	U	R		R	U		R	U
29	You have a continued high rate of sex, tactile contact throughout the relationship	U			R	R	U	R	R
30	You declare your love first, well ahead of partner		AN	R	AA		AA		
31	You consider love life your most important activity, even essential	AA	AN	R	AA		AA	R	R
32	You are prepared to "give all for love once under way"	U	AN	U	AA	R	AA	R	R
33	You are willing to suffer abuse, even ridicule from partner		AN	R	AA			R	AN
34	Your relationship is marked by frequent differences of opinion, anxiety	R	AA	R	AA	R	R		R
35	The relationship ends with lasting bitterness, trauma for you	AN	R	R	AA	R	AN	R	R

To diagnose your style of love, look for patterns across characteristics. If you consider your childhood less happy than that of your friends, were discontent with life when you fell in love, and very much want to be in love, you have "symptoms" that are rarely typical of eros and almost never true of storge, but which do suggest mania. Where a trait did not especially apply to a type of love, the space in that column is blank. Storge, for instance, is not the *presence* of many symptoms of love, but precisely their absence: it is cool, abiding affection rather than *Sturm und Drang*.

From J. A. Lee (1974). "The styles of love." Reprinted with permission from *Psychology Today Magazine*. Copyright © 1974 by the American Psychological Association.

Styles of Loving

As we indicated at the outset, there are many different ways to experience and express love. Eastwood Atwater (1986) reinforces this by saying some people plunge into new relationships with emotional intensity; others prefer to let love grow on a gradual basis. And, while some readily put their feelings into words, still others prefer to demonstrate their affection in deeds.

In an effort to distinguish its many forms, a number of categories of love have been constructed. These include **ludus**, **pragma**, **mania**, **eros**, **storge**, and **agape**.

Ludus   Derived from the word *ludicrous,* this type of love is playful and often self-centered and sexually permissive. Ludic lovers do not want long-range attachments from their partners. Most also do not want their partners to be dependent on them. Ludic love has often been described as playful love, a style that regards love as a game.

Pragma   Pragma comes from the Greek word *pragmatikos,* meaning practical and realistic. Pragma love is characterized by sensibleness and logic. Pragma lovers are realistic when they approach a potential partner and seek to match themselves with someone whose background is compatible with their own.

Mania   Manic love is intense and obsessive. Many manic lovers are overwhelmed by thoughts of their partners, so much so that they're always in a state of anxiety. They need continual affection and attention.

Eros   Eros is a style of love characterized by intense romance and the idealization of the partner. Often love is instant and partners are preoccupied with pleasing the other. Sexual intimacy is also strongly desired.

Storge   Storge (pronounced "stor-gay") is Greek in origin and means affectionate love. In its broadest sense, this type of love embodies companionship and the enjoyment of doing things together. Intense emotional involvement is usually avoided.

Agape   Agape is also Greek in origin and represents altruistic love. Agape lovers care deeply about their partners and seek to satisfy their well-being in a warm and kind fashion. This gentle style of loving also asks nothing in return.

TROUBLED RELATIONSHIPS: DATE RAPE

Date, or acquaintance, rape is a relatively recent topic of investigation. It concerns itself with the physical force used by a dating partner to have sexual intercourse. Karen Barrett (1984) reports that date rape, like wife-battering and other forms of assault against women, is a widespread phenomenon. It may also be the most unreported type of female sexual violation.

Because it is often unreported, it is difficult to ascertain how many women are victims of date rape. One source (Seligman, 1984), though, estimates that date rape accounts for approximately 60 percent of all reported rapes. Most date rape victims are between the ages of 15 and 25.

Another study (Lane and Gwartney-Gibbs, 1985) indicates that violence of a sexual and physical nature within the context of dating has dramatically increased in recent years. Based on their survey of college students, females reported using a wider array of violence than males—for example, they slapped, kicked, bit, or punched, or else threw some object at their partners. More male students, however, used more extreme forms of violence (such as beating up their partners), inflicted violence more frequently on their partners (and on more partners), and inflicted sexual aggression more frequently, than female students. Students from high-income families, whites, and those "living together" also reported more violence than did others.

According to Kenneth Jones and associates (1985), there are many reasons why women do not report date rapes. For instance, women may not regard such incidents as rape, believing that unwanted sex is the chance they take when dating. They may not want to report someone who is part

Physical assaults against women, including date rape, are increasing in contemporary society.

high level of force, was not threatened with a dangerous weapon, or was not seriously injured — she is less likely to see herself as a true victim, and is therefore less likely to report to the police. Of all the factors which influence a victim's decision to report, the most important appears to be the kind of relationship that exists between the victim and the rapist. Usually, a close relationship results in a less violent assault, which in turn means less likelihood of injury and medical treatment. Thus, women who are raped by a date or someone they know are more likely not to have the evidence which allows them to see themselves as true victims of a violent crime (Williams, 1984).

Similar to other types of rape, women who have been sexually violated within the dating context face a difficult recovery process. While few rape victims actually die as a result of the attack, most victims perceive the rape as a life-threatening experience. All victims find it acutely stressful, frightening, and humiliating, and afterwards typically express deep-seated fears of death. The crisis of rape upsets the victim's life physically, emotionally, socially, and sexually: in order to readapt to her environment and regain some sense of emotional equilibrium, she must work through the crisis of the sexual assault. Such working through becomes, in effect, a mourning process. As with the death of a loved one, the rape victim has lost a part of herself — albeit a psychological part — and the same unconscious process essentially operates. This is further complicated by concomitant mourning on the part of significant others in the victim's life, who may intrude and sometimes interfere with the victim's necessary mourning. Frequently there is blaming of or alienation from the victim by significant others as an unconscious manifestation of their own and separate mourning experiences (Matek and Kerstein, 1985).

of their own peer group or social set. Some feel that reporting such an incident is not worth the time and embarrassment. Also, there are those young women who may not want their parents to know that they allowed themselves to get into such a position. Finally, some may feel that they were perhaps responsible for what took place.

Females are more likely to report rape to the police if the circumstances of the rape correspond to the classic rape situation (that is, violent attack by a stranger). This is often because the classic rape provides the victim with the evidence she needs to convince both herself and others that she was indeed a true rape victim. Should this evidence be lacking — if she did not experience a

CHAPTER HIGHLIGHTS

Because of heightened levels of maturity, dating during the adulthood years is characterized by greater levels of mutuality and reciprocity. Gener-

APPLICATIONS

RECOGNIZING THE DANGER SIGNALS OF RAPE

Signs that a troubled relationship is about to erupt in sexual violence often go unheeded. According to Helen Benedict (1985) there are several ways to recognize the potential for physical abuse in a man. The key to a nonabusive relationship is an equal balance of love and respect between partners. The types of behavior listed below show a lack of both, even if they don't mean that the man is definitely going to end up beating or raping you. They are signs to be wary of.

- Has he ever forced sex on you? If a man has raped you or forced sexual acts on you in any way in the past, he'll almost certainly do it again. He has shown himself to be a man who doesn't care about your needs and desires, only about his. He won't improve.

- Does he seem to especially like sex when you don't? If so, then he's a potential rapist.

- Does he want you to perform sex acts you don't like? Is he particularly fond of bondage or violence in sex? His tastes won't change as your relationship progresses, so get out of it before his preferences turn to rape or torture.

- Has he ever threatened you with violence? If during a fight, he has threatened to hit you, beat you, or rape you, he'll probably actually do it one day. If he has ever raised a fist to you but not actually hit you, the same applies.

- Does he like to end fights by having sex, even if you are not in the mood? This tactic is not his way of making up, it's his way of winning the fight — he has made you give in to him.

- Is he overpossessive and extremely jealous? Someone who is obsessed by you is probably not stable. It may be flattering to be needed so much, but obsessive need is almost always unhealthy. Overpossessiveness can flare up into wild, groundless jealousy and from there develop quickly into violence.

- Does he have temper tantrums? There are appropriate and inappropriate ways to express anger. If he is angry at someone or something else but is in the habit of taking it out on you anyway, be warned. He is using you as a dumping ground for his fury. If he throws glasses or furniture around, beware. Someone with such little control over himself can be dangerous.

- Are you ever afraid of him? If so, then ask yourself what this means for your future together.

- Does he bully you? Is he able to compromise over your differences, or does he always insist on having things his way? If he won't compromise, take it as a sign of his lack of maturity and his lack of respect for you.

- Has he been violent toward previous wives or girlfriends? If you know he has — and he will probably try to hide it — there is little hope that he'll improve in his relationship with you.

- Does he drink too much and get violent when he's drunk? Drinking is frequently associated with domestic violence, and a drunk person is virtually impossible to reason with. He may drink in order to abuse you.   ▶

- Does he attack people physically? It is one thing to fight back in self-defense, but if a man is prone to losing his temper and suddenly lashing out at someone, he is not to be trusted. Even if you don't think he has hurt women — just other men — the potential is there. Again, he shows that he has an immature level of control over his temper.

- Has he ever hit or beaten you? Many women believe that once a man has made a commitment to them, he will change and treat them with more respect. This is not true. If he has hit you before, he will most likely hit you again.

- Does he want to control your money? This is a serious factor, because the person who controls the money usually controls the relationship. It is traditional for the man to "own" the money, even if the woman earns it, but for the sake of your self-respect and safety, this is a tradition worth changing.

- How do his parents behave? Take a look at his parents if you can, and see if they are abusive to each other. How does his father treat his mother? Is his mother subdued and dominated by her husband and son? Are the parents even together anymore? If not, what is the history of their separation? Also, look at how they communicate. If the parents don't get through to each other, the son probably won't know how to communicate either, and a relationship with him is likely to be difficult.

- Does he like violent pornography? This may be a sign that he will want to act out some of these scenes with you.

ally speaking, maturity refers to a state that promotes physical and psychological well-being. This chapter explored the many sides of maturity, including the research of Gordon Allport. Allport contends that maturity consists of seven important dimensions: (1) extension of the self; (2) relating warmly to others; (3) emotional security; (4) realistic perception; (5) possession of skills and competences; (6) knowledge of the self; and (7) establishing a unifying philosophy of life.

An intimate relationship involves the mutual exchange of experiences in such a way that a further understanding of oneself and one's partner is achieved. Intimacy embodies self-disclosure, the process by which individuals let themselves be known by others. Numerous forms of self-disclosure exist, such as through verbal means, body language, tone of voice, or by one's actions.

We also explored some of the components of intimate relationships: knowledge of oneself and one's partner, mutuality, interdependence, trust, commitment, and caring. And we examined bar-

riers to intimate relationships. Such barriers included possible rejection of one's self-concept, discovering that one's partner is not interested in having an intimate relationship, finding that information is used by one's partner to gain power or control of the relationship, betrayal of information to others, and inequity originating from a lack of equivalent input into the relationship.

George Levinger's model of relationship transitions embraces relatively broad, often diffuse changes over time. These changes in relationship properties emerge from a couple's personal, environmental, and relational causal conditions. The acquaintance, buildup, continuation, deterioration, and termination stages represent the transitions of a relationship. Against the backdrop of these stages, we examined the filtering agents that serve to narrow the field of potential partners: propinquity, physical attraction, homogamy, endogamous and exogamous factors, complementary needs, parental image theory, exchange, and role compatibility.

Love consists of a set of feelings, cognitions, and motivations that contribute to communication, sharing, and support. As we discovered, love is quite different from infatuation, and we found that close friendship and love also have similarities and differences. Different styles of love can exist: ludus, pragma, mania, eros, storge, and agape.

Date rape is the physical force exercised by a dating partner to have sexual intercourse. It is estimated that date rape accounts for about 60 percent of all reported rapes, and most victims are between the ages of 15 and 25. Date rape may also represent the most unreported type of female sexual violation.

KEY TERMS

agape love
complementary needs
date rape
endogamy
eros love
exchange theory
exogamy
filtering agent

homogamy
intimacy
intimate relationship
love
ludus love
manic love
maturity
parental image theory

pragma love
propinquity
role compatibility
self-actualization
self-disclosure
storge love

RECOMMENDED READINGS

Branden, N. (1981). *The psychology of romantic love.* New York: Bantam Books. A look at what love is, why it exists, why it sometimes grows, and why it sometimes dies.

Burns, D. D. (1985). *Intimate connections.* New York: Signet. A problem-solving approach to breaking out of loneliness and establishing intimate relations with others.

Cargan, L. (Ed.). (1985). *Marriage and family: Coping with change.* Belmont, CA: Wadsworth. The manner in which intimacy develops is explored in Chapter 5 of this book of readings.

Crosby, J. (Ed.). (1985). *Reply to myth: Perspectives of intimacy.* New York: Wiley. A wide assortment of perspectives are used to shatter myths related to intimate relationships.

Derlega, V. J. (Ed.). (1984). *Communication, intimacy, and close relationships.* New York: Academic Press. Among the topics are self-disclosure and intimate relationships, human motives and personal relationships, and the dangers of intimacy.

Fisher, M., and Dticker, G. (Eds.). (1982). *Intimacy.* New York: Plenum Press. A broad range of ideas about intimacy are presented, including theoretical concerns and matters of a technical nature.

Henslin, J. M. (Ed.). (1985). *Marriage and family in a changing society* (2nd ed.). New York: The Free Press. Sections five and six of this reader offer coverage of romantic involvements and dating.

Kelly, H. H. (Ed.). (1985). *Close relationships.* New York: W. H. Freeman. An excellent addition to the field and a valuable reference book for students of marriage and family. Includes many topics related to love and commitment.

Loudin, J. (1981). *The hoax of romance.* Englewood Cliffs, NJ: Prentice-Hall. An examination of the origins of romantic traditions and the manner in which ancient customs may adversely affect relationships today.

Murstein, B. (1986). *Paths to marriage.* Beverly Hills, CA: Sage. This noted scholar explores many facets of dating, from attraction and courtship to love and ultimate mate selection.

4

Sex-Roles and Relationships

CONTENTS

CONTEMPLATIONS

■ Want to take a little quiz on differences that exist between the sexes? Okay, answer true or false to the following statements:

1. During the first three to four months of prenatal life, there is no way that we can distinguish the sexual differences of males and females.
2. Biology, more than society or culture, is responsible for creating sex-typical behaviors.
3. Females, more so than males, tend to downplay intimate self-disclosure and the emotional closeness of a relationship.
4. Children rarely understand the sex-role stereotypes they see portrayed on television.

Want the answers? You'll discover them in the pages that follow.

■ Are males generally more physically active and more aggressive than females? Are females more emotional? Are males more independent than females? We hear so much about sex-role stereotypes today. But how much of what we hear is true? Where do these stereotypes originate and who accepts or rejects them? On a more personal note, are you guilty of clinging to sex-role stereotypes? You'll find out by the time you're done with this chapter.

■ Boys will be boys and girls will be girls. While a person is born male or female, the teaching of masculinity and femininity begins at surprisingly early ages. In this chapter, we'll discover that the societal agents responsible for sex-role transmission are numerous and diverse, from parents and siblings to teachers and the media. Have you ever wondered where your sex-role behaviors came from? You'll learn the answers in this chapter, and chances are you'll pause and reflect back on your own sex-role development while you read.

■ If you have ever been involved in a close relationship, past or present, this chapter is for you. We say that because we're going to examine close relationships and the impact that sex-role behaviors have on them. We're going to spend some time on how males and females tend to differ within the couple arrangement—how each falls in love, communicates, resolves conflicts, and so on. We'll also compare and contrast traditional sex-role relationships with liberated and balanced ones. As far as advantages to the latter are concerned, this chapter should give you some food for thought.

Say hello to Paul Jennings. Paul is a college junior, and, according to his father, he's a "chip off the old block." He's the star of the university football team, majoring in physical education. He's big, strong, and rugged—and has been for his entire life. Beyond the football field and his schoolwork, Paul has been known to enjoy an active social life. While he has a quick temper with fists to match, he also has the reputation of being a "lady's man." Although he doesn't talk openly about it, he confesses that some day he wants to find the "right" woman, someone who'll "settle him down" and turn him into a "family man."

We'd also like you to meet Donna Bradshaw, a junior at Paul's school. Donna is short, blond, and petite. Her friends call her sweet and innocent, but she has been known to sometimes whine to "get her way." She is extremely popular on campus and her friends often turn to her for advice and understanding when the need arises. She is warm and supportive and has the uncanny knack, with her sensitivity, of making others feel immediately at ease.

It was during their senior year that Paul and Donna met and they immediately became attracted to one another. They dated throughout the year and, after graduation, Paul and Donna got married. Fifteen years and two children later, old college chums say that married life has done little to change either one of them. Donna is an ideal mother and is supportive to the needs of her husband, standing loyally by his side as he carves out his career. Paul takes pride in the fact that at home he is "king of the castle" and that he tends to all of the family's economic needs. His occasional rowdiness as a college student has been replaced with coaching his eight-year-old son's Pee-wee football team. He likes to think that his little one is a "chip off the old block . . ."

SEX-ROLES AND SEX-ROLE DEVELOPMENT

While all of this may sound like an afternoon soap opera, our purpose in sharing it is to explore the nature of **sex-roles**, those attitudes and behaviors felt to be appropriate to males and females. **Sex-role development** is the process of socialization whereby such behaviors are acquired over time. As can be seen in the preceding passages, both of our characters have acquired their own unique sex-roles, be it Paul's physical aggressiveness and independence, or Donna's warmth and supportive nature.

In the last chapter, we explored the nature of intimate relationships, particularly how they form

and change over time. Now we want to examine the course of sex-role development and how it shapes the behavior of individuals within relationships. As we will learn, sex-role behaviors and expectations have numerous implications for relationships, be it within the realm of friendship, marriage, parenthood, or sex.

The study of sex-roles is an extremely important area of exploration because sex-roles permeate all areas of life, as we just observed with Paul and Donna. As Judy Long (1984) sees it, sex-role scripts prescribe "sex-appropriate" dress and bodily posture as well as emotional reactions, occupational choices as well as marital choices, and a myriad of expectations regarding who gets the

Sex-appropriate gestures and behaviors are evident in many facets of everyday life.

check in a restaurant and who gets the responsibility for the care of elderly parents.

Sandra Cirese (1985) adds that sex-roles are not only expected, but encouraged. This encouragement occurs during childhood and adolescence so that by adulthood, individuals are prepared to do what males *ought* to do and what females *ought* to do. Cirese offers the following elaboration regarding sex-roles and their development:

■ *Sex-roles are assigned; individuals don't choose them.* As soon as it is seen that we are either male or female, the cultural machinery goes into operation to teach appropriate behavior. We learn what is expected of us as boys or girls and, ideally, behave accordingly. Then, persons learn what is expected of them as men or women and again, ideally, behave accordingly. Sex-roles interact with other assigned roles, such as age roles.

■ *Sex-roles represent patterns of activity.* They comprise our behavioral responses to masculine or feminine expectations. Sex-role behavior embodies the characteristics of male and female images. Women, for example, take care of kids, wait for doors to be opened, and shave their legs; men support their families, open doors for women, and shave their faces. Sex-role behavior includes such subtle activities as posture, tone of voice, and ways of expressing concern for others.

■ *Sex-roles, similar to other roles, are often played in relation to other, complementary, roles.* A man acts as he believes a woman expects him to act in a particular situation — or at least he feels he should act that way. A woman does the same. Thus, sex-roles often reinforce each other, as do husbands and wives, mothers and children, doctors and patients.

■ *Sex-roles are defined by society, by the people among whom one lives and whose cultural traditions one shares.* An agreement exists, vague as it sometimes is, about the proper fit between role and image, activity and quality. Rebellion against this agreement is as predictable (but not as prevalent) as conformity to it. Whether it is more "masculine" to work in a steelmill or to stay home and knit cannot be established without reference to culture.

Now that sex-roles and sex-role development have been defined and explored, let's examine some other key terminology. **Sexual identity** refers to the biological differences that exist between males and females. **Gender identity** is the psychological awareness of being either a male or a female. It is generally accepted that gender identity occurs by age three.

One other term also needs to be understood: sex-role stereotype. A **sex-role stereotype** is a generalization of masculine and feminine characteristics and behaviors. An important dimension of sex-role stereotypes is that they reflect *expected* behaviors or characteristics, but these are not necessarily *desired* by males and females. Sex-role stereotypes represent oversimplified opinions or observations, such as all girls are emotional and dependent while all boys are aggressive and competent. Sex-role stereotypes abound in our society and, in this chapter, we will explore their impact on overall sex-role development.

RESEARCH HIGHLIGHT

FEMALES, MALES, AND SEX DIFFERENCES: SORTING FACT AND FICTION

Boys will be boys, and girls will be girls. Think about how often we hear reference to sex-role stereotypes, whether in reference to children or adults. Are any of these stereotypes founded in fact? For that matter, what about sex differ- ▶

ences in general? Are differences between the sexes inevitable in all walks of life? To find out, Susan Basow (1980) surveyed the literature and summarized the sex differences that exist within a number of developmental areas. Her findings included the following:

Cognitive

Learning and memory: No difference.
Intelligence: No difference in level of intelligence.
Verbal: Females tend to excel up to age 3 and after 11.
Quantitative: Males tend to excel after age 12.
Visual-spatial: Males tend to excel after age 8.
Analytic: No difference.
Concept mastery: No difference.
Cognitive style: Differences are unclear.
Creativity: No difference with nonverbal material; females tend to excel with verbal material.

Personality and Temperament

Self-description: Females are more people-oriented: males are more achievement-oriented.
Emotionality: No difference during childhood.
Fears: The evidence is contradictory; females report more fears.

Social Behavior (Communication Patterns)

Verbal: Males dominate.
Nonverbal: Males dominate; females may be more sensitive to cues.

Person-centered Interactions

Dependency: No difference depending on the definition used.
Affiliation: No difference during childhood. After adolescence, females tend to be more interested in people.
Empathy: No differences depending on experience and the person.
Nurturance: No difference depending on experience.
Altruism: No difference depending on the situation and the person.

Power-centered Interactions

Aggression: Males tend to be more aggressive after age 2.
Assertiveness: Differences are unclear; depends on the situation and the person.
Dominance: Differences are unclear; males may be more dominant depending on the situation.

▶

> Competition and cooperation: Differences are unclear, males may be more dominant depending on the situation.
>
> Compliance: No difference depending on the situation and the person from whom compliance is required.
>
> **Sexual Behavior**
>
> Response: No difference; females are capable of multiple orgasms.
>
> Interest: Males express more and have more experiences. Meaning of sex may be different for males and females.
>
> Response to erotica: No difference.
>
> Homosexuality: Reported more in males.
>
> Masturbation: Reported more in males.   ▬

EXPLORING MALE AND FEMALE SEX DIFFERENCES

At this point in our discussion, we'd like to explore the differences that exist between males and females. First, we'll spend some time examining biological distinctions between the two, including how chromosomes and hormones create physiological differences. Then, we'll show how the socialization process influences sex-role development and forges a person's sense of masculinity or femininity.

BIOLOGICAL SEXUAL DEVELOPMENT

Chromosomes

The most fundamental difference that exists between males and females lies in the nucleus of the human cell. Inside the nucleus are **chromosomes** —thin, rodlike structures that contain the directions for the cell's activity. Chromosomes occur in pairs which vary in number according to species. Human beings have 23 pairs of chromosomes per cell, or 46 chromosomes altogether.

Only two types of cells exist in organisms: somatic cells and sex or germ cells. The term *soma* means *body;* thus the approximately one trillion cells found in the human body, with the exception of the sex cells, are **somatic cells**. Chromosomes located in somatic cells contain genes that dictate many facets of development, such as hair and eye color.

The **sex** or **germ cells**, though, are the cells which govern reproduction and account for the biological uniqueness between male and female. If we were to line up the 46 chromosomes of the human female somatic or germ cell in two columns, each containing 23 chromosomes, we would observe that all 23 are in pairs; they are identical in appearance and they have the same function (for example, to determine eye color). The twenty-third set of chromosomes is sometimes called the sex chromosomes, for it determines the sex of the child (see Figure 4-1). In the female's cells, the twenty-third pair consists of two X chromosomes. However, when we look at the chromosomes in a male, the first 22 are pairs, but in position 23, we can easily see that it is not a pair at all—it is a mismatch. One chromosome is shaped like an X, the other like a Y.

Throughout history, many a queen lost her throne (or even her life) for not giving birth to a male heir. Note, however, that it is not the female but the male who determines the sex of the child. For the female the egg always—and only— contains an X chromosome. The male, however,

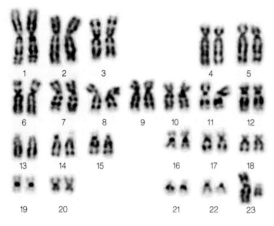

FIGURE 4-1   Human Chromosomes Grouped into 23 Pairs

can contribute a sperm cell that has either the X or the Y. If the X-carrying sperm penetrates the egg, the offspring will be a girl; if it is a Y, a boy will be conceived (see Figure 4-2).

FIGURE 4-2   How Sex Is Determined

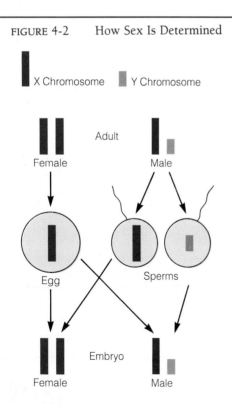

Hormones and Prenatal Sexual Differentiation

We've established the fact that there are genetic differences between males and females. However, during the first three or four weeks of prenatal life, there is no way to tell males and females apart. This is because those tissues that create sexual differentiation have not yet developed. Figure 4-3 illustrates how the **gonads** (sex glands) appear for males and females at this time.

By the fifth week of prenatal life, though, tissues begin forming that will differentiate the two sexes. More specifically, changes will be made in male and female genital ducts, gonads, and external genitals. Should the Y chromosome be present, the gonads will develop into testes. Once the testes develop, the organism will create hormones and direct the remainder of sexual differentiation. **Hormones** are internal secretions of the endocrine glands that are distributed by the bloodstream. The absence of testes enables the reproductive features of the female to develop.

However, the development of male and female sex organs is a bit more complicated than this. To understand the total process, we must examine some more complex developments during fetal life. The testes secrete **testosterone**, the major male hormone. Testosterone enables a group of cells called the **Wolffian ducts** to further differentiate male and female internal sex organs. However, also present at this time are **Mullerian ducts**, which have the potential of developing the female reproductive structure. To prevent this, the testes produce a **Mullerian inhibiting hormone**. The

FIGURE 4-3   Gonads at First Month of Prenatal Development

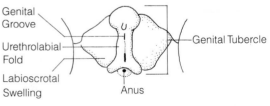

Male and Female Identical

SEX CHROMOSOME ABNORMALITIES

Sometimes, the union between the female egg and the male sperm does not result in the normal quota of 46 chromosomes, including the two sex cells (XX or XY). It is possible that one egg could have an extra chromosome, one less, or other combinations. When this happens, abnormalities typically result. The following are some of the more widely-known sex chromosome abnormalities:

Klinefelter's Syndrome (XXY)
These males have two normal X chromosomes plus the Y chromosome. They have small, external male sex organs but the general body contour of a female, including enlarged breasts. Those affected are sterile and often below average in intelligence. Older women more frequently give birth to males having this condition than do younger women.

Turner's Syndrome (XO)
This monosomic condition (only one sex chromosome) results in a female who looks somewhat normal at birth, but clinical signs appear at puberty. Physical characteristics include a webbed neck, short fingers (polydactylism), and short stature. No secondary sex characteristics appear at the time of puberty and those afflicted with this syndrome are sterile.

Triple X Syndrome
This syndrome affects females, many of whom are virtually normal physically except for menstrual irregularities and premature menopause. However, mental retardation is also common. Females possessing three, four and five X's have also been found. Usually the higher the number of sex chromosomes, the greater the level of retardation.

The XYY Syndrome
This syndrome, sometimes called the *Aggressive Syndrome* or the *Crime Syndrome,* was popularized by the news media when cases arose such as that of Richard Speck, who brutally killed eight nurses in Chicago in the 1970s. Persons carrying the XYY's (and sometimes XXYY) are generally taller than average (over 6'0") males, have personality disorders and below average intelligence. Sexual disturbances are common, as well as antisocial and occasionally violent behavior appearing early in life. As youngsters, those affected with this syndrome tend to be unmanageable, destructive, defiant, and fearless.

combination of both testosterone and the Mullerian inhibiting hormone enables male sexual organs to develop. The absence of the two enables the Mullerian ducts to develop into female sex organs (see Figure 4-4).

Just as we saw with genetic abnormalities, there can be hormonal errors that affect the course of sexual development. For example, **hermaphrodites** have both ovarian and testicular tissue and are the result of hormonal imbalances during pre-

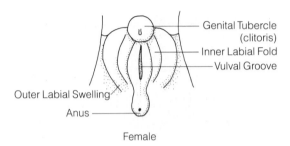

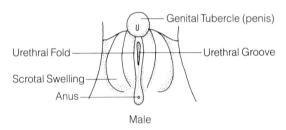

FIGURE 4-4   Gonads between Second and Third Month of Prenatal Development

natal development. One variation of this abnormality is having a penis as well as a vaginal opening. Another example of a hormonal accident are **pseudohermaphrodites**. Here, individuals have either ovaries or testes (not both), but their external genitals are characteristic of the opposite sex. An example of this is the **testicular feminizing syndrome**, a genetic male who has the external genitals of a female. Like hermaphrodites, this hormonal condition has its beginnings during prenatal development.

Hormones, Puberty, and Sexual Maturation

During the teenage years, at a stage called **puberty**, hormones exert a profound influence on the course of sexual development. Puberty marks a time when individuals become sexually mature and capable of reproduction.

Developing during puberty are primary as well as secondary sex characteristics. **Primary sex characteristics** are physiological features related to the sex organs. For males, these organs include the penis and the testes; and for females they are the ovaries, uterus, clitoris, and vagina. **Secondary sex characteristics** are not directly related to the sexual organs but nevertheless serve to distinguish a mature male from a mature female. Examples of secondary sex characteristics are the development of a beard in males and breasts in females. The gradual maturation of the primary and secondary sex characteristics signifies the end of childhood and the onset of reproductive maturity.

As we indicated, it is fairly well understood that the bodily changes associated with puberty are the result of hormones. Prior to puberty the part of the brain known as the **hypothalamus** stimulates the pituitary gland. The **pituitary gland**, often called the "master gland" because of its central role in the coordination of the endocrine system, then stimulates other glands (see Figure 4-5).

Puberty begins when the pituitary gland secretes increased amounts of the **human growth hormone** (somatotrophic hormone), which causes a rapid increase in body development, thus signaling the onset of a rapid growth spurt in the trunk, arms, and legs. Along with this growth spurt is the development of increased amounts of thyroxin and adrenalin to match the increase in cells or total body weight.

Gonadotrophins are also released by the pituitary gland. These hormones stimulate the testes and ovaries, which in turn secrete their own sex hormones. The male sex hormone, you'll recall, is called *testosterone,* while the female has hormones named **estrogen** and **progesterone**.

Cells within the testes secrete testosterone, which directs the development of the genital organs, pubic hair, and other features of sexual development. Estrogen is secreted by the follicles of the ovaries and controls, among other phases of growth, the development of the uterus, vagina, and breasts. Progesterone aids in the development of the uterine wall, particularly its preparation for implantation of a developing ovum and in placental development after implantation has taken place. Progesterone is also thought to be influential in breast development during pregnancy.

High levels of sex hormones in the bloodstream

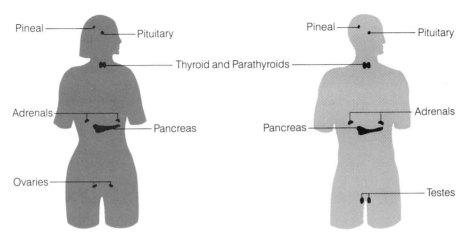

FIGURE 4-5   Location of Endocrine Glands in the Female and Male

are largely responsible for terminating puberty. Once a particular phase of physical or sexual development is complete these high levels of sex hormones signal the hypothalamus. The hypothalamus, in turn, ceases the further production of a given hormone (Doering, 1980; Higham, 1980).

Putting Biological Influences into Perspective

In light of the above material, and in reference to what's ahead, we must say that one's gender at birth does not automatically dictate future gender

---

SOME BIOLOGICAL DIFFERENCES BETWEEN THE SEXES

Average Male and Female Measurements

Males: The average male is five feet, nine inches tall and weighs 162 pounds. His chest measures thirty-eight and three-quarters inches; his waist is thirty-one and three-quarters inches.

Females: The average woman is five feet, three inches tall and weighs 135 pounds. Her bust is thirty-five and one-half inches; her waist is twenty-nine and one-quarter inches; and her hips are thirty-eight inches.

Blood, Amount of

Males: Men have about one gallon of blood.

Females: Women have approximately four-fifths of a gallon of blood.

Blood Pressure, Average Reading of

Males: The average blood pressure for a male is 140/88.

Females: The average reading for a female is 130/80.   ▶

Body Temperature

The average temperature of a man is slightly higher than that of a woman. It peaks at midday in both sexes.

Bones

The bones of a man are stronger, heavier, and larger than those of a woman. His shoulders are also broader, and his pelvic bone is narrower.

Brain, Blood Supply to

Women have a better blood supply to the brain than men do because of a more effective cardiovascular system.

Fat, Total

Males: Fifteen percent of a man's body is composed of fat.
Females: Twenty-seven percent of a woman's body is made up of fat.

Hearing

Males: On the average, men lose some hearing earlier than women do.
Females: Women can hear better than men but are less tolerant of loud noises and repetitive sounds. Sensitivity to sound persists throughout life for women.

Red Blood Cells, Average Number of

Males: A man has an average of 5 million red blood cells per cubic millimeter of blood.
Females: A woman has about 4.5 million red blood cells per cubic millimeter of blood.

Skull

A woman's skull is thinner than a man's, and smaller at the base, but greater in circumference at the crown.

Adapted from Stump, 1985.   ■

behavior. Other forces are in operation that shape, and sometimes even overshadow, one's biological disposition.

But this does not mean that physiological differences are unimportant. On the contrary, researchers exploring the complexities of genetics and the influence of the endocrine system on behavior are supplying sociologists with much "food for thought." For example, we've already seen in this chapter that a chromosomal abnormality (XYY) increases the risk of violent behavior and aggressiveness in males. Related to this, there is some speculation that among the lower animal species, the male hormone testosterone influences aggressive behavior and that the female hormone prolactin, secreted during pregnancy, stimulates protective and nurturing behavior among mothers.

Also, we are learning that the brain organization of males and females appears to be different, providing us with another possibile biological influence on behavior. Obviously, both males and females receive the same brain at birth, anatomically speaking. However, it seems that the sexes *process* information differently. Females, for example, excel in verbal skills while males have an advantage in visual-spatial reasoning. The nature of such differences, as well as their implications, is currently a "hotbed" for research activity (see Springer and Deutsch, 1985, for a review of the literature).

All of this suggests that we can't discount the impact of biology on differences between the sexes. However, sociologists turn to the impact of society to more adequately explain the process of sex-role development. While biological differences separate the two sexes, it is largely society and culture that mold one's sense of masculinity and femininity (Cargan, 1985).

SOCIALIZATION AND SEX-ROLE DEVELOPMENT

In the minds of many, such as James Henslin (1985b), the impact of society is much more influential than biology in creating sex differences. Henslin maintains that the sex-roles transmitted by society pervade our daily interactions. In some cases, such as dating, our sex is highly relevant to the interaction. However, in most situations in life, our sex is probably irrelevant to what we are doing, as, for example, being a student, a mechanic, or a checkout clerk in a supermarket. Yet others react to us as a male or female student, mechanic, or checkout clerk, and we ourselves fulfill such specific roles within the broader context of our sex-roles. Thus, we never stop being masculine or feminine, even when we are doing something that, in and of itself, is neither masculine nor feminine.

One's culture, too, affects the course of sex-role development. Our society and culture is competitive, hierarchal, and achievement-oriented, mea-

suring success in terms of power, prestige, and the accumulation of material wealth. Within America's present social framework, conventional masculinity embraces certain qualities: independence, competitiveness, aggression, leadership, task-orientation, courage, confidence, and self-control, among others. Conventional femininity in America, on the other hand, contains other qualities: dependency, passivity, fragility, nonaggression, sensitivity, nurturance, and noncompetitiveness (Bardwick and Douvan, 1980).

But what is characteristic of our culture may not be illustrative of others. For example, consider the observations of Margaret Mead (1950) in relation to three primitive New Guinea tribes. She reports that in one, the Arapesh, both men and women behaved in feminine fashions, at least as defined by our culture; among another, the Mundugumer tribe, both women and men revealed masculine traits; and, in the Tchambuli tribe, women were independent, dominant and managerial, while the men were emotional and dependent. Research such as this amplifies the point we're making: individuals receive their sexual identity at birth, but it is more apt to be one's society and culture that determines the course of sex-role development.

Theories of Sex-Role Development

Different theories have been proposed to explain how sex-roles develop throughout life. **Social learning theory** examines how boys and girls imitate sex-typed behavior displayed by parents and others in their surroundings. Also important is that children are rewarded and punished for certain sex-role behaviors. For example, girls are reinforced for engaging in feminine activities and not being aggressive, while boys receive encouragement for being the aggressors and participating in more physically oriented activities.

Cognitive-developmental theory postulates that sex-role development emerges through the child's growing cognitive awareness of his or her sexual identity. Early in life boys and girls become consciously aware of the fact that specific roles, activities, and behaviors are appropriate for their

CROSS-CULTURAL FOCUS

CULTURE, SEX-ROLES, AND FEMALE INEQUALITY

Sandra Cirese (1985) tells us that every society divides its tasks and specifies who does them on the basis of gender. This means that in every society, certain traits and roles are proper for females, and others for males. Most societies assign men more public and aggressive roles while women assume the domestic and nurturing duties. Another cultural universal is a difference in the status accorded males and females: women everywhere have a lower status than men. Men, on the other hand, are socially dominant.

But this does not mean that women in different cultures accept these conventional sex-roles. Indeed, in our society, Ronald Hardert (1984) and his colleagues remind us that the women's liberation movement repeatedly asserts how such traditional expectations work against, rather than for, human interest. Feminists have asserted their refusal to be treated as second-class citizens and instead want to be redefined on the basis of realities, not conventional stereotypes.

Despite the fact that growing numbers of women are entering the labor force and launching themselves in new directions, many are frequently confined to low-status occupations. Women continue to be discriminated against and remain a minority in professional and skilled careers, especially in managerial positions. The majority of women today work in office settings handling clerical chores while the more prestigious vocations are dominated by men. Compared to the white-collar, executive world of males, females are often relegated to the pink-collar world of the office secretary. Beyond significant pay differentials between men and women, such job placements also succeed in perpetuating unfair stereotypes of working women.

Women in our society are not alone. In fact, we can turn to both developed and undeveloped nations and find unique parallels to such unfair treatment and sex-role stereotypes. For example, consider the Larim women of East Africa. Because cattle are the economic base of pastoral societies in this region, it is often felt that men are the main breadwinners of such societies. Women are relegated to an inferior position. However, it may well be that by virtue of the cultivation of sorghum, millet, sesame, groundnuts, and vegetables, women provide much of the sustenance for Larim. A man's status, of which beer drinking is an important part, is contingent on his wife's provision of the beverage. In addition, women have responsibilities toward cattle and goats inasmuch as they tend to the calves and kids when they are in the village. All of this takes place as men, perceived as the heads of the households with responsibilities as breadwinners, a Western concept, are accorded the cash crops, the new breed cattle and aid. Thus, a type of inequality within the primitive culture of Larim is just as blatant as that which exists in modern-day workplaces (Langton, 1984).

Also, we can turn our attention to the Agta Negritos women of northeastern Luzon in the Philippines. In the minds of many, the work of these women is ▶

relatively unimportant and clearly lower in status than that of the male. However, fairly recent research (Estioko-Griffin and Griffin, 1981) indicates that Agta women are major contributors to the day-to-day subsistence of their families, and have a great deal of authority in decision-making in the family and in residential groups. Also, and in contradiction to one of the most fiercely held tenets of anthropology, women in one area often hunt game animals. They also fish in the rivers with men and barter with lowland Filipinos for goods and services. Thus, in their own unique culture and way, Agta women are doing that which their Western counterparts are also accomplishing. That is, they are clearly demonstrating their capability of doing those chores once thought to be the exclusive domain of the male. What they encounter, however, is the discrimination and inequality that faces women in all too many corners of the world. ■

own sex. As cognitive development increases, children are better able to understand and sort out these roles and behaviors. Awareness of sexual identity leads to natural identification with the same-sex parent, the adult typifying the sexual role the child has come to mentally recognize.

Identification theory proposes that sex-role development is the result of close interaction and emulation of one's parents. *Identification* is the manner in which parental behaviors serve as models for a child. Proposed by Sigmund Freud, this theory emphasizes how a boy assumes his fa-

Numerous theories have been proposed to explain early sex-role development, including children's play activities.

ther's sex-typed behaviors because of the *Oedipus complex*—the boy's romantic attachment to his mother. The attributes of the father are perceived as being those which captured the love of the mother, and are thus emulated by the boy. For girls, the *Electra complex* creates a similar situation, although in this case it is the daughter's romantic attachment to her father and imitation of her mother's behaviors.

In addition to the Oedipus and Electra complexes, Freud offered one other perspective on identification. That is, children develop strong emotional attachment and dependence on nurturant parents. The closeness offered by such parents leads to childhood identification and emulation.

The Transmission of Sex-Role Behaviors

Sex-role development has its beginnings early in life and originates from a variety of different sources. Among the more influential sources are parents, peers, early play behaviors, teachers and schools, and the media. Let's examine each of these a bit more closely and trace how it is that children learn sex-role behaviors.

Parents   From the very beginning, parents exert a significant influence on child's sex-role development. Should traditional sex-role stereotypes prevail, boys and girls receive differential treatment. Females are usually taught to be affectionate, gentle, and quiet, while males are often instructed to be aggressive, independent, and active. In time, boys will be taught that being employed and providing economic support to the family will be their primary adult tasks. Females are taught to engage in domestic activities, have babies, and handle most of the responsibilities associated with childrearing. Parents succeed in teaching many sex-typed standards through their own behaviors. Mothers are usually more nurturant and emotional, while fathers are traditionally more dominant, competitive, and unemotional (Plomin and Foch, 1981; Honig, 1983; Scanzoni and Fox, 1980).

RESEARCH HIGHLIGHT

INFANT CLOTHING: SEX LABELING FOR STRANGERS

Parents often remark that it is not important if strangers can tell at a glance if their infant is a boy or a girl. However, research conducted by Madeline Shakin and associates (1985) indicates that it is a rare infant whose clothes do not proclaim its sex. Indeed, the study involving 24 infant girls and 24 infant boys and their parents revealed that infant clothing is one more mechanism that separates the worlds of boys and girls.

The researchers found that almost no parent spontaneously admitted selecting baby clothes on the basis of masculinity or femininity. Virtually all insisted that "durability" was the chief criterion for purchase. Some commented on the unavailability of "neutral" baby clothes, although researchers found many either-sex garments on the market. Nevertheless, most dressed their babies in colors and styles that announced the wearer's sex and surrounded them with accessories that advertised gender.

Seventy-five percent of the girls in the study wore pink; most of the others, yellow or white. Blue was seldom seen on girls; red even more rarely. Seventy-nine percent of the boys were dressed in blue; red was the runner-up color.   ▶

The color of carriage pillows, blankets, rattles and pacifiers also tipped-off passersby to the baby's sex in the few cases where clothing did not reveal it. Ruffles on girls' socks, puffed sleeves, or ribbons informed onlookers that the occupant was a girl even when lack of hair or a neutral color outfit left sex in question. One person correctly identified a baby as feminine because her pacifier was pink, although she was wearing a red and blue outfit.

Strangers correctly identified the babies' sex 87.5 percent of the time and most were obviously dependent on external cues. Since the infants ranged from 1 month to 13 months old, passersby needed all the help they could get. The study was carried out in a shopping mall.

Why parents were so reluctant to admit that they picked baby clothes and accessories according to their child's sex is uncertain. Whether the parents in the study were unconscious of their strong labeling of their infants or felt some pressure to respond in a manner that would seem socially acceptable in these "liberal" days was not very clear to the researchers. They concluded that both of these explanations would seem to account for some of the conflict between the expressed lack of concern for labeling and the evidence of sex-typed clothing. ■

In regard to this latter point, the verbal behaviors of parents when interacting with children also contain unique sex differences. For example, Barry McLaughlin and associates (1983) recorded the speech of parents as they interacted with their children during free play situations. Mothers tended to provide more linguistic support for their children, tuning their language to the youngster's needs. Fathers were less sensitive to the child's linguistic abilities. Instead, they put more demands on their children during the play situations and, in so doing, raised performance levels. These findings are similar to those discovered in other studies. In one, (Bright and Stockdale, 1984), fathers were found to offer more demands and control to their children in structured play sessions. Mothers played a less active and demanding role.

One other study (Bellinger and Gleason, 1982) explored the differences in directives given by mothers and fathers to their children, ages two and one-half to five years old. The children engaged separately with each parent in a construction task. It was found that fathers produced more directives than mothers and tended to phrase them as commands ("Put the screw in") or as highly indirect "hints" ("The wheel's going to fall off") more often than mothers. Mothers had a tendency to rely more on relatively transparent indirect forms ("Can you put the screw in?"). There were no differences in the form of the directives addressed to girls and boys, nor were there any cross-sex effects. The authors concluded that parental *modeling*, rather than differential socialization of girls and boys, appears to be the mechanism by which children learn to request action in sex-associated ways.

Over time, there are several important variables related to parents and the transmission of sex-role stereotypes. It appears that fathers, more so than mothers, are concerned about transmitting appropriate sex-role behaviors to their offspring. Moreover, fathers usually take active steps to discourage cross-sex behavior in their children. As far as other findings related to parents are concerned, nontraditional rather than traditional parents are likely to rear children who resist sex-role stereotyping and are more flexible in their overall views of masculinity and femininity (Langlois and Down, 1980; Zuckerman and Sayre, 1982).

The imitation of parental behaviors contributes to sex-role learning.

WHAT TRADITIONAL PARENTS TELL BOYS AND GIRLS

What verbal messages and advice do parents give that encourage traditional sex-role behaviors? How do they encourage boys to become husbands and providers while encouraging girls to be wives and mothers? How is it that boys are raised to be *self*-oriented and girls to be *other*-oriented? Marjorie Hansen Shaevitz (1984) maintains that the parental messages boys and girls receive throughout their upbringing provide many of the answers. Consider the messages imparted to each:

For Boys:

"Be strong!"
"Don't be helpful; someone might get an edge on you."
"Argue, swear, show tension; it will keep the other guy on guard."
"Be competitive, even combative; nice guys never win."
"Take care of yourself; don't think the other guy is going to take care of you!"
"Figure out what you want and go after it."
"Don't do it if someone else can do it for you."

▶

For Girls:

"Be nice!"

"Be helpful; above all, don't be selfish."

"Help people feel good about themselves."

"Don't show tension — relieve it."

"Be collaborative, not competitive."

"Be warm, loving, nurturing."

"Be compliant, accepting, understanding."

"Don't say no; it's not nice."

"Don't bother people; if you want something, do it or get it yourself."

■

Play Behaviors   Another factor promoting sex-role development during the early years is playtime activity. Very often, stereotypes abound with children's toys and play behaviors. Females are frequently given dolls or engage in playing house, while males often indulge in aggressive games, are given masculine toys such as guns and trucks, and avoid "sissy" play activities. Female play behavior is usually more dependent, quieter, and less exploratory. Males often become preoccupied while playing with toys that require more gross motor activity, and are more vigorous and independent. Such sex-typed play behavior for both sexes is also frequently supported and reinforced by parents (DiPietro, 1981; Fagot and Kronsberg, 1982; Muller and Goldberg, 1980).

Consistent with our earlier point, fathers in particular seem to be more vocal about the selection of sex-appropriate toys and play behaviors. Further pressure to engage in sex-typed play emerges from the peer group, an increasingly important source of social approval and reinforcement (Pitcher and Schultz, 1983; Maccoby, 1980; Langlois and Downs, 1980; Lamb, Easterbrooks, and Holden, 1980).

An interesting aspect of sex-typed play is that boys seem to be more aware of sex differences than girls and avoid playing with objects that might be labeled feminine or "sissy." Girls, however, seem to be willing to engage in male-oriented activities. Although both sexes congregate in sex-typed play groups, boys seem to hold more rigid, stereotyped beliefs than girls (DiPietro, 1981; Fagot and Kronsberg, 1982).

There is some evidence that the traditional classification of "masculine" and "feminine" forms of

play may be changing. Society's attempt to promote a more unisexual definition of the sexes may be reducing the gap between male and female activities. Although girls still engage in "feminine" play, they now also enjoy types previously cast as "masculine," such as track and field competition, basketball, golf, and softball.

Girls are more involved in organized sports activities than ever before. Schools are enlarging their programs and encouraging females to participate more actively and more competitively. Furthermore, success in sports and the accompanying social prestige no longer appear to be the exclusive domain of the male (Murphy, 1983).

Peers   Peers also influence the course of sex-role development. As children experience greater amounts of socialization, they usually learn more about sex-role standards and behaviors from the peer group. Often, the failure to adhere to such expectations represents grounds for peer group rejection. The reinforcement of sex-appropriate behaviors from within the peer group also helps to explain the early sex-typed differences apparent in children's play (Lamb, Easterbrooks, and Holden, 1980; Harris and Satter, 1981; Reis and Wright, 1982).

During the preschool years children start to prefer same-sex peer groups. Close friends share the same interests. This will persist and even intensify throughout the years of middle childhood, although it is more pronounced in males than females (Fu and Leach, 1980; Reis and Wright, 1982). Often, opposite-sex play-groups openly torment one another, further solidifying gender boundaries. As Evelyn Pitcher and Lynn Schultz (1983) observe, when boys taunt and tease girls, the stage is set for the cat calls and whistles that will appear in the future.

Adolescence heralds the escalation of heterosexual development for most. Yet, while the sexes intermingle, sex differences persist, particularly in regard to friendships. The most striking of these is the emotional intimacy apparent in female friendships. Females tend to have more intimate and exclusive friendships than males. Moreover, the

Sex-role learning during adolescence is shaped by peer group relationships.

closer the female's friendships develop, the more intimate the amounts of self-disclosure will become. This is often true regardless of whether females are interacting with the same or opposite sex. Males, on the other hand, tend to downplay intimate self-disclosure and the emotional closeness of a relationship. Rather, their emphasis is on such elements as engagement in common activities (Berndt, 1982; Dickens and Perlman, 1981; Wheeler, Reis, and Nezlek, 1983).

The notion that there are sex differences in the intimacy of self-disclosure within friendships has received considerable research attention. In one study (Grigsby and Weatherley, 1983), female and male adolescents were involved in a deception which led them to believe that they were sharing self-disclosure with a stranger of the same sex whom they could later meet. The recorded comments revealed clear-cut gender differences in the tendency to self-disclose. Females were clearly more likely to disclose intimate information about themselves during the acquaintanceship process.

In regard to sex differences and amounts of self-disclosure, we should also acknowledge the viewpoints of Sharon Brehm (1985). She writes that *both* males and females need the same qualities in their interactions in order to avoid loneliness. Males usually desire emotional intimacy just as much as females. Unfortunately, it is difficult for them to disclose that need and achieve interpersonal comfort and acceptance with their partners.

There are other differences in regard to female and male friendships. For example, Thomas Berndt (1982) observes that females more so than males, *expect* the sharing of thoughts and feelings from their partners. Females are also more sensitive about rejection from friends. Carol Gilligan (1982) adds that females are also likely to be more selective and exclusive about their friendships. This may be because once they've found a friend, females are more apt to invest their emotional resources and offer a strong psychological commitment to their partner. The commitment from males is often not as great and shows more of an objective and rational nature.

Finally, there appear to be sex differences in regard to communication styles. Listening behavior, in particular, has been examined. In one study (Booth-Gutterfield, 1984), attention was focused on how the socialization process affects sex differences in listening. The authors contend that as boys and girls grow up, they are taught and reinforced in different styles of listening. The primary contrast appears in *task vs. interpersonal understanding*—that is, males are taught to listen for facts, and females are taught to listen for the mood of the communication. Males often encounter trouble listening for nonverbal cues, while females, who are listening for the mood of the communication, pick up on nonverbal cues much more readily. Later on in this chapter, we will more fully explore all of these sex differences and their impact on close relationships.

Teachers and Schools   Teachers also contribute to sex-role development. As significant others in the child's life, the behaviors and attitudes displayed by teachers are considered influential. Some may deliberately, others unwittingly, contribute to sex-role stereotypes. For example, George Morrison (1984) points out that some teachers may reinforce stereotypes taught at home or on the playground. This means that within the classroom, girls can water the plants but not empty the wastebaskets. They may also be rewarded only when they are passive, well-behaved, and well-mannered. Boys, on the other hand, may be reinforced for being assertive and asking questions, and are encouraged to use trucks, racing cars, and other physically oriented toys during play periods.

Teachers and schools exert other influences in later grades. Kevin Ryan and James Cooper (1980) tell us that some teachers may perpetuate stereotypes by advising students that certain professions are appropriate for women and not for men, and vice versa. Often, a school's curriculum may stamp a course as being masculine or feminine, such as requiring a course in home economics for females and automobile mechanics for males. In regard to the latter point, though, many of the nation's schools have removed the sex-based exclusivity attached to such courses. Indeed, some strongly

CROSS-CULTURAL FOCUS

ARE SEX DIFFERENCES IN CHILDREN'S FRIENDSHIPS UNIVERSAL?

Finding a friend to share meaningful experiences with ranks as one of life's greatest treasures. Cherished friends are important for young as well as old, and regardless of culture, friendships add a valuable dimension to the realm of human interaction. In this respect, friendships are a universal phenomenon.

For a moment, though, let's compare the sex differences apparent in the friendships of children from the United States with those in other cultures. To do this, we can turn to several representative investigations. One study (Tietjen, 1982) of 72 second and third graders from Sweden revealed that males had contact with larger groups of friends than females. Females, however, spent more time in close-knit friendship dyads and with their families. With age, there was a movement toward fewer and more intensive friendships with schoolmates, although the latter was more true for females. This was accompanied by gradual movement away from family members. Youngsters in father-absent homes had more limited peer networks than children from intact families. However, the former spent less time with their families.

Another study (Sharabany, et al., 1985) examined the nature of Israeli children's friendships and uncovered similar parallels to American children. In this investigation, males and females from fifth, seventh, ninth, and eleventh grades were studied. The youngsters were asked to rate their friendships with a same- or opposite-sex best friend.

These researchers discovered that a significant age difference in overall intimacy with same-sex friends existed. Spontaneity, sensitivity, attachment, and sharing were among the factors that changed with age; loyalty and trust, as well as taking and imposing, did not. Opposite-sex friendship revealed a significant increase with age. Males and females did not differ in reported opposite-sex friendship in the fifth and seventh grades, whereas females in the ninth and eleventh grades reported higher intimacy than did males. This sex-by-age pattern of interaction was especially apparent for attachment and for the dimensions of trust and loyalty. As with American youngsters, females were higher in sharing, giving, and sensitivity.

recommend that students enroll in a mixture of such courses.

Lucille Lindberg and Rita Swedlow (1985) emphasize the importance of teachers in downplaying sex-role stereotyping. From earliest schooling to the end of formal education, children and adolescents need to receive instruction in an objective and sexually unbiased fashion. To reach such a goal, teacher behaviors need to be carefully examined and the curriculum objectively assessed.

The Media   One other model for sex-role development is the media, particularly television. Television very often promotes sex-role stereotyping in its overall programming. Males are often portrayed as leaders, while females are cast as pas-

Teachers are often responsible for transmitting sexually appropriate behaviors to students in both subtle and direct ways.

sive, submissive, and defenseless characters. Also, males usually outnumber female cast members; indeed, many programs actually lack a regular female character. Similar types of sex typing and disproportion are evident in television commer-

cials as well (Downs, 1981; Feldstein and Feldstein, 1982; Williams, LaRose, and Frost, 1981).

We might consider several studies in support of these facts. In one research investigation of television (Stewart, 1983), 551 major speaking characters in 191 programs were examined. Males clearly outnumbered females in all program types. When family themes were portrayed, most males were employed in white-collar jobs while women were typically full-time housewives. In another investigation of older persons portrayed on television (Cassata, Anderson, and Skill, 1983), males outnumbered females in professional or managerial positions by a ratio of four to one. Females accounted for 100 percent of homemaker, service, or clerical positions.

How do children in the midst of their sex-role development perceive such stereotyped portrayals? Do they understand the sex-role stereotypes seen on television? Apparently so, at least according to one fairly recent investigation (Durkin, 1984). In this study, 17 children aged four and one-half and nine and one-half years were interviewed individually and asked to discuss features of a series of highly stereotyped male and female behaviors shown on television. The children displayed considerable knowledge of sex-role conventions and revealed a clear ability to relate this knowledge to their accounts of the excerpts presented. So we see that children are able to infer feelings and motives appropriately and offer plausible accounts of portrayed stereotypes by using their existent sex-role knowledge.

RESEARCH HIGHLIGHT

AND THE BEAT GOES ON . . . SEX-ROLE STEREOTYPING IN MUSICAL LYRICS

Today, music is delivered to us from an endless array of electronic gadgetry, from boom boxes and walkmans to sophisticated stereos and laser disks. Because of the pervasiveness of popular music among both young and old alike, it has long served as a socializing agent in the lives of its audience. But only recently have we begun to explore more carefully the sex-role portrayals in popular music.   ▶

Research reveals that popular music portrays men and women in unique ways. This was borne out in a study (Hyden and McCandless, 1983) that focused on the roles of men and women as portrayed in the lyrics of 110 popular songs. Overall 72 (68 percent) of the songs were sung by males, while 27 (26 percent) were sung by females. Of the 72 songs sung by males, 38 (53 percent) were descriptive of males and 29 (39 percent) were descriptive of females. Women, however, sang about men as often as they sang about women.

Interestingly, while men were pictured as possessing both masculine and feminine characteristics, women largely conformed to traditional stereotypic feminine attributes. While loving, faithful, and gentle are all stereotypic feminine characteristics, they were used frequently to describe men. Women were most frequently described as being young, childlike, and passive. Thus, it seems that while lyrics break down some barriers attached to sex-role stereotypes, they are guilty of promoting others. ■

Finally, let's acknowledge the role that children's literature plays in the transmission of early sex-role behaviors. Similar to other trends we've uncovered in this section, sex-role stereotyping is quite evident within the pages of children's books. Girls are often portrayed as passive and domestic, while boys are more active and adventurous. Boys also outnumber the females portrayed in many stories. Stereotyping also exists when certain careers are cast as exclusively masculine or feminine. In relation to all of this, Evelyn Pitcher and colleagues (1984) remark that all too often books portray "ferocious" daddy tigers and "gentle" mommy pussycats, and books about cars, trucks, and trains show only men at the wheels.

There is a growing movement to eliminate sex stereotyping in children's books, especially male chauvinism frequently manifested in character portrayals and language. Attempts to make books nonsexist may take several forms. Women may be portrayed as more confident and independent, and they may have occupations traditionally reserved for males. Removing females from the household and placing them in the world of nature, business, science fiction, or other male-dominated domains helps to remove sex stereotyping. Removing some of the stereotyping of males also helps to make books nonsexist. Instead of portraying males as cool, competent, fearless, and some-

times insensitive, more books are making an effort to show that boys can be sensitive, loving, and emotional. Some stories show that there are boys who do not fit the stereotype of the competent "superior" male, who is in control of every situation and every emotion.

What will be the outcome of efforts to remove stereotyping from children's literature? There are indications that nonsexist literature can change children's stereotyped images of the sexes. However, because sexist attitudes are woven through the whole fabric of society, we can hardly expect that books alone will produce children who are unbiased and unstereotyped in their attitudes. Also, while nonsexist books are important, many persons feel that literary quality should not be sacrificed to meet this need. Thus, a good novel should not be attacked because it has no female characters. Few people would suggest rewriting the classics or historical fiction, or discarding them altogether.

Contemporary Influences on Sex-Role Behaviors

Combined, the above factors serve to transmit sex-role behaviors to children in a mixture of subtle and direct ways. The result is that children learn to behave in sexually appropriate fashions within

APPLICATIONS

WHAT ARE LITTLE GIRLS MADE OF? SUPPLYING CHILDREN WITH ACCURATE ANSWERS

Sex-role stereotyping in children's literature begins very early for youngsters. Consider some of the rhymes that await children in Mother Goose tales alone: "What are little girls made of?" "Georgie Porgie . . . kissed the girls and made them cry." "Bobbie Shattoe went to sea . . . he'll come back and marry me." "Bye-baby-bunting, father's gone a-hunting." Even Jill comes tumbling down the hill *after* Jack.

In an effort to remove stereotyping in children's literature, a number of books stress sex-role equality. The following are representative of these books and may prove useful to adults wishing to teach children such lessons:

Author and Title	Age
Berenstain, S. & Berenstain, J. *He Bear, She Bear*	3–6
Delton J. *Two Good Friends*	3–6
Delton, J. *Rabbit Finds A Way*	4–6
Gaeddert, L. A. *Noisy Nancy Norris*	4–6
Goldreich, G. and Goldreich, E. *Who Can She Be? A Musician*	5–7
Gordon, S. *Girls are Girls and Boys are Boys*	5–7
Jacques, F. *Tilly's House*	5–7
Klein, N. *Girls Can Be Anything*	3–6
Krasilovsky, P. *The Man Who Didn't Wash Dishes*	4–6
Lasker, J. *Mothers Can Do Anything*	3–8
Lystod, M. *Jennifer Takes Over*	4–8
Merriam, E. *Boys and Girls, Girls and Boys*	4–8
Merriam, E. *Mommies at Work*	3–5

Adapted from Pitcher, Feinburg, and Alexander, 1984.

the framework of their society. Furthermore, these sex-typed behaviors become more deeply rooted as children mature (See Tavris and Wade, 1984; Fu and Leach, 1980; Basow, 1980; Harris and Satter, 1981).

Before leaving this topic, let us remind the reader that some rigid sex-role standards seem to be diminishing. Consider that there are adults sharing roles previously labeled as solely "feminine" or "masculine." Several factors account for this turnabout. The similarity of educational experiences that many males and females receive dur-

ing their early schooling, and the fact that males today engage in more "feminine" chores around the house (for example, cleaning or doing the dishes) are contributing factors. Females are also employed outside of the home more frequently, sometimes in jobs previously held down by males (and vice versa). Finally, more fathers are taking active roles in childrearing, a factor that may help to reduce traditional sex-role typing in the household. How all of this affects children is currently under the scrutiny of researchers.

Such role reversals are welcomed with open

RESEARCH HIGHLIGHT

CHILDREN, VOCATIONS, AND SEX-ROLE DEVELOPMENT

School-age children are usually able to perceive sex-roles in much the same way that adults do. Many also know which stereotyped occupations go with which sex, although this may not be as rigid as it once was. Indeed, one study (Archer, 1984) shows how role reversals occurring at home and in the labor force have influenced the perceptions of children. This was borne out when kindergarten, fifth grade, and eleventh grade children were given a questionnaire listing 44 adult occupations and activities. The children were asked to indicate (for each occupation) who they thought should be doing the job: male, female, or either one. The subjects were also asked to relate their own future career aspirations.

While the younger subjects were more sex-typed in their perceptions, liberality (conceptualized as the number of "either" responses) increased with age. In addition, a significant gender variance with kindergarten children existed — the females were more liberal than the males, although this was not apparent in the other grade levels. Females cited as many different potential adult occupations for themselves as did the males. Males and females also tended to select careers conventionally deemed suitable to their own sex, with some tendency for females to name traditional male occupations as well. Studies such as this show that stereotypes surrounding certain occupational roles seem to be diminishing.

arms by those concerned with society's sex-role stereotypes. Some have proposed that rigid standards of masculinity and femininity may be maladaptive to both child and adult, since they do not allow the full expression of one's personality. As Sarah Cirese (1985) sees it, sex-role stereotypes strip people of their individuality and pose awesome barriers to intimacy and genuine relationships between males and females.

To help overcome sex-role stereotyping, a concept known as **androgyny** has emerged. In addition to the previously mentioned sharing of roles and chores, this concept suggests that both male and female personality traits are beneficial and important to possess. Androgynous persons view themselves as human beings, not typecast males or females. Because of this, personality traits are not compartmentalized by sex. Both males and females are encouraged to be nurturant, assertive, sensitive, dominant, affectionate, and self-sufficient, to cite but a few examples.

Research suggests that the androgynous personality has many positive character traits. Compared to persons with traditional sex-role behaviors, androgynous individuals seem more competent and demonstrate higher levels of self-esteem. In addition, androgynous persons seem to deal more effectively with their surroundings. They are also more secure with themselves, more flexible in their behavior, and less anxious (Wiggins and Holzmuller, 1981).

Without question, the concept of androgyny is controversial (see, for example, Blitchington, 1984; Baumrind, 1982). There is also evidence (for example, Werner and LaRussa, 1985) that many sex-role behaviors and stereotypes in existence for years refuse to budge. However, proponents of androgyny maintain that the removal of sex-typed behavioral constraints would allow males and females to demonstrate the best qualities of both sexes. Children, especially, would benefit from a more tolerant acceptance of their

Androgynous couples swap chores as well as share them.

SEX-ROLE DEVELOPMENT AND RELATIONSHIPS

The Costs of Conditioning

Should traditional sex-role development occur, a male-female relationship follows a fairly predictable pattern. In fact, Herb Goldberg (1983) goes so far as to label it as a relationship between a machine and a child. The male is viewed as fearing intimacy and loss of control, while the female is seen as having a great capacity to commit herself, to love, and to be intimate. The more accurately he approximates the masculine ideal, the more machine-like the man is in his behavior and consciousness of himself and his life. The more closely she resembles the feminine ideal, the more child-like the female becomes psychologically. The relationship between the two produces guilt and hopelessness in the male, and feelings of rage, helplessness, and victimization in the female.

From the perspective of their conditioning, then, it is unlikely that either male or female has the capacity for genuine intimacy. His "fear" of it and her "desire" for it are both distortions based on their gender conditioning and expectations. He fears losing control by getting close because he is subconsciously aware that he will be engulfed by her needs and the pressure to perform and take care of her, and will feel guilty if he fails. What are the consequences of such relationships? Both males and females have expectations — of themselves and each other — that are psychologically impossible to meet, and that therefore give rise to a sense of failure and personal inadequacy. Because of the perpetuation of relationship myths men and women alike are haunted by the feeling that something is wrong with them, when actually failure is built into the basis and structure of these relationships. Those that survive it or, seemingly, succeed in it do so largely by denying and submerging their inner experience in obedience to their roles. A rare few find genuine and mutual satisfaction, because they have managed to free themselves from the defensive strictures of masculine and feminine role defensiveness (Goldberg, 1983).

total selves, rather than being continually told how society expects them to behave.

As far as relationships are concerned, androgynous couples would seek to transcend traditional sex-role boundaries, too. These sex-role boundaries, as Judy Long (1984) notes, facilitate the expectation that the female partner exists for purposes to be directed by the male. The wife and the household are satellites of the husband, and his wishes take priority. This would not be the case in an androgynous relationship, which interestingly enough, is the type of arrangement many of today's young adults want. Long's review of the research indicates that women and men admire the same qualities in others, and aspire to them in themselves. The kind of person they want to be and want to marry is both competent and tender, capable of interdependence and intimacy, and possesses strength and confidence. These are the "new generation." Will they live new marriages or old? The way they live their marriages will reveal the interplay of the individual and social factors — their personal desires versus societal patterns.

THE ALL-AMERICAN MALE AND FEMALE

Within the traditional couple framework, individuals may wonder—or no longer know—who they are or what they are like inside. This is because they've put boundless energy—knowingly and unknowingly—into maintaining an acceptable masculine or feminine image. Consider some of the following traditional sex-roles that are often brought into relationships:

Traditional Masculinity

- Rather than admitting that he needs anything from anyone, he often leads a life of exaggerated independence.
- He won't express his fears nor will he even allow himself to experience them.
- He doesn't disclose himself to women because he's afraid that he'll be regarded as unmasculine, especially if his inner core is seen.
- He will not make himself vulnerable and will keep his emotions to himself.
- He hides from failure and tries to always put on the facade of the successful man.
- He denies "feminine" qualities, such as expressing warmth and tenderness (Corey, 1986).

Traditional Femininity

- She has been trained to want and need intimacy in a relationship.
- She has been taught to "take care" of everybody but herself.
- She does not express negative feelings or emotions. She is not argumentative, attacking, rejecting, or challenging.
- She expresses herself by being proper, personal, open, emotional, and indirect.
- She has been trained to be psychologically "there" for her partner 24 hours a day.
- She has been taught to be sensitive to nonverbal cues so that she can "read" the men in her life (Shaevitz, 1984).

Implications for Relationships

Let's be more specific and examine gender patterns in traditional relationships. Letitia Peplau's (1983) review of the literature suggests that sex differences exist in the following areas: falling in love, self-disclosure, language and nonverbal communication, instrumental activities, decision-making and influence strategies, conflict and aggression, and reactions to relationship dissolution.

Falling in Love   Males are more apt to endorse "romantic beliefs," such as love comes but once, lasts forever, and conquers barriers of social class or custom. On the other hand, females are more likely to be "pragmatists," saying they can love many individuals, that some disillusionment often accompanies long-term relationships, and that economic security is as important as passion in relationships.

Differences also result when it comes to actual

love experiences. Both males and females seem to love their partners equally, but females are more apt to report emotional symptoms of love. The latter include such states as feeling euphoric or having trouble concentrating because of intense romantic involvement.

Self-disclosure Earlier, we mentioned that females demonstrate higher levels of self-disclosure in friendships. In regard to dating relationships and marriage, it is important to distinguish preferences about disclosure from the level and content of actual disclosure. Evidence indicates that women *prefer* greater self-disclosure in relationships than men. In actual interaction, however, a norm of reciprocity often encourages similar levels of disclosure between partners; the *amount* of actual disclosure may thus represent a compromise between the preferences of both partners. In marriage, equal disclosure between spouses is common. But, when asymmetries in disclosure do

occur, it is the wife who discloses more. Recent studies of college dating couples have uncovered few overall sex differences in level of disclosure, suggesting that younger educated couples may be moving away from the traditional pattern of silent men and talkative women. Let it be finally added that even when men and women disclose equal amounts, sex differences have been observed in the *content* of their self-disclosures. For instance, males are more likely than females to reveal their strengths and conceal their weaknesses.

Language and Nonverbal Communication We also pointed out earlier that males and females employ different forms of communication. In close personal relationships, this appears to be just as true for verbal communication as it is for nonverbal communication. Males do more verbal interrupting, claim greater personal space, initiate more touching, and are poorer at decoding nonverbal communication. Females also seem to be

Within traditional relationships, emotional sensitivity is more evident among females.

more supportive of males than vice versa. Among husbands and wives, the latter seem to be more adept at encoding nonverbal messages.

Instrumental Activities   The exchange of confidences and the execution of instrumental tasks are important for close relationships. The evidence indicates that husbands and wives perform different types and amounts of instrumental tasks and family work. Gender-based specialization in family work, such as males performing physical and mechanical forms of labor and females handling domestic chores, appears to be the norm in American marriages.

Decision-making and Influence Strategies Three general conclusions in regard to this topic exist. One, males and females in a close relationship specialize in different areas of decision-making. For instance, husbands are more likely to make decisions about the family car and insurance; wives are more likely to decide about meals and home decorating. Within the dating relationship, boyfriends may have greater say about recreational activities, and girlfriends may have more say about sexual intimacy.

A second conclusion is that many American couples perceive their relationships as egalitarian; these partners report that decision-making is mutual or divided equally. When dating and marriage are not seen as egalitarian, however, it is much more often the man rather than the woman who is dominant.

Finally, males and females may employ somewhat different tactics to try to influence each other. For example, wives are more likely to attribute *expert* power to their husbands than vice versa; husbands may say that their wives more often use *referent* power, appealing to the fact that they are all part of the same family and should see eye to eye. Also, men are more likely than women to report using direct and mutual power strategies, such as bargaining or logical arguments. In contrast, women are more likely to report using indirect and unilateral strategies, such as withdrawing.

Conflict and Aggression   Conflict situations bring different responses from males and females. In role-playing situations, for example, husbands are often motivated to resolve conflict and restore harmony, while wives are often rejecting, cold, or use appeals to fairness and guilt. Among young couples, both males and females expect women to react to conflict by crying, sulking, and criticizing the boyfriend's insensitivity. Often both sexes expect men to show anger, reject the woman's tears, call for a logical approach to the problem, and try to delay the discussion. As far as the use of physical force to resolve conflict is concerned, females are more apt to be the victims of physical abuse. (This latter topic receives in-depth focus in Chapter 15, "The Abusive Family.")

Reactions to Relationship Dissolution   The termination of a love relationship is often a difficult and stressful experience. Evidence suggests, however, that men tend to react more negatively to breakups than do women. Moreover, the association between marital disruption and a variety of illnesses and disorders is stronger for men than for women. There is also evidence that men may react more severely than women to the ending of a dating relationship. Research suggests that boyfriends are less sensitive to problems in their relationship, less likely to foresee a breakup, less likely to initiate a breakup, and tend to have more severe emotional reactions to the ending of the relationship. Thus, women tend to fall out of love more readily and easily than men.

Personal Attitudes and Values about Relationships   There is much commonality in regard to what Americans want in close relationships, regardless of their gender. Most people express a desire for a permanent relationship. Both sexes value companionship and affection and give relatively less importance to economic security and social status. In actual relationships, male-female similarity is usually further enhanced by the selection of a partner who shares compatible attitudes and a similar background.

As far as the sex differences that do exist, men in general have more conservative attitudes about roles in dating and marriage. Men also favor traditional sex-role specialization to a greater extent than do women. Women view verbal self-disclosure as more important in a relationship than do men. And, among educated young adults, women show greater concern than do men about maintaining personal independence outside their love relationships by having their own friends or career. Finally, men and women seem to value somewhat different qualities in an ideal love partner. Women more often value men's experience, intelligence, and occupational achievements. Men, on the other hand, more often seek partners who are youthful and sexually attractive. All of this points to the fact that men and women are likely to enter dating and marital relationships with somewhat different personal values and preferences. In turn, these factors may account for some of the gender-based role differences that occur in dating and marriage.

Breaking Down Sex-Role Barriers

Couples wanting to break down traditional sex-role barriers face a difficult, but not insurmountable, task. To begin with, partners need to be open-minded and sincerely interested in releasing themselves from stereotypical roles. Gerald Corey (1986) feels that men and women need to recognize that they're both after the same thing—a loosening of the sex-role rigidity that has trapped them. Many men recognize a need to broaden their views of themselves to include capacities that have been traditionally stereotyped as feminine and that they have consequently denied in themselves. And, there are numerous females who are seeking to give expression to a side of themselves that has been traditionally associated with males. As both sexes pay closer attention to attitudes that are deeply ingrained in themselves, they may find that they haven't caught up emotionally with their intellectual level of awareness. While couples might well be "liberated" intellectually and *know*

what they want, many have difficulty in *feeling* okay about what they want. The challenge is getting the two together!

In his critically acclaimed book *The New Male-Female Relationship,* Herb Goldberg (1983) writes that traditional couples wanting to change their sexist ways will not face an either-or situation. Indeed, change will more likely be an expansion process, one that is filled with stops and starts, forward and backward motion. Traditional gender defensiveness creates a world view to which people become deeply committed. To alter it is to shake a person's deepest frame of reference. Therefore, arriving at a new integration requires a slow methodical, trial-and-error approach. Goldberg suggests that couples will go through a transition process as they seek to implement changes. The following represents parts of this transition process:

- Trying to change one's partner as a way of improving the relationship is not the best way to start. Instead, the best and perhaps only effective way to create change in a relationship is to change that in oneself which allows for and reinforces the partner's "offensive" behavior. Attempting to modify one's partner rather than focusing on one's own behavior is a form of psychological one-upmanship that allows one to maintain a facade of wanting change while avoiding the actual risks involved in doing so.

- It is conceivable that changes in oneself will create a temporary crisis and alter the balance of the relationship. However, this will be overcome when a new understanding is achieved. During disharmonious times, blaming, provoking guilt, and threatening are common maneuvers designed to push the other person back to a formerly established position and avoid change.

- Couples should first decide what they *really* want, rather than what they *believe* they want, before change is attempted. This can help to avoid problems down the road. For example, many people see themselves as wanting more closeness or more autonomy in a relationship,

Heightened levels of satisfaction and contentment may greet those couples abandoning rigid sex-role behaviors.

but want that change to occur without jeopardizing their familiar security. A male may think that he desires more sexual assertiveness, independence, or direct and honest expressions of anger from a woman partner, and the woman may believe she wants greater expression of emotion, vulnerability, and need, with less success drive in the man. However, what is wanted in actuality is all of the old, safe, and known qualities, *in addition* to an idealized new person. This combination is often psychologically impossible.

■ The less need there is for a partner to change in order to reduce the other's insecurities, the more easily overall change evolves. This is because there is minimal resistance or threat between one another.

■ Traditional polarized relationships look okay on the surface; however, what looks good and always remains the same can eventually contaminate the relationship. Those couples wanting to change may have what appears to be a relationship filled with disequilibrium and conflict. It therefore may not look as good from a superficial standpoint. However, the transitional relationship is characterized by two persons trying to achieve a satisfying, dynamic balance — as opposed to the pseudopeace of traditional relationships, where the emphasis is on being "nice" and understanding while suppressing the negative. The new relationship involves a struggle between partners aimed at setting boundaries, retaining their individuality along with the relationship, and sharing responsibility, decision-making, control, and power. Conflict, therefore, rather than peace, becomes the norm, particularly in the initial stages of the relationship.

■ A balanced relationship is much less a matter of who does what than a matter of masculine-feminine nondefensiveness and of balanced interaction in all aspects of human expressiveness. In this sense, a man can be the primary breadwinner while the woman mainly stays at home, and the relationship can still be liberated in its process or essence. Likewise, the woman can be a corporation president and the man a househusband, and the relationship can be very traditional or sexist in its moment-to-moment interaction pattern. In general, a persistent pattern of blaming and feeling guilty is the sign of a polarized sexist interaction no matter what specific external role and chore division there is. Along the same lines, if the moment-to-moment process of being together is genuinely balanced, it will not matter what functions or tasks either one fulfills.

■ Couples should not be misled by thinking that relationships can be improved simply by making efforts to have good communication, or to hear each other accurately. The greatest intellectual awareness and most skilled efforts to communicate cannot transcend the impact of a relationship imbalance. Balanced interaction needs to be coupled with good communication to attain the best possible relationship.

■ Honest, nonsexist interaction is the key to balanced relationships. Nonsexist interaction means that the partners are responding to and satisfying each other's real needs, rather than assumed needs. In addressing assumed needs you are really only validating yourself, with the illusion of satisfying your partner's needs.

■ Within couples wanting to change, there are no victims or victimizers, only the appearance of such. Trying to figure out who is doing what to whom is an unending, ultimately futile task. Rather, partners should focus on what they want to change and what they're doing to avoid or block that change.

■ It is incorrect to base an intimate male-female relationship on the notion that each partner shares the same philosophy of liberation. People who enter into a relationship because of shared philosophies tend to relate to each other in overly self-conscious, critical, intel-lectualized ways, with a tendency toward oppressive seriousness, constant mutual vigilance, and accusations of hypocrisy or ideological weakness.

In summation, Goldberg proposes that to improve a relationship, partners must focus on the *being* rather than the *doing* aspects of it — put another way, this means the *rhythm* or *process* rather than simply the *content*. Techniques, or external how-tos, used to improve the relationship will just be transformed by its process. The greatest sex techniques in the world cannot create passion, and reversing roles will have no liberating effect if the same person still controls while the other reacts. Worse still, techniques (the *what* of a relationship) may drive partners crazy with the feeling, "I'm doing everything right; why does it feel so wrong?"

COMPONENTS OF LIBERATED MALE-FEMALE RELATIONSHIPS

The absence of masculine and feminine polarization enables males and females to choose each other based on the same kind of attraction and delight that motivates the development of a "best friends" relationship, and to avoid a relationship founded on gender defenses, which often creates rigidity and insecurity. Liberated relationships generate a type of playfulness between partners, a relaxed and enjoyable mixture of spontaneity and openness. The following are some of the components of liberated relationships:

Intrinsic Attraction   True relationships are motivated principally by the pleasure of the other person's presence and not his or her function. This person is an end, not a means.

Mutual Knowing   Partners feel known and recognized by one another, in the way they know themselves to be. There is no sense of being on a pedestal, of being idolized, distorted, or magnified by the other person's needs.

Stream-of-Consciousness Relating   In those relationships transcending sex-role barriers, verbal interaction flows. Conversations are personal, connected, unintellectualized, and engaged in easily and spontaneously. There is no conscious self-censorship or concern about avoiding certain topics, being misunderstood, or saying something that shouldn't be said.   ▶

Couples find there is no need to maintain an image, and therefore there is a sense of freedom in response and expression. This does not imply uncontrolled self-indulgence, but rather that any self-control will be based on voluntary restraint rather than fear of exposure of one's thoughts or feelings.

Transcendence of Gender Defensiveness   No behavior is repressed because of its reflection on the masculinity of the male or the femininity of the female. The interaction is gender free, person to person, as between two intimates of the same sex.

Authentic Attraction and Interaction   A couple's desire to come together and be together is based on the pleasure of being in each other's presence, rather than on defensive motivations. Sexuality, for example, becomes a spontaneous experience free of feelings of responsibility, defensive proving, and need for affirmation that one is loved that cause it to become work and eventually a source of fear and distress in traditional relationships. The greater the gender polarization, the greater the insecurity and defensive clinging, which make it impossible to come together out of passionate desire.

The Maintenance of Separate Identities   As the fusion of identities takes place, the energy and stimulation of being with another person is lost. Gender defensiveness produces the kind of fusion that results in feeling as if one is talking to oneself rather than to another person. As this occurs, boundaries disappear and the capacity for flow is lost. The degree of playfulness potential is correlated with the security and strength in the definition and maintenance of separate identities. Genuine interest in each other can only exist under such conditions.

Mutual Acceptance   The ability to know and be known is related to the absence of mutual judging and control. On the other hand, the need to present an image instead of the reality of oneself grows in proportion to the fear that one will be judged.

The ability to accept another person is also contingent on full awareness and acceptance of oneself. The more defensive one becomes in the quest to be "perfect" rather than fully real, the more critical one will be of others. As people become more authentically human and whole, the full complexity of inner experience will be found to be similar and available for all.

Objective Love and Admiration for One's Partner   If one's partner were not one's mate, one would want him or her as a friend anyway, because one objectively loves and admires that person—in terms of aesthetics, values, intellect, and the overall delight experienced in each other's presence.

From Goldberg, 1983. ■

CHAPTER HIGHLIGHTS

This chapter began with a description of key terminology related to the topic of sex-roles and relationships. Sex-roles are those attitudes and behaviors felt to be appropriate to males and females. Sex-role development is the process of socialization whereby such behaviors are acquired. Sexual identity refers to the biological differences that exist between males and females. Sex-role stereotypes are generalizations of oversimplified opinions of masculine and feminine behaviors and characteristics.

Different chromosomal structures represent one form of biological differences between the sexes. While both males and females have an identical number of chromosomes, it is the twenty-third pair that serves to differentiate a male from a female. We also explored how hormones operate to create sex differences. The influence of hormones on sexual development is especially apparent during prenatal life and puberty.

While it is important to study biological differences between the sexes, sociologists maintain that society and culture are largely responsible for shaping sex-role development. The three major theories of sex-role development are the social learning, cognitive-developmental, and identification interpretations. The agents of socialization responsible for transmitting sex-roles include parents, play behaviors, peers, teachers and schools, and the media. Androgyny is a concept that seeks to downplay the differences that exist between the sexes. Advocates of androgyny maintain that the removal of sex-typed behavioral constraints allows males and females to demonstrate the best qualities of both sexes.

The latter portion of this chapter focused on the implications of sex-roles on close relationships. We reviewed sex differences that exist in falling in love, self-disclosure, language and nonverbal communication, instrumental activities, decision-making and influence strategies, conflict and aggression, and reactions to relationship dissolution.

The chapter ended with ways to break down sex-role barriers and establish a balanced relationship. Favorable outcomes of the latter include intrinsic attraction, mutual knowing, stream-of-consciousness relating, transcendence of gender defensiveness, authentic attraction and interaction, the maintenance of separate identities, mutual acceptance, and the objective love and admiration for one's partner.

KEY TERMS

androgyny
chromosome
cognitive-developmental theory of sex-role development
estrogen
gender identity
gender-role
gonadotrophins
gonads
hermaphrodite
hormone
human growth hormone
hypothalamus

identification theory of sex-role development
Kleinfelter's Syndrome
Mullerian duct
Mullerian inhibiting hormone
pituitary gland
primary sex characteristics
progesterone
pseudohermaphrodites
puberty
secondary sex characteristics
sex cell
sex chromosome abnormality
sex-role

sex-role development
sex-role stereotype
sexual identity
social learning theory of sex-role development
somatic cell
testicular feminizing syndrome
testosterone
Triple X Syndrome
Turner's Syndrome
Wolffian duct
XXY Syndrome

RECOMMENDED READINGS

Berman, S. (1984). *The six demons of love: Men's fears of intimacy*. New York: McGraw-Hill. A unique and thoughtful account of how certain obstacles prevent males from experiencing intimacy with their partners.

Goldberg, H. (1983). *The new male-female relationship*. New York: Signet Books. This is must reading for anyone wanting to better understand the dynamics of sex-typed relationships and how to transcend them.

Heilbrun, A. B., Jr. (1981). *Human sex-role behavior*. New York: Pergamon Press. A thorough account of how sex-roles govern human behavior and our various social interactions.

Kammeyer, K. C. W. (Ed.). (1981). *Confronting the issues: Marriage, the family, and sex roles* (2nd ed.). Boston: Allyn and Bacon. This book of readings supplies ample coverage of sex-roles and their implications for all close relationships.

Kilgore, J. E. (1984). *The intimate man: Intimacy and masculinity in the 1980's*. Nashville, TN: Abington Press. In a very readable fashion, this paperback explores the concept of intimacy and how it can enhance the lives of all concerned.

Lengermann, P. M., and **Wallace**, R. A. (1985). *Gender in America: Social control and social change*. Englewood Cliffs, NJ: Prentice-Hall. Among the topics considered are sociological theories and the study of gender, the learning of gender roles in childhood, and social structures promoting gender equity.

Mitchell, G. (1981). *Human sex differences*. New York: Van Nostrand Reinhold. An authoritative and scholarly account of sex differences, with special emphasis on the psychology of women.

Pleack, J. H. (1981). *The myth of masculinity*. Cambridge, MA: The M.I.T. Press. Pleack focuses attention on the most commonly accepted myths concerning masculinity and then analyzes each, including why they have been upheld for years.

Rubin, L. B. (1983). *Intimate strangers: Men and women together*. New York: Harper & Row. An excellent analysis of how the differences between men and women arise and how they affect such areas as intimacy and sexuality.

Seward, J. P., and **Seward**, G. H. (1981). *Sex differences: Mental and temperamental*. Lexington, MA: Lexington Books. Sex differences from biological, sociological, and cultural perspectives are explored in detail by the authors.

5

Sexual Attitudes and Behavior

CONTENTS

CONTEMPLATIONS

■ Time for another one of our prereading quizzes. Ready? Okay, answer true or false to the following statements:

1. It is primarily the man's role to initiate sex.
2. Casual sex is more exciting than intimate sex.
3. If a couple loves one another and communicates, everything will go fine sexually.
4. Using sexual fantasies during intercourse indicates dissatisfaction with one's partner.

Now that we have your interest, read on for the "correct" answers.

■ Ever have a question about sex . . . and were afraid to ask? If so, maybe some answers you've always wanted await you within the borders of this chapter. For example, did you know that both males and females experience similar stages of sexual response? Ever wonder what teenagers think about when they masturbate? At approximately what age, with whom, and where one's first intercourse is likely to occur? What the primary reasons are for not engaging in premarital intercourse? Want to satisfy your curiosity on these questions? Read on.

■ Teenage pregnancy has often been called a social problem of epidemic proportions, and rightfully so when statistics from the 1980s are examined. Consider the following in support of this: about one million teenage females get pregnant each year, and 600,000 give birth to their babies. Approximately 30,000 adolescents *under* the age of 15 become pregnant annually. And, nearly half of all black females in the United States are pregnant by age 20. Why are these statistics so alarmingly high? What factors account for this problem? Such questions and numerous others will be addressed as we explore unwed pregnancy in the United States.

■ AIDS. . . . the very mention of it creates an immediate negative and uncomfortable feeling in most people. It is a rare but devastating disease, one that so far as we know, is invariably fatal. Each year, thousands continue to die from AIDS as it cripples the body's natural immunity against disease. In the concluding portion of this chapter, we'll explore AIDS and other sexually transmitted diseases, including what we know about them and what remains elusive to today's scientists.

Few topics related to marriage and family life generate more interest and curiosity than sexual behavior or human sexuality in general. As far as sexual behavior is concerned, this interest is as pronounced for the individuals engaging in sex as it is for the researchers exploring the activity, not to mention the general public wanting to learn of the results. Because of such unparalleled motivation to learn more, a flurry of publications have appeared on the topic. Today it seems that everything you've wanted to know about human sexuality is available just for the asking.

In Chapter 4 we focused on various dimensions of sex-roles and their impact on developing relationships. In this chapter, we'd like to share what has been learned about human sexuality. While the topic of sexual satisfaction and fulfillment will be discussed elsewhere (see Chapter 8), our emphasis here will be on sexual attitudes and behavior. Before doing so, though, several terms and concepts need to be clarified.

Sex refers to the biological aspects of reproduction, covering the *anatomy* (structure) and *physiology* (function) of the two sexes. Sex can also refer to biological mechanisms of sperm and egg production, mating, pregnancy, and sexual arousal. **Sexuality**, on the other hand, refers not only to reproduction and sexual pleasure, but also to one's need for love and personal fulfillment. Sexuality concerns the many cultural and psychological factors related to human sexual behavior (Jones, et al., 1985).

Herant Katchadourian (1985) writes that sexuality unfolds in unique ways at each phase of life. For the child, sex is a form of play; for the teenager, it becomes a source of intense yearning; for the adult, a bond of love and a means of procreation. For everyone it is a potential source of pleasure or sometimes suffering. Sex is a part of every culture, and sexual activity has taken place (obviously) since time began.

APPLICATIONS

HOW MUCH DO YOU KNOW ABOUT SEXUALITY?

The following self-quiz, designed by Barry and Emily McCarthy (1984), is designed to measure your knowledge about sexuality and sexual functioning. Read each of the following statements carefully, and then indicate whether each is "true" or "false."

T F 1. Sexual expression is purely natural, not a function of learning.

T F 2. Foreplay is for the woman; intercourse is for the man.

T F 3. Once a couple establishes a good sexual relationship, they don't need to set aside time for intimacy together.

T F 4. If you love each other and communicate, everything will go fine sexually.

T F 5. Sex and love are two sides of the same coin.

T F 6. Technique is more important than intimacy in achieving a satisfying sexual relationship.

T F 7. Casual sex is more exciting than intimate sex.

T F 8. If you have a good sexual relationship, you will have a fulfilling experience each time you have sex.

T F 9. After age 25 your sex drive dramatically decreases, and most people stop being sexual by 65.

T F 10. It is primarily the man's role to initiate sex.

T F 11. If one or both partners become aroused, intercourse must follow or there will be frustration.

T F 12. Men are more sexual than women.

T F 13. Having multiple orgasms is a sign of a sexually liberated woman. ▶

T F 14. Since men don't have spontaneous erections after age 50, they are less able to have intercourse.

T F 15. When you lose sexual desire, the best remedy is to seek another partner.

T F 16. The most common female sexual problem is pain during intercourse.

T F 17. The most common male sexual problem is not having enough sex.

T F 18. Penis size is crucial for female sexual satisfaction.

T F 19. Oral/genital sex is an exciting but perverse sexual behavior.

T F 20. Simultaneous orgasms provide the most erotic pleasure.

T F 21. Married people do not masturbate.

T F 22. Using sexual fantasies during intercourse indicates dissatisfaction with your partner.

T F 23. Clitoral orgasms are superior to vaginal orgasms.

T F 24. Male-on-top is the most natural position for intercourse.

T F 25. People of today are doing much better sexually than the previous generation.

To score this test, add the number of "true" statements. These statements are all incorrect since all items are false and were written to expose sexual myths or misconceptions. Don't feel guilty if you got some wrong; such misconceptions abound in our society. In support of this, the McCarthys maintain that the average person gets nine wrong. How do you compare to this total?

DIMENSIONS OF HUMAN SEXUALITY

How we respond sexually is not a unitary concept. Rather, each of us has three sexual response systems. Shirley Radlove (1983) observes that these systems are separate, but interrelated. The **biophysical system** originates from one's biological capacity to respond to sexual stimulation. This system determines the physiological limits of sexual response. The **psychosocial system** is based on the culture's sexual programming for appropriate male and female sexual behavior. The **sexual value system** is an individual's unique set of beliefs about sexuality. Combined, these three systems show how persons must learn scripts that tell them how to have sex, who to have it with, and even the extent to which they are allowed to take advantage of their biophysical capacity for responsiveness. Radlove offers the following elaboration of each of these systems.

The Biophysical System

As indicated above, this system comprises the body's natural capacity to respond to sexual stimulation. The biophysical system encompasses the internal sex organs, the genitals, the nervous system, the circulatory system, and every physiological structure and process involved in sexual response. The biophysical system tends to be a dominant one. It is not easily disrupted or susceptible to negative influences such as anger or resentment toward one's partner. However, negative attitudes and beliefs can diminish in part the body's natural tendency to respond to sexual stimulation. For example, a woman may experience high levels of physiological tension and excitement during sexual activity, but she may not be fulfilled if she is frightened or ashamed by the intensity of her sexual response. Obviously, this system is a multifaceted and complex one.

THE SEXUAL RESPONSE CYCLE

Noted sex researchers William Masters and Virginia Johnson (1966) conducted a ten-year investigation focusing on the physiology of the human sexual response. Among other findings, their research revealed that four phases exist in relation to male and female sexual responses.

The first phase is called the **excitement phase**, and may last anywhere from a few minutes to several hours. During this phase, arousal increases and the genital areas become engorged with blood. In males, the penis becomes erect and the testes enlarge. For females, the vagina begins to lubricate and widens.

The **plateau phase** is the second part of the response cycle, bringing an increase in heart rate, body tension, and blood pressure. In males the head of the penis becomes larger and in females the glands in the vagina continue to secrete lubricating fluid.

The third phase is labeled the **orgasm phase**, and is accompanied by rhythmic contractions in the genitals of both sexes and by ejaculation in the males. These contractions occur every eight-tenths of a second and last for varying lengths of time. The orgasm is experienced as a pleasurable sudden release of sexual tension for both males and females.

In the final phase of the cycle, called the **resolution stage**, the body gradually returns to its normal state. The penis loses its erection, and the vagina reduces in size. For males, Masters and Johnson noted that a **refractory period** takes place, during which the male is unresponsive to sexual stimulation. Thus, second ejaculations or more may be experienced, but only after a certain amount of rest. The refractory period varies in time from male to male. (The figure on page 128 depicts the male and female sexual response cycles.)

Masters and Johnson acknowledged that while these four phases of sexual response are experienced by both males and females, there are some notable differences between the sexes. For example, women are capable of having multiple orgasms in rapid succession, while most males do not. Women may also experience variation in the overall duration and strength of orgasm from one intercourse experience to the next. Most males, on the other hand, experience a similar form of orgasm each time ejaculation occurs.

▶

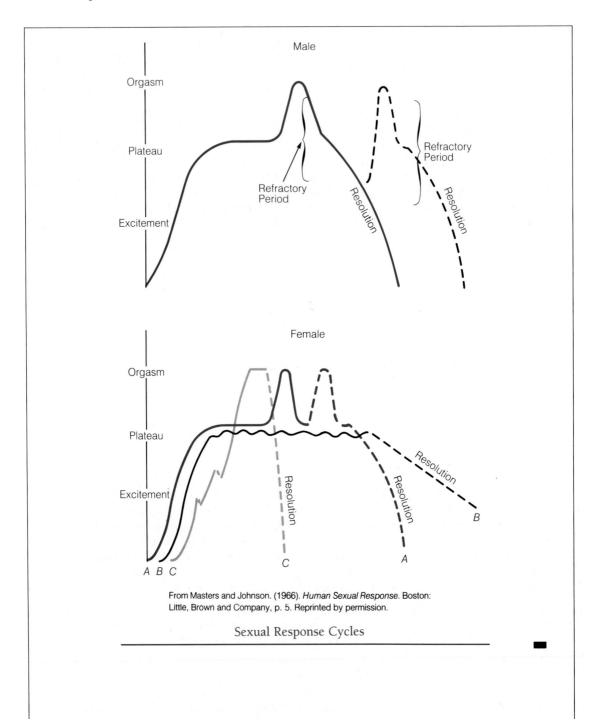

From Masters and Johnson. (1966). *Human Sexual Response*. Boston:
Little, Brown and Company, p. 5. Reprinted by permission.

Sexual Response Cycles

The Psychosocial System

The psychosocial system includes the learned and internalized messages and myths transmitted to men and women by their culture. For instance, in our society, men are told to value and explore their sexual feelings, while women are taught to hide their sexual feelings and remain naive. Men are directed to increase their sexual knowledge and sexual performance skills via multiple-partner experience, while women are advised to avoid multiple-partner experience unless they want to be labeled oversexed or promiscuous.

Radlove points out that the psychosocial system, including its culturally imposed stereotypes and myths, does not always lead to sexual problems for men and women. Difficulties arise, however, when the realities of individual experience fall short of cultural ideals. For example, if a man has not fully developed his sexual skill, it is unlikely that he will be able to effectively satisfy a naive and inexperienced woman who is completely dependent on him for sexual direction.

The Sexual Value System

The final sexual response system is the **sexual value system**, encompassing the person's sexual attitudes and beliefs. It consists of family attitudes and personal learning beyond that which is generally transmitted by the culture at large. For example, although the culture may approve and promote sexual skill-building via exploration of the male's sexuality, an individual man's religious beliefs may be such that he prefers to remain sexually inexperienced prior to marriage.

CULTURAL ROLE SCRIPTS FOR SEXUALITY

Role scripting, according to Lonnie Barbach (1984), is a term used for behaviors individuals learn in order to fill certain functions. Some scripts that males and females learn have changed over the years as social ideas and trends change. Others have remained relatively unaltered. As far as sexuality is concerned, these scripts can level a powerful effect on sexual functioning. Barbach shares some of the more common cultural role scripts for sexuality.

The "Sex Is Good/Bad" Script   This role script works most directly against women. Women are often told that sex is dirty or negative, but they are instructed to save it for someone they love. Women are also often taught that being a virgin is virtuous and that keeping one's genital area untouched is the greatest gift to give their husbands on their wedding night. Some religions teach that premarital sex leads to damnation, yet they never relate the pleasures of marital sex — except to say that producing children is a righteous act. Many women also rarely see sex as being for their own enjoyment; instead, they learn that it is a way to attract a man.

The "Fantasy Model of Sex" Script   Here, a fantasy model of sex as espoused by popular novels leads men and women to believe that the activity itself is filled with unrelenting excitement, arousal, and unparalleled satisfaction. Couples learn from this script that a sexual experience must keep building in intensity until it peaks and explodes in the ultimate simultaneous orgasm. Such descriptions are far from the typical sexual experience, which has its ups and downs. To believe in such a script, unfortunately, programs many men and women alike for sexual frustration and even failure.   ▶

The "Men Should Know" Script   This fantasy model of sex portrays the male as the sexual expert, someone in total control of the sexual activity. The male is responsible for "sweeping the female off her feet" against her better judgment and then thoroughly satisfying her sexually. This script portrays women as trying to remain pure, innocent, and unknowledgeable, while men are supposed to be totally responsible and sexually all-knowing.

The "Women Can't Talk" Script   This script implies that women are embarrassed to talk about sex and shouldn't be doing so anyway. Words relating to sex are awkward to say, especially since many women have learned that it is not ladylike to use them. Because of this script, women often remain inhibited when it comes to communicating their sexual preferences to their partners.

The "Media" Script   The media script gives men and women a different set of standards to live up to. For example, magazine covers dictate what is pretty and what is not. If we fall short of any glamorized physical qualities, we may worry about not being sexually desirable. These cultural pressures often make men and women alike self-conscious, and make them forget that beauty and appeal lies in one's uniqueness, not in a stereotyped image.

The "Sex Equals Intercourse" Script   When people talk about sex, they rarely refer to kissing, holding, or touching. All too often, the "real thing" is intercourse and nothing else for younger people. Expectations of intercourse also grow unrealistically high, and once it becomes an acceptable part of sex, other activities are often abbreviated, if not omitted entirely. There are many activities beyond intercourse that are sexual in nature and can succeed in giving both partners pleasure and satisfaction.   ▬

There are many restrictions in our culture as to what sexual behaviors are more appropriate for women or for men. North American culture, however, promotes the idea that sex is dirty, sinful, or painful for either gender. These negative perceptions are also often learned in a more personal context. For instance, a woman who is raped may come to devalue sex as painful and frightening. Similarly, men and women whose religion has taught them that nonreproductive sexual activity is dirty or sinful may bury their natural potential for sexual response and may associate sex with guilt and shame. It can be said that such individuals have a negative sexual value system.

In summation of these three systems Radlove states that although males and females are quite similar in their biophysical potential for sexual response, they tend to be dissimilar with regard to their cultural learning of sexual behavior norms. Differences may also exist in their sexual value system—the degree to which they value or devalue sexuality. For females, the research seems to suggest that cultural learning of feminine role behaviors may be implicated in female sexual problems. As far as males are concerned, sexual problems seem to be more often related to negative sexual values than to a stereotypic masculine role.

SEXUALITY IN CONTEMPORARY SOCIETY

How Sexual Values Have Changed

One of the most consistent research findings regarding sexuality is that today's attitudes toward

During the Elizabethan era there were those whose lives would have met with the full approval of today's Moral Majority. And, in Victorian England there were those whose sexual behavior makes today's "swingers" look rather prim. Sexual ethics have always been subject to change, and sexual behavior has always been difficult for society to dictate.

What is it that accounts for the change in sexual values in America over the past 20 years? What factors are there that might explain the nature of sexual activity that is permitted today, not to mention how society perceives this activity? Certain reasons can be cited, such as the multiple meanings sex has come to acquire in modern society. Rather than being seen as merely the means of procreation, sex has acquired new purposes, such as a form of communication, pleasure, or expression.

People have become more tolerant and permissive toward sexual attitudes and behaviors.

Sexual values are transmitted in many ways, including by the media.

sex have become more relaxed and tolerant. Studies repeatedly uncover the fact that American society has moved from an antisex to a prosex orientation. These liberal attitudes are part of the so-called sexual revolution America has been experiencing over the past 20 years or so.

In the Western world, sexual revolutions are not rare events. Sharon Brehm (1985) observes that from one culture to another, and from one time period to another, views on sexual behavior have changed drastically: the Romans were noted for orgies, the early Christians for celibacy, the Elizabethans for bawdiness, the Puritans for moral strictness, the Victorians for repressed sexuality, and the Edwardians for playboys. Also, there has always been conflict between the dominant cultural ethic about sex and people's actual behavior.

Sexual values have also changed because of greater equality between the sexes. And, there are more open discussions about sexuality—in the classroom, on television, and in books—helping to remove the taboo once surrounding the topic. More people today are comfortable with the topic of sex. Related to this is the fact that increasing affluence in America enables more people than ever before to have contact with sources of information. Finally, there are changing perspectives on virginity in contemporary society. While virginity is still important, for many it is not the single most important criterion behind mate selection.

Moral Standards Underlying Sexual Behavior

While today's sexual attitudes have become more liberal, it is incorrect to assume that all sexual behavior is equally liberal. It is true that we are experiencing a convergence of liberal sexual attitudes and behavior, but not everyone participates in permissive sexual activity. Furthermore, not everyone thinks it right. Therefore, actual sexual behavior needs to be more carefully examined, including the principles motivating sexual activity.

In this respect, Ira Reiss (1960) has proposed four basic principles or moral standards underlying sexual behavior. The **abstinence standard** holds that it is wrong for both unmarried males and females to engage in sexual intercourse. The **double standard** asserts that males can have sexual relations prior to marriage, but women are expected to remain abstinent. The **permissiveness-without-affection standard**, also called "recreational sex," means that sex by itself without emotional attachments is acceptable. The **permissiveness-with-affection standard** implies that sexual relations are acceptable if accompanied by emotional attachment between partners.

Of these four guiding principles, permissiveness with affection is the most popular today. This latter fact was borne out in a survey of over 300 young adults in a college setting. When questioned about their sexual standards, results clearly indicated that the more emotionally involved a person was in a relationship, the more likely were increasing levels of physical intimacy to be regarded as appropriate (Knox and Wilson, 1981).

Adults are least likely to favor the double standard and the permissiveness-without-affection value. The double standard is viewed as demeaning to women, and rejection of this standard may well be part of the social movement to remove all types of sexual inequality.

CROSS-CULTURAL FOCUS

EXAMPLES OF CONTRASTING SEXUAL IDEOLOGIES

James Garbarino (1985) observes that most of us familiar with North American views of sexual behavior dimly recognize that these are not the only perspectives. On the contrary, there are wide cultural variations in sexual attitudes and behavior. Consider the following two illustrations, which represent extremes in sexual permissiveness and repressiveness.

On the Polynesian island of Mangaia, anthropologist Donald Marshall (1971) observed that sexual permissiveness abounds. Children observe adult sexual activity throughout their lives, and both boys and girls masturbate as an accepted practice. Outside the family, children hear stories and jokes about sex, and the language is rich in sexual words. At age twelve, boys and girls are fully initiated into the world of adult sex. For boys, there are two weeks of intensive instruction in oral sex, the kissing and sucking of breasts, and techniques to achieve simulta- ▶

neous mutual climax. Also, they are taught how to bring the woman to climax several times before the male. The girls are often initiated into intercourse by an experienced male relative. Virginity is frowned upon by the islanders since virgins are not able to supply men with sexual pleasure and satisfaction.

Now consider the sexual repressiveness that John Messenger (1971) found on Inis Beag, an island off the coast of Ireland. The population of this small island appears to have little or no knowledge of numerous sexual activities such as hand stimulation of the genitals or open-mouthed kissing. Any woman who finds pleasure in sex is regarded as deviant. There are no sex education programs on Inis Beag and considerable ignorance regarding sexuality exists. For example, little or nothing is known about the physiology of menstruation, and the islanders maintain that intercourse is physically taxing and takes its toll on one's health. For this latter reason, the men of Inis Beag refrain from intercourse on the eve of sporting events or strenuous work days. When marital sex does take place (premarital sex is rare on Inis Beag) the husband always initiates the activity and it is always performed in the male-superior position. Foreplay is virtually nonexistent and the male does not seek to sexually satisfy his wife. Rather, he ejaculates as quickly as possible. Female orgasm is a relatively unknown experience on Inis Beag. ∎

Related to the permissiveness-without-affection standard, research reveals that young adults can be quite conservative about certain aspects of sexual activity. This was shown in a study designed to elicit college students' moral judgments of sexual situations. When asked about the morality of having sex with many partners, the respondents had a tendency to regard such behavior as immoral or sinful. While they viewed premarital sexual relations as tolerable, achieving this through a succession of partners was not (Robinson and Jedlicka, 1982).

In a more recent position, Ira Reiss (1981) maintains that two additional sexual ideologies may exist in society today. The first of these is what he calls the **traditional-romantic ideology**. The underpinning of this ideology is the belief in the primacy and rightfulness of the double standard. It suggests the following:

- Gender roles should be distinct and segregated with the male role being dominant.
- Bodily centered sexuality is to be avoided by females.

- Sexuality is an extremely powerful emotion and one that should be feared by females.
- The major goal of sexuality is heterosexual coitus, and that is where the male's focus should be.
- Sexuality entails guilt feelings for women, mainly because it violates their sexual prohibitions. However, females have learned to value romantic love, which therefore becomes partial justification for sexual behavior. Thus, love redeems sexuality from its guilt, particularly for females.

The second ideology, the newer of the two, is called the **modern-naturalistic ideology**. This ideology challenges all of the above, promoting equalitarian relationships of males and females rather than the double standard. The following are the key tenets of the modern-naturalistic view:

- Males and females should share similar gender roles and should promote equalitarian participation in society.
- Person-centered sexuality is of more worth than body-centered sexuality, but the latter

still has a positive value for both females and males.

- Both female and male sexual emotions are strong, but manageable in the same way other basic emotions are.
- The major goals of sexuality are physical pleasure and psychological intimacy. This can be realized in a variety of sexual acts for both sexes.
- A wide range of sexuality should be accepted without guilt by both males and females, provided it does not involve force or fraud.

Reiss maintains that this newer ideology reflects a naturalistic view of sexuality and its acceptability. The expression of sexuality is regarded as a good and proper part of much of human social life. The newer ideology is based upon a fundamental moral view of the genders which assumes equality. However, it should be clear that many people today are in transition and so they will adhere to elements of both the old and the new sexual ideologies. Also, there are others who will exhibit behaviors not falling within either category.

EARLY FOUNDATIONS OF SEXUALITY

Childhood

As we discovered in Chapter 4, gender identity begins very early in life. Children learn to behave in sexually appropriate ways and people around them typically reinforce sociocultural expectations. However, childhood also marks a time for learning about sexuality.

For example, John DeLamater (1981) writes that the foundations of sexual object choice are established at early ages. The child will learn that dyads comprised of one male and one female marry and/or have children. Couples "in love," or engaging in such behaviors as kissing or caressing each other, consist of one male and one female. Seeing such behaviors tells the child that members of the opposite sex are appropriate objects for such interaction.

DeLamater observes that childhood also marks a time when youngsters explore and manipulate their own bodies and the bodies of other children. For most children, these are simply forms of play. Youngsters lack the sexual scripts possessed by adults, thus exploring other children's genitals is not defined by them as a sexual act. Mutual exploration often occurs in a medical script such as doctor-patient, which is consistent with their experience in which doctors or nurses have examined their bodies and perhaps their genitals. Interestingly, parents may teach the child the moral significance of such behavior if they respond to such activities with moral outrage, which often happens.

Learning about sexuality is a process that begins early in life.

Sally Wendkos Olds (1985) emphasizes that during the early years of childhood, youngsters need to become aware of themselves as sexual beings and to become comfortable with their sexuality. One's sexuality is an intrinsic part of one's personality. Children need to feel good about their bodies, to appreciate their beauty and the pleasure they can give them. Early sex play with oneself and with other children is both a common and a normal way to develop pleasure. The feelings a child nurtures about these activities reach far into the future of the adult the child will become.

She adds that children also need to nurture healthy sexual attitudes if they are to feel comfortable within their own gender identity. The comfort attained often determines whether a child will act in appropriate male or female patterns and how that youngster will feel about his or her total self. Children learn these differences between themselves and others by exploring their own bodies and by seeing those of other children and of adults. They develop a sense of what sexuality means, of its relationship to love, to conception, and to pleasure. Moreover, they learn their culture's standards for sexual behavior in the process.

Unfortunately, these early sexual goals are often not fulfilled in healthy, satisfying ways. Consequently, individuals continue through life trying to make up for earlier interferences with healthy sexual development. For too many, sexual development has been hindered or blocked by ignorance, naivete, and embarrassment that gets passed down from generation to generation. For those who are even more unfortunate, development is further distorted because of such childhood traumas as molestation or incest. Such events leave scars that people may spend the rest of their lives trying to remove.

APPLICATIONS

HOW TO TALK WITH CHILDREN ABOUT SEX

Sex experts Lorna and Phillip Sarrel (1984) point out that even the most basic facts about sexuality can be confused in children's minds. They often spin their own fantasies about how babies get started, where they grow, and how they are born. They need to learn about sex and reproduction many times, not just once. Thus, an open flow of communication — one that permits questions to be asked and asked again — is important.

Parents need to introduce the topic of sexuality from time to time, in a way that is appropriate for the child's level of reasoning. To do this effectively, parents need to understand their own views on sexuality and decide what they will do and say in certain situations. Also, calling the parts of the body by their real names is highly recommended.

Sarrel and Sarrel feel that the manner in which we talk about sex and how it is described in books for adults and children usually shows the male as the active agent and the female as the passive recipient. Consider this for a moment. The penis *always* enters the vagina, and the sperm are pictured as swimming furiously toward and then penetrating the egg. The fact that the egg moves through the genital tract and plays an active role at the moment of fertilization is often omitted. Adults should say, "When the man and woman join together," or, "When the egg and sperm come together." Adults should try to avoid sex-role stereotyping in describing sex, and not make it something a male does to a female. ▶

Parents who are uncertain about how to describe sex to children might find suitable ideas within books. Books for children on the subject are extremely helpful for several reasons: pictures help children understand, having a book is reassuring and can help parents feel less anxious about what to say, and reading a book together is a common, everyday occurrence. Thus, this will be just one more reading time rather than a slightly tense "Talk about Sex." The following books may prove useful:

For Parents

The Eternal Garden by Sally Wendkos Olds (Times Books, 1985).

Talking with Your Child about Sex by Mary S. Calderone and James W. Ramey (Random House, 1982).

The Family Book about Sexuality by Mary S. Calderone and Eric W. Johnson (Harper & Row, 1981).

Getting Closer: Discover and Understand Your Child's Secret Feelings about Growing Up by Ellen Rosenberg (Berkley Books, 1985).

Raising a Child Conservatively in a Sexually Permissive World, by Sol Gordon and Judith Gordon (Simon & Schuster, 1983).

For Children

Did the Sun Shine Before You Were Born? by Sol Gordon and Judith Gordon (ED-U Press, 1982).

Making Babies by Sara Bonnett Stein (Walker, 1974).

How Was I Born? by Lennart Nilsson (Delacorte Press, 1975).

For Preadolescents

Am I Normal? (for boys) and *Dear Diary: An Illustrated Guide to Your Changing Body* (for girls), both by Jeanne Betancourt (Avon Books, 1983).

Ellen Rosenberg's Growing Up Feeling Good by Ellen Rosenberg (Beaufort Books, 1983).

What's Happening to My Body? A Growing Up Guide for Mothers and Daughters by Lynda Madaras and Area Madaras (Newmarket Press, 1983).

For Adolescents

Facts about Sex for Today's Youth by Sol Gordon (ED-U Press, 1983).

The Teenage Body Book Guide to Sexuality by Kathy McCoy (Simon & Schuster, 1983).

Changing Bodies, Changing Lives: A Book for Teens on Sex and Relationships by Ruth Bell (Random House, 1981).

Adolescence

Puberty, the onset of sexual maturity, heralds new levels of sexual responsiveness. With the maturation of secondary sex characteristics, puberty increases the salience of specifically sexual meanings and behaviors for the individual. These changes make the teenager more aware of sexual activity, reproduction, and the processes of dating and mate selection that are socially defined as integral aspects of these physical/biological processes. When individuals enter adolescence we expect them to begin the transition from childhood roles which emphasize submissiveness, nonresponsibility, and asexuality, to adult roles which emphasize dominance, responsibility, and sexuality. In this respect, there are both biological and social pressures toward sexual development (DeLamater, 1981).

Teenagers often become the recipients of inconsistencies and mixed messages regarding sexuality. For example, the media promotes adolescent sexuality by using young actors, actresses, and models dressed in provocative fashions. On the other extreme, parents try to restrict activity or limit opportunities for sexual engagement by curfews and other limitations. Both messages convey the expectation of adolescent sexuality, but they differ in their approval. Teenagers need to evaluate these messages, but must do so against the background of the overall changing cultural context of sexuality (Garbarino, 1985).

In many other cultures, children and teenagers alike have virtually no guilt, shame, or inhibition to overcome. By contrast, American children and teenagers have a dozen or more years of learning during which, typically, sex is shrouded in shameful mists. Hands are removed from genitals with outraged glares, and information is withheld or parceled out grudgingly. Perhaps a prolonged adolescent-youth phase in our culture is needed so that teenagers are allowed enough time to rid themselves of all the negative messages they have received over the years concerning sex (Sarrel and Sarrel, 1984).

Our discussion implies that the sexual outcome of the teenage years is based on the physiological turbulence of the body and the psychological changes that accompany it. Adolescents have to come to grips with the fact that they're now sexually mature. This implies an acceptance of one's physical changes — what a person looks like and what he or she is capable of. The teenager's new sexual capabilities of ejaculation or ovulation signal their untried fertility. These capabilities usually bring a heightened level of sexual responsiveness. While adolescents are coming to terms with what they look like and what they can do, they also need to come to terms with their sexual identity. This is the time of life when young people actively establish their sexual preference — usually heterosexual, sometimes homosexual; when they think seriously about their sexual values, deciding which of their parents' values they agree with and which they want to supplant; and when they think about being sexually competent (Olds, 1985).

Before leaving the topic of adolescence, let us acknowledge that much of the guilt and shame about sex originates from incorrect thinking about masturbation. **Masturbation** is defined as the manipulation of one's own sex organs to produce pleasure. Once regarded as a sinful and forbidden activity, masturbation today is generally recognized as a normal form of sexual expression. By age 21, research evidence indicates that masturbation has become almost universal, especially among males. This means that experiencing masturbation is the norm while the failure to masturbate by this time is the exception (Gold and Petronio, 1980).

Lorna and Phillip Sarrel (1984) point out that we are just beginning to emerge from a dark age of incredible misbelief about and terror of masturbation. Nineteenth-century books on the subject now sound absurd with their dire warnings about "self-pollution" causing everything from insanity to sallow complexions. However, such thoughts have persisted into our century. Until about 1920, there were still neuropsychiatric centers where people with nerve-degenerative diseases, and other as yet unclassified ailments, were treated in "Masturbation Clinics."

The onset of sexual maturity and heightened heterosexual interests confront teenagers with an assortment of adjustments.

Learning about one's body and discovering how to masturbate is regarded as a major sexual turning point in a person's life. If masturbation is followed by a sense that it is wrong or shameful, an ambivalence about sexuality often arises that can dominate an individual's life. Sally Wendkos Olds (1985) maintains that to combat this, teenagers and adults need to learn that masturbation is an acceptable form of sexual expression. For teenagers especially, acceptance of it can help to prevent the problems that arise from inhibitions against any self-stimulation at all. In a society such as ours, it's ironic that teenagers can be told about reproduction, but are rarely told anything about the kind of self-pleasuring they could be, or are already, doing.

RESEARCH HIGHLIGHT

TEENAGERS, MASTURBATION, AND SEXUAL FANTASIES

One of the areas of teenage sexuality explored by Robert Coles and Geoffrey Stokes (1985) was masturbation. The two researchers queried 1,067 teenagers and found the average age at which masturbation begins is 11 years and 8 months. Ninety percent of those who masturbated during adolescence started before they were 15.

Coles and Stokes found that considerable guilt and negative feelings were attached to masturbation. Fewer than a third (31 percent) said they felt no guilt when they masturbated, and one-fifth (20 percent) felt either "a large amount" or a   ▶

"great deal" of guilt. Overall, many of the respondents felt that masturbation was something that just shouldn't be talked about. Even among those who agreed intellectually that masturbation was okay, a degree of reticence about it remained.

Some interesting trends were uncovered in relation to sexual fantasies during masturbation. Fantasies about one's boyfriend or girlfriend were most common (57 percent), followed by TV or movie stars (44 percent), acquaintances (41 percent), strangers (36 percent), rock stars (28 percent), and made-up people (17 percent). Males were generally more likely than females to have fantasies—more than three-quarters (77 percent) of the males and only about two-thirds (68 percent) of the females. However, the objects of their fantasies were noticeably different.

It was found that males and females were about equally likely to have fantasized about their girlfriends or boyfriends, but males were much more likely than females (52 percent to 38 percent) to have had fantasies about strangers. At least among teenagers, the oft-repeated notion that women's fantasies are likely to focus on some mysterious figure who will force them to do all the things they won't allow themselves to admit wanting to do seems to be a myth. By a somewhat larger margin (56 percent to 38 percent), males were more likely than females to have fantasies about acquaintances. Though the sexes are equally likely to have fantasized about rock stars, this, too—given the relative paucity of female rock performers—may indicate a generally higher level of fantasies among males; they were certainly more likely (by 52 percent to 37 percent) to have fantasized about TV or movie stars. The sexes were approximately equal, however, when it came to fantasies about made-up persons.

Finally, the only fantasies that more than 15 percent of the teenagers had more than twice a week involved boyfriends and girlfriends. Here, however, almost a fifth of the adolescents (19 percent) fantasized at least once a day, and more than a third (36 percent) did so twice a week or more. Males and females did not differ significantly in terms of the frequency of these fantasies, and both genders had frequent fantasies about their boyfriends and girlfriends—more than twice as often as they did about other subjects. The researchers concluded that to a certain extent, it appears the chicken-and-egg question can be answered: having a sex partner is more likely to lead to sex fantasies than having sex fantasies is to having a sex partner. ■

PREMARITAL SEXUAL RELATIONSHIPS

Rates of Premarital Intercourse

Research supports the fact that a greater percentage of today's teenagers and young adults are engaging in premarital intercourse than in the past. A comparison of Alfred Kinsey's classic studies of male and female sexual behavior (Kinsey, Pomeroy, and Martin, 1948; Kinsey, Pomeroy, Martin, and Gebhard, 1953) with more recent investigations will illustrate this point. When Kinsey conducted his research, he discovered that approximately 20 percent of all females and about 40 percent of all males queried had experienced sexual intercourse by the time they were 20. More contemporary research provides us with an interesting comparison. Many of these studies report significant increases in the percentages reported by Kinsey and his colleagues. In fact, a glance at the findings reveals that it is not uncommon to find approximately 50 percent of the females surveyed, and about 70 percent of the males, engaging in premarital intercourse before age 20 (Kantner and Zelnik, 1980; Clayton and Bokemeier, 1980; Bell and Coughey, 1980; Robinson and Jedlicka, 1982).

In relation to the above, consider the findings of a fairly recent research study (Coles and Stokes, 1985). In this particular investigation, rates of premarital intercourse were about equal between the sexes: 53 percent of the females and 46 percent of the males reported having had intercourse by age 18. Interestingly, most of the teenagers had carefully planned this event. Well over half (57 percent) talked the matter over with their first partner before having intercourse. And, contrary to popular myth, females were more likely to have had

such discussions, hence are less likely than males to have been "swept away" — by a margin of 64 percent to 52 percent.

Rarely did any of the respondents (less than 5 percent) have their first intercourse with a stranger. Statistics revealed that for approximately a quarter (23 percent), the first partner was a friend; for more than two-thirds (68 percent), it was a boyfriend or girlfriend. Males seem to have been more casual than females, however, for about a third (32 percent) of them describe their first partner as a friend — more than half as many as the 61 percent whose partner was a girlfriend. By contrast, more than three-quarters of the females (76 percent) were with their boyfriends (only 13 percent were with friends). As these figures might lead one to expect, females tend to be significantly older at the time of their first intercourse.

Coles and Stokes also found that more than half the teens (54 percent) first had intercourse at their own or their partner's houses; another 15 percent were at a third party's house. Only 2 percent first had intercourse in a hotel or motel — not surpris-

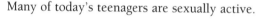

Many of today's teenagers are sexually active.

ing given the ages at which first intercourse took place — and 15 percent were outdoors. The traditional trysting place, a parked car, was actually used by only 12 percent of teenagers.

Finally, it was discovered that, in general, no matter what the degree of planning or of logistic difficulty, most of the teens regarded their first experience positively. Only five percent said they were "sorry they had the experience"; the rest were pretty evenly divided between "glad" (43 percent) and "ambivalent" (46 percent). Females, however, were *much* more likely than males to express sadness or ambivalence.

It should be noted, though, that females were also more likely than males to feel that their relationship with their first partner improved after intercourse. Their lingering regret, despite the improved relationship, suggests that females place a higher value on virginity per se. About half, for instance, want to be virgins when they marry, while only a third of the boys want to marry a virgin. Fifteen percent of the females who'd already had intercourse said they had wanted to be virgins when they married.

Motives for Premarital Intercourse

There are a variety of reasons for engaging in premarital intercourse. Among these are a desire for intimacy; feelings of trust, love, and caring; pressure from a desire to please one's partner; and an attempt to improve a couple's relationship. Other reasons include a physiological need for a sexual outlet or an experience to test the capacities, both sexual and physical, of two people seeking marital compatibility.

Beyond these, Roger Rubin (1985) adds that motivation often arises from loneliness, relief from tension and frustration, controlling and dominating others, getting revenge, escaping oneself, communicating, or conveying love and spiritual harmony. The use of sex is sometimes a way of trying to salvage a doomed relationship. Sex may also make a person feel wanted and loved even without a deep commitment. It may serve as an outlet for aggression or an expression of gratitude. Sexual activity may be a way to bolster an ego because of

an inadequate career or to flee the pressures of a family break-up. Finally, it may be a source of power, even for those who are often the weakest and most vulnerable.

A number of reasons are also given for *not* engaging in sexual intercourse. For females, two of the more common reasons are the fear of pregnancy and the guilt over loss of virginity. This is also a source of anxiety for males as far as responsibility is concerned. Some couples also fear public disapproval. For many, another important reason for refraining is the fear of contracting a sexually transmitted disease, a topic to be covered later in this chapter.

Factors Affecting Premarital Intercourse

Certain factors affect the rates of premarital coitus. As the aforementioned statistics imply, rates will increase as adolescents get older. Actual frequency of premarital coitus is also greater among lower socioeconomic, noncollege adolescents than among higher socioeconomic youths who attend college. Rates are greater for adolescents who do not attend church on a regular basis. And, Protestant, college females have higher rates of premarital intercourse than either Catholic or Jewish females. Finally, blacks more than whites, engage more frequently in premarital coitus (Lamer and Housker, 1980; Clayton and Bokenmeier, 1980; Bell and Coughey, 1980; Inazu and Fox, 1980).

As far as gender is concerned, rates of premarital intercourse are generally higher among males. However, research included in this discussion and other investigations (that is, Sack, et al., 1984) reveals that this isn't always the case. Finally, it seems that males generally want sexual intercourse before females do during the dating relationship. Almost half of the college-aged males surveyed in one study felt (Knox and Wilson, 1981) that intercourse was appropriate by the fifth date, in contrast to about 25 percent of females surveyed. Does this mean that individuals should circle their calendars and set their watches in anticipation of the fifth date? Hardly. This is strictly an average and should not be taken out of context.

Also related to gender, William Talmadge

Numerous reasons are cited for today's high rates of teenage promiscuity, including earlier sexual maturity and society's liberal sexual attitudes.

(1985) adds that males and females are becoming less different in relation to their sexual attitudes. The attitudes of both are becoming more permissive, and the degree of commitment in the relationship appears to be the key determining factor in sexual behavior. As we learned earlier, sex with casual strangers is much less acceptable among young people. Should conservative sex attitudes prevail, they are likely to originate from such factors as guilt or inaccurate sex information.

RESEARCH HIGHLIGHT

ETHNIC DIFFERENCES IN PREMARITAL SEXUAL BEHAVIOR

A recent longitudinal study of teenagers' sexual behavior has revealed interesting ethnic differences. The two-year ongoing study, conducted by Edwin Smith and Richard Udry (1985) examined 492 white males and 516 white females, and 183 black males and 178 black females. When the subjects were first surveyed, they were between the ages of 12 and 15. At that time, 29.3 percent of the white males and 11.1 percent of the white females had already had intercourse. Among the adolescent black males, 75.8 percent had experienced intercourse and 40.5 percent of the black females were no longer virgins. Two years later, 67.9 percent of the 28 virgins among the black males had experienced intercourse, compared ▶

with 30.7 percent of the white males. Twenty-three percent of the white girls who were virgins at the beginning of the study had intercourse during the two-year period, compared with 41 percent of the virgin black girls.

Beyond the obvious differences between rates of premarital intercourse, unique ethnic and cultural patterns of sexual behavior appeared. In general, young white males and females followed a predictable sequence of pre-coital petting stages. They progressed from kissing and necking to light petting (above the waist and over the clothing) to heavy petting before reaching the point of first intercourse. The sequence tended to extend over a long period and allowed youngsters time between dates to think about where they were headed and consider the consequences. They could also date others without feeling they were reneging on a sexual commitment.

Black teens, on the other hand, were likely to follow a much less predictable pattern of pre-coital behavior. Progression to intercourse was more rapid, with teenagers often moving directly from light necking to intercourse with no stops in between. In many instances, heavy petting was bypassed entirely.

The researchers felt that these different behavior patterns originated from different sets of cultural expectations. For example, white adolescents often grow up expecting to do a lot of necking and petting before eventually engaging in intercourse or rejecting it. This expectation allows a longer preparatory period before sexual commitment and can provide a rather long period of abstinence before "date" is ultimately transformed into "mate." The prolonged sequence also gives adolescents a chance to think about contraception and do something about it. Among black adolescents, however, the normative expectations often result in precipitous coitus.

It was also observed that the differences between black and white adolescents' approach to the physical aspects of dating obviously influenced the likelihood of contraceptive use. For white females, necking on one date was not likely to escalate into intercourse on the next. For black adolescents, however, necking might be one of the few behaviors engaged in before intercourse, the researchers felt. For white females, the "next move"—above the waist petting—was not affected by the lack of contraception. For black females, the next move might be unprotected intercourse and, as a result, unwanted pregnancy.

These different patterns of expectations and subsequent behavior may be a partial explanation for the differing pregnancy rates in the two groups, the researchers suggest. They add that the need to obtain contraception when the most intimate experience a black youngster has had is necking probably may seem pointless from the youngster's perspective. However, if counselors and sex educators are more aware of cultural differences in sexual patterns, they may be able to reach black teenagers and help them adjust to their growing sexuality and its consequences.

PREMARITAL PREGNANCY

The Problem and its Causes

Premarital pregnancies are rapidly increasing in the United States, most noticeably among teenagers. Approximately one million adolescent females become pregnant annually. Of this total, about 600,000 give birth to their babies. With birth rates for older women declining, statistics reveal that one out of every five new mothers today is a teenager. And perhaps the most shocking statistic is that approximately one out of every ten teenagers will become a mother by her eighteenth birthday (Nye and Lamberts, 1980). Figure 5-1 displays pregnancy rates of American teenage females with those from other nations.

These figures do not tell the whole story. Consider the following in relation to this social problem: many adolescents become pregnant in their early or middle teens, about 30,000 of them each year under age 15. Nearly half of all black females in the United States (whose pregnancy rate between the ages of 15 to 19 is almost twice that among white females) are pregnant by age 20. If present trends continue, it is estimated that 40 percent of all of today's 14-year-old females will be pregnant at least once before the age of 20 (Wallis, 1985).

Many reasons can be cited to explain why these figures are so high. The liberal sexual attitudes and behavior of today's youth culture is often quoted, as is the earlier sexual maturity of teenagers. And some adolescents do not care about the consequences of their sexual behavior; others become pregnant simply because they want to have a baby (Kelley, 1983; Oskamp and Mindick, 1981; Strahle, 1983).

The misuse of contraceptives, or the absence of any birth control whatsoever, is another important contributing reason. Gail Zellman and Jacqueline Goodchild's (1983) review of the literature indicates that many young women do not use contraception because they just don't believe that their sexual activity might result in pregnancy. Their stated reasons for failing to use birth control are often disconcerting: "I didn't expect to have sex," "I forgot," or "We only did it two times." This reasoning shows an interesting parallel to the feelings of children, who also believe that nothing can happen to them. Such denial of reality reflects cognitive immaturity, which makes it difficult for adolescents to think rationally about themselves. Teenagers also may, for all their sophistication, simply fail to understand elementary probability theory. Rather than realizing that each month an individual has the same probability of conceiving as in the previous month, teenagers may develop false notions about the probability of becoming pregnant. Gender-role stereotypes that make the female ultimately responsible for whether or not pregnancy occurs don't help the situation either. Many teenage males don't worry about impregnating a partner and don't feel the need to discuss contraception. It is no surprise, then, that girls rarely trust boys with any contraceptive responsi-

FIGURE 5-1   Pregnancy Rates of United States Teenagers, Compared to Selected Nations

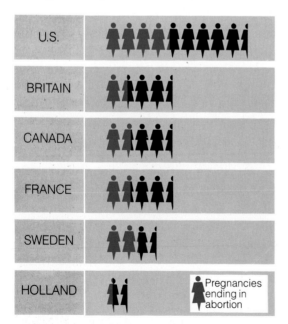

Alan Guttmacher Institute

If present rates continue, it is estimated that 40 percent of all 14-year-old females will be pregnant at least once before the age of 20.

bility because doing so would mean that they accept themselves as assertive, sexually active persons.

Despite the fact that some people blame teenage promiscuity on the widespread dissemination of contraceptives, the discussion above supports the fact that those who become pregnant do not use contraceptives. This is all the more reason, observes Vern Bullough (1981), to make accurate information on contraception more available. Unfortunately, he feels that our society has not yet accepted the fact that teenagers are biologically ready to have children. Instead, we pretend that if we do not tell them about contraceptives they will not know about sex. The result is increased pregnancy and abortion.

Implications of Unwed Pregnancy

There are numerous implications for teenage pregnancies. They introduce drastic disruptions into the lives of adolescents, their offspring, their parents, and the society as a whole. Lacking a supportive family and the requisite material and psychological resources for childbearing, the lives of the mother and of her child are disrupted from the start, and so are the lives of their families, parents, and grandparents. The problem is also passed on to the wider community and to public institutions. Teenage mothers cost the taxpayers large sums of money each year and, in addition, they face social disapproval and financial hardships. Those who marry have an exceptionally high divorce rate. The sexually transmitted disease rate for these adolescents is also high, with gonorrhea rating in the adolescents second only to the common cold (Smith and Kolenda, 1984).

There are numerous health risks, too, for the children of teenage mothers. The younger the mother is, the greater the chances of infant death. Teenage mothers are more apt to have premature births than older mothers and are more likely to experience labor and delivery complications, including toxemia and anemia. The babies themselves frequently suffer from neurological problems and birth defects. Children of teenage mothers also tend to have lower IQs and perform more poorly in school than children of older mothers (Broman, 1981; Chilman, 1980).

Teenage pregnancy has a variety of implications for both parent and child.

Our entire discussion highlights the magnitude of teenage pregnancies and their far-reaching implications. This represents a social problem demanding the attention of everyone. Beyond the need for information on birth control already mentioned, sex education as a whole needs to be stressed. This includes in the home, school, and within those institutional settings facing the problem. Making parents more aware of the problem and encouraging viable forms of communication with their teenage offspring also needs to be stressed. The emotional support that parents can offer is considered critical (Byrne, 1983; Fisher, 1983).

Finally, those teenagers who decide to keep their children need our help as well. Programs need to focus on the health-care needs of both mother and child. Attention also needs to be directed toward increasing the educational level of teenage parents, especially the mother, in addition to upgrading vocational skills (Schneider, 1982; Brown, 1982; Montgomery and Leashore, 1982). Without these measures, we will continue to see an increase in one of our most pressing social problems.

SEXUALLY TRANSMITTED DISEASES

Besides pregnancy, another risk for sexually active persons is contracting a sexually transmitted disease. A **sexually transmitted disease** (or *venereal disease*) is a contagious infection passed on by intimate sexual contact with others (coitus, oral-genital sex, or anal intercourse). Four of the more common diseases are gonorrhea, syphilis, genital herpes, and the acquired immune deficiency syndrome (AIDS).

Gonorrhea

Gonorrhea is the most common of all sexually transmitted diseases, afflicting more than one million individuals each year. The word gonorrhea means ''flow of seed'' and was used by the Greek physician Galen in A.D. 130 to describe the signs of the disease as it occurred in males. To this day, gonorrhea is much more common in males and is highly contagious.

Gonorrhea is caused by a bacterial infection and is spread by direct sexual contact with an infected person, usually affecting the penis in men, the vagina in women, and the throat and anus in both sexes. Left untreated, it can lead to a generalized blood infection, sterility, arthritis, and heart trouble. Moreover, in men it can spread throughout the prostate gland and the male duct system, causing painful inflammation.

Gonorrhea can also lead to infections if the eyes come in contact with genital secretions. This can happen, for example, if the person rubs the eyes after handling the infected genital organs. Also, during the birth process, a baby can contract this disease when it passes through the mother's infected birth canal. Today, most states require that a few drops of silver nitrate or penicillin be placed in the eyes of all newborns to prevent infection and possible blindness from this infectious disease.

Symptoms   For males, symptoms of gonorrhea include a yellowish discharge from the penis, usually within two to ten days after the disease has been contracted. Painful and burning urination is also commonly reported. For females, gonorrhea may exist in the early stages without any observable symptoms. However, in time it is often marked by a discharge from the vagina and urethra; frequent, painful urination; cloudy urine; vomiting; and diarrhea. Gonorrhea can also lead to a pelvic inflammatory disease which, in turn, can cause sterility.

If gonorrhea of the anus is contracted, symptoms often include bloody or mucus-filled discharges from the anus and pain during bowel movements. Gonorrhea of the throat may have no noticeable symptoms or may reveal itself only by a scratchy, sore throat.

Treatment   Gonorrhea can usually be controlled by antibiotics, with a single injection of penicillin effecting a cure in most males. While

Sharing sexual intimacy with a succession of partners increases the risk of contracting a sexually transmitted disease.

under treatment, the patient should abstain from sexual activity until further tests have confirmed that gonorrhea is no longer present. This is usually done one week after treatment begins and sometimes again two weeks later. The treatment of gonorrhea, similar to all forms of sexually transmitted diseases, requires that every sexual partner of the infected person also be examined and treated if necessary.

Syphilis

Syphilis claims an estimated 150,000 new victims each year. Syphilis is caused by *spirochetes,* thin corkscrew like organisms that thrive in warm, moist environments. This highly infectious disease enters the body through any tiny break in the mucous membranes and then burrows itself into the bloodstream. Besides sexual contact through intercourse, syphilis can be contracted through the use of contaminated needles.

Left untreated, syphilis can affect all parts of the body — the brain, bones, spinal cord, and heart, as well as the reproductive organs. Blindness, brain damage, heart disease, and even death can result. Syphilis can also be transmitted from a mother to her unborn baby, causing congenital syphilis in the child. This may eventually result in blindness and deafness, among other serious consequences. Syphilis in a pregnant woman must be treated prior to the eighteenth week of the pregnancy in order to prevent passage of the disease to the fetus.

Stages and Symptoms As a progressive disorder, syphilis passes through four stages: primary, secondary, latent, and late. **Primary syphilis** is marked by a painless, open sore called a **chancre**. This appears at the site where the spirochete entered the body and it is usually the size of a dime or smaller. The chancre typically appears between 10 and 90 days after exposure to the disease, and with or without treatment, disappears in three to six weeks. However, while the chancre has disappeared, the disease is still active within the body and will enter the second stage if left unchecked.

Within six weeks to six months after contact with the disease, **secondary syphilis** appears. The symptoms of secondary syphilis include a skin rash, whitish patches on the mucous membranes of the mouth, temporary baldness, low-grade fever, headache, swollen glands, and large moist sores around the mouth or genitals. These symptoms typically last from three to six weeks without treatment, and the disease then progresses to the third stage.

During the **latent stage**, all symptoms disappear and the patient appears healthy. However, the spirochetes are still in the bloodstream and at this point are burrowing themselves into the central nervous system and skeletal structure. This stage is a precursor to the highly destructive late stage.

During the **late stage** of syphilis, the symptoms are quite lethal and can appear up to 15 or 20 years after the initial exposure. Here, the entire body can come under siege of the disease. Damage to the bones and spinal cord, blindness, brain damage, heart disease, or even death can occur.

Treatment Despite its damaging effects, syphilis is fairly easily treated. Similar to gonorrhea, syphilis can be controlled with antibiotics, usually penicillin. Similar patterns of treatment in relation to sexual abstinence are also followed.

Genital Herpes

Genital herpes has created much public concern in recent years. An estimated ten million Americans currently suffer from it, with 500,000 new cases reported each year. Because a cure for genital herpes remains to be found, the number of cases continues to spiral upwards.

Genital herpes is caused by *herpes simplex* viruses. Herpes simplex comes in two varieties: *herpes I* — which causes cold sores and fever blisters — and *herpes II* — which causes lesions on the genitals. However, the two forms often mix, and herpes II may appear both in the mouth and on the genitals.

Genital herpes is spread primarily through intimate sexual contact. The virus itself rests in the cell center of specific sensory nerves (see Figure

Skin Surface

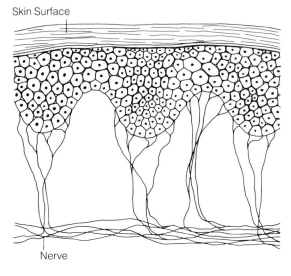

Nerve

Dormant Herpes Virus

Herpes Blister

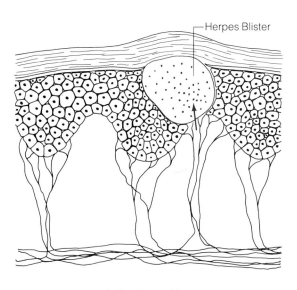

Active Herpes Virus

FIGURE 5-2   Herpes Simplex Type 2
Dormant herpes simplex type 2 lie within nerve cell (top). When activated by stress or illness, active herpes blisters result (bottom).

5-2). These viruses become inactive, or latent, when they reach the nerve cell center. However, herpes will "flare up" in a recurrence and the virus becomes reactivated. It is thought that the virus follows the same nerve and multiplies on the skin at, or near, the site of the original sore. Sexual contact is not necessary for a recurrence.

Symptoms Approximately 2 to 20 days after the virus enters the system, the person experiences a primary, or first, outbreak. The infection typically begins as a rash of red patches with white blister-like sores, usually appearing in clusters. Genital herpes will usually make an appearance on or around the penis in men, and the vagina in women. Internal sores can also occur in the mouth, vagina, cervix, or anus, or anywhere on the body where the virus first entered the body. Beyond the rash, one or all of the following may be present: pain and discomfort in the area of the infection, fever, headache, and a general feeling of ill health. Also common is pain or burning when urinating. Glands in the groin area may become swollen. Women may notice a vaginal discharge.

Within a month's time, the sores usually heal. To all outward appearance, the infection seems to have left the body, but this is not the case. Even though the sores disappear, the virus remains in the nerve tissue in the body and possibly in the skin. The virus can multiply at a later date and cause sores and a reoccurrence. However, generally, the symptoms of the first outbreak are the most serious.

Treatment As indicated, there is no cure for genital herpes. However, there is treatment now available for acute outbreaks that involves the use of either the antiviral drug cyclovir or laser therapy, both of which will heal blisters, reduce pain, and most importantly, kill large numbers of the herpes virus. For many, cyclovir can reduce the reproduction of the virus in initial outbreaks, thus possibly lessening the number of subsequent outbreaks. However, to be effective, laser therapy must be started immediately after the first sores appear.

APPLICATIONS

HOW TO AVOID SEXUALLY TRANSMITTED DISEASES

Bea and Byron Mandel (1985) warn that if you have sexual contact with someone who has a venereal infection, the risk of getting that infection is extremely high. One's ability to resist sexually transmitted diseases (STDs) may vary, depending on your overall state of health and how easy it is for you to resist diseases in general. The more people with whom you have intimate contact, the greater your risk of becoming infected. In an effort to provide as much information as possible on sexually transmitted diseases, the Mandels supply these answers to some commonly asked questions:

Can STDs Be Transmitted through Saliva?   Yes, saliva can carry organisms that cause some diseases. For example, the virus for oral herpes is present in saliva.

Can I Get STDs from Toilet Seats?   Generally speaking you cannot get infected from an inanimate object such as a toilet seat. Most organisms that transmit sexual disease need the human body to survive and multiply. Specifically, these organisms require the warmth and moisture found in mucous membranes such as the tissue inside the mouth, vagina, and urinary tract. A toilet seat, for the most part, does not provide this type of environment.

Can I Get an STD from Using Someone Else's Towel?   For the most part, STDs are transmitted from person to person. Disease-causing organisms generally cannot survive long enough on articles such as towels and washcloths to infect another person. Crabs, scabies, and other small parasites, however, can be spread in this way. For this reason, it makes sense to avoid using another person's towel or personal items whenever possible.

Can I Take Antibiotics or Other Medicine to Prevent STDs?   There is no medicine that you can take to prevent STDs. Taking antibiotics to prevent STDs is risky for several reasons:

- Each disease is different and requires a different type of antibiotic to treat it.
- Proper dosages vary from one person to another and, especially, from one disease to another.
- The overuse of antibiotics can actually make some infections more difficult to cure because organisms may become resistant to the drug's effect.
- Some people who take large quantities of antibiotics develop allergies or sensitivities to these drugs which can result in life-threatening reactions.
- Antibiotics may kill organisms that are beneficial to you, such as certain bacteria in the intestines.   ▶

Can Condoms Help Prevent STDs?   The condom is the best available means of preventing STDs. Anything that minimizes direct genital contact during sexual activity reduces the risk of getting STDs. While condoms do not provide 100 percent protection, when used according to the instructions provided, they are the best protection available. However, condoms will not protect you from scabies, crabs, or other diseases not restricted to the genital area.

Can Someone with No STD Symptoms Still be Contagious?   Yes. The absence of symptoms does not mean that a person is not contagious. For example, most women who have gonorrhea do not know they are infected but can still pass on their infection to another person. With some diseases — herpes, for example — there may be a period of time just prior to an outbreak of symptoms when the infected person is contagious. Usually, but not always, an outbreak will be preceded by warning signs such as tingling or burning in the genital area.

When Is It Safe To Have Sexual Contact with Someone Who Has an STD?   An infected person remains contagious until the STD is completely cured. Sexual contact is not safe until the infected person has undergone medical testing and has been given a "clean bill of health" by a health professional. Just because someone is taking medication does not mean that the infection is gone. In general, both partners (and anyone else who has had intimate contact with the infected person) should be tested and treated if necessary. Because symptoms do not always show up immediately, the partner who appears to be uninfected may later prove to have the infection and unknowingly pass it back to the originally infected partner. This cycle could go on indefinitely. If your partner has ever had herpes, he or she may have periodic outbreaks of the disease. You should not have any sexual contact during the contagious period, which includes several days before a flare-up, as well as the outbreak itself.

If I Have Pain when Urinating, Do I Have an STD?   Pain during urination is a very common symptom of STDs in men. However, this symptom also can be caused by other conditions, such as bladder infections. Any discomfort when urinating should be checked by a health professional.

If I Ignore STD Symptoms, Will They Go Away?   Symptoms may disappear temporarily, but the infection will not go away unless it is treated. Symptoms can reappear weeks or months later if the disease is still present. The disappearance of symptoms does not mean that an infection is gone; it may be present in your bloodstream or in other parts of your body. If symptoms are ignored, complications may develop later, making the disease more difficult to treat. If an infection goes untreated, it can result in serious, irreversible damage, the most common being sterility in both men and women; some untreated STD cases may even result in death.

Acquired Immune Deficiency Syndrome (AIDS)

The **acquired immune deficiency syndrome** (AIDS) is a serious disease caused by a virus. It is characterized by a specific defect in the body's natural immunity against disease. People who suffer from AIDS become susceptible to a variety of rare illnesses not often found in people whose immune systems are normal. If they do occur, they are relatively mild.

To date, no one has ever been cured of AIDS. And, as of 1985, nearly 5,000 people have died from the disease in the United States, and at least 25,000 Americans have been afflicted with it. By the end of 1991, it is estimated that 270,000 Americans will have received a diagnosis of AIDS, and 179,000 will have died of it (see Figure 5-3). Some 5,000 persons in ten European nations including West Germany, Belgium, Denmark, and Britain suffer from AIDS, and the number is rapidly growing. As many as 600,000 Europeans are

thought to be carriers of the AIDS virus (Wright and McCain, 1986).

It should be pointed out that nobody actually dies of AIDS. Its victims are not claimed by a single mysterious disease. Rather, they die of infections and cancers that are able to thrive in a body with a hopelessly weakened immune system. Most of these diseases are treatable, and in fact, AIDS patients often are cured of them. But they either return or are followed by other diseases until the body can simply no longer resist.

AIDS is caused by a recently identified virus called HTLV-III, which is thought to have originated in Africa about a decade ago. The virus may be a newly evolved variant of a virus that infects a number of monkey species, including the African green monkey, which is indigenous to Zaire and neighboring countries. Its proteins are similar to those of the monkey virus. AIDS has also been diagnosed among Zairians.

Analyses of blood drawn from Zairians over the years and kept frozen suggest the possibility that some time in the 1960s the monkey virus mutated into a form that could infect humans. Some Zairians are known to kill monkeys and eat the meat, activities that could have brought contaminated monkey blood into contact with human blood. No one knows how the virus may have traveled from Africa to the United States. It is known to have established itself among Haitians; and since Haiti and Zaire are both French-speaking countries, it may be that travelers between the two transferred the virus.

AIDS is spread primarily through sexual contact with an infected person, usually through anal intercourse. Because this practice is common among homosexual men, the disease has moved rapidly through the gay community. It might be worthwhile to note that Haiti has long been a favorite vacation spot for homosexual men from the United States. The virus cannot pass through unbroken skin; it must enter through an opening, such as the mouth, a wound, or other break in the skin. And, since anal intercourse often damages the lining of the rectum, an opening may be created through which the virus can enter the body. AIDS can also

---

FIGURE 5-3   Diagnosed and Projected AIDS Cases and Deaths, 1981–1991

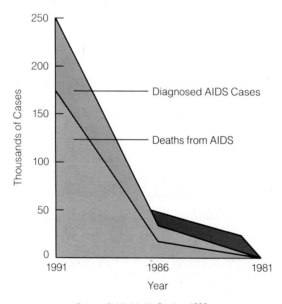

Source: Public Health Service, 1983.

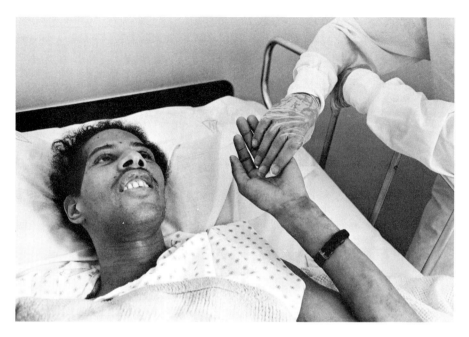

Although research is promising, a cure for AIDS has yet to be discovered.

be transmitted from men to women during anal sex, or vaginal sex when penetrating causes tiny abrasions in the vagina. And fairly recent research indicates that women may be able to pass the disease to men, since the AIDS virus could be present in menstrual blood and vaginal secretions — although it has not yet been found there. The risk of AIDS is increased by having multiple sexual partners.

There are other ways to contract AIDS. Needles shared by intravenous drug addicts can carry the virus from one person to another. AIDS virus has been found in blood donated to blood banks. Persons receiving a blood transfusion have picked up the virus in this way, but since the development of a blood test for signs of infection by the virus, blood banks now throw away donated blood that's found to be contaminated.

Symptoms   The symptoms of AIDS include low-grade fever, swollen lymph glands, weight loss, fatigue, night sweats, long-standing diarrhea, and a general sick feeling. Up to one-third of the victims develop a previously rare cancer known as **Kaposi's sarcoma**, which can appear as purplish bumps on the skin. Many develop a severe form of pneumonia. The main problem, however, is the inability of the body to fight many diseases that come along, including various cancers, skin infections, fungus growths, and tuberculosis.

Individuals with AIDS almost uniformly have reduced numbers of **lymphocytes** — specialized white blood cells that are critical in combating infectious diseases such as those caused by tuberculosis and viruses. Lymphocytes may also be instrumental in destroying malignancies in their early stages. There are two types of lymphocytes actively engaged in coping with infection — the **T-cell** and the **B-cell**. The T-cell is mainly concerned with direct cytotoxicity; that is, by a series of complex processes, it directly kills invaders. The B-cell, on the other hand, is concerned with the production of infection-fighting antibodies when stimulated. In AIDS the T-cells are greatly reduced; in fact, it is the "helper" T-cell (a further subdivision) that is most profoundly decreased.

WHO GETS AIDS? A PROFILE OF PATIENTS IN THE UNITED STATES

The Victims

- 73 percent are homosexual or bisexual men
- 17 percent are users of intravenous drugs
- 1.5 percent are blood-transfusion patients
- 1 percent are hemophiliacs
- 1 percent are heterosexuals
- 6.5 percent are unclassified

Racial Considerations

- 57 percent are Caucasians
- 26 percent are black
- 14 percent are Hispanic
- 3 percent are unclassified

Age Considerations

- The average age at diagnosis is 34
- 47 percent are between 30 and 39
- 22 percent are between 20 and 29
- 22 percent are between 40 and 49
- 9 percent are under 20 or over 50

Geographic Considerations

- Today, the disease is found throughout the United States
- New York has the highest concentrations of AIDS patients, followed by California
- Idaho, Montana, North Dakota, and South Dakota have the lowest concentration of AIDS patients

Adapted from Wright and McCain, 1986.

Treatment As we said at the outset, there is no cure for AIDS to date. Some AIDS patients with Kaposi's sarcoma are being treated experimentally with forms of interferon—a virus-fighting protein produced by the body. Although some success against Kaposi's sarcoma has been reported, interferon treatment does not appear to restore the immune system's functioning. There are other treatments, such as radiation, drugs, and surgery for many of the illnesses suffered by AIDS patients, and many biomedical investigators continue to work on methods for treating the specific immune defects found in AIDS patients.

Limited trials of a substance called interleukin-

2, which scientists believe may help fight the severe deficiencies seen in the immune systems of AIDS patients, will begin soon. Preliminary laboratory results are promising, but much more work remains to be done. Other experimental drugs include suramin, ribavirin, azidothymidine (AZT or compound S), and foscarnet. All are believed to interfere with a key step in the AIDS virus's action.

The Public Health Service (1983) has recommended that the following steps be taken to prevent the spread of this disease:

- Sexual contact should be avoided with persons known or suspected of having AIDS.
- Sexual promiscuity is a risk factor. Avoid having multiple sexual partners and avoid sexual contact with others who do.
- Members of high-risk groups should refrain from donating blood.
- Physicians should order blood transfusions for patients only when medically necessary. Health workers should use extreme care when handling hypodermic needles.

NATIONAL ORGANIZATIONS PROVIDING INFORMATION ON AIDS

- Public Health Service, Department of Health and Human Services, Washington, DC 20201 (800) 342-AIDS (A recorded message defines AIDS and gives information about how to avoid it) (800) 447-AIDS (The number to call if you wish to speak to a doctor for a personal consultation)
- Centers for Disease Control, Center for Prevention Services, Technical Information Services, 1600 Clifton Road, Atlanta, GA 30333 (Several pamphlets are available)
- Gay Rights National Lobby, Box 1892, Washington, DC 20013 (202) 546-1801
- KS Research and Education Foundation, 54 Tenth Street, San Francisco, CA 94103 (415) 864-4376
- National Coalition of Gay STD Services, P.O. Box 239, Milwaukee, WI 53201 (414) 277-7671
- National Gay Task Force, 80 Fifth Avenue, Suite 1601, New York, NY 10011 (212) 741-5800
  Crisisline: (800) 221-7044, (212) 807-6016
- National AIDS Hot Line: (800) 342-2437 for recorded information about AIDS, or call (800) 443-0366 if you have specific questions
- *Surgeon General's Report on AIDS*. Free from InterAmerica Research, 1200E North Henry Street, Alexandria, VA 22314, (InterAmerica Research is a private firm that distributes AIDS-related literature for the Red Cross and the U.S. Public Health Service.)
- *Answers About AIDS*. Free: Send a self-addressed business-size envelope with postage attached. Mail to AIDS Report, American Council on Science and Health, 47 Maple Street, Summit, NJ 07901
- Local or state health department: Information provided about where to go for confidential testing for the presence of the AIDS virus.

CHAPTER HIGHLIGHTS

The exploration of sexuality has attracted many researchers. Sexuality refers not only to reproduction and sexual pleasure, but also to one's need for love and personal fulfillment. Sexuality also embraces the many cultural and psychological factors related to human sexual behavior.

Related to the above, we reviewed three dimensions of human sexuality. The biophysical system encompasses the body's natural capacity to respond to sexual stimulation. The psychosocial system originates from a culture's sexual "script" for appropriate male and female sexual behavior. The sexual value system represents a person's unique set of beliefs about sexuality.

Today's attitudes regarding sexuality in general have become increasingly tolerant. Four major moral standards regarding sexual behavior have been proposed: the abstinence, double standard, permissiveness without affection, and permissiveness with affection principles. Of these, the permissiveness with affection standard is the most popular today. In this chapter, we also explored two other sexual standards: the traditional-romantic and modern-naturalistic ideologies.

After we examined how sexuality develops during childhood and adolescence, we explored the nature of contemporary premarital sexual relationships. Research supports the fact that a greater percentage of today's teenagers and young adults are engaging in premarital intercourse than in the past. There are many motives for and against premarital intercourse, and we pointed out those factors that affect the overall rates of premarital coitus.

One of the risks associated with sexual promiscuity is unwed pregnancy. This is glaringly evident among teenagers. Each year about one million adolescent females become pregnant, with approximately 600,000 giving birth to their babies. This chapter addressed the many problems posed by teenage pregnancy and stressed the importance of curbing this social problem.

Sexually transmitted diseases are contagious infections passed on by intimate sexual contacts with others. Four of the more common sexually transmitted diseases are gonorrhea, syphilis, genital herpes, and the acquired immune deficiency syndrome. While the first two can be controlled by antibiotics, there is no cure for the last two. Thousands continue to die from AIDS as it cripples the body's natural immunity against disease.

KEY TERMS

abstinence standard
acquired immune deficiency
  syndrome (AIDS)
B-cell
biophysical system of sexuality
chancre
double standard
excitement phase
genital herpes
gonorrhea
Kaposi's sarcoma
late syphilis
latent syphilis

lymphocytes
masturbation
modern-naturalistic ideology
orgasm phase
permissiveness with affection
  standard
permissiveness without
  affection standard
plateau phase
primary syphilis
psychosocial system of
  sexuality
puberty

refractory period
resolution phase
secondary syphilis
sex
sexual response cycle
sexual value system of
  sexuality
sexuality
sexually transmitted disease
syphilis
T-cell
traditional-romantic ideology

RECOMMENDED READINGS

Allgeier, E. R., and Allgeier, A. R. (1984). *Sexual interactions.* Lexington, MA: D. C. Heath. For those wanting more information on sexual anatomy and physiology, see Chapter 4 of this readable textbook.

Barbach, L. (1984). *For each other: Sharing sexual intimacy.* New York: Signet. Barbach supplies thoughts on how to enhance sexual relationships.

Coles, R., and Stokes, G. (1985). *Sex and the American teenager.* New York: Harper & Row. A thorough and extensive study of contemporary sexual behavior among adolescents.

Feldman, H., and Parrot, A. (Eds.). (1984). *Human sexuality: Contemporary controversies.* Beverly Hills, CA: Sage. A wide assortment of topics focusing on sexuality appear in this reader, including forms of sexual expression, sex education, and functions of intercourse.

Katchadourian, H. A. (1985). *Fundamentals of human sexuality* (4th Ed.). New York: Holt, Rinehart & Winston. Chapter 9 explores the course of sexual development.

Jones, K. L., Shainberg, L. W., and Byer, C. D. (1985). *Dimensions of human sexuality.* Dubuque, IA: William C. Brown. One of the better introductory texts in the field of human sexuality.

Maier, R. A. (1984). *Human sexuality in perspective.* Chicago, IL: Nelson-Hall. See Chapter 22 for a concise discussion of sexually transmitted diseases.

Olds, S. W. (1985). *The eternal garden: Seasons of our sexuality.* New York: Time Books. A sensitive and moving account of sexual development, from childhood and adolescence to the later years of adulthood.

Rathus, S. A. (1983). *Human sexuality.* New York: Holt, Rinehart & Winston. The sexual response cycle and implications for arousal receive attention in Chapter 8.

Sarrel, L. J., and Sarrel, P. M. (1984). *Sexual turning points: The seven stages of adult sexuality.* New York: Macmillan. This book is just plain good reading. Readers are bound to see themselves and those they love within this thoughtful portrait of sexuality.

6

Alternative Lifestyles

CONTENTS

CONTEMPLATIONS

■ Here's another quick quiz, something we'll continue to spring on you every now and then throughout the book. This one's on being single and we want to know if the following statements are true or false:

1. Singles are generally happier than married couples.
2. Singles have more social outings than married couples.
3. Singles are more likely than marrieds to be wealthy.

Want the answers? The first statement is false, the second is true, and the last is false. This chapter will fill you in on the details.

■ In Denmark, it's called "marriage without papers," and in nations such as France and Australia, significant increases of it have been reported in recent years. In the United States, it's called cohabitation, and as an alternative lifestyle, it's just as popular. In 1985, for example, about two million persons involved themselves in a cohabitating relationship. Who are the people who cohabitate? What is the appeal of this lifestyle? Are all cohabiting relationships the same?

■ Of all the nontraditional household arrangements that exist, one of the most misinterpreted is the communal lifestyle. Many incorrectly assume that the first communes were created in the rebellious 1960s. While many did emerge then, they were hardly the first. Indeed, we'll show you how the communal lifestyle is rooted in antiquity. In an effort to remove uncertainty about this lifestyle, we'll also explore how communes operate, the different types that exist, the problems they face, and the dreams they share.

Although marriage is the chosen path for a clear-cut majority of the population, not everyone chooses to exchange traditional wedding vows. On the contrary, numerous alternatives to married life exist. In this chapter, we'll explore some of the more popular alternatives: singlehood, cohabitation, communal living, homosexuality, and nontraditional marital arrangements.

How have these lifestyle alternatives evolved and what is their incidence? What do these lifestyles entail? Who chooses these alternatives and why? Questions such as these lie at the heart of this chapter. Join us as we explore those who opt for a nontraditional lifestyle, individuals who question and sometimes even reject the values of mainstream culture.

SINGLEHOOD

A growing number of adults in our contemporary society simply prefer not to get married. There are currently over 20 million never-married, single adults 18 years of age and older. Moreover, this figure has been steadily rising. Since 1960, the number of singles living apart from relatives has increased over 100 percent (U. S. Bureau of the Census, 1982a).

These statistics do not include the numbers of divorced and widowed persons also single, populations that are increasing as well. One out of every three married persons will be single within the next five years and the figure will inflate to about one in every two by the 1990s. They will join the ranks of the 67 million single adults in America, a group comprised of divorced and widowed individuals as well as those who have chosen to postpone marriage or never marry at all (Simenauer and Carroll, 1982).

Arland Thornton and Deborah Freedman (1983) add that in 1982, only 39 percent of women aged 20–24 were currently married and living with their husbands, compared to 64 percent of women this age in 1960. And single life is now particularly common for black adult Americans. Among women aged 30–54 in 1982, less than half of black women were married and living with their husbands, compared to more than three-fourths of white women.

Motivations toward Singlehood

Numerous factors account for the increase in single adults. One important motive is that there are growing career and educational opportunities for

---

THE DEMOGRAPHICS OF SINGLEHOOD

■ Between 1960 and 1983, there was a large increase in the percentage of women and men between the ages of 20 and 29 who remained single (see table at end of box). Among 20 and 24 year olds, 55 percent of females and 73 percent of males remained single; the corresponding figures for the 25 to 29 year olds were 25 percent for females and 38 percent for males.

■ Between 1960 and 1982, the percentage of never-marrieds between the ages of 25 and 34 maintaining their own households almost tripled. In 1982, 53 percent of never-married women and 43 percent of never-married men had their own households.

■ By 1990, 28 percent of all women between the ages of 25 and 29 will be unmarried, an increase of 16 percent since 1975.

■ By 1990, 46 percent of all men between ages 25 and 29 will be unmarried, an increase of 6 percent since 1975.

■ Among 30 to 34 year olds, 19.6 percent of men and 13 percent of women have never married.

■ In the 45 to 54-year-old group, 6 percent of men and 4.5 percent of women are never married.

Adapted from Stein, 1981; Masnick and Bane, 1980.

Men and Women Remaining Single in the
United States, 1960–83 (in percentages)

	1960	1970	1980	1983
Women				
20–24	28.4	35.8	50.2	55.5
25–29	10.5	10.5	20.8	24.8
Men				
20–24	53.1	54.7	68.6	73.2
25–29	20.8	19.1	32.4	38.2

Source: *Statistical Abstract of the United States*, 1982–83, p. 39;
CPR Series P-20, No. 382 (July 1983), p. 4.

women. Pursuing a career or a degree rather than marrying at an early age is today an attractive alternative for many. Another reason is that there are more women than men of marriageable age, thus creating a surplus of singles, and more individuals seem to desire freedom and autonomy. Also, many who choose this lifestyle are aware of today's gloomy divorce statistics (Macklin, 1980; Stein, 1981). Table 6-1 illustrates the "pushes" and "pulls" toward marriage and singlehood.

Peter Stein and Meryl Fingrutd (1985) maintain that **singlehood** is a lifestyle that offers considerable potential for happiness, productivity, and self-actualization. Among the most fundamental benefits of single life are its unfettered opportunities for development and change. The years following high school and college are typically a time for men and women to clarify career goals, lifestyle preferences, and political and sexual identities; by remaining single, an individual enjoys that much more freedom to reflect, experiment, and make significant changes in beliefs and values should he or she so desire. Put in sociological terms, the single has an enormous opportunity to construct new identities—or, of course, perhaps to be confused by finding too many new identities. Yet the friends and other support networks that singles can develop may help to redress some of those conflicts.

Stereotypes about Singlehood

In the past, singlehood has had various images attached to it. For some, singlehood was viewed with suspicion—singles were regarded by many as being different or lonely losers, the labels "old maid" or "spinster" capturing this image. Other societal images paint the swinging single picture—a jet-set lifestyle characterized by fast-paced excitement and risqué forms of entertainment and recreation.

These myths and stereotypes are not representative of the singlehood lifestyle. According to Leonard Cargan and Matthew Melko (1982), a clearer portrait of the single person needs to be

TABLE 6-1

Pushes and Pulls toward Marriage and Singlehood

Negative Influences	Positive Influences
Marriage	
Pressure from parents	Approval of parents
Desire to leave home	Desire for children and own family
Fear of independence	Example of peers
Loneliness and isolation	Romanticization of marriage
No knowledge or perception of alternatives	Physical attraction
	Love, emotional attachment
Cultural and social discrimination against singles	Security, social status, and prestige
	Legitimization of sexual experiences
	Socialization
	Job availability, wage structure, and promotions
	Social policies favoring the married
Singlehood	
Lack of friends, loneliness	Career opportunities or career development
Restricted availability of new experiences	Availability of sexual experiences
A negative one-to-one relationship, feeling trapped	Exciting lifestyle
	Psychological and social autonomy
Boredom, unhappiness, anger	Support structures, sustaining friendships, therapeutic groups, collegial groups
Poor communication with mate	
Sexual frustration	

Source: From *Single Life* by Peter Stein. Copyright © 1981 by St. Martin's Press, Inc., and used with permission of the publishers.

presented, one not tainted with erroneous beliefs. Their review of the literature indicates that the myths and realities regarding singlehood need to be exposed. The following discussion highlights some of the more important points made by the authors.

Myths about Singlehood

Singles Are Selfish People Here, it is believed that singles do not get married because they are too self-centered. However, the selfish single does not emerge from the data reviewed by the authors. Tests do show that singles are more likely to value success and personal growth, whereas marrieds are more likely to value love and community service. Singles, however, are more likely than marrieds to value friends and prove to be greater contributors to community service. Thus, even though marrieds are likely to value community service more, the singles follow through and deliver.

Singles Are Rich Many feel that singles ought to be richer than marrieds — they have no spouses and children to support, they live in fancy condominiums and they have active social lives. This image is not realized by most singles, though. Many are young and at the bottom of the economic ladder; others are divorced and trying to support children. On the whole, marrieds are better off economically than singles.

Singles Are Happier than Marrieds Certain tests indicate that singles are less happy than marrieds. For example, on items measuring loneliness, singles are more likely than marrieds to be depressed when alone and much more often feel they have no one with whom they can really share or discuss their lives. One study (Cargan and Melko, 1982) found that more singles worry and/or feel guilty, despondent, worthless, or lonely. However, it is the divorced that report feelings of despondency, worthlessness, sexual apathy, and loneliness more often than the never-married.

Being Permanently Single Is Totally Acceptable Interestingly, this is a myth advocated but not accepted by most singles. While we noted in Chapter 2 that singlehood has been met with greater amounts of social acceptance, such approval appears to be directed towards temporary rather than permanent singlehood. Books about mate finding are as popular and prevalent as ever in the stores, as are magazine articles about mak-

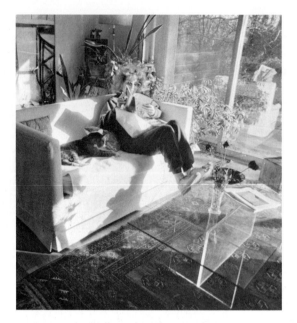

Numerous reasons exist for remaining single.

ing the best of singlehood, which implies that one must endure it if one cannot change it.

There Is Something Wrong with Singles This stereotype portrays singles as unhappy and lonely all of the time. This is obviously not the case. Also, there is nothing wrong with being lonely or sad some of the time. By measures of freedom, singles may be better off than marrieds, but that does not make it wrong to marry. Married couples may sometimes wish for freedom from the responsibilities of marriage, but on the balance they may consider it better to remain married. It is in this respect that singles remain single, even if loneliness is a price to be paid.

Realities of Singlehood

Singles Have More Time A popular image is that singles are "free" — they come and go as they please, sleep uninterrupted nights without being disturbed by the needs of children, and go on vacations when and where they like. In regard to time, it does appear that singles have more than marrieds. More of them are likely to be spending

The single lifestyle knows many variations, from moments of solitude to the crowded bar scene.

more time visiting friends, and more are likely to be spending more time on hobbies. Singles are also more apt than marrieds to go out socially twice a week and much more likely to be out three or more times a week.

Singles Are Swingers From the standpoint of variety, singles have had more sex partners than marrieds. Insight into the sexual lives of singles as well as their attitudes about sexual relationships has been supplied by Jacqueline Simenauer and David Carroll (1982). These two researchers surveyed 3,000 men and women residing in 36 states. Respondents ranged in age from 20 to 55 and included never-married as well as divorced and widowed persons. As far as the sexual lives of the respondents were concerned, the following information was uncovered:

- Almost two-thirds of men sleep with a woman on the first to third date; 80 percent sleep with a woman on the first to fifth date.

- Fifty percent of the women surveyed sleep with a man on the first to third date.

- Twice as many men in their early twenties (as compared with any other group) prefer a long courtship before actually having sex. Ten percent of men under 24 expect the same. Only 5 percent of all men over 25 prefer a long courtship before sex.

- One-third of women who have never married say it usually takes them several months and many meetings before they are ready for sex. Only 10 percent of women divorced twice or more feel the same way.

- Only 20 percent of single men and 6 percent of single women recommend casual sex or one-night stands.

- Absolutely no widows in the study recommended casual sex.

- Over three-quarters of the men felt it's acceptable for a woman to initiate sex.

- Two-thirds of single women have or would have intitiated sex with a date.

TABLE 6-2

Number of Sexual Partners of Single Male and Female Adults

	Men		
Number of Sexual Partners	Never Married	Divorced Once	Divorced Twice or More
NONE	5%	3%	2%
One	4%	10%	1%
2–4	14%	18%	9%
5–9	14%	14%	12%
10–19	19%	23%	26%
20–49	21%	17%	21%
50–100	12%	7%	8%
MORE	10%	7%	19%
Don't Know	1%	1%	2%
	Women		
NONE	10%	9%	3%
One	13%	16%	12%
2–4	23%	28%	21%
5–9	20%	15%	22%
10–19	15%	15%	9%
20–49	12%	10%	19%
50–100	4%	3%	4%
MORE	1%	1%	6%
Don't Know	2%	3%	4%

Source : Simenauer, Jacqueline, and Carroll, David. *Singles: The New Americans.* p. 150. C © 1982. Reprinted by permission of Simon & Schuster, Inc., New York, NY.

- Most singles do not think love is necessary for good sex.
- Approximately three-quarters of single men and almost 90 percent of single women feel it is difficult or impossible to be meaningfully and sexually involved with more than one person during the same period of time. The preceding table indicates the estimated number of sexual partners a person has had while single.

Singles Are Lonely   Singles are more likely than marrieds to feel that they have no one to share or discuss matters with. They are also more likely to feel that most people are alone. In addition, they tend to feel depressed just being alone and join social organizations because of their loneliness.

Life for Singles Is Changing for the Better Despite such continuities as a continued anticipation of marriage in the future, life and perceptions are qualitatively different for singles in the 1980s from what they had been earlier. The universal norm of marriage has been challenged and singlehood is a legitimate alternative lifestyle. Also, the singles population is a growing market, complete with products developed specifically for them including apartments, clubs, vacation spots, and tours.

COHABITATION

In addition to singlehood, many individuals choose cohabitation as a lifestyle in contemporary society. **Cohabitation** is defined as an unmarried man and an unmarried woman living together. While this form of alternative lifestyle did not gain prominence until the 1960s, today it is extremely popular.

The manner in which cohabitation burst into the scene during the 1960s was due to a combination of various social changes. On college campuses, administrators relaxed rules against opposite-sex visitors in response to student demands. Large numbers of students also took advantage of new options to rent off-campus apartments. At the same time, young adults began to liberalize their sexual attitudes and behaviors, making premarital sex more openly acceptable. These changes fell upon the fertile ground of a particularly large cohort of college students, products of the post-World War II baby-boom years (Atwater, 1985).

Statistics gathered in the 1980s further reveal the popularity of cohabitation. Unmarried couples living together have increased from nearly a million in 1977 to almost two million in 1985. This is

an increase of over 300 percent from the previous decade. Furthermore, it is projected that by 1990, 7 percent of all U.S. households will consist of unmarried couples living together (Thornton and Freedman, 1983; U.S. Bureau of the Census, 1982a; Population Reference Bureau, 1982). Figure 6-1 shows the increase in cohabitation in the United States since 1960.

Reasons for Cohabitation

There are many reasons behind a couple's decision to cohabit. Sexual modes and values are changing — consider, for example, the gradual weakening of the double standard. In addition, the availability of contraceptives and the relative ease of obtaining an abortion have reduced the risks of pregnancy

FIGURE 6-1   Increase in Unmarried Couples Living Together in the United States, 1960–1982

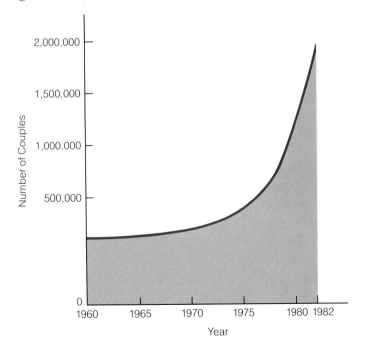

Based on data from Glick and Spanier (1980) and U. S. Bureau of the Census, 1982, 1984.

among sexually active cohabitants. Peer support for such a lifestyle represents an additional reason, and many cohabitants are today less concerned about the status of marriage. And adults who have seen their parents' marriages break down may also have less faith in formal marriage as an institution that can provide security and happiness (Oliver, 1982).

Most cohabitants are under age 35. This lifestyle continues to be popular among college students, due largely to the availability of off-campus housing, co-ed dormitories, and liberal student attitudes. In recent years, however, there has been an increase in the number of older cohabitants as well. It is estimated that there are approximately 350,000 persons over age 55 living together (Glick and Spanier, 1980).

Just as there are many types of marriages and diverse motives for people joining together in marriage, so, too, are there many types of living-together arrangements. Some couples live together for purely economic reasons. Some cohabit without any desire to become involved in an intimate relationship. For others, the opposite is true: cohabitation offers the opportunity to establish intimacy. The largest number of cohabitants, however, are those who believe marriage is on the horizon. In this sense, cohabitation is a precursor to marriage, not an alternative (Cherlin and Furstenberg, 1983).

The research of Jacqueline Simenauer and David Carroll (1982) indicates that age differences need to be taken into account when the above is considered. They found that older male and female singles perceive living together as a *transitory experience* rather than a preliminary to wedlock. Younger men and women, especially students, consider living together a trial marriage. The younger they are, the more likely they are to view things this way. Aside from age, few important characteristics differentiate the groups. To an extent, college-educated persons are more likely to judge living together as a permanent relationship than those who attended high school only. And professionals are less prone to live together than white- and blue-collar singles. These differences,

however, are not profound. What is profound is the fact that for the younger and hence statistically never-married single, cohabitation is thought to be part of the marriage process, while older and hence statistically more frequently divorced singles see it as an escape from marriage.

Along the same lines, Lynn Atwater (1985) adds that cohabitation can be distinguished by its overall duration. She identifies two forms of cohabitation: *courtship* and *long-term premarital cohabitation*. Courtship cohabitation, similar to the above, usually occurs between young adults who have never married. In this type of cohabitation, living together is not expected to be a permanent arrangement, nor is there a desire for children to be part of the relationship. Most of the participants in courtship cohabitation have defined themselves as not yet ready for marriage. This relationship typically lasts for only a few months and is best understood as an extension of the courtship stage, that is, a variation of steady dating but one that openly acknowledges sexual intimacy.

Long-term premarital cohabitation, on the other hand, offers a strong parallel to first marriages without children. Long-term cohabitation can last for years and fills the need for adults to test out their ability to relate intimately to another person, a necessary skill for survival in legal marriage. It enables couples to combine love and work and sex in a setting that is relatively free from their parents' control. This arrangement affords them the opportunity to continue to grow and change without forcing them to make a permanent commitment to another person before they are developmentally ready. Because they have not made a permanent commitment that they later find they cannot keep, they are free to separate without the burden of failure and guilt associated with divorce. Nor, of course, do they face the difficult chore of becoming one-parent families after divorce.

Problems and Pressures   While cohabitation has positive dimensions, it is not without its share of problems. Some cohabitants report guilt over their living arrangements and even more are fearful of their parents' reaction. Because of the latter,

Cohabitation is prevalent among students in many college and university settings.

many refuse to disclose their living arrangements to their parents. Another problem is that many couples feel closed in and stunted by their lifestyle. Finally, pregnancy often poses complications for those choosing cohabitation over marriage.

Types of Cohabiting Relationships

All cohabiting relationships are not the same. Indeed, the motives for cohabitation just described clearly indicate the diverse motivations to pursue such a lifestyle. From these motivations, Carl Ridley and his colleagues (1978) have developed four broad types of cohabiting relationships: the "Linus blanket," emancipation, convenience, and testing relationships. Let's explore each more fully.

The "Linus Blanket" Relationship This cohabiting relationship is characterized by a need for one member of the pair to have a relationship with *someone,* with little apparent regard for whom, or under what conditions. It is reasoned that to have someone to be with, even though this partner is a poor companion, is better than not having anyone at all. The need to feel secure through a relation-

ship overrides the importance of evaluating the circumstances of relationship formation, the motivations of the partner, or the conditions surrounding relationship continuation. Emotional security is the key to the "Linus blanket" relationship.

As long as the more secure partner does not feel trapped in this situation and their behavior remains predictable, the insecure partner's basic needs are likely to be met. The fragility of this relationship prevents the type of interaction between partners that increases the development of interpersonal skills important for maintaining heterosexual relationships. Open communication and successful problem solving do not take place and thus the experience does not serve as "practice" for improving the skills of the partners. Continued interaction is likely to be ritualized following traditional lines of male-female role behavior. In this case, the "Linus blanket" relationship provides an opportunity to learn sex-role stereotyped behaviors. When a "Linus blanket" relationship terminates, the insecure individual typically suffers a loss of self-esteem which neutralizes much of the potential gain of having lived with someone in an intimate relationship.

"Oh, Penny, will you, like, live with
me for a little while?"

Drawing by Wm. Hamilton; © 1971 The New Yorker Magazine, Inc.

The Emancipation Relationship   Evidence
indicates that some cohabiting relationships are
short-lived. Ridley and colleagues note that while
these abbreviated relationships are experienced
by both men and women, perhaps the clearest
example of this pattern is found among Catholic
females who start cohabiting early in their college
years and maintain a pattern of short duration, but
frequent, cohabiting relationships.

It is observed that females in this emancipation
situation experience pulls, pushes, and resistances
to becoming involved in cohabiting relationships.
Such resistances may rest primarily in socialization to strict sexual standards from family and
church, which deny guilt-free participation in sex-
ualized heterosexual relationships. The restrictions seem to be encountered by internal pushes to
loosen external controls and to demonstrate increased freedom by becoming sexually active. Peer
pressures which often support a liberalized set of
sexual norms place the females in a potentially
double binding situation. In other words, peer
pressure and the desire for more self control result
in her becoming involved in a cohabiting situation.
However, the subtle guilt feeling of "doing something wrong" makes it difficult for her to become
actively involved in a cohabitation, forcing her to
leave the live-in arrangement. Once the relationship terminates, the pulls and pushes return and

the cycle repeats itself. Another relationship is
begun, but the person has the same value system
—and conflicts—working against her. When the
pattern is left unchecked, reasons for exit from the
relationship are rarely understood and result in
confusion and self-doubt on the part of both
partners.

The Convenience Relationship   The convenience relationship is perhaps best exemplified in
the short-duration cohabiting relationships of the
freshman or sophomore male. This live-in arrangement allows the male to have regular sexual
contact with the luxuries of domestic living without the responsibilities of a committed relationship. The execution of domestic tasks falls to the
female simply because she is thought to be more
skilled and/or has been socialized to perform
them. The male's major task is to keep the female
interested when it appears that she is putting more
into the relationship than he is. If the male can
maintain this type of relationship (most do not), he
is probably exhibiting a fairly high interpersonal
skill level even though the inequity of the relationship may seem somewhat unjust.

The convenience relationship gives both males
and females the opportunity to learn the idea of
reciprocity—mutual giving and getting in a relationship. Females can learn that unconditional
giving can have limited long-range payoffs and
that assessments of what one is giving and getting
are important in certain contexts. At times it appears that the female is trying to make the male so
dependent on her that he would not think of leaving the relationship. On other occasions, she is
simply fitting into the culturally prescribed role for
women. It appears that the male is getting much
practice at strategic interaction by trying to maintain his freedom to interact with others (keeping
his options open), but at the same time presenting
to his partner a high level of involvement in the
cohabiting relationship. In a general sense, he
seems to learn a great deal about the day-to-day
aspects of domestic life (role behavior) and at least
some exchange skills. His *guarded openness* prevents the type of involvement that escalates the
relationship toward a premature commitment.

Cohabitants have the opportunity to learn about the routines and expectations attached to domestic life.

While it may seem that the male is getting the better end of the deal, it should be recognized that both the male and female are learning important aspects of "survival" within intimate relationships. This is true even though the learning experience may be painful for one or both of them. Interestingly, even though the researchers found that this situation is most typical with the male in the convenience role, the situation is sometimes reversed with a more assertive female forming and maintaining the relationship primarily for its convenience qualities.

The Testing Relationship   The testing relationship is the last major form of cohabitation outlined by Ridley and his associates. Individuals who are in the testing type of cohabiting relationship are typically well-adjusted people who exhibit a higher than average interpersonal skill level upon entrance into a cohabitation. A goal of this relationship is to develop a satisfying intimate relationship while, at the same time, maintaining individuality and autonomy. Partners use the relationship to get to know more about themselves — their likes and dislikes — and to learn more about how intimate relationships of this type apparently

lead to a deeper level of self-understanding for both individuals. But, when the relationship solidifies too quickly — prior to the development of individual interests and preferences — the partners feel overinvolved and dependent on the relationship, in the process experiencing a sense of loss of identity.

This combination of perceived loss of identity and high relationship cohesiveness *without* commitment increases the probability that many testing relationships will end at this point. However, the researchers point out that if the mutuality-autonomy issue is handled successfully, the relationship may develop in one of three directions:

- The relationship can terminate because the primary objectives for its formation (of which they may or may not have been aware) have been accomplished (increased self-understanding within a relationship context and increased knowledge of day-to-day intimate living).

- The relationship can evolve into an enduring cohabiting relationship similar to a marriage relationship, but without formal commitment and the ever-present possibility of terminating the relationship. According to Ridley and colleagues, the effects on the relationship of a lack of formal commitment and the availability of alternative sources of gratification is as yet unclear. They suggest that the persons involved would have to possess sufficient interpersonal skills to maintain this type of relationship without experiencing continuous crises arising from attempts to establish relationship predictability.

- The relationship goal can be extended from increasing self-understanding within the relationship context to developing a marital relationship which would involve further testing of compatibility and the ability to work together. If the cohabiting experience showed the couple that they could not work together, the relationship would most likely end. On the other hand, if compatability testing were positive, escalation toward marriage would be likely.

In summarizing these four typologies, the researchers conclude that numerous factors must be examined when exploring cohabiting relationships. Moreover, they stress that a specific answer to the question of whether cohabitation makes for a better marriage is elusive. A knowledge of the cohabitation typologies *and* an accurate understanding of the persons involved, however, makes it easier to assess the potential effects of cohabitation on the individuals. In order to do this effectively, several important factors must be considered, including:

1. Partners' motivations for cohabiting.
2. Partners' expectations for the cohabiting experience.
3. Partners' personal and interpersonal needs and goals.
4. Partners' interpersonal skill levels.
5. The present status of the relationship (for example, level of commitment).
6. The effects of the partners' previous heterosexual experiences.
7. The support structure of the partners' interpersonal networks.

APPLICATIONS

A CONTRACT FOR COHABITATION: ITEMS FOR CONSIDERATION

The much-publicized lawsuit involving actor Lee Marvin and his former live-in lover, Michelle Triola Marvin, has added a new dimension to the lives of cohabiting couples, and a legal one at that. The landmark ruling in 1976 by the California Supreme Court stipulated that all cohabitants have the right to claim a share of property and earnings, provided they can show that such an agreement existed while they were living together. Michelle Triola Marvin was able to prove this, and she received $104,000 in 1979 in the form of **palimony**, a type of alimony given to a partner after a cohabitation relationship terminates. The Marvin vs. Marvin case was a harbinger of things to come — in some instances there does not even have to be a written or spoken agreement between cohabitants. The fact of living together itself can imply a contract in the eyes of some legal advisors.

Because of such legal developments, couples contemplating cohabitation — and those within such living arrangements — need to draft an agreement that spells out the economic parameters of their relationship. Susan Macovsky (1983) writes that to draw up an informal contract, unmarried couples should begin before the beginning — by listing the major items each brought to the partnership. That ▶

makes it easier to walk out with them later on. If partners decide to make purchases together, and particularly if they buy a house, they need to spell out their proportionate shares of ownership. Both names should be on a deed, mortgage or rental agreement. They also need to state clearly what happens to property when they split up — whether the house will be sold and the proceeds split evenly, for example.

If one individual wants to keep the house, that person should have the option of buying the other out. In that case, the couple will need a way to put a value on the house. They could average three appraisals, or settle for just one. Couples should also specify how the rent or mortgage will be paid immediately after one moves out and the other is left with the bills.

It's important, too, that couples spell out who is responsible for which chores, especially if one is expected to do more to compensate for lower cash contributions. If one promises to support the other in case of separation, it should be stated how much and how long one is to pay.

However, the simplest agreement is a waiver of all financial claims on one another. The waiver should state clearly the following:

■ Neither person has any intention of sharing their earnings or property with the other.

■ Any property acquired while the couple lives together belongs to whomever paid for it.

■ Any future agreements to share earnings or property must be made in writing.

■ Neither person expects compensation for any services rendered the other.

■ Neither person has an obligation to support the other.

Adapted from Macovsky, 1983. ■

COMMUNAL LIVING

A **commune** is a self-supporting community in which residents dedicate themselves to cooperative living. The concept of communal living is not a recent development. Rather, communes are rooted in antiquity with some dating back to 103 B.C. In our own country, the Oneida Community of New York State was founded in 1848 by religious leader John Noyes, and other communes, also based on religious philosophies, have been around for as long, such as the Amish of Pennsylvania and the Hutterites of Canada. Some communes, though, are of more recent origin — consider the many ideological communes that sprang up during the 1960s and 1970s. Today, it is estimated that several thousand rural and urban communes are scattered throughout the United States, with about one million persons living within them.

Characteristics of Communes

As indicated, many communes are formed because of philosophical or religious beliefs. The commune often exists as a society whose life is governed by idealistic goals and a feeling of spiritual rebirth. This is attractive to those who wish to escape alienation and isolation. Other communes are formed for other reasons, such as economics.

Some communes, in an effort to encourage intimacy among their members, minimize the importance of marriage. Married couples are asked to

Children's activities were very much a part of the Oneida community in New York, founded in 1848.

give allegiance to the group as a whole. Frequently, communes use only first names, encourage emotional relationships among all group members, and take away property belonging to the couple as a means of spreading the love bond between husband and wife to the commune as a whole. Some also encourage sexual relationships among group members.

Many communes are characterized by equality, whether in the form of shared domestic tasks or in the provision of emotional support. Childrearing, for instance, is considered a community task. Work assignments are also equally dispersed. Men and women frequently work side by side and typically earn the same amount of money, which is channeled to the collective.

While some communes succeed and meet their goals, many fail. Relinquishing all of one's resources to the group becomes a stumbling block

for some. Others rebel at the loss of privacy. Many communes fail because the business enterprises undertaken, such as farming, are poorly planned and executed. Others fail because they have a loose overall organization, which often leads to a general lack of leadership and needed direction. These factors, coupled with frequent membership instability, often create internal disharmony and unsteadiness.

Types of Communes

Bernice Eiduson and Irla Lee Zimmerman (1985) stress the importance of distinguishing between the varieties of communes that exist. More specifically, one needs to understand the difference between religious communes and domestically based ones. Religious communes are founded mainly upon either Eastern philosophies and cul-

CROSS-CULTURAL FOCUS

COMMUNAL LIFE IN THE ISRAELI KIBBUTZ

In Israel, a form of communal lifestyle exists that provides unique contrasts to those originating in the United States. In existence for over 60 years, the Israeli **kibbutz** (from the Hebrew word for group) is a settlement where there exists a sharing of work and wealth and the communal rearing of children under a roof separate from that of their parents. The kibbutz was introduced to revolutionize Jewish society and prevent the development of social classes, an intention still persisting today.

Communal life within the kibbutz is based on socialistic ideology, an economic system under which the means of production and distribution are collectively owned. Initially, the kibbutz was characterized chiefly bv farming enterprises, but in recent years many have acquired an industrial character. Individual property ownership is discouraged and all members of the kibbutz take part in governance.

One of the more novel features of the Israeli kibbutz is the manner in which children are reared outside of their parents' homes. Shortly after birth until late adolescence, the children are reared in group settings, from the nursery to high school. The group of children that one is born into remains the same and as a result, close bonds of attachment usually develop. During infancy, a *metapalet*

The kibbutz encourages loyalty to the community as well as to one's family.

▶

(a childcare worker of the kibbutz) tends to the baby's basic needs. Parents visit the infant daily and the mother returns as often as necessary to feed the child. When the infant is weaned from the mother, the metapalet assumes full responsibility for feeding the youngster. As children get older, they move to other living arrangements and come into contact with other metapalets and teachers.

By the time they reach adolescence, teenagers are part of the "youth movement" that exposes them to the kibbutz and communal sphere with more intensity. They are encouraged to formulate group decisions and more fully develop such capacities as cooperation and sensitivity toward others. By the end of their teenage years, members of the kibbutz work with adults and contribute to the economy and governance of this unique communal lifestyle.   ■

ture or on the "Jesus movement," which seeks a new way to live out traditional Judeo-Christian convictions. A smaller number of religious groups are derived from allegiance to a charismatic leader who may espouse a personalized philosophical system.

The domestic commune, by contrast, is a less formally organized unit, developing spontaneously around shared crafts, political convictions, or identification with the natural rural environment or the small contemporary farm. In the latter, people who like each other decide to live in a small household or in close proximity and to share some quarters and tasks and some social and domestic activities, including childcare. Differences emerge in their family composition, structure, roles, and responsibilities. Keeping these points in mind, Eiduson and Zimmerman (1985) further distinguish five types of communal living arrangement: Christian religious family commune, Eastern religious family commune, leader-directed communal family, rural domestic commune, and the urban domestic commune.

Christian Religious Family Commune Many young adults joined these communes in the 1960s and 1970s in an effort to find meaning from a perceived drug-ridden, unstructured, and meaningless counterculture life. The communal lifestyle attracting them was energized by contemporary young people who sought ways of giving new

meaning to their lives in pledging themselves to Jesus.

Group cohesion within these communes is served by the philosophy as well as by shared daily practices. Members may live in individual nuclear family units to afford some private areas of family existence; however, functions of everyday life are determined by common practices of the group. When people wake, times of prayer, nature of work activities, and eating practices are all group decisions. Members demonstrate concern for each other, share knowledge and skills, and work toward common ends which reinforce shared values.

Children within the Christian religious family group occupy a special position. They are regarded as the future evangelists, and their growth and development is governed with this in mind. They pledge themselves to the Lord at an early age, already having regularly participated in prayer service. Parents expect that children will assume some group-assigned responsibilities by age two or three.

Parents soon realize that the overall communal philosophy determines their role. The Lord's will, for example, is perceived as dictating the child's personality and his/her response to parenting practices. The parent must work with children to make them responsive to the Lord's teachings. Spanking is used as a form of discipline but is followed by hugging to show the youngster that the

Communes consist of young and old and are bonded by a common ideology.

real purpose of discipline is teaching the child, with the parent as God's representative of love and care.

All of this shows that family life is structured by goals larger and more important than any individual aims. As parents live by certain group decisions, so children learn that lives will be regulated from the outside. Even when the children go to public school (since church schools are not always viable alternatives), scheduled chores and activities at home are also adhered to before and after school. "Proper" behaviors are usually sex-stereotypic, with both adults and children acting in traditional roles.

Eastern Religious Family Commune   Similar to the Christian family commune, the Eastern religion variation has a family life that is private and apart from the group experience, as well as a domain that is group-shared. A child's family structure begins as a nuclear unit, but if families separate, one parent remains in the group. In most communities, nuclear families have separate quarters or some private space (an apartment, a duplex, or a bedroom upon occasion) while sharing public spaces. Meals assume ritualistic features, sometimes around dietary restrictions, or convictions about prayer or interpersonal communication.

As far as childrearing is concerned, the parents are usually expected to nurture their own young, with support from group members who may babysit, run a preschool program, or carry out those activities that make it possible for the mother to play a role in the common activities of the group. Parents find all forms of personal and social assistance and resources from group members.

Youngsters are afforded some opportunity to partake of what the community environment offers: schools, companions, family friends, and relatives. As children grow older, special instruction geared towards religious beliefs is initiated. The spontaneity and creativity of the young, impulsive child are highly valued; thus, in a rigorous and ritualized family, the young child may be unfettered by most conventions as long as this does not conflict with movement toward the roles children must assume as young adults. Invariably, early orientation toward religious roles follows sex-stereotyped lines.

Leader-directed Communal Family   In a sense, religious family groups are leader directed. However, there are also family groups in which the leader is a tangible and charismatic figure. Leader-directed families are usually distinguished by their devotion to specified goals and are often considered religious with the members as devotees. However, their allegiance is to a belief system that is not structured around the concept of God. Instead, tenets of the leader show "The Way," with a search for self through goals shared in a hierarchically structured family organization with prescribed relationships within and outside the immediate family.

The development and practice of cult-like rituals is often nurtured by personal but shared philosophical views. Practices may include polygyny, in which a few powerful men in the group sire offspring with various women. Parents may also allow children to be separated from them and placed with group or infant-school caretakers. The latter will see that the child's special powers, or "energies," are used to group advantage. In a commune that believes that children are too age-graded in mainstream life, sensual group activities may involve children or teenagers. These types of sexual activities are rationalized as being in the psychological interests of healthy child adjustments. While the ideology of the group may more or less direct childbearing philosophy and practice, strategies for reshaping child development may turn out to be experimental, erratic, and radical.

This type of commune provides children with companionship and models for learning. Children are usually expected to find their own ways of using the social and cognitive environment. As with brothers and sisters in one very large biological family, the children learn to make their ways with each other and have personal attachments and rivalries.

The Rural Domestic Commune   In this commune, there is a desire to return to the land and a simple, traditional rural existence. This motivation usually brings the rural domestic commune to small, frequently hidden communities in remote areas. The family has usually gathered a group of interested friends to live in close proximity and thus share companionship, some meals, and some activities while maintaining the privacy of the private dwelling.

The overall process of building up one's own wherewithal for existence becomes the sum and substance around which family life proceeds. As with the pioneer farm family in the 1800s, there is little time or energy left for less-mundane, more-sophisticated activities. Pleasures include simple respites from hard work, but the greatest gratifica-

Many communes enjoy a simple, rural existence.

tions rest with the fact that the family is constantly renewing its vitality and viability by its own hands.

The youngsters of this commune have the freedom that has always been provided by farms, busy parents, and an almost-exclusive concern with the basics of life. They participate in the parent's activities and play with makeshift toys and spontaneously thought-up games. Lives are regulated by the needs of an early-to-rise, early-to-bed family.

Family life is not marked by an abundancy of ceremony. Informal games and get-togethers are as taken for granted as the slaughtering of animals for food or the continual rebuilding and improvising of homes. As these families find less need to prove their self-sufficiency in this lifestyle, they venture with their children into the nearby small towns, go to classes and lectures, see friends, and shop.

LIFE AT TWIN OAKS: A RURAL DOMESTIC COMMUNE

Twin Oaks lies at the foothills of Virginia's Piedmont Mountains, a picturesque and rambling 123-acre farm commune. It was begun in 1967 by organizers who wanted the communal living arrangement described by B. F. Skinner in his utopian novel, *Walden Two*. Buildings at Twin Oaks bear the same names as those in Skinner's book. For example, within the settlement is a farmhouse called Llano, a shop building called Harmony, and a dormitory called Oneida.

Twin Oaks strives to be a highly organized and systematic community, one that initially began as an anarchistic commune but evolved into a democracy. A board of planners and a manager for each of the work areas at Twin Oaks are elected by the resident population. And positive reinforcement abounds within the economic system. Work is allocated by a methodical system of labor credits so that none of the residents shoulder unequal burdens. Undesirable work receives more labor credits than desirable chores.

Titles and honorifics have been removed at Twin Oaks in an effort to accord everyone the same privileges, advantages, and respect. Even the personal pronouns "he" and "she" are frowned upon and replaced with "co" when speaking and writing. Members are discouraged from boasting of personal accomplishments and intolerance toward another member's beliefs is forbidden. Children at Twin Oaks are reared according to Skinner's principles of behaviorism.

No one owns private property at Twin Oaks. For that matter, members can only keep such personal items as clothing and books. Most end up selecting their attire from a massive community closet. Alcohol and tobacco are frowned upon at Twin Oaks and other forms of drugs are forbidden. Television, regarded as a form of cultural poison, is also not allowed

The commune is not without its share of problems. Financial hardships afflict Twin Oaks as they do other communes all across the United States. While the farm brings utopian rewards, it heralds monetary difficulties: members often find it necessary to work at other jobs or buy goods from outside sources because they're cheaper. Another problem is the high rate of turnover among the members. Each of the setbacks, in their own way, threaten the philosophical foundation of Twin Oaks. That is, the founders' effort to create — and sustain — a totally controlled environment.

Urban Domestic Commune   The final variety of commune identified by Eiduson and Zimmerman is the urban domestic commune. Within this arrangement, the child is also constantly with parents and their friends. Life has an informal, relaxed quality, with living as easy and flexible as possible. When the parents work away from home during all or part of the day, the child's day is shaped by the caretaking arrangements that the group has made: communal day care, nursery group, or baby-sitting. The parents place minimal demands on themselves, trying mainly to do the things they like to do, seeing the people they like to see, and interacting openly and without ceremony. •

Parental demands on their children for behavior or conformity are also light. The parents see themselves as supportive and meeting minimal needs without pressure. Children relate to their parents in a casual way, seeing other adults and children as important persons in their environment. Child-rearing has a casual, spontaneous, sometimes impulsive quality about it in contrast to the planned, scheduled milieu found in many traditional homes. Sharing is the most important principle as evidenced in decision-making, homemaking jobs, and baby-sitting.

HOMOSEXUALITY

Homosexuality refers to the love of one person for another person of the same sex. However, homosexuality is a broad term that needs to be further broken down. The terms **gay men** and **lesbian women** are preferred over homosexuality since they identify sexual orientation and affectional attraction to a member of the same gender. Moreover, these terms acknowledge nonsexual aspects of an individual's life (Parrot and Ellis, 1985).

Confusion about this chosen lifestyle, including sexuality and gender roles, abounds. Stereotypes often depict homosexuals as individuals who are uncomfortable with their gender identity and who want to change their gender. Cultural images of the effeminate gay man and the masculine, "butch" lesbian are still to be found. In relationships, ho-

mosexuals are thought to mimic heterosexual patterns, with one partner acting as the "wife" and the other partner playing the "husband." However, current research shows that these stereotypes are inaccurate and misleading. Although these stereotypes may characterize a small minority of homosexuals, they fail to fit the lifestyles of most gay men and lesbians (Peplau and Gordon, 1983).

Discrimination against Homosexuality

For many years, gay men and women have had to live with societal rejection and ridicule, not to mention discriminatory laws and practices. Andrea Parrot and Michael Ellis (1985) point out that this treatment of gay and lesbian Americans is still in evidence in the 1980s. For example, marriages between lesbian women and gay men are legally prohibited. Gay men and lesbian women are also prevented from adopting children. They are also barred from entrance to the armed services and various organizations and occupations. The educational system has frequently denied gay men and lesbian women teaching positions due to a fear that children will be corrupted and recruited to the so-called homosexual way of life or be abused by them in some way. This is an unfounded fear since the majority of those who sexually abuse and assault children are heterosexual men. The media also tends to depict homosexuality in an unfair and unrealistic light.

Parrot and Ellis (1985) further point out the discrimination that is leveled against gay men and lesbian women in regard to family life:

- Lesbian women and gay men are often perceived as a threat to family life. The real threat, however, is the ignorance and prejudice that cause family members to turn their backs on a gay or lesbian family member, destroying the family unit. Lesbian and gay children are often rejected by their families because the family is embarrassed by them.
- As previously indicated, gay marriages are not legal. Consider this inequality in regard to the following. The reasons often given for mar-

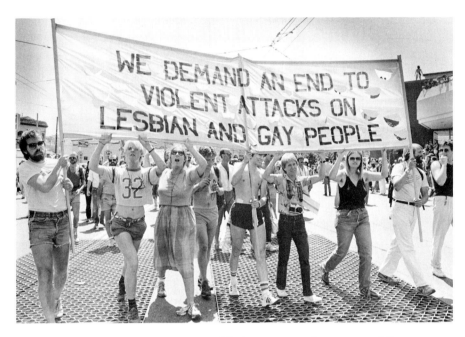

Discrimination against gay men and lesbian women has persisted for years.

riage of heterosexual couples include love, to have children, to attain the rights to make important decisions for the other person (such as life and death decisions in intensive care wards), to pass on inheritance, to be able to own things together (such as houses), to support each other financially, to gain cultural recognition as a couple, and to file joint tax returns. Most of these reasons are also important to gay and lesbian couples, but society discriminates against lesbian women and gay men by disallowing gay and lesbian marriages. Tax and insurance regulations also discriminate against homosexual couples. If one member of a married heterosexual couple is working and the other is not, their incomes are pooled and taxed based on two deductions rather than one. These tax savings are significant.

■ While most gay men and lesbian women do not become parents through traditional means, those who do are often discriminated against in child custody cases. They are also often discriminated against when attempting to become parents through nontraditional means. Because gay men and lesbian women do not usually have children by traditional means, "family planning" is not thought important for them (since family planning usually means postponing conception rather than planning how to have a family).

Relationships of Gay Men and Lesbian Women

Gay men and lesbian women often want the type of relationship heterosexual couples have, and they hold many of the same values. They are likely, however, to reject traditional roles in favor of an egalitarian relationship. As far as sexual relationships are concerned, gay men and lesbians, compared to heterosexuals, are more aware of their partners' sexual needs. This is probably because they possess more knowledge of their own sex (Peplau, 1981; Harmatz and Novak, 1983; Masters and Johnson, 1980).

The research of Letitia Ann Peplau and col-

Exploring the intimate relationships of gay men and lesbian women is a relatively recent research pursuit.

leagues (Peplau, 1981; Peplau and Gordon, 1983; Peplau and Cochran, 1980, 1981) has provided much insight into the intimate relationships of lesbians and gay men. Among other findings, she notes that most gays want to have steady relationships, although this is somewhat more important to women than men. Both gay men and lesbians, as well as heterosexual couples, desire certain elements in a close relationship: affection, companionship, and personal development. As far as qualities sought in partners, lesbians, gay men, and heterosexuals all value such traits as honesty, affection, and warmth.

In one study (Peplau and Cochran, 1980), matched samples of lesbians, gay men, and heterosexual women and men rated the importance of various features of love relationships. These included such issues as revealing intimate feelings, spending time together, holding similar attitudes, having an equal-power relationship, and having sexual exclusivity. The gathered results showed that remarkably few overall group differences existed between heterosexuals and homosexuals. For instance, on average, both groups gave greatest importance to "being able to talk about my most intimate feelings" with a partner.

The researchers found that one major difference between homosexuals and heterosexuals did emerge, however. Sexual exclusivity in relationships was much more important to heterosexuals than to homosexuals. Lesbians and gay men gave sexual fidelity an average rating of somewhat more than 5, compared with a rating of just over 7 for the heterosexuals (the highest possible importance rating was 9). Homosexuals were less likely than heterosexuals to endorse monogamy as an ideal for relationships. Two interesting gender differences also emerged. Whatever their sexual orientation, women gave greater importance than men to emotional expressiveness and the sharing of feelings. This finding is consistent with the emphasis in North American gender-role socialization that men should conceal their feelings and present a tough exterior. Second, lesbian and heterosexual women cared more than men about having egalitarian relationships. The researchers feel that perhaps because of the women's movement, women showed greater sensitivity to equal power in love relationships.

Such differences notwithstanding, this study shows that gay men, lesbian women, and heterosexual couples are more alike than dissimilar in terms of relationship dynamics. This prompts researchers such as Sharon Brehm (1985) to conclude that if we want to describe what goes on in a relationship between two gay men or lesbian

CROSS-CULTURAL FOCUS

HOMOSEXUALITY AMONG THE ZANDE

In Zande, Africa, unique sexual behaviors have been practiced throughout history, including incest and homosexuality. For example, history reveals institutionalized incestuous marriages between noblemen and their daughters as well as paternal half-sisters. Noblemen within Zande society also kept sizable harems, thereby creating a large scale monopoly of women. This monopoly of village women in the hands of a select few encouraged the widespread practice of homosexual acts by both men and women. However, such acts were institutionalized for men but condemned for women. The wives in a Zande harem might be sexually deprived, but because adultery was severely punished, young unmarried men were loath even to attempt it. Death for an adulterous wife and her lover was a distinct possibility. The minimum punishment for the lover was a very stiff fine. Some irate husbands, though, were not satisfied with this and demanded that the offender be physically punished.

Institutionalized male homosexual acts were associated with the military organization of the various Zande kingdoms. Before the coming of the Europeans, large numbers of adult males were organized into military units of either married men or bachelors. It was the custom of the men of the bachelor companies to take boy-wives, who could be as young as 12 or as old as 20. The relationship between the two was regarded as a legal union as long as it lasted. The older man had to pay a bride-price of five or more spears to the parents and performed services for them as he would if he had married a woman. If he proved to be a good son-in-law, he might later get one of their daughters as a wife to replace their son, who would in turn become a bachelor soldier and take a boy-wife. If another man had relations with the boy-wife, the husband could go to court with a charge of adultery.

The Zande thought the sole reason for such marriages was the shortage of women, not the lure of boys, but the custom was never spoken of as disgusting or abnormal. In post-European times it entirely disappeared, most probably because of a breakdown of the traditional morality, the suppression of the traditional punishment for adultery, and because it was easier for young men to marry women.

Adapted from Gregersen, 1983.

women—what makes for the success of that relationship and what may lead to problems—we do not have to use a different language. We can use the same terms as we would in describing a relationship between two heterosexuals. In our intimate relationships, we are all much more similar than we are different.

NONTRADITIONAL MARITAL ARRANGEMENTS

Before this chapter draws to a close, let us acknowledge two other possible lifestyles that are nontraditional in scope. Both occur within the general framework of marriage, but offer liberal options for partners. These two lifestyles are open marriages and swinging.

Open Marriages

In contrast to the traditional marriage, an **open marriage** is usually one that is flexible and stresses the importance of continual self-growth for both marriage partners. While we would expect this in any marriage, its underlying assumptions differ from the traditional marriage contract, which many couples still use to guide their individual marriages. Table 6-3 compares traditional marriages with open marriages.

In general, open marriages do not place the partners in bondage to each other, diminish the individual identity of the partners, create a "couple image," or enforce togetherness in the belief that only thus can the marriage be preserved. The open marriage does not substitute new regulations for old ones; rather, it suggests ways in which cou-

TABLE 6-3

Traditional vs. Open Marriages

Issue	Traditional Marriage	Open Marriage
Living for now and realistic expectations	Believe marriage will last forever	Values change in the marital relationship, even if the change results in ending the marriage
Privacy	Don't believe in separate vacations	Feel that it is important to spend some vacation time apart
Open and honest communication	Don't share fantasies or dreams that might hurt the other	Share all dreams; believe in self-disclosure
Role flexibility	Have ascribed roles	Exchange roles for sake of convenience
Open companionship	A caring relationship with someone of the opposite sex is a risk to the marriage	Caring relationship with someone of the opposite sex is acceptable
Equality	One partner has more freedom and responsibility	Freedom and responsibility are equally granted
Identity	Personal lifestyles are compromised to meet longterm needs of the marriage	Each spouse is free to pursue his or her own unique lifestyle
Trust	When one is away, the other is concerned about what the partner might do	Neither has any qualms about what the other might do

Source: Adapted from D. Wachowiak and H. Brag. "Open Marriage and Marital Adjustment." *Journal of Marriage and the Family*. February 1980, p. 59. Copyrighted 1980 by the National Council on Family Relations, 1910 West County Road B, Suite 147, St. Paul, Minnesota 55113. Reprinted by permission.

ples can learn to communicate openly with one another in order to arrive at a fully understood and mutual consensus for living (Wachowiak and Bragg, 1980).

Open marriages encourage freedom, open communication, and trust, both within and outside the parameters of marriage. If so desired, partners are free to engage in opposite-sex friendships and even extramarital sex. However, the latter is a controversial area and criticized by opponents of this marital arrangement. All points considered, this nontraditional lifestyle is not practical for most couples since it's likely to promote feelings of insecurity, resentment toward outside parties, and sexual jealousy (Watson, 1981).

Swinging

Swinging, also referred to as "mate swapping," is a relationship involving two or more married couples who decide to switch sexual partners or to engage in group sex. Swingers are usually upper-middle-class individuals who are employed in professional and white-collar occupations. Swinging is considered rare for persons under age 30, especially males.

Swingers often locate partners from a variety of sources—including newspaper ads, swinging bars, and "socials" sponsored by swinging magazines. Swinging takes many different forms—closed swinging refers to a situation in which several sets of couples pair off in separate rooms in order to engage in sex—open swinging refers to group sex, usually done in the presence of others, sometimes called an orgy. A wide variety of sexual activities are usually accepted. However, the recreation of sex, rather than the emotional aspects of it, is stressed (Dacey, 1982).

Research indicates that many couples turn to swinging in the hope that it will strengthen an otherwise strained relationship. Some regard it as a sexual adventure, a way to act out their inner fantasies. And, for those who are so inclined, swinging is but one of many ways to gain sexual satisfaction.

However, Robert Whitehurst (1985) points out that swinging, by its very nature, tends to have a short half-life, especially among males. He feels that the male's fantasy of a candy-store freedom to grab all the sex one can from anyone nearby is rapidly replaced by a more discriminatory approach to such casual sex. Male sexual appetites tend to be large in prospect but small in retrospect (wanting lots before the fact but becoming sated more easily than one had imagined). Thus, women may be more reluctant to begin swinging, but men are more reluctant to continue such behavior. Fear of diseases also gives pause to many males and females who otherwise might feel more free to participate.

CHAPTER HIGHLIGHTS

This chapter focused on the alternative lifestyles that exist beyond marriage in contemporary society. We began our discussion with an examination of singlehood, a lifestyle that is growing in popularity. There are about 67 million single adults in America, counting those who are divorced and widowed, as well as those who never married and those postponing marriage. Stereotypes abound about the single lifestyle, and we tried to dispel such inaccurate information.

Cohabitation is defined as an unmarried man and an unmarried woman living together. Cohabitation is extremely popular today, having increased over 300 percent from the previous decade. While most cohabitants are under age 35, there has been an increase in older cohabitants in recent years. Four types of cohabitation were described in detail: the "Linus blanket," emancipation, convenience, and testing relationships.

A third type of alternative lifestyle discussed in this chapter was communal living. A commune is a self-supporting community in which residents dedicate themselves to cooperative living. Communes are often formed around philosophical or religious beliefs and can be found in both rural and urban settings. We explored five unique types of communes and how they operate: The Christian religious family commune, Eastern religious family commune, leader-directed communal family, rural domestic commune, and the urban domestic commune.

Confusion has long abounded in relation to the lifestyle, sexuality, and gender roles chosen by gay men and lesbian women. These individuals have also had to live with societal rejection and ridicule, not to mention discriminatory laws and practices. The latter is particularly true in relation to marriage and family life. As far as intimate relationship dynamics are concerned, gay men, lesbian women, and heterosexual couples are more alike than dissimilar.

Two other possible lifestyles, open marriages and swinging, occur within the general framework of marriage but offer liberal options for partners. Open marriages encourage continual self-growth for both partners as well as an assortment of options and freedoms—including sexual freedom beyond one's partner, the most controversial facet of this lifestyle. Swinging, also known as mate swapping, involves two or more married couples who decide to switch sexual partners or engage in group sex.

KEY TERMS

Christian religious family
  commune
cohabitation
commune
Eastern religious family
  commune

gay men
homosexuality
kibbutz
leader-directed communal
  family
lesbian women

open marriage
palimony
rural domestic commune
singlehood
swinging
urban domestic commune

RECOMMENDED READINGS

Barkas, J. L. (1980). *Single in America.* New York: Atheneum. An excellent overview of the societal status of the single person in the United States. Types of successfully adjusted single persons and reasons for their success are among the topics explored.

Barton, C. (1985). *Cohabitation contracts.* Brookfield, VT: Gower Press. Among the issues raised are reasons for and against contracts, terms of cohabitation contracts, and the present law on cohabitation contracts.

Harry, J. (1984). *Gay couples.* New York: Praeger. A thorough and readable examination of male same-sex relationships.

Hart, J., and Richardson, D. (1981). *The theory and practice of homosexuality.* London: Routledge and Kegan Paul. The authors focus on the diversity of homosexual lifestyles and identities. Particular emphasis is placed on legal problems and the other difficulties that have to be overcome by gay men and lesbian women.

Kephart, W. M. (1982). *Extraordinary groups: The sociology of unconventional lifestyles* (2nd ed.). New York: St. Martin's Press. A leading contributor to the field explores a variety of unconventional lifestyles, from the Amish and the Mormons to the residents of the Oneida commune.

Macklin, E., and Rubin, R. H. (Ed.). (1983). *Contemporary families and alternative lifestyles.* Beverly Hills, CA: Sage. Among the topics in this collection of readings are singlehood, cohabitation, and the gay lifestyle.

Paul, W. (Ed.). (1982). *Homosexuality: Social, psychological, and biological issues.* Beverly Hills, CA: Sage. A total of 22 readings deal with the topic of homosexuality from a multi-disciplinary perspective.

Simenauer, J., and Carroll, D. (1982). *Singles: The new Americans*. New York: Simon & Schuster. A comprehensive analysis of what it's like to be single in America during the 1980s.

Staples, R. (1981). *The world of black singles: Changing patterns of male/female relations*. Westport, CT: Greenwood Press. Staples explores a number of issues related to black singles, including the mechanisms of dating, problems of finding and keeping a mate, and the prevalency of interracial relationships.

Stein, P. (1981). *Single life: Unmarried adults in social context*. New York: St. Martin's Press. Peter Stein enlightens readers on many topics related to singlehood, including styles of courting, living arrangements, and sexuality.

Part Three

EARLY MARITAL TRANSITIONS

1

The Path
to Marriage

CONTENTS

CONTEMPLATIONS

■ "Will you marry me?" The proposal of engagement comes in many forms, from discreet and romantic gestures to exotic and elaborate displays. Over the years, this question has been spoken, whispered, and even sung by suitors. It has been found printed on the front pages of newspapers, displayed on billboards, and even written across the sky. But as we'll see, the "popping of the question" from the male and the consideration given to it by the female may not be the most difficult chore attached to the engagement period. Rather, this is an important time for them to discuss expectations about marriage and maintaining a satisfying life together. Join us as we explore the engagement transition and its importance as a prelude to marriage.

■ In the United States most marriage ceremonies share many similarities, even though some differences among religions exist. For example, wedding vows are customarily spoken, wedding rings exchanged, and a reception traditionally follows the ceremony. In other cultures, though, an assortment of other customs characterize the marriage ceremony. For example, in Germany both bride and groom often hold candles trimmed with ribbons and flowers during the ceremony. In Morocco, the bride receives a ceremonial bath for ritual cleansing five days before the wedding. And in China, unlike the traditional color of white in America, the bride's dress is red, the color of love and joy in this nation. Later on in this chapter, we'll explore wedding customs from a cross-cultural and historical perspective. When we're done, we think you'll see American wedding customs, and those around the world, in a new light.

■ America is a rich mosaic of racial, ethnic, and religious diversity. As the many facets of our society converge and the differences between us become fewer, people are finding the barriers of race and religious training surmountable obstacles in marriage. Towards the end of this chapter, we'll take a look at intermarriages, particularly interfaith and interracial marriages. How widespread are these types of marriages? Why do individuals resist homogeneous pressures and marry others with dissimilar backgrounds? Do such marriages pose any special problems? The answers to these questions will become evident when you read about America's marriage melting pot.

I do. For the bride and groom, these two simple words symbolize the most important of all life commitments. Beyond its declaration of love, these words represent a public commitment, a social contract witnessed and endorsed by the community. And once the wedding ceremony has taken place, the agreement to live together as husband and wife also embodies a legal commitment. In the process, a new social status for the couple is created and a new chapter in their lives begins.

Few transitions over the course of the life cycle are as anticipated, talked about, or publicized as the decision to marry. Be it the engagement, public announcement, wedding ceremony, reception, or honeymoon, the event of marriage has become something of an obsession in American society. Narratives and descriptions of it — be they real life or fictionalized accounts — find their way into newspapers, magazines, soap operas, television, and the movies. The issue of who is marrying

Following the wedding ceremony, numerous transitions await the married couple.

whom, including all of the romantic intrigue, circumstances, and events surrounding it, sparks attention, interest, and just plain nosiness among many.

This interest is just as evident among contemporary social scientists wanting to explore the circumstances surrounding the decision to marry. Who decides to marry, why, the transitions that await the newly-married couple, and related issues provide fertile grounds for social science research. The nature of such investigative pursuits provides the foundation for this chapter.

CONTEMPORARY TRENDS IN MARRIAGE

Prevalence of Marriage

In the last chapter, we presented the alternatives to marriage that exist and showed how attitudes regarding the importance of marriage as a way of life have changed. Recall especially how the legitimacy of singlehood as a lifestyle is increasingly

recognized by young people and their parents. However, demographers such as Arland Thornton and Deborah Freedman (1983) tell us that despite such attitudes, marriage continues to be valued by a majority of young Americans. Most expect to marry, and, despite rising divorce rates, most also expect their marriages to be lasting.

Paul Glick's (1984b) analysis of marriage rates in the United States is supportive of this last point. He estimates that approximately 95 percent of the population above age 45 has married. However, he draws attention to some notable shifts among young Americans. In 1970, about 45 percent of males and 64 percent of females in their twenties had already married. By 1980, though, corresponding figures had dipped to 30 percent and 50 percent. Thus, while demographic trends indicate that most people marry, among modern Americans the decision is being postponed.

The total number of marriages in the United States soared to a record high in 1982. In that year, 2,456,278 Americans chose to exchange wedding vows. Such large numbers existed even in the presence of a declining **marriage rate**, the number of marriages each year per 1,000 members of the population. This is because the maturing of the large post-World War II baby boom generation increased the number of people in the most common marriage ages (National Center for Health Statistics, 1986). Table 7-1 displays the number of marriages by state in 1985, along with percentage decreases or increases from 1984.

Marriage rates peaked in the United States in 1946 in the surge of marriages that occurred following World War II. During that time, the marriage rate was 16.4 per 1,000 people. Marriage rates remained relatively high throughout the 1950s and then started to show a decline in the 1960s and 1970s. In 1983, the marriage rate per 1,000 persons was 10.5 (National Center for Health Statistics, 1986).

Timing of First Marriage

Earlier we mentioned that the timing of marriage has changed from past eras. Because of the growing numbers who are postponing marriage, the

TABLE 7-1

Number of Marriages by State, 1985, and Percentage Decreased or Increased from 1984

State	Marriages		State	Marriages	
	1985	*Change*		*1985*	*Change*
Alabama	45,816	−3.5%	Nebraska	12,185	−8.7%
Alaska	6,182	−5.2%	Nevada	106,922	−0.5%
Arizona	35,567	+12.9%	New Hampshire	11,159	−1.8%
Arkansas	30,496	−3.0%	New Jersey	60,915	−2.1%
California	226,150	−0.2%	New Mexico	14,585	−3.9%
Colorado	33,938	−2.0%	New York	164,864	−2.4%
Connecticut	27,206	+8.5%	North Carolina	50,575	−3.0%
Delaware	5,345	−2.2%	North Dakota	5,467	−5.8%
District of Columbia	5,040	−8.2%	Ohio	94,176	−4.6%
Florida	127,930	+3.1%	Oklahoma	35,536	−8.0%
Georgia	73,541	−3.0%	Oregon	22,414	−0.8%
Hawaii	15,319	+2.9%	Pennsylvania	88,687	−4.2%
Idaho	12,542	+0.2%	Rhode Island	7,963	+0.3%
Illinois	97,912	−4.5%	South Carolina	52,776	−5.6%
Indiana	52,688	−0.0%	South Dakota	7,836	−2.5%
Iowa	24,720	−8.3%	Tennessee	54,942	−0.5%
Kansas	23,571	−4.9%	Texas	213,766	+3.0%
Kentucky	46,949	+6.7%	Utah	17,077	−2.9%
Louisiana	39,666	−3.9%	Vermont	5,622	+4.6%
Maine	11,257	−9.4%	Virginia	66,670	+1.1%
Maryland	47,069	+0.5%	Washington	44,514	−0.5%
Massachusetts	51,648	−2.9%	West Virginia	14,649	−5.2%
Michigan	80,813	−9.6%	Wisconsin	40,072	−2.5%
Minnesota	34,458	−6.5%	Wyoming	5,355	−6.4%
Mississippi	24,733	−5.4%			
Missouri	49,014	−9.5%	Total	2,435,476	−1.8%
Montana	7,179	−6.5%			

Source: National Center for Health Statistics, 1986.

median age at first marriage has increased (median age means that one-half of the people marrying for the first time in a given year gets married before the given age, and one-half after).

The following statistics help show how the median age at first marriage has changed over the years. In 1890, the median age was 26.1 for men and 22 for women. In 1976, it was 23.8 and 21.3 for men and women, respectively. In 1983, it was 24.4 for grooms and 22.5 for brides. Statistics gathered for 1984 indicate that the median age has increased once more: 25.4 for men and 23 for women. This represents the highest median age ever recorded for American women, and the high-est for men since the median age of 25.9 in 1900 (National Center for Health Statistics, 1986).

What factors account for the postponement of marriage? Paul Glick (1984b) feels that a strictly demographic factor during the last two decades has been the "marriage squeeze." Given that women are usually two or three years younger than men at marriage, the marriage squeeze developed as a consequence of the upward trend of births during the baby boom. Because of this, a female born in 1947, when the birth rate had risen, was likely to marry a male born in 1944 or 1945, when the birth rate was still low. Consequently, about 20 years later, there was an excess of women in the primary ages for marriage, and this phenomenon continued for the length of time that the baby boom lasted. Therefore, by 1970, the number of men 20 to 26 years of age was only 93 percent of the number of women 18 to 24. The corresponding figure for black males was 82 percent.

This meant that by 1970, there was a shortage of men in the primary marriageable ages for women. This was true for young adults regardless of race. By 1980, this percentage had escalated somewhat, to 98 percent for all races. By 1995, the figure is expected to reach 108 percent, as the declining birth rates of the 1960s and early 1970s create a reversal of the marriage squeeze phenomenon.

Beyond this demographic phenomenon, there are other reasons for marriage postponement. More persons, especially women, are enrolling in college, graduate school, and professional schools. There are also expanding employment and career opportunities for women, and many men and women are placing their careers ahead of marriage plans. Finally, the high divorce rate in this country has prompted some to seriously question the traditional appeal of marriage and family life (Stein, 1981).

WHY PEOPLE MARRY

While the motives for entering married life are multiple and diverse, it is possible to identify some of the more popular reasons. The following represents some of these motives.

Love   The love and commitment shared by partners is often the driving reason for getting married. Couples desire to share themselves in an enduring and intimate relationship, one that they feel is best represented within the institution of marriage.

Conformity   For many, marriage represents the "thing to do" or the "natural progression." After courting and the engagement period, getting married is viewed as the final stage of the mate selection process. Contributing to this motive are the social pressures, both subtle and direct, from family, friends, and others prompting the couple to marry.

Companionship   The opportunity to spend one's life with someone in a permanent and visible institution looms as another motive. The prospect of a regular companion also tends to generate emotional and psychological well-being, which in turn breeds feelings of security and comfort. Relatedly, companionship provides couples with the opportunity to share, be it the routines attached to domestic life or recreation and leisurely pursuits.

Legitimization of Sex   Married status still provides social approval for many with respect to sexual behavior, although we noted in Chapter 5 that a large proportion of men and women engage in nonmarital intercourse. Also, many of today's Americans have adopted a more tolerant attitude toward premarital sexual relationships.

The desire for companionship is a strong motive for marriage.

Legitimization of Children Children born into a marital relationship have a legitimate identity. Some segments of society strongly feel that a child born out of wedlock is immoral. We should acknowledge, also, that many couples would never consider getting married unless they wanted to have a child.

Sense of Readiness Many couples report that a decision to marry occurred when they felt "ready." The couple had done the things they wanted to accomplish before marrying. This might have included finishing an education, launching a career, or tending to personal or family matters.

Legal Benefits This may not be one of the strongest motives for marriage, but it deserves to be acknowledged. Married status does have its share of tax advantages, as we'll presently see, and for couples concerned with the economic welfare of their relationship, this motive may receive more than cursory notice.

Before closing this particular part of our discussion, we should add that there are motives for not getting married. For example, some may feel that many of the above goals are possible through cohabitation, particularly the attainment of love, companionship, and sharing. Other motives against marriage include a perceived reduction of freedom and loss of independence.

There are also numerous "wrong" reasons for getting married. That is, some people may choose to marry for selfish reasons—for instance, to acquire a sexual partner or to obtain economic or emotional security. Some marry to escape the loneliness of a solitary existence or because they want to get away from an unhappy home situation. While the above reasons may be important to an

MARRIAGE AND TELEVISION PROGRAMMING: HOW CLEAR IS THE PICTURE?

Television is often guilty of transmitting inconsistent and inaccurate images of marriage. On the one hand, commercials and programming alike portray society as a two-by-two arrangement, always showing the couples' scene and deemphasizing the singles' lifestyle. Moreover, newly married couples are often portrayed in an atomosphere of total romantic bliss, never confronted with problems or frustrations of any sort.

Inconsistencies develop, though, when programming takes a different stance on marriage. For example, one source (Pollner, 1982) sees television as being guilty of portraying married men as incompetent husbands and parents as either fools or temperamental tyrants. And while husbands are verbally castrated, their wives are often portrayed as controlling bosses or mothering martyrs. Certainly most television commercials that portray domestic situations reflect the image of an inept husband whose wife tells him what to wear, eat, or take for various ailments. While husbands and fathers are continually demeaned on television, their single counterparts, when they do appear, maintain a heroic posture.

The implied message seems unmistakable with this type of programming: being single is better. To be single is to be free, while to be married is to be vulnerable or trapped. Yet, this theme competes with that of the perfect relationship, and both are fraught with false stereotypes and sweeping generalities.

individual, they are not sound reasons when they represent the major motivation for marriage (Berkley, 1981).

TRANSITIONS FROM SINGLEHOOD TO MARRIED LIFE

Getting married will of course bring many changes into the lives of couples. But according to James Henslin (1985a) these changes are often more extensive than partners imagined. Indeed, the transition from singlehood to married life may bring surprise and even confusion. Henslin identifies seven changes that characterize this transition.

Marriage Represents a New Public Identity This identity can be bestowed only by the community, and the community does this on a selective basis. When the community proclaims that the couple is married, it does so on the basis of its own particular rules. The parameters are typically based on sex and age, in some instances social class, race, and property, and in all societies the avoidance of incest.

The notion that it is the community proclaiming the marriage may appear backwards. After all, isn't it the partners announcing to the community that they are married? In one sense, of course, it is indeed the couple making such an announcement. From a sociological standpoint, though, it is the community that establishes the rules regarding who is eligible to marry whom. The community also bestows the public identity of marriage on those members meeting these qualifications, at the same time withholding such status from those who fail to meet these standards.

Marriage Creates a Legal Unit For many practical purposes in society, the married couple is regarded as a single legal unit. For instance, they are now one when it comes to bank loans (even despite modifications and changes in procedures, bank officials usually require both spouses' signatures on loan applications). The Internal Revenue Service also regards the couple as one unit. At their discretion, they may file jointly or singly, an option not available to the unmarried.

Marriage Changes the Couple's Social Relationships The two are considered one when it comes to relatives and friends. Invitations to social gatherings are extended to the couple, rarely to the husband or wife alone. Along similar lines, cards and gifts are usually addressed and given to Mr. *and* Mrs. as a unit. The married couple is reacted to as a pair in a wide assortment of social situations.

Marriage Changes the Couple's Relationship to One Another They no longer see each other on an optional basis. No matter how committed they were to each other prior to the wedding, an option or alternative existed in their relationship. That is, they could decide whether or not they were going to have contact with one another. If they so desired, they could also forego their agreements and understandings made as a couple and dissolve the relationship. Of course, the relative ease of today's divorce laws makes this also possible within the structure of marriage. However, the difference is that, because the community has bestowed a public identity, the married couple's relationship is no longer a private matter. An unmarried couple can separate and be done with it. With marriage, however, there is an assumption of permanence, and the couple must take into account their changed legal status and public identity. At a minimum, they must fill out papers and engage in a legal process that represents the community's termination of the relationship.

Marriage Creates Changes in a Couple's Legal and Social Relationships Marriage embodies nurturance and obligations of support that must be fulfilled, regardless of whether or not partners wish to fulfill them. For instance, for most it is no longer an option to share money, cook a meal, or visit relatives. The new relationship expects these activities, transforming them from options into responsibilities. Those who choose to abandon such expectations are typically married for only a short interval.

Marriage Creates Changes in How Each Partner Perceives and Evaluates the Other The roles of husband and wife represent a major change in status, one whose dictates are largely

Marriage gives couples a new public identity as well as a changed legal status.

determined by others. The rewards and responsibilities of these roles are also not constant throughout society, and the partners' understanding of them is always filtered through membership and participation in smaller social groups. However, both husband and wife have a set of expectations about how the other should act. One's marital partner is now seen on the basis of these expectations and performances are judged accordingly.

Marriage Leads to Changes in the Way Each Partner Perceives and Evaluates the Self The ideas that individuals have of marital roles also apply to one's own role in marriage. For example, the husband has specific ideas about how a husband ought to act, and the wife has thoughts about a wife's ideal behavior. Each judges his or her own self based on how one feels these expectations are being fulfilled. Amidst this self-reflective process, change in self-evaluation typically takes place.

Henslin feels that, combined, these changes represent important transitions for the newly married couple. Indeed, nothing is really the same after wedding vows are exchanged. Couples do not merely enter a new social status nor are superficial changes made in their lives. Instead, newly marrieds enter a different world, one that is often filled with the unexpected. Because this entry requires major adjustments, fundamental and taken-for-granted aspects of one's existence radically change for most. Adapting to a world that alters basic assumptions requires making changes in basic facets of the self as well as in one's significant relationships.

RITUALS, CUSTOMS, AND CEREMONIES

The Engagement

In contemporary society **engagement** is a rite of passage usually characterized by the presentation of an engagement ring to the fiancée, a shower for the bride, a party for the groom, and an announcement in the newspaper. The announcement is a remnant of the earlier historical posting of **banns**, a public notice of intent that was posted several weeks prior to the marriage at the church and other locations in the surrounding community. The purpose was to enroll the community behind the marriage and to afford persons who knew of legal or ecclesiastical impediments the opportunity to come forth (Murstein, 1986).

The engagement is an important transitional period between single and married status. As such, it represents a time for the couple to discuss their expectations and ideas about marriage, their values, and their desired lifestyle. It is an important trial period to test each other's basic ideas about marriage in order to create a mutually satisfying relationship.

The engagement period is also a time to become aware of those factors that make a marriage work. Indeed, the best time to consider these factors is before vows are exchanged, and then periodically review them as the relationship progresses. Along these lines, one source (Cadogan, 1982) proposes that at least 12 key questions should be examined:

1. Can I accept his/her faults and shortcomings?
2. Can I visualize and accept him/her in the various roles he/she must play during our marriage, that is father/mother, provider, companion, lover and so on?
3. Would I be willing to give up things or provide things that would be important to the satisfaction of his/her needs?
4. Is there the tender feeling that comes from knowing that he/she is on my side and is interested in satisfying my needs?
5. Is there a feeling of solid and enduring friendship?
6. Is he/she sexually attractive to me?
7. Do we enjoy many of the same things, and share similar or compatible goals?

Psychological and symbolic commitments usually go hand in hand for engaged couples.

8. Do I feel comfortable when I am in the company of his/her family and friends?

9. Do I like who I am, or the way I feel about myself when I am with him/her?

10. Has our courtship and relationship in general been relatively smooth and enjoyable?

11. Are his/her personal and household hygienic standards similar to, or compatible with, mine?

12. Am I willing to accept the responsibility, as far as is reasonable, for making the relationship work?

The Wedding

Couples have gotten married for centuries. Historically, the wedding has always symbolized what the marriage means to the couple as well as to the community: commitment, sharing, and happiness. For the couple, family, and friends, the wedding represents a festive ceremony and celebration. All of this is true today, and each culture has its own unique wedding customs. In addition, old wedding traditions are often updated by couples to accommodate changing ideals and values. And

CROSS-CULTURAL FOCUS

THE WEDDING CEREMONY IN OTHER CULTURES

Wedding ceremonies differ widely from culture to culture. For example, before a Hindu wedding ceremony begins, a holy fire is lit to the fire god, Agni, who traditionally will bear witness to the wedding. Customs during the service are both religious and cultural. A tree is planted because of the ancient belief that plants and

The wedding ceremony has many cross-cultural variations.

▶

animals are representations of the gods, and this will insure their presence. The bride's father gives her hand to the groom, then sprinkles her with holy water to indicate that his ties with her are washed away. A *thali*, a gold ornament threaded on a yellow string, is tied around the bride's neck. She will wear it for all her married life, its three knots reminding her of her duty to serve her parents, husband, and sons. The ceremony concludes when the couple circle the holy fire three times, throwing offerings of rice and flowers into the air.

In Japan, many wedding ceremonies take place before a Shinto shrine, even though a marriage is not regarded as a religious service. The ceremony brings the bride into the family of the bridegroom, and ancestors are honored in the ritual by bowing, ringing bells, and offering food before family shrines. Nine sips of sake are the essence of the ceremony, for there are no vows. Later, sips of sake are exchanged with the parents, both to honor them and to mark their formal acceptance of the marriage. A Shinto priest officiates.

Other examples illustrate the diversity that exists in wedding ceremonies. In India, the groom's brother sprinkles flower petals on the bridal couple at the conclusion of the ceremony to ward off evil. On the island of Fiji, the groom presents the bride's father with a *tabua* — a whale's tooth symbolizing status and wealth. In Bermuda, islanders top off their tiered wedding cake with a tiny tree sapling, which is planted by the newlyweds at the wedding reception. Finally, in Lithuania the wedded couple are served a symbolic meal by their parents — wine for joy, salt for tears, and bread for hard work.

Adapted from Tober, 1984.   ■

new customs are sometimes created to accentuate or add a different dimension to the wedding.

As far as this last point is concerned, American culture often goes to great lengths to provide innovations in ceremonies, as well as ritualizing and commercializing the wedding. While many couples cling to tradition, some work hard at making their wedding different or special. For example, in recent years, couples have been married in hot air balloons, on television programs, on horseback, before athletic events, on chartered yachts, barefoot on the beach, in midair flight on airplanes, in firehouses, on mountain tops, underwater, and in garden settings.

Other wedding variations are more subtle, but still reflect a couple's desire for innovation and a personalized ceremony. For example, the ceremony might include personally written vows, selected readings, poetry, or guitar-accompanied soloists. Some couples choose contemporary songs to be sung, and others have wedding booklets printed to share as souvenirs with their guests. Some may even design their own wedding invitations or wedding cake.

The expenses attached to weddings have skyrocketed in recent years. In 1985, the average cost of a wedding with a guest list of 200 was over $6,000. For the same type of wedding in 1980, the fee was about $3,000, while in 1970, estimated costs were only $1500. Of course, costs differ depending on the style of the reception and the region of the country. (Figure 7-1 shows the escalation of wedding costs since 1960.)

These costs do not take into consideration those expenses associated with the honeymoon. The honeymoon traditionally follows the reception

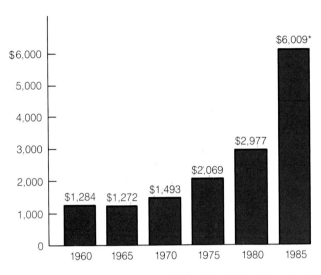

Breakdown of Costs	
Bride's gown	$ 426
Bride's veil	104
Invitations, announcements, thank-yous, etc.	200
Bouquets and other flowers	324
Photography	470
Music	369
Clergy, rabbi, church, chapel, synagogue fees	83
Limousine	58
Attendant gifts (bride's and groom's)	149
Wedding ring(s)	808
Mother of the bride's apparel	121
Bridal attendants' apparel	319
Men's formalwear	230
Groom's attire	55
Rehearsal dinner	293
Reception	2,000
TOTAL COST	$6,009

Source: Adapted from information in Tober, 1984.

*1984 dollars

FIGURE 7-1   U.S. Wedding Costs (in dollars)

and represents a period for partners to enjoy the exclusive company of each other. For some couples, the honeymoon lasts for a week while in other instances it may last for a month. Of course, financial considerations largely determine the duration of the honeymoon.

The Wedding Ceremony: Rituals and Customs   Many of today's wedding ceremonies and receptions are filled with customs which, when you think about them, appear to make little sense. The fact is that most of them are remnants of earlier customs and even superstitions. Barbara Jo Chesser (1980) offers the following analysis of the more popular wedding rituals.

The Wedding Ring   As we mentioned in Chapter 2, the Romans used wedding rings, and rings have also been found in ancient Egyptian tombs. From the times of these early civilizations, the wedding ring has symbolized the highest form of trust and commitment. Wearing the ring on the third finger of the left hand is a custom dating back to Egyptian pharoahs. They believed that a vein in that finger ran directly to the heart.

The Bridal Veil   The bridal veil has long been worn by Christian, Jewish, Moslem, and Hindu brides, to name but a few cultures. Over the centuries, the veil protected the bride against malicious spirits, from the "evil eye," and from the stares of curious outsiders to the ceremony. The veil also represented the bride's purity. Pulling the veil back after the vows were exchanged symbolized the bride's new status as a wife.

Color of the Wedding Gown   Throughout history, people have considered a marriage as a union of two families, not just a union of two individuals. The bride's family had to guarantee her virginity because it represented their honor. To do this, white wedding gowns were most often chosen, the purity of white symbolizing the bride's virginity. In support of this, as well as some other thoughts regarding wedding gown colors, consider the

ELOPEMENT AND THE CIVIL MARRIAGE CEREMONY

For various reasons, some couples avoid large, formal wedding ceremonies and instead choose to elope. This may be due to financial considerations, pregnancy, a health problem in the family, and so on. A civil wedding ceremony is often chosen by those who elope. Such a ceremony is usually performed by a Justice of the Peace and is relatively simple. The following fictionalized wedding of "John" and "Mary" illustrates the steps in the civil ceremony:

"We are gathered here in the presence of these witnesses for the purpose of uniting in matrimony John and Mary. The contract of marriage is most solemn and is not to be entered into lightly, but thoughtfully and seriously and with a deep realization of its obligations and responsibilities.

"John, do you take this woman, Mary, to be your lawful wedded wife?"

"I Do."

"Mary, do you take this man, John, to be your lawful wedded husband?"

"I Do."

"Do you each promise to love and comfort one another, to honor and keep one another, in sickness and in health, in prosperity and adversity, and forsaking all others, be faithful to each other as long as you both shall live?"

"We Do."

(For ring ceremony) "John, place the ring on the ring finger of Mary's left hand and repeat after me, to her: Mary, with this ring I thee wed." (Repeat Mary to John for double-ring ceremony)

(For no ring ceremony) "Join hands.

"John, repeat after me to Mary: I, John take thee Mary, to be my lawful wedded wife.

"Mary, repeat after me to John: I, Mary, take thee John, to be my lawful wedded husband.

"By virtue of the authority vested in me, I now pronounce you husband and wife."

following anonymous Victorian verse:

Married in white, you have chosen all right;
Married in grey, you will go far away;
Married in black, you will wish yourself back;
Married in red, you wish yourself dead;
Married in green, ashamed to be seen;
Married in blue, he will always be true;
Married in pearl, you will live in a whirl;
Married in yellow, ashamed of your fellow;
Married in brown, you will live out of town;
Married in pink, your fortune will sink.

The Kiss at the Altar   Like other traditions, this wedding custom has been with us for some time. For centuries, the purpose of the kiss was to seal or affirm the wedding vows. But the kiss is not required today to make the marriage legal. In earlier times, the priest gave the groom the "benediction kiss," the "kiss of peace," or the "holy kiss," as some called it, and the groom in turn kissed the bride. The priest's assistants then solemnly kissed each of the wedding guests. Today, the wedding participants and guests seem to prefer to do their own kissing.

Cutting the Wedding Cake Years ago, it was believed that the breaking or cutting of the wedding cake increased the wife's fertility and aided in the birth of the first child. Often, this was done by breaking or cutting the cake over the bride's head until the milder and less messy practice of sprinkling some of the crumbs on her seemed sufficient. There is speculation that this was where the practice of throwing rice on the couple developed.

Children in the Wedding Party Children were often added to the wedding party to encourage fertility and to serve as a reminder of the purpose of marriage. In Roman wedding ceremonies, an offering was made in the form of a wheat cake to the god Jupiter. They also repeated prayers to Juno, the goddess of marriage. An altar boy participated in these rituals, and he seems to be the obvious predecessor of today's ringbearer in symbolizing the desired male child.

The Honeymoon Centuries ago, brides were often captured and carried off to locations where they couldn't be found by relatives. When the moon went through its 30-day phase, the couple drank a fermented honey brew called metheglin or mead. Honey has long been a symbol of life, health, and fertility; combined with the lunar cycle, the word honeymoon thus evolved.

THE LAW OF MARRIAGE

Fundamentally speaking, marriage exists as a contract between a man and a woman. For a contract to be valid, R. Barry Ruback (1985) contends that several factors must be present. One, mutual assent must exist. By this, there must be an offer (some expression of a commitment or a promise to make a contract) followed by an acceptance of the offer. Two, some consideration for the contract must exist. Consideration means some bargained-for change in the legal position of the contract. Three, there cannot be any defenses to the creation of the contract. Two general types of defenses to a contract exist:

- Evidence that the two parties did not form an agreement due to some misunderstanding about the nature of the contract or other mistake.

- General considerations of public policy that prohibit certain types of contracts from being created. Two common examples of public policy considerations are that the contract involves something illegal and that one or both of the parties lacked the capacity to make a contract (for example, being underage, intoxicated, lacking mental capacity, or lacking volitional assent).

Ruback observes that analogously, for a marriage contract to be valid, there must be an offer and acceptance, consideration, and no defenses to the contract. In general, offer, acceptance, and consideration are not problems in determining the validity of a marriage agreement. But, the public policy considerations to a marriage, such as minority of one of the parties or a lack of mental competency, can be a defense to the marriage. Also, although marriage is a contract between two individuals, it is different from most contracts in that the state places some limitations on who may enter into the contract and, once the contract is made, the state takes a strong interest in preserving the relationship between the two individuals. With this in mind, let's turn our attention to the manner in which each state establishes its own requirements for a marriage license.

The Marriage License

Before two people can marry, they must meet certain legal requirements established by the respective state. To begin with, both parties must be of a certain minimum age, which varies from state to state. In most states, the legal age is 18 for the male and 16 for the female with parental consent, and 21 for the male and 18 for the female without parental consent. Marriages between close blood relatives are forbidden and proof of citizenship in the United States is required. Another requirement prior to the marriage is that the couple must obtain a **marriage license**. Also, most states require a

TABLE 7-2

Marriage Information*

State	With Consent		Without Consent		Blood Test**		Wait for License	Wait after License
	Men	Women	Men	Women	Required	Other State Accepted		
Alabama (b)	14	14	18	18	Yes	Yes	none	none
Alaska	16 (i)	16	18	18	Yes	No	3 days	none
Arizona	16 (i)	16	18	18	Yes	Yes	none	none
Arkansas	17	16 (j)	18	18	Yes	No	3 days	none
California	18 (i)	18	18	18	Yes (n)	Yes	none	none
Colorado	16	16	18	18	Yes (n)		none	none
Connecticut	16	16 (i)	18	18	Yes	Yes	4 days	none
Delaware	18	16 (o)	18	18	Yes	Yes	none	24 hrs (c)
District of Columbia	16	16	18	18	Yes	Yes	3 days	none
Florida	18	18	18	18	Yes	Yes	3 days	none
Georgia	16	16	18	18	Yes	Yes	none (k)	none
Hawaii	16	16	18	18	Yes	Yes	none	none
Idaho	16	16	18	18	Yes (n)	Yes	none (k)	none
Illinois (a)	16	16	18	18	Yes (p)	Yes	none	1 day
Indiana	17 (o)	17 (o)	18	18	Yes (p)	No	72 hours	none
Iowa	16 (o)	18 (o)	18	18	Yes	Yes	3 days	none
Kansas	14	12	18	18	Yes	Yes	3 days	none
Kentucky	— (o)	— (o)	18	18	Yes	No	3 days	none
Louisiana (a)	18 (o)	16 (j)	18	16	Yes	No	none	72 hours
Maine	16 (j)	16 (j)	18	18	No	No	5 days	none
Maryland	16	16	18	18	none	none	48 hours	none
Massachusetts	— (o)	— (o)	18	18	Yes	Yes	3 days	none
Michigan (a)	18	16	18	18	Yes	No	3 days	none
Minnesota	16 (e)	16 (e)	18	18	none		5 days	none
Mississippi (b)	17 (q)	15 (q)	21	21	Yes		3 days	none
Missouri	15	15	18	18	none	Yes	3 days	none
Montana	15	15	18	18	Yes (n)	Yes	none	3 days
Nebraska	17	17	18	18	Yes (n)	Yes	2 days	none
Nevada	16	16	18	18	none	none	none	none

State							
New Hampshire (a)	14 (e)	13 (e)	18	Yes	18	Yes	5 days	none
New Jersey (a)	—	12	18	Yes	18	Yes	72 hours	none
New Mexico	16	16	18	Yes	18	Yes	none	24 hrs (g)
New York	16	14	18	Yes (p)	18	No	none	none
North Carolina (a)	16	16	18	Yes (p)	18	Yes	none	none
North Dakota (a)	16	16	18	Yes	18		none	none
Ohio (a)	18	16	18	Yes	18	Yes	5 days	none
Oklahoma	16	16	18	Yes	18	No	none (f)(h)	none
Oregon	17	17	18	Yes	18	No	3 days	none
Pennsylvania	16	16	18	Yes	18	Yes	3 days	none
Rhode Island (a) (b)	18	16	18	Yes (n)	18	No	none	none
South Carolina	16	14	18	none	18	none	24 hrs	none
South Dakota	16	16	18	Yes	18	Yes	none	none
Tennessee (b)	16	16	18	Yes	18	Yes	3 days	none
Texas	14	14	18	Yes	18	Yes	none	none
Utah (a)	14	14	18	none	18	Yes	none	none
Vermont (a)	18	16	18	Yes	18		5 days	5 days
Virginia (a)	16	16	18	Yes	18	Yes (m)	none	none
Washington	17	17	18	(c)	18		3 days	none
West Virginia	18	16	18	Yes	18	No	3 days	none
Wisconsin	16	16	18	Yes	18	Yes	5 days	none
Wyoming	16	16	19	Yes	19	Yes	none	none
Puerto Rico	18	16	21	(f)	21	none	none	none
Virgin Islands	16	14	18	none	18	none	8 days	none

* Marriageable age, by states, for both males and females with and without consent of parents or guardians. But in most states the court has authority to marry young couples below the ordinary age of consent, where due regard for their morals and welfare so requires in many states, under special circumstances, blood test and waiting period may be waived.

** Many states have additional special requirements; contact individual state. (a) Special laws applicable to nonresidents. (b) Special laws applicable to those under 21 years Ala., bond required if male is under 18, female under 18. (c) 24 hours if one or both parties resident of state. 96 hours if both parties are nonresidents. (d) None, but both must file affidavit. (e) Parental consent plus court's consent required. (f) None, but a medical certificate is required. (g) Marriage may not be solemnized within 10 days from date of blood test. (h) If either under 18, 72 hrs. (i) Statute provides for obtaining license with parental or court consent with no state minimum age. (j) Under 16, with parental and court consent. (k) If either under 18, wait 3 full days. (l) If under stated age court consent required. (m) Va. blood test form must be used. (n) Applicant must also supply a certificate of immunity against German measles (rubella). (o) If under 18, parental and/or court consent required. (p) Statement whether person is carrier of sickle-cell anemia may be required. (q) Both parents consent required for men age 17, women age 15, one parent's consent required for men 18–20 years, women ages 16–20 years.

Source: Compiled by William E. Mariano, Council on Marriage Relations, Inc., 110 E. 42d St., New York, NY 10017.

TERMS OF ENDEARMENT . . . AND OTHER LEGAL CONSTRAINTS

In the United States, laws governing marriage are based on English common law, which regards husband and wife as one person, with the woman the one to surrender her property and identity. Until recently, a bride was required to change her surname to that of her husband, to live where her husband chose, even to give over her earnings to him. The husband, in turn, had a responsibility to support his wife as well as to compensate for any debts she incurred or crimes she committed.

Laws in every state change almost from day to day. In general, legislatures are relaxing restrictions and equalizing the statutes in favor of women. The movement toward humanization of the laws is strong, although some ridiculous ones governing marriage remained on the books until very recently. These may still be in effect:

- A married couple in Michigan must live together or be imprisoned.
- In Kentucky, a wife must have her husband's permission to move the furniture in her house.
- A judge in Michigan decided that a woman's hair is the property of her husband.
- In Minnesota, a hug and a kiss in the presence of a girl's parents, combined with several gifts of candy, is considered a proposal of marriage. (Tober, 1984)

blood test to insure that neither partner has a sexually transmitted disease. Most states have a three-day delay between the time of the blood test and the actual issuance of the marriage license. Presumably, this delay represents a "cooling off" period, a time span that affords couples one last chance to change their minds. Table 7-2 on pages 202 and 203 displays the requirements that exist for marriage, by individual state.

The Marriage Certificate

The wedding ceremony itself must be performed by someone legally permitted to do so by the state, and it must be witnessed by two persons of legal age. Following the ceremony, the couple, the witnesses, and the official performing the ceremony must sign the marriage license. Finally, the completed license is sent to the state's capital where it is recorded and filed. At this point, the state will issue a **marriage certificate**, a copy of which can be secured by the couple.

Prenuptial Agreements

A **prenuptial agreement**, or **personal marriage contract**, is a document drafted by some couples before they marry. In its most common form, a prenuptial agreement spells out how assets will be divided if the marriage dissolves. It is very similar to the cohabitation contract discussed in the last chapter.

Prenuptial agreements may also include other items, including the expectations partners have of one another, and might range from how household tasks are to be handled and role responsibilities assigned, to how many children the couple will bear. (The box beginning on page 205 illustrates the many diverse areas that can be included.)

Besides recognizing that divorce is a possibility in their lives, couples cite other reasons for drafting prenuptial agreements. Some feel that love is often blind during early stages of the relationship and want to clearly assess the union in writing. Others seek a written commitment to go along

APPLICATIONS

DRAFTING A MARRIAGE CONTRACT: ELEMENTS FOR CONSIDERATION

1. Process: Persons planning to wed usually feel the great pull of attraction and the ectasy of a new love; a field ripe for the growth of unchallenged assumptions. The act of the contracting process provides an opportunity for each person to communicate and negotiate. Before and after each negotiating session the couple may wish to quietly focus inward.

    a. Centering: It is recommended that each person sit in a balanced position directly across from the other. Each may breathe deeply, behold the other's eyes, and attune to each other by either holding hands or placing the right hand on the heart and the left hand on the partner's right hand.

    b. Communication: It is preferable for each to use "I sense," "I think," and "I want" language rather than "you are" language, thus taking responsibility for personal behavior. Awareness of the communication process is important; repeated defensiveness and dependent statements may be indicative of a relationship that could be more mature. Throughout the negotiation sessions each person will want to be aware of any changes in body tension, breath, and eye contact.

2. Relevant History: Each partner will want to relate the history that could have a possible effect on the intended union. Past marriages and the existence of children could affect the legality of a marriage if untold. The health history of the intended and the intended's family is important, especially for couples desiring to procreate.

3. Economic Provisions: Over 95 percent of contracts contain economic provisions

    a. Assets held prior to marriage: The contractors may opt to continue to separately hold and manage assets acquired before marriage. Other contractors may opt to merge and jointly manage such assets to give each partner an equal start.

    b. Property, Debts, and Living Expenses after Marriage:
    Partners may wish to reject the concept that superior earning power should not increase the burden on the lesser earner. Couples choosing to adopt the practice of keeping resources separate and contributing to expenses in amounts proportional to income will place neither partner in the dependent position of begging economic favors.

4. Name: The name bespeaks identity. Each partner may wish to retain her or his own birth name. Such a partner would not suffer loss of identity, confusion of professional record and reputation, or embarrassment of bearing the name of an exhusband. Partners may wish to choose a joint or new name consciously.

5. Legal Domicile: It is currently presumed that the husband's domicile could be decided jointly. Individuals (such as those in commuting dual-career couples) could choose to maintain separate domiciles. ▶

6. Career: Individuals could agree to attach equal importance to the careers of the wife and the husband. Subprovisions arising from this would concern prospective choice making regarding career opportunities in other geographical locations. The partners could indicate their preference for and not for joining in career-social obligations that could enhance a career—for instance, the image of the corporate spouse. The role of homemaker would be deemed to be as valuable as outside employment.

7. Relationships with Others: Partners may wish to contract guidelines regarding their relationships with others. These may be general relationships, sexual relationships, and relationships with the spouse and other relatives from a previous marriage.

   a. General Relationships: The partners may wish to address their preference to present or not to present an inseparable couple front at social functions. Partners may want to affirm the extent and time commitments that each may spend with others, so that individual needs are fulfilled and potential capacities are developed.

   b. Sexual Relationships: Some marital partners may want the security and exclusive commitment of sexual monogamy, specifying in the contract penalties to be imposed for failure to live up to the agreement. Other marital partners may indicate that sexual access be subject to the consent of individual participants, thus eliminating the current doctrine that a husband cannot rape his wife. The contracting couple may choose to permit sexual relationships, specifying boundaries, time commitment, and communications.

   c. Relationships with Spouse and Relatives of Previous Marriage: Separation or divorce does change day-to-day relationships; however, kin is always kin, and children especially always need parents. The limits of such relationships are established depending on whether or not there are children from the former marriage; the level of hostility or affection experienced during the divorce process; the general conditions of the separation; and quality of ties with kin, especially in-laws. The contracting couple may specify the length of time periods that children of a previous marriage may live with them so that there is less interference in the development of the new dyadic relationship.

8. Children: The contracting couple first indicates a preference to bring or not to bring children into the union. With the choice to bear children, other contract options may be considered.

   a. Partners may anticipate having children only as a result of mutual and deliberate agreement. Responsibility for birth control will be shared or mutually assigned; abortion at the woman's discretion is occasionally stipulated in case of accidental pregnancy.
   b. Responsibility for parenting may be outlined with attention to general guidelines for child rearing and social control (discipline) to specific responsibilities. The type of religious training as well as type of education (parochial, state, or private) may be specified.

▶

c. Contracting parties may elect to indicate that support for the children will be provided in the same proportion to the earnings, even after divorce, irrespective of custody. Other rules for determining support payments, division of assets, and payment of alimony or its waiver could be set.

d. Provisions for support of the children and a partner when death of a provider occurred: life insurance beneficiaries could be designated.

9. Ritual: The intending partners will want to reflect on and indicate the significance of ritual to their individual lives and to their relationship. The observation of ritual or rites of passage stimulates naturally occurring "highs" in the celebrants. It reunites the couple across the fabric of seasons with past and future generations of families.

10. Renewability and Change of Contract: Partners may plan a periodic evaluation of the partnership or of any specific issue to be initiated by either partner. The other partner is expected to cooperate. In case of unresolved conflicts, partners may agree to accept arbitration by an objective third party. The contract may hold for a limited time (for example, until birth of the first child) to acknowledge the fluid, changing, "living contract."

11. Provisions Affecting Termination: The partnership may be terminated by mutual consent, desire of either partner, or breach of a substantial provision. If one partner supports the other through school and the marriage then terminates, the receiving partner is obligated to reimburse the first one for the educational expense. Should one partner have agreed to forgo further education and career opportunities and stay home and care for children and the household, a lump sum for compensation for loss of earning ability for the sake of the marriage could be negotiated.

Jeter K., and Sussman, M. B. "Each couple should develop a marriage contract suitable to themselves," pp. 287–290 in *Current controversies in marriage and family,* edited by H. Feldman and M. Feldman. Copyright © 1985 by Sage Publications, Inc. Reprinted by permission of Sage Publications, Inc.

with the psychological commitment. Still others use prenuptial agreements as a way to periodically examine the health and growth of their relationship. Over time, the agreement is reviewed to see whether goals, ambitions, and related aspirations have been met.

Those prenuptial agreements focusing on financial divisions are starting to be recognized in court and do have legal substance. However, for this document to be upheld in court, it must be shown that it is fair, that it was executed voluntarily, and that it was entered into in good faith. To meet these criteria, the prospective bride and groom must each have a lawyer. Because this is a contract being

negotiated, both parties must be represented by counsel or the contract may later be ruled invalid. Both partners must also make a full financial disclosure, and negotiation must take place without coercion or threat (Totenberg, 1985).

From a legal standpoint, there is growing support for prenuptial agreements. Such agreements are seen as providing the parties some degree of certainty regarding their estates in the event of divorce or the death of one of the parties. Also, it is expected that making prenuptial agreements valid should reduce the amount of litigation and the acrimony that often follows a divorce. In addition, it has been suggested that such agreements may force parties who are about to marry to realize the seriousness of marriage and may actually reduce the number of divorces, since the parties know from the start of their marriage what will take place if a divorce occurs (Ruback, 1985).

Common-Law Marriages

In some states, **common-law marriages** are recognized by the courts. In such marriages, no formal ceremony has taken place nor has the couple complied with the legal requirements for a license. Rather, the couple has agreed to live together as husband and wife.

At one time, common-law marriages were particularly useful, such as during the settlement of the American Frontier. At that time, individuals who could marry two people were few and far between. Contrary to the thoughts of many, there is usually no minimum time interval required for a common-law marriage, even today. Interestingly, the effect of a common-law marriage parallels that of a ceremonial marriage. That is, the marriage is regarded as valid and requires a legal divorce to dissolve it (Ruback, 1985).

INTERMARRIAGES

As we learned in Chapter 3, homogamous pressures encourage the selection of a partner having a similar background, including that of religion and race. While most persons choose to stay within these parameters we'd like to briefly examine the marriages of those who do not. The numbers of those marrying outside of religious and racial boundaries have been increasing in recent years and add a unique flavor to America's melting pot.

Interfaith Marriages

Interfaith marriages are much more common than **interracial marriages**. One source (Glenn, 1982) indicates that 15 to 20 percent of all marriages are of the interfaith variety. About 18 percent of all Catholics marry non-Catholics, 11 percent of all Jews marry non-Jews, and 7 percent of all Protestants marry non-Protestants. A more recent study of Jewish intermarriages (Gruson, 1985) indicates an even higher percentage. According to this source, as many as one in four Jews choose to marry outside of their religion.

Bernard Murstein (1986) proposes that several factors account for why interfaith marriages are more popular than interracial ones. There is apparently less of a barrier to marriage when there are no visible signs of intermarriage, such as skin color. In addition, the decline in religious prejudice and the lessening of ethnic and cultural differences, present among immigrants, has created an increasingly homogamous American culture.

Interestingly, interfaith marriages have unique demographic variations. For instance, in New York where there are large Catholic and Jewish populations, there is a high incidence of Catholic-Jewish marriages. In Iowa, Minnesota, and Pennsylvania where the religious makeup is about fifty-fifty Catholic and Lutheran, a higher than average rate of intermarriage between those two faiths exists. Catholic-Lutheran marriages are the most stable, with a 90.5 percent survival rate (Pace, 1986).

Although they do not encourage interfaith marriages, there is at present a greater acceptance of them by the clergy. In Louisiana, Mississippi, New York, and California, an agreement exists between the Roman Catholic and Episcopalian churches dispensing with the requirement of obtaining written permission from a bishop before allowing an interfaith couple to be married in the church. The agreement also encourages the couple to continue worship in their respective faiths.

We should also add that with the changing attitude of society toward greater acceptance of inter-religious marriages, a number of congregations are devising activities and programs to reach out to these families. For example, many synagogues now offer workshops on Jewish holidays and life cycle. The Roman Catholic church also offers a marriage preparation course that includes special counseling for intermarried couples.

APPLICATIONS

MEETING THE CHALLENGES OF AN INTERFAITH MARRIAGE

Stephanie Dahl (1984) writes that interfaith marriages have the potential of creating problems for partners. No area is more sensitive or personal than that of religion. And, since religious faith goes to the very core of our identity, to who we are and what we believe, it is not an issue that can be compromised and discussed in quite the same way as other issues might be. Beyond this, one's religion extends into the realm of family identity and, sometimes, ethnic heritage. Because of this, a religious difference between partners raises significant issues for the future of the families involved: the celebration of holidays, the raising of children, and the transmission of values and traditions. For the interfaith couple then, a life together demands more than finding workable solutions for themselves; it requires finding solutions for their families as well. In this vein, Dahl proposes that couples need to explore a number of issues:

■ How much do you know about each other's religious background? Knowledge brings understanding. Discuss religious experiences, visit each other's clergy, and consider premarital instruction programs as ways to learn more about another faith.

■ What are your faith's laws regarding marriage? Visit the clergy as soon as you decide to marry, and find out what changes can be made in the wedding ceremony for interfaith couples. If both faiths will sanction the marriage, and if the ceremony can reflect elements of both traditions, you and your families and friends will feel more comfortable.

■ What values and beliefs do the two of you share? No matter how disparate your religious backgrounds, it is essential that you, as an interfaith couple, find a common ground of values and beliefs.

■ What holidays and religious occasions are important to you and your families? Alienation of children is what families dread the most. You can minimize these fears by planning in advance how you will celebrate Hanukkah, Christmas, Easter, Passover, and other holidays in your home and with your families.

■ How will your children be raised? Most couples agree that youngsters need to be raised with some religious beliefs; how they are implemented may be the single greatest issue that interfaith couples face. You need to be honest with each other regarding your children's religious future.

■ Are you willing to shoulder your religious responsibilities in the home? When one partner is essentially nonpracticing, the other may not only have to continue practicing his/her faith alone, but may also have to take primary responsibility for the religious training of children. It can be a heavy burden.

Adapted from Dahl, 1984.

Interracial Marriages

Miscegenation is the technical name given to interracial marriages. As late as 1966, 17 states had formal prohibitions against one or more forms of interracial marriage. The United States Supreme Court overturned the 16 existing state **anti-miscegenation statutes** (laws prohibiting mixed marriage) with a decision rendered June 12, 1967. At one point or another, 40 of the 50 states have had laws which prohibited blacks from intermarrying with whites. Pennsylvania, in 1780, was the first state to repeal its anti-miscegenation law, while Indiana and Wyoming took this action as recently as 1965 (Cretser and Leon, 1982).

Interracial marriages are not widespread in the United States. They amounted to less than 2 percent of all marriages in 1982, and were most common between white females and black males. Demographer Barbara Wilson (1984) observes that such marriages accounted for 0.5 percent of all marriages between 1968 and 1970. Marriages between black females and while males accounted for 0.2 percent of all marriages during the same period. Marriages between a white spouse and a partner of another race, or a black spouse and a partner of another race, constitute the remaining percentage of interracial marriages.

According to Wilson, brides and grooms who marry interracially are usually older than average. In 1980, for example, ages at first marriage for brides and grooms regardless of race were 22.1 and 24.1 years, respectively. In a first marriage, for both, white brides were 21.5 years old at marriage to a white groom, 23.4 when marrying a black groom, and 22.4 at marriage to a groom of another race. Black brides pairing with black grooms were 23.1 years old, but 23.8 when marrying a white groom, and 23.6 at marriage to a groom of another race. When both bride and groom were of other races the average bride was 23.6 years old, while brides of other races who married white grooms were 23.9, and those who married black grooms were 23.7.

Interracial marriages are not widespread in the United States but have shown an increase in recent years.

While black brides or grooms who marry white spouses tend to have a higher level of education than those who marry black spouses, members of other races who marry interracially have less education than is average for their group. In 1980, white grooms who married interracially were more likely to have completed college than those who married white brides. While 18 percent of white grooms whose spouses were also white held college degrees, 24 percent who married black brides and 25 percent who married brides of other races had finished college. In contrast, only 5 percent of black grooms paired with brides of other races had completed college, while 13 percent of black grooms of white brides and 9 percent of black grooms whose spouses were also black held college degrees. One quarter of the grooms of other races who married brides of other races were college-educated, while 22 percent of such grooms whose spouses were white had finished college (Wilson, 1984).

Beyond those reasons for marriage discussed earlier, what motivates individuals to marry outside of their race? What are some of the characteristics of those involved? Since the black-white marriage is the most popular form of interracial marriage, let's turn to the research of Ernest Porterfield (1982) to answer such questions. Porterfield's review of the literature indicates that at least six general patterns of motivation exist. One, the participants tend to be nonconformists and do not let racial homagamy control their selection of a mate. Two, some whites marry nonwhites for idealistic or liberal reasons (that is, to defy the prevalent cultural prejudice of society). Three, there may be the "lure of the exotic." That is, the individual may experience a profound psychosexual attraction to the "otherness" of someone who may be physically different. Four, there is also the notion that a white peson may marry a nonwhite to rebel against parental authority. A fifth motive is repudiation, a possible indication that the person either has not been thoroughly integrated into his/ her social group or has repudiated it for some reason. Finally, the idea of neurotic self-hate or self-degradation (by marriage to an "inferior") also looms as a possible motive.

Porterfield sounds a note of caution with all of these motives. While they do give us clues as to why persons choose interracial marriage, they are unsystematic, fragmentary, and speculative. In many instances, they are derived on the basis of individual cases or small samples. Therefore such information should not be accepted as a valid reason for all mixed marriages.

Over the years, interracial marriages have posed their share of problems. While there are many experiencing marital happiness and satisfaction, it appears that many more suffer from external as well as internal conflict. Externally, disapproval from parents and family almost always heads the list, although this seems more prevalent among white than black kin. Some couples face discrimination in housing and many experience social discomfort when out in public. Despite the fact that society is more tolerant toward interracial marriages, a fairly recent survey (Gallup, 1983) shows that a majority of Americans still oppose it. Internal disharmony also punctuates interracial marriages. Statistics show that divorce rates are higher among interracial marriages than same-race ones (Price-Bonham and Balswick, 1980).

CHAPTER HIGHLIGHTS

Despite rising divorce rates, most people expect to marry at some point in their lives. Today, however, many are choosing to postpone marriage. We explored a number of motives for marriage: love, conformity, companionship, legitimization of sex and children, a sense of readiness, and legal benefits.

The transition from single to married life brings numerous changes. Specifically, marriage represents a new public identity and creates a legal unit. It also changes the couple's social relationships and patterns of interaction with each other, including perceptions as well as evaluations. Each of these changes requires adjustment and adaptation.

The engagement is a rite of passage usually characterized by the presentation of an engagement ring to the fianceé, a shower for the bride, a party for the groom, and an announcement in the newspaper. The engagement period affords couples the opportunity to explore their expectations and ideas about marriage, their values, and their desired lifestyle. The wedding has always symbolized what the marriage means to the couple as well as to the community: commitment, sharing, and happiness. This chapter explored the many innovations and rituals surrounding weddings in the United States as well as in other nations. Many of the rituals followed in wedding ceremonies are rooted in antiquity.

We also examined how marriage exists as a legal contract between a man and a woman. Individual states, rather than the federal government, determine marriage requirements. As such, procedures for obtaining a marriage license differ from state to state. Many couples today are drafting prenuptial agreements, personalized marriage contracts which spell out how assets will be divided if the union dissolves. These may also include the expectations partners have for one another. In common-law marriages, the couple has not been "legally" married but chooses to live together as husband and wife. In some states such marriages are recognized by the courts.

This chapter concluded with a discussion of intermarriages, particularly interfaith and interracial marriages. Couples entering such marriages have chosen to resist homogamous religious and racial pressures. Of the two types of intermarriages, interfaith marriages are more common. As we learned, both types pose numerous adjustment challenges to the couple.

KEY TERMS

anti-miscegenation statute	interfaith marriage	marriage rate
banns	interracial marriage	miscegenation
common-law marriage	marriage certificate	personal marriage contract
engagement	marriage license	prenuptial agreement

RECOMMENDED READINGS

Carey, A. (1984). *In defense of marriage.* New York: Walker and Company. Carey explores the popularity of marriage and explains why he regards it as the best arrangement for structuring relationships and organizing family and kin.

Chambers, W. and Asher, S. (1983). *The celebration book of great American traditions.* New York: Harper & Row. History buffs will enjoy reading about the manner in which wedding ceremonies have evolved into their present-day form.

Cheser, B. J. (1980). Analysis of wedding rituals: An attempt to make weddings more meaningful. *Family Relations, 12*(4), 73–77. This interesting article explores wedding symbolisms, customs, and pageantry.

Crester, G. A., and Leon, J. J. (Eds.). (1982). *Intermarriage in the United States.* New York: The Haworth Press. This sophisticated collection of articles covers the many facets of interracial marriages.

Feldman, H., and Feldman, M. (Eds.). (1985). *Current controversies in marriage and family.* Beverly Hills, CA: Sage. Part One of this book reveals the pros and cons of intermarriages.

Greenblat, C. S., and Cottle, T. J. (1980). *Getting married: A new look at an old tradition.* New York: McGraw-Hill. This work covers such topics as the desire to marry, the decision to marry, the engagement, and the quest for the "perfect" wedding.

Lamm, M. (1980). *The Jewish way in love and marriage*. New York: Harper & Row. Lamm provides good coverage of the Jewish marriage ceremony and compares it with other rituals, symbols, and wedding practices in Western civilization.

Leonard, D. (1980). *Sex and generation: A study of courtship and weddings*. New York: Methuen. This paperback explores the process of courtship and marriage among young couples in a provincial town in South Wales.

Ruback, R. B. (1985). Family law. In L. L'Abate (Ed.), *The handbook of family psychology and therapy*. Homewood, IL: The Dorsey Press. Ruback clearly explains the legal aspects of marriage in this article.

Weitzman, L. (1981). *The marriage contract: Spouses, lovers, and the law*. New York: The Free Press. For those couples wanting more information on marriage contracts, this is one of the better books available.

8

Developmental Tasks of Married Couples

CONTENTS

CONTEMPLATIONS

■ We've only just begun . . . . For newly married couples, starting out in life together has enormous and exciting potential. But many couples find that the images they've attached to married life are filled with myths and misconceptions. For most, idealistic dreams are quickly replaced by the realities of day-to-day living. What are some of these myths? How do such idealistic dreams originate? What must couples do to overcome such misconceptions? We'll explore some of the more prevalent myths that exist about married life, and we'll replace them with factual information. In the process, we'll also take a look at the many adjustments needed to create marital harmony and stability.

■ HUSBAND: You wouldn't believe what a tough day I've had. I'm exhausted.
WIFE: *You're* exhausted? You wouldn't believe the type of day I've had.
HUSBAND: I didn't even get a lunch break.
WIFE: I had to catch the late commuter train home because the office was so busy.

As the above dialogue illustrates, the labor force is no longer the exclusive territory of the male. On the contrary, the dual-earner marriage has come to occupy the prominent position once held by the traditional family, in which the husband was the "breadwinner" and the wife the "homemaker." What is life like in dual-earner marriages? What adjustments have to be made when both husband and wife work? What are the benefits and drawbacks? These and numerous other questions will be addressed when we explore the two-paycheck marriage of the 1980s.

■ The Harrisons have been married for almost 20 years, which is a surprise to many who know them. They quarrel on a regular basis and always seem to nag and irritate each other. The Donovans have been married almost as long, but their marriage is different. While once deeply in love, they've drifted apart over the years, and although they don't fight, they spend little or no time together. And then there's the Thompsons, married for 25 years and still as romantically attached to one another as the day they were wedded. Each of these marriages has endured over the years, but they're all obviously different. What factors account for such disparate marital relationships? Are these differences a reflection of the conceptions partners have of marriage? If this is the case, is it possible to categorize the different conceptions that exist? The latter portion of this chapter will supply some answers.

Marriage is one of the most complex institutions in the world. Yet, two people fall in love and marry with surprisingly little knowledge of the depth and variety of the network of relationships they are being integrated into. Many have inherited a hope chest of taken-for-granted misinformation which they bring to their household and may carry with them for the rest of their married lives. Complicating the situation is that partners typically know just a little about the family background or the personality subleties of their partner. Unfortunately, many couldn't care less since they are in love (Krantzler, 1981).

Reality quickly comes into the lives of newly married couples. In simple terms, partners discover that living together on a permanent basis can cause problems. People who have lived together for a decade or so may have forged solutions and resolutions to some of the problems they encountered. But for the newly married couple, such interpersonal abilities and adaptations do not yet exist. Rather, they must be nurtured and developed (Pocs and Walsh, 1985).

MYTHS AND REALITIES OF MARRIED LIFE

In the minds of many there is an idealistic image attached to the early phases of marriage. Some tend to picture the young couple as always engulfed in romantic bliss, perfectly attuned to each other's needs and responding favorably to every marital challenge. We have a tendency to look at young married couples and think "and they lived happily ever after"—further perpetuating the idealistic dream.

Contributing to these idealistic perceptions are a number of marital myths. Irene and Herbert Goldenberg (1985) write that these myths are usually ill-founded, self-deceptive, and destructive. Borrowing from the earlier work of Glick and Kessler (1980), the Goldenbergs provide a synopsis of the more common myths that many couples tend to believe. These myths are presented in Table 8-1.

TABLE 8-1

Common Marital Myths

Myth	Reality
1. Marriage and families should be completely happy; each member should expect all or most gratifications to originate from the family	This is a "romantic" myth; it overlooks the fact that many of life's satisfactions are commonly found outside the family
2. "Togetherness" through close physical proximity or joint activities creates a satisfactory family life and individual gratification	"Togetherness" varies greatly from one family to another; close contact or joint activities cannot be considered ideal patterns for all families under all conditions
3. Marital partners should always be totally honest with one another	While openness is usually desirable—especially in the service of a constructive, problem-solving approach—it may also be damaging if used in the service of hostile, destructive feelings
4. Happy marriages have no disagreements; when family members fight it means they hate each other	Differences between family members are inevitable and often create arguments; if these clarify feelings and are not personal attacks, they may be constructive and preferable to covering up differences by always appearing to agree
5. Marital partners should always see eye to eye on issues and work toward an identical outlook	Differences in background, experiences, and personality make this impossible to achieve; actually, different outlooks, if used constructively, may provide families with more options for carrying out developmental tasks
6. Marital partners should be unselfish and not think of their own needs	Extremes of self-absorption or selflessness are undesirable; but satisfactions are needed as an individual; you are not merely an appendage to others (for example, mother lives only to serve the family)
7. Whenever something goes wrong in the family, it is important to determine who is at fault	Rather than blaming a single individual, dysfunction in family interactions should be examined so that all members accept responsibilities

TABLE 8-1. *(continued)*

Common Marital Myths

Myth	Reality
8. Rehashing the past is helpful when things are not going well at present	Endless recriminations about past errors usually escalate present problems, not reduce them, since they usually invite retaliation from your partner
9. In a marital argument, one partner is right and the other wrong; the goal is to see who can score the most "points"	Marriages generally suffer when competition rather than cooperation characterizes marital interactions
10. A good sexual relationship inevitably leads to a good marriage	A good sexual relationship is an important component of a satisfactory marriage, but it does not preclude the presence of interpersonal difficulties in other areas
11. In a satisfactory marriage, sexuality will more or less take care of itself	Not necessarily; sexual difficulties may be brought into the marriage or be related to stresses outside of the marriage
12. Marital partners understand each other's nonverbal communications and therefore do not need to discuss matters with one another	This is less likely to be true in dysfunctional families, where misperceptions and misinterpretations of each other's meanings and intent are common
13. Positive feedback is not as necessary in a marriage as negative feedback	Positive feedback (attention, compliments) increases the likelihood that desirable behavior will reoccur, rather than taking for granted that it will and focusing on what's wrong with the other's behavior
14. Good marriages simply happen spontaneously requiring no effort	Another romantic myth; good marriages require daily input by both partners, with constant negotiation, communication, and mutual problem solving
15. Any spouse can (and often should) be reformed and remodeled into the shape desired by the partner	A poor premise in marriage, and one likely to lead to frustration, anger, and disillusionment. Working on improving the relationship should make partners more compatible and more sensitive to each other's needs
16. In a stable marriage, things do not change and there are no problems	All living systems change, grow, and develop over time. Fixed systems sooner or later are out of phase with current needs and developments
17. Everyone knows what a husband should be like and what a wife should be like	This is especially untrue in modern society, where new roles are being explored
18. If a marriage is not working properly, having children will rescue it	On the contrary, children usually become the victims of marital disharmony
19. No matter how bad a marriage, it should be kept together for the sake of the children	Not necessarily true; in marriages where partners stay together as "martyrs" for the children's sake, children usually bear the brunt of the resentment partners feel for one another
20. If a marriage does not work out, an extramarital affair or divorce and marriage to another spouse will cure the situation	Occasionally true, but without gaining insight, similar choices will be made, and the same nongratifying patterns will be repeated

Source: Adapted from Goldenberg and Goldenberg, 1985 and Glick and Kessler, 1980.

The realities of day-to-day living soon temper the idealistic images attached to married life. This is as true today as it was long ago.

While the attainment of marital happiness is an admirable goal, believing such myths or feeling that a perfect relationship is possible is unrealistic. Sooner or later, most couples discover that the romance and happiness attached to the wedding and honeymoon do not last forever. Indeed, reality quickly asserts itself and they see that the world is less than ideal. Ups and downs will begin to punctuate the relationship. As Sander Breiner (1980) writes, the first misunderstanding or fight leads the couple to realize that each partner is only a human being, complete with weaknesses and differences. On a larger scale, they come to realize that their marriage does not fit into the "perfect" mold. Rather than continuing the search for an idealistic and unattainable relationship, couples learn that they must focus instead on the many adjustments that characterize day-to-day married life.

MARITAL ADJUSTMENTS

Relationship Adjustments

The happiness and harmony that a couple generates are determined by the quality of interaction between the two partners. A relationship is not simply the sum of two individuals; rather, it is a unity of two interacting personalities. To state it another way, no single type of personality causes a failure in marriage; instead, two individual personalities, through interaction with one another, can fail or succeed in marriage. Consequently, the successful marriage relies on the desire of the husband and wife to make their relationship work. How committed they are to meeting one another's expectations will ultimately decide whether a marriage is successful (Ammons and Stinnett, 1980).

In the last chapter, we explored the major changes that accompany the transition from single to married status. Newly married couples find that some reevaluation of old patterns of interaction is needed at this time. Many couples find that marriage brings new levels of commitment and a need to redefine expectations for one another. According to Marie Kargan (1985), the latter is especially important since unfulfilled expectations lead to disenchantment, disappointment, and unhappiness. Early on in a marriage, a string of unfulfilled expectations can deliver devastating damage to the trust and faith needed in a relationship. Couples need to carefully examine and fine-tune their mutual expectations for consistency, fairness, and clarity.

Pauline Boss (1983) relates that newly married couples also need to clearly define the boundaries that exist in their relationship and remove any ambiguity surrounding them. By boundaries, Boss refers to who is performing what roles and tasks within a relationship. These parameters need to be clearly identified and, in the best interest of the relationship, mutually agreed upon.

In recent years, growing numbers of married couples are adopting an **egalitarian** orientation to their relationship, emphasizing equality between partners, particularly within the realm of role-sharing. According to Linda Haas (1980), fully developed egalitarian relationships share each of the following traditionally segregated family roles:

- *The Breadwinner Role* The husband and wife are equally responsible for earning family income; the wife's employment is not considered more optional or less desirable than the husband's. As a result, the spouses' occupations are equally important and receive equal status. Minimally, the occupation which has more status is not determined by notions of the intrinsic supremacy of one sex over the other.

- *The Domestic Role* The husband and wife are equally responsible for performing housekeeping chores such as cooking, cleaning, and laundry.

- *The Handyman Role* The husband and wife are equally responsible for performing traditionally masculine tasks such as yard work and mechanical repairs.

- *The Kinship Role* The husband and wife are equally responsible for meeting kinship obligations, like buying gifts and writing letters, which have traditionally been the wife's responsibility.

- *The Childcare Role* The husband and wife are equally responsible for doing routine childcare tasks and for the rearing and disciplining of children.

- *The Major/Minor Decision-Maker Roles* The spouses have generally equal influence on the making of major decisions which males have traditionally dominated and the minor decisions traditionally delegated to the female.

Haas feels that specialization within any of these roles (for example, husband cooks, wife launders) would be compatible with role-sharing, as long as specific tasks are not assigned to a spouse on the

Reprinted with special permission of King Features Syndicate, Inc.

basis of sex (that is, because they are deemed more appropriate for someone of his/her gender) and as long as the overall responsibility for the duties of each role is evenly shared.

While increasing in popularity, egalitarian marriages are still in the minority — roles are assigned on the basis of traditional sex-typed expectations. Thus, for example, the husband becomes the principle breadwinner and handyman while the wife is responsible for the domestic chores and childcare.

Audrey Smith and William Reid (1986) maintain that couples who are attempting to achieve a role-sharing marriage are struggling to define and implement emerging values about marital relationships. These values embrace equality of opportunity for career development and fairness in division of domestic and parental responsibilities. As we saw in Chapter 4, egalitarian values often run counter to long-held traditions concerning the institution of marriage. Because of these traditions, a man and woman are not entirely free to form a relationship based on egalitarian values. They enter it with abilities, expectations, and attitudes molded by their earlier socialization, discover their choices constrained by market-place realities, and face continuing pressures from society at large to maintain traditional conceptions of marital roles. The result is usually a set of compromises between the modern and traditional marriage.

Gayle Kimball's (1983) research reveals that egalitarian relationships tend to fall into three categories: those that began traditionally and changed to role-sharing after the woman returned to paid work (these were the most troubled relationships), second marriages that successfully react against a traditional first marriage, and intact marriages that began equally (usually younger couples influenced by feminism). She also found that two different styles of egalitarian marriage emerge: one that is easygoing, casual, and low key — in which, for example, whoever feels like doing a task does it with no specific assignment; and the other more structured, with specific division of tasks and financial responsibilities and specific times set aside for talk and leisure. The structured style is sometimes accompanied by more interpersonal

intensity, more visible ego, more willful personalities, more ups and downs, and more conflicts than the low-key style.

The benefits of egalitarianism to a relationship are numerous. For both spouses, there is typically a greater opportunity to develop abilities and pursue personal interests without being limited by traditional role expectations. Partners also report relief from the stress and overwork that originates from having primary responsibility for a broad area of family life. And egalitarianism promotes greater levels of independence for husband and wife. Aside from these benefits, though, many couples report problems shifting to a role-sharing relationship. For example, there is often a disinclination among both husband and wife to do non-traditional chores. Discrepancies may also exist between partners in housekeeping standards, such as in the orderliness and cleanliness of the tasks executed. Many wives are also reluctant to delegate domestic responsibility to their husbands. Finally, a lack of non-traditional domestic skills frequently exists for both spouses (Haas, 1980).

Work-Related Adjustments

The vocational arena is no longer the exclusive and private domain of men. Over the past decade or so, the dual-earner family has come to occupy the prominent position once held by the traditional family — in which the husband was the breadwinner and the wife the homemaker. While there have been other changes effecting the family structure, none has been as significant as the growing prominence of dual-earner marriages (Hayghe, 1982).

In **dual-earner marriages**, the majority of women (and many of the men) work at **jobs**, positions that are not a major life interest and are undertaken primarily to provide family income. However, there is a developing minority of families in which both the husband and wife pursue **careers** while maintaining a life together. Denise Skinner (1983) emphasizes that the word career refers to occupations which require a high degree of commitment and have a continuous developmental character. A person usually pursues a career by obtaining the education and relevant experience which enable him or her to perform with expertise. This individual tends to view his or her career as a primary source of personal satisfaction. **Dual-career marriages** then, are a subtype of the larger category of dual-earner marriages.

Women in the Labor Force The history of women's involvement in the paid work force has been characterized by considerable resistance. This resistance has been expressed by many, including women themselves. Females who left home to work were often regarded as unfeminine, immoral, or negligent in their mothering duties. Employers and society in general often did not take the working woman seriously. Without question, the increase in women entering the labor force has helped to change these attitudes, and in turn, has encouraged more women to seek employment (Nieva and Gutek, 1981).

Women account for 43.5 percent of the total labor force. And between 1982 and 1985, women accounted for 64 percent of all new workers. Today, about 60 percent of all women over the age of 16 work, and this figure is expected to rise to 75 percent by 1995 (U. S. Bureau of Labor Statistics, 1984). Figure 8-1 shows the proportion of women in the labor force by age and generation in 1985.

The contemporary female worker is succeeding in removing traditional sex-role barriers, not only by the work she does, but also by the fact that she often operates from a set of carefully cultivated career goals. Such careful planning was virtually unheard of in previous generations because yesterday's females were not expected to have career goals. For many today, this is a societal expectation that still lingers. There are also those who feel that success in a career is something to fear, since they have been taught that being competitive and successful is unfeminine (Lipman-Blumen, 1984; Steers and Porter, 1983; Scarf, 1980).

Joyce Slayton Mitchell (1982) proposes that a

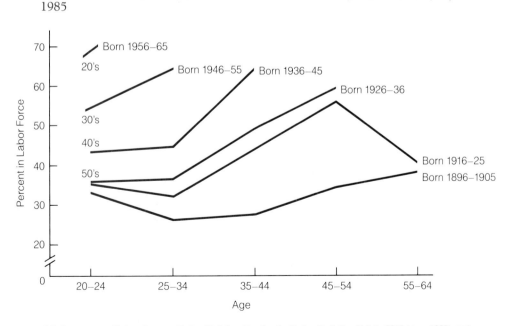

FIGURE 8-1   Proportion of Women in the Labor Force by Age and Generation, 1985

U.S. Department of Labor, Bureau of Labor Statistics, *Handbook of Labor Statistics*, Bulletin 2217 (June 1985), and other Bureau of Labor Statistics publications (Washington, D.C.: Government Printing Office).

woman is often in a different position than a man, particularly when the career-selection process begins. Along traditional lines, she is expected to be financially supported by someone else when she grows up. He is expected to financially support himself and perhaps others when he grows up. She is often programmed to be assessed on the basis of the salary her husband earns; he on his own earnings. He has been programmed to discover his worth through his vocation. She is often programmed to find her worth through her family. He has been programmed as a success object; she, a sex object. Note the sex-role stereotypes that abound with each of these perceptions.

Although some of these traditional stereotypes are changing, the process is slow and difficult. The going is not easy for a woman who is faced with fears, insecurities, and misconceptions that are the result of being brought up as a woman in our society. Sylvia Senter (1982) adds that many females today have been raised to be nurturing, subservient, and supportive. Such conditioning will not help those women who want to climb the occupational ladder. It's acceptable if females want to be mothers or housewives, but traditional "feminine" responses usually fail when women want to function with men in more prestigious positions. Senter believes that certain problems among modern-day career women often emerge because of

their "traditional" childhood conditioning. These include the following:

- Fear of taking risks.
- Passivity; waiting for someone else to do things for them.
- Inability to give orders.
- Fear of competition.
- Panic in the face of authority.
- Inability to cope with rejection.
- Confusion about sexuality and its place in the office.
- Not knowing how to use criticism to one's advantage.
- Needing to nurture and to be indispensable.
- Failing to understand the subleties of teamwork.

All of these, though, can be overcome. Just as males learn the behavior that enables them to function successfully, so too can women. What women need to do is *uncondition* themselves. This is not, however, as simple as it may sound. In the end, what a woman has to say is that she wants a career and that she is willing to confront the problems that she will have because she is a woman (Mitchell, 1982; Petit, 1983; Douglas, 1982).

While large numbers of females are entering the workplace, many are frequently confined to low-

CROSS-CULTURAL FOCUS

WOMEN IN THE INTERNATIONAL LABOR FORCE

Around the world, women comprise more than one-third of the total paid labor force, with 47 percent of all women aged 15 to 64 working. However, this percentage shows variation depending on the nation under study. For example, while 60 percent of all United States women are in the labor force, Russia heads the list with 71 percent of its women being employed. And only 30 percent of Latin American females are in the paid workplace. (The figure at the end of this box displays the percentage of women in the labor force, by selected nations.)

World-wide, women continue to earn less than men. In 1982 women working in the manufacturing industry earned an average of 70 cents for every dollar earned   ▶

by men. Inferior pay is also accompanied by other negative working conditions. Compared to their male counterparts, women work at lower-paying, unskilled types of occupations. Moreover, their chances for advancement are fewer. Inequality and discrimination are thus not exclusive problems for American women.

While female labor force participation rates are available, the housework and childcare carried out by women around the world is largely invisible. It is not included in countries' labor or economic statistics. However, if the value of the cooking, cleaning and nursing activities that make up this work was calculated, it would equal half the gross national product in many countries. Consider, for example, that a woman in rural Pakistan spends 63 hours a week on domestic work, and in the developed world, women spend about 56 hours per week on housework.

This means that on a world-wide basis, women spend more hours working and have much less free time than working men. In support of this, consider that females in rural Rwanda do three times the amount of work men do. In Java women work over 20 percent more than men, and in Europe a working woman has less than half the free time her husband has.

Cancellier and Crews, 1986.

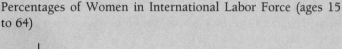

Percentages of Women in International Labor Force (ages 15 to 64)

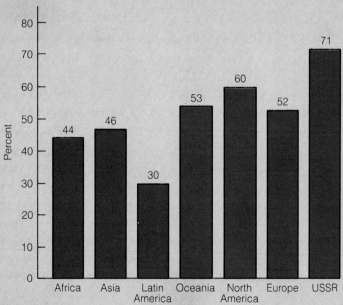

Source: Mary Mederios Kent, Carl Haub, and Keiko Osaki, "The World's Women: A Profile," Population Reference Bureau, 1985.

status occupations. Women continue to be a minority in professional and skilled careers, especially managerial positions. Most women today work in office settings, handling clerical chores, while the more prestigious vocations are dominated by males. Compared to the white-collar, executive world of males, females are often relegated to the pink-collar world of the office secretary (Miller and Garrison, 1984).

The lopsided distribution of men and women in various careers can be seen by examining occupational groupings. For example, 95 percent of dentists, 89 percent of physicians, and 87 percent of lawyers are males. On the other hand, 96 percent of nurses, 84 percent of elementary-school teachers, and 78 percent of librarians are women (U.S. Bureau of the Census, 1980a).

Even when they hold the same jobs as men, women receive substantially lower salaries. On the average, women in the United States earn about 65 cents for every dollar that a man is paid. Contrast that with Sweden where women earn over 81 cents to the male dollar. In Italy and Denmark, it's 86 cents, and in France, 78 cents (Hewlett, 1986). In some fields, such as science and engineering, the salary gap widens as one gets older. Retirement benefits are also far lower for females. In 1980, for instance, the average retirement benefit for a woman was less than 40 percent of that for a retiring male. But perhaps this next fact will let you know where women stand in earning ability: on the average, women with college degrees earn less pay than men who only finish the eighth grade. In support of this, the average income for female college graduates in 1982 was $12,347. Males who never had even one semester of high school had an average income of $12,965 (Mitchell, 1982, National Research Council, 1981; Porter, 1980; Russo and Cassidy, 1983).

It should be emphasized that vocational inequality begins almost immediately in the career cycle. A survey of over 3,000 tenth- and eleventh-graders starting their first job bears this out. Adolescents' first jobs are already significantly segregated by sex. On the average, females work fewer hours per week than males and earn lower hourly wages. In addition, hourly wages are higher in job types that are dominated by males. In general, these differences are maintained over young people's early job histories (Greenberger and Steinberg, 1983).

To fight such financial inequality for women of all ages, the U.S. Supreme Court decreed in 1981 that females must be paid the same amount as males for "equivalent" work. Equivalent work is defined as work that fulfills essentially the same function or requires the same amount of training or education. Whether this ruling can be uniformly enforced, though, is questionable.

It is our contention that as a nation, we need to reexamine the total structure of the labor force and remove those forms of segregation, inequality, and discrimination that have persisted. As it now stands, the labor force often exploits women. Females are frequently trapped in work that is tedious, low-paying, unchallenging, and sometimes even degrading. This is as true for single women as it is for those married, for young females as well as for those older (Dixon, 1983; Roos, 1983).

Adjusting to the Two-Paycheck Household
Now that we have examined the impact that women have had in the labor force, let's turn back to the household. What effect has the high rate of paid employment among women had on marriages? Does the dual-earner marriage create special needs and adjustments? What are the advantages and disadvantages of this lifestyle?

At the outset, we'd like to say that a dual-earner marriage has the potential of promoting considerably high levels of happiness, satisfaction, and accomplishment. Many dual-earner couples report stability in their marriages and contentment in their career pursuits. Indeed, some say that the involvement and sacrifices required in a vocation make marriage and domestic life more meaningful. Thus, two time-consuming, bustling vocations may bring considerable enrichment and contentment, not to mention elevated levels of finance.

However, there are two sides to every coin. Because of its demands, a two-paycheck marriage may also snap the patience of even the most dedicated couples. Such a domestic arrangement has the potential of bringing headaches and sacrifices, the pressures of which often overwhelm marriage partners.

Let's first acknowledge the fact that in all too many marriages it is necessity alone that forces a wife to work. Granted, some couples have the economic security that allows them to be concerned about their careers, rather than jobs. But for those without this luxury, two paychecks are merely a means of making ends meet. Many couples have to run faster and faster to try to remain in the same economic place. The presence of female discrimination in the workforce certainly doesn't help the situation. His job may be more gratifying and is certainly better paying. But both are likely to regard their work as ordinary jobs rather than careers, something they are forced to do for a paycheck (Krantzler, 1981).

The household division of labor among dual-earner couples also poses problems. While many women are employed, most of the traditional sex roles attached to them are still in place. Recall that the egalitarian relationship exists in many homes, but is still overshadowed by conventional orientations to household chores. This means that in addition to vocational demands, working women still carry the brunt of household chores. Consequently, the problem is that a dual-earner marriage is really a three-earner marriage, with the wife typically holding down two careers. As we'll see in Chapter 12, this situation worsens during parenthood when childcare chores are added to the woman's domestic routines and responsibilities.

In reference to this, Sylvia Hewlett (1986) points out that modern-day women face two persistent and unfair forms of inequality: in the workplace and on the home front. As she sees it, the average workweek of American women is 21 hours longer than that of men, yet men do less than a quarter of all household tasks. The average time a married man spends doing family tasks has increased only 6 percent in 20 years, despite the massive shift of women into paid employment.

Joseph Pleck (1985) adds that a woman's high level of time in household and paid work has nega-

The two-paycheck household requires special adaptations and adjustments.

tive consequences for the marital relationship. Low participation by the husband typically leads the wife to be dissatisfied with the division of labor. This, in turn, has negative consequences for her overall adjustment and well-being. On the other hand, greater husband participation in household chores promotes more healthy adjustment and domestic stability.

There are variations to all of this, of course. For example, Pleck (1985) observes that some wives are content with their husbands' low level of domestic participation. The belief that housework and childcare are ultimately the wife's responsibility (no matter what her employment status) is widely and deeply held. In addition, some wives may not want their husbands to do more because they feel that the home domain is their territory, and they derive a sense of psychological identity from this role.

Another problem associated with dual-earner marriages is the pressure and competition it often creates. The husband's psychological identity with his work is often the underpinning to this problem. Phillip Blumstein and Pepper Schwartz (1983) write that with both partners working, some men feel threatened because traditional sex-typed boundaries have been crossed. Having a wife who works is contradictory to those who grew up in homes where only the husband worked.

This becomes particularly evident in dual-career households where wives are earning close to, or even more than their partners. This is unsettling to many men because money translates into power, and men are unaccustomed to yielding power to women. Not only are men unused to having a partner with a high income, they are not familiar with women in prestigious jobs. Many

---

APPLICATIONS

HOW COUPLES CAN DEEMPHASIZE WORK-RELATED COMPETITION

Mel Krantzler (1981) maintains that important marital challenges face couples who must resolve career and economic dilemmas. One of these is the reduction of work-related competition. The manner in which couples respond to the following questions can often provide clues to how this challenge is being handled:

- Do you tell each other what happened during your working day?
- Do you really listen and care about what has happened to your spouse on the job?
- Does only one person ask or tell the other?
- Do you refuse to share your concerns about your job because you think your spouse wouldn't understand the problem you are facing at work?
- Are you too embarrassed to tell your spouse that your boss reprimanded you, or that you are terrified about making a presentation at a company meeting?
- Do you try to put yourself in your spouse's shoes and understand that what might prove to be no problem to you might be a great problem to your partner, requiring your helpful feedback?
- Do you admire your spouse's strengths on the job as you would a colleague's, or are you secretly envious that he or she possesses these qualities?
- Do you feel you are entitled to a greater say in family economic decisions and in household management because you are earning more money than your spouse?

The degree to which couples share vulnerabilities and strengths, as well as empathy and the willingness to care about one another's welfare are indicators of healthy and satisfactory modes of adjustment. These factors will also determine whether or not partners have avoided setting up a competitive husband-wife relationship in which power based on self-centeredness prevails. Should couples bring the competition of their vocations into the marriage, the relationship may become little more than an extension of the workplace, rather than a sanctuary from it.

take pleasure in a woman's success, but only as long as it does not challenge their own. Conflict is likely to increase unless men learn how to accept their partner's achievement without feeling threatened.

Barbara Berg (1986) amplifies this last point, adding that when communication and interaction are marked by one-upmanship, bickering and bad feelings must surely follow. Working couples need to talk about their competitive feelings openly with one another. Comparisons between them are natural and expected. Angry competition and the unhappy feelings it arouses are not. Couples should try not to view each other's professional gain as a personal loss. Being allies rather than adversaries will turn a threat to a relationship into an opportunity for growth.

Financial Adjustments

Closely allied with work-related adjustments are those of a financial nature. Money is a powerful influence on human behavior, and it creates its share of pressure on the marital structure. Indeed, as we just learned, the lack of it usually transforms the traditional family model into the dual-earner arrangement. Learning how to save, manage, or invest money—along with a multitude of other financial issues—tests married couples from the very beginning.

The role that money plays in the lives of individuals and couples alike is complex. It can be a kind of bartering device that gives one control or power over other people and situations. Money can represent love when we spend it and hostility when we withhold it. Unfortunately, money represents more than economic security to many people. Money is closely related to status and to our self-esteem. People who lack money may feel inadequate. Also, couples who are disappointed with the amount of money they have often find their relationship less satisfying (see Figure 8-2). In addition, when we confuse what we have with who we are, money affects our emotional security (Dinkmeyer and Carlson, 1984).

Carol Colman (1983) tells us that financial

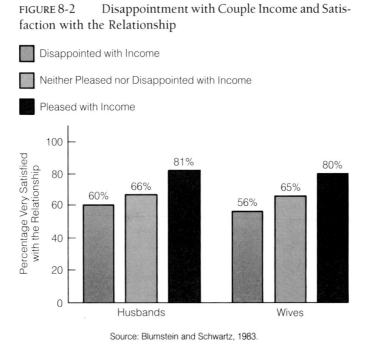

FIGURE 8-2   Disappointment with Couple Income and Satisfaction with the Relationship

Disappointed with Income

Neither Pleased nor Disappointed with Income

Pleased with Income

Source: Blumstein and Schwartz, 1983.

arrangements between couples almost always reflect their personal relationships. Couples don't just stumble into a system of handling money. The way they divide financial responsibilities is based on their expectations of the role and duties each partner performs in the marriage. For example, a husband who gives his wife an allowance and a wife who is happy with the arrangement have a dramatically different marriage from that of a couple in which both spouses have equal control over the family finances. Two people who live together and keep painstaking track of who pays for what have a very different future from that of live-in lovers who have a more casual attitude about money. A working couple with egalitarian ideas about the roles of men and women will not handle their paychecks the same way as a working couple with a more traditional outlook.

Sylvia Porter (1985) stresses that from the very beginning, couples need to deal realistically and competently with money matters. This means learning how to manage both love and finances through mutual planning and open communication. Couples can best do this when various financial steps are followed.

Establish a Financial Plan   It's possible to get by without a financial plan, but it's not advised.

Since the future is uncertain, it makes sense for couples to protect themselves against any setbacks that may lie ahead. A good financial plan takes care of the couple: it allows them to live well at present, enables them to make the most of life's opportunities, and provides a safety net when one is needed.

Philip Rahney (1982) stresses that financial planning is an active process which should not be confused with *budgeting,* a passive process. In budgeting, the emphasis is on stretching financial resources to meet predetermined expense needs over which the budgeter exercises little if any control. There are predetermined expense needs in financial planning, but the emphasis is on active, determinant control over the way financial resources are managed. Budgeting suggests specific limitations in every aspect of spending, limitations that many couples disavow as useless at the first sign of budgetary failure. Financial planning, on the other hand, promotes financial freedom within specific spending categories because two of the most important objectives of money management are actively planned for and pursued: improving the family financial position through savings, investments and insurance; and of equal importance, coping with and hedging against the effects of inflation.

FINANCIAL PLANS AND STRATEGIES: SOURCES OF INFORMATION

Apilado, V. P., and Morehart, T. B. (1980). *Personal finance management.* St. Paul, MN: West.

Bailard, T. E., Biehl, D. L., and Kaiser, R. W. (1982). *Personal money management* (4th Ed.) Chicago: Science Research Associates.

Colman, C. (1983). *Love and money.* New York: Coward-McCann.

Freeman, M. H., and Graf, D. (1980). *Money management: A guide to saving, spending, and investing.* Indianapolis: Bobbs-Merrill.

Porter, S. (1985). *Love and money.* New York: William Morrow.

Stein, B. (1985). *Financial passages.* New York: Doubleday.

Wolf, H. A. (1981). *Personal finance* (6th ed.). Boston: Allyn and Bacon.

Keep Informed about Finances The world of finance is constantly changing, and couples owe it to themselves to keep alert. They need to make a deliberate attempt to understand basic financial concepts. As tax rules change, couples may discover ways of saving many tax dollars. As circumstances change, partners may want to adopt approaches to handling finances that were not appropriate before. All options should be investigated. It makes sense to make an effort, because the cost of ignorance can be very high.

Be Realistic about Finances Couples need to be realistic and practical with their wallets. For example, an objective look at each other's spending habits could save a couple's credit rating. When money is mixed up with strong emotion — not just devotion but guilt, for instance, or hostility — the results can be most unfortunate.

Communicate on a Regular Basis about Finances This is the key to all healthy financial relationships. Across the board, communication is the single most important element in harmonious cooperation on money matters. Without open discussion, small differences over the handling of finances can soon turn into major problems. But seemingly irreconcilable differences can usually be whittled down to manageable size when all the sides of the issue are examined.

APPLICATIONS

HOW TO DEVELOP A BUDGET SYSTEM

A budget does not tell you how to use your money. You are the one who makes that decision. How you spend your money is a very personal value judgment; you decide the benefits you get from your spending. No matter what your values or your lifestyle, a budget can assist you in obtaining the maximum satisfaction from your income. Lawrence Lang and Thomas Gillespie (1984) propose that the development of a budget proceeds through four steps.

Step One: Estimate Available Income   What you get paid is your *take-home pay*. The difference between your *earnings* and your *take-home pay* is caused by deductions from your salary. Some of those deductions you agreed to when you took the job; these are voluntary deductions. But some of the deductions are the opposite: you must accept them. These nonvoluntary deductions result from certain policies in the city or community and state and country where you live and the company you work for.

Voluntary deductions represent contributions from your earnings to things such as a bond-a-month plan, a stock-purchase plan, a savings plan, and the like. They all represent income that would become available to you should you decide or need to discontinue these kinds of savings and investments.

Nonvoluntary deductions represent taxes on your earnings — regular federal income taxes, state income taxes, and local income taxes — which your employer is required by law to deduct from your earnings and send to various government units on your behalf. Also included among your nonvoluntary deductions are payments to Social Security and any deductions for pension plans and medical insurance premiums.

Your *available income* is the total amount of money you have available if you need it. You use it to budget or plan with, because it is what you currently have. ▶

The largest component in available income is usually your salary. In addition to salary, available income includes all interest and dividends received on savings accounts, bonds, common stocks, and mutual funds.

Step Two: Define the Major Expenditure Categories   Here, persons must decide how detailed they want their budget to be. It can be a very simple statement with a few major expenditure categories such as food, rent, and clothing. Or, it can be far more elaborate, containing detailed breakdowns of each of the major categories. A word of caution: a lot of detail will provide a great deal of information, but it will take you more time and make the budget more work. Too little detail will make your budget easy to prepare, but it won't enable you to analyze your expenditures very well.

Many budgeting systems categorize expenses as either *fixed* or *variable*. However, this is somewhat unrealistic since very few expenses are fixed amounts. Even food expenses vary somewhat. Therefore, the terms *regular* and *occasional expenses* more accurately describe the breakdown of normal expenditures. Regular expenses are the costs of everyday living: food, housing, transportation, entertainment, regular savings, and monthly payments on installment debts such as auto loans. Occasional expenses are bills for insurance and major purchases that may occur only once or twice a year. Make sure that these expenses are considered in your budget. An amount of money sufficient to cover the annual totals for these occasional expenses should be included as a major expense each month.

The next step in budgeting is deciding and setting amounts for each expense category. Everybody has a limited income and must decide how that income should be spent. How much for food? Clothes? Housing? Transportation? Recreation? Savings? You must answer these questions in order to develop a workable budget. How you divide your income will depend on what you think is most important.

Step Three: Prepare The Budget Summary Sheet   A budget summary sheet is designed to highlight three things. First, it shows what you planned to do — your budgeted income and budgeted expenditures. Second, it lists what your actual income and actual expenditures were during the budget period. Last, for each income item and expenditure, it spotlights those times when the actual amount was different from the budgeted amount. When actual income exceeds budgeted income, the difference is defined as a *surplus*. Conversely, a *deficit* occurs when actual income is less than budgeted income. (The table on page 231 exhibits a hypothetical budget summary sheet.)

Step Four: Review and Analyze the Budget Summary Sheet   The initial purpose of a budget is to help you plan your expenditures. Once that is done, you will want to review how well your financial plan is doing. This review and analysis period involves comparing the actual results with your planned results on your budget summary sheet in order to judge your progress. If the two amounts are significantly different, you may want to analyze the surpluses and deficits to see what caused the gap.   ▶

Sample Monthly Budget			
	Budgeted Amount	Actual	Surplus (Deficit)
Available Income	$1875	$2075	$200
Expenses			
Food	263	273	(10)
Housing			
Mortgage or rent	525	525	—
Real estate taxes	75	450	(375)
Utilities	120	160	(40)
Homeowners insurance	14	—	14
Maintenance	44	—	44
Clothing	90	15	75
Medical expenses	26	—	26
Automobile			
Gas, oil, maintenance	110	80	30
Repairs, insurance, other	53	—	53
Contributions	60	40	20
Life insurance	32	—	32
Personal	38	20	18
Entertainment and travel	124	14	110
Miscellaneous	70	20	50
Total expense	$1644	$1597	$ 47
Monthly Savings			
Short-term goals	$ 71	$ 71	—
Long-term goals	50	50	—
Total savings	$ 121	$ 121	—
Loan Payments			
Auto	$ 110	$ 110	—
Expenses, Savings, and Loan Payments	$1875	$1828	
Emergency Cash Reserve:			
Deposits (withdrawals)	$ 0	$ 247	

Source: From L. R. Lang and T. H. Gillespie. *Strategy for personal finance*. Copyright © 1984 by McGraw-Hill. Reprinted by permission.

Sexual Adjustments

The impact of sex on the marital relationship is varied. Sexual interaction can be the icing on the wedding cake, or it can be the sore point in an otherwise comfortable relationship. Couples who enjoy a stable and harmonious relationship are more apt to share sexual pleasures; a rewarding sex life also works to endear partners to one another. Thus, good sex serves to make a good marriage even better. On the other hand, poor sex tends to worsen a relationship (Katchadourian, 1985).

Whether or not a marriage is sexually successful depends on both the individual characteristics of the partners and how the partners interact with each other. Significant individual characteristics include *self-esteem, assertiveness, concern for the partner, and freedom from sexual anxieites or inhibitions.* Important features of the partnership include *open and honest communication, shared emotional intimacy, and freedom from hostilities and conflicts,* such as struggles for dominance. Generally speaking, a good sexual relationship results when two partners are relatively free of individual emotional conflicts and enjoy a mutually rewarding "total" relationship (Jones, Shainberg, and Byer, 1985).

Marital Sexuality Myths

Marital sexuality is a dynamic, on-going process. Over the years, we have learned a great deal regarding its expression and importance to couples. However, certain myths surrounding marital sexuality have managed to persist and have generated inaccurate and distorted information on the topic. William Talmadge (1985) summarizes the more prevalent myths as well as the facts to dispel them.

Sex in Marriage Comes Easy   If this myth is true, then marital sexuality is essentially an end and not a process. Those who believe in this myth expect that they will have sex whenever they want it and that there will be no problems. Because of the institution of marriage, there is a belief that sexuality or the expression of it will be unencumbered with problems. This myth denies the developmental changes of the individuals and of the marital relationship, such as those accompanying the vocational work cycle or the experience of aging.

Sexual Frequency Is a Prime Indicator of Sexual Compatibility and Marital Happiness   There tends to be a decline in coitus rates during the first year of marriage. However, over the duration of the marriage, rates of intercourse usually decline and rise according to the mood of the relationship. In this respect, frequency of coitus is not an indicator of marital satisfaction. Sexual satisfaction is instead highly correlated with marital satisfaction. Moreover, the *mutuality* of enjoyment appears to be the key factor in marital sexual compatability.

RESEARCH HIGHLIGHT

SEXUALITY IN THE EARLY YEARS OF MARRIAGE

Limited research has focused on the frequency of sexual interaction during the early years of marriage or what the meaning and importance of sex is in these years. In an effort to learn more about these and related areas, Cathy Greenblat (1983) conducted in-depth, structured interviews with 30 males and 50 females (not married to one another). The respondents had been married for five years or less.

The most striking finding was the degree of decline in frequency of intercourse. Both first-year and current rates were available for 62 persons who had been married for more than one year. The current frequency was divided by the first-year frequency for each of them, yielding a percentage. This revealed that (a) 6 percent reported current rates higher than their first-year rates; (b) 24 percent reported current rates the same as their first-year rates; (c) 32 percent reported rates from 60 to 90 percent of their first-year rates; and (d) 37 percent reported rates of less than 60 percent of their first-year rates (including 6 percent for whom   ▶

the rates were less than 30 percent of the first-year rates). Men's and women's distributions were similar.

Although a steady pattern of decline from year to year did not become apparent, less than one-half of the respondents said they were presently having intercourse with their spouses more than twice a week. While approximately 75 percent had reported such rates for the first year, only 40 percent reported such current frequencies. However, there was considerable variation in the reports, which ranged from once a month to 20 to 25 times a month.

In analyzing this data, Greenblat feels that in all likelihood a pattern, or habit associated with marital sexual relationships establishes itself in the first year. From then on almost everything—children, jobs, commuting, housework, financial worries—that happens to a couple conspires to reduce the degree of sexual interaction. Thus, some couples with children have high rates while others have low rates, but most couples who have children experience a decline in the frequency of intercourse. They are not likely to know whether their initial rates or their current rates are high or low in comparison to others, nor are they likely to realize that others without children are also experiencing a decline in the frequency of intercourse. Instead, for them as for most persons, their own prior experience represents the only known and relevant comparison.

Despite declining rates of frequency, respondents enjoyed the satisfactions and intimacies that sex brought. The most frequent type of response on this topic dealt with positive elements of a couple's sex life: "It's a way of expressing your love," "We have a relaxed feeling about it," and "We still have a need for each other—it's a way of expressing our love—it's fun and we enjoy it." Greenblat also notes that most of the respondents regarded sex as important to the overall marriage. Interestingly, this included not only intercourse, but other forms of expression as well: closeness, tenderness, love, companionship, and affection. Some said they found that just cuddling or lying together was rewarding and they didn't require the specifically sexual interaction much of the time. Others remarked that when intercourse did take place, it existed as a form of intimacy and strengthened the bond between husband and wife.

Poor Sex Leads to Unhappy Marriages and Extramarital Sexual Affairs   Related to the previous myth, the basis of this misconception is that if a person only has high rates of sex, uses many varied techniques, and therefore keeps their partner happy with sex, then the marriage will be happy. Once again in operation is a belief that high sexual frequency creates good marriages. As we've already seen, this is not the case. Neither high nor low rates of sexual frequency create marital happiness or unhappiness. Sexual incompatibility is a symptom of marital unhappiness or an imbalance within the relationship and is not the causative factor for the difficulty within the relationship. More often than not, the difficulties within the relationship (poor communication style, an imbalance of power, lack of equity, and so on) are the reasons for the difficulty within the sexual relationship as well as the marital unhappiness. Relatedly, extramarital sexual affairs usually do not result because of inferior marital sexuality, but rather from the quality of the relationship itself.

The Sexual Relationship and the Marriage Relationship Are Separate Entities   This myth implies that no relationship exists between marital factors and those that contribute to the couple's sexual satisfaction. On the contrary, marital and sexual satisfaction are highly related variables. Factors which seem to be particularly related between the two are the degree of communication, affective tone within the relationship, self-disclosure, prior experiences with premarital sex, and degree of intimacy.

Sex in Marriage Creates Intimacy   According to this myth, coital contact or sexual expression between partners automatically creates intimacy within the relationship. However, research reveals that effective communication and self-disclosure are more apt to generate intimacy. Equally important is the ability of the couple to express affective sexual behaviors.

Happily Married Couples Do Not Have Sex Problems   This is a misconception, for one, because it overlooks developmental changes in the marital relationship. For instance, research supports the fact that there is a decline in sexual frequency during the first year after a child's birth. Research also shows that happily married couples do, at some point during their marital relationship, experience specific types of sexual difficulties. But what makes this a problem for which the couple seeks therapeutic intervention or not is determined by the marital relationship. For those couples who have sexual difficulties but do not seek help, these difficulties do not seem to become significant problems within the relationship. Factors such as the ability to communicate, problem resolution, and the affectional quality within the relationship play an important part in resolving the couple's sexual difficulty.

If I Am Only Handsome or Pretty Enough and Do All of the Things That My Partner Wishes, Then a Satisfying Marital Sexual Relationship Will Result   The individual within the relationship is denied by this myth. It implies that if one partner only is and does what the other

Establishing and maintaining sexual intimacy are important dimensions of married life.

partner wants, then they will find marital sexual satisfaction with one another. This misconception denies that one partner may possibly have changes occurring outside of the relationship which have an impact upon the relationship. These intervening factors may not be subject to change by the partner within the relationship. Unfortunately, many couples have accepted this misconception, which is often portrayed in the media. Television, popular magazines, and the movies lead persons to believe that if only they will act as romantically as possible — wearing the "right" type of cologne or perfume, drinking the "right" type of beverages, and going to the "right" places — then they will find marital sexual happiness with one another.

Marital Sex Is Always Exciting, Romantic, and Orgasmic   Particularly among newly marrieds there is an expectation that sex will always be pleasurable, fun, easy, and delightful. But, as we learned in Chapter 5, these sexual expectations are unrealistic and often lead to harsh disappointment within the marriage. Unless these high expectations can be resolved, the couple soon finds itself in a state of disappointment and resentment. This misconception simply denies the developmental stresses and strains which couples experience. It discounts other reality factors such as physical health, personal and career crises, and self-image which may disrupt the stability of the relationship.

Rather than accepting these myths, Talmadge stresses that couples should view marital sexual functioning as *a complex set of interacting variables operating within the overall relationship.* It is the couple's total relationship which determines sexual adequacy and satisfaction. Factors such as communication, affection, intimacy, problem resolution, commitment, work, play, sex drive, and perception of one's problem, play a significant role in determining the marital sexual compatibility of the couple. In addition, marital sexual compatibility is greatly determined by the couple's commitment to engage in a long-term process of interacting with one another, expressing affection, needs, desires, likes, and dislikes in a trusting, caring, and vulnerable atmosphere.

APPLICATIONS

HOW COUPLES CAN IMPROVE THEIR SEX LIVES

Noted sex researchers William Masters, Virginia Johnson, and Robert Kolodny (1986) believe that many marriages suffer from sexual distress, ranging from disinterest to outright dysfunction. Yet, too many couples merely drift along and let their problems become caught in a downward spiral of frustration and anxiety. While some may need professional help, many couples can learn to increase their sexual satisfaction on their own. To accomplish this, the researchers suggest the following:

■ **Don't Make Sex a Fragmented Experience**   As long as sex is viewed as an isolated activity, it will remain a fragmented experience rather than part of a couple's total life. The escalation of desire relies on what happens over the hours or days preceding a sexual interlude. Getting "in the mood" need not be a deliberate playing of romantic music or dining by candlelight (although there's nothing wrong with such activities); it can and should be part of a continuing nonsexual closeness.

Seek to create times for togetherness, instead of letting children, work, or social life crowd out private moments. Allow your feelings and needs to dictate what you do with this quality time together. Without shared moments of nonsexual affection, it is difficult to create a sense of intimacy the instant you're ready for lovemaking.

■ **Take Responsibility for Your Own Sexual Pleasure**   You — not anyone else — are responsible for your own eroticism. While men tend to have an easier time accepting this aspect of sex, women often slip into a culturally dictated role of passivity; that is, they expect that their partner will be the "expert" when it comes to sex, relieving them of any responsibility except to respond on command. This idea of sex as something one person does to or for the other can create problems. By taking responsibility for your own sexual ▶

needs, you are actually paying your partner a terrific compliment, saying in effect, "I care enough about you to want to keep you from having to guess what I want and what can make me happy."

■ **Express Your Feelings and Needs Effectively**   When done in a constructive fashion, talking about sex can promote understanding — from how to handle differing degrees of desire to establishing signals that convey what is and isn't pleasurable. Also, talking about sex isn't something to do once and then put aside. Similar to other forms of intimate communication, it benefits from a continuing dialogue that permits a couple to learn more about each other.

■ **Don't Let Sex Become Routine**   Boredom is one of the greatest threats to long-term sexual satisfaction. With some creativity, though, couples can keep sex from becoming dull. The result will usually be a renewed appreciation of one's partner and new dimensions to sexual interaction and pleasuring.

■ **Find New Pleasures through Fantasy**   Sexual fantasizing can be used in many ways to enhance excitement and variety. Whether used to whet sexual appetite or incorporated into your lovemaking directly, your imagination can help transform ordinary sex into something far more erotic. Reliance on fantasy also does not indicate sexual or psychological problems or personality flaws. On the contrary, people with recurrent sexual fantasies feel neither the desire nor the need to act on them in real life.

■ **Don't Bring Anger into Sexual Activities**   This suggestion is often ignored by many couples; the result being that sex often gets turned into a power struggle. This is not to say that sex can't be used to end an argument, because it can. However, those who try to settle a score from an unresolved issue by withholding or demanding sex are asking for trouble, no matter how satisfying it may be to gain a temporary sense of revenge. The most effective way to deal with anger is to recognize its source and discuss it with your partner in its early stages. It is important to realize that occasionally getting angry with your partner is no sign that your relationship is doomed. If your anger is not easily dissipated, however, it is usually best to acknowledge it and temporarily avoid sex.

■ **Don't Always Wait To Be "In the Mood"**   It's perfectly reasonable to accomodate your partner's needs when you're not feeling in the mood. While you may not feel sexy at the moment, you may find that your feelings change rapidly if you give yourself a chance. Otherwise, you will prevent yourself from being able to enjoy this facet of your sexuality — having your appetite arise when you least expect it.

■ **Don't Be Too Serious**   It is natural to try to deal with sexual anxieties or frustrations by working harder to overcome them. This usually does not work, however, because it makes sex so goal-oriented that it loses its spontaneity. Experiencing sex as fun or adventure, rather than a task with predetermined objectives such as exciting your partner or reaching orgasm, will reduce performance anxiety and trivialize shortcomings. Worrying about sexual inadequacy can become a self-fulfilling prophecy. This does not mean that you should totally ignore sexual problems. But carrying a mental checklist into every encounter and analyzing your performance as a spectator is not the way ▶

to solve them. Rather, set no goals that must be immediately attained. This will create far less pressure to perform, and more opportunity for enjoyment.

- **If Problems Persist, Get Help**   The significant majority of people have times when they are temporarily out of commission sexually. This may be for physical reasons (fatigue, infection, acute illness) or because of psychological factors (stress, depression, job or family problems). These transient episodes usually disappear within weeks. However, if difficulties persist longer than a few months without showing signs of improvement, it's probably best to seek professional advice.

- **Be Realistic**   Expecting every sexual encounter to be sheer ecstacy is setting yourself up for failure. But, if instead you accept the fact that sex isn't always the great passionate joining of souls that Hollywood would have us believe — that it's sometimes feeble, awkward, and even unsatisfying — then you won't be a prisoner of unrealistic standards. Keep in mind that we're human beings, not machines.   ∎

EMERGING MARITAL TYPES

There is no blueprint for marital relationships. The dynamics exhibited by couples differ tremendously, including the variations that are known to exist in meeting all of the adjustments just described. However, it is possible to observe general types of marriages that develop over a period of time. Five such types have been identified by John Cuber and Peggy Harnoff (1965) in their study of 211 couples who had been married for ten years and who felt committed to one another. The five types included **conflict-habituated, devitalized, passive-congenial, vital,** and **total**.

The Conflict-Habituated Marriage

The conlict-habituated marriage tends to be the most prevalent type of relationship. Its overt behavior patterns are readily observable and the relationship presents some obvious contradictions. Within this marriage, there is much tension and conflict, but it is largely controlled by the partners. At worst, there is some private quarreling, of which members of the immediate family, and more rarely close friends and relatives, have some awareness. At best, the couple is discreet and polite, but given the right circumstances, disagreements will surface. The intermittent conflict is also rarely kept

from the children. Husband and wife usually privately acknowledge that incompatibility is pervasive, that conflict is ever-potential, and that a climate of tension permeates the relationship.

Valence in these marriages is so subtle that it is often missed by casual observers. Indeed, the couple's desire to control conflict and curb hostility preoccupies much of the interaction. Paradoxically, it may be possible that this deep need to do psychological battle provides cohesion to the relationship and extends its longevity. Whatever the explanation, the existence of habituated attention to handling tension and concealing it is definitely a dominant force. And, for some, it can last an entire lifetime.

The Devitalized Marriage

The devitalized marriage is also common. It exists as a marriage of contrasts, usually between middle-aged reality and the earlier years. Partners describe themselves as once being deeply in love, particularly being romantically attached to, and having a close identification with, one another. Over time, though, they have drifted apart. Little time now is spent together, and interests and activities are not shared to the extent they once were.

Many couples report that time spent together is more or less "duty time"; that is, entertaining together, planning and sharing activities with children, and community responsibilities. They do as a rule retain, in addition to a genuine interest in the welfare of their children, a shared attention to their joint property and career pursuits. But even in the latter case the interest is contrasting. Despite a common dependency on each other's success and the benefits which flow therefrom, there is typically very little sharing of the intrinsic aspects of jobs.

In general, the emotional dimension of these marriages has become a void. The enthusiasm, vitality, and zest characterizing earlier years has disappeared. There is usually little overt tension or conflict, but the interplay between partners has become lifeless. However, no serious threat to the continuity of the marriage is generally acknowledged. It is intended, usually by both, that it continue indefinitely despite its numbness. Continuity and relative freedom from open conflict are fostered in part because of habit.

Marriages vary considerably in terms of internal and external dynamics.

The Passive-Congenial Marriage

Similar to the devitalized marriage, this relationship lacks emotion and enthusiasm. However, unlike the devitalized arrangement, the passive-congenial marriage has been this way since the very start. Consequently, couples give little evidence that they had ever wished for anything much different from what they are currently experiencing. Existing modes of association between partners are comfortably adequate and there is usually little conflict in this relationship.

Couples often arrive at this way of living and feeling by drift. There is so little which they have cared about deeply in each other that a passive-congenial mode is a deliberately intended arrangement. That is, two people have interests and creative energies that are directed away from the dyad—into careers, or in the case of women, into children or community activities. Many say they know this and want it this way. These people simply do not wish to invest their total emotional involvement and creative effort in the male-female relationship. Thus, the passive-congenial marriage enables people who desire a considerable amount of personal independence and freedom to realize it with a minimum of inconvenience from or to the spouse. It also spares the need to give a great deal of personal attention to "adjusting to the spouse's needs." The passive-congenial relationship thus emerges as a *mood* as well as a *mode*.

Let's pause just for a moment to further compare the devitalized and passive-congenial marriages. Beyond outward similarities, partners' evaluations of their present situations are also largely the same —the accent on "other things," the emphasis on civic and professional responsibilities, the importance of property, children, and reputation. The key difference lies in their diverse histories and often in their feelings of contentment with their current lives. The passive-congenials had from the beginning a life pattern essentially consistent with what they are now experiencing. However, when the devitalized reflect, they often see the void in their lives created by earlier satisfactions.

The Vital Marriage

Partners within the vital marriage can easily be overlooked as they move through their worlds of family activities, work, and recreation. They do the same things, publicly at least, and when talking for public consumption, say the same things — they are proud of their homes, love their children, and gripe about their jobs, while being quite proud of their career accomplishments. However, when an intimate look is taken, the key feature of the vital relationship becomes evident: the mates are intensely bound together psychologically in important life matters. Their sharing is genuine and can be readily observed, such as in the mutuality of feelings or the participation together in important "life segments."

Couples in vital marriages find happiness and satisfaction with and through each other. Their marriages consume their interest and dominate their thoughts and actions. This does not mean that people in vital relationships lose their separate identities. When conflict does occur, it results from matters that are important to them, such as which college a daughter or son should attend, and it is also devoid of the trivial. Compared to the conflict-habituated relationship, conflicts between couples in vital marriages are also settled quickly and, whenever possible, avoided.

The Total Marriage

The total marriage is a rare relationship, but it can exist and has enduring qualities. This marriage resembles the vital relationship but is more multifaceted. The points of vital meshing are more numerous — in some cases all of the important life foci are vitally shared. Also, there is practically no pretense between persons in the total relationship or between them and the world outside.

There are also few areas of tension, mainly because the items of difference which have arisen over the years have been settled as they arose. There often were serious differences of opinion but they were handled, sometimes by compromise, or sometimes by one or the other yielding. It is important to note that these outcomes were of sec-ondary importance because the primary consideration was not who was right or who was wrong, only how the problem could be resolved without creating instability within the relationship. When confronted with differences, couples can and do dispose of the difficulties without losing their feeling of unity or their sense of vitality and centrality of their relationship. This is the pivotal feature of the marriage.

Cuber and Harnoff caution that these five marriage types are not to be interpreted as degrees of marital happiness or adjustment. Respondents in the study within all five types were currently adjusted and most said that they were content, if not happy. The five types instead represent different kinds of adjustment and different conceptions of marriage.

Also, the five types of marriages described do not necessarily represent stages in a cycle of initial happiness and later disillusionment. It is true, though, that many marriages begin in the passive-congenial stage; in fact, quite often people intentionally enter into a marriage for the acknowledged purpose of living this kind of relationship. To many, the simple amenities of habit are not disillusionments or even disappointments. Instead, they are sensible life expectations which provide an altogether comfortable and rational way of having a "home base" for their lives. Finally, while each of these types tends to persist over time, there may be movement from one type to another as circumstances and life perspectives change. The authors point out that this movement may go in any direction from any point, and a given couple may change categories more than once. However, these types of fluctuations are relatively infrequent. The critical theme is that relationship types tend to persist over relatively long periods of time.

CHAPTER HIGHLIGHTS

For many, an idealistic quality is attached to married life. Contributing to this are a number of myths and misconceptions, many of which portray marriage as a perfect, carefree existence. Couples soon learn that these myths must be abandoned and attention must be focused on the many adjustments that accompany married life.

The happiness generated by the couple is determined by the quality of interaction between the two partners. Newly marrieds find that some re-evaluation of old patterns of interaction is needed, including expectations for one another. Clearly defining the roles that exist within the relationship also needs to be undertaken. In recent years, growing numbers of couples are adopting an egalitarian orientation to their marriages.

Many marriages today are dual-earner in scope and a developing minority are dual-career. This chapter explored the impact of women in the labor force, including the marital adjustments that are needed when both partners work. We also spent some time examining the role that money plays in the lives of couples. Learning how to save, manage, or invest it are formidable challenges for both young and old couples alike. Among other things, couples need to establish a financial plan, keep informed and be realistic about finances, and communicate on a regular basis about monetary issues.

Couples who enjoy a stable and harmonious relationship are more apt to share a rewarding sex life. A number of myths tend to generate inaccurate ideas about marital sex: sex in marriage comes easy; sexual frequency is a prime indicator of sexual compatibility and marital happiness; poor sex leads to unhappy marriages and extramarital sexual affairs; the sexual relationship and marriage relationship are separate entities; sex in marriage automatically creates intimacy; happily married couples do not have sex problems; if individuals fulfill their partner's sexual wishes, a satisfying sexual relationship will result; and, marital sex is always exciting, romantic, and orgasmic. In this chapter we dispelled each of these myths, in addition to supplying suggestions for improving a couple's sexual relationship.

Over time, it is possible to observe general marital types or categories. These include the conflict-habituated, devitalized, passive-congenial, vital, and total. These five types represent different kinds of adjustment and different conceptions of marriage, not the degree of marital happiness or adjustment.

KEY TERMS

career

conflict-habituated mariage

devitalized marriage

dual-career marriage

dual-earner marriage

egalitarian

job

passive-congenial marriage

total marriage

vital marriage

RECOMMENDED READINGS

Aldous, J. (Ed.). (1982). *Two paychecks: Life in dual-earner families.* Beverly Hills, CA: Sage. An excellent collection of articles focusing on the dual-earner household.

England, P., and Farkas, G. (1986). *Households, employment, and gender: A social, economic, and demographic view.* New York: Aldine Publishers. Sex roles in the family and the labor force are fully discussed in this paperback.

Hewlett, S. (1986). *A lesser life: The myth of women's liberation in America.* New York: William Morrow. This is must reading for any woman struggling in the face of career inequities and demands as well as heightened family responsibilities.

Kargan, M. (1985).*How to manage a marriage.* Boston: Foundation Books. A down-to-earth look at how marriage can be practiced and managed in the 1980s.

Kimball, G. (1983). *The 50-50 marriage.* Boston: Beacon Press. This book explores how 150 couples moved from traditional ways of thinking and behaving to egalitarian orientations.

Krantzler, M. (1981). *Creative marriage.* New York: McGraw-Hill. Readers will enjoy Krantzler's narrative of the developmental passages that exist within a marriage.

Lazarus, A. A. (1985). *Marital myths.* San Luis Obispo, CA: Impact Publishers. Lazarus explores how the road to wedded happiness is littered with myths.

Pepitone-Rockwell, P. (Ed.). (1980). *Dual-career couples.* Beverly Hills, CA: Sage. Of special interest are the effects of wives' employment on marital role structure and the benefits and costs of dual-career relationships.

Pleck, J. (1985). *Working wives, working husbands.* Beverly Hills, CA: Sage. Topics include role overload, wife's employment and the division of household work, and husbands and their family role.

Smith, A. D., and Reid, W. J. (1986). *Role-sharing marriage.* New York: Columbia University Press. An in-depth look at couples who equally share breadwinning, home care, and childrearing responsibilities.

Communication and Conflict

CONTENTS

CONTEMPLATIONS

■ A chilling silence . . . a rude gesture . . . an affectionate hug . . . a passionate kiss. In this chapter we're going to explore how some actions do speak louder than words and how "the sounds of silence" convey many messages. Nonverbal language is an extremely important facet of the total communication process and being aware of it will make you more adept in your relationships with others. Want to learn more? If you just nodded your head, frowned, or changed your posture to begin reading, we get the message.

■ "Do you hear me?" How often we come across that expression, particularly as far as the marital relationship is concerned. As we'll learn, though, a more accurate inquiry would be "Are you *listening* to me?" While both hearing and listening work together, it is the latter that determines whether or not messages have been accurately understood. The concept of effective listening will be one of our focal points, including what it takes to sharpen this important capacity. Good listening is partially an art, but also, like any skill, it can be developed. To discover how, read on.

■ It was a fight to end all fights, a verbal tirade laced with insults, accusations, and the most colorful of language. Chris and Donna Freemont launched into it over a seemingly minor issue: she needed more money in the family budget for children's clothes but, unexpectedly, this request hit a nerve for Chris. He flew into a relentless rage about money and Donna's inability to operate the family budget within its limits. While she cowered at first, it wasn't long before Donna took to the attack and fired back some of Chris' own medicine. What is it that prompts such behavior in relationships? Is conflict an inevitable part of being married? Do conflicts represent a barometer of the psychological health and well-being of the relationship? By the time this chapter concludes, you'll have the answers to these questions.

Most people today are aware of the importance of sincere and effective communication between spouses, between parent and child, or between any persons who want to share meaningful ideas or make plans together. However, often at the heart of marital strife is the fact that couples are unable to effectively communicate with one another. Indeed, many are able to talk with others more comfortably than they can talk to their own wife or husband.

Providing testimony to this are the many couples who share the same house and bed but feel they are strangers. They want to share and be intimate, but they find themselves growing apart. They communicate ideas and facts but rarely share their personal feelings about each other. For these couples, intimacy, empathy, and honest caring are at best shallow and superficial (Dinkmeyer and Carlson, 1984).

It seems that a successful marriage, and the effective communication that should go with it, are areas in which most people are ill prepared. As Howard Waters (1980) points out, there are no required courses or diplomas that must be earned before we marry. We know a little from what we have experienced in a family relationship with our parents, and the rest we must often learn by trial and error.

In this chapter, we'd like to explore the concept of communication and how couples can develop meaningful patterns of interaction. In the process, we'll explore the importance of listening and its relation to the overall communication process. Attention will also be focused on how conflicts can punctuate a relationship, the impact they have, and the strategies than can be employed to help curb them.

COMPONENTS OF COMMUNICATION

Communication entails the exchange of information, signals, and messages between people.

The process of communication is effected by a number of factors including attitudes, personalities, and relationships. For instance, happily married couples are better able to pick up each other's nonverbal messages, like the readiness for sex, than unhappily married couples. Moreover, individuals communicate for different purposes, which is not always apparent in their words (Atwater, 1986).

Communication is a multifaceted process and at least four related propositions regarding it can be made. First, human communication is guided by socially established rules, the knowledge of which

---

APPLICATIONS

WHAT KIND OF A COMMUNICATOR ARE YOU?

If you have difficulty understanding people or being understood, it's likely that you've ignored or overlooked some part of the communication process. It is up to you to try and find the problem and correct it, which is no easy chore. The following self-evaluation can help you assess your particular areas of need and interest and provide you with a standard by which you can measure your progress. Circle the number that best represents the frequency of each item in your experience.

(1 = seldom, 2 = sometimes, 3 = often, and 4 = usually)

1 2 3 4   1. People understand my thoughts and feelings.

1 2 3 4   2. When communication problems arise, I am determined to solve them.

1 2 3 4   3. I know the major causes of communication breakdown.

1 2 3 4   4. I demonstrate personality qualities to which people are attracted.

1 2 3 4   5. In difficult situations, I consciously choose how I express myself.

1 2 3 4   6. The tone of my voice and the words I say communicate precisely how I feel about my conversational partner.

1 2 3 4   7. I am able to listen deeply to the feelings expressed by my spouse and friends.

1 2 3 4   8. My friends tell me I am a good listener.

1 2 3 4   9. I can tell whether a communication problem is basically caused by the one speaking, the message itself, or the listener to the message.

1 2 3 4   10. I am able to analyze accurately the thoughts and feelings of the person talking to me.

1 2 3 4   11. When I talk, people listen.   ▶

1	2	3	4	12.	People tell me I am a good conversationalist.
1	2	3	4	13.	I say no when I want to say no.
1	2	3	4	14.	I assert myself because I value my opinions as well as the opinions of others.
1	2	3	4	15.	I handle hassles with children effectively.
1	2	3	4	16.	I talk with children the way I want them to talk with me.
1	2	3	4	17.	I allow loved ones and friends to know me as I really am.
1	2	3	4	18.	I am able to tell people close to me how much I really care about them.
1	2	3	4	19.	When I experience a conflict with someone, I know how to resolve it.
1	2	3	4	20.	I know what to say in tense situations.
1	2	3	4	21.	I know how to gain the cooperation of others.
1	2	3	4	22.	When I ask people to do something that I want them to do (within reason), they do it.
1	2	3	4	23.	I enjoy the highest level of communication with my partner, family, and friends.
1	2	3	4	24.	Because I know the value of successful communication, I look for ways to improve my communication skills.

To arrive at your total, add together all of the point values for the items you've circled. Once this is done, check your total with the following:

92–96 Excellent   This is an extremely high point total. It reflects outstanding communication skills and expertise in human relationships.

78–91 Good   You are well on your way to becoming a skilled communicator. Focus your attention on the areas where you feel you need to refine your skills.

50–77 Fair   You are missing a significant amount of satisfaction which could be experienced through better communication. With concentrated work on your communication abilities, you will achieve greater rapport with your partner, family, and friends.

24–49 Poor   Your basic communication skills are in need of attention. Quite likely, this means developing new skills and strategies as well as examining how it is that you relate to others.

Adapted from Swets, 1983. ∎

permits interacting persons to exert influence over the outcome of their interactions. Second, self-concepts are formed and sustained as people interact with others. Third, the formation of sustained interpersonal relations depends on the attraction resulting from reciprocal self-concept support. Finally, organizations and the cultural system establish the boundaries within which self-concepts and interpersonal relations are formed. Individuals are born into cultures, work in organizations, and meet individuals from other cultures. Together, each of these interactional systems exerts a major, lasting influence on who an individual is and how he/she relates to others. Knowledge of the principles, processes, and skills involved in interacting in such systems permits persons to control presentation, growth, and validation of self and interpersonal relationships (Cushman and Cahn, 1985).

Kinds of Expression

Our communication to others can be broken down into four types of expression: **observations, thoughts, feelings,** and **needs.** Each type entails a different style of expression and in many instances, a very different vocabulary. Matthew McKay, Martha Davis, and Patrick Fanning (1983) expound upon these four kinds of expression.

Observations   In a general sense, observation means reporting what your senses tell you. This kind of communication contains no speculations,

inferences, or conclusions. It can best be described as factual communication.

Thoughts   Thoughts are conclusions, inferences drawn from what a person has observed, heard, or read. Thoughts are attempts to synthesize observations so that persons can perceive what's taking place and understand why and how events occur. Thoughts may also incorporate value judgments in which a person decides that something is good or bad, wrong or right. Beliefs, opinions, and theories are all varieties of conclusions.

Feelings   The communication of feeling involves the expression of emotion and for the most part, this does not reflect observations, value judgments, or opinions. The expression of feelings is probably the most difficult part of communication. Some people don't want to hear what others feel. Or, some may decide to keep their many feelings to themselves.

Needs   When needs are expressed, statements reflect what would help or please the person. Needs are not judgmental or pejorative and they do not blame or assign fault. As we'll see, relationships change, accomodate, and grow when partners can clearly and supportively express what they need.

Nonverbal Communication

Not all human communication is linguistic or verbal. Rather, **nonverbal communication** also exists, which is communication without words. Such forms of communication include gestures, mannerisms, eye contact, body language, and the like. Noted social psychologist Roger Brown (1986) writes that nonverbal channels are continually attended to and serve to communicate information that is primarily affective in quality and connected with personal relationships.

While nonverbal communication is especially effective at communicating feelings and attitudes, the verbal channel is normally used to communicate information about events external to the speaker. However, this does not mean that nonverbal communication is superior and better

Developing effective communication skills is essential for couples of all ages.

adapted to the expression of affect and relationship than the verbal channel. The two are better viewed as components of the total communication process, and their effectiveness or ineffectiveness rests with the individual speaker.

However, Judy Burgoon (1985) points out that adults tend to place greater reliance on nonverbal than verbal cues when interpreting communication. This pattern has been confirmed under such varied circumstances as job interviews, assess-

WHOLE VS. CONTAMINATED FORMS OF EXPRESSION

Whole messages contain all four types of expression: what a person sees, thinks, feels, and needs. Whole messages are at the foundation of intimate relationships. Partners cannot get to know one another unless they share their experiences. That means not leaving things out, not covering up anger, and not squelching needs. It means giving accurate feedback about what a person sees, clearly stating inferences and conclusions, saying how it all makes one feel, and if something is needed for change, making straightforward requests or suggestions.

A **partial message** occurs when some facet of expression is omitted. Partial messages typically generate confusion and distrust. People sense something is missing, but often they don't know just what. They're turned off when they hear judgments untempered by your feelings and hopes. They resist hearing anger that doesn't include the story of your frustration or hurt. They are suspicious of conclusions without supporting observations. Also, persons are uncomfortable with demands growing from unexpressed feelings and assumptions.

Not every relationship requires whole messages, though. Effective communication with your garage mechanic probably won't involve much deep feeling or discussion of your emotional needs. For that matter, even with intimates, the majority of messages are informational. But partial messages, with something important left out or obscured, have potential danger. They become relational boobytraps when used to express the complex issues that are an inevitable part of intimacy.

Contaminated messages are forms of expression that are mixed or mislabled. Contaminated messages are usually confusing and alienating. For instance, the message, "I see your wife gave you two large apples for lunch" is confusing because the observation is contaminated by need. The need is only hinted at, and the listener has to decide if what he heard was really a covert appeal. The message, "While you were feeding your dog, my dinner got cold" is alienating because what appears to be a simple observation contains undercurrents of anger and judgment —"You care more about your dog than me."

Contaminated messages differ from partial messages in that the problem is not merely one of omission. The anger, the conclusion, or the need have not been left out of it. They are there, but in a disguised form. As an example of a contaminated message, suppose a wife says to her husband, "Why don't you act a little human for a change?" In this message, a need is contaminated with a value judgment (thought). A whole message might have been, "You say very little, and when you ▶

do it's in a soft, flat voice (observation). It makes me think that you don't care, that you have no emotions (thought). I feel hurt (emotion) but what I really want is for you to talk to me (need)."

The best way to contaminate messages is to make the content simple and straightforward, but to say it in a tone of voice that betrays one's feelings. As a result, the message can have multiple meanings and prompt confusion and uncertainty. The key to avoiding contaminated messages is to separate out, and clearly express, each part of the communication.

Adapted from McKay, Davis, and Fanning, 1983. ■

ments of leadership, therapeutic sessions, attitudinal expressions, and judgments of first impressions. In addition, nonverbal cues are especially likely to be believed when they conflict with the verbal message.

Sarah Cirese (1985) proposes that nonverbal communication transmits a unique flow of steady messages. Our movements and actions as well as our expressions and silences all have something to say about us. She estimates that from 65 to 93 percent of the social meaning in face-to-face communication is carried by nonverbal messages. However, Cirese points out that nonverbal communication poses special problems:

"I know you're listening—your knuckles are turning white."

- Nonverbal messages are highly ambiguous. Thus, are difficult for others to interpret accurately because they are only implicit indicators. For example, a frown may signal displeasure, concentration, disagreement, a headache, or simply be a reaction to bright light. All of this means that nonverbal messages are revealing, but they have many possible meanings. Some suggested meanings for certain gestures appear in Table 9-1, but the reader should take into account the cross-cultural, ethnic, and religious variations that can exist.

- Relative to verbal messages, nonverbal forms of communication are very limited in what they can express. You can prove this easily by trying, without using any words, to find out from your instructor when the next assignment is due. Words must be employed to clearly express most of our thoughts, our plans, and our needs.

- Verbal and nonverbal messages are sometimes contradictory. We may say one thing with words (It's all right. I'm fine.") and another with our actions (holding stubbed toe, grimacing in pain). This is *double-talk,* and it creates confusion for our receivers (Well, is she hurt or not?).

With all of this in mind, individuals as well as couples need to realize that one of our most important conversational skills doesn't come from the tongue, but from the body. Nonverbal language communicates our feelings and attitudes often be-

TABLE 9-1

Communication Without Words: Some
Translations of Gestures

Gesture	Possible Meaning
Hand-wringing	Thinking over an idea
Rubbing the nose	Rejection, disagreement
Patting the hair	Approval
Steepling of fingers	Feeling of superiority
Rubbing the eyes	An inner desire not to see something that might change one's mind
Fingers interlocked, elbows on the desk	Inward struggle to keep silent
Tugging at shirt cuff	Self-satisfaction
Hitching up trousers	Concern over making a decision
Legs crossed, one foot swinging	Desire to walk away

Source: Adapted from Bedeian, 1986.

fore we speak, and it projects our level of receptivity to others. Most poor conversationalists do not realize that the non-receptive communication given off by their body (poor eye contact, closed posture, bored expression, and so on) is often the cause of short-lived and unsustained dialogs. We are judged quickly by the first signals we give off, and if the first impressions are not positive, it will be difficult to engage in meaningful forms of communication (Gabor, 1983).

Paralanguage and Metamessages

Two other components of communication worthy of our attention are paralanguage and metamessages. According to Matthew McKay and colleagues (1983), **paralanguage** is the vocal component of speech, considered separate from the verbal content. Paralanguage incudes **volume**, **pitch**, **articulation**, **resonance**, **tempo**, and **rhy-**

HOW TO READ THE GLEAM IN THE EYE

Anthropologist David Givens (1983) maintains that the first rule of body language is that a person cannot *not* behave. Even if a partner tries not to show anything, the body's very immobility will speak. In time, couples will learn to understand the wide assortment of nonverbal behaviors that exist. This is as true for reading expressions of boredom as it is for those accompanying anger and hostility.

How it is that potential partners show nonverbal attractions and interest in one another was the focal point of Givens' research. While no single recognition sign is 100 percent accurate, he discovered that a number of signals are surprisingly uniform, including pupil size in the eye. Many are aware that the pupil constricts and dilates in reaction to light and dark. However, there's a psychological component to pupil size, too. That is, pupil dilation correlates with liking, and constriction with disliking. For example, a man's pupils will enlarge when he looks at photos of nude women. A woman's eyes will also dilate when she views attractive-looking men in bathing suits, but interestingly, they will constrict when she sees nude men.

Other clues provided by the eyes are the blink rate and gaze. As far as the former is concerned, both sexes blink more with partners they like. Eye contact is also a positive sign. The telltale signal of interest is given when a stranger looks at another person for longer than two seconds. This is not the "bold stare" which is ▶

Nonverbal communication conveys many moods, emotions, and feelings.

universally threatening and hard to take. Rather, it is a slightly lingering look that typically ends with a shy glance downward.

Another positive sign of attraction is mirroring. Mirroring is imitation of the posture or gestures of another during a conversation. Crossing the legs or leaning back when a partner does reveals a mutual fondness, such as when friends act alike or move in unison. Generally, the listener mirrors the speaker.

Synchrony provides yet another signal. During friendly conversations, listeners move their heads, shoulders, arms, and hands in time with a speaker's words. It's almost as if speaker and listener "dance," so to speak, to the same beat. Synchrony comes from overall sensory awareness, and once a person "feels" the presence of a partner, the greater the visible synchrony. For example, a man lifts his glass, a woman lifts hers; she brings her fork to her mouth, and he follows suit.

Other potentially positive forms of nonverbal communication include the forward lean and body alignment. In general, the forward lean connotes interest and people regard it as a warm, friendly one. The alignment of the upper body before talking may be the most intentional signal of all. Here, two people will "aim" themselves, square up chest-to-chest for several moments, as if to show that their conversation is imminent. In other words, they demonstrate a willingness to talk before actually doing so by adopting postures that speakers use. Should a little nod or friendly smile follow, the conversation will undoubtedly begin.

Just as there are positive nonverbal signals that couples give one another, so too ▶

are there negative ones. Classic among these is the cold shoulder, the body's automatic reaction of turning away when threatened. Both the head and the body instinctively avert to the side away from danger. Known as a "cut-off," this gesture is partly protective and partly an "ignore it till it goes away" or an "out of sight out of mind" response.

Tensed lips and arm-crossing represent other negative signals. Men and women can hide a lot of feelings, but can't keep tension from showing in their lips. Even tiny distresses can trigger tightness and strain in the intricate musculature around the mouth. A person's lips will thin and roll inward as they contract. The greater the anxiety, the greater the tenseness, until the lips actually curl in and almost disappear. As far as arm-crossing is concerned, people tend to hang onto themselves in anxious settings. While it sometimes can serve as a barrier gesture, it more often than not is used to console and comfort oneself. It is a sign that a person is definitely affected by another party, and the cross shows that this person is not being taken for granted.

Finally, the absence of any reaction whatsoever deserves mention. Those who choose to exhibit no outward forms of expression communicate a signal loud and clear: indifference. A blank face, expressionless eyes, and casual notice send a bland, matter-of-fact attitude. It is characteristic of the typical waiting-line, bus-depot, and airport "nonperson" treatment. ■

thm. It is through paralanguage that speakers betray their true attitudes and moods. **Metamessages** represent intentional alterations of speech rhythm or pitch for emphasis, or the use of special verbal modifiers. Metamessages add another level of meaning to a sentence, often a disapproving one.

Let's explore paralanguage and metamessages as researched by McKay and associates a bit more closely. Consider first the elements of paralanguage and their impact on the communication process:

Volume　Volume refers to the loudness of one's voice. On the positive side, loud volume is usually associated with enthusiasm and confidence. Negative connotations include aggressiveness, or an exaggerated belief in the importance of a message. A person of higher status often raises the volume of his or her voice over that of a subordinate.

Pitch　When the vocal cords are tightened, the pitch of one's voice is raised. Intense feelings of joy, fear, or anger make a voice go up. When de-

pressed, tired, or calm, the muscles of the vocal cords relax and pitch of the voice goes down. Though pitch varies in normal conversations, it will move towards the extremes when intense feelings are expressed.

Resonance　The shape of one's vocal cords and chest determine resonance. Resonance is the richness or thinness of the voice. A man with heavy vocal cords and a large chest is likely to have a deep, full voice. A woman with tight, thin vocal cords is apt to have a thin, high voice. With some practice, both pitch and resonance can be controlled — as singers and public speakers regularly do. Deep chest tones communicate firmness, self-assurance and strength. Thin, high-pitched voices suggest insecurity, weakness, and indecisiveness.

Articulation　This refers to the *enunciation* of words. Different levels of articulation are appropriate in different situations. A slight slur or drawl may contribute to an atmosphere of comfort or intimacy. However, slurred words would be inappropriate in a board meeting where clear, decisive speech is expected.

Tempo   The tempo or speed at which words are spoken reflects emotions and attitudes. Fast talkers usually convey excitement and can be expressive and persuasive. Speaking too fast, however, can make the listener nervous. Rapid speech can also signal insecurity. A slow, hesitant speaker may give an impression of laziness or indifference. To another listener, the slow speaker may sound sincere, thoughtful, and interested.

Rhythm   Just as every song has its unique rhythm, so, too, does every language. Rhythm determines which words will be emphasized in a sentence. In the question, "What time is it?" the emphasis is normally on the word "time." If you were to place the emphasis on "what," you would upset the rhythm. As we'll see, the words emphasized in a sentence make a vital difference in the meaning of that statement.

Many of the sentences we use have two levels of meaning. One level is the basic information being communicated by a series of words. The second level, or a metamessage, communicates the speaker's attitudes and feelings. The metamessage is largely communicated by rhythm, pitch, and verbal modifiers. As an illustration, examine the sentence, "You're late tonight." Should the word "late" be emphasized with a slightly rising inflection, the sentence communicates surprise. It may also imply a question about the cause of the delay. If the word "you're" is emphasized, note how the metamessage now communicates irritation.

Metamessages are often at the center of interpersonal conflict. At the surface level a statement may seem reasonable and straightforward. At its second level, though, the metamessage communicates blame and hostility. Consider the statement, "I'm trying to help." If the verbal modifier "only" is inserted, and given the emphasis of a rising inflection, then the metamessage becomes very different. "I'm *only* trying to help" communicates hurt feelings and defensiveness. Note how the message has now transformed itself into an attack.

There are many components to the communication process, including the sounds of silence.

It is a difficult chore to defend against the disapproval in negative metamessages. Often, the attack is so subtle that persons don't realize that they've been hurt. For instance, Tom recently moved out of a college dormitory into his own apartment. When his mother visits she remarks, "Of course, it *is* your first apartment." By adding the modifier "of course" and emphasizing the verb "is," the metamessage becomes, "This place isn't very nice, but what can you expect from a novice homemaker?" Tom feels irritated for the rest of her visit, but has no idea how he has been put down.

Many compliments also have hidden metamessage barbs in them. For example, the sentence, "You're sweet" changes considerably, depending on the speaker's use of rhythm and pitch. When "you're" is emphasized with a rising inflection, the metamessage is surprise, perhaps distrust. The statement reads, "You're being sweet, but that's an unusual occurrence." When "sweet" is emphasized the message is clearly appreciation or affection. A sarcastic, cutting metamessage is achieved by giving both words a strong emphasis and "sweet" a falling inflection.

Using Paralanguage and Metamessages to Your Advantage   Individuals and couples can be better communicators if they expand their awareness of paralanguage and metamessages. As far as paralanguage is concerned, an understanding of its various dimensions is a step in the right direction. Tape recording one's voice can shed light on how the elements of volume, pitch, resonance, articulation, tempo, and rhythm are used. Individuals can discover whether their voice reflects what they want to say, if the voice is congruent with the words spoken, or if there is something about the voice that is disliked and needs to be changed.

Since speakers use metamessages to say something covertly that they're reluctant to say directly, there is little chance for overt retaliation. When a metamessage is heard, though, it can be repeated in one's mind and analyzed for rhythm, pitch, and any verbal modifiers that are used. More importantly, a person can say what a metamessage is thought to be out loud, asking the speaker if that

was the intention of the message. If an interpretation is not examined, then a person is forced to mind-read the other person's intent, or behave as if the assumed metamessage was true. Examining metamessages is also a good way of teaching metamessagers to talk honestly and directly. When questioned about their covert attack, they are more likely to be direct. The thoughts and feelings hidden in the metamessage can then be looked at openly and sincerely (McKay, Davis, and Fanning, 1983).

THE PROCESS OF COMMUNICATION

Steps in the Transmission of Messages

Now that we have explored the various components of communication, let's turn our attention next to the actual process of communication. Arthur Bedeian (1986) reminds us that communication is successful only when a mutual understanding results; that is, when one transmits information and makes oneself understood by another.

Communication thus represents a vital and dynamic process. The complex nature of this process must be understood if effective, meaningful communication is to occur. Bedeian, among others, analyzes the communication process by breaking it into various steps (as seen in Figure 9-1). In doing so, we must realize that any attempt to diagram the sequence of communication between two individuals is necessarily an oversimplification. Moreover, it should be kept in mind that the steps in a communication episode not only occur individually, but also interact with each other. By discussing the steps separately, the communication process tends to be distorted.

The first step in the communication process is **ideation**. A sender has information for, or needs information from, another person. This information, as we know, can consist of observations, thoughts, feelings, and needs. Whatever the form of expression, a decision is made to communicate.

The second step is **encoding**. At this point in the communication process the sender translates the message to be conveyed into a set of symbols, which it is believed the intended receiver will understand. To be most effective, the symbols selected are adapted to the medium used to transmit the message. Words represent the most obvious symbols, and this step is characterized by the sender selecting the appropriate words to convey the message.

The third step is the actual **transmission** of the message as encoded. Messages can be transmitted in a number of different forms. They may be presented orally or in writing. Remember, too, that messages may be communicated through body movements such as gestures, facial expressions, and posture.

In the fourth step **(reception)** the person with whom communication is intended *receives* the message. Obviously, if there is to be any communication at all, the intended receiver must perceive the message. If the message is oral, for example, the receiver must be listening. If the intended receiver is not listening, the message will be lost.

The fifth step is **decoding**. Here the receiver interprets the message. Thus, the receiver perceives certain words or sees certain actions and interprets them as having a particular meaning. Depending on the skills of the sender in encoding and transmitting, and the receiver in receiving and decoding, the meaning may or may not be that intended.

FIGURE 9-1   Steps in the Communication Process

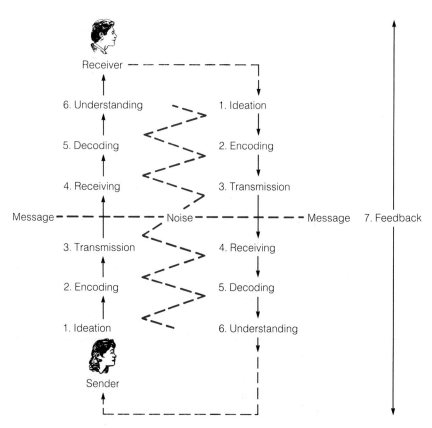

Source: Adapted from Bedeian, 1986.

Understanding is thus the sixth step in the communication process. Should an accurate message be sent and successfully decoded, comprehension should take place at this time.

The final step is **feedback**. This allows the sender to determine if the intended message has been accurately received. A message may not be accurately received because of *noise* that exists when it is sent. Noise is *any factor that disturbs or distorts a message*. It can range from actual "noise" that makes a message difficult to hear, to a receiver not paying attention. Feedback is thus necessary for verifying the degree to which a message has been understood. It can occur orally, in writing, or nonverbally through body movements. The feedback loop in Figure 9-1 recognizes that communication involves a two-way flow of information. Thus, the above steps also must be followed in the communication of a return message.

THE ROLE OF LISTENING IN COMMUNICATION

The effectiveness of the communication process hinges on good listening skills. Peak communication is a two-way street that requires both clear talking and refined listening. Effective listening is not merely a matter of being passive and quiet while the other is talking; listening is an active skill, and is also hard work. It involves communicating *empathy, confirmation, clarification, and attention* (Holland, 1985).

Unfortunately, many individuals are poor listeners. Some lack the motivation to listen, others are inaccurate in what they translate, and still others have never been taught the importance of using this skill. Disheartening is the fact that *the average person grasps only 25 percent of what is spoken, and remembers only about one-half of this total* (Fallon, 1981).

Other reasons for poor listening range from the presence of distractions to tuning out what was said in self-defense. Another reason for poor listening is that people rely on selective listening; that is, they pick out bits and pieces of conversations that interest them and turn a deaf ear to the

rest. The sheer volume and complexity of the noise around us also contributes to the problem.

As far as sex differences are concerned, women appear to be better listeners than men. One study (Booth-Gutterfield, 1984) focused on how the socialization process affects such sex differences. The authors contended that as boys and girls grow up, they are taught and reinforced in different styles of listening. The primary difference is in task vs. interpersonal understanding—males are taught to listen for facts, and females are taught to listen for the mood of the communication. Males thus often have trouble listening for nonverbal cues, whereas females, who are listening for the mood of the communication, pick them up much more readily.

This latter point was among the central findings reported in another study (Hall, 1984). Not only were females better decoders of nonverbal cues, they were also superior to males in the recognition of faces and the expression of emotions by means of nonverbal communications. Women also used body movements and positions that seemed to be less restless, less expansive, more involved, more expressive, and more self-conscious than those of men.

Hearing vs. Listening

All too often, the words hearing and listening are used interchangeably. This is inaccurate. **Hearing** refers to *the physiological process by which auditory impressions are received by the ears and transmitted to the brain*. More specifically, the outer ear catches sound waves and guides them into the auditory canal. At the end of the canal, the waves vibrate the eardrum, sending vibrations across the three bones of the middle ear and moving the innermost bone in and out. Then a fluid translates sound waves into nerve impulses and stimulates nerves to send "messages" to the hearing center in the brain (Swets, 1983).

Listening is *the psychological procedure involving the interpretation and understanding of sensory experience*. Be it the whisper of a lover or the whimper of a baby, listening requires that we interpret what is heard around us and give it significance and meaning. Without this, messages are not under-stood and communication becomes fatally flawed.

These two processes should work together to help create maximum communication. However, it is possible to hear and not listen. Perhaps, then, the appropriate question to ask a "distant" spouse is not, "Do you hear me?", but rather "Are you listening to me?"

APPLICATIONS

HOW EFFECTIVE ARE YOUR LISTENING SKILLS?

What kind of listener are you? Complete the following self-rating listening scale to evaluate your strengths and to identify where you might need to fine-tune your listening skills. Circle the number that applies to your listening:

Do most of the listening	5	4	3	2	1	Do most of the talking
Focus on other person	5	4	3	2	1	Talk about myself
Maintain good eye contact	5	4	3	2	1	Maintain little eye contact
Listen carefully to what the other person is saying	5	4	3	2	1	Always think of what I'll say next
Sit face to face	5	4	3	2	1	Sit across desk, table, or other barrier
Mostly use the word "you"	5	4	3	2	1	Mostly use the word "me" or "I"
Talk flows like a conversation	5	4	3	2	1	Talk is mostly question and answer
Often use other person's name in conversation	5	4	3	2	1	Rarely use other person's name in conversation
Keep things confidential	5	4	3	2	1	Tend to tell others what I know
Help others to make own decisions	5	4	3	2	1	Give too much advice
Keep questions simple and understandable	5	4	3	2	1	Tend to ask multiple questions
Keep things positive	5	4	3	2	1	Tend to encourage negative feelings
When others slighted or criticized, I emphasize the good	5	4	3	2	1	When others slighted or criticized, I add fuel to the fire
When there is silence, I allow it without fear	5	4	3	2	1	When there is silence, I rush in to fill the void
Ask questions that require a thoughtful response	5	4	3	2	1	Ask questions that can be answered "yes" or "no"
Lean forward to show atten-tiveness	5	4	3	2	1	Slouch when listening carefully

▶

Use humor to break tense moments	5 4 3 2 1	Don't know how to handle tense moments
When criticized, listen to discover feelings	5 4 3 2 1	When criticized, get defensive
When asked for advice, tend to probe for more information	5 4 3 2 1	When asked for advice, tend to respond with snap judgments
Try to sense how other feels about sensitive issues	5 4 3 2 1	Tend to think how I feel about sensitive issues
Ask short questions	5 4 3 2 1	Ask long questions
Tend to be supportive and affirming of other	5 4 3 2 1	Tend to be assertive and confronting with other
More interested in being helpful to other	5 4 3 2 1	More interested in being liked by other
Sensitive to feelings behind what is said	5 4 3 2 1	Respond only to facts of what is said
Wait for other to finish even if I have something to say	5 4 3 2 1	Tend to interrupt a lot or finish other person's sentences

SCORING: Add the numbers that you circled to determine your score. The highest score possible is 125 (25 items). Once you've understood what your score means, have your partner or a close friend take the test and compare the two totals.

100 or More   You are a truly exceptional listener, gifted in conversing with others and helping them to make their own decisions and to solve their own problems. You are able to suppress your own needs for attention in order to focus on the other person. You are an affirming person, probably very unselfish, and you are likely to be called upon by your friends in their time of need.

85 to 99   You are a strong and effective listener, although you may sometimes draw the conversation back to yourself too much. You help others to work problems through and are a good partner in any conversation. Try to put yourself in the other person's shoes a bit more and work on making your talk less of an interview and more of a conversation.

70 to 84   Your listening skills show potential but need some fine tuning. How do you learn to be a good listener? Often by studying others who are good listeners and identifying their good qualities. Try to put yourself more in the background and focus on the other person. It's okay to give your advice and opinions, of course, but remember that sometimes people just need someone to help them to "think out loud." Work on developing conversational skills that are other-directed rather than self-directed.   ▶

70 or Less	Your listening skills need some hard work. Perhaps you view listening as doing the talking and providing your views on a subject rather than helping other people to express themselves. Practice by refraining from talking even when you want to and by asking others for their views and feelings. Study the techniques of people whom you feel are good listeners. Don't give up or think you can't become a good listener, but don't shy away from the hard work needed to succeed either.

Adapted from Zehring, 1986. ■

The Sounds of Silence

Often hampering the listening process, as well as communication in general, is silence. Silence is an important element of conversations that is very often misinterpreted, neglected, and even ignored. For many people, according to Howard Waters (1980), it's the most difficult of all things to handle. It may seem unusual to consider silence important in a relationship — because our society places so much importance on "polite conversation" and discourages thoughtful silence, most of us have learned to feel uncomfortable with silences and to regard long pauses in conversation as being impolite or showing a lack of interest. But, as we've learned in this chapter, talking is not the only way to communicate, and often it isn't even the best way. Silence can communicate quite eloquently. Socially, we often use the "silent treatment" as a form of rejection, defiance, or condemnation. Fortunately, there are many ways that silence can be used as a positive, constructive force.

Waters feels that when silence is used constructively, it can prompt another person to communicate. It can effectively shift the responsibility for verbal expression to the other person in a relationship. Oftentimes a partner can be "drawn out" in this way and made more communicative.

Silence may also help the less articulate partner to feel accepted. By feeling accepted as a shy and quiet person, he/she may be able to accept oneself. As a result, communication often becomes more confident and direct.

Another value of silence in a relationship is that remaining silent after a partner's serious expression of feelings often allows that person to think and to come up with new insight into these feelings. One value of silence, then, is that it forces depth of thought about one's affective side.

Finally, Waters notes that silence can reduce the pace of the conversation. Many times, that pace is directly related to the amount of anxiety being felt by both people. Often silence can help to eliminate some of that tension. Above all, it is important to be sensitive to what the other person is communicating to you through silence. For example, is one's partner merely wondering what to say next? Or, is the person feeling something that is difficult to express? Is one pausing in expectation of something? Or, is one's partner collecting his/her thoughts and thinking over what was just said? These are but a few of the many reasons for silence. Skilled listeners are adept at pinpointing the motives for silence and are aware of the many messages that this behavior can communicate. Indeed, the sounds of silence can be very revealing.

Listening Techniques and Strategies

Listening is a skill that can be improved. With practice, couples can sharpen their ability to listen to each other and in the process, enhance the overall relationship. The following are some ideas.

■ *Don't Interrupt*   Nothing is accomplished when two people talk at the same time. Also, acknowledge the importance of silence in a conversation. Don't jump in too quickly with comments, reactions, or observations.

■ *Pay Attention to Nonverbal Communication*   Listen with your eyes as well as your ears. We've examined how body language can reveal many facets of a person, and this information can give you a more complete picture of the total situation. Also, examine your own body language. Good eye contact and posture idicates that a person is receptive to communication. Pay attention, too, to paralanguage and metamessages.

■ *Listen Objectively*   Your emotions should not interfere with the conversation. Avoid judging and criticizing, and don't "label" either the speaker or the topic. Evaluations and mental responses to the issues raised should be suspended until the speaker is finished.

■ *Beware of "Tune-out" Words*   Some words are generally disliked and tend to produce negative reactions. When used, these words work against effective communication, for speakers as well as listeners. Table 9-2 lists words that people tend to like and those they dislike.

■ *Pick the Right Time for Conversations*   Little is accomplished when only one person wants to talk. Find a time that is suitable for both parties, taking into consideration such factors as peak fluctuations of energy. Attentive listening is usually heightened when the proper moment is chosen.

■ *Minimize Distractions*   Just as there is a time for everything, there is a place, too. Find a location that is conducive to conversation. Also, clear away those things that prevent giving someone your undivided attention such as pens or paperclips.

■ *Keep the Tone Positive*   Make a deliberate effort to avoid negative suffixes and prefixes as well as negatively worded phrases or sentences. For example, rather than saying "Mary

TABLE 9-2

Sweet and Sour Words

Most People Like These Words:

advantage	ease	integrity	responsible
appreciate	economy	justice	satisfactory
benefit	effective	kind	service
capable	efficient	loyalty	success
confidence	energy	please	superior
conscientious	enthusiasm	popularity	useful
cooperation	genuine	practical	valuable
courtesy	helpful	prestige	vigor
dependable	honesty	progress	you
desirable	honor	reliable	yours

Most People Dislike These Words:

abuse	decline	ignorant	squander
alibi	discredit	imitation	superficial
allege	dispute	implicate	tardy
apology	exaggerate	impossible	timid
beware	extravagance	misfortune	unfair
blame	failure	negligent	unfortunate
cheap	fault	opinionated	unsuccessful
common-			
place	fear	prejudiced	waste
complaint	fraud	retrench	worry
crisis	hardship	rude	wrong

Source: Adapted from Pollack, 1984.

APPLICATIONS

SKILLS TO SHARPEN YOUR LISTENING ABILITIES

According to John Zehring (1986) attentive listeners distinguish themselves by using a variety of skills. These skills enhance a conversation and forge a bridge of understanding between speaker and listener. Among these skills are the following:

Probing   This is used for digging for more information and deeper feelings. Be concerned with who, what, when, where, why, and how. "How do you feel about going back to work, Paula?"

Clarifying   Ask the other person to explain something they said. "I'm not sure I fully understand what you mean, Cathy. Could you say a little more about . . ."

Summarizing   Sum up your understanding of what the other said. "So what we've decided, Sam, is that . . ."

Confronting   Ask another to explain inconsistent remarks. "Now, Claire, didn't you say before that you. . . . How do you reconcile those two things?" Be gentle; confronting responses can lead to defensive reactions.

Supporting   Make it clear that you agree, or at least support a person's statement. "Bill, if that's what you really want, I think you ought to get it."

Affirming   An affirming statement or nonverbal gesture is a positive indication of your approval or understanding. It is often done by nodding, grunting approval, or interjecting short comments. "Sure . . .That makes a lot of sense, Anne!"

Restating   Repeat back what another has just said. This provides an opening for them to continue, or it allows them to hear what you think they said. "So you told Ron, 'I don't care if you are the manager, you can't talk like that to employees.'"

Reflecting   Look back and analyze what has been said. This adds insight or speculation to the conversation. "If you started a small business like that, Rita, it sounds like you wouldn't only make a good living, but you'd also have loads of fun."

Bouncing   Make a statement or quote another and ask the person to react to the statement. "Bill thinks the economy will be a lot brighter next year. How do you feel about that, Paul?"

is wasting her time here at the university," you might say, "Mary needs to find some direction in her life." Such positive orientations to topics helps to reduce the speaker's potential for defensiveness.

ANATOMY OF A CONFLICT

It is a myth that most couples do not engage in conflict. Indeed, conflict is inevitable over the many transitions that characterize the marriage and family life cycle. Marie Kargan (1985), for one, perceives these conflicts as constructive challenges to the couple. While the struggle to overcome them sometimes means taking one step forward and two steps back, they present opportunities to strengthen a relationship.

Joanna Cole and Holly Laibson (1983) concur with this and add that not fighting at all is destructive, particularly since it can promote boredom and even depression. Dorrine Turecamo (1980) adds that a couple can grow together more through adversity than placidity. The task-facing couple, though, must learn to overcome conflict as a caring and giving partnership, not as opposing armies on a battlefield.

What exactly is a conflict as it exists within the relationship? Donald Peterson (1983) regards **conflict** as an interpersonal process that occurs whenever the actions of one person interfere with the actions of another. While partners can come into conflict over practically any kind of issue, not all experience this interference in the same areas and at the same levels of intensity. In seeking to analyze the dynamics that exist in conflicts, Peterson identifies three components: *initiating events*, *middle stages*, and *termination*.

Initiating Events

For a conflict to take place, some type of precipitating event must occur. Behavioral expressions of incompatible interests kindle the conflict, followed by the goal-directed activity of one person interfering with the goal-directed activity of another. The events that usually trigger conflict reflect four possible conditions: criticism, illegitimate demand, rebuff, and cumulative annoyance.

Criticism Conflicts evolve when verbal or nonverbal acts on the part of one individual are regarded as demeaning or unfavorable by the other. In short, behavior is interpreted as critical. The criticized party feels offended and is likely to retaliate with aggression or withdrawal.

Illegitimate Demand Usually, a demand of any kind by one person upon another is likely to be interfering. However, the demands likely to produce the most serious conflict are those beyond the normative expectations that each person holds toward the other. The demand is thus perceived as being unfair.

Rebuff A rebuff occurs when one party appeals to the other for a desired reaction, and the other fails to respond as expected. The individual experiencing the rebuff usually feels devalued and angry with the other. A common reaction to feeling rebuffed is withdrawal.

Cumulative Annoyance This is a buildup of annoyances until some threshold is exceeded. A first act may go unnoticed, and a few more may be ignored. When the offended reaches his or her limit, though, no further acts are tolerated and the conflict begins.

After an initiating event has taken place, the couple may decide to either avoid the conflict or engage each other in it. Should avoidance be chosen, it must be mutual. This usually occurs when the issues are seen either as insufficiently important to outweigh the distress conflict brings or as intractable, at least for the moment. The couple regards the risk of open conflict to be greater than the uncertain gains to be obtained through active dispute.

If the couple decides to engage in the conflict, it is probable that at least one person perceives the issue imposing enough to require action and believes that a favorable outcome can be attained. Generally speaking, powerful partners appear more likely than those with less power to engage in conflict rather than to avoid trouble. By engaging in conflict, they may reestablish the generally superior position that the conflict threatened to upset. But, if successive violations become intolerable, even a dependent partner may be willing to endure whatever punishment the conflict entails. By the act of engagement itself, greater influence over future interactions is acquired. Once the weaker partner takes a stand, the dominant one must thenceforth deal with the costs of active conflict in pursuing personal aims at the expense of the other.

WHAT COUPLES FIGHT ABOUT THE MOST

While we've indicated that not all couples experience conflict in the same areas, certain topics are more prevalent than others. The following represents the major areas of marital conflict:

Money   How much money do we need? Who should make the money? How do we decide who spends the money? What do we purchase? How much money should we borrow?

Sex   How often do we have sex? When? Where? Who should initiate sex?

Work   Can both partners work? Who decides what job to take? How much work is too much?

Children   Should we have children? How many? When? What type of discipline should we use? What goals or hopes for the children do we share?

In-laws   With whose parents shall we spend holidays? How often and how long should we visit? How shall we deal with parental interference?

Religion   What church should we attend? How can we resolve our different religious backgrounds? What religion should be taught to the children? How often should we attend church? Should we pray at the dinner table?

Friends   Can we have different friends? What about friends of the other sex? How much time can we spend with our friends? Do I have to like your friends? What if I don't like them?

Alcohol and Drug Usage   How much shall we drink? When? Where? How much money should be spent on alcohol? Is alcohol or drug use adversely affecting our relationship?

Recreation   How much time shall we spend on recreation? Do we have to pursue recreation together? Where do we spend our vacations? How many trips should we take each year? Should we spend vacations alone or take the children with us?

Power   How should lines of authority be established? What should this be based on? How does the division of power relate to the regulation of household affairs? The disciplining of children?

Adapted from Dinkmeyer and Carlson, 1984.

Middle Stages

Once it has been activated, a conflict can move in two directions: *direct negotiation and resolution,* or *escalation and intensification.* Should direct negoti- ation be chosen, partners settle their disagreement. Each party states his or her position and obtains validation of the position by the other, and a straightforward problem-solving exchange follows. Information relative to the conflict is expressed and received without distortion. Both parties work toward a solution until some acceptable outcome is attained. (The major conflict resolution strategies used by couples will be presented a bit later in the chapter.)

Intensification of the conflict brings intensely angry fighting. Usually, biased perceptions and hostilities based on unvalidated beliefs about another intensify the conflict. This often brings along strategies of power along with tactics of threat, coercion, and deception. Manipulation techniques also emerge: the attribution of blame to the other rather than to oneself, sexual withdrawal, and name-calling are popular forms.

A heated conflict does not go to a rational problem-solving stage, particularly if insulting remarks have been exchanged or if physical abuse has taken place. Rather, an intermediate step is needed before negotiation can begin. This component of conflict takes the form of a conciliatory act and is intended to reduce negative affect. More-

over, it expresses a willingness to work toward a remedy for the conflict. A conciliatory act may be a partner saying, "This problem has gotten out of hand; let's get it back in perspective," or "This problem is at least partly my fault; I'll do what I can to solve it."

It is possible that conciliatory gestures will be followed by reciprocal conciliation from the other. When this happens, anger tends to dissipate on both sides, and the combatants are able to move rationally and cooperatively toward resolution of the issue. In resolution of severe conflicts, the least that happens is a reversal of the process of escalation. Personal attacks are stopped and coercion, as well as threats of it, are withdrawn. Concern that had been generalized across a range of issues is redirected toward more specific issues. Then the couple can attend to solving the problem rather than injuring each other, and chances for a satisfactory outcome are improved.

Termination

Most conflicts end one way or another, either destructively or constructively. A destructive outcome is one that has a damaging effect on later interactions, while those with positive outcomes have positive benefits. The following five forms of resolution reflect such outcomes, roughly from most destructive to most constructive.

Separation This termination is characterized by the withdrawal of one or both parties without the immediate resolution of the conflict. Separation may be a useful act towards later resolution; time away from one another may prompt more creative solutions to the problem and provide a "cooling off" period. However, more often than not, withdrawal brings with it damaging effects. For example, it is often accompanied by a "parting shot" or aggressive gesture that leaves partners feeling worse about each other and the relationship as a whole.

Domination The termination of some conflicts embodies conquest. That is, one partner gives way and the other continues to pursue the

"Ah! The eye of the storm, I presume."

Drawing by Geo. Price; © 1980 The New Yorker Magazine, Inc.

line of action leading to personal goals. Chronic domination is destructive for the loser as well as for the winner. The latter has ignored the partner's wishes in order to gain victory at any cost, and has failed to take advantage of the opportunities that conflict offers for positive and constructive change.

Compromise   This approach is marked by both partners reducing their aspirations until a mutually acceptable alternative is discovered. This type of trade-off results when interests are diluted rather than reconciled. It often represents the best possible outcome in those competitive situations where one partner gains only at the expense of the other.

Integrative Agreements   When the goals and aspirations of both partners are simultaneously met, the result is an *integrative agreement*. Purely integrative agreements are rare because it is difficult to reconcile genuinely divergent interests. Most agreements range somewhere between compromise and integration, with the creation of an alternative that satisfies somewhat modified goals and aspirations for one or both partners.

Structural Improvement   At the outset, we said that conflicts have the potential of strengthening a relationship. If this is realized, the treatment accorded to one another often comes to be guided by different rules. The affection of each partner for the other may grow stronger, and the understanding of one for the other may be deepened. A severe conflict that has revealed previously unrecognized characteristics of the partners or of the relationship may be resolved through open communication. This, in turn, may lead to a beneficial change in the casual conditions governing the dyad.

CONFLICT RESOLUTION STRATEGIES

Don Dinkmeyer and Jon Carlson (1984) feel that the way a couple deals with conflict determines whether or not the conflict will be harmful to their marriage. The inability to deal with conflict constructively is a potent force in dampening marital satisfaction. Moreover, when conflict occurs, it often tends to be repeated. It thus becomes important to learn to handle conflict appropriately. Dinkmeyer and Carlson offer the following ideas to resolve marital conflict.

Demonstrating Mutual Respect

Rather than the issue itself, the attitude of one or both partners is often at the center of the conflict. In a relationship with mutual respect, each partner seeks to understand and respect the other's point of view. Should verbal fighting take place, couples also need to fight fairly.

Clarifying the Problem

Most couples have difficulty focusing on the *real* issue. Along these lines, who does what around the house, how money is spent, or whether or not to have sex usually are not the true issues. While these disagreements do have to be resolved, the purpose or goal the partner is trying to achieve is the central issue. Following the clarification of the real issue, it becomes easier to resolve surface disagreements. The concern usually centers around one of the following issues:

- A partner feels a threat to his/her status or prestige ("Why should I give in?" or, "What will they think?").
- A sense that one's superiority is being challenged ("If I'm not on top, I feel inadequate.").
- One's need to control or one's right to decide is at stake ("If I don't boss them, they won't do it right," or, "Why should I let him/her decide for me?").
- A feeling that one's judgment is not being considered or that treatment is unfair ("Whose way is the best way?").
- One feels hurt and needs to retaliate or get even ("He/she won the last one," or, "I'll get even this time").

Once the central issue has been identified—such as who controls, who resents control, who

APPLICATIONS

RULES FOR A FAIR FIGHT

- Make an appointment and name the topic.
- When you are beginning, state your complaint with an "I" statement. For instance, "I feel lonely when you come home late."
- Don't make "you" statements, which assign blame and cause defensiveness. For instance, don't say, "You wouldn't come home late if you cared about me."
- Be very specific in your criticism.
- Don't bring up the past. Stay current.
- Be assertive and express your anger directly instead of using abuse, sarcasm, blame, or hostile comments about the other person.
- Don't use words like "always" or "never."
- Before the other person speaks he or she should restate what the first person has said, to his or her satisfaction.
- Be accepting of the other person's feelings.
- Once all feelings are out and the issue is clear, each person should state what changes would be satisfactory to him or her.
- Negotiate a compromise and stick with it for a week.
- At the end of a week, if the solution isn't working, try another solution for a week.
- Agree to "call" each other on infractions of these rules.
- If you lose control and start breaking all the rules, take an hour's break and go off by yourself to cool off. Then resume the argument.

Adapted from Cole and Laibson, 1983.

feels a lack of respect—the couple can discuss alternative ways to behave, and reach a new agreement.

Agreeing to Cooperate

When conflicts take place, the easiest solution that often comes to mind is to suggest how one's partner could change to alleviate the problem. This may not be the best route, though. A more effective approach is to ask, "What can I do to change our relationship?" By focusing on what you are willing to do and by not requiring your partner to change, you generate an atmosphere in which agreement can be reached. While the ultimate solution to conflict involves mutual change of behav-

ior, the desire to change is responsibility of each person.

Mutual Decision-Making

Once the problem is confronted and the issues become clear, either partner may propose a tentative solution. Either may respond by accepting the proposed solution, modifying it, or making a counter suggestion. An atmosphere of give-and-take and compromise, as earlier discussed, is most effective. When an agreement is reached, the role of each partner in executing the decision should be clarified. Also, what should be done if either partner doesn't follow through needs to be decided.

Couples need to exercise mutual respect and co-operation when confronted with conflict.

Now, it is important to allow a partner the option of not being involved in a decision, providing the partner was given a choice to be involved or uninvolved. Conflict may surface when a decision is made without giving a partner the option to be involved. When both partners mutually participate in conflict resolution, they can develop creative agreements that are acceptable to both and that are in line with their common goals. When this is accomplished, power and responsibility are shared equally, and cooperation replaces resistance within the relationship.

CHAPTER HIGHLIGHTS

Communication embodies the exchange of information, signals, and messages between people. Communication can be broken down into four types of expression: observations, thoughts, feelings, and needs. Each of these entails a different style of expression and, in many instances, a very different vocabulary.

Nonverbal communication shows how not all forms of human communication are linguistic in nature. Nonverbal communication includes gestures, mannerisms, eye contact, body language, and the like. As a type of communication, it is especially effective in conveying feelings and attitudes.

Paralanguage is the vocal component of speech, considered separate from the verbal content. It includes the elements of volume, pitch, articulation, resonance, tempo, and rhythm. It is through paralanguage that speakers betray their true attitudes and moods.

Metamessages are intentional alterations of speech, rhythm, or pitch for emphasis, or the use of special verbal modifiers. Metamessages serve to add another level of meaning to a sentence, usually a disapproving one.

The communication process is best understood when its individual components are explored. These components include the ideation, encoding, transmission, reception, decoding, understanding, and feedback steps. Each of these occur individually, but interact with one another as messages are transmitted and received.

Effective communication between partners requires good listening skills. Broadly defined, listening is the psychological procedure involving the interpretation and understanding of sensory experience. Listening is a skill that can be improved and this chapter supplied techniques to elevate its effectiveness.

Conflicts begin when a precipitating event triggers four possible conditions: criticism, illegitimate demand, rebuff, or cumulative annoyance. A conciliatory act from one, or even better, both partners, is usually needed to start problem-solving strategies. Five possible forms of conflict resolution are known to exist. Separation, domination, compromise, integrative agreements, and structural improvement. Finally, we examined some conflict resolution strategies that often prove helpful to couples. These included the demonstration of mutual respect, problem clarification, cooperation, and mutual decision-making.

KEY TERMS

articulation	ideation	reception
communication	listening	resonance
conflict	metamessage	rhythm
contaminated messages	needs	tempo
decoding	nonverbal communication	thoughts
encoding	observations	transmission
feedback	paralanguage	understanding
feelings	partial message	volume
hearing	pitch	whole messages

RECOMMENDED READINGS

Atwater, E. (1986). *Human relations.* Englewood Cliffs, NJ: Prentice-Hall. Chapter 7 of this softback explores the concept of effective communication, while Chapter 8 examines conflict resolution strategies.

Burley-Allen, M. (1982). *Listening: The forgotten art.* New York: Wiley. Readers will find many valuable tips on how to sharpen their listening abilities in this book.

Cushman, D. P., and Cahn, D. D., Jr. (1985). *Communication in interpersonal relationships.* Albany: State University of New York Press. An excellent investigation of communication principles, processes, and skills.

Galvin, K. M., and Brommel, B. J. (1982). *Family communication: Cohesion and change.* Glenview, IL: Scott, Foresman & Co. An in-depth look at how communication affects, and is in turn affected by, the family unit.

Hall, J. A. (1984). *Nonverbal sex differences: Communication accuracy and expressive style.* Baltimore, MD: The Johns Hopkins University Press. A documentation of the sex differences that exist in the realm of nonverbal behavior and skill.

Knapp, M. L., and Miller, G. R. (Eds.). (1985). *Handbook of interpersonal communication.* Beverly Hills, CA: Sage. Among the topics in this reader are the management of conversations, nonverbal behavior, and communicator characteristics and behavior.

Kramarae, C. (1981). *Women and men speaking.* Rowley, MA: Newbury House. An interesting look at the interaction between language and the sexes.

McKay, M., Davis, M., and Fanning, P. (1983). *Messages: The communication skills book.* Oakland, CA: New Harbinger Publishers. A highly readable and encompassing look at how interpersonal communication can be refined and enhanced.

Roloff, M. E. (1981). *Interpersonal communication: The social exchange approach.* Beverly Hills, CA: Sage. See Chapter 4 for a thorough discussion of interpersonal conflict.

Sieburg, E. (1985). *Family communication.* New York: Gardner Press. Sieburg provides a scholarly interpretation of important communication topics, including metamessages and relational needs.

Part Four

PARENTHOOD
AND FAMILY
TRANSITIONS

10/FAMILY PLANNING

11/CONCEPTION, PREGNANCY, AND CHILDBIRTH

12/CONTEMPORARY PARENTHOOD

10

Family Planning

CONTENTS

CONTEMPLATIONS

■ Robert and Joyce Champlain have been married for almost nine years and want to have children . . . someday. At present, though, they are each busy with their careers and are setting their immediate sights on vocational fulfillment. Bob and Joyce's decision to delay parenthood stands in distinct contrast to those couples wanting children as soon as possible. At a greater extreme are those couples deliberately choosing to remain childless. This chapter will address itself to these trends in family planning, as well as to why birth rates are declining in the United States and other nations in the 1980s.

■ In the People's Republic of China, birth rates are declining, but not as fast as government officials would like. So the government has implemented a drastic birth control policy in an effort to overcome its massive overpopulation problem. Hoping to attain zero population growth by the year 2000, the government has raised the legal age of marriage, stipulated that couples can have only one child, and experimented with a male birth control pill. How successful have these measures been? Will China resolve its overpopulation crisis? As this nation calculates its progress, the rest of the world pays close attention.

■ They are called the birth control methods of the future: "morning after" pills, contraceptive vaccines and nasal sprays, and subdermal implants, to name but a few. While they are still in the experimental stage, many experts predict that these sophisticated contraceptive measures will soon be available to the public. As you read this chapter, you'll see how these contraceptives will offer a different dimension to those birth control devices already being used.

■ In the United States, about 1.5 million abortions are performed each year. This is a very large total, but other nations have higher abortion rates, including Rumania and Cuba. Leading the world in abortion rates is the Soviet Union, where the average woman has six abortions in the course of her lifetime. The latter portion of this chapter will explore abortion in the United States as well as abroad, including what it entails, the public policies that surround it, the controversy that it creates, and why it touches the lives of so many.

What is the best family size? This is a tough question, one depending on a multitude of factors. Robert Coles (1985) writes that some men and women, well before marriage, have already decided upon the ideal size for their families. The reasons for such a decision, often enough, are quite personal: fond memories of growing up in a large family, or unpleasant memories of being an only child. Sometimes those reasons might be reversed: a man or woman liked being an only child, or emphatically didn't enjoy being one of eight or nine brothers and sisters. Then, too, there are those who represent a new breed of married couples—husbands and wives preferring voluntary childlessness.

More couples than ever before are grappling with the issue of **family planning**, the voluntary decision making about how many children they want and when, or if they are wanted at all. Family planning embraces contraception to space and prevent pregnancy, as well as infertility therapy to help couples achieve wanted conceptions. In this chapter we'll explore the concept of family planning as it exists in the 1980s and in the process examine past historical trends, as well as international parallels.

TRENDS IN FAMILY PLANNING

There are several unique trends happening in family planning today that offer interesting contrasts to past historical periods. Among these are declining birth rates, delayed parenthood, and voluntary childlessness. Let's examine each more closely.

Declining Birth Rates

The current emphasis placed on overpopulation and deliberate family planning has reduced the number of children in today's homes. Statistics reveal that there are just about two children per household in the United States. It is projected that by 1990 there will be approximately 60 million American homes without children under the age of 15. It is also projected that the average family size in 1990 will be three, including parents and children (U.S. Bureau of the Census, 1984; Masnick and Bane, 1980). Figure 10-1 displays how the average family size is shrinking in the United States.

Why are birth rates declining? One obvious reason is that more people today are deciding not to get married. Another is that more marriages are child-free, which we'll discuss momentarily. As mentioned earlier, more couples today are also aware of the problems attached to overpopulation and are more deliberate in planning their families. Another reason is that children are expensive to raise. Once an economic commodity, children have become an economic liability. Recall from Chapter 2 that while many children were an asset to families living in preindustrial societies, this is not the case with families of the industrial age. Children today must be loved and wanted for rea-

sons other than the work they can perform (Saal, 1982).

The total cost of housing, feeding, and clothing one child, as well as educating him or her through college, are between $80,000 and $150,000 (Price, 1982). As schooling has lengthened, the financial drain of maintaining children within the home may be prolonged to almost 20 years. Consequently, few couples can afford large families anymore. Other reasons for having fewer children include greater numbers of women pursuing careers, the fact that females are becoming less emotionally dependent on males, the greater diversity of contraceptives now available, and the practice of abortion.

Delayed Parenthood

Another trend in family planning is delayed parenthood. Not only are the numbers of couples choosing to postpone parenthood increasing, they are also having fewer children. Delaying parenthood provides couples with the opportunity to develop their personal, career, and marital lives before they take on the responsibilities of parent-

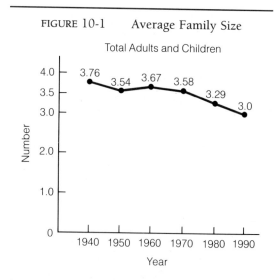

FIGURE 10-1   Average Family Size

Source: Adapted from the U.S. Bureau of the Census, (1986). *Statistical Abstract of the United States, 1986.* Washington, DC: U.S. Government Printing Office.

CROSS-CULTURAL FOCUS

DECLINING FAMILY SIZE REPORTED IN MANY NATIONS

The United States is not alone in its shrinkage of family size. On the contrary, it has been reported (Gallup, 1980) that small family size is a trend in many other nations. The results of this study show a decline since 1975 in the proportion of the public, in many countries, favoring large families. In Brazil, for example — a developing country whose population passed the 100-million mark in the 1970s — the percentage favoring families with four or more children has dropped sharply. A decline in the appeal of large families — although not so pronounced as in Brazil — is recorded in most other nations for which comparative data are available — Australia, Japan, and Italy, for example.

The survey showed that large families are found to be most popular in the Philippines, where 25 percent of those interviewed say the ideal number of children for a family to have is four or more. Australians are next most likely to favor large families, with 18 percent saying the ideal is four or more children. Large families tend to be less popular in Europe and the United States than in other parts of the world. In Belgium, one of the most densely-populated nations, only 4 percent of the public say four or more is the ideal number of children for a family to have and 6 percent believe a childless family is desirable.

Demographers and others concerned about the world's population growth and its attendant problems are heartened by these changes in family size. However, as the size of households shrinks in more and more nations, a unique demographic situation can develop: *negative population growth*. That is, rather than a population increase, a decrease results instead. Joseph McFalls (1981) projects that barring increased immigration, which is unlikely, or government intervention, the United States will reach zero population growth around 2020, and thereafter the number of individuals in the United States will actually decline, creating a negative population growth situation.

McFalls maintains that few societies face negative population growth with equanimity. Regardless of their objective circumstances, they believe it is in their interest, if not to grow, at least to remain stable in size. The family institution is almost always assigned the task of reproduction. If the family cannot accomplish this task satisfactorily, two alternatives exist: it can farm out the task in whole or in part to another institution such as the economic institution, or it can shore up the family institution, by making reproduction there more attractive.

This second option has already been tried by several populations who are at or near zero population growth. East and West Germany, Austria, Luxembourg, and Britain have already reached zero population growth and depopulation. Others, such as Czechoslovakia, Hungary, Denmark, Norway, and Sweden are on the verge of zero population growth or at least nearer to it than the United States is. The figure below displays those nations at, or approaching, zero population growth.   ▶

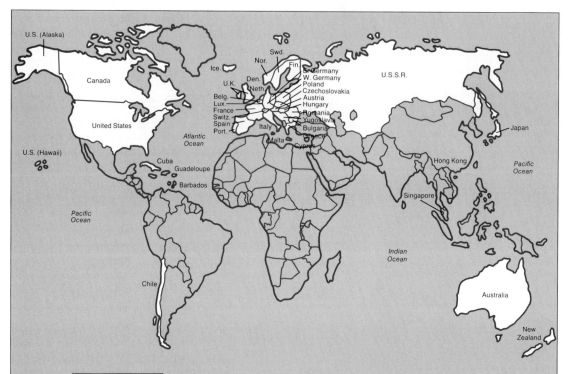

*Thirty-seven countries, indicated on white, are at or near zero population growth.
Source: Schaefer, 1986

Zero Population Growth Worldwide*

   The governments of many of these nations have already intervened in many ways to encourage couples to have more children, such as offering an interest-free credit of $10,000, excused entirely on the birth of the third child; reducing a mother's work week, but not her pay; giving preference on housing; providing free day-care centers; child bonuses; paid maternity and paternity leaves; and supplementary income for working mothers. In Sweden, despite many of the incentives, the birth rate for citizens fell below replacement level in the 1970s. Moreover, deaths have exceeded births since 1975. These programs have been more successful in Eastern Europe, however, due primarily to the tightening of abortion laws, a powerful pro-natalist tactic.

   As other nations deal with possible approaches to the problem, the United States must devise its own set of strategies. McFalls feels that the U.S. government will be heavily subsidizing reproduction within the family by the year 2000. He maintains that by then European nations will probably have devised the most cost-effective approaches. It is to be hoped that the United States will profit from the experience of its overseas neighbors.

hood (Ford, 1981; Wilkie, 1981; Knaub, Eversoll, and Voss, 1983).

The Demographics of Delay   David Bloom's (1984) review of the literature indicates that certain demographic factors can help to explain the scope of delayed parenthood. These factors include:

■ A woman who is white, highly educated, and pursuing a career is most likely to delay the birth of her first child. Educational level is the most critical variable influencing the age at which a woman begins childbearing. The more education a woman has, the older she will be when her first child is born. Also, as the educational level of American women increases, more women are delaying parenthood.

■ While black women tend to start their families at earlier ages, the effect of a woman's race on the age at which she bears her first child becomes less significant when aspects of her socioeconomic background, and especially her education, are considered.

■ Females in high-status occupations tend to be older than other women when they have their first child. Also, the closer a wife's earnings parallel her husband's, the more likely she is to delay parenthood.

■ Women raised in urban settings, Catholic women, and those whose parents are well educated and whose fathers have relatively high-status occupations tend to be older when they have their first child. However, when the woman's education level is held constant these associations lose their significance. In a similar sense, the number of siblings a woman has, or the instability of her parents' marriage are not as important in determining the age at which she begins childbearing as the number of years she attended school.

■ The age at which a woman becomes a first-time parent depends on when she herself was born and when she married. Events such as wars and fluctuations in the business cycle caused by unemployment, inflation, and recession also explain some variation in the timing of a woman's first child.

■ Since there are a limited number of childbear-

ing years (typically ending in a woman's late 40s, the longer a woman remains childless, the smaller the probability that she will have a child. And, the longer women postpone having children, the more health risks they face. Females over age 30 are more susceptible to circulatory problems, kidney ailments, and problem pregnancies than their younger counterparts.

■ Mortality rates associated with pregnancy and childbirth are substantially higher for women in their 30s and 40s than they are for younger women. The risk of Down's syndrome escalates with the age of the mother. Furthermore, while a female is waiting for the "right" time to bear children, she is exposing herself to deleterious health consequences associated with certain kinds of contraception and with abortion. Bloom also points out that chance must be taken into consideration. Even after a woman decides—on the basis of her preferences, financial situation, and physiological condition—when to have children, chance occurrences can cause her to give birth before or after she planned to. Overall contraceptive failure occurs at an average rate of 7.7 percent per year, a topic to be discussed later in this chapter. The probability of conception itself varies with age and the individual. Other random factors include the age at which a woman begins intercourse and the fecundity of her sexual partner.

Pros and Cons of Delayed Parenthood   Older women who have developed competence in the world before bearing children often bring to the mothering experience strengths different from those of their younger counterparts. Older mothers with established careers are often more accepting and less conflicted in the parenting role than younger professional women. They have a tendency to reveal strengths concomitant with their level of maturity that are generally advantageous for their children's development. Research has indicated that levels of marital satisfaction are higher among women postponing parenthood and childless women than among young mothers (Polonko, Scanzoni and Teachman, 1982).

Growing numbers of couples today are choosing to postpone parenthood.

There are also forces that may work against the couple who delay parenthood. Perhaps the biggest risk, as we've indicated, is that a woman's fertility will decrease with age and health risks will increase. Another problem is that older parents may not have the helping services of *their* aging parents. Also, parents delaying parenthood may find the tasks associated with childcare physically exhausting, maybe even more so than younger parents (Wilkie, 1981; Daniels and Weingarten, 1981).

Voluntary Childlessness

A third trend in family planning is **voluntary childlessness**. For these couples, a conscious decision has been made not to have children. Unlike couples wanting a family, voluntarily childless couples do not regard parenthood as a necessary ingredient for marital happiness or satisfaction.

It is estimated that 25 to 30 percent of young married women will elect not to have children (U.S. Bureau of the Census, 1980a, b). This is an interesting trend when compared to the high premium placed on having children during early historical periods. Recall that in the Old Testament, God's directive to Noah was, ''Be fruitful and multiply.'' Often, parents faced certain consequences if they did not bear children and produce large families. In the classical age of Greece, barrenness was sufficient grounds for a man to divorce his wife. And remember that in colonial America, single men were viewed with suspicion and penalized with special taxes for not doing their share to increase the population. This is a far cry from the sentiment expressed today in certain countries, such as the People's Republic of China, where parents are required to limit family size to one child.

Those couples choosing voluntary childlessness tend to be well educated, financially well off, and live in urban settings, although there are exceptions. In addition, they enjoy the company of one another and are very involved in their careers.

Marian Faux (1984) maintains that many childless couples believe that their parents were limited by the chores of parenting. Women, in particular, view their own mothers as never having the careers they longed for or believe that careers were cut short, once they became mothers.

The decision to remain childless is usually a difficult one. Recently an organization called the National Alliance for Optional Parenthood was formed to help couples in their decision making. Its central theme is that parenthood is a life option for couples, not a duty. The organization seeks to promote the idea that it is perfectly acceptable not to have children.

Research undertaken by Jean Veevers (1980) indicates that many couples who remain childless initially have no strong feelings either for or against parenthood. Many make the conventional assumption that, similar to others, they will probably eventually have one or two children. Veevers discovered that the transition from wanting to not wanting children typically evolves through four stages. These stages can be separated, but they are not discrete and discontinuous categories. Rather, they represent overlapping foci of the marriage at various times.

Postponement for a Definite Time   This initial stage involves postponing childbearing for a set amount of time. During this stage, the voluntarily childless are difficult to distinguish from the conventional and conforming couples who will eventually become parents. In most groups, it is not necessarily desirable for the bride to conceive during her honeymoon. It is considered understandable that, before starting a family, a couple might want to achieve certain goals, such as traveling, buying a house, or simply getting adjusted to one another. The reasons for waiting vary, but there remains a clear commitment to have children as soon as conditions are right.

During this stage, childless couples practice birth control conscientiously and continuously. Should the couple manage to postpone pregnancy deliberately for even a few months, they have es-

tablished a necessary but not a sufficient condition to voluntary childlessness, namely the habit of effective birth control within marriage. Once this happens, habit and inertia tend to make them continue with the same behavior. The couple now has the task of deciding whether or not they wish to stop using birth control so as to have a child. Although for the first few months of marriage the postponement of pregnancy is widely accepted, even at this stage the permanently childless are somewhat different from their preparental counterparts. Many conventional couples — even those who approve of birth control and have access to it — do not seriously try to control their own fertility until they have had at least one child.

Postponement for an Indefinite Time   During this stage, postponement for a *definite* time is replaced by an *indefinite* time frame. Couples often cannot recall exactly when they shifted into this second stage. They continue to remain committed to being parents, but become increasingly vague about when the blessed event is going to take place. It may be when they can ''afford it'' or when ''things are going better'' or when they ''feel more ready.''

Veevers found that some couples postpone parenthood until they feel that they can give children all the things they think children should have. Under these circumstances, this stage closely parallels the reticence felt by many parents who do not want children too soon. Often, couples are concerned with being able to spend enough time with their children, having an apartment or house big enough for them, or the couple's readiness to manage on one salary. These kinds of reasons are generally relatively acceptable, in that they are attempts to maximize the advantages available to children rather than to minimize the disadvantages that accrue to parents. A common consequence of such reasoning, however, is that the standards to be achieved before one is truly ''ready'' to have a child can escalate indefinitely, resulting in a series of successive ''temporary'' postponements.

Voluntary childlessness is a recent trend in family planning and offers a unique comparison to earlier historical eras.

Deliberating the Pros and Cons of Parenthood   Here, there is a qualitative change in the thinking of childless couples. For the first time there is an open acknowledgement of the possibility that, in the end, the couple may remain permanently childless. The only definite decision is to postpone deciding until some vague and unspecified time in the future.

Veevers found that husbands are often less articulate about their rationale for avoiding parenthood because they have tended to think about it considerably less than have their wives. Since wives most often raise the issue of the advantages of a child-free lifestyle, the husband interestingly enough often ends up in the role of the devil's advocate, articulating the advantages of children in order to encourage his mate to consider both sides of the issue.

Acceptance of Permanent Childlessness   At this time, a definite conclusion is reached that childlessness is a permanent rather than a transitory state. For most couples, there is never a direct decision made to avoid having children. Instead, after a number of years of postponing pregnancy until some future date, couples become aware that an implicit decision has been made to forego parenthood.

Overall, Veevers found that movement within a stage, or through the entire sequence, is affected by certain factors. For example, pregnancy "scares" tend to accelerate a couple from one state of postponement to the next. Other factors provide ample opportunity for continued delay. For instance, reasoning related to the advancing age of the mother is often employed. Here, a couple may feel that after a number of postponement years, childbearing is too great a medical risk for both mother and child. Or, a couple may feel that their tolerance of young children has been reduced because of their advancing age.

HUMAN REPRODUCTIVE SYSTEMS

Male Sexual Physiology

As we learned in Chapter 4, the male sex is determined at the moment of conception by the union of the egg containing the X chromosome with a sperm carrying the Y chromosome. Genetic messages contained on the Y chromosome are responsible for programming maleness throughout the course of sexual development.

The male reproductive system consists of the two testes, a network of ducts, a set of glands, and the penis. The **testes** are two oval-shaped glands located in the **scrotum**, a thin-walled pouch of skin hanging behind the penis. The function of the testes is to manufacture male sex hormones (**testosterone** and **androgen**) as well as **sperm** cells. Earlier, we discovered how sex hormones dictate the course of male secondary sex characteristics, such as body hair growth, voice change, and increased muscle mass.

CROSS-CULTURAL FOCUS

CHINA'S ONE-CHILD LIMIT

Family planning is not always a voluntary decision by couples. Indeed, in the People's Republic of China, where the population in 1984 hovered over the one billion mark, it is the government that dictates family planning. In an effort to reduce overpopulation, couples in this nation are allowed to have only one child. Furthermore, the government has raised the minimum age for marriage to 20 for women and 22 for men. Even later marriages are encouraged to reduce the couple's risk of having more than one child.

China's one-child limit represents one of the most dramatic family planning programs ever attempted in the world. China also becomes the first nation to ever restrict a couple's right to procreate. It seeks to accomplish this through incentives, peer pressure, and attempts to persuade newly married couples that their rational fertility decisions will mean a better future for their own families, their communities, and their nation. The government hopes to limit 95 percent of its urban families and 90 percent of rural families to the one-child limit. Such measures

The one-child limit in the People's Republic of China has attracted worldwide attention.

▶

would stabilize the population at 1.2 billion by the twenty-first century. Government officials fear that if this goal is not reached, China's ability to feed its people is in jeopardy, among other consequences (David, 1982).

Interestingly, China's family planning began with a two-child limit and an emphasis on later marriages and long intervals between births. The one-child limit was imposed in 1979, though, when government officials found that more drastic family planning measures would be needed. Demographics showed that with large numbers of young people due to reach marriage age in the next two decades, even a two-child average would mean continued population growth.

If Chinese couples follow such family planning legislation, the government awards a one-child "certificate." This special document entitles couples to numerous benefits including increased income levels, greater living space, large pensions, free education, lower-cost health care, and better nursing intervention. Eventually, the only child receives preferential treatment in the school system as well as in the labor force. Should couples give birth to a second child, the family forfeits all of these benefits. In some regions of China, the birth of more than one child leads to a 10 to 20 percent reduction in the parent's wages and a loss of promotion opportunities.

Complicating these family planning policies is the fact that Chinese families have traditionally preferred male children. Should a firstborn be female, couples may try to conceive again in an effort to bring a male into the world. This places couples at odds with the aforementioned policies, not to mention their consequences. Indeed, in one province of China, couples expecting a second child will have their wages docked if the woman decides not to have an abortion. In 1984, about one in every three pregnancies in China was aborted, bringing the total to about 8.9 million.

Adjacent to each testis is the **epididymis**, the first part of the genital duct system through which the sperm will pass (see Figure 10-2). Inside the epididymis are several ducts which direct sperm from the testes into the **vas deferens**. The vas deferens, or continuation of the epididymis, loops up into the body before descending into a duct in the **seminal vesicle** gland. This duct from the seminal vesicle joins the **ejaculatory duct**. The ejaculatory duct lies on the superior end of the prostate gland. From here, the duct stretches through the prostate gland and enters the upper segment of the **urethra**, the tube that connects the bladder to the outside of the body. At different times the urethra functions as an exit tube for urine as well as for sperm.

During their journey through the duct system, sperm combine with fluids from the male glands. The two main types of male glands are the seminal vesicles and the prostate gland. **Seminal vesicles** each lie near the underside of the bladder (storage depot for urine elimination from the body). They discharge a sticky, thick fluid that unites with the sperm cells emerging from the testes. The **prostate gland** is a small doughnut-shaped organ positioned so that it completely surrounds the urethra. The prostate gland secretes a substance that makes up the major portion of seminal fluid, which carries sperm outside the body. The secretions of the prostate gland also protect sperm cells from acid present in both the male urethra and the female vagina.

The **penis** is the external organ that propels

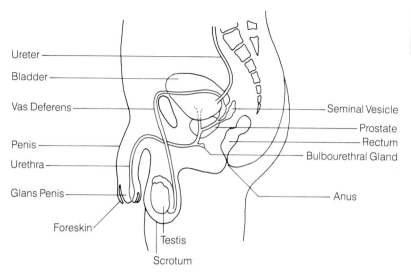

Ureter
Bladder
Vas Deferens
Penis
Urethra
Glans Penis
Foreskin
Testis
Scrotum

Seminal Vesicle
Prostate
Rectum
Bulbourethral Gland
Anus

FIGURE 10-2   Male Sexual Physiology

sperm into the female during sexual intercourse. In the nonexcited state, the penis is pendulous and flaccid and measures about 5 to 10 centimeters in length. When sexually excited, the large internal spaces, or *corpora cavernosa*, within the penis fill with blood. As the penis engorges, it becomes rigid enough to enter the female vagina. During ejaculation, semen formed in the urethra travels out of the penis.

Female Sexual Physiology

The female reproductive system consists of the ovaries, fallopian tubes, uterus, cervix, and vagina, The **ovaries**, two pinkish, almond-shaped glands located in the lower abdomen, monitor the cyclic functions of the reproductive system, which is based on ovulation. **Ovulation** is the monthly production and release of a mature egg or **ovum**. This action and other reproductive functions result from stimulation of hormones — estrogen and progesterone — secreted by the ovaries. As we learned in Chapter 4, **estrogen** regulates the secondary sex traits of body hair growth and breast development, as well as ovulation and menstruation. **Progesterone** contributes to reproduction, as

well as to enlargement of the breasts during pregnancy and milk production after childbirth. Both hormones coordinate to control the menstrual cycle. When an egg is released, it travels along the **fallopian tube** (see Figure 10-3). There are two fallopian tubes and they extend from each ovary into the uterus. Their reproductive function is to contain the egg until fertilization with the male sperm occurs. Fallopian tubes direct the sperm to the egg and then propel the fertilized egg, or zygote, into the uterus.

The **uterus** is a pear-shaped hollow organ about the size of a lemon. It is situated in the pelvis between the urinary bladder and the rectum. Its muscular walls are lined with rich, soft tissue called the **endometrium**. Each month the lining adds layers in anticipation of receiving and nourishing a fertilized egg. Should conception occur, the lining nourishes the fertilized eggs in the uterus until birth. However, if the egg remains unfertilized, the uterus sheds the endometrium and the unfertilized egg, which leave the body as menstrual discharge.

The lowermost portion of the uterus is called the **cervix**. The cervix is a narrow opening to an inch-long canal. This passageway connects the lower

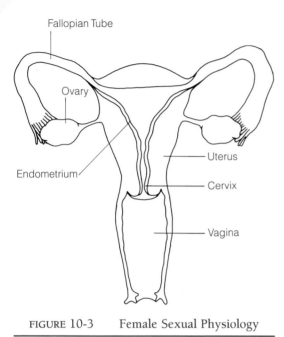

Fallopian Tube

Ovary

Endometrium

Uterus

Cervix

Vagina

FIGURE 10-3   Female Sexual Physiology

end of the uterus to the upper portion of the vagina. This canal carries sperm on their way to fertilize an egg and is the passageway for menstrual discharge and babies leaving the uterus.

The **vagina**, or birth canal, is a passageway leading from the uterus to the outside of the body. In the average adult female, it measures four to five inches in length. Although vaginal walls are normally close together, they separate to accomodate a descending baby during childbirth and the erect male penis during sexual intercourse. The vagina produces natural secretions that provide continual lubrication and cleansing of the organ.

CONTRACEPTION

Contraception, also known as birth control, is the voluntary prevention of pregnancy. The number of unwanted pregnancies each year (see Chapter 5) is clear evidence that nature stacks the odds heavily in favor of pregnancy when an effective form of contraception is not used. It is estimated that couples who use no contraceptive have a 90

percent chance of achieving pregnancy over the course of a year. The following discussion focuses on the more prevalent forms of birth control practiced today, the most popular of which are displayed in Figure 10-4.

Oral Contraception

Oral contraceptives, known more popularly as birth control pills, or "the pill," are the most effective method of contraception. When used properly, oral contraception is almost 100 percent effective. It is available by prescription only.

The pill uses synthetic female hormones, estrogen and progestin, to override the natural hormonal regulation that results in the release of an egg. The pill signals the pituitary gland, which directs hormonal activity in the body, not to release the hormones that would normally stimulate the ovary to release an egg. Another type of oral contraceptive, called the "mini-pill," is also available. The mini-pill contains progesterone alone and changes the female's cervical mucus so that no sperm can enter.

Oral contraceptives are preferred by many because of their effectiveness and because there is no interruption in lovemaking. For some, the pill also provides relief from painful periods. However, oral contraceptives do have disadvantages. They are not recommended for women with a history of high blood pressure, blood-clotting problems, hepatitis, or any cancer of the uterus or breast. And, a woman over age 35 who smokes heavily is advised to stop smoking if she wants to take the pill. Also, oral contraceptives should not be taken by a woman who suspects she may be pregnant. In addition, women with diabetes, epilepsy, heart or liver disease, and thyroid disease may be advised not to take the birth control pill, depending on the nature and severity of the disease.

Intrauterine Devices

An **intrauterine device (IUD)** is made of plastic, usually coated with copper wire, and designed in a variety of shapes. It is inserted in the womb by an obstetrician (see Figure 10-5) and can remain in

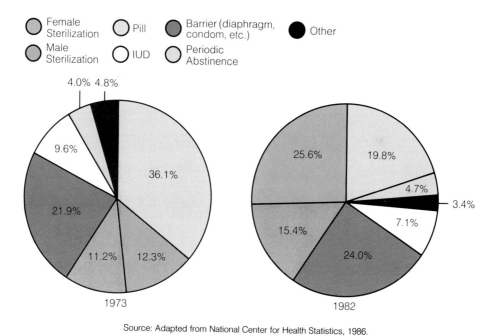

Female Sterilization · Pill · Barrier (diaphragm, condom, etc.) · Other
Male Sterilization · IUD · Periodic Abstinence

1973

1982

Source: Adapted from National Center for Health Statistics, 1986.

FIGURE 10-4 Popularity of Birth Control Methods

place for several years if no difficulties arise. The IUD prevents pregnancy by not allowing a fertilized egg to implant itself in the uterine lining.

Intrauterine devices are about 95 percent effective, making them a reliable method of contraception. The IUD is often chosen because it does not disrupt lovemaking and because one need not worry about contraception each day. In recent years, however, there have been increasing numbers of problems with intrauterine devices. For example, if you use an IUD you risk perforation, which may result in intestinal obstruction, infection, or bowel strangulation. Severe menstrual cramps and increased menstrual bleeding may also follow the insertion of an IUD. In addition, the IUD may be expelled, creating discomfort and bleeding. Because of these combined health risks, the manufacture of IUDs has almost disappeared in America.

FIGURE 10-5 The Intrauterine Device (IUD)

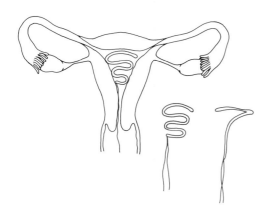

The Diaphragm

The **diaphragm** is a thin sheet of rubber or latex stretched over a collapsible spring rim. The diaphragm is coated with a spermicidal (an agent that kills sperm) jelly or cream and inserted into the vagina so that it covers the entrance to the uterus; thus, no sperm can enter (see Figure 10-6).

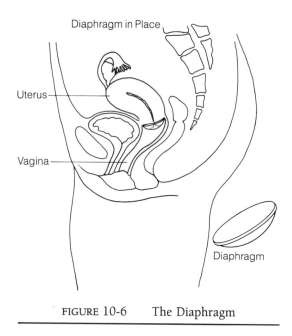

Diaphragm in Place

Uterus

Vagina

Diaphragm

FIGURE 10-6   The Diaphragm

The diaphragm requires a doctor's fitting and prescription.

Diaphragms are quite effective, leaving only a 3 to 5 percent chance of pregnancy. The diaphragm and spermicidal jelly or cream are also considered very safe, having essentially no health risks. However, a diaphragm can become dislodged, and lovemaking must be interrupted for insertion. Added cream or jelly is also needed prior to repeated intercourse, a factor that may inhibit sexual spontaneity.

The Condom

The **condom** is the only current form of contraception directly under the male's control. The condom is a thin rubber or synthetic sheath that is fitted over the penis prior to intercourse. The sheath catches semen so that it cannot enter the vagina.

The condom is as effective as the diaphragm when used correctly, especially with the use of a spermicide. There are also no health risks with the condom; indeed, the use of a condom can help prevent the transmission of venereal diseases.

However, interruption in lovemaking is necessary and tiny holes or tears in the condom can cause leakage of sperm. In addition, when the penis is withdrawn from the vagina, the condom can sometimes break or partially unroll inside the vagina, thus releasing its contents.

Spermicides

Spermicides are available in aerosol foams, creams, jellies, tablets, or suppositories. They are used by injecting a premeasured amount of the desired foam into the vagina no more than an hour before intercourse. The spermicide acts to immobilize the sperm, thus preventing pregnancy.

Spermicides are between 75 and 85 percent effective when used correctly. While health risks are at a minimum, spermicides have to be applied before every act of intercourse, and the application tends to be somewhat untidy. Some spermicides also have a chemical odor.

Contraceptive Sponge

The **contraceptive sponge** is a fairly recent innovation and represents a variation on spermicides. It is a disposable, sponge-like device saturated with spermicide. The sponge is inserted into the vagina up against the cervix where the device works by continuously releasing spermicide for up to 24 hours. Additional applications of spermicide are not necessary even for multiple acts of intercourse.

The contraceptive sponge is approximately 85 percent effective. Unlike a diaphragm, it does not have to be fitted and can be inserted ahead of time, allowing greater sexual spontaneity. However, sensitivity to chemicals may cause irritation and there is some speculation that the inserted sponge may become a breeding ground for infection if used improperly.

The Rhythm Method

The **rhythm method,** or **natural family planning method,** of birth control requires refraining from intercourse on days when pregnancy can occur.

CROSS-CULTURAL FOCUS

BIRTH CONTROL AROUND THE GLOBE

Societies throughout the world have developed a number of ways for regulating the size of their population. Coitus interruptus, or penis withdrawal prior to ejaculation, is supposed to be the most widely used contraception method cross-culturally. It is also the least effective method of birth control. However, on the small Pacific island of Tikopia, it was once part of a conscious population control policy and was used by the married and unmarried alike.

Attempts to remove the semen from the vagina are also reported from a few societies. Kavirondo women stand up after coitus and shake their bodies in a quick jerky rhythm. Sande women try to get rid of the semen by slapping their backs.

Some Navaho believe that certain drugs will render even men sterile, but for the most part *all* drugs are taken by women. Certain indian tribes in Nevada make use of a plant *Lithospermum ruderale*, which has been subject to scientific investigations and found to inhibit the functioning of rats' ovaries.

Contraceptive charms are also not rare. A "snake girdle," made of beaded leather and worn over the navel, was used by certain Plains Indians. And ancient Roman charms included the liver of a cat placed in a tube and worn on the left foot, or a part of a lioness's womb kept in an ivory tube.

Considerably more effective than these devices is abortion, which is tolerated and even institutionalized in a great many societies, and practiced in a great many others. Hunting and gathering groups know numerous plant and animal poisons that are effective in inducing miscarriages. Other means include the tying of tight bands round the stomach, beating the stomach or inserting sharp sticks into the vagina.

Adapted from Gregersen, 1982.

This is the only method of birth control approved by the Roman Catholic Church. Couples using the rhythm method calculate when the woman ovulates, determine her fertile period, and structure their sex lives accordingly. The abstinence period before, during, and after ovulation is usually between seven and ten days.

The effectiveness rate for this kind of natural family planning is about 70 to 80 percent, depending on extreme planning and care. It obviously does not require the use of mechanical aids or drugs, considered by many to be a big advantage. However, even in women with regular cycles, illness, fatigue, stress, or even a vacation can delay ovulation and throw off the most deliberate and carefully planned calculations. Figure 10-7 illustrates the failure rate of the rhythm method compared with other forms of birth control.

Future Contraceptive Possibilities

Researchers throughout the world are exploring a variety of contraceptive devices beyond those just described. The ultimate goal is to provide men and women with a contraceptive device that combines safety, effectiveness, and ease of use. Among the more promising devices, although still in experimental stages, are the following:

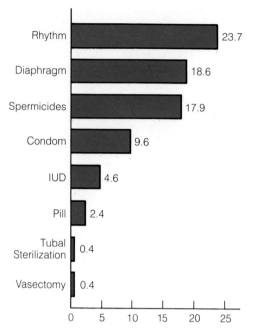

FIGURE 10-7   Unexpected Pregnancy and the Birth Control Methods Used

---

"Morning After" Pill   This form of oral contraceptive, known more technically as RU-486, induces a miscarriage in the early weeks of pregnancy. The pill, designed to be taken after a woman has missed her first period, is about 70 percent effective when given to women in the first 40 to 50 days of pregnancy. However, recent studies indicate that when RU-486 is combined with another drug, *prostagladin,* the success rate increases to 90 percent.

Male Oral Contraceptive   The possibility of a male oral contraceptive may lie in *gossypol,* a cotton-based extract. This substance has been given in pill form to men in China in an effort to curb that nation's overpopulation problem. We know that it inhibits sperm mobility and production. However, while it has been effective in preventing pregnancy, it has produced serious side effects including infertility after discontinuing use and a loss of potassium in the body. The World Health Organization is currently working on modifications of the drug.

Contraceptive Nasal Sprays   Another contraceptive possibility for both women and men is a special nasal spray. For females, the spray contains a synthetic hormone that mimics the pituitary gland and is used once each day to inhibit ovulation. Early testing indicates the hormone is effective but dosage is difficult to regulate. Side effects include some irregular bleeding and postmenopausal symptoms. The nasal spray for men is less promising. In men, the hormone inhibits sperm production, but they need much larger doses and a sustained release form needs to be developed.

Contraceptive Vaccines   This is a possibility, once again, for both women and men. The vaccine for women is made from the urine of pregnant women and produces antibodies that interrupt the hormone action that would support a pregnancy. For men, the vaccine originates from a pituitary gland hormone that interferes with sperm production but not male sex hormone production. The contraceptive vaccine for both women and men is still very much in the experimental stage.

Levonorgestrel Releasing Intrauterine Device   This special IUD is inserted and removed in the same way as those currently used, but contains a steroid that is released into the uterus. It can remain in place for up to five years, and in clinical trials, users showed less of the heavy bleeding problems associated with the present IUD.

Subdermal Implants   With this form of contraception for women, six small rubber capsules implanted under the skin of the arm slowly release small doses of progesterone to block ovulation. These implants, which can be inserted and removed in a doctor's office, are supposed to block pregnancy for five years. Because the implants do not contain estrogen, they are considered safer and avoid some of the side effects found in the pill. However, they do cause some irregular menstrual bleeding. The implants are currently available in Finland and Sweden.

Vaginal Ring   The vaginal ring is shaped like a thin donut and secretes hormones designed to prevent pregnancy. It can be worn in the vagina for

21 days, then removed for seven days to allow for menstrual bleeding. Rings containing both progestin and estrogen, and progestin alone are currently being evaluated. Side effects are minimal and the pregnancy rate in clinical research is 2 percent, about the same as the pill.

STERILIZATION

Sterilization is a surgical procedure that interrupts the reproductive tracts of either the male or female so that fertilization is prevented. In recent years, voluntary sterilization has increased in popularity. Among the reasons for this are the simplification of surgical procedures, the female's desire for a career beyond that of a homemaker, and consciousness of the world population problem.

Male Sterilization

A **vasectomy** is a relatively simple surgical procedure in which the vas deferens are cut to prevent the passage of sperm. In the surgery, a tiny incision is made in the scrotum on either side (or sometimes a small incision in the midfrontal area) and each vas deferens is cut and cauterized (see Figure 10-8). The surgery can be done in 15 or 20 minutes in a doctor's office under local anesthesia. The vasectomy does not interfere with ejaculation, since the sperm constitute only a very small portion of the semen. The sperm that are still produced by the testes degenerate and are reabsorbed by the body.

Following the vasectomy, a male is considered sterile when two consecutive semen examinations are found to be negative and when three weeks have transpired. The recovery period from a vasectomy is about two days of relative inactivity. Sexual relations can usually be resumed within a week or so, and the male's sexual response and orgasm are normal.

The vasectomy operation itself is considered almost 100 percent effective. Surgical reversal of a vasectomy is quite difficult and failure rates are high. The primary reason for this is because sperm counts remain low following surgery. Sperm anti-

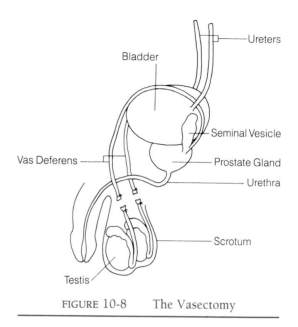

FIGURE 10-8   The Vasectomy

bodies produced by the body also account for low sperm counts.

Vasectomies have become more acceptable to men because the once common, erroneous idea that such surgery would destroy a man's sexual power has been dispelled and most people are now aware that it in no way affects or changes sexual desire or the ability to satisfy it. A vasectomy does not effect the man's capacity to have an erection or ejaculate, as we noted. Other reasons for its popularity are that it is simpler and less costly than female sterilization.

Female Sterilization

The most popular form of female sterilization is a type of surgery called **tubal ligation**, more commonly referred to as "tying the tubes." New instruments and surgical procedures permit tubal ligation to be done under local or short-acting general anesthesia. Two of these procedures are **minilaparotomy** and **laparascopy**.

Minilaparotomy, sometimes called "minilap," involves a small abdominal incision of less than 3 centimeters. Each fallopian tube is gently pulled to this incision, blocked by cutting and tying the cut ends or by applying clips or rings, and allowed to

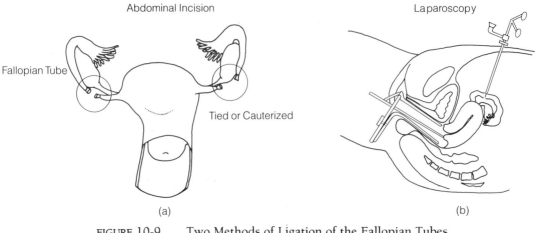

FIGURE 10-9   Two Methods of Ligation of the Fallopian Tubes

slip back into place (see Figure 10-9). Laparoscopy involves inserting a telescope-like instrument into the abdomen, through which a doctor can see the internal organs and block the tubes by cauterizing them or by applying rings or clips. Either procedure can be performed on most women in about 10 to 20 minutes, usually without an overnight hospital stay.

The minilaparotomy and laparoscopy are both highly effective. Pregnancy rates after one year are usually less than one per 100 women. Among the more common reasons for pregnancies after sterilization are a pregnancy already conceived but too early to recognize, a surgical error in identifying a fallopian tube, spontaneous rejoining of a severed tube, or formation of a new passage in the tube that allows sperm and egg to join.

As with the vasectomy, these surgical procedures do not decrease feelings of sexuality. Patients are advised to rest at home for a few days, and to refrain from sexual intercourse for about five weeks. Menstruation will continue and the ovaries will still release eggs, but they are trapped in the blocked-off tubes and reabsorbed by the body.

ABORTION

One other form of family planning is **abortion**. Abortion was first outlawed in the 1800s to protect women from primitive methods and unskilled practitioners of pregnancy termination. Prior to this country's law, based upon the Common Law of England, the death rate from abortions rivaled that of major operations.

In 1973, the Supreme Court ruled that a state cannot interfere with the decision of a woman to effect an abortion during the first trimester of pregnancy (a woman's pregnancy is divided into three, three-month segments called *trimesters*). The court further ruled that during the second trimester the state could impose only those regulations relating to the pregnant woman's health and safety, and that abortion could be prohibited during the third trimester only if such prohibition posed no threat to the woman's life or health. This decision gives a woman the freedom to choose whether or not to continue a pregnancy and, if she decides to terminate it, the right to do so safely, legally, and with dignity.

Definitions and Procedures

An **induced abortion** should not be confused with a **spontaneous abortion**, or miscarriage. The latter occurs when pregnancy terminates before the developing organism is mature enough to survive outside the womb. Physiologically, this happens when the embryo separates from the uterine wall and is expelled by the uterus. It is estimated that 10 percent of all pregnancies end in spontaneous abortion, usually during the first two or three months. Precipitating factors that have been identified include severe trauma, abnormalities of the reproductive tract, and maternal viral and bacterial infections.

Induced abortions are deliberate, external attempts to remove the organism from the uterus. Rates of induced abortion are quite high in the United States, as they are in other nations such as the Soviet Union, Rumania, Cuba, and Japan. The following are the more common forms of induced abortion:

Vacuum Aspiration   This is a first trimester procedure that involves a local anesthesia and dilation of the cervix. A small, hollow tube attached to a vacuum machine is inserted through the cervix into the uterus, which is emptied by gentle suction. This procedure generally takes a few minutes and the patient recovers in a few hours.

Dilation and Curettage   This is also a first trimester procedure. Following local or general anesthesia and dilation of the cervix, fetal material is removed from the uterine wall with a small, spoon-shaped curette. This procedure takes a few minutes and the patient recovers the same day.

Dilation and Evacuation   Dilation and Evacuation is a fairly recent medical innovation and can be performed between the thirteenth and twentieth weeks of pregnancy. It involves local anesthesia, a slow and gradual dilation of the cervix, and removal of the fetal material by an alternation of suction and curettage. This procedure requires only a few hours' recovery period.

Amniotic Fluid Replacement   This technique is a second trimester procedure usually performed between the sixteenth and twentieth weeks of pregnancy (18 to 22 weeks from the last menstrual period). A small amount of amniotic fluid is withdrawn from the uterus and replaced with a concentrated saline solution which causes contractions within 12 to 24 hours and eventual miscarriage. Another technique of inducing miscarriage is by injecting a hormone called *prostaglandin* into the uterus. Both of these procedures may require a hospital stay.

Hysterotomy   This procedure is carried out at between the sixteenth and twenty-fourth week and major surgery is required. An incision is made through the abdominal wall and the fetus is removed. A hysterotomy may require a hospital stay of four to seven days and full recovery may take up to several weeks. Once a hysterotomy is performed, all future deliveries are usually by caesarian.

The earlier an abortion is performed, the safer the procedures. After an abortion, regular menstrual periods usually start again in a month or two. It is incorrect to think that pregnancy does not occur for extended lengths of time beyond abortion. Indeed, pregnancy can occur before a woman's next period if birth control is not used. If the pill is the method of choice it can generally be used right away. An IUD can also be iserted at the

CROSS-CULTURAL FOCUS

PRIVATE LIVES, PUBLIC POLICIES

In the Soviet Union, where contraceptives are both unpopular and hard to obtain, the average woman has six abortions in her lifetime. In Kenya, where a man's wealth is often measured by the number of his children, the average woman bears eight children. In Mexico City, where herbal abortifacients are sold in markets, four out of five beds in the Woman's Hospital are filled by women suffering complications after illegal abortions. In Italy, where abortion has been ▶

legal since 1978, Pope John Paul II condemns even contraception, fueling fierce political debate.

An endless variety of laws, restrictions, customs and traditions affects the practice of abortion around the world, although the general trend is toward liberalized laws. In the study, *Induced Abortion: A World Review*, 1981, by Dr. Christopher Tietze, we see the following findings: 9 percent of the world's 4.4 billion people live in countries that totally forbid abortion (among them: Spain, the Dominican Republic, and Indonesia); 38 percent live in nations where abortion on request is allowed, at least in the first trimester of pregnancy; the rest live under laws that allow abortions under conditions that range from saving the mother's life to economic hardship. In the past 15 years, 17 countries (including Canada, India, Norway, and Great Britain) have liberalized their abortion laws; in the same period, seven nations (Bulgaria, Czechoslovakia, Hungary, Rumania, Iran, Israel, and New Zealand) have adopted tougher legislation.

There are still some anomalies in generally liberal Western Europe. In Belgium, abortion is allowed only to save a mother's life. As a result, thousands of women travel a few miles north to the Netherlands, where 75 percent of the legally restricted but officially tolerated procedures are performed on foreigners. Among their own citizens, the conservative Dutch have the lowest abortion rate of any West European nation.

In Latin America, abortion is legal only in Cuba, but law does not necessarily determine practice. Argentines routinely weekend in Uraguay to shop — and to have illegal but readily available abortions. In Brazil, the government is slowly introducing a national family planning program (in deference to the church, the words "birth control" are not used), while a morbid and lucrative illegal abortion business thrives. The United States provides, through various aid programs, 16 percent of the world's family planning funds. No U.S. aid goes for abortions, but right-to-life groups, claiming that family planning promotes abortion, are demanding further restrictions.

Antiabortionists in New Zealand succeeded in passing legislation in 1977 that required cumbersome review procedures by medical consultants to determine the extent of physical or mental danger to the mother. The abortion rate dropped briefly as 3,000 women a year flew to Australia for legal abortions. Recently, New Zealand women have learned to present the required symptoms (mainly psychiatric) for abortion, and the rate has returned to about 4,000 a year.

Adapted from Jane O'Reilly, Private lives, public policies, *Time*, 1981, April 6, p. 27. Copyright 1981 Time Inc. All rights reserved. Reprinted by permission from TIME. ■

time of early abortion. A diaphragm can be fitted at a woman's follow-up visit after her uterus has returned to its normal size. The contraceptive sponge can only be used after all bleeding stops, preferably after the first normal menstrual period. Foam, condoms, and abstinence can always be used. And rhythm methods may be used beginning with the first normal menstrual period.

Before closing, let us also acknowledge the psychological implications of abortion. For the female, the termination of a pregnancy can be a devastating emotional experience. Depression, loneliness, and guilt are common reactions not only before the operation but also afterwards, While competent and qualified medical care is needed for the operation, attention should also be directed to the woman's psychological needs.

CHAPTER HIGHLIGHTS

In the recent past, we have seen several trends in family planning: declining birth rates, delayed parenthood, and voluntary childlessness. This chapter explored these trends and how they contrast with past eras. In order to better understand fertility and patterns of family planning, we also explored male and female sexual physiology and how conception takes place.

Contraception, also called birth control, is the voluntary prevention of pregnancy. The more popular methods of birth control include oral contraception, the intrauterine device, diaphragm, condom, spermicides, contraceptive sponge, and the rhythm method. Of these, oral contraception is the most effective, while the rhythm has the highest rates of failure. Future contraceptive possibilities include a "morning after" pill, male oral contraceptives, birth control in the form of nasal sprays, contraceptive vaccines, a levonorgestral releasing intrauterine device, subdermal implants, and a vaginal ring.

Sterilization is a surgical procedure that interrupts the reproductive tracts of either the male or female so that fertilization is prevented. For males, a vasectomy is the procedure in which the vas deferens are cut to prevent the passage of sperm. For females, a tubal ligation can be performed with the surgical procedures known as a minilaparotomy or laparascopy.

We concluded with a discussion of abortion. An induced abortion is a deliberate attempt to remove the organism from the uterus. Induced abortion procedures include vacuum aspiration, dilation and curettage, dilation and evacuation, amniotic fluid replacement, and hysterotomy. It is generally recognized that the earlier an abortion is performed, the safer it is.

KEY TERMS

abortion
amniotic fluid replacement
androgen
cervix
condom
contraception
contraceptive sponge
contraceptive vaccine
delayed parenthood
diaphragm
dilation and curettage
dilation and evacuation
ejaculatory duct
endometrium
epididymis

estrogen
fallopian tube
family planning
hysterotomy
induced abortion
intrauterine device (IUD)
laparascopy
levonorgestrel releasing
  intrauterine device
male oral contraception
minilaporatomy
"morning after" pill
oral contraceptive
ovaries
ovulation

ovum
penis
progesterone
prostate gland
rhythm method
scrotum
seminal vesicles
sperm
spermicide
spontaneous abortion
sterilization
subdermal implants
testes
testosterone
tubal ligation

urethra   vagina   vasectomy
uterus   vaginal ring   voluntary childlessness
vacuum aspiration

RECOMMENDED READINGS

Chen, P. C. (1984). Birth planning and fertility transition. *Annals of the American Academy of Political and Social Science* (Vol. 476), 128–141. The author describes government policies in the People's Republic of China related to birth control.

Faux, M. (1984). *Childless by choice.* New York: Doubleday. A good overview of voluntary childlessness, including a personal look at those couples preferring this lifestyle.

Fox, G. L. (Ed.). (1982). *The childbearing decision: Fertility attitudes and behavior.* Beverly Hills, CA: Sage. This reader explores fertility decision making from diverse disciplinary perspectives.

Garfield, J. L., and Hennessey, P. (Eds.). (1984). *Abortions: Moral and legal perspectives.* Amherst, MA: University of Massachusetts Press. Readers wanting to explore the moral and legal complexities of abortion will find this to be an excellent collection of articles.

Goldstein, M., and Feldberg, M. (1982). *The vasectomy book.* Boston: Houghton Mifflin. This book provides a good analysis of the vasectomy decision, including what it surgically entails.

Jones, E. F. (1984). The availability of contraceptive services. *Comparative Studies,* No. 37, London: World Fertility Survey. The types of birth control services available in 21 countries are reviewed in this comprehensive report.

Planned Parenthood. (1981). *Family planning in the 1980's: Challenges and opportunities.* New York: Planned Parenthood Federation. The accomplishments of family planning in 63 nations highlight this volume.

Polit-O'Hara, D., and Berman, J. (1984). *Just the right size: A guide to family planning size.* New York: Praeger. The authors present a guide to individual parents to assist them in developing guidelines for deciding the number of children best suited to their needs.

Shostak, A. B., McLouth, G., and Seng, L. (1984). *Men and abortion: Lessons, losses, and love.* New York: Praeger. This book shows how men are concerned about abortion, their responsibility for pregnancy, and their involvement in the decision to go ahead with the abortion.

Tucker, T. (1981). *Birth control.* Wynne, PA: Banbury Books. A good overview of the major forms of contraception and how they should be used.

11

Conception, Pregnancy, and Childbirth

CONTENTS

CONTEMPLATIONS

■ Frank and Louise Henderson have always wanted to have children, but can't because of infertility. The problem, according to the doctors, is that Louise has a defective fallopian tube, the result of scarring from a past infection. Undaunted, the Hendersons are now turning to sophisticated medical technology to help them conceive a child: in-vitro fertilization. This chapter explores this and other modern-day techniques that add a new twist to conception and pregnancy. Read on and learn more about high-tech pregnancies in the 1980s.

■ A child is born—we call it a miracle of life. Yet even more remarkable are the prenatal developments that occur in the womb before birth. During these first nine months, a single fleck of tissue transforms into a fully developed fetus. What factors account for such profound growth and development? What observations can be made about the earliest beginnings of life? Join us as we search for answers.

■ How do you plan to deliver your baby? This is a question unasked in bygone eras, since virtually all babies entered the world in a traditional birthing fashion. Today, though, this is not the case. Increasing numbers of couples are selecting nontraditional birthing techniques, such as the Lamaze approach to natural childbirth. What does this approach, and others like it, entail? What factors account for the popularity of nontraditional childbirth approaches? Toward the end of this chapter, we'll direct our attention to these topics.

Congratulations Mr. and Mrs. Jones. . . . It's a girl! Each year, about 3,500,000 babies are born in the United States. When this moment arrives, parents from all walks of life experience a myriad of emotions, from joyous awe and delight to serene satisfaction and contentment.

Couples report many reasons for wanting children. For some, children represent an extension of the self. They are also a source of personal fulfillment and represent an enhancement of a couple's identity. Some adults want children because they look forward to the companionship that they'll bring. Others maintain that children will provide security to them when they're old. Finally, many want children because of social expectations. In other words, it's the thing to do when you're married.

Of course, just as with marriage, there are many wrong reasons for having children. Having a baby because one's parents want grandchildren should not be the only motivation. Furthermore, a baby is not the cure for a marriage void of meaning. Some couples use the exclusive measure of financial stability before they have children, but financial security by itself is not a sound motive for having children. Neither is the singular motive that a baby will give a totally bored couple something to do. Although a child will certainly be a source of activity, couples with this underlying motive often become just as bored with childcare chores.

In this chapter, we'd like to examine the earliest beginnings of life, starting with the moment of conception. We have a tendency to regard birth as one of life's most cherished miracles, and rightfully so. Yet, even more remarkable is the process whereby a single fertilized egg develops into a fully functioning infant—complete with arms, legs, eyes, internal organs, and a personality all its own. Equally compelling is the physiological and psy-

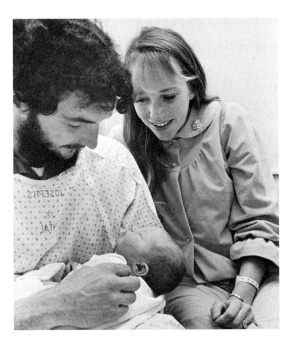

Parenthood yields many experiences of pride and satisfaction, but few surpass life's early beginnings.

chological impact that pregnancy has on the mother, climaxed by the delivery itself—a shared event for a growing number of couples today.

But not all couples are successful in conceiving a child; infertility stands in the way for many couples wanting to have children on their own. Let's begin then with a discussion of infertility, including some pretty sophisticated measures used to overcome this problem.

INFERTILITY

Infertility is defined as *the inability to carry pregnancies to live birth.* It is estimated that about 15 percent of the population—approximately one in six couples—is infertile at any given time. However, patience is sometimes the answer for many of these couples. Statistical evidence reveals that for normal women who aren't using birth control and are sexually active, 25 percent will be pregnant within one month, 63 percent will be in 6 months, and 80 percent will be in one year. An additional 5 to 10 percent will become pregnant the following year (Hotchner, 1984).

Physiological Causes of Infertility

For other couples, though, infertility represents a physiological problem. About 40 percent of infertility problems can be traced to the male. Among the more common causes are *poor sperm quality, low sperm count,* or *poor sperm motility (movement)*. Another 40 percent of infertility difficulties originate from the female: *irregular ovulation, damaged fallopian tubes,* or *the presence of cervical mucus,* which acts as a barrier to sperm. Twenty percent of the time, couples share the problem or infertility and the reasons often remain unknown.

Aging also contributes to infertility. Females under age 25 have about a 7 percent chance of being infertile, but by the age of 40, one out of every three females is unable to have a child. A woman in her thirties does not have many fertile years left. There are no equivalent figures for male infertility, but once again, it is partly determined by age; a man of 50 generally has a lower sperm count than a man of 20, although the natural decrease in his sperm count may not prevent him from having children if enough of his remaining sperm are healthy (Lauersen, 1983).

High-Tech Pregnancies

In about 75 percent of the cases involving infertility, pregnancy is possible with the use of new drugs and/or microsurgery. Other methods, although in the experimental stages, offer hope to the remainder of couples facing this problem. These techniques, often dubbed "high-tech" pregnancies, include **in-vitro fertilization, artificial insemination by donor, surrogate motherhood,** and **embryo transfer.**

In-vitro Fertilization (IVF)   Originally called "test-tube pregnancies," in-vitro fertilizations are one of the most popular forms of high-tech pregnancies. The first successful in-vitro fertilization took place in July 1978 in Oldham, England. For John and Lesley Brown, parents of baby Louise, the birth was a triumphant event that ended years of frustration at not being able to conceive a child. Mrs. Brown's primary problem was a malfunctioning fallopian tube. For Patrick Steptoe and Robert Edwards, the two British physicians who masterminded this dramatic medical breakthrough, the birth was the successful culmination of over 12 years of intensive research and experimentation. Since that first birth, an estimated 900 babies have been conceived this way, including 300 in the United States.

In-vitro fertilization involves a unique medical procedure. First an incision is made in the woman's abdomen. With a special device called a laparascope, the physician is able to see inside the abdomen and remove the egg from the ovary. The egg is then placed in a dish where it is fertilized

with the male sperm. After this is done, the **zygote** (fertilized egg) is placed in another dish of life-sustaining serum for approximately five days. Here it develops into a cluster of cells and is technically called a *blastocyte*. After the mother receives hormonal treatments to prepare the uterine wall for implantation, the blastocyte is placed in the uterus, where it embeds itself and continues its normal prenatal development. From conception in the laboratory, life continues in the womb of the mother.

Artificial Insemination by Donor This technique is used when the male experiences infertility but the female is fertile. Sperm donors are screened and matched as closely to the husband as possible for such characteristics as ethnic background, stature, complexion and blood type. Special screening is also given to prevent genetic de-

In the technique of in-vitro fertilization, sperm is added to the mature ovum.

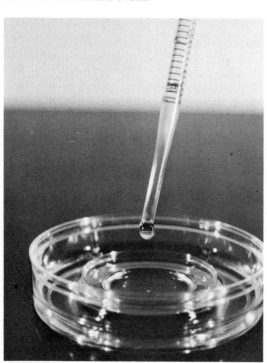

Once conception takes place, early cell division takes place.

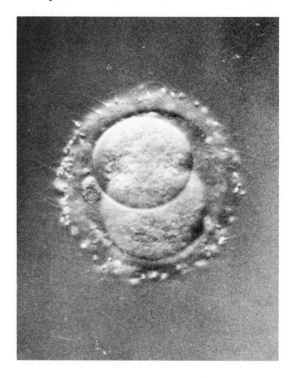

fects, sexually transmitted diseases, and other potential problems.

Total anonymity exists between the donor and recipient. The donor's sperm is placed in the female's cervix at the fertile part of her ovulation cycle. While fresh sperm is preferred, frozen sperm can also be used, and in about 75 percent of the cases, pregnancy occurs by the third attempt.

Surrogate Motherhood   Surrogate motherhood is usually the last resort for females who cannot conceive a baby on their own. Here, a chosen surrogate mother is artificially inseminated with the husband's sperm. The surrogate mother carries and bears the child, which is then given to the couple.

It is estimated that about 200 babies have been born via surrogate motherhood. Costs for such a service, usually sponsored by a clinic or center, are approximately $25,000. This often includes a $10,000 fee outright to the surrogate mother; the remainder goes for the center's expenses, including medical and legal fees. Often these specialized centers advertise on a continual basis for new surrogate mothers (see the accompanying box for a representative newspaper advertisement).

SURROGATE MOTHERS — Wanted. Couples unable to have children are willing to pay $10,000 fee and expenses to a woman to carry husband's child. Conception by artificial insemination. All replies are strictly confidential. Contact: Patricia L. Meade, Administrator; Howard B. Jones, Executive Director. The Infertility Center of San Diego, 14 East 57th Street, Suite 1262, San Diego, CA 92101. (619) 699-6475.

Embryo Transfer   Somewhat related to surrogate motherhood is embryo transfer, although it is a much more experimental procedure. Women with ovulation problems are usually the candidates for this technique. In embryo transfer, a female is designated to become impregnated with the father's sperm. After several days, the fertilized ovum is removed from her womb (rather than through surgical incision, the ovum is flushed from the womb) and placed within the wife's uterus. This is done when the menstrual cycle of the wife indicates that she is prepared to accept a pregnancy.

Reactions to High-Tech Pregnancies   Without question, high-tech pregnancies represent important medical breakthroughs. However, we need to acknowledge that along with critical acclaim has come considerable controversy. For example, the Catholic church and other groups oppose these scientific advancements for religious reasons. Other controversy originates from the legal front. For instance, very few medical problems have arisen with artificial-insemination-by-donor offspring, but only 25 states recognize their legitimacy.

To date, no clear-cut and comprehensive laws cover the surrogate motherhood arrangement, perhaps the stormiest controversy of all. Among the more heated issues include the following:

- The baby is actually produced for the couple's benefit, not the child's.
- The "substitute" mother intends to abdicate all parental responsibility — to transfer the child as in adoption, but this is intended prior to conception.
- Transfer is not like adoption since one does not know ahead of time how the infant will turn out, and some people tend to reject what does not meet their initial expectations.
- The creating of a newborn child is, in the surrogate model, too detached a process; the rearing mother is not emotionally attached because she did not bear it within her own body. Therefore, the child may suffer rejection by the couple who initiated the process.
- The newborn becomes just another "consumer item" and is a commodity for use by those who merely have to pay for its birth.
- Other siblings may fear being given away by parents, especially the children of the gestational mother. Since the couple are not the biological parents (when the ova of the woman who will raise the child is not involved), the

FOR MORE INFORMATION ON INFERTILITY AND PROBLEM PREGNANCIES, SEE . . .

Andrews, L. B., J. D. (1984). *New conceptions.* New York: St. Martin's Press.

Lifchez, A. S., M. D., and **Fenton, J. A.** (1980). *The fertility handbook.* New York: Clarkson N. Potter.

Nofziger, M. (1982). *The fertility question.* Summerton, TN: The Book Publishing Company.

Older, J. (1984). *Endometriosis.* New York: Charles Scribner's Sons.

Silber, S., M. D. (1980). *How to get pregnant.* New York: Charles Scribner's Sons.

Stigger, J. A. (1983). *Coping with infertility.* Minneapolis, MN: Augsburg Publishing House.

White, K. (1981). *What to do when you think you can't have a baby.* New York: Doubleday.

parents-to-be may not be psychologically ready for raising the baby.

- Surrogate bearers may change their minds and seek to retain the baby who, earlier, was "fathered" by someone other than the surrogate's husband.
- Problems of lineage may compromise the social status of the baby.

At present only a few states are even considering legislation to settle such issues. Combined, all of these techniques bring us to the larger issue: how far are we, as a society, willing to let technology go in aiding conception—and where do we draw the line? Single women use artificial insemination—should IVF be available to them as well? Should homosexuals use surrogate mothers? Should government funds support research on human embryos? The questions far outnumber the available answers, and acceptable solutions may be years away. In the meantime couples who want a child must research their options on their own—considering all the issues involved very carefully (Isaacs, 1986).

PREGNANCY

The Moment of Conception

As we learned in Chapter 10, the physiological mechanisms responsible for reproduction are fairly well understood. Recall that alternately each month (approximately halfway through the 28-day menstrual cycle), one of the ovaries in the female releases a mature egg, or ovum, which contains chromosomes. The ovum then begins about a week's journey along the 4-inch fallopian tube into the uterus. Here the uterine walls have been accumulating a large supply of blood vessels to nourish the egg should it be fertilized. Should the ovum remain unfertilized, it continues past the uterus and eventually degenerates. The uterine walls also begin disintegrating and the menstrual flow begins.

However, if a sperm cell penetrates the ovum during an approximate 24-hour critical time period while the ovum is in the fallopian tube, conception takes place (see Figure 11-1). The ferti-

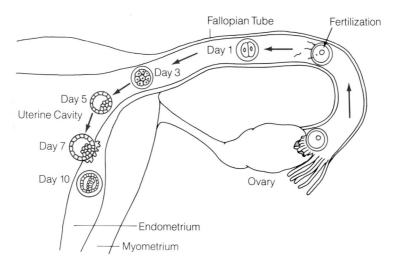

Fallopian Tube   Fertilization

Day 1

Day 3

Day 5

Uterine Cavity

Day 7

Day 10

Ovary

Endometrium

Myometrium

FIGURE 11-1   Conception in the Fallopian Tube and Implantation

lized egg, containing its own complement of 23 chromosomes plus 23 chromosomes from the sperm, is now referred to as a zygote. Pregnancy commences at this point and prenatal development begins.

The average full-term pregnancy lasts about 280 days from conception to full term, about 40 weeks. However, the duration of pregnancy has wide variations—it may be as long as 300 days or as short as 240 days.

Because of these wide variations, determining one exact due date is difficult. Ways of computing approximate due dates, though, have been proposed. The due date can be computed as 280 days from the first day of one's last period. Women should take the begining day of their last period, count back 3 months, and add 7 days. This is the same as saying that the baby takes 9 months and 7 days—280 days—to reach full term. This is called predicting the due day "by dates." A second method of determining the due date is having the doctor listen for the sound of the fetal heart. The

APPLICATIONS

METHODS OF DETERMINING PREGNANCY

The Home Pregnancy Test   This is the least accurate but most private of pregnancy tests. Similar to the lab urine test described below, the home pregnancy test diagnoses pregnancy by detecting the presence of the hormone HCG (Human Chorionic Gonadotropin) in the urine. The test can show if one is pregnant as early as nine days after a missed menstrual period, or about three and one-half weeks after conception. If it's done correctly—and that's an important "if"—the at- ▶

home test is about as accurate (95%) as a urine test done in a doctor's office or laboratory, with a positive result more likely to be correct than a negative one. But there are drawbacks to this test. For one thing, it can be more expensive than a lab test. Also, a person is less likely to feel confident in the results and more likely to want another test, adding further to the cost. The major risk is that if the test is negative (and incorrect), a woman may postpone a visit to the doctor and not begin taking proper care of herself and her baby until weeks later. If one does decide on a home test, it should be bought on the day before one plans to use it (it requires a first-of-the-morning urine sample) and women need to follow the instructions carefully.

The Lab Urine Test   This test can also detect HCG in the urine with an accuracy of about 95% — and as early as 20 days after conception. Unlike the home test, it is performed by a professional, who is more likely to do it correctly. (Of course, labs have been known to make mistakes, too.) If a woman plans on taking the test, she should call the lab the day before and ask for instructions on collecting her urine. This is sometimes the least expensive pregnancy test, but it is less reliable than a blood test.

The Blood Test   The serum pregnancy test can detect pregnancy with 95% plus accuracy as early as eight to ten days after conception, and with virtually 100% accuracy (barring lab error) six weeks after conception. Now that they're in common use, blood tests often cost no more than urine tests, and their accuracy renders the necessity of a retest less likely.

Regardless of the test chosen, the chances of a pregnancy being correctly diagnosed is enhanced when the test is followed up by a medical examination. The physical signs of pregnancy—an enlarging and softening of the uterus, and a change in the texture of the cervix—may be apparent to a doctor by the sixth week of pregnancy. The following table lists the probable signs of pregnancy.

Adapted from Eisenberg et. al., 1984

Probable Signs of Pregnancy

Sign	When it Appears	Other Possible Causes
Softening of uterus and cervix	2–8 weeks after conception	A delayed menstrual period
Enlarging uterus and abdomen	8–12 weeks	Tumor
Intermittent painless contractions	Early in pregnancy, increasing in frequency	Bowel contractions
Fetal movements	First noted 14–20 weeks of pregnancy	Gas, bowel contractions

fetal heart can be heard at 18 to 20 weeks, which gives a date that has a 2-week leeway. This method is less exact than the menstrual data above.

The duration of a woman's pregnancy will tend to follow a woman's menstrual cycle. If one has periods every 21 days, the baby will probably be early. If a woman has a 28-day cycle the baby may be late. Women with consistently regular periods are more likely to have their baby on the 280th day than women with irregular periods. A woman's age, race, size, and previous number of children have no influence on the length of her pregnancy (Hotchner, 1984).

Multiple Conception

Conception usually takes place when a single sperm cell penetrates the female ovum to create a zygote. When this happens, a single child is conceived. It is possible, though, for more than one child to be conceived at one time, known technically as **multiple conception**.

Multiple conceptions are not nearly as common as singletons. About 30,000 sets of twins are born in the United States each year. Twins occur approximately once in every 90 births; triplets about once in 9,300 births; quadruplets once in 490,000; and quintuplets once in every 55,000,000 births. As far as cross-cultural differences are concerned, blacks give birth to the most twins. Orientals, on the other hand, give birth to the fewest number of twins.

While the conception of twins is relatively infrequent, they are the most common of multiple births. Two major types of twins have been identified (Figure 11-2). **Identical twins** result when a single fertilized egg splits after conception. Identical twins are genetically alike, having the same physical characteristics, including sex, blood type, and eye color.

Fraternal twins result when two female eggs are fertilized by two separate sperm cells. About two-thirds of all twins are fraternal. Fraternal twins are no more alike than any two singletons born to the same parent. They may or may not be of the same sex, and each possesses individual characteristics.

FIGURE 11-2   Fraternal and Identical Twins

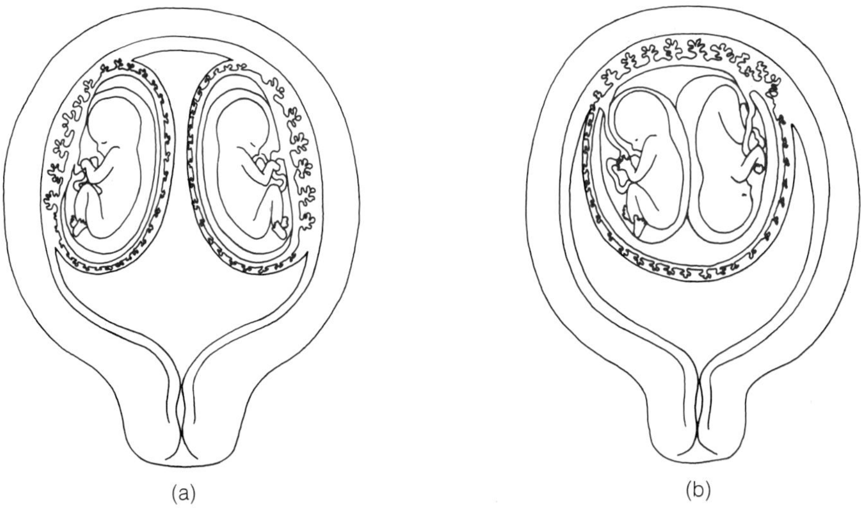

Fraternal twins (a) have separate placentas even though they come into close apposition. Identical twins (b) share a common placenta.

CROSS-CULTURAL FOCUS

BELIEFS ABOUT CONCEPTION

Research undertaken by Edgar Gregersen (1983) indicates that theories about how babies are made vary by culture. Some societies, such as the Áranda of Australia, the Trobriand islanders off the coast of New Guinea, and the Yapese on an island in Micronesia in the Pacific, reportedly deny that men are necessary for procreation. Some anthropologists discount these reports, but there are other beliefs that are equally astonishing. The Buka of the Solomon Islands in the Pacific believe that a child is conceived only from the mother's blood — semen playing no role in procreation. However, inserting a penis inside the woman is necessary; it somehow starts the process of conception.

Other cultures maintain that conception requires continual sexual intercourse, even after pregnancy! The Wogeo of Papua, New Guinea, for example, contend that a fetus consists of a combination of menstrual blood and semen. Copulation has to be repeated so often so that the passage leading from the womb will be blocked up with semen to prevent the blood from escaping. The Yanomamo of Venezuela and Brazil believe that for a child to grow healthy and strong, many men should copulate with the mother frequently during her pregnancy. This has its problems, since if she is discovered with a lover, her husband will invariably challenge him to a duel and will abuse her. However, mothers apparently know their obligations and risk even the wrath of their husbands for the sake of their children.

The notion of the need for many acts of coitus is taken one step further by the Ngonde of Malawi: should a woman become pregnant after having had sexual intercourse only once with her husband, she would be accused of adultery — without any further evidence. On the other hand, the Mam of Guatemala may accuse a woman of adultery if she has copulated with her husband regularly for two or three years and does *not* become pregnant — they believe that having sex with more than one man prevents conception.

A society that recognizes that men are necessary for procreation and that one act of intercourse is enough to cause pregnancy may still hold to other inaccuracies. For example, the Kubeo of Brazil insist that a pregnant woman stop having sex altogether because continued intercourse will pile up the number of fetuses within her and she may explode! Somewhat less dramatic is the conviction in a number of societies that twins are a sign of adultery.

All of this tends to be amusing to us, in part because such examples are culturally remote. However, some Westerners have held equally wrong ideas. Among the uninformed in such countries as Jamaica and Puerto Rico, an earlier European belief that a woman must experience orgasm if coitus is to lead to conception is still held. The fact of the matter, as we know, is that women need not enjoy sex at all to get pregnant.

Finally, a belief held throughout much of western history is that a woman is ▶

simply the greenhouse in which a man's seed grows to become a child. Of course, this myth was not restricted to the West: the Trukese of the Pacific and the Tupinamba of South America still believe it. Without scientific technology people will create such explanations not only to account for biology but probably also to justify other aspects of their society. For example, those societies that play down paternity tend to play up the woman's role in the culture and trace descent, inheritance, and succession through women. The opposite is true when maternity is deemphasized.   ■

To determine whether twins are fraternal or identical, certain tests such as fingerprinting or blood-typing are undertaken (results should be the same for identical twins).

Cojoined twins("Siamese") are considered an obstetrical rarity. The ratio of Siamese to normal twin births is approximately 1 in 1,000. Siamese twins are always identical and usually female.

Twins have an average gestation period that is about 25 days shorter than normal, and almost half of all twin births are premature. When delivery takes place, the first twin is usually born head first while the second is often a breech (buttocks first) delivery (Noble, 1980; Abbe and Gill, 1981).

PRENATAL DEVELOPMENT

The duration of pregnancy can be divided into three equal segments called **trimesters**. Each trimester is three months long and reflects distinct phases of prenatal growth and development. Let's examine each of these periods and the changes that take place in the developing organism.

The First Trimester

The First Month Following conception, the zygote begins the first of many cell divisions. While this happens, the cluster of cells will travel down the fallopian tube and, on or about the fourth day, reaches the uterus. It then drifts about for another three or four days before embedding itself in the spongy-vesseled wall of the uterus. At this time *the entire cluster of cells is no larger than the*

head of a pin. When the fertilized ovum becomes implanted in the uterine wall and the cells begin to exhibit marked differentiation, the organism is called an **embryo**. The embryonic period will last until the second month of pregnancy.

After eighteen days, a primitive heart structure begins to appear, and by three weeks the heart is functional, undergoing muscle contractions, although it is not under neural control. The heart beats and blood pulsates through a small enclosed bloodstream that is separate from the mother's. A backbone also encloses a spinal cord; and such internal organs as the lungs, liver, kidneys, and endocrine glands also begin to form. In addition, the digestive system has begun to develop. Small "buds" which will eventually become arms start developing on day 24 and on day 28 leg "buds" appear. Throughout development, the legs lag behind the arms.

By the end of the first month of prenatal life, the embryo measures only 3/16 of an inch in length, but is 10,000 times larger than a zygote. The specialization of cells produces an embryo that has a short, pointed, curled-up tail and a primitive umbilical cord through which it will eventually be nourished.

The Second Month The rapid cell division and specialization that characterized the first month of prenatal life continues to occur. By the end of eight weeks the embryo measures about an inch in length and weighs 1/30 of an ounce. Facial features and a neck are forming and the limbs are elongating, showing distinct division of knee and

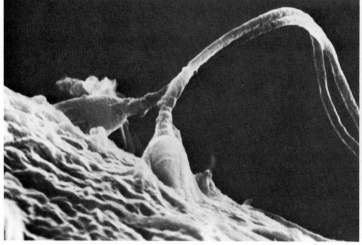

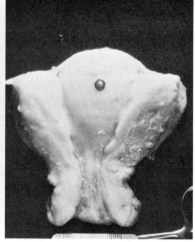

| The moment of conception. | Implantation in the uterine wall. |

elbow, although they are less than 1/4 inch long. More specifically, about day 31 the shoulders, arms, and hands develop; on day 33, the fingers; and on days 34 to 36, the thumb completes its development. The internal organs also continue to develop quite rapidly, not only in form and structure, but also in functional properties. The nervous system becomes functional, the kidneys are capable of moving uric acid from the bloodstream, and the stomach is capable of manufacturing some digestive juices.

While only one inch in length, the organism is already exhibiting some genetic characteristics which have been inherited. For example, the ear lobes will be attached or unattached, and certain nose types will make their appearance on day 37. These, as well as fingers and toe shapes, are just a few of the inheritable traits that express themselves as early as the embryonic period.

The Third Month   The third month of prenatal life marks the start of the *fetal period*. During this time, progressive maturation of both nerves and muscles, which leads to generalized movements in response to external stimulation, occurs. Fetal turning and rotation will also occur, perhaps as early as the ninth or tenth week (although the

Rapid cell division and specialization characterizes the first trimester of prenatal development. By the end of the second month, the organism is about an inch long and weighs 1/30 of an ounce.

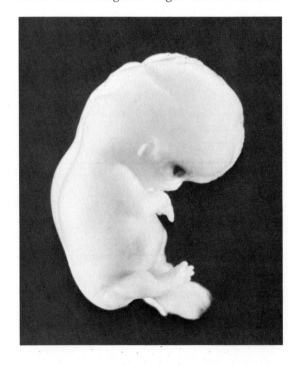

EXPLORING THE INTRAUTERINE WORLD

Within the mother's womb, the fetus experiences secure and safe surroundings. A transparent membrane called the **amniotic sac** envelops the fetus. **Amniotic fluid** within the sac holds the embryo or fetus in suspension and protects it not only from being jarred, but also from any pressures exerted by the mother's internal organs. The fluid also provides a constant temperature for the fetus. The amniotic sac thus allows the fetus safe and free movement, while protecting the mother from potentially harmful kicks and pushes.

The **placenta**, or afterbirth, is attached to the uterine wall, and is the membrane that allows nourishment to pass from mother to embryo and waste products to be channeled from embryo to mother. It should be noted here that there is no direct connection of blood vessels between mother and embryo. Substances are transmitted to and from the mother's and child's blood vessels via the placenta. The placenta — sole source of food, oxygen, and water for the unborn — must grow in relation to the organism's needs. Originally microscopic in size, it becomes three or four inches in diameter by the fourth month and at birth weighs about a pound and measures eight inches in diameter.

Connecting the placenta to the fetus is the **umbilical cord**. The umbilical cord contains three blood vessels: one vein carrying oxygenated blood from the placenta to the infant and two arteries that carry blood and waste products from the infant to the placenta. Since the umbilical cord is without nerves, the severance and tying into the "belly button" at delivery is a painless matter. (The figure below illustrates the basic intrauterine structures.)

Basic Intrauterine Structures

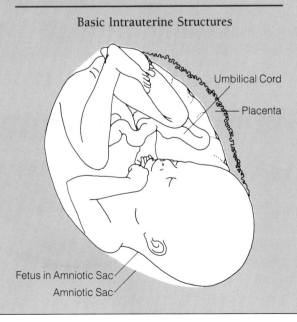

Umbilical Cord

Placenta

Fetus in Amniotic Sac

Amniotic Sac

mother will be unaware of all this activity). By the end of 12 weeks, the fetus can also curl the toes and fingers, kick, and even squint in response to external stimulation. The fetus is now 3 inches long and weighs about an ounce. Arms, hands, fingers, legs, feet, and toes have fully developed. Even nails are forming on the 20 digits. Tiny tooth sockets, with the "buds" of future teeth, are present in the jawbone. The eyes are almost fully developed and have lids that remain fused.

At the conclusion of the third month, a tiny but highly complex organism exists. The nerves and muscles have tripled in number during the final stages of this trimester. The heart can be heard by use of special instruments; the kidneys become operable; and sexual development is such that sex can be noted by a cursory examination. Meanwhile, the soft cartilaginous substance of the ribs and vertebrae turns to bone.

The Second Trimester

The Fourth Month   The fetus now measures seven inches in length and weighs approximately four ounces. The head appears disproportionately large in comparison to the rest of the body. A strong heartbeat is evident, along with a fairly well-developed digestive system. The eyebrows and genital organs are now quite noticeable. Because the fetus is also quite active, there is an increase in intake of food, oxygen, and water. The placenta has increased from three inches to four inches in diameter, allowing for a more rapid exchange of nutrients and waste products between mother and child. In appearance the transparent fetal body is bright pink or red. This red coloration is due to blood flowing through the circulatory vessels, since there is no pigmentation in the fetus skin.

The Fifth Month   The fetus is now about a foot long and may weigh anywhere from a half to a full pound. The eyelids are still fused shut and a fine downy growth of hair, termed **lanugo**, appears on the entire body. The skin is also usually covered with a wax-like substance called the **vernix ca-**

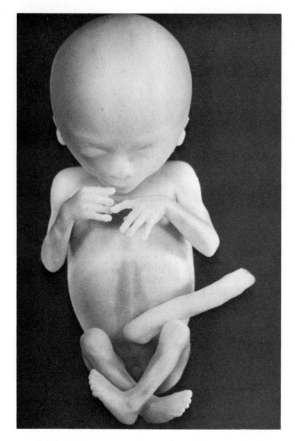

Marked differentiation has taken place as the fetus enters the third month of prenatal life. Note the development of the appendages as well as the facial features.

seosa, the purpose of which is to protect the fetus from constant exposure to the amniotic fluid. The internal organs are also rapidly maturing, with the exception of the lungs, which lag behind in development. The size and movement of the fetus is such that the mother is now very much aware of the ripplings and flutterings inside her. The fetus now has both sleeping and waking moments. During wakefulness there is crying, kicking, thumb-sucking, and hiccuping, and even head-over-heels somersaults.

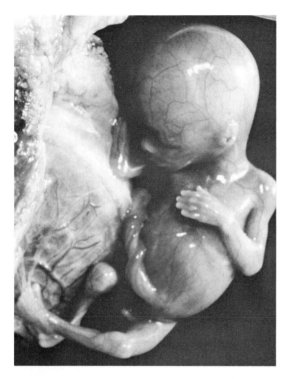

The fetus alternates periods of sleep with periods of activity.

rated and tiny eyelashes can be observed, and the fingernails extend to the end of the fingers. A hardening of the bones has also begun. But even with all this development, there is only a poor chance of survival should the fetus be born now.

The Third Trimester

The Seventh, Eighth, and Ninth Months Prenatal development at this time is marked primarily by rapid gains in growth and weight. The fetus grows in length by 50 percent and gains nearly six pounds in these final three months. During the last two months of prenatal life the fetus gains an average of a half pound a week. In the seventh month there is rapid development of the reflexes that will be observed at birth. As prenatal growth increases (much of the weight gain is subcutaneous fat), and the uterus becomes cramped, the fetus's movement is somewhat curtailed. Periods of sleep and inactivity now alternate with longer periods of activity than before.

Fetal organ development, for the most part, is rapid during the final trimester. This allows the organs to operate independently of the prenatal environment. However, independent respiration is one of the last bodily mechanisms to fully develop. Until there is appropriate neural functioning, respiration remains inefficient. Thus respiratory problems are among the major difficulties to be faced in keeping the prematurely born infant alive.

The Sixth Month The six-month fetus has started accumulating subcutaneous fat and now weighs about one and one-half pounds and measures over a foot in length. The eyelids have sepa-

---

APPLICATIONS

MATERNAL CHANGES DURING PREGNANCY: ADJUSTMENTS AND ADAPTATIONS

During the course of a normal pregnancy, most women feel as well as they have at any other time in their lives. In fact, many feel even better than ever before. However, there are certain minor, common, everyday symptoms and problems which are shared by a significant number of pregnant women. Here are some of these problems and what can be done about them: ▶

Morning Sickness, Indigestion, and Nausea

Eat small meals every two to three hours rather than three larger meals. Avoid liquids with meals, acid- or gas-producing foods, and an empty stomach. Dry foods such as crackers usually stay down better than liquids such as soups.

Shortness of Breath

Concentrate on good posture, pulling in your abdominal muscles and tilting your pelvis, to give the stomach and lungs more room. Try sleeping on extra pillows to elevate your head and chest.

Pelvic Pressure; Thigh-Hip Pain; Heaviness in Legs; Backache

Practice good posture while sitting, standing, and lifting. Using your abdominal muscles, try to lift the baby up off the big blood vessels in the pelvis and nerves that might be pinched. Relieve strain on your back with ample rest periods. Try pillow support under your top leg (when lying on your side) and arms and uterus to relieve the pull on your back.

Stretch Marks

These may be reduced by good posture, which reduces pressure on and stretching of the abdomen.

Swelling of the Feet; Varicose Veins

Good posture and ample rest will help. You can improve circulation by raising your legs to drain fluid from them. Lie on the bed or floor with a pillow under your hips. Raise your legs up on the wall with your knees bent and slowly make circles with your feet to the right and left. Point your heel rather than your toe. If you wear elastic support hose, drain your legs this way *before* putting on your stockings. Change your body position often; wear sensible shoes and clothing that does not bind.

Swelling of the Hands

Slight swelling of the fingers is common. Drink six to eight glasses of water daily and maintain a good diet, high in protein. Restrict salt only if instructed by doctor.

Leg Cramps

These are common in the last three months because of the drain of calcium from your system for the baby's bone growth and decreased circulation as a result of the pressure of the growing baby. Adequate calcium in the diet — from dairy products, dark green vegetables, or calcium lactate (only if prescribed by your doctor) — is essential. Practice good posture. Straighten cramped muscles by standing up. Try warm baths, loose covers over your feet, pillows under your legs.

Constipation

Moderate exercise will help. Maintain intake of roughage in diet (fruits, whole ▶

grains, bran, raw vegetables). Increase fluids. Establish regular bowel habits, responding quickly to the urge to eliminate. Try relaxation and deep breathing during elimination to relax the anal sphincter. Use stool softeners only if prescribed by physician.

Fatigue/Insomnia
Try deep breathing for relaxation and good pillow support for comfort. Sleep on your side with pillows under your top leg and arm and under your uterus, or try a semi-sitting position, with pillows under your back, knees and arms. Keep your feet up as much as possible during the day.

Dizziness
Get up slowly, moving your arms and legs to increase blood flow. Roll over onto your side and push yourself up with your hands to avoid back strain.

Feeling of Warmth; Heavy Body Secretions; Oily Hair
These are all caused by hormonal changes and increased metabolism. Wear cool, loose, comfortable clothing. You may feel more comfortable if you bathe and wash your hair more frequently.

Adapted from Hales and Creasy, 1982; Hall, 1983. ■

PROTECTING THE PRENATAL ENVIRONMENT

Over the course of nine months, the fetus must develop from a single cell to a complex organism weighing approximately seven pounds. As this development takes place, the fetus is influenced by its external and internal environment. The external fetal environment is the amniotic fluid. The internal environment consists not only of the proteins and enzymes manufactured within the organism but also of a continuous inflow of nutrients, hormones, oxygen, chemicals, and other substances from the mother's bloodstream.

We noted earlier that there is no direct connection between the blood vessels of mother and child. Because of this, a mixing of blood in the placental region never occurs. Instead, molecules of many substances are released by the maternal bloodstream and pass through the placenta. If small enough, these substances are assimilated by

the blood vessels within the umbilical cord, thus making the placenta an area of exchange. The placenta is not, however, a filtration system. The environmental impact, then, comes from the substances exchanged in the placenta. Obviously, a physically healthy mother who is eating the proper foods for herself and her baby, which we'll discuss presently, will help provide the proper environment. Beyond maintaining a well-balanced diet, the mother should be free of disease and under the care of a physician who can offer qualified prenatal care (Krause, 1984; Hamilton and Whitney, 1982).

Maternal Nutrition

The ability of the fetus to develop normally depends on nourishment supplied by the mother. Poor maternal nutrition may either directly affect the fetus by not meeting its nutritional needs or indirectly affect the fetus by increasing the

Pregnant women need to pay close attention to proper nutrition and maintain good physical health.

mother's susceptibility to disease. Not only can malnutrition cause poor health, rickets, scurvy, physical weakness, miscarriages, and stillbirths, but it can also produce mental subnormality in the fetus. One source (Winick, 1981) estimates that a seriously malnourished fetus has as many as 20 percent fewer brain cells than the normal fetus. However, maternal nutrition is not considered the only deleterious condition influencing prenatal development. Malnourished mothers frequently come from an environment of poverty, inadequate medical care, and inferior sanitation conditions.

We cannot emphasize too strongly the importance of eating balanced, sensible meals during pregnancy. Paula Hillard and Gideon Panter (1985) state that such meals must supply enough energy and nutrients to satisfy the mother's needs as well as those of her unborn child. Pregnancy is not a time for weight reduction, nor is it a time for massive weight gain beyond what is necessary for appropriate growth of fetal and maternal tissues.

Diets for pregnant women can vary widely, es-

pecially for those who plan to breast-feed their child as opposed to formula feeding. However, certain basic guidelines are usually contained within all diets, including:

- Seventy-five to one hundred grams of protein are needed daily.
- Five hundred calories are needed over a normal diet; that is, a total of about 2,600. Calorie needs will be greater if the mother is underweight, under severe emotional stress, has had a previous miscarriage or still birth, is having a baby within one year of another baby, or any combination of these. Also, if the mother is breastfeeding, a few extra pounds of weight gain is recommended.
- No sodium restriction is necessary—use iodized salt ad lib. Also, calcium—1200 mg. daily—four cups of nonfat milk is suggested.
- Toward the end of the pregnancy, five or six small meals should be eaten instead of three large ones—for increased comfort and easier digestion.

■ Daily prenatal vitamin supplements are required: 30 to 60 mg. of elemental iron and 400 to 800 ug. (0.2 to 0.4 mg) of folacin.

■ The nearer foods are to their natural state, the higher their food value — fresh is best, frozen next, canned foods last. (Hotchner, 1984)

Nicotine

While it is known that nicotine affects fetal development, exactly how much nicotine produces which prenatal effects remains unknown. Researchers have weighed and measured newborns of smokers vs. nonsmokers and found that the average weight of a baby born of a mother who smokes tends to be smaller than that of a nonsmoking woman. But, while statistical evidence indicates this, it is not known how or why this phenomenon occurs. An educated guess would be that the fetus of a nonsmoker is receiving its full quota of oxygen, while a smoking mother, having various gases, tars, and nicotine in her system, passes along these unhealthy substances through the placenta. The fetus receives these chemicals possibly at the expense of oxygen and/or other nutrients (Hillard and Panter, 1985).

Nicotine apparently has other effects as well. Just as adult heavy smokers experience an increase in heart rate, it has been suggested that smoking not only increases the fetal heart rate, but that it may even lead to fetal hyperactivity. In addition, women who are heavy smokers (as opposed to nonsmokers) are more likely to give birth to premature babies. Finally women who smoke are

WEIGHT GAIN DURING PREGNANCY

Most pregnant women will experience an average 24 to 29 pound weight gain over nine month's time. This weight gain will be gradual and steady, but will be distributed differently (see the figure below). The first pounds will go into building up stores of fat and protein than can be used by the baby later in the pregnancy. Some of these stores will be held in reserve even longer to help meet the mother's nutritional requirement after pregnancy and to help produce breast-milk. Nature assumes that humans, like other mammals, will breastfeed and wisely stores energy and nutrient supplies in the mother's changing body.

Normal Changes in Abdominal Contour during Pregnancy

20 Weeks   24 Weeks   28 Weeks   32 Weeks   36 Weeks   40 Weeks   7 Days Postpartum ▶

Other parts of the mother's body will also be growing during the early months of pregnancy. Blood plasma will increase in quantity by almost fifty percent, as will other body fluids. Breasts will begin to grow in anticipation of feeding the baby after birth and by midpregnancy will weigh about a pound more than before pregnancy. The uterus will also become bigger.

During the second half of pregnancy, stores of fat will decrease as the fetus uses them for growth, but other parts of the mother's body will be changing and making up that lost weight. The amniotic sac will fill with about two pounds of amniotic fluid. The placenta will also grow significantly during the last half of pregnancy. And, of course, the fetus itself will be getting bigger daily (Brown, 1983).

The following table shows how weight gain is distributed over the normal course of pregnancy for a woman who gains 29 pounds.

	Weight in Pounds
Baby	8.5
Stores of fat and protein	7.5
Blood	4.0
Tissue fluids	2.7
Uterus (womb)	2.0
Amniotic fluid (bag of waters)	1.8
Placenta (afterbirth) and umbilical cord	1.5
Breasts	1.0
Total	29.0

Adapted from Brown, 1983.

more likely to give birth to infants having life-threatening complications (Naeye, 1981; Fribourg, 1982).

Drugs

The specific effects of drugs on the developing organism will vary, dependent not only on which drug is involved, but also on the quantity used and the time during pregnancy when it is taken. If a pregnant woman is given a sedative during labor, the pattern of electrical activity in the brain of the infant decelerates following birth; in fact, if the sedation is excessive, asphyxiation or even permanent brain damage can result.

We also know that addictive drugs such as heroin and methadone pass through the placenta readily, causing mothers who are hard addicts to give birth to babies who are also addicted (that is, they have developed a physiological dependence upon the drug). Consequently, an addicted newborn must pass through all of the withdrawal symptoms (tremors, fever, convulsions, and breathing difficulties) that adults do when they "dry out." While most evidence indicates that no abnormalities exist in addicted infants, these babies are generally smaller (heroin babies seldom weigh *more* than five and one-half pounds) than average.

Heavy intake of alcohol can lead to what researchers label the **fetal alcohol syndrome** — a condition in which infants are often born undersized, mentally deficient, and with several physical deformities (such as abnormal limb development, facial abnormalities, and heart defects). Other complications also develop later in life for the

APPLICATIONS

REDUCING PREGNANCY RISKS

Good Medical Care   Even a low-risk pregnancy is put at high risk if prenatal care is absent or poor. Seeing a qualified practitioner regularly, beginning as soon as pregnancy is suspected, is vital for all expectant mothers. Select an obstetrician experienced with your particular condition if you are in a high-risk category. But just as important as having a good doctor is being a good patient. Be an active participant in your medical care — ask questions, report symptoms — but don't try to be your own doctor.

Good Diet   A good diet gives every pregnant woman the best odds of having a successful pregnancy and a healthy baby. It may also help to prevent gestational diabetes and hypertension.

Fitness   It's best to begin pregnancy with a well-toned, exercised body, but it's never too late to start deriving the benefits of fitness. Regular exercise prevents constipation and improves respiration, circulation, muscle tone, and skin elasticity, all of which contribute to a more comfortable pregnancy and an easier, safer delivery.

Sensible Weight Gain   A gradual, steady, and moderate weight gain may help prevent a variety of complications, including diabetes, hypertension, varicose veins, hemorrhoids, low birth weight, or difficult delivery due to an overly large fetus.

No Smoking   Quitting as early in pregnancy as possible reduces the many risks to mother and baby, including prematurity and low birth weight.

Abstinence From Alcohol   Drinking very rarely or not at all will reduce the risk of birth defects, particularly of fetal alcohol syndrome, the result of high alcohol intake.

Avoidance of Drugs   So little is known about the effects of drugs on fetal development that it is best to avoid taking any during pregnancy that are not absolutely essential and prescribed by your doctor.

Prevention of, and Prompt Treatment for, Infection   All infections — from the common flu to urinary tract and vaginal infections to the increasingly common venereal diseases — should be prevented whenever possible. When contracted, however, infection should be treated promptly by a physician who knows you are pregnant.

Being Wary of the Superwoman Syndrome   Often well established in their careers and highly motivated in everything they do, many of today's mothers tend to be overachievers and overdoers. Getting enough rest during pregnancy is far more important than getting everything done, especially in high-risk pregnancies. ▶

> Don't wait until your body starts pleading for relief before you slow down. If your doctor recommends that you begin your maternity leave earlier than you'd planned, take the advice. Some studies have suggested a higher incidence of premature delivery among women who work up until term, particularly if their jobs entail physical labor or long periods of standing.
>
> Adapted from Eisenberg, Murkoff, and Hathaway, 1984. ■

children of alcoholic mothers, including poor attention skills and reaction times (Streissguth, 1984).

One study (Streissguth, Barr, and Martin, 1983) examined the effects of maternal alcohol use during midpregnancy and neonatal habituation. Maternal alcohol consumption was obtained by self-report during the fifth month of pregnancy and newborns were evaluated by means of a specialized infancy assessment test. It was found that maternal alcohol consumption was significantly related to poorer habituation and increased low

arousal in the newborns, even after the researchers adjusted for smoking by mothers, maternal age, nutrition during pregnancy, sex and age of the infant, and obstetric medication.

Teratogens

A **teratogen** is any substance that creates a change in normal genetic functioning, which in turn produces an abnormality or malformation in the developing organism. The development of fetal organs and appendages is especially vulnerable to

TABLE 11-1

Teratogenic Agents and Their Effects

Category	Cause	Effect
Physical	Irradiation (X-rays)	Malformation of any organ; the organ involved depends on the organism's state of development
Infectious	Rubella (German measles)	Brain damage (mental retardation), sensory and cranial nerve damage (especially vision and hearing)
Chemical	Quinine (?)	Possible deafness and congenital malformations (not totally substantiated). Note: quinine water lacks sufficient quinine to be included in this group
	Cortisone	Possibly contributes to formation of cleft palate
	Paint fumes (?)	Suspected of causing mental retardation. Pregnant women would probably have to be in unventilated paint area for substantial length of time to be affected
	Thalidomide	If taken 21–22 days after conception may cause absence of external ears, cranial nerve paralysis: 24–27 days, agenesis of arms; 28–29 days, agenesis of legs
	Vitamin A	Large doses taken throughout pregnancy may cause cleft palate, eye damage, congenital abnormalities
	Vitamin D	Large doses taken throughout pregnancy may cause mental retardation
	Alcohol	New evidence indicates possibility of heavy drinkers (pregnant females) producing infants with subnormal IQs

Adapted from Turner and Helms, 1987.

teratogens. The most dangerous time for the developing organism is the first two or three months after conception since this is a critical time for these fetal developments. Teratogenic agents can be classified as physical (X-rays), infectious (rubella), or chemical (thalidomide). Table 11-1 displays examples of some teratogenic agents and their effects.

Maternal Emotions

How the pregnant woman's environment affects the fetus has generated many misconceptions, myths, and even old wives' tales. For instance, if a pregnant woman had been frightened, some believed that the child would be born with a birthmark shaped like the object that had upset the mother. Another misconception was that happy mothers will give birth to happy babies, while worried mothers will bear children who are emotionally upset. While there is little factual evidence in support of these old superstitions, there are some closely associated biological factors that must be taken into consideration.

For example, while maternal emotions do not directly influence the developing organism, there is evidence that the hormones released while the pregnant woman is under great stress do affect the unborn. In support of this, women who are subjected to severe or prolonged emotional stress during their pregnancies are more likely to give birth to infants who are hyperactive, have low birth weights, exhibit irritability, and have feeding problems and digestive disturbances. Moreover, highly anxious women tend to have more spontaneous abortions and a higher percentage of premature infants, and they spend an average of five more hours in labor. They also tend to have more complicated and abnormal deliveries (Bloomberg, 1980).

Sex During Pregnancy

Before we leave the topic of safeguarding the prenatal environment, we'd like to say a few words about sex during pregnancy. We do so because in the minds of many, considerable confusion exists regarding what effect sexual activity has on prenatal development. For many, sexual relations during pregnancy are anxiety-ridden experiences.

Traditionally, physicians have advised that intercourse be avoided during the last month or six weeks of pregnancy and during the six weeks after the baby is born, but these recommendations are based on little factual information. The medical literature itself contains conflicting reports. During an uncomplicated pregnancy, however, sex is not harmful. A persistant fear, though, is that intercourse will cause a miscarriage or harm the fetus. There is no medical evidence that any of this is true for normal pregnancies, but a physician may advise a woman who has had a miscarriage to avoid sex. If a woman has had spotting during early pregnancy or has had a previous miscarriage, she should ask her doctor whether intercourse should be avoided and, if so, for what period of time. Sometimes spotting results from a cervical irritation, and intercourse can aggravate the condition. However, in the absence of bleeding, ruptured membranes, cervical weakness (incompetent cervix), or threatened premature labor, there is no reason that couples should not continue to pursue normal sexual activity throughout the duration of pregnancy (Hillard and Panter, 1985).

COMPLICATIONS AND PROBLEMS

Miscarriage

A **miscarriage** is the termination of a pregnancy before the embryo or fetus has the opportunity to fully develop. About one out of ten pregnancies results in a miscarriage. It is estimated that 90 percent of all miscarriages occur during the first three months of pregnancy (Hall, 1983).

In many miscarriages, the cause is a genetic abnormality. This creates a defective embryo that is unable to develop normally. Early miscarriage is viewed by some (for example, Hales and Creasy, 1982) as a natural selection process in which the defective organism is rejected before it has a chance to fully develop.

Certain factors are believed to increase the risk of miscarriages. For example, miscarriages occur more often in women who smoke and consume large amounts of alcohol. Other factors suspected of triggering a miscarriage include rubella, x-rays, or severe infections such as pneumonia. These latter factors are regarded as one-time events, though, and usually do not affect future pregnancies (Eisenberg, Murkoff, and Hathaway, 1984).

Ectopic Pregnancies

During its journey to the uterus, it is possible for the fertilized egg to become lodged in the wall of the fallopian tube (see Figure 11-3). Called an **ectopic pregnancy**, this happens once in about 200 pregnancies, and it produces an untenable situation. The tubes were not designed to harbor pregnancies. If a fertilized egg does become stuck in the tube it will continue to grow normally for a while; but sooner or later the tube (as opposed to the flexible muscular uterus) will be able to expand its delicate wall no further and will burst. This invariably happens sooner rather than later — sometime during the first three months, producing bleeding directly into the abdominal cavity which must be stopped by an abdominal operation to remove the tube (Hall, 1983).

FIGURE 11-3   Ectopic Pregnancy

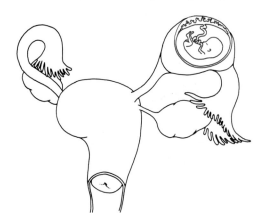

Combating Prenatal Problems

Because of advancements in modern-day technology, several new methods have been devised to detect and study problems within the prenatal environment. The result of these advancements has been a better understanding of the disorders that can exist early in life, as well as ways of dealing with them. Among these are genetic counseling and amniocentesis, sonography, and fetoscopy.

Genetic Counseling and Amniocentesis
While it is true that some genetic defects occur randomly, usually there is a pattern to their occurrences. As researchers discover more about the way defects are transmitted genetically, they are able to counsel couples about the potential risks to their unborn children. Today, numerous genetic counseling centers exist, staffed by physicians or specially trained "genetic associates" and equipped with computerized information-retrieval systems that provide immediate access to the facts and statistics about certain genetic problems. **Genetic counseling** is recommended for certain groups of parents most likely to have children with defects, including:

- Women over age 35.
- Parents of a child with a single-gene abnormality or another form of physical or mental impairment.
- Women who've had three or more miscarriages.
- Couples with chromosomal abnormalities.
- Women who may be carriers of X-linked disorders.
- Couples whose family members have a high incidence of certain diseases or unusually frequent cases of cancer or heart disease.
- Couples whose ethnic or racial backgrounds increase the likelihood of a particular problem. (Hales and Creasy, 1982)

One of the laboratory techniques employed in genetic research is **amniocentesis**. Amniocentesis allows for the detection of chromosomal abnormalities in the fetus. Amniotic fluid is sampled by

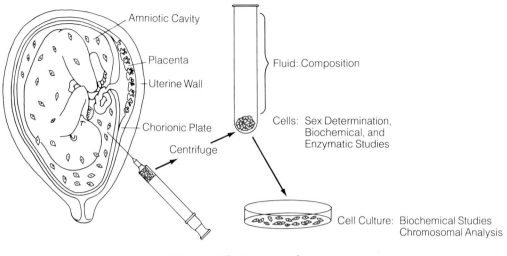

Amniotic Cavity

Placenta

Uterine Wall

Chorionic Plate

Centrifuge

Fluid: Composition

Cells: Sex Determination, Biochemical, and Enzymatic Studies

Cell Culture: Biochemical Studies Chromosomal Analysis

FIGURE 11-4   The Process of Amniocentesis

inserting a hollow needle through the mother's abdominal wall and into the amniotic sac. A syringe is then attached, and amniotic fluid withdrawn. This fluid contains discarded fetal cells, which can be observed, measured, and analyzed for size, shape, and number (see Figure 11-4).

This procedure has been used since the early 1960s, and currently, more than 50 chromosomal abnormalities can be tested for (more than 1,600 known human diseases exist). Amniocentesis is generally used on pregnant women who have a family history of heredity defects.

For women wishing to undergo amniocentesis, the fourteenth to sixteenth week of pregnancy seems optimal. At this point there are sufficient fetal cells in the amniotic sac, which is now large enough to lessen the likelihood of a needle puncture being injurious to the fetus. This also allows time for a safe abortion, if necessary (Kaye, 1981).

Sonography   Another technique used to explore the prenatal environment is **sonography**, or ultrasound. Figure 11-5 illustrates the ultrasound examination. With this method, ultrasonic waves are transmitted to and from the mother's abdomen through a cluster of quartz crystals placed inside a

small hand-held transducer. When this transducer is moved over the surface of the skin, the ultrasound waves are directed against the placenta and the amniotic sac containing the baby. Once the

FIGURE 11-5   Ultrasound Examination

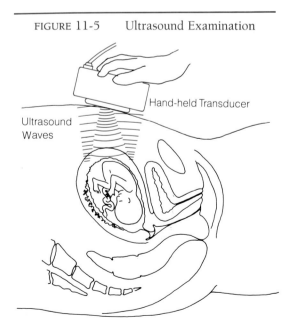

Hand-held Transducer

Ultrasound Waves

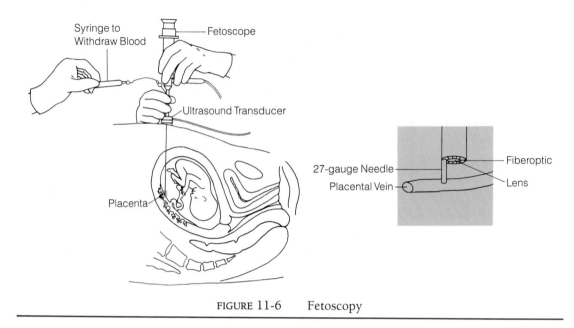

FIGURE 11-6   Fetoscopy

waves hit a permanent organ they are deflected outward and can be picked up through a special receptor, which, in turn, feeds the transmitted impulses of sound into a scanning machine that projects them onto the ultrasound screen. A clear picture of the various fetal organs can be put together by moving the transducer over different areas of the abdomen. The size, location, and contour of various organs can then be measured and analyzed (Lauersen, 1983).

Fetoscopy This technique of analysis involves a fetoscope, a viewing instrument with a diameter slightly greater than a large needle. It is inserted through the abdominal wall into the amniotic cavity in much the same manner as in amniocentesis (see Figure 11-6). The fetoscope contains a high-powered fiberoptic light source which allows a view of the fetal and placental surfaces; but due to the small diameter of the fetoscope, the area observed at any one moment is quite limited. The fetoscope is also equipped with a biopsy forceps which can be used to obtain a small piece of the baby's skin for chromosomal and biochemical studies, also making possible the prenatal diagnosis of a variety of congenital skin diseases. And

by inserting a tiny needle into the placenta and umbilical cord, doctors have been able to obtain samples of fetal blood for analysis (Shapiro, 1983).

LABOR AND DELIVERY

When Labor Begins

Physical development of the fetus is complete by the end of the third trimester of pregnancy. The first stage of birth begins when the mother begins to experience signs of labor, particularly uterine contractions. The first of these is often a feeling of discomfort in the lower part of the abdomen, usually described as a menstrual-like pain. Less commonly, it may be felt in the lower back and the legs. Another sign is a characteristic pinkish discharge from the vagina, commonly known as the "bloody show," which is caused by the release of the mucous plug from inside the neck of the cervix. A typical "show" is a small quantity of blood, similar in amount to the blood loss at the beginning of a menstrual period, mixed with mucus. Occasionally there is an initial discharge of clear watery material instead of the show, which indicates the imminent rupture of the fetal membranes. The release of the mucous plug is often a sign that labor is on the way, but it can occur a few days before the onset of progressive labor. A third sign that labor is beginning is the rupture of the membrane containing the amniotic fluid; although once again, this may take place a few days before labor begins, or during labor itself (Lauersen, 1983).

During early stages of labor, uterine contractions are mild and infrequent. But as labor progresses, contractions become more painful and frequent. The duration of contractions is an individual phenomenon and highly variable. At their peak, contractions will occur about every 2–3 minutes and last approximately 45–60 seconds. These contractions cause the cervix to open until it reaches full dilation, at which time the baby begins to move out of the uterus.

Delivery of the Baby

The second stage of labor is the delivery of the baby. Most fetuses will be in a head-downward position for delivery. About ten percent, though, will engage themselves in what is called a **breech** position.

The breech is the lower part of the fetus and three kinds of breech presentations are possible. The most common is the *frank breech*. In the frank breech, the legs of the fetus are bent straight up at the hips, with the knees straight. Fortunately, fetuses are very flexible, since in the frank-breech presentation the feet of the fetus are all the way up by the fetus's cheeks. Less common is the *complete breech*. In the complete breech, the knees of the fetus are flexed; the fetus is in a sitting position,

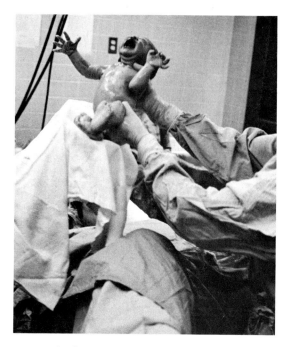

The long-awaited moment of birth.

with the legs folded in front. The third type of breech presentation is the *incomplete breech*, or *footling breech*. In this type, one or both feet or knees lie below the buttocks of the fetus. This can occur as either a single footling or a double footling, depending on whether one or both feet are coming first (Hillard and Panter, 1985).

During the delivery stage, uterine contractions push the baby into the birth canal and out of the mother's body. This stage, on the average, lasts approximately one hour. If the position or size of the baby is a concern, or if the mother develops

SOME SIGNS OF ABNORMAL LABOR AND DELIVERY

- *Continuous and severe lower abdominal pain,* often accompanied by uterine tenderness.
- *Discontinuance of good strong contractions* during first-stage labor.
- *Excessive vaginal bleeding* sometimes caused by a cervical laceration or delivery before full cervical dilation. ▶

- *Abnormality in fetal heart rate,* in which case the mother is usually moved onto her left side to take pressure off the major blood vessels on the right.
- *Abnormally slow dilation of the cervix,* which is a subjective judgment made by attendants based somewhat on the mother's pain tolerance and the strength of the contractions.
- *Abnormal presentation or prolapse* of the cord, placenta, or an extremity of the fetus.
- *Adverse change* in the condition of the mother (fever, high blood pressure) or the fetus (fetal heart rate).

Adapted from Hotchner, 1984. ■

physical problems, a **caesarean section** may be performed. This means that the baby is delivered through a surgical incision made in the abdominal and uterine walls. It is estimated that 15 percent of all births are of the caesarean variety (National Institute of Health, 1981).

Expulsion of the Placenta

The last stage of labor is the expulsion of the **placenta**. Usually within five minutes after the baby has been delivered, uterine contractions expel the placenta and the remaining portion of the umbilical cord. In some instances, the placenta is removed by the physician since it does not easily disengage from the uterine wall.

DELIVERY TECHNIQUES

Today, growing numbers of couples are pursuing alternatives to conventional or traditional hospital delivery procedures. Many are doing so because they object to the deemphasized role of the father in the delivery of the baby. Others object to the use of anesthesia during the delivery and to other medical intrusions on the mother and the baby.

An alternative to traditional procedures is **natural childbirth**. Natural childbirth avoids the use of anesthesia and allows both husband and wife to play an active role in the delivery of their baby.

Couples choosing this approach attend special classes that stress special breathing exercises and relaxation responses, since fear during delivery may cause women to tense their muscles, delaying the birth process and increasing the mother's pain. If women know what to expect and learn how to relax, proponents of this approach feel that discomfort can be significantly reduced.

The **Lamaze method** is one of the most popular natural childbirth approaches. Mothers are taught the importance of *prepared childbirth,* including breathing techniques and muscular exercises, prenatal development, and the stages of labor. The Lamaze method and others like it represent a conditioned learning technique that teaches the mother to replace one set of learned responses (fear, pain) with another (concentration on relaxation and muscle control). Fathers are encouraged to attend Lamaze classes and participate in the actual delivery as a supportive "coach."

The **Leboyer method** emphasizes the importance of a gentle delivery and minimal trauma for the newborn. The baby is born into a dimly lit delivery room that is kept relatively silent. Loud noises are minimized, including conversations. Immediately after birth the infant is placed on the mother's stomach to be gently massaged, the belief being that tactile stimulation and contact soothe the baby and possibly enhance early bonding and attachment. The infant is further soothed by receiving a warm bath, perhaps minimizing the sep-

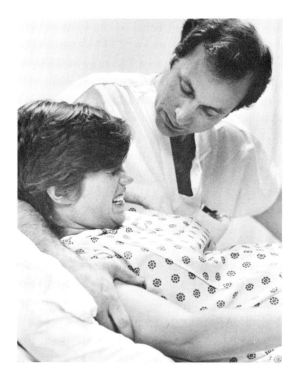

Many contemporary fathers share in the birth experience.

aration from the liquid surroundings of the prenatal environment. Only after this is the baby given a routine medical examination.

It is suggested that the foregoing procedures minimize the trauma of birth and the sudden and abrupt departure of the fetus from the womb. This delivery approach has not, however, gained universal acceptance. Critics maintain that it is dangerous to postpone the examination of the neonate after birth, especially when dim lighting may prevent the detection of vital life signs.

Another option for couples today is **home birth**. Home births are likely to increase in years to come, since parents are rebelling against increased hospital costs and impersonal neonatal and postpartum care. Home births are usually performed by licensed **nurse-midwives**, trained delivery specialists who provide qualified medical care to expectant mothers. Usually the midwife has earned a bachelor's degree in nurse-midwifery and works on a medical team consisting of a gynecologist and an obstetrician. The nurse-midwife spends considerably more time with the mother than traditional care dictates before, during, and after the delivery. Moreover, such care and attention can be offered in a personal relaxed, and comfortable setting.

Two other alternatives to conventional delivery procedures are **rooming-in** and **birthing room** hospital facilities. Hospitals offering rooming-in facilities allow couples to care for their newborn in their own private room. The infant is usually brought to this location within the first few hours after birth and remains there (rather than in the nursery) for the duration of hospitalization. A birthing room provides couples with homelike surroundings within the hospital delivery unit. Labor and delivery takes place in this room rather than in the hospital's conventional delivery room.

CROSS-CULTURAL FOCUS

HAVING BABIES IN THE NETHERLANDS

At one point in American history, almost all babies were born at home. Necessity dictated such a practice since hospitals and physicians were few and far between. As the United States advanced its health-care system, though, things changed. Hospitals emerged to combat disease and mortality risks, and as a result, home ▶

deliveries became less common. Today, almost all babies are born within a hospital setting.

The Netherlands offer an interesting comparison to the United States. Here, approximately 35 percent of all Dutch women deliver their babies at home. While the Netherlands is a medically advanced nation, it leads the industrialized world in the proportion of women having babies at home. Midwives perform virtually all home and hospital births.

Among the Dutch, there is a higher rate of infant mortality within a week after birth in hospitals than at home. However, this is because virtually all problem births are detected in advance and take place in the hospital setting. National health insurance policies cover most Dutch deliveries and regard home births as so safe that they will not pay for a hospital birth unless it is medically indicated.

Why are home births so popular? One major reason is the importance of the home in Dutch social life. Also, the small geographic size of the Netherlands and its above-average roads enable expectant couples from any location to be at a hospital within half an hour, if need be. Should delivery take place in a hospital, a "short-stay" policy adds further testimony to the importance placed on the home. Barring any complications, most mothers and their newborns are back to their homes within five hours after delivery.

APPLICATIONS

PLANNING YOUR BIRTH: SOME CONSIDERATIONS

Obstetrical practices vary widely throughout the country, in scope, character, and quality. Couples wanting to deliberately plan the birth of their child should be aware of choices related to the place of birth and type(s) of attendants, as well as procedures used during labor. Given the mutual distrust that sometimes exists between doctors and home birth attendants, couples should avoid accepting advice from either group at face value. Instead, they should judge for themselves the risks and benefits of all available options in their communities. Here are a few of the areas worthy of attention and consideration:

■ Most births, perhaps as many as 90 percent, are normal and occur without complications, but birth does entail risks, no matter where it occurs. Where would you feel most comfortable in the event of a complication? Who would you want to be there?

■ Birth attendants' philosophies vary. How much control do you want over the events during labor? How do you want to divide responsibility for what happens?

■ What role do you want technological equipment to play in your labor and birth?

- Many facets of the medical establishment consider home births unsafe and often disdain midwifery as a profession. How would you feel about going against conventional medical advice?
- Even the most deliberate planning of couples may have to be altered if labor does not proceed as expected. How flexible are your plans? How would you feel about changing birth environments in mid-labor?

The individual you select to attend your birth will be crucial during labor and delivery. Compile a list of the things that are important to you, then search for a person who not only agrees with you, but also with whom you can develop a trusting relationship. Here are some questions you might want to ask prospective birth attendants:

Questions for Doctors
(Consumer fears: loss of control, too much technology and intervention.)

- What are their experiences with and attitudes toward the practices you have chosen for labor and delivery? How do they feel about labor-inducing drugs, electronic fetal monitoring, episiotomy, and anything else you would like to include or exclude?
- What have been their caesarean section rates? The national average is in the 10 to 20 percent range, but this is considered excessive by some health workers.
- Who are their back-up doctors and do they share your attitudes toward your birth choices?

Questions for Midwives
(Consumer fears: informal training, the issue of legal status, less access to technological tools, and the possible need for mid-labor transfer to a hospital.)

- How broad is the training and experience they have had?
- How have they handled emergencies?
- What kind(s) of back-up do they have? Some midwives have a doctor who will assist or take over if a complication arises. Others have informal relations with the staff of a local hospital.
- How would they handle a transfer to a hospital, if it became necessary? Would they stay with you?

Adapted from Levinson, 1984. ■

There are numerous advantages and rewards from these nontraditional delivery approaches, including the sharing of the birth experience, the greater attention and care directed to the newborn, and the opportunity for both husband and wife to more directly assume their new role as parents.

CHAPTER HIGHLIGHTS

While there are many couples who want to have children, there are those who can't because of infertility. Infertility, a physiological problem, is the inability to carry pregnancies to a live birth. This chapter explored some of the techniques available to those couples who cannot conceive on their own, including in-vitro fertilization, artificial insemination by donor, surrogate motherhood, and embryo transfer.

As far as pregnancy is concerned, the moment of conception occurs when the male sperm penetrates the female egg to create a zygote. The average pregnancy lasts about 280 days, from conception to full-term. Pregnancy is divided into three equal segments called trimesters. As we learned in this chapter, distinct phases of prenatal growth and development take place during these three trimesters.

Throughout all of pregnancy, a mother must take steps to safeguard the prenatal environment. Among other health considerations are those re-

lated to nutrition, nicotine, drugs, teratogens, and maternal emotions. We also acknowledged complications and problems that can exist, such as miscarriages and ectopic pregnancies. Modern-day technology has supplied new techniques to help safeguard the prenatal environment: genetic counseling and amniocentesis, sonography, and fetoscopy are but a few.

Three stages of the birth process have been identified: the onset of uterine contractions, the actual delivery of the baby, and the expulsion of the placenta. Today, a number of delivery options are available for expectant couples. Among these are the Lamaze and Leboyer methods, home births, and rooming-in and birthing rooms within hospital settings.

KEY TERMS

amniocentesis
amniotic fluid
amniotic sac
artificial insemination by
  donor
birthing room facility
breech delivery
caesarean delivery
cojoined twins
ectopic pregnancy
embryo
embryo transfer
fetal alcohol syndrome

fetoscopy
fetus
fraternal twins
genetic counseling
home birth
identical twins
infertility
in-vitro fertilization
Lamaze method of childbirth
lanugo
Leboyer method of childbirth
miscarriage

multiple conception
natural childbirth
nurse-midwife
placenta
rooming-in facility
sonography
surrogate motherhood
teratogen
trimester
umbilical cord
vernix caseosa
zygote

RECOMMENDED READINGS

Bradley, R. A. (1980). *Husband-coached childbirth.* New York: Harper & Row. The emphasis of this book is on the active participation of the father during pregnancy and birth.

Brown, J. E. (1983). *Nutrition for your pregnancy: The University of Minnesota guide.* New York: Signet. Topics include eating well during pregnancy, fundamentals of nutrition, and nourishment for newborns.

Eisenberg, A., Murkoff, H. E., and Hathaway, S. E. (1984). *What to expect when you're expecting.* New York: Workman. One of the better pregnancy guides for mothers- and fathers-to-be. Loaded with practical suggestions and supportive guidance.

Hales, D., and Creasy, R. K. (1982). *New hope for problem pregnancies.* New York: Harper & Row. Chapter 6 provides an excellent discussion of how to protect the prenatal environment from drugs, chemicals, and other contaminants.

Hall, R. W. (1983). *Nine months reading.* New York: Bantam. A highly readable and thorough medical guide that explores pregnancy from conception to postnatal care.

Hillard, P. A., and Panter, G. G. (1985). *Pregnancy and childbirth.* New York: Ballantine. Particularly well-done are the chapters dealing with problems during pregnancy, from ectopic pregnancies to miscarriages.

Hotchner, T. (1984). *Pregnancy and childbirth.* New York: Avon. An extremely comprehensive account of pregnancy and birth, filled with numerous charts and tables as well as practical advice for expectant couples.

Lauersen, N. H. (1983). *Childbirth With Love.* New York: Berkley Books. Readers will find chapters on fetal development, genetic counseling, and the birth process to be especially informative.

Loader, A. (Ed.). (1980). *Pregnancy and parenthood.* Oxford, England: Oxford University Press. This collection of articles includes pregnancy problems, prematurity, twins, expectant fathers, and the anatomy and physiology of labor among its many topics.

Shapiro, H. I. (1983). *The pregnancy book for today's woman.* New York: Harper & Row. New obstetrical technology is given full coverage in Chapter 10 of this book.

12

Contemporary Parenthood

CONTENTS

CONTEMPLATIONS

■ The modern American mother. It may well be that she is putting in more hours than her grandmother did in running the household and almost all of her role commitments have expanded: wife, mother, home manager, community participant, breadwinner, and household decision maker, among others. In light of such an increasing workload, many label today's mothers "supermoms." With modern conveniences and technological advancements in the home, how is it that the mother's work load has increased? How do mothers balance all of their roles and maintain domestic harmony? What about the father's involvement? This chapter will look at these and other issues as parenthood in the 1980s is explored.

■ Upon the birth of a baby, the mother *or* father in Sweden can stay home with the newborn for almost a year and receive about 90 percent of their salary. In Hungary, a childcare grant that equals 40 percent of the mother's wages exists and lasts until the child is three. In Czechoslovakia and East Germany, a supplementary leave is available after the birth of the second and subsequent children. These are examples of federally funded maternity and paternity leave programs, varying in design and coverage, but available in over 100 countries around the world. A glaring exception to such programming is the United States. Why are such government programs lacking? How have these other nations designed such policies? A look at international maternity leaves will reveal some interesting findings.

■ How to bring the kids up right. This has been a concern of parents for years and an issue that has sparked a mixed batch of opinions from the so-called childrearing experts. These experts have given advice to parents on every conceivable aspect of childrearing from temper tantrums to toilet training. How might these strategies be classified? Is one more effective than the others? What if children don't follow what the "book" says? When you're done reading this chapter, you'll be in a position to better answer such questions.

The transition from a dyad to a triad relationship is usually the most complex and dramatic change most couples will ever face. Few other experiences will produce as many personal or social adaptations as becoming a parent. For that matter, no single circumstance in the growth and development of children will be as influential as parental interactions.

Doris Entwisle (1985) adds that little formal socialization exists for first-time parents. This is discouraging since parenthood signifies full entrance into adult society, including all of the responsibilities that such a status brings. The woman must integrate the mother role with her roles as wife, daughter, and possibly employee. The man must integrate the father role with his other roles: husband, son, employee, and so on. Moreover, parenthood has profound psychological and social implications for men and women, for their relations to each other and to the larger society.

EARLY ADJUSTMENTS AND ADAPTATIONS

Parenthood brings the need for considerable adjustment and adaptation, to say the least. Some researchers (Miller and Sollie, 1980; Waldron and Routh, 1981) view early parenthood as a stressful period and expound upon the many required adjustments and adaptations. The married couple is perceived as an integrated social system that requires a major reorganization when new members are added. With the arrival of a newborn, patterns of intimacy and affection are altered and need to be redefined. Some research even suggests that the addition of children lowers the overall marital happiness of the parents (Campbell, 1981; Glenn and McLanahan, 1981).

This does not mean that parenthood exists as a negative experience. On the contrary, not all experts contend that it is a stressful period. While it has its share of demands, most parents are able to successfully adapt. And even though some researchers find that the addition of children reduces marital happiness, most parents express overall satisfaction with their children and the parenting role in general (Chilman, 1980).

Right from the very beginning, parents need to reject the idealistic myth of creating and maintaining the perfect family. Like marriage, parenthood has its share of triumphs, but it also has its share of ups and downs, heartaches, and headaches. Too many parents strive for perfection and in the process program themselves for failure.

To say this even stronger the myth of the perfect family has greatly hindered human relations. To live in a family today is to be subjected to an ever-rising and broadening image of perfectionism. The family, however, is one of the facets of modern life in which perfectionism stands the least chance of attainment, no matter what the standards may be. This is because standards applied to the family prescribe inner states for people, rather than behavior. If a family is to be regarded as normal and stable, regardless of the ideal image within which it is housed, it is supposed to experience emotional states such as love and happiness. This emphasis

The transition from dyad to triad brings numerous challenges.

on inner experience intensifies the strains of family relationships. Probably as a result of this heightened strain, parents experience widespread guilt and anxiety over childrearing. The expectations for families must be reduced — their emotional lives depend on that. The family represents a perfectly imperfect world that is peaceful one moment and engaged in battle the next, simultaneously creative and stifling.(Morrison, 1983).

The adjustments posed by parenthood are numerous. Mothers must learn to adjust to loss of sleep and frequent physical fatigue. Many express concern about their personal appearance, changes in their figures, and the fact that they frequently feel edgy or emotionally upset. Fathers typically report such adjustments as additional domestic chores and, like mothers, sleepless nights. Many worry over financial matters, and some report irritation toward in-laws concerning proper childcare. Both mothers and fathers also report uneasiness about the unknown aspects of parenthood

MYTHS AND MISCONCEPTIONS ABOUT PARENTHOOD

The decision to have children should be founded on sound, rational principles. However, even during these enlightened times, many couples believe an assortment of folk tales that do nothing more than romanticize parenthood.

Here are some of the more common myths and misconceptions:

- *Modern-day parents are not as effective as those of yesterday.* This misconception is impossible to prove or disprove, of course, but it is prevalent in the minds of many. It is true, however, that higher standards are applied to today's parents, and the modern world in which parents have to function is more complex than it was in bygone eras.

- *Children will turn out okay if they have "good" parents.* Children and society are so complex that parents simply do not have the "quality control" one finds in industrial production. Effective parents usually turn out a more reliable "product" than those with more modest talents — even for good parents there is no such thing as "zero defects." Along these lines, almost everyone knows of at least one nice family with a black sheep in the fold.

- *Today's youngsters are appreciative of all the things their parents are able to give them.* Conversely, the opposite seems apparent: many children are today less appreciative than those of an earlier era, not more so. A similar attitude seems to be characteristic of all who live in modern society; we take for granted such things as painless dentistry and religious freedom and complain when the system fails to deliver.

- *Childrearing is all fun and little work.* The reality of the situation is that raising children is probably the most draining and thankless task in the world. While few parents would deny that it is rewarding and interesting, the tasks associated with childrearing are not always leisurely and amusing.

- *Bringing up youngsters today is easier because of modern medicine, modern appliances, child psychology, and the like.* While some claim that contemporary parents have an easier time because they have access to such things as dishwashers and diaper services, the truth of the matter is that parents are in much more of a "rat race" today with their busy schedules than their grandparents ever imagined.

- *Love is all that's needed to be effective parents.* While love is certainly needed, it is not enough. It must be guided by knowledge and insight and tempered with self-control on the part of the parent.

- *All married couples should have children.* This is a questionable proposition and one that few (if any) experts would support. Many married couples enjoy their own exclusive company and can sustain their marriage without the addition of children.

- *There are no bad children — only bad parents.* This may well be the most destructive bit of folklore related to parenthood. In addition to parents, numerous factors affect the destinies of children, including genetic heritage and the actions of siblings, peers, teachers, and other agents of socialization.

Adapted from LeMasters and DeFrain, 1983.

and the lack of preparation for this new role (Roman and Raley, 1980; Sollie and Miller, 1980).

As adjustments are made and routines are established , anxieties and unsettled feelings about childcare usually diminish. Many parents develop confidence in their abilities and take pride in their daily accomplishments. Fears and anxieties also usually subside when parents learn that they don't have to do everything by the "book." Because of the practical experiences gained and lessons learned first-hand, parenthood over time begins to acquire a less tense and more relaxed, quality.

THE SCOPE OF PARENTHOOD

Parenthood brings numerous responsibilities — primary among which is financial security. Most couples find that the costs of rearing a child begin innocently enough, but soon mount. Food, clothing, furniture, toys, and the like make it an expensive venture (Brooks, 1981; Jaffe and Viertel, 1980).

The provision of care and supervision of the baby is an especially important responsibility. For many parents this seems to be a never-ending chore. Even the baby's sleep time has to be monitored to some degree. Childcare needs often mean that both subtle and distinct changes have to be made in household routines. During the course of feeding, napping, or diapering the baby, parents find that much of their day revolves around the infant's needs. Consequently, non-childcare–oriented chores and general household activities often have to be fitted in around the baby. With adaptation and adjustment, however, the needs of the baby, the parents, and the home can be juggled and routines usually established.

Let us acknowledge, though, that many young mothers do report feeling overwhelmed by the seemingly unending flow of infant-oriented tasks, that have to be performed. Feeding and bathing of the baby and laundering clothing, added to the regular household routines of cleaning, cooking, and shopping, make for a full day's work. Numerous other chores and responsibilities can be added to this list. However, if the father shares in the household work, the mother's load is reduced considerably. With the current emphasis on **egalitarianism**, the picture may be changing. Growing numbers of fathers are discovering satisfaction in caring for their children and sharing household chores.

Often, new parents find it difficult to enjoy each other's exclusive company. In addition, interactions and visits with friends become restricted. First-time parents also learn that the child's needs often compete with their own. Because of this, it is

TRANSITIONS OF PARENTHOOD

Becoming a parent is a key transition in the marriage cycle. Husbands and wives now become fathers and mothers, and married life acquires a new dimension. From the moment the infant enters the world to the time when maturity is reached, parents and children alike experience significant growth and development. Moments of happiness and pride directed toward one's offspring are interwoven with such feelings as sadness and frustration. Parents and children become partners for life and share a diverse assortment of experiences.

The dynamics that unfold between parent and child have prompted Ellen Galinsky (1980) to suggest that parenthood unfolds in a seemingly predictable series of stages. She proposes six stages in all, based upon interviews with over 200 parents from all parts of the country. Unlike most researchers who emphasize the   ▶

parents' influence on the growing child, Galinsky describes the effects of the developing child on the parents themselves.

At the foundation of her theory is the notion that parents experience a progressive transformation of their self-images. Parents mentally picture the way they think things should be, particularly in terms of their own personal behavior and that of their children. If such images are successfully achieved, satisfaction and happiness are experienced. If they are not attained, parents usually experience anger, resentment, and even depression. As a result, parents' self-images — not to mention parental development — are molded by interactions with their children. Because of this, it is the child who leads the parent from one stage of development to the next.

The **parental-image** phase occurs when the baby is born. At this time, parents seek to treat their children as they would have liked their parents to treat them. Images of parenthood center around a desire for perfection, even though most new parents acknowledge that childrearing perfection is nearly impossible.

The **nurturing stage** is the second phase of parental development and lasts approximately through the second year of the child's life. Developing bonds of attachment to the baby is the major task at this time, as well as learning how much and when to give, not only to oneself, but to one's spouse, job, and friends.

The **authority state**, between two and four years, represents a time when adults critically question their effectiveness as parental figures. For the youngster, this is a time of newly discovered social autonomy, testing of new powers and saying "no." Witnessing such developments may cause parents to discover flaws in their images of parental perfection. Parental growth during this stage may well be measured by rejecting the images that are simply unrealistic.

The **integrative stage**, embracing middle childhood, is the fourth phase proposed by Galinsky. Further childhood gains in independence and initiative, as well as expanding social horizons, often force parents to reexamine and then test their own implicit theories about the way things should be ideally and how they are in fact. Discrepancies between these two polarities are difficult for adults groping for effective parenting skills to accept.

The **independent teenage years** are a time for adolescents to seek greater levels of freedom, responsibility, and, in some cases, emancipation from the home. In perhaps one of parenthood's most impactful stages, adults must learn to redefine authority regarding the teenager's growing independence, while at the same time trying to ease the growing pains characteristic of the adolescent years.

The **departure stage**, around age 18, occurs when adolescents leave the home. For the parents, this final stage becomes a time for the assessment and evaluation of their overall past performances. Evaluating the entire experience of parenthood usually reveals positive as well as negative dimensions: the loose or crumbling pieces and the cracks, in addition to the cohesiveness, of their whole lives. Such an overview at this time in the family cycle, coupled with the assessments inherent in each of the previous stages, provides adults with a thought-provoking analysis and narrative of their performance as parents. ■

not uncommon for parents during stressful times to feel angry, jealous, and resentful.

This means that parents need to support one another and openly discuss their everyday needs, concerns, and problems. Just as accomplishments are shared, so too should the hardships and difficulties. Parents also need to periodically get away from the baby and enjoy their own private space, even though it often seems that too much work and effort are required for a night out on the town. In the final analysis, it's worth it. Husband and wife need to maintain a loving, harmonious relationship so that they can better fill the roles of mother and father.

One additional responsibility is developing childrearing approaches suitable for nurturing the youngster's healthy growth and development. The strategies employed and the parent-child relationship in general are important throughout all phases of childhood and adolescence. Regardless of the strategies chosen, an atmosphere of love,

trust, and security must be added and maintained during the formative years. Later in this chapter we will explore a representative number of childrearing theories that have been proposed for parents to consider.

PARENTAL ROLES

The Role of the Mother

American parents today, especially mothers, operate under higher standards than their historical counterparts. As mothers tend to family needs, they are expected to perform duties that did not exist in the past. For example, they are supposed to stay informed about new medical findings, such as new vaccines, making sure their children receive proper care. The same holds true for their involvement in community child-centered organizations: today's mother is expected to be alert to new programming for children, get their offspring

Children will alter the lives of parents in many ways.

interested, and get them enrolled. Examples such as this abound in modern society (LeMasters and DeFain, 1983).

The workload of the mother is clearly a formidable one. In addition to caring for their children, mothers often have to handle the father's needs. And, besides managing most of the domestic chores, many women also work outside of the home, a topic to be discussed presently. Suffice it to say that mothers need to balance all of these demands and needs, in the process maintaining positive self-regard.

Certain factors serve to complicate the role of mothers in contemporary society. As we saw with marriage, motherhood is often portrayed in an unrealistic light. Many accept the myth of the perfect mother and set their sights accordingly; expecting a totally happy home, perfect children, smoothly functioning schedules, and a blissful relationship with one's spouse. In seeking to attain such idealistic goals, mothers tend to overlook the day to day realities that constitute parenthood.

Another complication is that despite living in a home usually equipped with every modern convenience imaginable, the mother's work load actually increases. It may well be that women's workloads have paradoxically increased with the

introduction of each new invention originally intended to save time. For example, when the cast-iron stove replaced the open hearth, a variety of foods took the place of the one-pot dinner. Corn bread once was sufficient, but then milled flour came along making cakes and pastries possible. While cooking, cleaning, and taking care of the needs of the family have become more complex and time-consuming endeavors, the alternatives — such as communes, hot-food delivery systems, and commercial vacuum cleaning — have never been accepted, because they conflict with the family's desire for privacy and individuality (Cowan, 1983).

During the early stages of parenthood mothers typically discover just how much their lives have been altered. Almost immediately, the mother is thrust into her new role and will have to make decisions regarding her offspring. For example, choosing to breast-feed or bottle feed one's infant quickly puts the mother in a decision-making situation. It is also during these early stages of parenthood that many mothers report feelings of inadequacy, especially if they have had limited prior contact with children. With experience and a meaningful support system, though, such feelings gradually subside.

EARLY MOTHERING DECISIONS: FORMULA OR BREAST-FEEDING?

The breast or the bottle? A woman is almost immediately confronted with an important decision in her new role as mother: deciding between infant feeding alternatives. Indeed, this may be her most important decision. Most new mothers will find that this issue existed for years and has generated numerous opinions from a multitude of diverse sources — from watchful grandparents and in-laws to psychologists and anthropologists. In addition, this topic is almost always a focal chapter in every how-to book on childrearing, from Spock to Brazelton.

Prior to the 1930s, about the time when formula feeding was perfected, there was really no safe and reliable substitute for breast milk, although a woman could hire a wet nurse instead of nursing the baby herself. Today, though, most mothers have a choice — and a chance to weigh the supporting evidence for each alternative. The proponents of breast-feeding, supported by an international organization ▶

called the LaLeche League (from the Spanish word for milk), stress the close physical and psychological bonding that results between mothers and infants. It is maintained that nursing is the "natural" way to nourish an infant and prevent most feeding problems, constipation, and some allergic reactions. The mother's milk also contains antibodies that protect the infant from infectious diseases.

Many nursing mothers also report a calm peace during feeding times, and this serenity may have psychological support. Research indicates that breast-feeding inhibits the mother's menstrual cycle, as well as the mood swings associated with menstruation. The apparent lack of tension, irritability, and restlessness, frequently related to the menstrual cycle, may enable nursing mothers to respond to the needs of the baby in a more relaxed fashion.

There is also support, though, for bottle feeding. Proponents point to the greater mobility and freedom that bottle feeding offers to the mother after birth. The growing numbers of mothers rejoining the labor force within relatively short periods of time usually cannot do so without relying on formula feedings for the baby. We might add, though, that increasing numbers of working mothers continue to breast-feed via the use of breast pumps and infant-care nearby their work sites. Bottle feeding also allows the father to become involved in feeding times and the mother to spend more time with her other children, who might resent the continual contact that the breast-fed baby receives. And some mothers find nursing to be physically annoying and painful, while others report a general dislike of the practice or varying degrees of social embarrassment.

At the present time, scientific evidence states that neither approach is more effective than the other, a factor which may make the decision all the more difficult for the mother. Since no perfect choice exists, though, it may relieve a sense of guilt for choosing one approach over the other. What seems to be more important than the issue of breast or the bottle is the manner in which the mother interacts with the infant during feedings. Her love, care, and attention — as well as the trust that she conveys while meeting life's most basic need — may determine her success in this area, rather than the approach chosen.   ■

Working Mothers   Years ago, mothers were expected to remain at home and care for their children, particularly during their offspring's early years of development. Many felt that this was the only way a mother could love and properly rear her children during this important life stage. To venture away from the family in search of a paycheck was viewed as uncaring and unwise.

In contemporary society, escalating numbers of women are removing this traditional stereotype of mothering and working outside of the home. In addition, there is growing acceptance that a

woman can handle the multiple roles of breadwinner and mother. Far from being perceived as indifferent or uncaring, many are perceived as having established quality time with their children.

In support of the increasing proportion of mothers returning to the workplace, consider the following statistics:

■ In 1985, 54 percent of the women with children under age 6 were working, only 1 percent below the rate for all women.

■ In over 50 percent of the marriages where the husband is present and there are children under age 18, the mother works at least part time outside of the home.

■ In 1981 the number of children below age 18 who had working mothers totaled 31.8 million.

■ Since 1970 the number of children with working mothers has grown by 6.2 million, despite a 6.6 million decline in the children's population.

■ Compared to other historical eras, when women left the labor force for years for childbearing, the modern mother will return to work after not more than one year for each birth.

■ It is estimated that by 1990, 85 percent of American homes will consist of dual-earner couples. (Grossman, 1982; Children's Defense Fund, 1982; Masnick and Bane, 1980.)

(Figure 12-1 charts female participation rates within the overall labor force.)

It is generally acknowledged in the literature that the dual-earner family reaps its share of benefits and personal satisfaction (see Pleck, 1985; Voydanoff, 1984; Gilbert, Holahan, and Manning,

1981; Maracek and Ballou, 1981). However, certain sacrifices are common in homes with younger children. The responsibilities of childrearing and tending to domestic chores appear to be the biggest obstacles for women to overcome in pursuing careers. In many instances, the woman still performs the majority of household tasks. As a result, the two-career marriage is really a three-career marriage, with the mother typically holding down two jobs.

While more men than ever before offer help and assistance around the house, it is the wife who typically carries out most of the chores. Thus, despite gains in a more egalitarian work orientation, household chores still bear a sexist dimension. According to one study (Ferber, 1982), men even acknowledge the fact that they could do more household chores.

Working mothers may face other difficulties. Many report a degree of anxiety about their children's well-being and wonder if they've made the right choice about returning to the labor force. Many full-time mothers, on the other hand, wonder if they shouldn't return to the labor force.

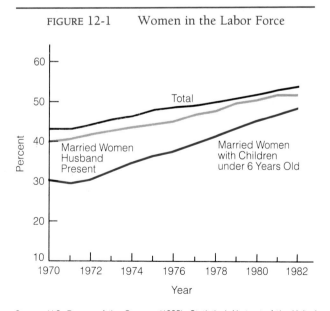

FIGURE 12-1   Women in the Labor Force

Source: U.S. Bureau of the Census. (1985). *Statistical Abstract of the United States.* Washington DC: U.S. Government Printing Office, p. xxi.

Thus, a type of "Catch-22" situation exists. Working mothers may also be satisfied with their chosen professions but feel inadequate in their mothering roles. This is a situation often breeding role conflict. Still others report guilt and mixed feelings if they happen to earn more money than their husbands (Rubenstein, 1982; Gilbert, Holahan, and Manning, 1981).

Finding quality childcare is an important concern for today's working parents. Whereas in earlier historical times mothers remained at home to care for their young, today's dual-earner couples must turn to the outside for childcare assistance. The relinquishment of the youngster to childcare facilities thus offers a new twist to childrearing practices and may place contemporary parents at odds with their parents. Many of the older generation strongly believe that a woman's place is in the home. The modern woman's removal of these "chains" sometimes produces ambivalence on the older generation's part. A growing acceptance of women entering the employment world is apparent in modern society, though, and we're likely to see increasing approval of childcare assistance in years to come.

In the United States, daycare facilities for the children of working parents are scarce. This is in marked contrast to the federally sponsored daycare programs available in such nations as the So-viet Union, France, and Sweden. The scarcity of childcare facilities is illustrated by the following statistics. Daycare centers, nursery schools, and other early childhood education facilities account for only 15 percent of working parents' children under the age of five. Forty percent are cared for at someone's home, and about 31 percent are watched by someone within the parents' home. Nine percent care for their youngsters while working (U. S. Department of Commerce, 1982).

Working parents able to enroll their youngsters in an early childhood education facility are usually well-educated, employed full time, and have a high family income. Lower-income couples find female relatives to care for their young, with grandparents an especially popular choice. (Figure 12-2 displays childcare arrangements of working mothers with children under five years of age).

In recent years, attention has been focused on those children not having adult care and supervision during the day. About 1.8 million youngsters between the ages of 3 and 13 fall into this category and are called "latchkey children." These youngsters care for themselves at home, in school yards, or on the street for several hours each day. What is happening to these children while their parents are at work? The most accurate answer is that, as a nation, we are unsure (Children's Defense Fund, 1982; Kamerman and Kahn, 1981).

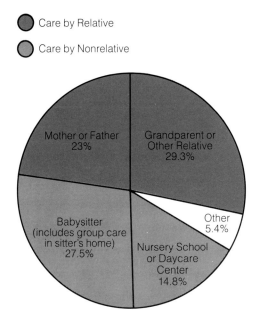

Care by Relative

Care by Nonrelative

Mother or Father
23%

Grandparent or
Other Relative
29.3%

Babysitter
(includes group care
in sitter's home)
27.5%

Other
5.4%

Nursery School
or Daycare
Center
14.8%

Source: U.S. Bureau of the Census. (1982, June). *Daytime care of children.* Current Population Reports, Series p-20.

FIGURE 12-2 Childcare Arrangements of Working Mothers with Youngsters under Five Years of Age

Beyond the difficulties working parents encounter in finding quality daycare, we also need to acknowledge that the United States offers mothers an inadequate maternity-leave system. Most European nations have adopted extended – maternity-leave policies in the last few decades. They vary from one to three years, with complete job security and some pay for the entire duration. In these nations, there is often a declining birth rate and labor shortages. The United States, conversely, has an abundance of workers and high rates of unemployment. In the United States maternity leaves usually vary from company to company and are, for the most part, quite short in comparison to other nations. In many instances maternity-leave pay is nonexistent.

European maternity leaves do not exercise any negative impact on the situation of women in the labor force. Maternity leave in itself is not a threat to a woman's job identity. Hungarian women, for example, never doubt their work role as full workers; Swedish women, in the vast majority, reenter the labor market and hold their jobs. If anything, maternity leaves of greater length contribute to a stable work identity; women know when and where they are going back if they choose to, whereas in the United States women often drop out or are forced to do so and then have a problem finding another job afterward (Erler, 1982).

The Children of Working Parents Within dual-career homes, how do the children fare? Contemporary research indicates that children of working parents are no more problem-prone than others. Indeed, many are better organized and more independent than those children with the mother or father at home, and many children of working parents take on greater levels of household responsibilities (Petersen, 1982).

CROSS-CULTURAL FOCUS

MATERNITY LEAVE POLICIES AROUND THE WORLD

In addition to a lack of government-sponsored daycare, the United States has no federal law giving working women a maternity leave of absence. Unlike over 100 countries around the world, there is no program that guarantees them the same or a comparable job on their return, or the provison of at least part of their earnings while they are on leave. (The figure on the following page displays maternity and paternity leave programs in other nations.) ▶

Some countries offer benefits even beyond these. For example, Hungary provides a childcare grant that equals about 40 percent of the mother's wages and lasts until the child is three. In Czechoslovakia and East Germany, supplemental leave is available after the birth of the second and subsequent children. Countries such as France, Norway, and Sweden permit either parent to take an unpaid, job-

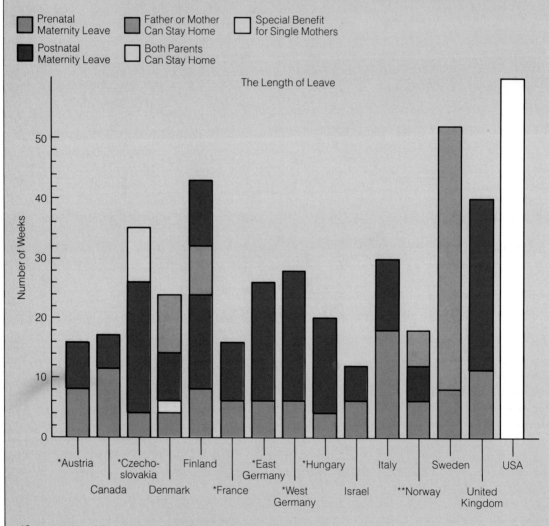

Legend:
- Prenatal Maternity Leave
- Postnatal Maternity Leave
- Father or Mother Can Stay Home
- Both Parents Can Stay Home
- Special Benefit for Single Mothers

The Length of Leave

Number of Weeks (y-axis: 0, 10, 20, 30, 40, 50)

Countries: *Austria, Canada, *Czechoslovakia, Denmark, Finland, *France, *East Germany, *West Germany, *Hungary, Israel, Italy, **Norway, Sweden, United Kingdom, USA

*Some portion of the pre- and/or postnatal leave is mandated. In other countries, women are permitted flexibility in how they divide their total leave between the pre- and postnatal periods.

**Father can use up to 12 weeks of the total benefit if mother uses less of the prenatal leave.

Source: Kamerman, S. B. (1985). Time out for babies. *Working Mother, 4* (9),80–82.

protected leave, ranging from one to two years, when the paid leave ends. And in West Germany, Sweden, and Norway, the government also sponsors paid leave when care for a sick child is needed.

How are all of these benefits paid for? These programs represent a type of "social insurance" and are similar in scope to Social Security and unemployment benefits in the United States. For example, in eight nations (Canada, France, Finland, East Germany, Hungary, Israel, Italy, and the United Kingdom), employers and employees each contribute a small percentage of their wages for such programming. In Sweden and Czechoslovakia, employers and the government finance the benefits. In Austria, West Germany, and Norway, financing originates from employer, employee, and government contributions, while in Denmark, general tax revenues from national and local governments pay for it.

Adapted from Kamerman, 1985; Kamerman, Kahn, Kingston, 1983) ∎

One researcher (Crouter, 1982) discovered that the child's sex and the socioeconomic status of the family are two important variables to consider when evaluating the issue of working parents and children. For girls, having a mother who works outside the home is especially beneficial. Girls are more likely to admire their mothers, to have a positive view of being female, and to be more independent than their peers whose mothers work at home. However, this trend is not apparent among boys. In middle-class families, sons of employed mothers perform less well in school than boys whose mothers work at home. But this pattern does not hold for low-income families, perhaps because the income brought in by the mother is so important to the family economy that it offsets any negative consequences her working might have for her sons.

Joseph Pleck (1981) views the dual-career household in a positive light because of the role equality it nurtures. He maintains that children experience the healthiest growth and development when both parents share in the upbringing. He feels that more balanced childrearing occurs when parents' job lives are more equal. In this respect, equal employment policies benefit not only women, but also children to the degree that fathers, whose wives' earnings are important to the family, take more active roles with their children.

Recently, attention has been focused on the effects of daycare on children. Working parents often turn to daycare because of its convenient programming. It offers full day sessions, often from 7:00 A.M. until 6:00 P.M.. Some specialize in infant and toddler care, offer meals and structured learning sessions. For the children of working parents, daycare can represent a home away from home.

However, daycare centers have sparked considerable controversy among child psychologists, educators, social workers, and parents. While such facilities offer supervision and care to children and enable mothers to work, concern is frequently voiced over the effects of daycare on youngsters. Maternal separation and the disruption of attachment bonds to the caretaker are critical issues for many. Some argue that the daycare center cannot provide this essential early social relationship except under ideal conditions. Most youngsters must share the attention of a daycare worker with other children, and in the typical ten-hour center day, work shifts change at least once. Add to this vacations and job turnovers, and a child may well have no one special person to be close to. Sometimes the mother complicates the problem of an unhappy child by blaming the center and switching the child to another (White, 1981; Zigler and Turner, 1982).

Not everyone agrees on the potential negative

Meeting the needs of children while sustaining a vocation requires special talents.

effects of daycare, though. It is argued that children are fully capable of adjusting to daycare situations at an early age, and many also believe that these institutions offer rewarding learning experiences. In a review of the literature, Susan Kontos and Robin Stevens (1985) observe that quality daycare can promote more sociable and considerate children, not to mention enhancing cognitive and linguistic competencies.

A critical issue for working parents, is finding a quality program and not settling for a mediocre operation. This is not an easy task, but one well worth the effort. Parents need to look for centers with such positive features as low adult-to-child ratios, good nutrition programs, excellent sanitation conditions, and adequate staff training. A successful daycare experience goes beyond the center's qualifications, though. The parental warmth, acceptance, and care that the child receives in the home may greatly influence the youngster's response to the overall daycare experi-

ence (Peters, Hodges, and Nolan, 1980; Auerbach, 1981).

The Role of the Father

The role of the father in childcare has been overlooked until recent years. While his importance in the home has always been generally recognized, American society has traditionally been "mother-centered" in its philosophy of childcare. With more of today's households being characterized as dual-earner, however, and with society's increasing deemphasis of sex-role differences, this focus may be changing. The father's influence on various aspects of the developing child is now being affirmed. Modern-day researchers are actively exploring the father's role and have uncovered a wide range of information (see Robinson and Barret, 1986; Lewis and Salt, 1986; Hanson and Bozett, 1985; Pederson, 1980; Lamb, 1981; Parke, 1981).

Contemporary fatherhood offers a unique contrast to earlier historical times. More men today are sharing a larger portion of the parenting role that had previously been reserved for women, for example, a more active participation in childbirth is common today. Also, in a growing number of cases, fathers are given custody of their children when there is a divorce. Such illustrations of the father's changing status is indicative of a trend involving the father more deeply in the task of parenting and overall family development (May and Perrin, 1985; Beer, 1982; Keats, 1981). As Bryan Robinson and Robert Barret (1986) put it, more men than ever before are sharing the breadwinner and nurturing roles, and, more are speaking out about the rewards of both.

Fathers' increased family participation was the main finding in a research study examining the role of men in 309 suburban families. In 71 of the families surveyed, fathers had the major responsibility for the day-to-day care of their children. Some had this responsibility because they were unemployed and their wives were in the work force; others because they had deliberately chosen this lifestyle. One of the contentions of this study

APPLICATIONS

SELECTING A QUALITY EARLY CHILDHOOD PROGRAM

Specialists working in early childhood education and child development have identified several indicators of quality care for preschoolers. These are important to identify since quality care can benefit your child, your family, and your community. Your youngster's educational, physical, personal, and social development will be nurtured in a well-executed program. The following represents important areas of concern:

Staffing Considerations

■ *The adults should enjoy and understand how young children learn and grow.* Are the staff members friendly and considerate to each child? Do adult expectations vary appropriately for children of differing ages and interests? Do the staff members consider themselves to be professionals? Do they read or attend meetings to continue to learn more about how young children develop? Does the staff work toward improving the quality of the program and obtaining better equipment?

■ *The staff should view themselves positively and therefore continually foster children's emotional and social development.* Do the staff help children feel good about themselves and their activities? Do the adults listen to children and talk with them? Are the adults gentle while being firm, consistent, and yet flexible in their guidance of children? Do the staff members help children learn gradually how to consider others' rights and feelings, to take turns and share, yet also to stand up for personal rights when necessary? When children are angry or fearful are they helped to deal with their feelings constructively?

■ *There should be enough adults to work with a group and to care for the individual needs of the children.* Is there at least one teacher and an assistant with every group of children? Are infants in groups of no more than 8 children? Are two- and three-year-old children in groups of no more than 16? Are four- and five-year-olds in groups of no more than 22 children?

■ *All staff members should work together cooperatively.* Does the staff meet regularly to plan and evaluate the program? Are they willing to adjust daily activities for children's individual needs and interests?

■ *The staff should observe and record each child's progress and development.* Does the staff focus on children's strengths and show pride in their accomplishments? Are records used to help parents and staff better understand the child? Is the staff responsive to parents' concerns about their child's development?

Program and Activity Considerations

■ *The environment should foster the growth and development of young children working and playing together.* Does the center have realistic goals for children? Are activities balanced between vigorous outdoor play and quiet indoor play? Are children given opportunities to select activities of interest to them? Are ▶

children encouraged to work alone as well as in small groups? Are self-help skills such as dressing, toileting, resting, washing, and eating encouraged as children are ready? Are transition times approached as pleasant learning opportunities?

■ *A good center should provide appropriate and sufficient equipment and play materials and make them readily available.* Is there large climbing equipment? Is there an ample supply of blocks of all sizes, wheel toys, balls, and dramatic play props to foster physical development as well as imaginative play? Are there ample tools and hands-on materials such as sand, clay, water, wood, and paint to stimulate creativity? Is there a variety of sturdy puzzles, construction sets, and other small manipulative items available to children? Are children's picture books age-appropriate, attractive, and of good literary quality? Are there plants, animals, or other natural science objects for children to care for or observe? Are there opportunities for music and movement experiences?

■ *Children should be helped to increase their language skills and expand their understanding of the world.* Do the children freely talk with one another and the adults? Do the adults provide positive language models in describing objects, feelings, and experiences? Does the center plan for visitors or trips to broaden children's understandings through first-hand contacts with people and places? Are the children encouraged to solve their own problems, to think independently, and to respond to open-ended questions?

Staff, Family, and Community Considerations

■ *A good program should consider and support the needs of the entire family.* Are parents welcome to observe, discuss policies, make suggestions, and participate in the work of the center? Do staff members share with parents the highlights of their child's experiences? Is the staff alert to matters affecting any member of the family which may also affect the child? Does the staff respect families from varying cultures or backgrounds? Does the center have written policies about fees, hours, holidays, illness, and other considerations?

■ *A good center should be aware of and contribute to community resources.* Does the staff share information about community recreational and learning opportunities with families? Do they refer family members to a suitable agency when the need arises? Are the volunteers from the community encouraged to participate in the center's activities? Does the center collaborate with other professional groups to provide the best care possible for children in the community?

Health and Safety Considerations

■ *The health of children, staff, and parents should be protected and promoted.* Is the staff alert to the health and safety of each child and of themselves? Are the meals and snacks nutritious, varied, attractive, and served at appropriate times? Does the staff wash their hands with soap and water before handling food and after changing diapers? Are children's hands washed before eating and after toileting? Are surfaces, equipment, and toys cleaned daily? Are they in good repair? Does each child have an individual cot, mat, or crib? Are current medical records and emergency information maintained for each child and ▶

staff member? Is adequate sick leave provided for the staff so they can remain at home when they are ill? Is at least one staff member trained in first aid? Does the center have a health consultant? Is the building comfortably warm in cold weather? Are the rooms ventilated with fresh air daily?

- *The facility should be safe for children and adults.* Are the building and grounds well lighted and free of hazards? Are furnishings, sinks, and toilets safely accessible to children? Are toxic materials stored in a locked cabinet? Are smoke detectors installed in appropriate locations? Are indoor and outdoor surfaces cushioned with materials such as carpet or wood chips in areas with climbers, slides, or swings? Does every staff member know what to do in an emergency? Are emergency numbers posted by the telephone?

- *The environment should be spacious enough to accommodate a variety of activities and equipment.* Are there at least 35 square feet of usable playroom floor space indoors per child and 75 square feet of play space outdoors per child? Is there a place for each child's personal belongings such as a change of clothes? Is there enough space so that adults can walk between sleeping children's cots?

Adapted from the *National Association for the Education of Young Children,* 1983, pp. 28–32. ■

was that fathers and mothers are equally important to their children and are equally able to care for them, right from birth (Russell, 1983).

As we learned in the last chapter, growing numbers of fathers are participating in natural childbirth classes, as well as assisting the mother during the delivery of the baby. Such involvement appears to have numerous positive consequences, in many instances extending beyond the delivery room. Fathers who have involved themselves in the delivery process tend to interact more with the newborn child and participate more in infant care than uninvolved fathers (Miller and Bowen, 1982; Cordell, Parke, and Swain, 1980).

Fathers are also able to establish strong bonds of attachment to their children and vice versa. Moreover, infants regularly turn to fathers in times of distress. Such father-infant interaction debunks the myth that attachment with one's offspring is the exclusive domain of the mother. However, what appears to be different in family relationships are the activities of the parents that foster attachment. The infant's more intense levels of attachment toward the mother may be attributable to her caretaking functions. Fathers offer other types of

stimulation such as play activities and exploration of the environment (LaRossa and LaRossa, 1981; Fein, 1980).

It is also fairly well-known that fathers have significant influences on the child's emotional, social, and cognitive development. His presence, and the attention that he directs toward his children, has short- and long-term benefits. The absence of his care also seems to affect the development of the child. For example, academic achievement and IQ levels in children may be adversely affected by the absence of a positive father-child relationship. The father can affect how well children progress in school, which subjects they prefer, and even the kinds of occupations they eventually choose. Fathers also influence social and sex-role development. As far as sex-role development is concerned, fathers influence children through their personalities, by serving as role models, and in their daily interactions (Parke, 1981; Radin, 1981).

Clearly, the father's influence on the family cannot be overstressed. However, whether or not this influence becomes positive is another issue. This depends on a number of factors, including

Compared to past historical periods, fatherhood has changed in breadth and scope.

involvement in childcare and family activities, the father's own upbringing, the quality of his other relationships, and the natural characteristics of his offspring (Lamb, 1982, 1983; Adams, 1984). Michael Lamb and colleagues (1986) add that fathers influence their children by the way they behave toward their offspring and the manner in which they interact with their wives.

Even though many fathers look forward to childcare, there are those who do not think that they should be spending more time with their children. Some maintain that the care, supervision, and entertainment of children are provinces of the mother. Many also feel that they are poorly prepared for the traditional tasks of parenting, let alone increased childcare responsibilities. In this respect, many fathers experience considerable anxiety, confusion, and uneasiness over the multi-

ple needs of their children (Spieler, 1982; Nannarone, 1983).

However, anxiety and confusion over children's needs and parenting in general are normal for *both* fathers and mothers. Our society is lacking in its preparation of adults for parenthood. The need for such preparation becomes especially obvious during a child's infancy, as many parents anxiously tend to the intense, multiple needs of their offspring. The adjustment and demands required by both father and mother are numerous (Roopnarine and Miller, 1985; Waldron and Routh, 1981; Clark, 1981; Miller and Sollie, 1980).

CHILDREARING TECHNIQUES AND STRATEGIES

The Child Experts Speak

We mentioned at the outset of the chapter that one of the most important responsibilities of parenthood was adopting suitable childrearing standards. Beginning around the turn of the century, the United States experienced an unparalleled interest in this topic. While child psychologists were scientifically exploring the many complexities of growth and development, childcare experts began to focus on the practical aspects of rearing children. In time, their ideas and viewpoints would find their way into books, magazines, professional journals, newspapers, and an assortment of parenting seminars and workshops.

The guidance offered by the so-called childcare experts focused on every conceivable aspect of childrearing, from discipline and toilet training to temper tantrums. Generally speaking, though, these experts addressed themselves to parenthood's most persistent challenge — how to guide children so that they become healthy, well-adjusted adults.

There is no question that this diverse assortment of childrearing guidance has helped to better educate parents about children and their many needs. The range of differing opinions and philosophies has, however, produced its share of confusion, too.

CROSS-CULTURAL FOCUS

RATES OF CHILDCARE PARTICIPATION AMONG AUSTRALIAN FATHERS

Increasing numbers of today's fathers are more involved with their youngsters and participate in greater amounts of childcare. This is apparent not only in the United States but in such countries as Australia. Let's explore some research focusing on Australian fathers and their families to see if any differences exist in the two nations.

One representative investigation was launched by Graeme Russell (1982). He studied 71 Australian households in which fathers were highly involved with their youngsters. These fathers, who had the primary responsibility for their children for an average of 26 hours per week, were compared with fathers from traditional families. In these homes, mothers bore the sole responsibility for their youngsters. A number of patterns became evident in the two domestic settings.

For instance, rates of father participation were greater in those homes having higher-status occupations and higher levels of education, and with families with fewer and older children. However, while highly participant fathers were the primary caregivers during the day, overall they spent less time at specific childcare tasks than did either their spouses or the mothers in traditional families. It was also discovered that mothers and fathers in highly participant–father families placed greater emphasis on interpersonal sensitivity and expressiveness, independence in thought and action, and less emphasis on conformity to social norms. Russell found tentative support for the notion that high father-participation enhances the affective nature of the father-child relationship.

This is as evident today as it was when the child experts first began to present their opinions.

For example, consider the conflicting childrearing advice that abounds on the issue of how much freedom to give a child. The swing of the pendulum on this particular issue has historically been extreme. Popular at the turn of the century was a **restrictive parenting** approach that stressed strict parent-child relations. Considerable emphasis was placed on the development of self-control, respect, and disciplined character. Parental affection was generally discouraged, since it was believed that excessive amounts would create childhood immaturity and irresponsibility.

During the 1940s a **permissive** approach to childrearing emerged. This approach emphasized greater levels of freedom with children and was popular among middle-class parents. Parents were advised to generate a loving attitude toward children that encompassed understanding, sensitivity, and affection. As far as disciplining measures were concerned, parents were encouraged to move away from physical punishment and adopt more relaxed but firm measures. They were also urged to develop confidence in their roles as parents. The permissive approach is evident in many books, the most notable being Benjamin Spock's *Baby and child care,* first published in 1945. This is an enormously popular book on childrearing, still used by many parents today.

These two contrasting childrearing approaches are good illustrations of the range of advice available to parents. While educational and informative, the differing opinions and philosophies often have a tendency to create parental confusion, frustration, and even anxiety. For instance, parents may ask which approach is better? Will it work for my child? Why isn't my child following the prescribed schedule or doing what "the book" says?

We want to add, too, that even in contemporary times a scientifically proven means of childrearing has yet to emerge. Although ideas and suggestions are bountiful, precise answers remain elusive. Consequently, it seems likely that parents will continue to be swept into a crossfire of opinion, as they seek out the best way to raise their children.

Theories of Childrearing

Because of the diverse assortment of childrearing strategies that are available to parents, it is helpful to categorize approaches according to their oper-

---

RESEARCH HIGHLIGHT

HEALTHY FAMILIES SPAN COLORS, INCOME LEVELS

Emotionally healthy families share the same characteristics whether they are black or white, affluent or struggling, according to a study conducted by John Looney and Jerry Lewis (1984). At the end of a three-year study of 18 black families, the investigators concluded that they — like the 45 well-functioning, well-off white families among 120 middle-class households in an earlier study — had two outstanding characteristics; that is, they created a family system that helped the parents feel nurtured and supported, and the system enabled children to go out in society and become independent human beings.

While differences in income inevitably produced differences in lifestyles, the healthy black working-class families and the healthy white middle-class families had amazingly similar structure, values, and goals. All the households were marked by:

■ Shared parental leadership. Neither the mother nor the father dominated, and the marital partnership was strong.

■ Clear generational boundaries between parents and children. There was no doubt as to who the parents were in these homes.

■ Clear, responsive communications between family members.

■ The freedom to be open about feelings.

■ Reliance on negotiation to solve problems.

■ Smooth functioning as a family unit.

The black families in this study did not have the rigid, autocratic framework some researchers have found in working-class minority families fighting for financial survival. Neither parent exercised power over the other, and the matriarchal pattern observed in other studies did not exist here.

Income for the family ranged from $6,600 to $15,320 a year. Mothers had attended school for ten years on the average; fathers, for nine. Mothers' jobs ▶

included machine operator, telephone operator, domestic worker, baby-sitter, and in one instance, social caseworker. Fathers' employment included construction workers, clerks and semi-skilled workers.

As indicated, the emotionally healthy households of both races and economic levels had common values. Both groups gave top priority to being honest, loving, and forgiving. They ranked education, religious values, family security, happiness, self-respect, and wisdom high among their family aims.

The researchers add that emotionally healthy families experience all the ordinary domestic disappointments and hurts. The families were thus healthy, but not perfect.

ating philosophy, so a better understanding of the rationale behind a suggested guideline or opinion can be developed. Let's look at some of the more popular childrearing strategies to emerge.

Parent-Effectiveness Theory   Developed by Thomas Gordon (1978), parent-effectiveness training (P.E.T.) teaches parents how to enhance children's self-images and reach their full potentials in life. Gordon's techniques include reflecting positive images back to the child, engaging in mutual negotiation when problems arise, and "active listening" or verbally feeding back to the youngster that which has been expressed. Gordon proposes that this latter communication technique enables children to better understand what they've said and assists them in solving their own problems. Gordon also advocates the use of "I"

rather than "you" messages ("I get upset when you disturb me like that," as opposed to, "You're a very rude child to bother your poor father like this."). He feels that "I" messages are more likely to impart facts, while "you" messages have a tendency to attach blame, promote rebellion, and reduce the child's self-concept.

Developmental-Maturational Theory   This approach was developed by Arnold Gesell (1940) and is called an age-stage theory of childrearing. Such an approach acknowledges that while individual variations exist, most children experience developmental milestones at fairly predictable ages. Gesell spent considerable time exploring this principle, leading him to devise numerous norms of infant and child development. Gesell emphasizes that parents should have an understanding of

childhood's developmental sequences and structure their expectations and childrearing techniques accordingly.

Democratic Theory   This approach is evident in the writings of many childrearing experts, the most notable of whom is Rudolph Dreikurs (1964). Dreikurs maintains that the family unit is the primary force in shaping children's behavior. Consequently, parents should seek to integrate children as fully as possible into the family network, so they can benefit from everyone's observations, feedback, and encouragement. Children are encouraged to participate in family decision-making processes, including the establishment of rules and expectations. By so doing, Dreikurs believes they will learn "logical consequences" of their behavior, those expected behavorial standards that will ensure the fair treatment of all family members. The promotion of such a collective and cooperative atmosphere will promote security, trust, and a sense of belonging within the child.

Humanistic Theory   The humanistic approach was developed by Haim Ginott (1965) and stresses the development of parental empathy, sensitivity, and insight into the needs of children. Parents are encouraged to improve their communication abilities so that they can better appreciate their children's feelings and motivations. Among other suggestions, Ginott suggests the practice of preceding statements of advice with statements of understanding, the resolution of conflicts without attacks on personalities, and the abolishment of all threats and sarcasm.

Transactional-Analysis Theory   Developed by Eric Berne (1964), the transactional-analysis approach stresses the importance of three *ego states* and their relation to effective communication. The three states are the child (source of spontaneity, but also the source of fear, helplessness, and intimidation), adult (source of reason, but also the source of emotionless responses), and parent (the source of nurturance, but also the source of emotional response). Berne suggests that the adult

psyche is capable of expressing these three unique ego dimensions when communicating with others. The analysis of communication patterns (called transactions), therefore, reveals interesting and complex dynamics. In connection with childrearing, parents may inappropriately respond to a youngster's problem by activating helplessness within their own child state. Or both parents may be striving to solve the same childrearing issue, but are unproductive because their ego states are incompatible (the father may be utilizing the nurturance facet of his parent state, while the mother's communication embodies the oppressive-adult ego state). Throughout his writings, Berne emphasizes the importance of ego-state recognition and the compatibility of exchange patterns, as well as the parental nurturance of the adult ego state in children.

Behavior-Modification Theory   Those stressing the behavior-modification approach place an emphasis on the child's surroundings and exercising some control of them. Should this be accomplished, then parents are capable of shaping a child's behavior. Practitioners advocate the use of *positive reinforcement,* or the rewarding of a desired behavior (a child is given a toy for good behavior), or *negative reinforcement,* giving children the opportunity to behave in a way that reduces or eliminates an aversive stimulus (children are sent to their rooms because of a temper tantrum, but can return as soon as they calm down). Proponents claim that when consistently adhered to, these principles enable parents to nurture desired behavioral patterns in their children.

Putting Childrearing Theories into Perspective   These theories provide us with a great deal of insight into the nature of childrearing. However, we must stress that these theoretical positions do not have to be examined or weighed in an either-or manner. They are not mutually exclusive or independent of one another. Several of them could be operating at different times or under different conditions. For example, the fact that child may be at a specific norm of Gesell's developmental-maturational theory does not mean that principles of reinforcement are not operating or that the youngster's interaction with the family unit becomes non-existent. Thus, while each theory is an effort to explain childrearing techniques, it is not uncommon for two or more of them to be operating simultaneously.

This is the primary reason why many parents today choose to be eclectic when viewing childrearing theories. They pick and choose the bits and pieces of theories that they can accept, and then develop their own strategies. Moreover, theories need to be adapted and modified to take each individual child into account. Generalized childrearing theories without individual modification downplay the uniqueness of both child and parent.

Finally, while each of the theories has broadened our understanding and offers us new areas of exploration, we have not yet been able to answer all our questions about childrearing. As we indicated earlier, no theory has yet to explain the ''best'' way to rear youngsters. This underscores the need to further investigate this field of study, as well as the need for reassessing the theories and viewpoints generated thus far.

AN OVERVIEW OF CHILD AND ADOLESCENT DEVELOPMENT

Efforts to chart the course of child and adolescent development have attracted the attention of many researchers. Emerging from these investigative pursuits, according to Judy McKee (1986), are a number or organizing concepts: the issues of nature vs. nurture, orderly development, ages and stages, and individual variation.

Nature vs. Nurture   The nature vs. nurture issue suggests that heredity (maturation, temperament, and nature) and environment (nurture, including learning) interact, resulting in the organization of growth, behavior, and adaptation over time. When observing children and adolescents, one can see that a second concept—*orderly development*—follows a sequential order. For example, while the age for walking varies by several

months, every child goes through a number of predictable steps such as rolling over, moving on hands and knees, and pulling up to a standing position before finally walking.

Ages and Stages   The ages and stages concept proposes unique periods of development when certain abilities are most observable. Stages refer to predictable, sequential, developmental periods that are qualitatively different from each other. They serve to describe what can be reasonably expected of children and what is beyond their abilities during a time period.

Individual Variation   Finally, the concept of individual variation suggests that there are general developmental patterns and stages. However, their emergence varies widely for individuals. There is ample evidence that children follow the genetic principles of orderly development through stages, but variation within a wide spectrum of individual differences is the norm. For example, the loss of baby teeth and understanding of mental concepts are different for youngsters of even the same age.

With these concepts in mind, let's turn our attention to the course of childhood and adolescent development. While we can't possibly explore the many complexities of development in the confines of one chapter, we can supply a few observations regarding these life stages. Let us acknowledge, too, that only for scientific convenience do we identify stages of development. Life does not stop or start at the beginning or end of stages or age classification systems.

Infancy and Toddlerhood

During the years of infancy and toddlerhood, numerous developmental challenges appear. For example, developing control in physical expression, such as walking, as well as refining mental concepts to clarify one's surroundings are important tasks. Personality and social demands are equally significant, particularly interactions with one's parents and other family members.

It is from early interactions within the family that children develop a better understanding of themselves and their environment. Heightened cognitive powers blend with early personality and social forces to help youngsters realize that they are separate, unique individuals. These processes combine to foster the development of such feelings as trust or mistrust, autonomy or self-doubt, and a range of other behaviorial expressions.

Socialization is a multi-faceted process that begins early in life. As infants begin to spend more hours of the day awake, they usually have more interactions with parents, from the rituals of feeding, diaper changing, and other custodial chores, to recreational and playtime activities. These early interactions are the seeds of social development for the child.

Meaningful parent-infant interaction is important because adults can provide critical stimulation to the youngster's linguistic, cognitive, social, and physical capacities. Indeed, the lack of adult interaction and stimulation will retard growth in these areas. Through interactions with parents, infants also gradually develop a sense of the home's emotional climate. Interactions frequently reveal how parents feel about themselves and each other. Without question, the feelings parents have toward the child will also ultimately surface in direct or indirect ways (Roman and Raley, 1980; LaRossa and LaRossa, 1981).

Today, growing numbers of fathers share child-rearing chores, and unique bonds of attachment form between fathers and their children. However, the mother is usually the dominant influence in the infant's life. From the earliest feedings and handlings to verbal exchanges and eye contact, the mother has an unremitting influence on the infant's personality and social growth. During the early months the two will develop a bond of attachment that provides support and comfort to both.

Some researchers feel that attachment begins during the hours immediately following birth and that early interaction between parents and infants intensifies the overall strength of attachment. However, reactions to this point of view are mixed

Attachment behaviors are expressed in many different ways.

(see Lamb, 1982; Chess and Thomas, 1982; Herbert, Sluckin, and Sluckin, 1982; Marano, 1981), and no one has yet proved that such early attachment stimulation yields long-lasting results. However, we do know that, generally speaking, bonds of attachment strengthen over time. To observe this, one has only to watch the intense and unblinking gaze of the infant toward the mother, the clinging behavior of a two-year-old, or the upset face of a preschooler unexpectedly separated from mother. Witness, too, the intense reciprocal attachment behaviors from the mother to the infant as she tends to her child's needs.

Attachment is an important dimension of healthy personality and social functioning, promoting such positive behaviors and feelings as trust and security. Its absence, on the other hand, can trigger anxiety, anger, and inner turmoil. For instance, insecurely attached children seem to be less adept at overall social relations than securely attached children. For some, absence of attachment even results in grief and depression (Bowlby, 1980; Londerville and Main, 1981).

Early as well as later social development appears to be affected by attachment experiences during the first years. One's general outgoingness, social independence, and emotional investment in others may even be traced to the outcome of these early social experiences. Also, we must not forget that our need for security, reassurance, or nurturance, while most intense during infancy and toddlerhood, is never really left behind. These are important needs that persist even into adult life.

ERIK ERIKSON'S EIGHT STAGES OF HUMANITY

Erik Erikson (1982; 1980; 1963) contends that the process of socializing the child into a given culture occurs by passing through innately determined sequential stages, or what he calls psychosocial development. Each stage of life has a crisis related in some way to an element in society. The successful resolution of these life crises is important throughout all of development, from the months of infancy through the later years of adulthood.

The first of Erikson's eight psychosocial crises is called **basic trust vs. mistrust** (ages 0 to 1). During this stage, the nature of parental interactions with the infant is critical. If infants receive proper care, love, and affection, they develop a sense of trust. If these basic needs are not met, they become suspicious, fearful, and mistrusting of their surroundings.

During **autonomy vs. shame and doubt** (1 to 3), developing motor and mental abilities give the child the opportunity to experience independence. If their growing urge to explore the world is encouraged, children grow more confident in themselves and more autonomous in general. However, if their developing independence is met with parental disapproval or discouragement, children may question their own abilities and harbor doubts about their own adequacy.

During the third stage, children experience the psychosocial crisis known as **initiative vs. guilt** (3 to 5). Increasingly refined developmental capacities prompt the child to self-initiate enviromental exploration and discovery. Parental reinforcement will encourage such initiative and promote purpose-and-goal-directiveness. Parental restrictiveness, on the other hand, is likely to promote guilt whenever children seek to discover the world on their own.

Industry vs. inferiority (6 to 11) is characterized by the child's desire to manipulate objects and to learn how things work. Such an industrious attitude typically leads to a sense of order, a system of rules, and an important understanding about the nature of one's surroundings. Inferiority feelings may result, however, if adults perceive behavior as silly, mischevious, or troublesome.

The fifth psychosocial crisis, perhaps the most famous, is **identity vs. role confusion** (adolescence). The task at this time is to develop an integrated sense of self, one that is personally acceptable and, it is hoped, distinct from others. Failure to nurture an accurate sense of personal identity may lead to the dilemma of role confusion. This frequently leads to feelings of inadequacy, isolation, and indecisiveness. ▶

The task of **intimacy vs. isolation** (young adulthood) is to develop close and meaningful relationships with others. Having attained a sense of personal identity in the previous stage, individuals are now able to share themselves with others on a moral, emotional, and sexual level. Intimacy may mean marriage, the establishment of warm and nurturant friendships, or, of course, both. Those unable or unwilling to share themselves with others suffer a sense of loneliness or isolation.

Erikson's seventh stage is called **generativity vs. self-absorption** (middle adulthood). The positive pole of this stage, generativity, means that adults are willing to look beyond themselves and express concern about the future of the world in general. The self-absorbed person, on the other hand, tends to be preoccupied with personal well-being and material gains.

The final stage is **integrity vs. despair** (old age). Those persons nurturing a sense of integrity have typically resolved previous psychosocial crises and are able to look back at their lives with dignity, satisfaction, and feelings of personal fulfillment. Those who have not successfully resolved previous crises are likely to feel a sense of despair. These individuals usually view their past lives as a series of disappointments, failures, and misfortunes.

Early Childhood

During the years of early childhood, youngsters expand their social horizons and develop considerable independence and autonomy. Once socially restricted and dependent, preschoolers become more involved with their environment and venture into new and challenging social situations with peers and adults. These new experiences — originating from the neighborhood, school, or other socialization agents — are integrated into the child's total sense of being and contribute immensely to developing personality and social awareness (Walsh, 1980; Blatchford, Battle, and Mays, 1983).

Of critical importance to the youngster during these early years is entry into an early childhood education program. Beyond the educational benefits described earlier, preschool programming offers a rich terrain for growth and development. From these early schooling experiences, youngsters will further develop their autonomy and ability to adjust to change. Moreover, they will broaden feelings of competency and trust.

In joining the company of others, children emerge as individuals, gaining insight into their own unique personalities. Socially, children can see what effects their behavior has on others, a developing cognitive power that enables them to nurture concepts of right and wrong. Their social experiences also enable them to slowly understand rights and privileges of others. In addition, social experiences help children develop a self-concept — that is, the manner in which they perceive themselves.

The family continues to transmit appropriate behaviors, knowledge, and values to children; but it also provides them with an emotional setting that makes them feel accepted and loved. It should be noted that the child must experience and learn to deal with negative emotions as well as the so-called positive emotions in order for psychological growth to occur. Along these lines, favorable home environment and a positive emotional climate become critical influences in the child's total personality and social development. This is as true now as it is for later years.

Certain factors in the child's interaction with

the family are of particular importance during early childhood. For example, parental support, guidance, and fulfillment of the child's needs for security, trust, and understanding are extremely significant when one examines the quality of family relationships. Equally important are the methods of parental control in operation as well as relations with siblings. Stable personality and social growth in general are greatly affected by one's sense of identity and belonging to the family unit, not to mention the warmth and acceptance accorded by others (Westlake, 1981; Smith, 1982).

Middle Childhood

Middle Childhood is an active period of growth and development. During this time, the interaction between child and society (which constitutes socialization) expands and becomes more complex. Observers of this age group will see that youngsters wish to be with others and that social relations acquire many new dimensions, whether in peer-group relations, school activities, sports, or family activities.

With the expansion of social horizons, children discover that they must adjust their behavior to meet the numerous expectations and demands of society. This is an ongoing process and requires considerable adaptability. Socially acceptable or tolerable behavior in toddlers, such as clinging dependency, may not be acceptable in school-age youngsters. Modification of behavior is thus necessary to meet the changing expectations of society.

Children acquire insight into themselves and their developing personalities from the social relations of the school year. Indeed, the child's sense of self grows through interactions with others and from inferences about personal experiences. While certain degrees of self-awareness were evident earlier in life, they were frequently based on

The path to social maturity begins early in life.

the youngster's physical qualities or possessions. Children are now likely to include in their self-appraisals other facets of themselves, such as how they are perceived by others and their general competencies (Perry and Bussey, 1984; Harter, 1983; Damon and Hart, 1982).

The fact that children now attend school full-time, have greater interaction with their peers, and display heightened levels of independence places the family in a new perspective. Children still need and rely very much on their parents, but their contacts with the outside world have expanded. As a result, their social relationships with other adults are considerably broader, including, for example, interactions with teachers, den mothers, coaches, or summer camp leaders.

The negotiation of new social boundaries and parents' reactions to the youngster's strivings for independence make these years especially challenging. Many children want to spend more time away from the family. This may threaten many parents, who need to be assured that this is a completely normal phase of child development and that they will remain special and unique in the wake of their social strivings. It is interesting to note that admidst these desires for social independence, many school-age children periodically tend to slip back to dependency, although usually in private and on their own terms. This age also marks the time when many want to spend more time alone doing private things or to keep secret what they do both within and away from the family.

Children's greater interactions with others enable them to bring back to the home an abundance of social experiences, whether it be tales about school or sports exploits or neighborhood news. Their increasing powers of social cognition also enable them to compare their home environment with those around them. As a result, what other children have or do is weighed against what they have or are allowed to do, a comparison likely to breed a fair number of questions and possible disagreements with parents. (How many parents have heard, "Everyone else does it; why can't I?") Parents' values and standards are also tested when children bring home ideas, language, and attitudes different from those taught at home.

APPLICATIONS

HOW TO BE AN EFFECTIVE DISCIPLINARIAN

Youngsters need to experience a favorable home climate throughout all of childhood, but this is especially true during the school years. Children unquestionably need the support and guidance of parents as they seek to meet the challenges of this age. This is as true for achieving personal independence as it is for other facets of growth, such as developing a sense of morality, establishing healthy relations with siblings, learning appropriate sex roles, and building self-esteem.

Favorable home environments provide warmth and acceptance to children and employ effective discipline. Unfortunately, learning how to master the latter is a stumbling block for many parents. Much of the problem is due to uncertainty regarding what the term discipline entails. **Discipline** is the establishment of limits in an effort to teach acceptable forms of conduct or behavior. The ultimate goal of discipline is to produce responsibility in children. Moreover, children must learn ▶

that they are accountable for the consequences of their behavior. The following guidelines will assist adults confronted with the task of disciplining children:

■ *Realize that there are motivations for misbehavior.* Misbehavior doesn't just happen on its own; the child may be motivated in some way to engage in disruptive behavior. Some of the more common reasons for misbehavior include boredom and desire for attention, revenge, power, and control.

■ *Act with confidence.* Adults must believe in themselves and their ability to promote responsible behavior. They should adopt a take-charge attitude and handle disciplinary situations with self-assurance and confidence. Children are quite adept at spotting adults unsure of themselves.

■ *Relate the discipline to the situation at hand.* Adults should focus on the central issue and not stray into unrelated problems. It is also important to tell children that it is the misbehavior that is being rejected, not them as individuals. Furthermore, adults need to explain why they are upset with the misbehavior ("You broke the vase, and I'm angry because it was special to me"). This helps teach youngsters that misbehavior has implications for others.

■ *Be consistent.* Erratic discipline confuses children and seems unlikely to prevent similar problems in the future. If adults are going to discipline the child for one particular type of misbehavior, the recurrence of this misbehavior must also be disciplined. If there are two or more children in the home, discipline should be consistent among them as well.

■ *Don't make discipline a public spectacle.* Discipline can be a sensitive affair, especially among older children. Talking with children alone rather than in front of others reduces embarrassment and other painful emotions. Adults should also respect children's feelings after discipline has been administered. Shame and guilt are fairly common reactions. Understanding adults do not attempt to increase the child's guilt after the situation has been confronted, and they are also open to whatever resolution the youngster wants to make.

■ *Avoid angry emotional outbursts.* No evidence exists indicating that yelling, screaming, or other emotional tirades promote effective discipline. In fact, it is conceivable that youngsters listen less when this sort of adult behavior occurs. Adults should take the time to organize their thoughts. Speech should be deliberate, controlled, and firm. Children also seem to listen better when adults talk *with* them, not *to* them.

■ *Establish limits in a clear, precise fashion.* Children need to know what is acceptable and what is not. Adults should spell out acceptable behavior limits so that there is no question about what misbehavior is or what it can encompass. Many children naturally test limits, which is all the more reason to be clear and consistent about behavioral expectations.

■ *Make the discipline fit the misbehavior.* Adults need to examine the type and degree of disciplinary measure employed in relation to the misbehavior at hand. The discipline administered should be compatible with the nature of the misconduct and not too lenient or too extreme.

■ *Discipline should be administered as close in time as possible to the misbehavior.* Once adults have gathered their thoughts, discipline should be administered quickly. Children have a tendency to remember better and more clearly ▶

associate events occurring together in time and space. Misbehavior and discipline should be yoked together, the latter not being put off for hours or until day's end.

■ *Follow through at an appropriate time.* Discussing the disciplinary situation during a follow-up conversation often helps ensure that a lesson has been remembered. This does not mean dwelling on the misconduct or accentuating the negative; it implies that both adult and child have the opportunity to reflect on the issue and the role that discipline plays in creating a more harmonious living arrangement.

These suggestions should help parents develop effective disciplinary strategies and move away from negative discipline. The early seeds of responsibility sown by parents will likely blossom in the form of adult accountability and maturity. Parents will discover that they can gradually relinquish the teaching of responsibility and allow children to become the architects of their own lives. Better yet, children will come to view their parents not as harsh disciplinarians, but rather as supportive guides preparing them for life. Parents thus emerge as partners *with* children, helping them meet the challenges and demands of everyday life.

Adapted from Turner, 1986.   ■

Adolescence

Adolescence is the bridge between childhood and adulthood. It is a stage of life characterized by numerous and complicated developmental tasks and physical, psychological, and emotional changes. Adapting to these changes places great demands on the teenager, in some instances causing anxiety, apprehension, doubt, and even guilt. Yet one cannot deny that adolescence is also a time of happiness, growing independence, new and exciting perceptions of the world, and satisfying social relationships.

While growth during the elementary school years is relatively calm, during adolescence males and females experience pronounced physical developments that change them from children to sexually mature young adults. This point in development, during which biological changes begin to give the first indications of sexual maturity, is known as **puberty**. Adjusting to the many biological changes brought on by puberty is a formidable challenge, one that often heralds preoccupation with the changing physical self. How teenagers react to such biological changes will greatly affect the manner in which they ultimately perceive themselves.

Personality and social development acquire new dimensions during the adolescent years. Observers of this age group will discover that teenagers demonstrate heightened levels of self-awareness and intensified desires to be accepted by their peers. Establishing a personal sense of identity; examining one's values, beliefs, and attitudes; and developing personal and intimate social relationships are all important. The latter provides an outlet for new feelings and experiences, a source of support and security, and a mirror to one's own generation.

Personality developments in adolescence affect and are affected by social growth as they are in other stages of life. This means not only that the accuracy, stability, and acceptance of the self-concept affect the nature and degree of social relationships but also that feedback and reinforcement of others influence how adolescents ultimately perceive themselves. Other developmental forces also

Socialization acquires new dimensions during adolescence.

blend with personality and social growth. Heightened social cognitive skills, for example, give teenagers the mental prowess to examine themselves and others around them with greater understanding and awareness. Adolescents' acceptance of their changing physical selves and achievements in other developmental areas will affect sexual interests and social development, particularly if the teenager is an early or late maturer.

By adolescence, the overall climate of the home environment may be affected not only by the method of control employed but also by the degree to which parents and teenagers seek to understand one another. Lack of understanding and empathy between parents and teenagers is likely to disrupt family harmony and create conflicts. However, when parents seek to promote open discussions, democratic decision making, and explanations for rules around the house, domestic disputes are usually minimized. Also effective in maintaining harmony is seeking to understand and appreciate

the position of the other party. The ability to take the perspective of another person into account is higher in homes fostering support, nurturance, and affection (Adams et al, 1982).

As the adolescent searches for a sense of identity and the need to be accepted and recognized, the peer group emerges as a critical agent of socialization. For many, security is found among friends who share the same feelings, attitudes, and doubts. Teenagers turn to their peers for approval of various activities and behaviors (Kandel, 1980).

This does not mean that a dichotomy suddenly appears between peer and parental influences. Indeed, most peers come from the same social class as the teenager's family and are thus likely to share the same values. Furthermore, while adolescents rely on peers for ordinary day-to-day decisions, they tend to lean toward parents in more critical matters. The perceived competence of parents and peers, though, is a critical element in determining the adolescent's eventual choice between the two (Larson, 1980).

CHAPTER HIGHLIGHTS

The transition to parenthood is a complex one. In the minds of many, there is an idealistic myth attached to parenthood, and striving to have the perfect family is an unattainable goal. In addition, the required adjustments to a baby are many, although we pointed out that domestic disruption and anxieties lessen over time.

It was suggested in this chapter that six stages of parenthood can be charted. These six stages are the result of the dynamics that take place between parent and child. The stages are parental image, nurturing, authority, integration, independent teenage years, and departure.

Parenthood makes it necessary to reorganize daily routines and carry out new responsibilities. Most obvious among these responsibilities is the provision of food, shelter, and clothing for the new arrival. Other responsibilities include providing the newborn with continual attention, executing infant-oriented tasks, allocating domestic chores, reorganizing and adapting to changes in the power structure of the marriage, and developing proper parental emotional attitudes and suitable standards of childrearing.

A considerable amount of time was spent in this chapter exploring the contemporary roles of the mother and father. Society has a tendency to generate a perfect image of the mother, much as it does with parenthood as a whole. The general impression this chapter conveyed is that motherhood is rewarding, but is a physically and psychologically taxing job. Often the mother is overcommitted in her ever-expanding roles: wife, mother, community participant, breadwinner, and household decision maker. Despite the fact that more husbands are helping around the house, the mother still does the bulk of the housework.

Many mothers are returning to the labor force. While most women enjoy working outside of the home, there are some problems. Household tasks, in addition to career obligations, physically wear down many women. Many feel the roles of woman, mother, and laborer are in conflict. Also, the lack of an adequate number of childcare facilities in the United States raises serious questions concerning who is going to watch working parents' children. In the case of "latchkey children," no one is providing supervision.

A relatively recent research pursuit among marriage and family researchers is the role of the father in childrearing. More fathers than ever before are participating in childcare responsibilities. Studies indicate that the father is influential in shaping overall emotional, social, and intellectual growth. Whether or not this influence becomes positive depends on a number of factors, including his involvement in the home, his upbringing, the quality of his relationship with his wife and others, and the natural characteristics of his children.

We also examined the nature of contemporary childrearing. Parents today are the recipients of much advice and guidance from parenting experts. We pointed out, however, that with such a massive barrage of recommendations, many parents become confused, frustrated, and even anxious. We also examined some of the major childrearing approaches employed today, such as developmental-maturational, behavior-modification, humanism, parent-effectiveness, democratic, and transactional-analysis.

We concluded with a discussion of child and adolescent development. To understand the concept of individual growth, we explored several key concepts: the nature vs. nurture controversy, orderly development, ages and stages, and individual variation. The manner in which development proceeds was examined by reviewing several important life stages: infancy and toddlerhood, early childhood, middle childhood, and adolescence.

KEY TERMS

authority stage	egalitarianism	integrity vs. despair
autonomy vs. shame and doubt	generativity vs. self-absorption	intimacy vs. isolation
basic trust vs. mistrust	humanistic theory	nurturing stage
behavior modification theory	identity vs. role confusion	parent-effectiveness theory
democratic theory	independent teenage years stage	parental-image stage
departure stage	industry vs. inferiority	permissive parenting
developmental-maturational theory	initiative vs. guilt	puberty
discipline	integrative stage	restrictive parenting
		transactional analysis theory

RECOMMENDED READINGS

Arnold, L. E. (1984). *Parents, children, and change (2nd Ed.).* Lexington, MA: D. L. Heath. A good assortment of articles focusing on many facets of parent-child relationships.

Brooks, J. (1981). *The process of parenting.* Palo Alto, CA: Mayfield. A very practical approach to parenthood, covering all of the stages of childhood and adolescence and the problems that might arise from each.

diGiulio, R. (1980). *Effective parenting.* New York: Follett. An interesting analysis of parenting, especially the styles that adults adopt.

Hanson, S. M., and Bozett, F. W. (Eds.). (1985). *Dimensions of fatherhood.* Beverly Hills, CA: Sage. An excellent collection of readings related to contemporary fatherhood. Topics include transitions to fatherhood, househusband fathers, and stepfathers.

LaRossa, R., and LaRossa, M. M. (1981). *Transition to parenthood: How infants change families.* Beverly Hills, CA: Sage. The title of this book says it all. A good narrative of family life and how it changes with a baby's arrival.

LeMasters, E. E., and DeFrain, J. (1983). *Parents in contemporary America (4th Ed.).* Homewood, IL: Dorsey Press. A well-referenced and topical text that should be on the bookshelf of any serious-minded student of psychology or sociology. Particularly well done are chapters on the roles of the mother and the father, folklore about parenthood, and minority-group parents.

Mercer, R. T. (1986). *First-time motherhood: Experiences from teens to forties.* New York: Springer. The experience of motherhood, particularly how children are perceived and managed, highlight this volume.

Olson, D. H., and McCubbin, H. I. (1983). *Families: What makes them work.* Beverly Hills, CA: Sage. An analysis of families, the stresses they encounter, the resources employed that promote coping, and the factors that produce marital and family satisfaction across the life cycle.

Robinson, B. E., and Barret, R. L. (1986). *The developing father.* Beverly Hills, CA: Sage. An up-to-date examination of fatherhood, not only from the perspective of current research, but through the personal accounts of men describing their own parenting experiences.

Segal, J., and Segal, Z. (1985). *Growing up smart and happy.* New York: McGraw-Hill. Written for parents, this book explores how adults can nurture children's development and foster a healthy environment.

Part Five

TROUBLED TRANSITIONS

13

Family Stress
and Crises

CONTENTS

CONTEMPLATIONS

■ Stress . . . . The very mention of it often generates images of intense anxiety, turmoil, chaos, and strain. For some, stress within the family context means the path to destruction and ruination, a downward spiral of heated tempers, unending frustration, and sleepless nights. But are such images accurate portrayals of what stress really is and what it encompasses? Does stress automatically mean negative consequences for the affected parties? If your answer is "yes," we believe you'll change your thinking by the time this chapter draws to a close.

■ Crisis resolution is one of the more interesting topics in the marriage and family literature — one of the most puzzling as well. For years, sociologists have struggled with how some families are faced with crisis situations and weather the conflicts and challenges with relative ease. Others, though, faced with the same pressures, succumb to the crisis and find themselves in a state of disequilibrium. What accounts for such differences? Why are some families better equipped than others to handle crises? Are there traits that can be associated with crisis management?

■ For the Greenwood family, the nagging problem was financial in scope. The Mattisons never seemed to recover from the accidental death of their nine-month-old son. Around-the-clock care for their aging parents placed the Thompson household in a continual state of sorrow and depression. And for Donna Blackstone, the problem persisting for years was her alcoholic husband. Often, outside help in the form of therapy is needed to assist a troubled family. In this chapter, we'll explore the nature of therapeutic intervention — be it individual therapy for the principally affected family member, for the entire family unit, or some segments of it. We'll also explore prevention and enrichment programs, innovative and popular forms of intervention designed to improve family systems and the well-being of each member.

Throughout this text we have emphasized the transitional nature of marriage and family life. As stages progress in the family life cycle, successful adjustment involves the mastery of those tasks, challenges, and stresses that occur. For example, the young married couple faces such developmental tasks as establishing and maintaining intimacy, adjusting to parenthood, and launching careers. These are all life changes that bring along their share of stress.

Other changes persist into middle and late adulthood. As far as midlife is concerned, coping with the departure of grown children or caring for aging parents are but two examples of potentially stressful life situations. During late adulthood, adjusting to retirement, adapting to a lowered income, and dealing with the death of one's spouse are also stressful.

And, throughout all of life, crises not limited to any developmental period appear. They are sudden and abrupt: the accidental death of a child, hospitalization, the loss of a job, or a natural disaster. Such crises bring along their own potential for chaos, disharmony, and instability. Learning to adjust to these and all other forms of stress and turmoil test the very foundation of marriage and family life.

Stress is an active research topic among contemporary researchers. At the heart of this research is the notion that changes in family life are normal, and necessary adjustments have to be made by all concerned, both physically and psychologically. While certain levels of stress accompanying life changes are minimal and can be easily handled, other levels are not so easily managed and can create a crisis situation. In this chapter we'll explore how a crisis can occur, but more importantly, how it can be avoided.

DIMENSIONS OF STRESS

Stress and Stressors

Before we explore how stress affects the family, we need to first explain some basic terminology and concepts. **Stress** is the common, nonspecific response of the body to any demand made upon it, be it psychological, sociological, or physiological. **Stressors**, on the other hand, are external events or conditions that affect the equilibrium of an organism. Stressors are thus situations which place the person or family in a stressful state. For some people, stress is self-imposed; that is, there are those who worry about what never happens. Examples of stressors include emotional turmoil, fear, disease, physical injury, and even fatigue. Everyday stressors may include domestic tensions, personal tensions, noise, interpersonal relationships, indecision or anxiety about work-related issues, and so forth. Obviously, stressors become very individualized. What is one person's stressor may be viewed with indifference by someone else (Breznitz and Goldberger, 1982; Coyne and Lazarus, 1980; Endler and Edwards, 1982).

A number of stressors may work together at any one time. They may be big, small, nagging, or acute; and there are even stressors that remain uncategorized. In all, five major types of stressors

have been identified. First there are **social stressors**, such as noise or crowding. Second, **psychological stressors** include such elements as worry and anxiety. Then, there are **psychosocial stressors**, such as the loss of a job or the death of a friend. Fourth, **biochemical stressors** include heat, cold, injury, pollutants, toxicants, or poor nutrition. Finally, **philosophical stressors** create value-system conflicts, lack of purpose, or lack of direction (Curtis and Detert, 1981).

Mark Fried (1982) believes that another type of stressor can be added to this list offering a reflection of life in contemporary society—the **endemic stressor**. Endemic stressors are long-term in scope and have become so prevalent that we have learned to live with them. Instead of trying to deal with them head on, most of us passively integrate them into our lives, and consequently there is often a sense of hopelessness about them. Examples of endemic stressors include inflation, the existence of income tax, and fear of nuclear war.

Stressors are thus conditions producing bodily turbulence or some type of reactive change that triggers bodily reactions. But it should be pointed out that both good and bad can interfere with the body's equilibrium and create stress. Whether you're fired or promoted, hit with a brick or caressed by a lover, a state of stress is experienced. One's body has a similar reaction every time (Schwartz, 1982).

It is important to recognize, therefore, that stress has both positive and negative qualities. **Eustress**, or positive stress, occurs when the body's reactive change is put to productive use. For instance, athletes often use the anxiety and tension in their bodies before a game as a method of "psyching themselves up" for the competition. It may well be that humans function best at moderate levels of stress or, as they say, "healthy" tension. In fact, the lack of stress often creates a reaction known as "cabin-fever syndrome," where there is too little stimulation, variety, and challenge (Rathus and Nevid, 1983).

Distress, on the other hand, is negative and unpleasant stress. It occurs when the body and

▲ Stress surfaces in many different ways for individuals and couples alike.

mind are worn down from repeated exposure to an unpleasant situation. Stress of this nature can affect the body's overall immunity, nervous system, hormone levels, and metabolic rates. When one's emotional state leads to real physical illnesses, the disease is called *psychosomatic* (psycho = mind; somatic = body). Such disorders include hypertension, headache, arthritis, rheumatism, peptic

HOW STRESS TAKES ITS TOLL

- One out of every six Americans takes some form of tranquilizer regularly.
- The most prescribed drug in the United States is Valium; the second most prescribed drug is Librium.
- About 34 million Americans have high blood pressure.
- An estimated 8 million Americans have ulcers.
- Coronary disease has increased 500 percent in the last 50 years.
- Cardiovascular disease is responsible for nearly one million deaths per year — amounting to 52 percent of deaths from all causes.
- Cardiovascular disease is responsible for a loss to national productivity of more than 53 million man-days per year.
- There are approximately 12 million migraine-headache sufferers.
- Americans spend a greater share of their resources on health care than do the people of any other nation. ▶

- Americans spend $1 out of every $9 on health care.
- Hospitals have an increased cost average of 17 percent per year.
- Approximately 12 million Americans are alcoholics.
- A conservative estimate is that 10 percent of the work force can be labeled as either alcoholic or as problem drinkers.
- Alcoholism costs $13 billion for health and medical costs, and $20 billion for lost production costs.

Adapted from Nuernberger, 1981. ■

ulcers, obesity, backache, skin disorders, impotence, menstrual irregularities, and possibly even some types of heart ailments.

Primary vs. Secondary Stressors

Researchers John Curtis and Richart Detert (1981) maintain that stressors can be either primary or secondary. A **primary stressor** is one that initiates the stress response. **Secondary stressors** are events that result from the first stressor and keep the stress response activated. This typically creates a vicious cycle that continues to trigger the stress response.

To understand the primary-secondary stress cycle, consider the following situation proposed by Curtis and Detert. A wage earner has been fired from a job (primary stressor). Emotions such as frustration and anger elicit the stress response that facilitates adjustment. Then worry (as a secondary stressor) is likely to begin—"How will I support my family, pay bills?" It may also be expressed as concern about what "I" did wrong, where "I" went astray—as self-blame. Worry is a special kind of stressor. It raises anxiety levels and keeps the stress response activated long after the primary stressor initially activated that response. The individual who begins to consume alcohol as a means of coping adds another secondary stressor. If this person also becomes apathetic and depressed, the apathy and depression are additional secondary stressors. All of these secondary stressors keep the stress response activated. It is easy to see how an individual's life can quickly get out of control because of this cycle.

THEORIES AND MEASUREMENT OF STRESS

Several noteworthy theories of stress, as well as techniques for measuring it, have been proposed. Understanding individual reactions to stress is important, particularly since we'll examine how the family unit reacts to it later in the chapter.

Hans Selye's Theory

Hans Selye (1982, 1980a, 1980b, 1976), developed the concept of the **general adaptation syndrome** (GAS) to help explain the physiological changes that occur when prolonged physical or emotional stress is experienced. The general adaptation syndrome consists of three successive stages: alarm reaction, resistance, and exhaustion.

Alarm reaction occurs when the body's defenses prepare for the stressful situation. Hormones that arouse—for example, epinephrine (adrenalin)—are produced and the person switches from the *parasympathetic* nervous system (the system that controls internal organs on a day-to-day basis) to the *sympathetic* nervous system (the system that is a "backup" or "reserve" emergency system). For short spurts of energy, the backup nervous and hormonal (endocrine) system are quite remarkable.

Everyday life brings its share of stressful moments.

Should a person remain under stress, the stage of **resistance** is encountered, wherein the body continues to produce huge amounts of energy. An individual could remain in this stage for hours, days, months, or even years. Since the person is in high metabolic gear, the wear and tear on the organism can be phenomenal. However, each of us experiences these two stages regularly with no significant impact on our health and well-being. This is because most stressors are encountered and removed with regularity.

Exhaustion is the final stage of the general adaptation syndrome. Exhaustion hits us when a counterreaction of the nervous system occurs, and the body's functions decrease to abnormal levels. Continued exposure to stress at this time may create stress-related diseases such as high blood pressure and ulcers, or even depression and death. Whether or not one reaches the stage of exhaus-

tion depends on a number of factors, including the intensity of the stressor and the amount of time spent in the resistance stage.

Selye's three stages should be viewed as a cycle of adaptation. When used repeatedly, the human machine runs the risk of breakdown. Our reserves of adaptation energy can be compared to an inherited bank account from which we can make withdrawals, but cannot make deposits. Following exhaustion from stressful activity, sleep can restore resistance and overall adaptation almost to previous levels, but total restoration is probably impossible.

Karl Menninger's Theory

An interesting contrast to Selye's general adaptation syndrome has been developed by Karl Menninger (1963). Menninger introduces a psychological continuum that includes five levels of emotional problems. Each level represents a progressive degree of emotional dysorganization.

Level 1 of dysorganization is commonly called "nervousness," tension that is produced when we are experiencing coping difficulties. Feelings of anxiety, fear, frustration, and even anger escalate. These feelings are also usually accompanied by psychosomatic disorders. Everyone at one time or another enters Level 1.

Level 2 of dysorganization is characterized by neuroses such as phobias, hysteria, obsessions, and physical disorders. Individuals at this level typically withdraw by fainting or developing amnesia; and may become infantile, dependent on drugs, or hypochondriacs. Because of individual differences, there may be an assortment of other debilitating or semi-debilitating disorders.

Level 3 of dysorganization often includes aggressive behavior (homicide, assault and battery, and other social offenses) with no evidence of conscience. *Level 4* often triggers psychotic behavior. That is, the person loses contact with reality, sometimes becoming paranoid and delusional. Finally, at *Level 5,* there is a loss of will to live, and the dysorganized person may become severely lethargic or even suicidal. Physical death typically follows this final level.

The Social Readjustment Rating Scale

Although different types of stress have been identified and theories have been developed to explain its origins, it is a difficult concept to measure. However, several noteworthy attempts have been made in recent years. One of the more popular ways to measure stress is to explore the life events creating it (see Perkins, 1982; and Dohrenwend et al., 1982, for a review of this mode of assessment and an evaluation of its effectiveness). Of the techniques available , one of the most widely accepted is the **Social Readjustment Rating Scale** (Holmes and Rahe, 1967).

The Social Readjustment Rating Scale ranks the life events creating stress, 43 in all, and places them on a scale from low to high levels of intensity. The ranking of stressful life events was the result of interviews and observations with over 400 people who experienced such situations. Table 13-1 shows how these life events are ranked.

The various life events on the Social Readjustment Rating Scale have a certain number of points called "life crisis units." The more serious the life event, the greater the number of points allotted; the death of one's spouse carries 100 points while minor violations of the law have a total of only 11 points. The more points accumulated over a year-long period, the greater the risk for illness. For instance, a total under 150 is considered safe, but a score near 300 may indicate that one is nearing a serious health problem. A total over 300 places a person in a "high risk" category. Individuals in this category have nearly a 90 percent chance of experiencing a serious health change within the next few years.

This measurement device is but one way to assess the stress that exists around us. We remind the reader again that life changes can be negative as well as positive in scope. Both, however, succeed in creating stress. Persons experiencing many life changes must take special care of themselves, particularly since they are vulnerable to health problems. For that matter, all of us should manage our lives so that the number of major life changes at any one time are kept at a minimum.

Type A and Type B Personalities

Why is it that some persons are more susceptible to stress than others? How can one person's pleasure be another person's poison? Again, individual differences account for wide variations in stress reactions. For example, some persons can be classified as "hot reactors." Their psychological and physical makeup is such that stress causes disruptions in physical well-being. Others react to the same situation without physical or psychological harm, or they react with only a brief disruption in their stability and well-being (Wilding, 1984).

Personality dynamics may help to explain why stress reactions vary from person to person. Research conducted by Meyer Friedman, Ray Rosenman, and Margaret Chesney (Friedman and Rosenman, 1974; Rosenman and Chesney, 1982; 1980; Chesney and Rosenman, 1981a,b) shows how a stressful personality type known as the **Type A personality** is prone to cardiovascular disease. Individuals with a Type A personality are extremely competitive and impatient, and always seem to strive to accomplish more than is feasible. Type A behavior also includes difficulty in controlling anger and aggression, which usually persist beneath the surface and are expressed in the form of fist-clenching, facial grimaces and nervous tics, and tensing of the muscles. Also, Type A traits include hurried speech, no compassion for other Type A's, and feelings of guilt during periods of relaxation.

The **Type B personality** is in contrast to Type A behavior. The Type B personality is characterized by a generally relaxed attitude toward life, no hostility, and competitiveness only when the situation demands it. Type B personality types have no sense of urgency about them and do not have free-floating hostility. Unlike Type A personalities, Type B's have the ability to relax without guilt.

Research indicates that not only are Type A personalities more likely than Type B's to suffer coro-

TABLE 13-1

The Social Readjustment Rating Scale

Life Event	Mean Value	Life Event	Mean Value
1. Death of spouse	100	23. Son or daughter leaving home	29
2. Divorce	73	24. Trouble with in-laws	29
3. Marital separation	65	25. Outstanding personal achievement	28
4. Jail term	63	26. Spouse begin or stop work	26
5. Death of close family member	63	27. Begin or end school	26
6. Personal injury or illness	53	28. Change in living conditions	25
7. Marriage	50	29. Revision of personal habits	24
8. Fired at work	47	30. Trouble with boss	23
9. Marital reconciliation	45	31. Change in work hours or conditions	20
10. Retirement	45	32. Change in residence	20
11. Change in health of family member	44	33. Change in schools	20
12. Pregnancy	40	34. Change in recreation	19
13. Sexual difficulties	39	35. Change in church activities	19
14. Gain of new family member	39	36. Change in social activities	18
15. Business readjustment	39	37. Mortgage or loan less than $10,000	17
16. Change in financial state	38	38. Change in sleeping habits	16
17. Death of close friend	37	39. Change in number of family get-togethers	15
18. Change to different line of work	36		
19. Change in number of arguments with spouse	35	40. Change in eating habits	15
		41. Vacation	13
20. Mortgage over $10,000	31	42. Christmas	12
21. Foreclosure of mortgage or loan	30	43. Minor violations of the law	11
22. Change in responsibilities at work	29		

Interpretation

Refer to the score range below to classify your life change score.

Score Range	Interpretation	Susceptibility
300+	Major life change	Major illness within year
250–299	Serious life change	Lowered resistance to diseases
200–249	Moderate life change	Depression
150–199	Mild life change	Colds, flus, occasional depression
149–0	Very little life change	Good health

Reprinted with permission from T. H. Holmes and R. H. Rahe. "The Social Readjustment Rating Scale," *Journal of Psychosomatic Research* 11 (1967):213–218. Copyright 1967, Pergamon Press, Ltd.

nary heart disease, but fatal heart attacks occur almost twice as frequently. The relationship between Type A behavior and heart disease is reported to be especially significant for individuals in their thirties and forties, and it affects both males and females. As far as women are concerned, the most prominent group of Type A personalities are those who have changed their lifestyle to fit executive careers (Hymes and Nuernberger, 1980). Research such as this illustrates that although cardiovascular disease is related to many factors, such as obesity and smoking, the role of the stressful personality cannot be overlooked.

APPLICATIONS

STRESS AND PERSONALITY MAKE-UP: ARE YOU TYPE A OR TYPE B?

Now that the meanings of Type A and Type B personalities have been explored, let's get more personal. Have you given any thought as to how this applies to you? How is it that you react to stress? Rate yourself on the scales below by circling the number (1–8) that best characterizes your personality and habits. For instance, if your approach to keeping appointments is fairly casual, but you're usually on time, a "4" more than likely would be your choice.

1. Attitude about appointments:
   Very casual   1 2 3 4 5 6 7 8   Never late or missed
2. Degree of competitiveness:
   Not competitive   1 2 3 4 5 6 7 8   Extremely competitive
3. Usual working pace:
   Never rushed   1 2 3 4 5 6 7 8   Always rushed, pressured
4. Number of projects attended to at once:
   Always one at a time 1 2 3 4 5 6 7 8   Several at once
5. Speed of daily activities (eating, walking, driving, etc.):
   Always slow   1 2 3 4 5 6 7 8   Always fast
6. Openness in expressing feelings of affection, anger, and other emotions:
   Always open   1 2 3 4 5 6 7 8   Never open with feelings
7. Number of interests outside of work:
   Many   1 2 3 4 5 6 7 8   Few

Your Total Score _____

Interpret your score by using this scale:

Score	Personality Type	
Less than 30	Low stress level	B
30–33		B+
30–39		A
40 or more	High stress level	A+

Adapted from Holland, 1985.

In addition to the personality types mentioned, a third category has been recently recognized: the **Type C personality**. Type C personalities are individuals who sustain considerable stress, but have learned to cope with it. Whether or not they are bothered by cardiovascular illness depends on how effectively they have learned to cope. Many of us tend to be in this category, since nearly all of us share, to a certain degree, some characteristics of the Type A personality. The more involved we are with these characteristics, the more involved we are with stress (Nuernberger, 1981).

FAMILY STRESS AND CRISES

The Structure of Family Crises

Now that we have explored the nature of stress, let's apply what we've learned to the family unit. As we indicated at the outset, families rarely experience life without complication or strain. A **family crisis** occurs when members face an obstacle to their goals that, at least for some period of time, appears insurmountable by means of their customary problem-solving strategies. Since its ordinary coping behavior is inadequate, the family restructures itself in some way. Usually, the moment of crisis is followed by a period of disorganization and emotional upheaval during which the family makes various abortive attempts to solve their problems. In the end, some adaptation is achieved for better or worse. This outcome is frequently governed by the way in which the family organizes itself and by its interaction during the crisis period (Goldenberg and Goldenberg, 1985).

Developmental Crises

A **developmental** (or normative) **crisis** originates from predictable developmental changes over the family life cycle. This crisis is related to the devel-opmental tasks faced by the family at a given point in time. The family unit needs to adapt to individual changes (human development) and family system changes (roles, relationships, organization, and so on) as a natural consequence of performing its function of evolving a family unit over time. Operating together, family and individual changes may create psychological and interpersonal disturbances that call for coping and adaptation (McCubbin, Cauble, and Patterson, 1982).

Developmental crises are regarded as normal. If the crises is handled advantageously, it is assumed that the result is some kind of maturation or development. If the crisis is not handled well, old tensions may be renewed and new conflicts may arise. It should be noted that the developmental crises carry no stigma or label of deviancy (Mederer and Hill, 1983).

Situational Crises

A **situational** (or non-normative) **crisis** is not predictable or normal. Rather, this type of crisis is sudden and abrupt and can occur at any point in the family's development. Because of its unforeseen nature, families often do not have the psychological, social, or material resources needed to manage the situation (McCubbin, Cauble, and Patterson, 1982).

Situational crises, similar to those of a developmental nature, require family members to develop new styles of coping. While the stress may cause the family's regression to ineffective behavior pat-

---

EXAMPLES OF DEVELOPMENTAL CRISES

Getting married	Retiring from the labor force
Becoming a parent	Adjusting to the "empty nest"
Child starting school	Becoming in-laws
Entering the labor force	Adjusting to widowhood
Raising adolescent children	Entering a nursing home
Launching grown children	Mother re-entering labor force
Oldest child getting married	Caring for aging parents
Becoming a grandparent	Adjusting to the death of one's parents

---

EXAMPLES OF SITUATIONAL CRISES

Death of a child	Alcoholism/Substance abuse
Financial problems	Separation
Divorce	Medical hospitalization
Domestic abuse	Mental illness
Unemployment	Rape
Adultery	Abortion
Suicide	Miscarriage
Desertion	

---

terns, the crisis also presents the family with an opportunity to grow through adaptive strategies. Should ineffective strategies persist, the suffering of families would be long-lasting. And, situational crises run the risk of never being resolved (Goldenberg and Goldenberg, 1985).

Situational crises are also called *catastrophic crises*— they are often life-threatening and, due to the circumstances, give survivors a feeling of extreme helplessness. Charles Figley (1983) writes that catastrophic crises disrupt the lifestyle and routine of survivors, cause a sense of destruction and loss, and leave a permanent and detailed memory of the event which may be recalled voluntarily or involuntarily. Figley also proposes that compared to developmental crises, those of a catastrophic nature share the following characteristics:

- *Limited Time to Prepare* Victims typically have little or no time to prepare because of the catastrophe's sudden onset. Because of this, the individual victim or family is prevented from planning and rehearsing a survival strategy.

- *Limited Sources of Guidance* There is information available on coping with family life situations. However, sources of guidance are limited for those families who must cope with the stress of sudden unemployment, war, death, abandonment, and other catastrophes.

- *Experienced by Few* Families who are victims of catastrophe are relatively small in number and typically have limited access to one another. This underscores the need for fami-

lies in similar situations to offer mutual support and guidance.

- *Slight Previous Experience* For most, the crisis is a new experience. For those who do have repeated exposure to the same type of crisis, the amount of stress experienced has a tendency to decline. For example, frequent flood and coastal storm victims demonstrate fewer stress symptoms than new inhabitants.

- *Interminable Time in Crisis* As indicated earlier, catastrophic crises may last days, months, and even years. Recovery is difficult and victims often feel that the worst is not yet over.

- *Lack of Control/Helplessness* Compared to developmental crises, families trapped in catastrophic crises are often unable to modulate the sources of stress, and are powerless to remove or postpone them. Consequently, there is a sense of being out of control and helpless.

- *Disruption and Destruction* While developmental crises are disruptive, in the presence of change they usually bring new roles, routines, and responsibilities. Catastrophic crises, on the other hand, have the potential of disrupting and destroying a family's entire lifestyle, including deep and permanent changes.

- *Sense of Loss* Loss as a result of catastrophic stress can embody more than death. Indeed, there can be a loss of time, loss of innocence, loss of a role or function, or loss of a sense of invulnerability.

- *Emotional Impact* Developmental stressors are usually emotionally upsetting, but they

Feelings of helplessness and devastation are often experienced in the face of catastrophic crises.

tend to be acute for only limited durations. Catastrophic stressors more often than not are acute as well as chronic.

■ *Medical Problems* The early part of this chapter explored health problems caused by stress. Research indicates that such disorders are found more frequently among victims of catastrophe, although we remind the reader

of such variations as the Type A or Type B personality.

■ *Dangerousness* It may well be that the most significant feature of catastrophic stress is the degree of danger it poses. The threat of physical harm or death causes the most intense of human reactions and leaves behind an emotional imprint, which often never disappears.

STRESS AND THE BLACK FAMILY

According to Harriette McAdoo (1983), black families share many of the same characteristics and problems as white families. For example, they experience the developmental changes in children and parents as they grow older, the problems attached to single parenthood, as well as the stressors of unemployment and inflation. However, a racist environment often intensifies and changes the impact ▶

and meaning of these sources of stress. Black families often do not have the same opportunities and experiences as white families, thus creating unique stressors and patterns of coping.

Paramount among the stressors confronting black families is the denial of economic opportunities. Blacks often face job discrimination and experience inadequate education, higher unemployment rates, and inferior incomes. The national unemployment rate for blacks is twice the rate for whites. About 41 percent of black children live in families with poverty level incomes, many headed by single mothers.

Also, the national youth unemployment rate among young black men in urban areas hovers near 60 percent. In relation to all of this, McAdoo writes that too many people feel that their conditions are the result of things wrong with blacks themselves. She maintains that these stressful conditions are instead the result of a long continuing history of inequities. These inequities, in turn, have led to the development of groups who do not nurture the skills or who lack the personal and social connections enabling them to assist themselves out of their impoverished conditions.

Other stressors, a direct result of the above, are inferior housing and health care. The cost of housing often restricts black families to living in public housing projects and high-crime neighborhoods. Black families with a poor income level cannot afford proper health care, particularly that of a preventative nature.

Combined, such stressors prevent blacks from living without a high degree of stress. However, McAdoo feels that effective and functional coping strategies are emerging from this stress. In particular, Blacks find strength and support within their own families and kin networks. To deal with day-to-day stressors, black families turn within, in the process providing help and assistance to those in need. Black families also receive support from a network of friends as well as the broader black community.

McAdoo acknowledges another coping strategy emerging in black families: flexibility of family roles. In traditional white families, roles are clearly and, until recently, rigidly defined: the husband was the wage earner and the wife handled the domestic chores, including childrearing. While there are more dual-employed white couples than ever before, both black partners have had to almost always work outside the home to make ends meet. Black families also tend to be egalitarian with both husband and wife sharing in the authority to make decisions and other family responsibilities. This role flexibility also tends to reduce the strains associated with dual-earner families. Moreover, black women report less ''helplessness'' when divorced or widowed and are often better able to deal with the role changes required in single-parent or stepfamily households.

McAdoo feels that these features of black family stress and coping have important ramifications for public policy as well as stress research in general. The origins of social discrimination and the stressors described need to be attacked and eliminated. Social service agencies also should make an effort to support and increase ▶

the existing helping networks to black families instead of replacing them. In addition, agencies and policymakers should not take for granted that black families will "take care of their own," so much so that they do not need services. Rather, those involved need to be aware of the needs and diversity of experiences in black families and avoid stereotyping, even if the images generated are positive. ▬

FAMILY ADJUSTMENT TO STRESS AND CRISES

All families do not react to stress and crises in the same fashion. Rather, the adaptation process for each is unique and knows wide variation. In an effort to understand how it is that families differ, two models of family stress and crises have been proposed—the ABCX and Double ABCX models

The ABCX Model

Reuben Hill (1949) was one of the earliest researchers to explore the effects of stress on the family. His theory—referred to as the **ABCX model**—is an older, yet nonetheless relevant, contribution to the field of sociology. It is an excellent illustration of how a meaningful theory can withstand the test of time and still have contemporary application. Hill's model consists of four component parts, indicated by the letters ABCX:

The Stressor (A) This part of the model refers to the event and its hardships. Recall that a stressor is a condition that usually triggers change and brings the potential for instability and disharmony. Hill maintained that family stressors can be classified according to their impact: *dismemberment,* the loss of a family member (for example, death), which in turn affects the unit's social structure; *accession,* the addition of new family members (birth, adoption), which changes the family's structure; *loss of family morale and unity* (alcoholism, abuse); and *changed family structure and morale* (divorce, desertion). Note how all of these stressors can change many facets of family life, including roles and patterns of interaction.

The Resources (B) This facet of the model represents the family's resources for dealing with the stressor. The successful application of these resources will provide resistance and ultimately, prevent the disequilibrium of the family system. Two primary forms of family resources have been identified: *integration* and *adaptability*. Family integration refers to unity and strength in such areas as affection, interests, and economic interdependence. Family adaptability embodies the concept of flexibility; that is, the family's ability to implement an assortment of problem-solving strategies as needs dictate.

The Family's Definition of the Stressor (C) Here, the magnitude and severity of the stressor is assessed by the family. This will be a subjective analysis of the stressor rather than the community's objective and cultural definition of it. The family typically explores the hardships that the stressor will bring, including sacrifices to be made and lifestyle changes that will have to be implemented. Also affecting the family's overall assessment of the stressor will be how successful it was dealing with past changes and challenges.

The Actual Crisis (X) This last feature of Hill's model represents the amount of disequilibrium, instability, and disorganization that a crisis brings. Whether or not the stressor triggers a crisis depends on the preceding factors: the magnitude of the stressor, available family resources, and the ultimate definition given to the stressor. If a family is durable and resourceful, stress may never reach this crisis point. Should this not be the case, the family will not be able to maintain stability and harmony.

RESEARCH HIGHLIGHT

STRESS-EFFECTIVE COUPLES: WHAT MAKES THEM CLICK?

What goes on inside the healthy spousal relationship that enables some couples to deal more effectively with stress than others? In an effort to isolate commonalities among stress-effective couples, Dolores Curran (1985) interviewed and studied the behavior and interactions of 32 couples. Certain attitudes and characteristics surfaced and shed light on the concept of healthy stress management:

■ *The healthy couple views stress as a normal part of family life.* Healthy couples do not equate family life with perfection. Indeed, their goals and expectations are frequently lower than those of other couples. These couples also don't correct problems with self-failure. Rather, they anticipate stresses like children's behavior and occasional disagreements over money as a normal part of married life. Furthermore, they develop ways of coping that are both traditional and unique.

■ *The stress-effective couple shares feelings as well as words.* Healthy couples openly communicate, in the process employing honesty and sincerity. They employ nonthreatening techniques that enable them to get in touch with their own and their partner's feelings. These couples also emerge as friends, not just spouses or lovers. They share ideas, activities, and emotions without the feeling of being owned or judged.

■ *The healthy couple develops conflict-resolution skills and creative coping skills.* The couples best able to deal with everyday stresses are those who develop workable ways of solving their disagreements and an assortment of coping skills. Conflict-resolution skills depend largely on communication, while coping skills depend upon creativity, ingenuity, and perseverance. Also, self-esteem is usually equal, with neither partner allowing himself or herself to be manipulated or pushed around by the other. In this respect, healthy communicating spouses rarely exhibit a boss-employer relationship. In addition, they employ compromise in order to resolve conflict as well as collaboration, exploring underlying issues and arriving at solutions that best meet mutual needs.

■ *The healthy couple makes use of support people and systems.* Stress-effective families and stressed families perceive support systems quite differently from one another. Stress-effective families see relatives, friends, groups, and community as valuable supports in dealing with stresses and therefore turn to them when the need arises. On the other hand, highly stressed families view such support systems as evidence of their own inability to deal with stresses.

■ *The stress-effective couple is adaptable.* Healthy couples adapt and borrow each other's techniques in resolving conflict and dealing with stress. When confronted with a stressor, they are able to modify attitudes and habits to best meet it. These types of behavior reflect the flexibility that healthy couples possess, a skill that enables them to cope with the many transitions and demands that characterize married life.

The Double ABCX Model

Stimulated by the work of Hill, Hamilton McCubbin and Joan Patterson (1983a,b; 1982) developed a theory that complements and expands the ABCX model. It is distinguished from Hill's model by its emphasis on the additional life stressors influencing the family's adaptation ability. The **Double ABCX** model also describes those psychological and social factors families use in managing crises, the processes families engage in to attain satisfactory resolution, and the eventual outcome of these efforts.

The Pileup of Family Demands (aA Factor)
More than likely, families are not dealing with a single stressor. Rather, there is a pileup of stressors and strains, referred to as the aA factor in this model. These demands or strains may result from individual family members, the family system, and/or the community. Five general types of stressors and strains contributing to a pileup can be identified:

- *The Stressor and Its Hardships* The stressor brings hardships which often increase and intensify as the situation persists or remains unresolved. When hardships such as anxiety, insecurity, or frustration persist, they become additional sources of strain contributing to family distress.
- *Developmental Crises* Occurring concomitantly, but independently of the initial stressor, are developmental or normative crises. Recall that such crises are normal and can be expected, but their presence along with other stress adds to the demands placed on the family.
- *Prior Strains* Many families carry some residue of strain, often the result of some unresolved demands from earlier stressors or transitions. When a new stressor is introduced, these prior strains usually complicate the situation by adding to the pile-up of demands.
- *Consequences of Family Efforts to Cope* Separate stressors and strain can evolve from the coping behaviors employed by the family. Suppose, for example, that in a household facing financial hardship the husband takes a second job. While this type of coping will reduce the financial difficulties, the second job might create others: loneliness of the wife, disruption of lifestyle, physical and psychological demands placed on the husband, and so on.
- *Intra-family and Social Ambiguity* Every stressor embodies ambiguity because change creates uncertainty about the future. Within the internal framework, the family may feel uncertainty about its structure. This is particularly evident with such situations as the death of a family member, a young adult leaving home, or a divorce. Who is inside the family system's boundaries and who is outside may be cloudy. Social ambiguity can also result when the community's prescriptions for crisis resolution are unclear or absent.

Family Adaptive Resources (bB Factor) Resources are an integral part of the family's ability for meeting demands. Resources include characteristics of individual members, of the family unit, and of the community. In response to a crisis situation over time, two general types of resources evolve: existing resources and expanded family resources.

- *Existing Resources* Such resources are already in place and will typically minimize the impact of the initial stressor. Moreover, existing stressors will reduce the probability that the family will enter into a crisis. Examples of existing family resources include togetherness, role flexibility, and shared values.
- *Expanded Family Resources* These include new resources (individual, family, and community) strengthened or developed in response to the strain and demands. Examples would include the reallocation of family roles and responsibilities, or the seeking of community resources. The authors emphasize that one of the most important resources comprising the bB factor is social support. Those families able to develop it through friends, relatives, and the like tend to be more resistant to major crises and better able to restore stability to the family system.

Family Definition and Meaning (cC Factor) The cC factor represents the meaning given

APPLYING FAMILY RESOURCES TO CRISES: PATTERNS OF SUCCESSFUL COPING

Earlier, we described some traits characteristic of stess-effective couples. But what about coping techniques used by the family unit? Are certain approaches more effective than others? Certain characteristics do differentiate functional and dysfunctional modes of family crisis management. More specifically, stress-effective families share at least 11 elements of functional coping:

- Ability to identify the stressor.
- Viewing the situation as an entire family problem, rather than merely a problem of one or two of its members.
- Adopting a solution-oriented approach to the problem, rather than simply blaming.
- Showing tolerance for other family members.
- Clear expression of commitment to and affection for other family members.
- Open and clear communication among members.
- Evidence of high family cohesion.
- Evidence of considerable role flexibility.
- Appropriate utilization of resources inside and outside the family.
- Lack of overt or covert physical violence.
- Lack of substance abuse.

Adapted from Figley, 1983.

to the *total* crisis situation. This includes the stressor believed to have initiated it, the added stressors and strains, old and new resources, and estimates of what needs to be accomplished to restore balance and stability. All of this requires considerable work: clarifying the hardships and issues so that they are more manageable and responsive to problem-solving strategies, decreasing the intensity of the emotional burdens accompanying the crisis, and encouraging the family unit to continue with its task of promoting each member's social and emotional development. Also, family coping and eventual adaptation is often facilitated when members view crisis situations as a challenge or an opportunity for growth.

Family Adaptation Balancing (xX Factor)
We stated earlier that adaptive resources emerge from individual family members, the family sys-

tem, and the community. Each of these elements has both capabilities and demands. Family adaptation occurs through reciprocal relationships; that is, demands of one of these elements is met by the capabilities of another. When this is accomplished, a simultaneous balance is achieved at two primary levels of interaction. In relation to this, consider the following forms of balance:

- *Balance of Member to Family* The balance sought here is between individual family members and the family system. Family stress often emerges when there is a demand-capability imbalance at this level of family functioning. More precisely, the demands an individual member places on the family may exceed the family's ability to meet these demands, thus creating the imbalance. To cite an example, the stressor of a family member going through adolescence may create an imbalance because of the family's rigid rules and inability to alter expectations, which would allow for the autonomy a teenager often needs for personal development. To remedy this, a new "balance" between the individual member and the family unit is needed.

■ *Balance of Family to Community* A "fit" must also exist between the family and the community of which it is a part. McCubbin and Patterson observe that two institutions in particular — the family and the work community — compete for the involvement and commitment of family members. Often, this creates a demand-capability imbalance, which in turn produces stress. As an illustration, the stressor of a mother returning to work may create an imbalance if the family demands that she make a priority commitment to her husband and children. To resolve this, the family must reestablish and achieve a balance between its demands and capabilities and those of the work community.

In relation to adaptation balancing, families need to realize that there is no perfect fit between demands and resources. Family coherence and stability does not revolve around such an unattainable goal. Family coherence is instead based on the ability to balance two other dimensions: control and trust. For certain life circumstances and events, a family can influence and shape the occurrence and/or the final outcome. Conversely, many life experiences of families cannot be directly controlled by them, and they must trust that things will be effectively handled elsewhere. By this, the family must trust that other persons, institutions, or a higher power will act with their best interests in mind. Coherence is being able to differentiate when the family should take charge from when it should trust and believe in and support legitimate authority and/or power.

The concept of family adaptation is regarded as the central concept in the Double ABCX model (see Figure 13–1). It is used to describe a contin-

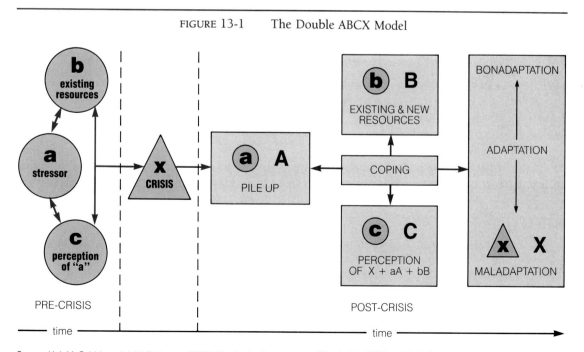

FIGURE 13-1   The Double ABCX Model

Source: H. I. McCubbin and J. M. Patterson. (1983). The family stress process: The double ABCX model of adjustment and adaptation. In H. I. McCubbin, M. B. Sussman, and J. M. Patterson (Eds.), *Social stress and the family*. New York: The Haworth Press.

uum of outcomes which reflect family efforts to achieve a balance fit at the member-to-family and the family-to-community levels. The positive side of the continuum of family adaptation is labeled *bonadaptation* and is characterized by a balance at both levels of functioning. This results in the maintenance or strengthening of family integrity, the continued promotion of both member development and family unit development, and the maintenance of family independence and its sense of control over environmental influences. At the negative end of the continuum is family *maladaptation,* which is characterized by a continued imbalance at either level of family functioning or the achievement of a balance at both levels. However, this comes at a price in terms of a deterioration in family integrity, a curtailment or deterioration in the personal health and development of a member or the well-being of the family unit, or a loss or decline in family independence.

THERAPEUTIC INTERVENTION

Prolonged exposure to a crisis may herald the depletion of internal resources and the family's inability to perform basic functions. Such a state usually means that therapeutic intervention is needed. At this point, the family needs outside assistance so that its equilibrium can be restored and the stressors creating the crisis can be effectively managed. For some families, help is sought only for the principally affected individual. For others, the entire family unit, or segments of it, are the focus of therapeutic intervention.

Individual and Family Therapy Compared

Michael Nichols (1984) offers a succinct and methodical comparison of individual and family therapy. Individual therapies recognize the primary importance played by family life in shaping the personality. However, they assume that these influences become internalized, and that intrapsy-

chic personality dynamics become the dominant forces that determine behavior. Because of this, treatment is directed at the person and his or her personal makeup. Family therapy, on the other hand, acknowledges that past experiences are encoded in individuals, but considers these influences to be weaker than current intepersonal interactions. From the family perspective, treatment is most powerful and effective when it is applied directly to the organization of the family.

Individual therapies also perceive personality formation as an internal process. As a result, symptoms are seen as the result of conflicts within the person. The environment is considered only as a contributory source of stress, activating latent inner conflicts, and treatment is carried out in isolation, in a private relationship with the therapist. Individual therapy is designed to change the way a patient handles his or her own internal experience, to equip him or her to go forth better able to negotiate the environment.

In family therapy, the dominant influences on behavior are thought to be located externally, in the ongoing life of the family. To the extent that personality is shaped by early experiences, these are viewed as real interactions and perceptions rather than distorted fantasies. What happens to the developing person is thought to be the result not of internal conflict but of the realities of family living. Symptom formation is also viewed as the result of conflict between the individual and the environment, but with a different emphasis. Individual therapies consider symptomatic individuals to be inadequately equipped to deal with the environment, and so they try to change the individual. Family therapy regards dysfunctional families to be inflexible in responding to the natural strivings of the developing person, and so tries to change the family.

Family therapy is best understood as an *orientation* to problems such as crisis management, not as a method. Once this is understood, the conceptual dichotomy between individual and family therapy dissolves. From a family therapy point of view, all psychological treatment is treatment of families,

To deal more effectively with stress, couples often turn to counseling and the assistance of trained therapists.

whether one, two, or several people are present, and whether or not the therapist includes the whole family in the actual assessment.

Goals of Family Crisis Therapy

This chapter has emphasized how crises can vary in magnitude, duration, and frequency. Irene and Herbert Goldenberg (1985) tell us that since the crisis period is a time of increased vulnerability as well as an opportunity for growth and change, prompt action-oriented intervention focused on resolving the urgent problem may have great benefits for all concerned. Designed for just such emergency situations, family crisis therapy seeks to help the family resolve the crisis through a process of systematic change and to restore its functioning to its previous adaptational level. In some

APPLICATIONS

HOW PARENTS CAN HELP CHILDREN HANDLE STRESS

Stress is no stranger to the lives of children. On the contrary, Alice Honig (1986) writes that stress is to be expected throughout the entire course of development. She maintains that an assortment of situations throughout childhood produce stress, including physical illness; pain; concentration; overexertion; anxious anticipations of failure due to overly strict or high parental expectations; fear and tension before a test or during a visit to the dentist; being a latchkey child after school; being teased about facial features, allergies, or asthma; humiliation; fear of abandonment; feelings of being unloved; racial slurs; living in a dangerous neighborhood; heavy doses of violent television; physical abuse; and even joyous overstimulation.

Honig points out that childhood stress surfaces for identifiable reasons. For example, stress can originate from *internal* factors. It can develop from an illness or from the painful stomachaches of a young child lying in bed and listening each night to parents' violent quarreling in the next room. Stress can also emerge from *external* factors. For instance, a kindergarten child, forced by a recent family move to attend a new school, finds walking the new route alone a terrifying experience. He may arrive home with soiled pants because he loses bowel control.

Stress can also be *acute* as well as *chronic*. Acute stresses arise suddenly, are usually isolated episodes, and their impact may not last long. An infant's sudden fever after a DPT shot or a preschooler's first days of adjustment to a high-quality nursery school program are examples of acute stress. Some acute stresses, if isolated, such as a single hospitalization for a child, are associated with short-term emotional disturbance, but not with long-term upset years later. Chronic stresses, on the other hand, may be cumulative even for the most well-adjusted child and can lead to long-term disturbances. An alcoholic or an unpredictably abusive parent are examples of chronic stresses that may impair even the psychologically sturdiest child's functioning.

Lorraine Stern (1986; 1985) feels that a certain amount of stress in a child's life isn't necessarily bad. Coping with it helps a child learn to overcome obstacles, react to change and develop into an effective, mature person. But too much stress or poorly handled stress can undermine a child's emotional and perhaps even physical health. The following suggestions are designed to help parents reduce the stress in their children's lives:

- *Set aside plenty of quiet time with your child.* Children and parents need time just to be together. Any uninterrupted period is important, and affection is good therapy for the day-to-day stresses your child faces.

- *Be a strong source of support for your child.* A child under stress needs more than the usual amount of warmth and closeness. Children are not spoiled by being held and comforted at times of need.

- *Treat your child's distress as real, even if it seems inappropriate to you.* Sometimes children have traumatic reactions to seemingly minor experiences. This is perfectly normal, and the best way for you to respond is to treat such a reaction just as you would one you considered legitimate.

- *Keep discussions of adult uncertainties out of your child's hearing.* A discouraged remark about not having enough money or the inevitability of a divorce can severely upset a child. Children not only take these problems to heart but often feel responsible for them as well. If your child does overhear a disturbing ▶

conversation, give immediate, optimistic reassurance that the problem can be solved.

■ *If possible, prepare your child for future stressful experiences.* Sometimes you can soothe fears and correct misconceptions about a coming event in an even more concrete fashion. Many hospitals, for example, now have special programs that use tours, games, or books to prepare children for hospitalization. You could use children's books to ease the impact of other upcoming events too.

■ *Don't hesitate to seek psychological help.* As we've indicated, acute stressful life events alone rarely cause long-term problems. Rather, stress leads to trouble only when it occurs in the midst of ongoing difficulties such as poor self-image or pressure to perform in school. Early psychological counseling can not only solve an immediate problem but also strengthen the child's ability to cope in the future.

■ *Examine your own ability to manage stress.* How you control stress has a lot to do with how your child will. Do you have an optimistic attitude, or do you feel overwhelmed by circumstances? Are you constantly running from one activity to another? Do you have enough time for yourself as well as your family? If you're not coping well, you can help both yourself and your child by obtaining professional help in stress management. ■

cases, immediate aid to the family on an outpatient basis may prevent the hospitalization of one or more of its members. The Goldenbergs further point out that family crisis therapy aims to help a distressed individual and his or her family actively define the crisis in terms of the family system. They then utilize the family's combined coping skills to deal with the existing, as yet unresolved, situation. It is time-limited (typically no more than six sessions) and highly focused on the management of the current crisis and the prevention of future crises. In reviewing the literature on successful family crisis therapy, the following overlapping steps can be identified:

■ Immediate aid is offered any hour of the day or night.

■ The crisis is defined as a family problem and all relevant family members are involved in the treatment from the outset.

■ The focus remains on the current crisis, placing immediate responsibility for change on all of the family members.

■ A nonspecific treatment program (offering hope and reassurance, discouraging regression, lowering the family's tension level, prescribing medication for the identified patient for symptom relief) is initiated.

■ Specific tasks are assigned to each family member in an effort to resolve the crisis.

■ Resistances to change are negotiated, as are role conflicts that have hampered the member's ability to deal with the crisis.

■ Therapy is terminated, but with the understanding that further assistance is available in the event of a future crisis. Should it be necessary, referral for long-term family therapy may be made at this time.

Prevention and Enrichment Programs

Let's look now at family problem prevention and enrichment programs. Such efforts are relatively recent innovations and have gained increasing popularity. Moreover, the number, scope, and types of such programs are expanding rapidly.

A distinction exists between prevention and enrichment programs. Bernard Guerney and his associates (1985) point out that prevention is concerned with dealing with problems on a community-wide basis rather than an individual basis. Prevention does not, however, mean that one works only with people or families who have no problems or difficulties. Early and efficient treatment programs and programs dealing with aftermath problems also fall into the category of prevention programs. Whether it is before, during, or after a problem arises, effective prevention programs are designed so that they are applicable to large numbers of people. Their impact must also be broad enough to make a substantial difference when the rate of the problems on a community-wide basis is examined.

Enrichment programs, on the other hand, are typically targeted to strengthen families not at risk. However, as Guerney and associates point out, in the wake of such problems as divorce and drug abuse in society today, it seems fair to say that all families are at risk. Because of this, enrichment programs should not be sharply distinguished

EXAMPLES OF FAMILY INTERVENTION PROGRAMS

Family Programs

Family Structured Enrichment (SE)   The goals of family structured enrichment programs are to build personal skills into daily living. Couples and families participating in this approach receive programmed instruction from a group leader and participate in structured exercises on a wide range of topics. Depending on the issues relevant to the particular family, the specificity of the program may vary. For example, it could include such topics as problem solving and feeling awareness, or more specific areas such as adoption, alcoholism, sexuality, or widowhood. In general, the program focuses on family development and its transitions, family needs, and the needs of special families such as those experiencing divorce or the stresses of dual careers.

Family Relationship Enhancement (FRE)   This program can be used by individual family members, a subgroup from a family, an entire family, or groups consisting of any of these combinations from different families. The primary teaching techniques are skill training and practice. Among the skills taught are those designed to enhance greater personal awareness, appreciation and understanding of others, problem solving, openness and compassion, and self-changing capacities; as well as skills to help others change, and skills designed to *maintain* all of these desired behaviors.

Marital Programs

Marriage Encounter (ME)   Originally conceived by the Roman Catholic Church, Marriage Encounter has been altered to fit both Protestant and Jewish faiths. The program is designed as a retreat which typically involves large numbers of couples. Usually beginning on a Friday evening and ending on a Sunday afternoon, it covers a wide range of topics designed to enhance the marital arrangement: self-disclosure, empathy, self-awareness, tolerance, love, marital unity, and ▶

> the marital sacrament. Typically, a religious ceremony and a renewal of marriage vows concludes the weekend.
>
> The Minnesota Couples Communication Program (MCCP)   This marital enrichment program is widely used and is based on a theory of growth-oriented systems. That is, the marital or family system is seen as having a number of potential patterns and structures. Couples receive training on how to develop strategies that will enable them to experience various levels of interaction. Emphasis is placed on such areas as accurate self-perception, improvement of communication skills, flexibility in interactional styles, and adjustment to situational constraints.
>
> Adapted from Guerney, Guerney, and Cooney, 1985. ∎

from prevention programs. Rather, enrichment programs should be viewed as belonging at the lower end of the at-risk continuum, not off the continuum entirely. But types of interventions need not be sharply segregated with respect to whether they are prevention vs. enrichment vs. therapy. Instead, any particular program may define as its target population families anywhere or everywhere on a continuum of risk or on a continuum of strength or satisfaction. In addition, all intervention programs (whether they be prevention, enrichment, or therapy programs) may be viewed as having a common purpose: improving the family as a system and improving the psychosocial well-being of each member of that family system.

CHAPTER HIGHLIGHTS

Successful adjustment over the family life cycle involves the mastery of tasks, challenges, and stresses that often occur. In this chapter, we carefully examined the concept of stress and how it affects both the individual and the family unit. Stress is defined as the common, nonspecific response of the body to any demand made on it, be it psychological or physiological. Stress can have both positive (eustress) or negative (distress) dimensions. Stress is a response to stimuli called

stressors, which may range from fear and fatigue to physical injury and emotional conflict.

We also discovered how there can be a variety of stressors working together at any one time. Stressors can be social, psychological, psychosocial, biochemical, philosophical, and endemic in scope. Recall, too, that we need to make a distinction between primary stressors, ones that initiate the stress response, and secondary stressors, the events that result from the first stressor and keep the stress response activated. Research has revealed that having Type A behavior or a susceptibility to a stressful personality, can lead to cardiovascular disorders, especially during middle adulthood.

Stress has been studied by numerous researchers. Hans Selye describes what he calls the general adaptation syndrome, which is a sequence of physiological events that occur when one is under stress. The three stages are alarm, resistance, and exhaustion. Karl Menninger distinguishes five levels of emotional dysorganization: nervousness, neurosis, aggressive behavior, psychosis, and the loss of one's will to live. The Social Readjustment Scale is a test that seeks to measure and rank life events that produce stress.

A family crisis occurs when members face an obstacle to their goals and there is a period of disorganization and upheaval. A developmental crisis is a normal crisis and originates from predictable changes over the course of the family life cycle. A situational crisis is not predictable, but instead, sudden and abrupt. Also called catastrophic crises, they are often life-threatening and due to the circumstances, give survivors a feeling of helplessness.

Two of the more prominent theories of family stress and crisis were explored. Reuben Hill's ABCX model consists of four components; the stressor (A), resources (B), family definition of the stressor (C), and the actual crisis (X). The Double ABCX model, developed by Hamilton McCubbin and Joan Patterson, expands upon Hill's earlier work. It consists of four components: the pileup of family demands (aA), family adaptive resources (bB), family definition and meaning (cC), and family adaptation balancing (xX).

The family's depletion of resources and the inability to perform basic functions usually means that therapeutic intervention is needed. Some families seek help for the principally affected individual while others choose therapy for the entire family unit or segments of it. We described the differences that exist between individual and family therapy, as well as the dynamics of family crisis therapy. We concluded with a discussion of prevention and enrichment programs, complementary forms of intervention designed to improve the family as a system and the well-being of each member.

KEY TERMS

ABCX model

biochemical stressor

developmental crisis

distress

Double ABCX model

endemic stressor

eustress

family crisis

general adaptation syndrome

philosophical stressor

primary stressor

psychological stressor

psychosocial stressor

resistance

secondary stressor

situational crisis

social stressor

Social Readjustment Rating
  Scale

stress

stressors

Type A personality

Type B personality

Type C personality

RECOMMENDED READINGS

Barker, R. L. (1984). *Treating couples in crisis: Fundamentals and practice in marital therapy.* New York: The Free Press. The stresses that couples face and how they can be resolved in therapy are presented in this well-written text.

Curran, D. (1985). *Stress and the healthy family.* Minneapolis, MN: Winston Press. Curran explores the turmoils of the modern family, with special emphasis on stress management advice.

Goldenberg, I., and Goldenberg, H. (1985). *Family therapy: An overview (2nd ed.).* Monterey, CA: Brooks/Cole. See Chapter 2 for a good exploration of functional and dysfunctional family systems.

Kennedy, E. (1984). *Crisis counseling.* New York: Continuum Publishing. This paperback explores, among other topics, what a crisis is, the types that exist, and how they can be approached.

McCubbin, H. I., and Figley, C. R. (Eds.). (1983). *Stress and the family.* New York: Brunner/Mazel Pub. This two-volume set of scholarly and timely readings focuses on normative and catastrophic crises, respectively.

McCubbin, H. I., Sussman, M. B., and Patterson, J. M. (Eds.). (1983). *Social stress and the family.* New York: The Haworth Press. Chapter 1 offers a detailed analysis of the Double ABCX model of family adjustment and adaptation.

Rossman, **P**. (1984). *Family survival: Coping with stress*. New York: Pilgrim Press. This book is loaded with practical advice on how to reduce stress and avoid crisis situations.

Rubin, **T. I.**, **and Rubin**, **E**. (1984). *Not to worry: The American family book of mental health*. New York: Viking. A focal point of the authors is the importance of stability and equilibrium in family life.

Shaffer, **M.**, (1983). *Life after stress*. Chicago: Contemporary Books. Chapters include stress reduction in the family, the signs of stress, and effective family support systems.

Strommen, **M. P.**, **and Strommen**, **A. I.** (1985). *Five cries of parents: New help for families on the issues that trouble them most*. New York: Harper & Row. The authors focus on the special stressors that accompany parenthood.

14

Marital Dissolution

CONTENTS

CONTEMPLATIONS

■ "Do you promise to love, honor, and cherish . . . until death do you part?" How often we've heard these traditional wedding vows exchanged, but in the wake of escalating divorce rates, how realistic are they? We'd like you to consider that question as we explore the magnitude of divorce; consider that in 1985 nearly two and one-half million adults had experienced marital dissolution. Why are divorce rates so high? Who chooses to divorce and what are some of their motives? Join us as we explore what it is that transforms romance at the altar into marital unhappiness, disappointment, and eventual dissolution.

■ They are called the children of divorce and their ranks swell each year. In 1985, for example, their number totaled over one million and all indications are that this figure will continue to grow. Who are these children and how are they affected? How does the experience of divorce change their lives? Might they fare differently if their parents remained together? These are difficult and complicated questions, but we'll try and supply some answers.

■ Pay close attention to the following facts. The fastest growing household in the United States is not the nuclear or blended family. Rather, it's the single-parent family. If you're surprised, read on: About 60 percent of *all children born in this decade* may expect to live with only one parent for at least a year before reaching age 18. What factors account for such a phenomenal pattern? What problems if any, do single parents and children face within this household structure? Later on in the chapter we'll focus in on these and related issues.

■ For years, the blended family has been portrayed on television in a multitude of different formats, from the "Brady Bunch" to "Eight is Enough." Just how realistic are these portrayals? Do they capture an accurate image of this family living arrangement? Are the blended family's strengths and weaknesses accurately conveyed? Material in this chapter will help you be better informed about the blended family of the 1980s.

For Bill and Laura Tucker, it started out as a match made in heaven. They fell in love in high school and dated steadily throughout their formal schooling. Shortly thereafter, they married and in time, started their own family. Over the next twelve years, the Tuckers brought up three children in what neighbors called a happy and loving household. That's why it came as a total surprise when Bill and Laura first filed for a legal separation and six months later, obtained a divorce.

The marriage of Rick and Joan Cummings didn't even last that long. The two conceived a child before they completed high school and reluctantly agreed to get married. Without a high school education, Rick had to settle for tedious and low paying jobs while Joan became a full-time teenage mother. Mounting bills created financial pressure, which didn't help the marital strife that had begun to appear on a regular basis. As the conflicts escalated, both Rick and Joan knew their relationship was going nowhere. Within two years, they called it quits and obtained a divorce. Rick has since moved away, while Joan — still in her teens — has custody of their child.

The dissolution of a family by divorce or separation can occur at any stage of the marriage cycle and can be a major crisis for all its members. Although death is the leading cause of family breakup in the United States, divorce rates are at an astronomically high level. Consider that in 1985, 1,187,000 divorces were granted in this country. Such a total involves nearly two and one-half million adults and over one million children (National Center for Health Statistics, 1986).

THE SCOPE OF DIVORCE

Statistical Trends in Divorce

One way to discover the frequency of divorce is to examine the crude divorce rate. The **crude divorce rate** indicates the number of divorces per 1,000 members of the population in a given year. In the United States in 1983, there were 5.0 divorces per 1,000 population. This is considered to be a high rate of divorce. Compare this to Poland, for example, where the divorce rate is 1.3, while in El Salvador it is only 0.3. The U. S. crude divorce rate of 1983 is also double the rate recorded in 1965 and now ranks among the world's highest (Population Reference Bureau, 1985).

It should be noted that the crude divorce rate in the United States has shown a decrease in recent years. In support of this, the crude divorce rate was 5.0 in 1983, but dipped to 4.9 in both 1984 and 1985. In 1986, the crude divorce rate was 4.8 (National Center for Health Statistics, 1986).

It has been reported by some that almost 50 percent of all marriages end in divorce. This is a misleading statement, and such a statistical analysis must be placed into a proper perspective. This percentage was arrived at by comparing all divorces granted in one year with the marriages performed in that same year. In 1984, for example, there were 50.5 divorces for all new marriages (National Center for Health Statistics, 1986). This is quite different from the crude divorce rate and tends to be somewhat misleading. This is because divorces granted in any year are the result of marriages performed in earlier years; that is, marriages contracted either one year or fifty years previously are compared to the number of current-year weddings (Crosby, 1980). To avoid such misinterpretations more accurate methods for computing divorce rates are needed, such as the longitudinal method discussed in Chapter 1. Figure 14-1 displays marriages and divorces in the United States, 1960–1982.

One must also be careful not to generalize about divorce statistics; divorce does not affect all social groups equally. For example, divorce rates are higher for blacks than for whites (see Table 14-1).

TABLE 14-1

Married and Divorced Persons among Population Aged 18 and Over: 1960–1984 (in percent)

Sex and Race	1960	1970	1980	1984
		Married		
Males	76.4	75.3	68.4	65.8
White	77.3	76.1	70.0	67.7
Black	68.4*	66.9	54.6	50.6
Females	71.6	68.5	63.0	60.8
White	72.2	69.3	64.7	62.8
Black	66.3*	61.7	48.7	44.5
		Divorced		
Males	2.0	2.5	5.2	6.1
White	2.0	2.4	5.0	6.0
Black	2.2*	3.6	7.0	7.0
Females	2.9	3.9	7.1	8.3
White	2.7	3.8	6.8	8.0
Black	4.8*	5.0	9.5	11.0

* 1960 black data are for nonwhites.

Sources: Bureau of the Census, *Statistical Abstract of the United States: 1985,* 105th edition (Washington, D.C.: 1984) Tables 44 and 46, and "Marital Status and Living Arrangements: March 1984," *Current Population Reports,* Series P-20, No. 399, July 1985, Table 1.

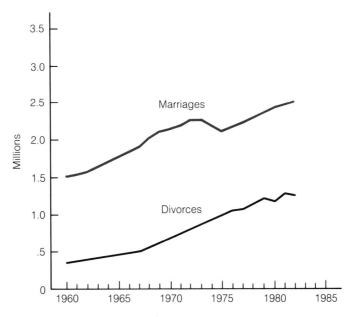

Source: U.S. Bureau of the Census. (1984). Statistical Abstract of the United States, p. 60.

FIGURE 14-1   Marriages and Divorces in the United States, 1960–1982

Also, the higher the educational level, the lower the divorce rate will generally be. However, one interesting exception to this latter trend is women with graduate degrees. They have disproportionately high divorce rates, due perhaps to increased social independence and economic security. Another variation to consider in regard to divorce is its timing in the marriage cycle. Those who divorce tend to do so relatively early in their marriages. Divorce rates are at their highest two to five years after marriage, a statistic that has changed little over the years (Spanier and Thompson, 1984).

John Crosby (1980) also cautions that divorce statistics only tell us one thing: how many marriages were legally dissolved in a given period of time. They do give justification for claiming that the statistics represent the number of failures in marriage. Conclusions drawn from present-day statistics are invalid unless they are contrasted with a referent period of time with due considera-tion given to the social-cultural milieu of the referent period.

Divorce and the Changing Family

All cautions about statistics considered, there is no mistaking the fact that divorce rates over the past two decades have markedly increased. However, this does not mean that the institution of marriage is deteriorating. Nor does it mean that persons have lost faith in it. The latter is evidenced by the sheer number of individuals who continue to choose marriage over all of the other possible life-styles as well as those who opt to remarry.

Marriage does have a future, but we need to acknowledge that its present form differs from its past. According to Andrew Cherlin (1981), this is due at least in part to changes in marrying, divorc-ing, and remarrying. He observes that a smaller proportion of families today than in the 1950s resemble the two-biological-parents-with-children family which has been the norm in the United States. Rather, a larger proportion consists of single parents and their children or families formed by remarriage after divorce. Because of the sharp rise in divorce, the common assumption that a family occupies one household is increasingly incorrect. While separation and divorce sever the ties between father and mother, the ties between children and parents tend to remain intact.

Because of this, Cherlin feels that an increasing number of families extend across two or three or more households, linked by the continuing ties between parents and children who live apart. Thus, kinship ties are more complex and far-reaching than in families formed by first marriages. Also, even the definition of a family can become problematic. For example, a child whose mother and father have divorced and remarried may define the members of his family differently from either of his parents.

Beyond the structural changes of modern-day marriage and family life, the very nature of divorce also needs to be placed within a proper contemporary perspective. While divorce is a social problem that needs to be reckoned with, it also needs to be objectively examined. Along these lines, Graham Spanier and Linda Thompson (1984) write that it is easy to fall into traps that shroud our objectivity. For example, many feel that marriage and family life has never been as healthy as nostalgic reminiscences would have it. But, as researchers examine past trends and reconstruct American family history, we discover that none of our current problems are new. Indeed, many of them are less burdensome today than they were yesterday. What has been uncovered is a strong argument that marriage and family life is changing, not deteriorating. Put another way, it is different, not deficient.

In Chapter 2, we indicated that the rising divorce rate is suggestive of a change in the ways Americans perceive their lives. This is also the sentiment expressed by Matthew McKay and his colleagues (1984). They note that the fear of social disapproval attached to divorce has declined. Fur-

Compared to earlier times, divorce today has reached widespread proportions.

thermore, while past generations of women were deterred by the stigma and financial hardships of divorce, women today live in a climate of increased personal freedom and economic independence. The guiding ethic of this age for women and men is choice, autonomy, and the freedom to change one's life. Many no longer feel compelled to wither in a marriage because they once vowed "till death do us part." Fewer are willing to endure the heavy, unremitting weight of bitter years.

It may well be, then, that how one views the rapidly rising divorce rate depends on how one views the role of marriage and family in society—this is how Leonard Cargan (1985) approaches the matter. Those who view the nuclear family as the norm regard the escalating divorce rate as an indicator of the breakdown of the social structure and a sign of moral decay. However, those who perceive marriage as a choice for personal fulfillment may see the divorce increase as an indication that this goal is being better met.

Cargan proposes that it is expectations, then,

that define what is acceptable and desirable in marriage. As we've indicated, these expectations are changing toward an emphasis on self-fulfillment, personal happiness, personal growth, and sexual satisfaction. Couple this with our immense romantic expectations of marriage, along with our lack of preparation for it, and it is not surprising that few anticipate the conflicts that occur, not to mention being ill-prepared to resolve them. It is thus conceivable the divorce rate is high, not because we regard marriage so little, but rather because we expect so much of it—affection, companionship, empathy, and self-actualization, to name but a few areas.

Reasons and Motives for Divorce

The reasons and motives for divorce are diverse. We are hindered in our attempt to pinpoint all of the reasons, however, since the legal act of dissolution for the most part is no longer an adversary proceeding. That is, nearly all states permit some variation of **no-fault divorce**, a legal proceeding we'll presently explore. The no-fault divorce concept does not regard divorcing couples as opponents nor does it require extensive reasons for marital dissolution. Rather, the basic requirement is to satisfy the court that "irreconcilable differences" have created an "irremediable breakdown" of the marriage.

Legal grounds for divorce, though, vary from state to state (see Table 14-2). Sixteen states regard irremediable breakdown as the sole ground for divorce. Another seventeen states also use this criterion, but the traditional fault grounds of cruelty, desertion, and adultery are also available. For the remaining states, the major no-fault grounds for divorce are incompatibility, mutual consent, and living apart for a specified period of time.

While legal grounds may shroud the actual reasons for securing a divorce, we can speculate on some of them. One source (Albrecht and Kunz, 1980), for example, lists a variety of reasons contributing to marital dissolution. In descending order, some of the major reasons include personal unhappiness, a desire to get out of a negative situation, opportunities for alternative financial support, being involved with someone else, and the relative ease of divorce laws.

Going a step further, James Henslin (1985c), believes that six trends reflecting contemporary society often contribute to divorce. First, incompatible sex roles abound all around us. As we learned in Chapter 4, many facets of the sex-role learning that males receive conflict with those taught to females, and vice versa. Because of this, the couple's adjustment to married life is often difficult.

A second reason, closely related to the first, is the separation of the sexes that exists. Females and males are placed in different life locations, each of which constitutes a unique world of experience. As a result, both husbands and wives undergo a continuing socialization process during which each acquires a somewhat different way of handling problems, of evaluating what is important and what is irrelevant, and of approaching life in general. Because the husband and wife share the same time/space/relational/income/sexual/emotional dimensions of life-space, it is almost inevitable that these differences will produce some conflict.

The pressures of adult life represent a third contributing factor. Those pressures that demand immediate satisfaction, such as monthly bills, are especially frustrating to married couples. Other stresses are employment-related or originate from the complex set of necessary chores. Given such an abundance of demands, there is often little energy or attention left to direct toward one's spouse.

The routines that develop within married life are a fourth factor. When the newness and novelty of marriage evaporates, many couples begin to engage in monotonous routines. Partners often become predictable as more time is spent together. While the latter can be healthy if it fosters security and constancy, it can also create boredom. Boredom needs to be relieved, but many couples tend to it by quarreling, having an affair, or engaging in some other destructive behavior.

TABLE 14-2

Grounds for Divorce in the United States

| State | Irremediable Breakdown Only | Fault Grounds* Plus | | | | Fault Grounds Only* |
		Irremediable Breakdown	Incompatibility	Living Apart	Mutual Consent	
Alabama		•	•	•		
Alaska		•	•		•	
Arizona	•					
Arkansas				•		
California	•					
Colorado	•					
Connecticut		•	•	•		
Delaware	•					
District of Columbia				•		
Florida	•					
Georgia		•				
Hawaii		•		•		
Idaho		•		•		
Illinois						•
Indiana		•				
Iowa	•					
Kansas			•			
Kentucky	•					
Louisiana				•		
Maine		•				
Maryland				•		
Massachusetts		•				
Michigan	•					
Minnesota	•					
Mississippi		•			•	
Missouri	•					
Montana	•					

TABLE 14-2 (*Continued*)

Grounds for Divorce in the United States

State	Irremediable Breakdown Only	Fault Grounds* Plus				Fault Grounds Only*
		Irremediable Breakdown	Incompatibility	Living Apart	Mutual Consent	
Nebraska	●					
Nevada			●	●		
New Hampshire		●		●		
New Jersey				●		
New Mexico			●			
New York				●	●	
North Carolina				●		
North Dakota		●		●		
Ohio		●		●	●	
Oklahoma			●			
Oregon	●					
Pennsylvania		●		●	●	
Rhode Island		●		●		
South Carolina				●		
South Dakota						●
Tennessee		●		●	●	
Texas		●		●		
Utah				●		
Vermont				●		
Virginia				●		
Washington	●					
West Virginia				●		
Wisconsin	●			●		
Wyoming	●					

* Major fault grounds are adultery, mental or physical cruelty, and desertion.

Source: Adapted from *Consumer Reports,* June, 1981.

A fifth contributing factor is changes in the basic functions of marriage and family. Recall from Chapter 2 how traditional functions kept the family together, such as the farming and domestic chores that couples performed. The husband and wife depended on one another and the household functioned as a total family unit. Today this is not the case.

The increasing emphasis on personality and emotional fulfillment is a sixth reason accounting for soaring divorce rates. In American marriage, there is an increasing expectation that couples need to fulfill the personality needs of their partner. When one partner feels "unfulfilled," he or she often blames the other for not meeting this need. Obviously, this type of need creates pressure

RESEARCH HIGHLIGHT

THE IMPACT OF AGE AND RELIGIOUS DIFFERENCES ON DIVORCE

Sociologists have long been interested in what factors present at the beginning of marriage tend to create divorce later. Two of these factors, age and religious differences, have often been cited as contributing reasons for divorce. The research of Tim Heaton, Stan Albrecht, and Thomas Martin (1985) has shed light on how these factors change over the course of the marriage cycle.

Interestingly, the researchers found that the problems of age and religion at the start of marriage do not diminish even 10 to 20 years later! As a result of their survey of almost 5,000 persons, they noted that each of four central problems existing initially continues to be problems throughout marriage:

- **Early Marriage**   Couples who marry at an early age are more likely to divorce than those who marry later, particularly women who marry before age 20. What is surprising, however, is that the problems created by age persist throughout the duration of the marriage.

- **Husband's Age Relative to Wife's**   Marriages are more unstable when husbands are several years older than wives or when wives are older than their husbands. The most stable marriages are those in which the husbands are about one to three years older than the wives. Again, this risk factor of age differences continues to be a problem later in marriage.

- **Religious Affiliation**   As expected, divorce is lower in religions where divorce is discouraged, with the lowest rates found among Catholics, Jews, and Mormons. The highest rates are among Protestants and those with no religious preference. Here, too, the problems created by religious differences persist throughout the duration of the marriage.

- **Husband's Religion Relative to Wife's**   Religious intermarriage adds additional tensions to marriage because basic values of the spouses are likely to differ. Again, this difference does not really get resolved as the marriage progresses.

The researchers propose several reasons as to why couples do not adjust over time. First, let's consider age. Early marriage is often linked with lower educational ▶

attainment, earlier childbearing and low incomes. Often, those who marry young miss out on "normal" life-course experiences, and once married, it becomes very difficult to compensate for missed experiences. Difficulties associated with lower socioeconomic status may also persist throughout the marriage. In short, the disadvantages of an early marriage may not be surmountable within the context of married life. Similarly, marrying late, after adult life patterns have been established, appears to create higher risk that is not reduced.

As far as religion is concerned, the values, ideology, and social pressures that discourage divorce seem to be effective throughout the duration of the marriage. Rather than disappearing, these factors persist and create marital turbulence. Finally, religious and abnormal age differences between brides and grooms may create fundamental differences that cannot be resolved completely at any stage in the life cycle. These two factors combined create multiple risks that threaten the stability of a marriage.

on both parties, particularly when you examine the complex and demanding needs of security, comfort, love, and the like.

The increased institutional support for divorced women looms as a seventh factor. Henslin feels that three features of this factor are apparent: the greater economic independence of women and their employability, the reduced stigma associated with divorce, and the expanded welfare system. Such institutional support means that a woman trapped in an unhappy marriage may feel less compelled to remain within it.

Finally, the social roles of husband and wife can be cited as a factor. For many people, assuming the role of husband or wife means forcing unthinking, automatic expectations and demands onto the other. This, in turn, creates resentment. This is illustrated by the woman who remarks, "Before marriage he treated me as someone special. Now he treats me like a wife." Henslin acknowledges that this last factor overlaps previous ones, but he regards it as a feature of marriage that creates many problems.

Alternatives and Barriers to Divorce Despite a miserable marriage, there are many couples who decide not to divorce. Several reasons may account for this decision. For example, some may feel that they have a bad marriage, but a divorce would be worse. Others acknowledge the fact that happy marriages exist, but have resigned themselves to the idea that theirs is not one of them. Still others play down the importance of certain parts of the marriage (love and intimacy, for example) and emphasize others (the children, material wealth, and so on). Also, there are couples trapped in a poor marriage who escape the situation by filling their private lives with a multitude of activities, both inside and outside of the home. For these couples, the less time spent together the better off they think they are.

Couples who eventually divorce encounter various barriers along the way. This was one of the central findings of a study launched by Stan Albrecht and Phillip Kunz (1980). The two surveyed 500 men and women who had divorced noting several patterns that became evident.

They discovered that the single most important hurdle was financial in nature. But this obstacle was clearly a much more important problem for females than for males. Of all the barriers to divorce noted by females, 36 percent dealt with financial constraints; this was true of only 10 percent of those noted by males. For the females, especially those with young children, a major fear was how they would be able to support themselves

TABLE 14-3

Perceived Barriers to Obtaining a Divorce

Barrier	Overall Frequency of Mention	Male Respondents	Female Respondents
No financial support	156	20	136
Children	102	54	48
Personal religious beliefs	102	29	73
Difficulty of divorce laws	64	34	30
Parents	56	23	33
Friends	36	17	19
Negative counsel from religious leaders	25	11	14
Fear of unknown	14	3	11
Spouse didn't want divorce	8	2	6
Neighbors	4	1	3
Other	16	7	9

Source: Albrecht, S. L., Kunz, P. R. (1980). The decision to divorce: A social exchange perspective. *Journal of Divorce, 3*(4), 329. Reprinted by permission of The Haworth Press, Inc. 75 Griswold St., Binghamton, NY.

and their families without a husband. This finding presents us with an interesting contrast to the thoughts of Henslin (1985), presented earlier. While his claim that growing numbers of women are becoming financially independent is supported in fact, this study clearly shows that this is not true for all females.

Contrary to what one might expect, males, rather than females, were more likely to cite their children as a barrier to divorce. Albrecht and Kunz suggest that this might reflect the nature of divorce settlements. Traditionally, women are more likely to receive custody of the children, an important concern for the males.

Another barrier to divorce is religious constraints. While less significant today than in previous years, many respondents had internalized beliefs saying that divorce was bad and indicative of failure or even of personal sinfulness. (Table 14-3 lists these three and other perceived barriers to obtaining a divorce as researched by Albrecht and Kunz.)

DIVORCE LEGALITIES

Obtaining a divorce today is simpler than it was years ago. However, divorce proceedings do have legal complexities, something we'd like to briefly explore in this part of the chapter. Before doing so, though, let's first explore the concepts of annulment and legal separation.

Annulment

Annulment is the invalidation of a marriage on the basis of some reason that existed at the beginning of that marriage. (Annulment is less common than divorce.) Some of the acceptable reasons for a legal annulment are insanity, fraud, being underage, and being under duress. Other reasons pertain to marriages prohibited by law—such as incestuous and bigamous relationships (Ruback, 1985).

Legal Separation

A **legal separation** often occurs before the actual court proceedings and allows couples to live apart. More specifically, it entails a contract between the two that focuses on the issues that have to be resolved before a divorce is granted—such issues as property division, alimony, and child custody. Typically, the contract is submitted to a judge, who has the power to modify parts of it if the terms are unfair to one of the parties.

Divorce Law

For centuries, divorce law centered around the concept of *fault*. There was the requirement that one party had done something wrong while the other party was without fault. Thus, traditional divorce law represented an *adversary* process. We should add that once fault was determined, financial terms of the divorce were directed to this party.

R. Barry Ruback (1985) notes that fault originally included only adultery and physical cruelty. Later, though, it came to include such other fault grounds as willful desertion, habitual drunkenness, and mental cruelty. Because divorce was an *action in equity*, it could be granted only if the party seeking the divorce was innocent of any wrongdoing. If both parties were at fault, the doctrine of recrimination prohibited the granting of a divorce. Also, proof that parties colluded to obtain a divorce would bar a divorce.

Traditional divorce law perpetuated the sex-typed division of roles and responsibilities apparent in traditional marriages. That is, in traditional marriage a woman presumably agreed to devote herself to being a wife, mother, and homemaker in return for her husband's promise of lifelong support. If the marriage did not endure, and if the wife were virtuous, she would be granted *alimony*. Alimony represents the husband's continued economic support. Traditional divorce laws also per-

petuate the sex-typed division of roles as far as the children are concerned; the wife is typically responsible for their care, while the husband is responsible for their economic support (Weitzman and Dixon, 1986).

No-Fault Divorce In 1970, California became the first state to recognize the breakdown of a marriage as a ground for divorce. Called the *Family Law Act*, this legislation heralded the concept of no-fault divorce. It does not accuse either party of creating the marital breakdown, a factor that makes divorce proceedings simpler. No-fault divorce often reduces the bitterness associated with adversarial proceedings, not to mention the complexities often arising with property settlements, alimony, and the like. As we mentioned earlier, since its inception in 1970, nearly every state has some form of no-fault divorce proceedings.

Lenore Weitzman and Ruth Dixon (1986) feel that the concept of no-fault divorce changes four basic elements of traditional divorce legislation. One, it *eliminates the fault-based grounds for divorce*. Two, it *reduces the adversary process*. Three, *financial settlements no longer originate on the concept of fault or sex-based role assignments*. Rather, the financial aspects of the divorce are based on equity, equality, and economic need. Four, no-fault divorce *redefines the traditional responsibilities of husbands and wives* by implementing a new norm of sexual equality. No-fault divorce attempts to institutionalize sex-neutral obligations between

Reprinted with special permission of King Features Syndicate, Inc.

CROSS-CULTURAL FOCUS

DIVORCE COURT IN CHINA

The scene is a divorce proceeding in the People's Court for the Chang Tong District of Shanghai. The bailiff has called the court to order and has informed observers that there will be no noise, spitting, or recording. The three uniformed judges, two men and a woman, file in and take seats behind a high wooden bench. The husband and wife sit facing the judges in straight-back chairs.

The trial begins. Although this is the last of several hearings for this couple, the presiding judge asks each of them a number of questions to determine whether there is any hope in saving the marriage. In China, the court has an alternative duty to encourage reconciliation. The judges probe, ask about details of the relationship, and continue to look for any cracks in the firmness of the couple's desire to divorce. While lawyers are present, they are traditionally not involved in divorce cases. Among other reasons, there just aren't enough to go around: there's about one for every 50,000 people, while in the United States the ratio is about one for every 365. Lawyers are also not apart of the dialogue between the judges and the couple. Rather, they only speak toward the end of the proceeding, making recommendations for custody of the children or property division.

In a sense, the judges also mediate. They attempt to influence the couple to agree on as much as possible. They want to achieve settlement on the issues and will decide only what the couple can not.

Following a recess, the presiding judge announces the court's decision. The father, with whom the child has been living for the past year, shall have custody. The personal property is divided. The mother must pay 12 yuan a month ($4 in the U.S. currency) support. This marriage is now legally ended, as are about 500,000 annually in the People's Republic. With four times more people, China has half the number of divorces as the United States.

Divorce is frowned upon in China, although about 80 percent of those cases that get to court are granted. To help combat divorce, community resources are available for troubled couples. Paramount among these resources are *mediators*. In China, there are more mediators that lawyers; ten times more cases are resolved through mediation than by litigation. A successful family mediation is one which leads to continuing the marriage, not to the courthouse steps.

In Beijing, a mediation committee exists for the sub-district of Zi Chang the western district of the capital. This committee is responsible for a neighborhood comprised of 2,600 people. Its members, elected for their reputation for fairness and warmheartedness, deal with squabbles between spouses, in-laws, and other family members. Within the mediation committee, there is a delegate to whom conflicts must first be brought. His or her job is to make big conflicts smaller, to nip them early before they are brought to the Mediation Committee. But this courtyard problem solver has status. He or she is a delegate, a representative — a member of the government.

▶

Beyond their role in conflict resolution, mediators also play a role in monitoring behavior. For example, in some disputes the mediation committee may call in family members or neighbors to gather information on the conduct of couples. In effect, a type of supervision is in operation—tell family members and neighbors what the disputants must do, and they will usually assist in monitoring behavior. Even in cases where divorce has been granted, family and peers see to it that an individual's responsibilities to child custody, alimony, or other settlements are met.

Adapted from Bishop, 1986. ■

partners, including those related to economic support, division of property, and child support.

Divorce Mediation   A relatively recent development in divorce proceedings is mediation. **Divorce mediation** is a conflict resolution process in which the disputants meet with a third-party mediator whose role is described variously as that of a facilitator of communication, an impartial guide to negotiation, a balancer of power, or a provider of perspective. Divorce mediation differs from the traditional adversary process, be it the public judiciary or private arbitration, in several important

ways. Most important, mediation is generally informal and less structured than either of the alternative procedures. Because it is private, it encourages an openness that is impossible in a public setting. The disputants retain control of the outcome rather than turning the decision-making power over to a judge or an arbitrator (Vroom, Fassett, and Wakefield, 1982).

Divorce mediation offers several distinct advantages to couples. First, mediation is often cheaper than a traditional adversary divorce. Second, proponents maintain that disputes are settled faster when there is a mediation rather than an adversar-

PRINCIPLES OF DIVORCE MEDIATION

■ The couple is the client, not the husband or wife as individuals. Protection of the family is the highest priority. Mediators are committed to doing what is in the best interest of the children.

■ Mediation respects and supports the participants' ability to make decisions that affect their lives. The separating partners control the results, taking responsibility for the final outcome, rather than handing decisions over to the courts or the attorneys.

■ Mediation provides a forum for cooperative solutions in which everyone can have his or her needs considered. This is especially important where children are involved and joint custody (shared parenting) is anticipated.

■ Mediation allows for maximum exploration of all options and alternatives and requires full disclosure. It encourages brainstorming, compromise, and unique solutions that are handcrafted to fit the needs of a particular family.

■ The mediator serves as an advisor who suggests options and can describe the range of decisions that courts are likely to make about a given issue. ▶

■ The mediator is an advocate for each party's well-being, but carefully maintains neutrality. Neutrality is important, since a mediator who is perceived as biased can no longer work effectively with the couple.

■ All proceedings are subject to full confidentiality. The legal consultant/educator will not testify on either partner's behalf in the case of a court hearing.

■ Personal growth is a secondary goal of mediation. In the process of working out an equitable dissolution agreement, couples often learn how to cooperate for their mutual interest and how to avoid past mistakes.

Adapted from McKay et al., 1984. ■

ial process. Third, participants are more likely to perceive a mediated settlement as fairer than a court resolution to the divorce (Ruback, 1985).

There are different styles of divorce mediation, although each strives for the same goal: agree to a settlement and avoid the cost of a court suit. In general, mediation can be performed by (1) a single mental health professional; (2) a single lawyer and a single mediator; (3) a lawyer-therapist interdisciplinary team; (4) through structured mediation, another type of interdisciplinary approach but more extensive in its use of family mediators and attorneys; and (5) through a court-sponsored public mediation program (McKay, et al., 1984).

TRANSITIONS IN THE DIVORCE PROCESS

Divorce is a difficult life task to deal with, largely because couples and families must confront a number of diverse processes and mentally taxing decisions. Paul Bohannon (1970; 1985a; 1985b) has examined some of the divorce processes that couples must undergo while Constance Ahrons (1983) has focused her studies on the divorce transitions that affect the entire family unit. Examining these two theoretical positions will give us a more complete picture of the various divorce transitions that exist.

Paul Bohannon's Theory

Paul Bohannon outlines six components or processes of divorce. These components are not sequential and can overlap. Bohannon feels it is important to understand these processes in order to find order and direction in the emotional chaos that frequently accompanies divorce.

Psychological Divorce The **psychological divorce** often begins before the actual break. It is centered around the deteriorating marriage, and the initial motivation for considering divorce has already appeared. In many instances, one or both partners have psychologically departed long before the actual physical separation.

As far as the psychological breakdown of a marriage is concerned, one source (Argyle, 1983) suggests that distressed couples often have similar behavioral characteristics. The partners usually make fewer pleasant remarks to each other (such as compliments) and more unpleasant ones (such as criticisms). They also engage in fewer pleasing acts (such as being helpful, a kiss, or a gift) and more displeasing ones (making a mess around the house, or offering expressions of disapproval). Unpleasant remarks are apt to be reciprocated; that is, one unkind remark leads to another. Distressed couples are inclined to be unresponsive to what the other says, often ignoring them. They are also more likely to avoid self-disclosure of their feelings or problems.

Legal Divorce The **legal divorce** entails going to court to sever the legal ties of marriage. As we've seen, the legal grounds for obtaining a divorce vary from state to state, and many couples find themselves lost in the shuffle of courtroom proceedings. While couples typically experience relief once the legal separation is final, many exhibit varying levels of emotional sensitivity during this stage.

Economic Divorce The **economic divorce** means that couples have to decide how they are going to divide their money and property. This is no simple task since complications arise due to tax laws. Legal assistance is usually needed, and couples frequently feel resentment, anger, and hostility concerning the redistribution of wealth. Bo-

hannon states that the economic divorce can be difficult for two reasons. First, there is never enough money or property to go around. Second, people get attached to certain objects and may need them to support their image of themselves.

Coparental Divorce The **coparental divorce** deals with the issue of child custody. Which party gets custody and responsibility for rearing the children is determined by the court on the basis of the children's well-being. Visitation rights for the noncustodial parent must also be determined. Worry and concern about the effects of the divorce on the children are frequently expressed during this stage. Bohannon points out that the issues of custody and economics represent the two greatest

WHO GETS CUSTODY?

When parents decide to separate, they must also decide who is to receive custody of the children. This has been a controversial issue for years, and even today ideas about the best custodial arrangements remain in a state of flux.

Historical judicial decisions regarding child custody reflect the uncertainty that has plagued this issue. For example, until the middle of the nineteenth century, children automatically went to their fathers. However, as economic conditions changed, the laws were modified to award custody to mothers as the natural nurturers of children during their "tender years." In most states, judges now make custody decisions on the basis of the child's best interest. Mothers still obtain custody in about nine out of ten cases, but fathers seek custody more often. Grandparents can also go to court to obtain the right to visit with their grandchildren (Thornton and Freedman, 1983).

Joint custody is one way to help reduce the problems and headaches associated with custodial decisions. Joint custody provides for the sharing of parental rights and responsibilities after divorce. Joint custody actually has two meanings. One is that both parents retain the rights they always have had as parents; for instance, the right to participate in decisions about schooling or health/medical considerations. The other meaning of joint custody is that evey week, month, or year parents will alternate in providing the child's shelter. This is called *joint residential custody* (Weiss, 1984).

Joint custody is becoming more and more popular today. Among the reasons for this increase in popularity are its similarities to the original marital household and its reduction of adjustments children have to make. Joint custody may also reduce the bitterness that often exists under sole custody arrangements, particularly ▶

among fathers who pay child support but have only limited access to their children. Finally, joint custody reduces the loss that a noncustodial parent often experiences under traditional sole-custody arrangements (Ruback, 1985).

However, joint custody may not be right for everyone. For instance, children and adolescents often want a single home as a base and find alternating homes confusing; moving from place to place can disrupt a child's education. In addition, joint custody does not insure that each parent is capable of handling the responsibilities of childrearing. Current research suggests that children might be best served if their parents have joint custody in the legal sense, but are not required to alternate residences. At the same time, children should have easy access to the parent with whom they do not live. All of this points to the fact that while joint custody poses an alternative custodial arrangement, whether it is the final word has yet to be decided (Weiss, 1984; Gardner, 1982). ■

difficulties divorcing couples face. Also, more divorces fail in the coparental aspect than in any other way.

Community Divorce   The **community divorce** implies that a person's status in the surrounding neighborhood changes in certain ways. Separated individuals must learn to adapt to the varying perceptions of those around them. Sometimes relationships with friends are altered and many divorced persons report feelings of isolation and loneliness. Some feel degrees of social disapproval. Others regret that divorcing one's spouse involves "divorce" from one's in-laws. Sometimes, in-laws become "out-laws." However, many divorced persons keep in touch with those they now call "the children's relatives."

Divorce from Dependency   The final component of divorce involves regaining individual autonomy. The shift from being in a couple-oriented situation to being a single person requires role realignment and considerable mental adjustment. Interestingly, those couples who maintained high levels of independence in their marriages are likely to regain autonomy more rapidly than are those marriage partners who were very dependent on one another.

These components illustrate the many complexities of divorce — the interacting forces that may be operating. Consider the anger that many

feel before, during, and after divorce. Between the separation and final decree, many may be angry because they have been rejected in the psychic divorce, cheated in the economic divorce, and misrepresented in the legal divorce. Beyond this, they may be lonely in the community divorce, afraid in the divorce from dependency, and enraged and bitter because they are still tied together in coparental divorce. Truly, divorce is a complex and multifaceted experience.

Constance Ahrons' Theory

The focus of Constance Ahrons' theory is on the family changes that accompany divorce. She regards divorce as a normative family transition that consists of five stages or transitions. These five stages represent a process through which family members acquire new roles and the family itself takes on a new definition.

Individual Cognition   During the stage of **individual cognition**, there is an awareness that something is wrong in the marital relationship. Individual reactions vary in the early phases of this stage — blaming one's partner, anger, depression, or even denial of the problem. Any resolution chosen at this stage depends on the couple's history of coping strategies. Some couples may decide to stay in the marriage until the children are grown. Others may decide to spend time and energy on

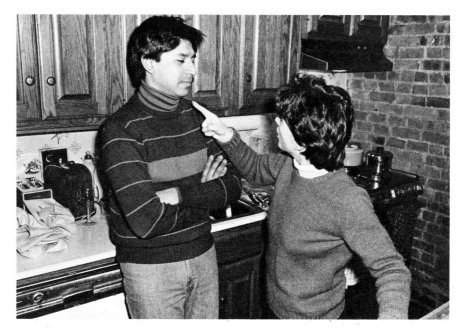

The decision to separate or divorce is triggered by many forces, including constant conflict and disharmony.

interests outside the family while attempting to maintain the facade of an intact marriage. This process of *emotional divorce*, the withdrawal of emotional investment in the marital relationship, is self-protective and may have some positive benefits for the individual. However, this withdrawal will have implications for the entire family system.

How long this stage lasts hinges on the coping behaviors used and other factors related to the family's vulnerability to stress. Equilibrium in the family is usually maintained, although precariously, during this transition. Role patterns may remain stable even in the midst of the growing family tension. Families may deal with internal stress by assigning one member the role of family scapegoat, and he or she is then blamed for any trouble. Thus, the coping strategies families use to alleviate feelings about the parents' marital difficulties often elevate family stress in other ways.

Family Metacognition   In the second stage, **family metacognition**, the entire family begins to realize that the marriage is deteriorating, and the family system begins to change in recognition of the problem. The problem is typically discussed by the family and the dialogue often sums up each member's anxieties. This is also a time for potential solutions and consequences of the problem to be discussed.

If the family has not demonstrated adequate and rational problem solving in past crisis situations, it is not apt to do so at this time, and for many families, this stage marks the time of greatest disequilibrium. Wife and husband roles are fading, and new ones (divorced coparents) have yet to develop. The future seems uncertain and ambiguous, and the family often searches for role models. For example, old rules and rituals may be sought by the family to preserve stability, but these usually fail to provide unity or comfort. Or children may begin to seek information about divorce by looking for friends who have experienced this crisis.

Separation   The third transition proposed by Ahrons is **separation**. During this stage, one parent moves out of the home and away from the family.

The family is in a state of flux, and family members often express more doubt in regard to family roles and boundaries. For example, a youngster may wonder if his/her parents are both still part of the family.

The typical separation involves the father moving out while the mother and children remain as one unit. Ahrons feels that the mother-headed household faces a difficult situation — should it reorganize and fill roles once enacted by the now absent father, or should it maintain his psychological presence in the system by not reorganizing? If the unit attempts to reassign roles, the father's return is usually met with resistance. Or, if they deal with the father as psychologically present, they perpetuate family disequilibrium and stress. The children face a difficult transition if the family remains in a state of disequilibrium characterized by the father's intermittent exit and return.

The family typically faces stress at this time, even if it has successfully coped with earlier stages. However, it may not experience serious disruption if its coping strategies are successful. Also during this transition, the family typically shares its marital separation with extended family, friends, and the community as it begins the tasks of the economic and legal divorce. (Note the connection to Bohannon's theory.) Ahrons believes these mediating factors can help and/or hinder the transitional process. The family typically encounters the legal system now and faces additional stress in confronting the hard realities of economic hardships (that is, splitting money, selling home) and child-focused issues of custody and care. All of this may heighten the sense of crisis.

Family Reorganization   During earlier stages, the lack of clear boundaries caused much of the family's confusion and stress, but in the **family reorganization** stage the clarification of boundaries itself creates distress.

As Bohannon suggests, and Ahrons reinforces, one of the most stressful chores confronting divorcing parents is that of redefining their coparental relationship, the relationship that permits them to continue their childrearing obligations and re-

sponsibilities after divorce. Ahrons takes this a step further by saying this task requires them to separate their spousal roles from their parental roles, terminating the former while redefining the latter. This complex process of ceasing to be husband and wife while still continuing to be mother and father creates the foundation for divorced family reorganization.

Divorcing spouses need to form new rules to redefine their continued relationship. For example, the divorced family needs to develop new structural rules which will guide its patterns of transactions (who relates to whom, when, and under what conditions). This type of arrangement can help clarify responsibilities and, by eliminating possible disagreements, minimize conflict between ex-spouses. Such rules are also critical to the child's understanding and to the stabilization of his or her relationship with each parent. How divorced parents define the ways in which they will share parenting can be critical to the child's psychological adjustment. Without a clear understanding of the relational rules, the child may become a victim in unresolved spousal or parental conflicts.

Family Redefinition   Ahrons feels that the **family redefinition** depends on the relationship between the divorced parents. Although a continued and cooperative relationship between divorced parents reduces the crisis potential associated with divorce, its dynamics remain largely unexplored. As we've indicated already, the growing debate about custody rights reveals our lack of knowledge about the time-honored concept ''best interests of the child'' and brings the custom of sole custody into serious question. The recent trend toward shared custody and coparenting represents an alternative, and would thus play a role in family redefinition.

A major feature of the redefinitional process appears to be the parents' ability to maintain a child-centered relationship. For some this includes maintaining a continuing friendship. For others, though, the relationship becomes less intimate and more task-oriented. Finally, components of

TABLE 14-4

A Comparison of Bohannon's and Ahrons'
Theories

Bohannon's Components of Divorce	Ahrons' Divorce Transitions
Psychological divorce	Individual cognition transition
Legal divorce	Family metacognition transition
Economic divorce	Separation transition
Coparental divorce	Family reorganization transition
Community divorce	Family redefinition transition
Divorce from dependency	

this stage include the processes of remarriage and the introduction of stepparents into the post-divorce family, topics we'll explore later on in this chapter. As we'll see, these processes represent further adjustments for all concerned and ongoing transitions of family redefinition.

SEQUEL TO DIVORCE

Adjustments and Adaptations

Divorce often forces people to critically examine themselves and what they want to do for the rest of their lives. The aftermath of divorce proceedings, however, may be a difficult time to think clearly and employ good judgment and logic. The legal battle may have been long and tiring. And, following a divorce, it is not uncommon to experience many psychological states, including a sense of failure, loneliness, sadness, and fear. Of course, amidst the disruption which often characterizes the rebuilding process, many feel relieved and glad to be starting over.

Diane Vaughan (1983) feels that divorce involves redefinition of the self as persons move from mutual identity toward autonomy. The uncoupling process is a status transformation which

is complete when the individual defines his/her salient status as "single" rather than "divorced." When one's newly constructed separate subworld attains a sort of order and life is experienced as making sense, the uncoupling process is completed. But, the completion of uncoupling does not occur at the same moment for each participant. For either or both of the participants, it may not happen until after the other has created a coupled identity with another person. With that step, the tentativeness is usually gone. But the uncoupling process for some may never be completed. One or both of the participants may never be able to construct a new and separate subworld that becomes self-validating.

Men, more than women, deny that they need help or support after a divorce. The man, however, faces considerable changes in his lifestyle. In addition to alimony and other court-related expenses, he is usually faced with the economic burden of finding a new place to live. Chores he might not have previously concerned himself with now become everyday realities: cooking, laundering, cleaning, and so on (Price-Bonham and Balswick, 1980; Rosenthal and Keshet, 1980; Oakland, 1984).

Women have their share of adjustments and adaptations, too. This is particularly true if children are involved. Women have to find a job and they usually carry the brunt of childcare responsibilities. Rebuilding a social life is especially hard when a woman has children needing continual care and attention. A divorced woman also often encounters difficulty establishing credit, a factor hampering her financial independence. Frequently banks, oil companies, and stores treat her differently than her male counterpart in similar economic situations.

A study launched by Stan Albrecht (1980) shows that women, compared to men, regard the divorce experience as more stressful and traumatic. Surveying 500 ever-divorced persons, Albrecht found that 27 percent of the female respondents attributed a very high degree of stress to the experience, while only 16 percent of the males, felt this way. On the other hand, 20 percent of the

Post-divorce life brings many role realignments.

males, compared to 13 percent of the females, described the divorce experience as relatively painless.

Most of the literature points to the fact that despite the adjustments cited, most divorced parties do find happiness and satisfaction. Elizabeth Cauhape (1983), for example, writes that divorced men and women are capable of weathering the stormy stages of the divorce experience and finding stability. For men and women alike, this path involves costs and tradeoffs, and identifying the tradeoffs that exist as possibilities is a critical factor in the transitional period following a divorce. Cauhape feels that success and happiness at this time depends on a person's ability to turn problems into opportunities for new self-definitions, and most individuals are equipped to do so.

Despite the trauma, then, divorce can be an opportunity for growth, a time for yet another transition. In the process of adapting to a new life, many people discover strengths and emotional re-

sources they never knew they possessed. They find they can survive loneliness and loss. They use the new freedom to learn about themselves, seek new interests, change lifestyles, pursue other careers, and find more fulfilling relationships (McKay et al. 1984).

Effects of Divorce on Children

Many of the homes stricken by divorce include children. As we indicated at the outset, it is estimated that nearly one million children each year will see their parents' marriage collapse. Should current rates hold, one of every three white children and two of three black children born after marriage will experience a parental marital dissolution by age 16. Most children of divorced parents live with their mother, and the majority will experience living in a fatherless home for at least five years. Moreover, the divorce experience is not necessarily over when the mother remarries.

RESEARCH HIGHLIGHT

THE EMOTIONAL AFTERMATH OF DIVORCE

Unfortunately, society tends to paint a rather bleak portrayal of divorced persons: completely unhappy, lonely, dissatisfied with their lives, and mentally crippled from the divorce experience itself. Such a portrayal is inaccurate and needs to be debunked, according to Helen Weingarten (1985). In her study of first-married, divorced, and remarried adults, she found that the divorced were not the mortally wounded victims some believe. Indeed, the divorce experience provided many of them with new and resourceful ways of handling day-to-day living.

This does not mean that divorced persons emerge from the divorce experience emotionally unscathed; many report bouts of unhappiness. However, on measures of well-being that do not involve evaluations of personal happiness, divorced and remarried adults are not significantly different. That is, the divorced report similar levels of self-esteem, perceived internal control, self-acceptance, and zest; and no higher levels of dissatisfaction, perceived shortcomings, worry, anxiety, immobilization, physical health symptoms and substance abuse than remarried respondents. Also, the divorced are even more likely than the remarried to mention having personal strengths when asked, "What would you say are your strongest points?".

Compared with first-marrieds, divorced persons are less zestful, less satisfied and more anxious. However, they are equally positive in their level of self-acceptance, equally high in self-esteem, and no higher in their reports of immobilization or frequency of worrying than are their first-married peers. In analyzing these results, Weingarten writes that one should remember that positive and negative feelings do not necessarily exclude one another. For example, it is possible to feel somewhat anxious but not feel depressed, and it is possible to feel dissatisfied but not be self-rejecting. By the same token, it is possible not to feel very happy without feeling very unhappy.

About one-third of white and one-half of black children whose mothers remarry will experience a second parental marital dissolution before they reach adulthood (Thornton and Freedman, 1983).

As one might expect, the problems encountered and adjustments required by children of divorce are numerous. Some children feel personally responsible for the divorce. Many are persuaded by their parents to take sides. Others may bear the brunt of displaced parental aggression. Coping with divorce may also spill over to other aspects of the child's life and create additional problems, such as in schoolwork (Wallerstein and Kelley, 1980; Hetherington, 1981; Berger, 1983).

Some people believe that a divorce should never occur while dependent children are at home. Advocates of this position realize that the stresses of marital discord may force children into roles that can exact a tremendous emotional toll. However, as Mary Jane Van Meter (1985) points out, this course of action has exceptions. Family violence

Children react to divorce in diverse fashions.

and sexual abuse, in which the abuser is unwilling to seek help or is unresponsive to help, are examples where it is unhealthy for families to remain together.

Others feel that under no circumstances should embittered parents stay together just for the sake of the children. Unhappy parents should get a divorce, thus ending the marital war and removing the children from the crossfire. As Matti Gershenfeld (1985) puts it, couples do have a right to their own happiness, even when they have children.

We need to acknowledge that either of the above courses of action may pose problems to the children. They may be subjected to continual quarreling and tension if the parents stay together, or they may be brought up by a single parent who is frequently beset by numerous adjustment problems. What appears to be critical in the overall transition are psychologically healthy parents with empathic attitudes, cooperation, and open lines of communication with children (Kurdek, 1981; Ahrons, 1984; Goldstein and Solnit, 1984).

Reactions to Divorce: Ages and Stages   The trauma of divorce affects children in a multitude of different ways. By examining an impressive longitudinal study headed by Judith Wallerstein and Joan Kelley (1980) we can establish some insight into children's reactions and behaviors. The two researchers traced 131 children from 60 divorcing families in northern California. Four age groups of children were studied: preschoolers, six- to eight-year-olds, nine- to twelve-year-olds, and adolescents.

One of the most important findings was that children's reactions to divorce vary according to age. Among the preschoolers, for example, there was a distinct fear of being abandoned. Many exhibited anxiety, including clinging activity and disturbed sleep patterns. Regression was also common (thumb-sucking, bed-wetting) as was increased aggressiveness toward other children.

Six- to eight-year-olds exhibited the most sadness of all four age groupings. Many grieved openly and expressed a great yearning for the departed parent. Also, few expressed anger or leveled criticism toward the separated figure. In school, about 50 percent of this age group declined in academic performance.

Among the nine- to twelve-year-olds, the most pervasive reaction was anger. More often than not, this anger was channeled toward the parent perceived to be responsible for the divorce. Often, children were encouraged to take sides and form an alliance with one parent (usually the alliance was with the mother against the father). This age group also felt lonely and anxious, but to a lesser degree than the anger.

Anger was also expressed by the adolescents, but it was directed more toward their parents' dating. The authors surmise that perhaps the teenagers regarded this as competition with their own emerging heterosexual development. The adolescents also experienced a sense of deep loss and emptiness. Many had difficulty concentrating and some suffered from chronic fatigue. However,

many of the teenagers demonstrated positive behaviors following the divorce. For example, about one-third took on more household responsibility and displayed more sensitivity and understanding in their own relationships.

Five years after the study was launched, Wallerstein and Kelly conducted a follow-up. Thirty-four percent of the children were doing extremely well and 29 percent were adjusting adequately. However, 37 percent were found to be in poor psychological health. Problems associated with the latter group included (among others) depression, anger, and rejection.

Fairly recently (Wallerstein, 1984) another follow-up was conducted on the subjects who were preschoolers at the time of the initial study. Few conscious memories of the intact family or of the divorce were seen to have been retained, although all of the youngsters had been distressed and frightened by the family crisis at the time. It would appear to be a strong possibility that children who

APPLICATIONS

HOW TO TALK WITH CHILDREN ABOUT DIVORCE

Almost every parent fears the inevitable pain that children will feel when they learn about an impending divorce. David McKay and associates (1984) write that no matter how hard it is to face the children, it is a job that must be done. Furthermore, it can not be done in the form of a simple announcement. The dialogue between parent and child is the beginning of a process in which youngsters can express feelings, get reassurance, and gradually integrate this important change into their lives. The authors offer the following guidelines to parents:

- Tell the children *clearly* and *directly* what divorce means. Tell them in an understandable way what problems and issues have led you to the decision. Be prepared to repeat this information several times before the younger children really acknowledge what's happened.

- Attempt to show them that your decision comes from much careful thought about the marriage and not from whim or impulse.

- Seek to describe any changes the children can expect in their day-to-day experience.

- Describe some of your attempts to protect and improve your marriage. ▶

- Emphasize that both parents will continue to love and care for the children. Be specific. Share your tentative decisions about visitation or shared custody.
- Do not assess blame. If the children are told that there was an affair, acknowledge that it was a symptom of the marital unhappiness. Emphasize that each parent has been hurt in his or her own way and that each has felt pain. If you're angry, acknowledge it, but don't express your rage and blame to the kids.
- Emphasize that the children in no way caused the divorce and are not responsible for problems between their parents. Explain that you are divorcing each other, not your kids. It is equally important to let children know that nothing they can do can bring about a reconciliation. Little children often harbor fantasies of mending your broken marriage.
- Assure children that they will always remain free to love both parents. No pressure will be brought to reject one parent in order to continue getting nurtured by the other.
- Encourage children to ask questions, not just at the beginning, but throughout the long process of adjusting to a separation. Also, let them express their feelings. Let them know you are listening by repeating back in your own words the concerns they express to you.

Beyond these suggestions, Elin McCoy (1984) points out that a number of good books on divorce are available for both parents and children. The following are representative:

For Parents

McKay, M. (1984). *The divorce book*. New Harbinger Publications.

Ricci, I. (1980). *Mom's house, dad's house: Making shared custody work*. Macmillan.

For Preschoolers

Perry, P., and Lynch, M. (1978). *Mommy and daddy are divorced*. Dial books.

Sinberg, J. (1978). *Divorce is a grown-up problem*. Avon Books.

Ages 5 to 9

Hazen, B. (1978). *Two homes to live in: a child's eye view of divorce*. Human Sciences Press.

Helmering, D., and William, J. (1981). *I have two families*. Abingdon Press.

Preteen and Adolescents

Blume, J. (1982). *It's not the end of the world*. Dell Press.

Danziger, P. (1983). *The divorce express*. Dell Press.

are very young when a divorce occurs are much less burdened in the subsequent years than are those who were older at the time of the divorce. While in fantasies they are no less attached to the intact family, they do not seem to be troubled by intensely cathected memories of parental conflict or of their own fear and suffering at the time — and they may be optimistic about the future.

Single-Parent Households

Following a divorce, it is conceivable that the child's custodial parent will remain single. Indeed, the single-parent family is the fastest growing family form in the United States today. Approximately 12 million children live in single-parent families. In the 1980s almost one out of every five families is of the single-parent variety. This represents about a 50 percent increase since 1970 (Furstenberg and Nord, 1982; Grossman, 1981).

About 85 percent of all single-parent families are headed by women. Let us point out, though, that while the single-parent family often consists of a divorced mother and her children, divorce does not represent the only reason for family dissolution. Rather, single parents may also be widowed, separated, or never married men or women. Others may have had their children naturally, through adoption, or through artificial means (see Chapter 10).

Statistics also tell us that black children are more likely than white children to live with their mother alone because of blacks' higher rates of marital dissolution, out-of-wedlock childbearing, and lower rates of marriage and remarriage. Fifty-seven percent of black children, compared to 20 percent of white children, who were six and under in 1970 experienced family living without a father for some time in the 1970s. Nearly 20 percent of black children spent the entire decade in a family headed by the mother, and only a third lived continuously in a two-parent home (Thornton and Freedman, 1983). (Figure 14-2 compares black and white single parent families from 1970 to 1982.)

Single mothers shoulder many extra responsibilities.

There are numerous problems reported by single-parent families, and financial difficulties almost always top the list. Many single-parent families are poor, especially if a female is head of the household. Research obtained in 1980 reveals that almost 40 percent of female-headed single-parent households were living in poverty. Conversely, only 16 percent of male-headed families were in the same category (Payton 1982; Johnson, 1980).

Janice Hogan and colleagues (1983) note that this economic plight reflects the problems associated with job discrimination against women, conflicts between employment and home responsibilities, and a reluctance by both ex-husbands and community agencies to help the female head

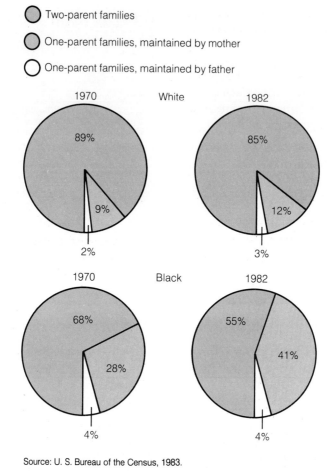

Source: U. S. Bureau of the Census, 1983.

FIGURE 14-2   Single-Parent Households among Blacks and Whites, 1970–1982

of household. Because of the generally low incomes of single-parent families, a small cash flow imposes a serious economic constraint on the managment ability of the single mother. Reduced income may mean a change in buying patterns, increased debt, and a change in housing to a less expensive neighborhood.

Another major problem is that court-ordered child support, important for single mothers, is not large and is frequently not paid. In 1981, only 75 percent of the divorced and separated women legally due child payments received any money from

the children's father, and only one-half of those got the full amount. It is expensive, time-consuming, and stressful for mothers to collect unpaid child support from their former husbands, and few are successful (Thornton and Freedman, 1983).

Care and supervision of the children is an additional financial problem, not to mention the quest itself for reliable daycare. This is difficult for couples and magnified even more for single parents, particularly if one considers absorption costs, transporation, teacher conferences, and the like. Role realignment, loneliness, and stigmatization are other commonly reported adjustment problems. Furthermore, both parent and child have to adapt to a changed family structure.

Fairly recently, a wave of publications have focused on the needs of single parents (see, for example, Grief, 1985; Renvoize, 1985; Bustanoby, 1985; Murdock, 1980). Most of these publications stress the importance of minimizing guilt and ambivalence toward single-parenthood and generating positive acceptance about this new social role. Many, such as Knight (1981), emphasize the positive features of rearing children this way, from the establishment of a single and consistent standard of discipline within the home to the encouragement of more self-reliance within one's offspring. While single parenting is a draining and often thankless task, it is not without its rewards.

RELATIONSHIP RECONSTRUCTION

Remarriage

Most divorced persons remarry and for the most part, this is done rather quickly. More specifically, 83 percent of divorced men and 75 percent of divorced women remarry. The average interval between divorce and remarriage is approximately three years (Sager, 1983; Glick, 1984, 1980b; Furstenberg, 1980).

Arland Thornton and Deborah Freedman (1983) note that remarriage rates generally exceed the first marriage rate in this country. Remarriage rates are also higher for younger than for older divorced persons. In addition, black Americans are both more likely than whites to remain separated without divorcing and less likely than whites to remarry after a divorce.

Contrary to what one might expect, divorce rates among the remarried are quite high. Statistics show that of the approximate 79 percent who choose to remarry, about 44 percent will divorce again (U. S. Bureau of the Census, 1982). Why is this so? Shouldn't there be a lower divorce rate based on what was learned the first time around? While these may be valid questions to ask, most experts point to a new set of problems confronting remarrieds. For example, frequently cited difficulties include the economic drain of providing for two families, stepchildren, and lingering emotional problems (anger and guilt, for example) related to one's ex-spouse. Figure 14-3 displays the statistical probabilities of marriage and divorce.

The Six Stations of Remarriage   Ann Goetting (1982) has borrowed the model of divorce developed by Paul Bohannon (1970, 1985a, 1985b) and fashioned six "stations" or components of remarriage. She feels that each of these stations require adaptation and adjustment. As in Bohannon's model, these stations may not occur to all remarried people with the same intensity and in the same order.

The **emotional remarriage** involves the reinvestment of emotions in a relationship so that

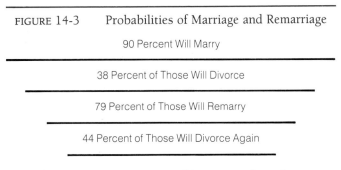

FIGURE 14-3   Probabilities of Marriage and Remarriage

90 Percent Will Marry

38 Percent of Those Will Divorce

79 Percent of Those Will Remarry

44 Percent of Those Will Divorce Again

Source: U. S. Bureau of the Census. (1982, December). *Current Population Reports*. Washington, DC: U. S. Government printing office.

comfort and love can be secured. This may be fear-provoking for some, since loss and rejection loom as distinct possibilities. Obviously, failure can lead to disappointment, as well as damage one's identity and self-concept.

The **psychic remarriage** is the process of changing one's conjugal identity from individual to couple. This means giving up the personal freedom and independence established by the psychic divorce, and resuming a lifestyle in which a person is expected to be viewed as one component of a relationship.

The **community remarriage** involves reentry into the world of couples. In the process, unmarried friends especially those of the opposite sex, may be lost for lack of a common lifestyle. Married life is often intolerant of relationships with former friends, and is thus an obstacle that has to be faced.

The **parental remarriage** occurs if children are involved, either from one side of the marriage or both. The process of combining children to form a new family is a task formidable in scope. Later on in this chapter we'll explore a number of issues confronting the blended family, each requiring considerable adjustment and adaptation.

The **economic remarriage** is the re-establishment of a marital household as a unit of economic productivity and consumption. The existence of children from a former marriage often complicates matters and creates financial instability. The remarriage also creates the problem of resource distribution; in other words, how the household's money is to be spent and who gets how much of what is available.

The **legal remarriage** involves the legal complexities associated with this new lifestyle. Beyond the child support, alimony, and property division that were associated with one's first marriage, other legal ramifications await remarrieds. For example, it must be determined which spouse — past or present — legally deserves the life and accident insurance inheritance, medical coverage, or pension rights. For that matter, one's financial obligations to children from a previous marriage, such as support for a college education, also need

to be determined. As one can see, the new marriage can often create legal complications, particularly when the former marriage is considered.

Assessing the Well-Being of Remarrieds   Is remarriage the best way of adjusting to post-divorce life? Are levels of well-being greater among remarrieds than singles? These are valid questions to ask, especially in light of the high divorce rates among remarrieds. Unfortunately, research studies focusing on these issues have produced mixed findings. For example, one longitudinal study undertaken by Graham Spanier and Frank Furstenberg (1982) examined 180 divorced men and women from Pennsylvania. The subjects' behavior was assessed from their post-separation periods of two and one-half years. From the collected data, the authors concluded that remarriage after divorce was not associated with enhanced well-being. Moreover, no other variables were identified which were able to predict well-being following divorce. However, limited evidence indicated that the likelihood of remarriage may be related to an existing state of well-being after divorce. Should these people remarry, the quality of the second marriage is positively related to well-being.

Other research investigations have produced different findings, though. One (Mitchell, 1983) compared a matched sample of divorced and remarried mothers. The latter group reported a higher sense of both competency and well-being than divorced mothers. This well-being was significantly related to feelings of competence and satisfaction in areas of love, community, and homemaking. There were no differences in other areas such as work and parenting.

Other studies on the topic produced just as many contradictory findings. Helen Weingarten (1980), for example, found that the level of content and well-being among remarried couples was about the same as first-married couples. Several researchers (Glenn, 1981; Yoder and Nichols, 1980) have noted that remarried women tend to rate their marriages and levels of well-being slightly lower than first-married women. In addition, a study (Saul and Scherman, 1984) comparing remarried couples with divorced persons showed no significant differences in regard to well-being and personal adjustment in general.

Before leaving this topic, we also need to take into account the emotional tension that frequently accompanies the remarriage process. This certainly has an effect on the well-being of remarried persons. Monica McGoldrick and Elizabeth Carter (1982) maintain that emotional tension is apparent at predictable points: at the time of serious commitment to the new relationship; at the time the plan to remarry is announced to families and friends; at the time of the actual remarriage and formation of the step-family; and as the logistics of stepfamily life are put into practice.

Beyond this, the family emotional process during the transition to remarriage consists of struggling with fears about investment in a new marriage and a new family: one's own fears, the new spouse's fears, and the children's fears (of either or both spouses); dealing with hostile or upset reactions of the children, the extended families; and the ex-spouse; struggling with the ambiguity of the new model of family structure roles and relationships; and a reawakening of intense parental guilt and concerns about the welfare of children. Any assessment of well-being among remarrieds would have to take all of these concerns into account. Table 14-5 shows some of the dynamics and developmental issues related to the remarried family.

Admidst such mixed findings and complicated issues, perhaps the best way to approach the topic of well-being in marriages is to assess such a psychological state in both partners before the union takes place. Similar to first marriages, it may well be that the quality of well-being and adaptive ability that two partners have beforehand should be stressed, not the institution of remarriage per se. With such a perspective in mind, numerous studies have focused on how persons can realign their lives after divorce and elevate overall levels of well-being and adaptation (see Wald, 1981; Furstenberg and Spanier, 1984; Sager, 1983; Cherlin, 1981; Whiteside, 1982). A recurrent theme is that divorced men and women can come to terms with

their circumstances and assume control over their lives, not to mention reaching suitable levels of well-being. Reordering one's life after divorce requires intense effort and considerable trial and error, along with numerous costs and trade-offs. But the rewards are great in terms of realignment and newly created identities. Should remarriage be on the horizon, the successfully adjusted are more likely to bring stability, harmony, and happiness to the new relationship.

Blended Families

Without question, remarriage requires a number of adjustments. One of the biggest occurs when a parent having physical custody of the child remarries. This creates what is known as a **blended** (or *reconstituted*) **family**. Approximately 60 percent of all remarriages fall into this category. Another 20 percent of remarriages involve noncustodial parents. Overall, it is estimated that 6.5 million children live in blended families (Jacobson, 1980; Glick, 1980b; Weingarten, 1980).

Emily and John Visher (1983) feel that remarriage with children is part of a process of family redefinition. It begins with a loss: a spouse or parent has died or there has been a divorce. A once-existing love relationship is gone. Children and parents have been separated either totally or partially, depending on the custody and visitation arrangements. In some situations, brothers and sisters have been separated. There may have been a severing of relationships with grandparents, or alienation from friends and a familiar community. For numerous adults in a remarriage, many cherished dreams of marriage have been lost in the chaos of instant children and former spouses. In this sense, remarriages, unlike first marriages, are born of many losses. Persons differ in the time it takes them to mourn the losses, and frequently adults form new and meaningful relationships while children are still adjusting to a new home, a new school, new friends, or separation from a parent.

The Vishers add that many adults enter a remarriage expecting the impossible of themselves and

TABLE 14-5

Remarried Family Formation: A Developmental Outline

Steps	Prerequisite Attitude	Developmental Issues
1. Entering the new relationship	Recovery from loss of first marriage (adequate "emotional divorce")	Recommitment to marriage and to forming a family with readiness to deal with the complexity and ambiguity
2. Conceptualizing and planning new marriage and family	Accepting one's own fears and those of new spouse and children about remarriage and forming a stepfamily Accepting need for time and patience for adjustment to complexity and ambiguity of the following: 1. Multiple new roles 2. Boundaries: space, time, membership, and authority 3. Affective issues: guilt, loyalty conflicts, desire for mutuality, unresolvable past hurts	a. Work on openness in the new relationships to avoid pseudomutuality b. Plan for maintenance of cooperative coparental relationships with ex-spouses c. Plan to help children deal with fears, loyalty conflicts, and membership in two systems d. Realignment of relationships with extended family to include new spouse and children e. Plan maintenance of connections for children with extended family of ex-spouse(s)
3. Remarriage and reconstitution of family	Final resolution of attachment to previous spouse and ideal of "intact" family; acceptance of a different model of family with permeable boundaries	a. Restructuring family boundaries to allow for inclusion of new spouse-stepparent b. Realignment of relationships throughout subsystems to permit interweaving of several systems c. Making room for relationships of all children with biological (noncustodial) parents, grandparents, and other extended family d. Sharing memories and histories to enhance stepfamily integration

Source: McGoldrick, M., and Carter, E. A. (1982). Remarriage and the family life cycle. In F. Walsh (Ed.), *Normal family processes.* Reprinted by permission of The Guilford Press, New York, NY.

of the rest of the family. For example, stepmothers try to be super-moms so they can overcome the "wicked stepmother" image. Stepfathers rush in and try to take command immediately, while stepchildren balk and drag their heels in resentment at being asked to participate in this new venture that has been no choice of theirs. Many grandparents feel somewhat isolated and uncertain of their roles, while ex-spouses may compete for the love and loyalty of their children. Add to this mosaic of emotions and unrealistic expectations the ways in which stepfamilies are different from biological families, and it is easy to see why remarried families experience their own particular tensions.

Blended families must work at building domestic solidarity and harmony. The successful assimilation of new family members and the definition of new family roles and relationships is especially difficult. Older stepchildren, in particular, often have difficulty accepting their new stepfather or stepmother. The issue of "turf," or who owns which possessions in the redesigned family network, is difficult for many. In the face of such complex developments, children may experience divided loyalties (Visher and Visher, 1982; Kompara, 1980; Johnson, 1980; Lutz, 1983).

Despite the energy required to meet these challenges, research indicates that stepchild-steppar-

APPLICATIONS

THE TEN COMMANDMENTS OF STEPPARENTING

Sharon and James Turnbull (1983) observe that the natural family contains plenty of its own stresses and conflicts. When one or two stepparents are added, along with a set of ready-made brothers and sisters, added pressures begin. The Turnbulls offer the following guidelines for stepparents:

1. Provide Neutral Territory   Even the very young children recognize that the prior occupation of a territory confers a certain power. When two sets of children are brought together one regards itself as the "main family" and the other as a subfamily. The determining factor, of course, is whose house gets to be the family home. One school of thought suggests that when a couple remarries they should move to a new house, even if it means selling family heirlooms. If it is impossible to finance a move to neutral territory, it is important to provide a special, inviolate place which belongs to each child individually.

2. Don't Try to Fit a Preconceived Role   When dealing with children the best course is to be honest right from the beginning. Each parent is an individual with all his or her faults, peculiarities and emotions, and the children are just going to have to get used to this parent. Children have excellent radar for detecting phoniness, and are quick to lose respect for any adult who will let them walk all over him or her.

3. Set Limits and Enforce Them   One of the most difficult problems for a natural parent and stepparent living together is to decide on disciplinary measures. It is important that the parents themselves work out the rules in advance and support one another when rules need to be enforced.

4. Allow an Outlet for Feelings by the Children for the Natural Parent   It is often hard for the stepparent to accept that his or her stepchildren will maintain a natural affection for their natural parent who is no longer living in the household. The stepparent may interpret this as a personal rejection. Children need to be allowed to express feelings about the natural parent who is absent. This needs to be supported in a neutral way so that the children do not feel disloyal.

5. Expect Ambivalence   Stepparents are often concerned when children appear on successive days or successive hours to show both emotions of strong love and strong hate toward them. Ambivalence is normal in all human relationships, but nowhere is it more accentuated than in the feelings of the stepchild toward their stepparent.

6. Avoid Mealtime Misery   For many stepfamilies, meals are an excruciating experience. This, after all, is the time when the dreams of blissful family life confront reality. In some instances, rejection of the food prepared by the stepmother takes place; other times the dinner table represents an ideal location for family members to clash. Obviously, constant fighting at the dinner table is not conducive to good digestion; but children can master the prerequisite etiquette with reasonable speed when both parents reinforce the message that table manners are expected.   ▶

7. Don't Expect Instant Love   One of the problems facing a new step-parent is the expectation of feeling love for the child and for that love to be returned. It takes time for emotional bonds to be forged, and sometimes this never occurs. All stepparents must acknowledge that eventuality.

8. Don't Take All the Responsibility . . . The Child Has Some Too   Ultimately, how well the stepparent gets along with the stepchild depends in part upon the kind of child he or she is. Children, like adults, come in all types and sizes. Some are simply more lovable than others. If the new stepmother has envisioned herself as the mother of a cuddly little tot and finds herself with a sullen, vindictive twelve-year-old who regards her with considerable suspicion, she is likely to experience considerable disappointment. Like it or not, the stepparent has to take what he or she gets. But that doesn't mean taking all the guilt for a less than perfect relationship.

9. Be Patient   The words to remember here are "things take time." The first few months, and often years, have many difficult periods. The support and encouragement of other parents who have had other similar experiences can be an invaluable aid.

10. Maintain the Primacy of the Marital Relationship   Many stepparenting relationships have resulted from divorce by one or both members of the couple. There is a certain amount of guilt left over about the breakup of the previous relationship which may spill over into the present relationship and create difficulties when there are arguments. The couple needs to remember that their relationship is primary in the family. The children need to be shown that the parents get along together, can settle disputes, and most of all will not be divided by the children.   ▄

ent relations are characterized by considerable happiness and satisfaction. Furthermore, stepchildren are generally regarded as a well-adjusted lot. Compared to children from natural families, most are just as happy and emotionally stable. Also, they do as well in such areas as academic achievement and problem-solving resourcefulness (Skeen, Robinson, and Flake-Hobson, 1984; Albrecht, Bahr, and Goodman, 1983; Santrock et al., 1982; Einstein, 1982; Knaub and Hanna, 1984; Jensen and Jensen, 1981).

CHAPTER HIGHLIGHTS

Divorce can occur at any stage of the marriage cycle and is a crisis for all concerned. To say that the divorce rates have risen in contemporary society would be an understatement. In 1985, nearly two and one-half million adults and over one million children were involved in the divorce experience. The divorce rate in the United States ranks among the world's highest.

This chapter explored some of the reasons behind divorce today, although the no-fault concept or variations of it disguise some of these motives. Primary among the reasons examined were personal unhappiness, a desire to get away from a negative situation, wanting to find opportunities for alternative financial support, being involved with someone else, and the relative ease of divorce laws. However, we also examined a number of trends evident in contemporary society that may influence the decision to divorce: incompatible roles, separation of the sexes, pressures of adult life, marital routines, changing functions of marriage and family, the emphasis of personality and emotional fulfillment, increased institutional support for divorced women, and the social roles of husband and wife. Barriers to divorce also exist, such as financial considerations, the presence of children, and religious constraints.

We also spent some time examining divorce legalities and related concepts. An annulment is the invalidation of a marriage on the basis of some reason that existed at the beginning of that marriage. A legal separation often occurs before the court proceedings and allows couples to live apart. More specifically, though, it represents a contract between the spouses that focuses on the issues that have to be resolved before a divorce is granted. No-fault divorce changes four basic elements of traditional divorce legislation: It eliminates fault-based grounds for divorce, removes the adversary process, stipulates that financial aspects of the divorce are to be based on equity, and redefines the traditional responsibilities of husbands and wives. Many couples seeking a divorce today employ what is called divorce mediation, a conflict resolution process in which a third party serves as an impartial guide to negotiation.

Two models of the divorce experience were examined. Paul Bohannon proposed six components or processes of divorce: the psychological, legal, economic, coparental, and community divorces, as well as the divorce from dependency. Constance Ahrons explored the family transitions that accompany divorce; including the stages of individual cognition, family metacognition, separation, family reorganization, and family redefinition.

As with any crisis, adjustments have to be made by divorced parties. The woman is frequently faced with having to get a job and parenting at the same time, since she typically receives custody of the children. The man, among other adjustments, encounters financial difficulties and must undertake a variety of domestic chores. Children face numerous problems when divorce occurs, especially confusion over why their parents have separated. Divorce may create a state of disorientation for children, which can leave many unpleasant memories. This chapter also explored how certain negative behaviors are expressed at different ages. As we stated, what appear to be critical in the child's transition to divorce are psychologically healthy parents who are empathic, open, honest, and cooperative when it comes to the youngster's interests.

Following divorce, it is very possible that a child's custodial parent will remain single. As we saw, there are approximately 12 million children living in single-parent homes in the United States. Approximately 85 percent of single-parent families are headed by women. Of all the problems facing these households, financial difficulties are the most prevalent.

Finally, we dealt with relationship reconstruction. Most divorced persons remarry, many within three years of the actual divorce. Ann Goetting, borrowing from the model developed by Paul Bohannon, has shed light on the adjustments required during remarriage. These adjustments become more complex if a blended or reconstituted family is created. Blended families must work especially hard at building domestic solidarity and harmony, especially since children often experience divided loyalties. Research indicates that for the most part, blended families are able to make the adjustments necessary for stability and happiness.

KEY TERMS

annulment
blended family
community divorce
community marriage
coparental divorce

crude divorce rate
divorce from dependency
divorce mediation
economic divorce
economic remarriage

emotional remarriage
family metacognition stage
family redefinition stage
family reorganization stage
individual cognition stage

joint custody	no-fault divorce	separation stage
legal divorce	parental remarriage	single-parent household
legal remarriage	psychic remarriage	
legal separation	psychological divorce	

RECOMMENDED READINGS

Berman, C. (1986). *Making it as a stepparent: New roles, new rules.* New York: Harper & Row. A sensitive and very applied account of the stepparent experience. Separate chapters focus on financial concerns, household arrangements, and discipline, among other areas.

Cauhape, E. (1983). *Fresh starts: Men and women after divorce.* New York: Basic Books. An interesting look at the divorce experience at midlife, including the disruptions that occur and the fresh starts that people make.

Cherlin, A. J. (1981). *Marriage, divorce, remarriage.* Cambridge, MA: Harvard University Press. A noted sociologist reflects on the many complexities of divorce in contemporary society.

Einstein, E. (1985). *The stepfamily: Living, loving, and learning.* Boston: Shambhala Publishers. See Chapter 8 of this paperback for the needs of children within the blended family structure.

Furstenberg, F. F., Jr., and Spanier, G. B. (1984). *Recycling the family: Remarriage after divorce.* Beverly Hills, CA: Sage. The results of a longitudinal study focusing on the social, psychological, and economic adjustments that transpire from divorce to remarriage.

Greif, G. L. (1985). *Single fathers.* Lexington, MA: D. C. Heath. An in-depth analysis of single fathers who are raising children following the breakup of their marriages.

McKay, M., Rogers, P. D., Blades, J., and Gosse, R. (1984). *The divorce book.* Oakland, CA: New Harbinger. Chapters 9 and 10 of this readable book deal with divorce mediation and divorce legalities, respectively.

Renvoize, J. (1985). *Going solo: Single mothers by choice.* Boston, MA: Routledge and Kegan Paul. A thought-provoking look at those women who choose to have children and rear them outside of a permanent relationship.

Spanier, G. B., and Thompson, L. (1984). *Parting: The aftermath of separation and divorce.* Beverly Hills, CA: Sage. Spanier and Thompson trace the lives of men and women involved in the divorce experience. Readers will find the movement toward separation as well as the emotional reactions surrounding divorce particularly interesting.

Weitzman, L. J. (1985). *The divorce revolution: The unexpected social and economic consequences for women and children in America.* New York: The Free Press. The impact of such decisions as alimony and child support on the lives of women and youngsters are examined and critically assessed.

15

The Abusive Family

CONTENTS

CONTEMPLATIONS

■ Domestic abuse has reached widescale proportions in contemporary society. Consider the following, not only in regard to the extent of the problem, but how violent the family has become: a person runs a greater chance of being killed by his/her spouse than any other individual encountered throughout life. Also, the family looms as the most violent and assaultive group or institution in the country, with the exception of the police or the military at war. Why has the family become so prone to physical violence? What factors ignite the powder keg of domestic abuse? Our task in this chapter is to find out.

■ Agree or disagree with the following statements. (1) Most abusers are mentally ill or have maladaptive personalities. (2) Alcohol and drug abuse are the primary causes of domestic violence. (3) Abusers lack the ability to love other people and are not sensitive to their needs. (4) Youngsters who are abused will definitely grow up to be child abusers. If you agreed with any of these statements, you're wrong. Want to find out why?

■ Marilyn L. is an abused wife. She has been battered about twice a month, by her husband, for eleven years. The physical abuse started six months after the wedding and her husband has become more violent over time. Over the years, Marilyn has had three broken bones, contusions all over her body, and on one occasion, a gaping wound that required sixteen sutures to close. How is it possible that assaultive behavior such as this continues for so long? Are there many women like Marilyn who choose to remain in the very home that fosters violence? We'll explore these issues and many similar ones as we examine the nightmares that abuse victims experience.

■ We have long recognized the presence of child and wife abuse in the domestic setting. Recently, though, researchers have made new additions to the list of victims: husband, parent, and elder abuse. At first glance, it may seem that abuse against these parties isn't possible, or that at best, a minimal number of victims are involved. However, such forms of abuse are a reality every day for *millions* of husbands, parents, and elders . . . and the numbers are increasing.

*H*ome sweet home. For countless Americans, the family unit still remains the provider of love, care, and security. Yet for a growing number of persons, the household has been transformed into a battleground filled with violent assaults, beatings, and even death for those living under the same roof. For the abused, there's no place worse than home.

At the onset, we need to emphasize that family abuse does not restrict itself to physical measures. On the contrary, pain and suffering can be inflicted on others in a number of different ways. Beyond physical abuse is neglect and abandonment, as well as verbal, emotional, and sexual abuse, to name but a few major forms.

We also need to stress that there is never just one victim in family abuse. Rather, abuse reverberates throughout the entire family structure. In support of this, Murray Straus and his colleagues (1980) report that violent spouses are likely to be abusive towards their children, and wives who are battered are more likely to strike their youngsters. Also, the more violent parents are to children, the more abusive the child is toward brothers and sisters. Finally, the more the parents hit a youngster, the more likely the child is to hit the parents.

THE VICTIMS: THE TRAGIC AFTERMATH OF VIOLENCE

The number of abused family members each year resembles a casualty list from a world war, famine, or natural disaster. In support of this, consider the following:

- In a given year, almost one million children are abused or neglected (Helfer, 1982). However, other sources (for example, Turner, 1980) place this figure closer to two million victims each year. If the latter is the case, this total amounts to nearly twice the population of Rhode Island or almost double the number of wounded in World War II and the Vietnam War combined.

- Approximately 2,000 American children will die each year from parental abuse and neglect. In West Germany, 1000 children will suffer the same fate, as will 700 youngsters in England and 100 in Canada (Straus, Gelles, and Steinmetz, 1980; Turbak, 1984).

- In 1983, 45 out of the 50 states experienced an increase of child abuse. Thirty-eight states also indicated that the severity of cases had increased (Stone and Cohn, 1984).

- It is estimated that some 1.8 million wives are severely attacked by their husbands each year. Almost the same number of husbands are attacked by their wives, although the injuries inflicted are not as severe (Straus, Gelles, and Steinmetz, 1980).

- Overall, there are approximately 28 million wives and 12 million husbands in this country who have been abused at one point or another during their marriages. Combined, these figures amount to almost five times the population of New York City (Turner, 1980).

- As many as 2.5 million parents are violently attacked at least once a year. About one million have been severely slugged, kicked, or whipped by their offspring. Often, a gun or knife is used against a parent (Cornell and Gelles, 1982).

- Between one and two million aged persons are abused or neglected each year (U.S. Dept of Justice, 1980). This is considered a conservative figure since the elderly's social isolation allows for many cases to go unreported. Also, many elderly persons, more so than younger persons, are afraid to notify authorities.

FROM THE HOUSEHOLD COMES A CRY FOR HELP

Real-life episodes of physical violence in the household are enough to make proponents of family unity shudder. In California, a 23-year-old unemployed father was arrested for battering his two preschool children. To the horror of his neighbors, who heard piercing screams in the night, one of the youngsters was hospitalized with a broken arm while the other suffered extensive internal injuries. She later lost the use of one kidney. In Texas, an eight-year-old girl tearfully told a child protective services worker how her stepfather forced her to perform oral sex almost every night for two years. In Idaho, a woman knifed and killed her husband in an effort to protect herself against his continual violent attacks. She was later acquitted of murder on the grounds of self-defense. In New York, a 19-year-old male punched and kicked his mother repeatedly before he stole twelve dollars   ▶

from her purse. Convicted in court, he admitted to similarly attacking his mother twice before.

More intense cases of domestic violence, although less common, still manage to make newspaper headlines with shocking regularity. A four-year-old died on the way to the hospital after her mother forced detergent and soap powder down her throat. A 26-year-old housewife was rushed to a rural Pennsylvania medical center and immediately placed in a critical care unit because her husband had used a torch to singe her hair; she lost sight in one eye and had to undergo extensive plastic surgery. In Louisiana, a sick and bedridden 79-year-old man was left to die by his daughter, who claimed that she could no longer handle the pressures of providing care. In Georgia, a 12-year-old boy was locked in a closet for over a month by his parents and given minimal food and water. He lost nearly 30 pounds during his terrifying ordeal and was hospitalized for two weeks. Incidents such as these illustrate how the family looms as the most violent group or institution in the country, with the exception of the police or the military at war.

The weapons used by physical abusers are a cross between instruments from medieval torture chambers and armaments from modern-day arsenals. Rope, chains, clubs, pins and needles, and straps of all shapes and sizes are fairly commonplace. So too are knives, razors, and assorted firearms. Of course, whatever household items happen to be nearby during the heat of the battle, such as lamps, chairs, silverware, and glassware, are usually grabbed as weapons. One repeated male offender from New Jersey had a habit of searching his workbench for an appropriate tool whenever an intense domestic outburst with his wife took place. When brought to court, the prosecuting attorney displayed an appalling array of tools used by the man: screwdrivers, hammers, pliers, and sheet metal scissors. When suitable weapons are unavailable, other abusers resort to biting, kicking, choking, clawing, gouging, or pulling hair.

Those choosing nonphysical forms of abusive behavior are just as shrewd and devastating, from verbal and emotional assaults to barbaric forms of neglect and abandonment. Be it physical or mental, verbal or emotional, the arsenal of abusive tactics is endless. Each, in their own way, make the nightmares and fears of the abused just as endless.

Adapted from Turner, 1980.   ■

MYTHS ABOUT FAMILY VIOLENCE

Richard Gelles and Claire Cornell (1985) maintain that a number of myths about family violence tend to hinder both effective professional practice and the public's awareness of the problem. These myths need to be replaced with factual knowledge gleaned from scholarly research on family vio-

lence. The following represents the more popular myths:

■ *Family Violence Is Rare* With any luck, we've already debunked this myth with our earlier statistical portrait of family violence. Family violence is widespread and has become a major social problem in contemporary society.

■ *Family Violence Is Confined to Mentally Disturbed or Sick People* The truth of the matter is that the majority of family abuse cases are carried out by "normal" people. Unfortunately, the media often perpetuates the myth by seldom showing normal or average family members resorting to abusive behavior.

■ *Family Violence Is Confined to the Lower Classes* This myth is as pervasive as the mental illness one. Family violence cuts a path through all socioeconomic levels, not just lower classes. However, read on for a clarification regarding the distribution of abuse within social classes.

■ *Family Violence Occurs in All Groups, and Social Factors Are Not Relevant* While abuse can be found among the wealthy and the poor, its concentration is greater among the poor. It might be added that by virtue of being in the lower class, families run a greater risk of being correctly *and falsely* labeled abusers if their children are seen with injuries

■ *Children Who Are Abused Will Grow Up To Be Child Abusers* There is some substance to this, but the wording is wrong. It is more accurate to say that children who are abused are *more likely* to become abusive, not preprogrammed. The wording makes it a de-

RESEARCH HIGHLIGHT

ABUSIVE MOTHERS FEEL THEY ARE GOOD PARENTS

Many abusive mothers think they are good parents doing what is necessary to raise good kids, according to research undertaken by Pat Crittenden (1983). Even some mothers already under supervision for abusive childrearing practices are self-confident. They think the daily punishment they inflict on their children, which includes bruises, burns, and occasional broken bones, are part of responsible parenting. If anything, abusing parents are too intensely involved with their youngsters. Overpunishment is chronic. These parents' standards for obedience are very high, and they can't tolerate any sign of rebellion or rejection.

Crittenden made such observations after working with 38 abusive and neglectful mothers who had children under two years of age. The mothers were predominantly low-income; 50 percent were white and 50 percent were black. Using three-minute videotapes of mothers playing with their children, she also found significant differences between responses of abusive and neglectful mothers. Abusive mothers used the same behavior as adequate mothers. They talked to their youngsters — but the timing was off. Careful observation revealed that the mothers were misusing appropriate behavior. For example, the mothers smiled after they irritated the child, and smiled when the baby showed discomfort. Superficially these mothers seemed supportive, but actually they were showing covert hostility.

In contrast, neglective mothers generally did not maintain the facade of appropriate maternal behavior. They didn't smile or talk or play with their babies. Neglective parents seemed to be personally overwhelmed, depressed, and hopeless. Many didn't expect anything to work in regard to childcare approaches.

Finally, Crittenden did not find any racial differences in child abuse patterns, nor did she find that any of the mothers were sadistic.

terministic statement rather than a probabilistic situation. Furthermore, perfect associations, such as this myth implies, rarely exist in social science.

■ *Battered Wives Enjoy Being Abused, Otherwise They'd Leave the Situation*   No one enjoys being abused and to think so is especially erroneous. Frequently, battered wives are forced to remain in the very home that produces violence for predictable reasons: economic dependence, guilt, shame, fear for their lives, and learned helplessness.

■ *Alcohol and Drug Abuse Are the Primary Causes of Domestic Violence*   In many cases of domestic abuse, drinking and/or drug usage has taken place. However, there is little evidence that alcohol and drugs are disinhibitors which unleash violent behavior. It is more accurate to say that alcohol and other drugs are *components* of the abusive relationship. Their effects need to be more fully studied before the above association can be made.

■ *Violence and Love Do Not Coexist in Families*   Many tend to believe that since family members are violent, they must not love one another. In reality, abusers are often loving, sensitive people. In addition, the abused frequently love their batterers in spite of the pain inflicted

COMMON ELEMENTS OF FAMILY VIOLENCE

Now that we've explored the more prevalent myths regarding family abuse, let's turn our attention toward some common elements. Even though child, spouse, parent, and grandparent abuse represent separate abuse syndromes, they all share a surprising number of common features. David Finkelhor (1981) expands upon these elements.

Abuse Is An Abuse of Power

All forms of family abuse are typically an abuse of power. Within the family, abuse has a tendency to gravitate toward the relationships of greatest power differential. This can be seen very clearly in

the sexual abuse of children. The most widely reported form of sexual abuse consists of authoritarian males who choose to victimize girls in subordinate positions.

Physical child abuse shows a similar pattern, as does spouse abuse. In regard to the former, the greatest volume of abuse is leveled against the most powerless of children, those under age six. As far as spouse abuse is concerned, again the strongest victimize the weakest. (Abuse of the elderly would be yet another illustration of this commonality.)

Abuse Is a Response to Perceived Helplessness

While abuse is an act of the strong against the weak, it is an act carried out to compensate for a perceived lack or loss of power. In incidents of childhood sexual abuse and spouse abuse, this attempt to compensate is often bound up in a sense of powerlessness, especially in regard to society's masculine ideals.

Furthermore, it has often been observed that men start battering their wives when the latter try to assert themselves or strive to establish independence. Also, many women resort to battering when they sense that they have lost control of their children and/or their own lives.

Victims Share Many of the Same Effects

Before, during, and after abuse, victims share a number of common experiences. For instance, all forms of family abuse typically occur in the context of psychological abuse and exploitation, referred to by many victims as "brainwashing." This means that victims are exploited mentally as well as physically; abusers use their power to control and manipulate the victim's perceptions of reality. Thus, elderly victims are told that they're unloved and a burden to all, and child victims are constantly reminded that they're bad or uncontrollable.

Victims also come to believe the abuser's accusations and blame themselves for their predicament. Many see themselves as having provoked the abuse — or having deserved it. Another com-

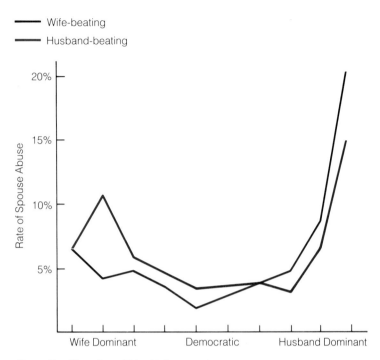

Source: From Murray Straus, Richard J. Gelles, and Suzanne K. Steinmetz, (1980). *Behind closed doors: Violence in the American family*. Achor/Doubleday, p. 194.

FIGURE 15-1   Marital Violence by Marital Power

monality is that both young and old victims alike suffer extreme shame and humiliation, so much so that they believe others could not possibly understand their predicament. Finally, many victims have trouble stopping, avoiding, or escaping abuse. As far as the latter is concerned, many don't even try.

Abusing Families Share Certain Characteristics

Often, the type of family situation in which one kind of abuse occurs is the same for all others. We've already learned in this chapter, for example, that abuse rates are higher in lower socioeconomic households. In addition, all forms of abuse are more common in homes afflicted by unemployment or economic deprivation. Evidence also

exists that abuse is more prevalent in families having a patriarchal power structure (see Figure 15-1). Finally, all forms of abuse are more prevalent in households that are isolated, have few community ties, friendships, or organizational affiliations

Family Abuse Shares Similar Social Response Histories

Finally, we can point out that the various forms of family abuse have emerged over the years in similar fashions. Their evolution as social problems contains similar misconceptions, such as initial underestimates for each. Also, each type of abuse was initially seen as a set of extreme pathological behaviors, a misconception we earlier corrected. Another similarity was the tendency to implicate the abused as well as the abuser. In other words,

WHY IS THE FAMILY VULNERABLE TO ABUSE?

What is it about family life that generates violence and abuse? A number of factors related to the family's social organization may help to answer this question:

- Having more time together under the same roof allows for more opportunities for conflicts to take place.
- Most families have diverse activities, which in turn offer more opportunities for conflicts.
- Family members are more intensely involved with one another.
- Time and money limitations may make it impossible for family members to do everything that they want to do.
- Spouses as partners or parents assume a greater right to control or influence each other as well as other family members.
- The family consists of age and sex differences. This often permits members to identify with age, sex, or other nonfamily groups against their own family members.
- Roles may be assigned to family members on the basis of age or sex or other physical characteristics instead of interests or abilities. This may lead to conflict.
- Except for marriage, family membership is involuntary through birth, adoption, or legal changes. Consequently, it is difficult to leave one's family.

Adapted from Gelles and Straus., 1979.

victims were often viewed as having provoked the offender.

All forms of family abuse share another commonality: *social scientists have had trouble defining the normative boundaries of each.* For example, there still is much controversy over when the line is to be drawn between strict discipline and child abuse. For spouse abuse, a similar controversy exists in regard to the normative boundaries of family violence.

CATEGORIES OF FAMILY ABUSE

Child Abuse

Child abuse, referred to more specifically as the **battered child syndrome**, is perhaps the most alarming type of domestic violence. This is because of the acute vulnerability of children, their inability to escape the trauma of the situation, and the degrees of physical punishment that they suffer. Broken bones, lacerations, concussions, limb dislocations, and abrasions are commonplace. So, too, are instances of sexual and emotional abuse, neglect, and abandonment.

Child abuse is most common among children six years of age and younger. Several reasons account for this. For one, the child at this time is especially susceptible to parental frustration as adults have to adjust to the rather tedious chores of early childcare. Early economic hardships also cause tensions, and frustration on the parent's part may develop because of the child's inability to interact with the adult in a socially meaningful manner. Finally, abuse is most prevalent under six years because the child is most defenseless and unable to absorb the amounts of physical violence that an older youngster can.

What factors cause parents to abuse their children? Pressures from work, the home, financial

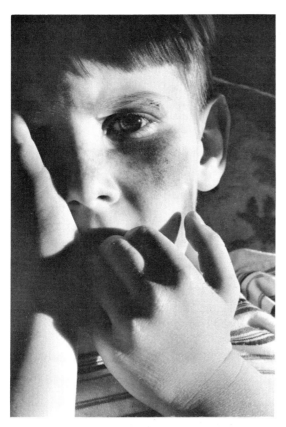

The scars of child battering are psychological as well as physical.

- Both parents are verbally aggressive to the children.
- More than the average amount of conflict between the husband and wife exists.
- The husband is verbally aggressive toward his wife.
- The husband is a manual worker.
- The husband is dissatisfied with his standard of living.
- The wife is a manual worker or a full-time housekeeper.
- The wife is less than thirty years old.
- There are two or more children in the home.
- The couple has been married less than ten years.
- The couple has lived in the neighborhood fewer than two years.
- The father participates in no organized community groups. (Straus, Gelles, and Steinmetz, 1980)

Many parents also abuse their children in an effort to enforce discipline. Some have an overpowering need to impress other adults with a well-behaved child. Still other child abusers identify with the youngster and consider every fault and mistake of the child to be their own. Then there are those who perceive themselves as failures in life, who believe they are attaining superiority and command by exerting such forceful dominance.

A particularly bothersome feature of child abuse is the consequences of battering in later life. Many abused children run a risk for self-destructive behaviors, school failure, and delinquency. Many are insecure, with poor self-concepts, and have low overall levels of self-confidence and self-reliance. An adult who has been abused as a child often lacks trust, has low self-esteen, poor communication skills, and has difficulty making decisions (Leehan and Wilson, 1985; Straker and Jacobson, 1981; Reidy, 1980; Kinard, 1980).

Sibling Abuse   Children who have been abused by their parents are also at risk for assaulting siblings. **Sibling abuse** in the form of slapping, pushing, or the like, is the most common form of

difficulties, a history of maltreatment in the parent's background, and low levels of self esteem are frequently cited as reasons behind violence. Many abusers are lonely, frequently depressed, and have never learned how to contain their aggression (Ulbrich and Huber, 1981; Steele, 1980; Gelles, 1980). James Garbarino (1984) adds that physical illness, untimely childbearing, and a parent's poor ability to empathize with youngsters can substantially increase the likelihood of child maltreatment. This is particularly true when social stress and social isolation characterize the family.

There also appear to be certain elements of family activity and structure that foster child abuse. For example, homes having the following characteristics may run a greater risk of child abuse:

domestic violence today. One estimate places the number of children abusing a sibling in the course of a year at 36 million. As many as 19 million children employ more violent measures ("beating up," hitting with an object, biting, and so on) against siblings (Straus, Gelles, and Steinmetz, 1980).

Reasons for sibling abuse range from jealousy and aggression to acting out socially learned forms of behavior. Arthur Green (1985) feels that sibling abuse frequently takes place when an abused, scapegoated older child is exposed to a baby or younger sibling who receives a disproportionate share of the parents' limited caregiving. As parents

CROSS-CULTURAL FOCUS

SWEDEN OUTLAWS PARENTAL CHILD-SPANKING

In Sweden, parents are forbidden to spank, beat, or harm their children in any way. If they do, they are breaking the law and can be arrested by local police. In addition, Swedish children have access to an emergency phone network, and an ombudsman has been hired by the government to protect children's rights. Such legislation and progressive change, enacted in 1979, made Sweden the first nation to legally protect children within the home.

The antispanking law informs parents that any act which, for the purpose of punishing, causes the child physical injury or pain, is prohibited. This includes pain that is even mild and passing. It is also meant to include psychological punishment, but Swedish legal experts feel that this aspect of the law is vague and much more difficult to enforce. Actually the punishment for spanking does not parallel any consequences for breaking the law in the United States. Social pressure and the threat of social ostracism, though, seems to be law enforcement enough in Sweden.

This law has produced mixed responses. Many social workers, doctors, and psychologists hail it as a tool to curb child abuse and maltreatment. Many parents, though, are annoyed with the new legislation. Some firmly believe that spanking is a good disciplinary technique. Others report that while they would not spank their children under any circumstances, a parental right has been arbitrarily taken away.

Despite the antispanking law, child abuse is no stranger to Sweden. In fact, recent research undertaken by Richard Gelles (in press) indicates that Swedish children may be abused just as often as American children. However, the intensity of abuse may not be as great as it is for American youngsters. For example, Swedish children are less apt to receive injuries from physical assault or require hospitalization.

Other nations have also initiated programs to curb child abuse. West Germany, for example, has a government-sponsored 24-hour abuse hotline and an information center located in Hamburg. Poland employs a protective court system to separate abused or neglected children from their parents. As one other example, some Australian states provide a 24-hour reporting center and offer extensive protection to those who register complaints (Turbak, 1984).

Sibling abuse is prevalent in many families.

ignore the target child, they simultaneously burden him with excessive and inappropriate care-taking responsibilities for a ·younger rival perceived as a favorite. During the physical attacks on their siblings, the abusers make use of the defensive maneuver of "identification with the aggressor" and treat their victims in the same manner as their own parents treated them.

Green also feels that sibling abuse may have some adaptive value for the child-perpetrator. Besides getting even with the more highly valued sibling, it might act as a safety valve for pent-up rage toward the parents, which cannot be expressed directly. Sibling abuse may offer children a means of actively mastering the physical and psychological trauma endured at the hands of their parents; that is, they can re-enact the abuse by acting as the aggressor rather than the victim. Finally, it might be the only way the child can impact on and be recognized by the parents. In the ab-

sence of intervention, children who abuse their siblings will be at risk for extending their violent behavior toward peers, and ultimately toward their spouses and children.

Child Sexual Abuse and Incest   The sexual abuse of children, including incest, has received considerable attention from all factions of the media in the 1980s. Each year, sexual molestation occurs to a shocking number of children. However, it needs to be stressed that because most victims usually do not disclose what has happened to anyone, reported cases do not tell the whole story.

Estimates can be made, though, about the epidemic proportions of child molestation. One reseacher (Stark, 1984) proposes that as many as 15 million individuals in the United States have been victims of incest, and it has been estimated that the reported cases of childhood sexual abuse have increased over 200 percent since 1976 (Kempe and Kempe, 1984). So the problem is very much with us today, and no solution is in sight.

As far as nonfamily sexual abuse is concerned, boys are more often molested than girls. But a stranger is not likely to be the offender; indeed, assaults on children by strangers represent only a slight percentage of child sexual abuse cases. The perpetrator is more apt to be someone who has developed a close relationship with the child and is someone the child probably trusts.

In support of this latter point, Diana Russell (1984) found that only 15 percent of the perpetrators of extrafamilial child sexual abuse were strangers to their victims. Forty-two percent were acquaintances and 41 percent were more intimately related to their victims (friends of the family, neighbors, teachers, and so on). Of these perpetrators, 40 percent were labeled authority figures. Two-thirds of them were so classified because they were much older adults.

David Finkelhor's (1985) review of the literature uncovered the following facts about extrafamilial sexual abuse:

■   Estimates drawn from surveys of men in the general American population suggest that perhaps 2.5 to 5.0 percent of men were sexually victimized before age 13.

- Girls as well as boys are most commonly victimized by men.
- Boys are more likely than girls to be victimized by someone outside the family.
- The abuse of boys is more likely to be reported to the police than to a hospital or child protective agency.

Incest is defined as sexual intercourse or sexual relations between persons so closely related that they're forbidden by law to marry. In one study (Russell, 1984), 40 percent of incestuous abuse occurred within the nuclear family, and the father (biological, step, foster, or adoptive) was the leading perpetrator. Girls are much more likely to be victims of incest. Father-daughter incest typically begins when the daughter is between the ages of 6

APPLICATIONS

HOW PARENTS CAN HELP PREVENT CHILD SEXUAL ABUSE

There are numerous things that parents can do to help prevent the sexual abuse of their children. The Children's Protective Society (1981) offers the following suggestions.

What To Teach Children:

1. No one has the right to touch the private parts of their body or make them feel uncomfortable. They have the right to say no.
2. To tell you if anyone asks to, or has, taken their picture.
3. Adults do not come to children for help. Adults ask adults for help.
4. To never get in a car without your permission.
5. To make you aware of any unusual discussions or strange requests.
6. To tell you when any adults asks them to keep a "secret."
7. To tell you of gifts or money given to them.
8. Never to go into someone's home without your knowledge.
9. When away from home, scared, or uncomfortable, they have the right to use the telephone without anyone's permission.
10. To tell you of any situation where a statement or gesture is made about sex or love.
11. Never to answer the door when alone.
12. Never to admit to anyone over the telephone that they are home alone.
13. That you will always believe them about a molestation and will protect them from further harm. (Children do not lie about molestation.)

Parents Should Pay Attention to the Following:

1. Question any money or gifts your child brings home.
2. Ask your child who he or she is spending time with and of the activities they engage in.
3. Find out who their best friend is, and why.   ▶

4. Be watchful of any strong bond that seems to develop between your child and an adult figure in their life (including friends, teachers, coaches, clergymen, and so on).

5. Avoid male babysitters unless you are thoroughly familiar with them. Also avoid overnight trips alone with an adult.

6. Maintain constant and regular telephone contact with your child whenever one of you is away from home.

7. Never leave your child unattended, day or night.

8. Never leave your child alone in a car; molestation only takes a minute.

9. Be involved in any sports or activities your child has.

10. Beware of coaches or leaders who do not have a child of their own in the same group.

11. Listen when your child tells you he or she does not want to be/go with someone. There may be a reason why.

12. Never make your child submit to physical contact (that is, hugs and kisses, and so on) if he or she does not want to. Children have the right to say no.

13. No one should want to be with your child more than you. When someone is showing your child too much attention, ask yourself why.

14. Be sensitive to any changes in your child's behavior or attitudes. Encourage open communication with your child. Never belittle any fear or concern your child may express to you. Never compromise any private or confidential matter your child may share with you. ▬

and 11, and although wide variations are reported, it is generally acknowledged that the average relationship lasts about two years (Stark, 1984).

While the use of extreme physical force is seldom used in sexual contacts with children, mild to moderate amounts of parental force occur frequently. Also, extensive use is made of psychological pressures, such as verbal threats, bribes, intimidation, trickery, and outright seduction. The psychological force most often brought to bear is the natural authority of adults over children. In this sense, the existence of this powerful psychological force obviates the need for physical force (Geiser, 1982).

The victim's fear, reluctance, and hesitance to report incest contributes to the conspiracy of silence that exists all too often. The victim's suffering may be expressed in physical ailments such as chronic pelvic pain or the psychological disturbances of depression and hysterical seizures. Vic-

tims are usually left with a strong feeling of guilt, a trauma that often requires intensive therapy (DeChesnay, 1983; Renvoize, 1982).

Much like other disturbing events, incest often destroys the victim's perception of daily living. One investigation (Silver, Boon, and Stones, 1983) reveals that following such experiences, searching for the meaning of one's existence is a common adaptive process. In this study, such behavior of 77 adult women who as children were victims of father-daughter incest was studied. There was no concise answer as to whether the women in this sample were able to discover meaning in their victimization; more than half of the women who were actively searching for meaning, an average of twenty years after the incest had ended, reported that they could make no sense of it whatsoever. However, it is felt that the ruminations and remembrances that are part of the search for meaning do serve an adaptive function. They are likely

Childhood sexual abuse is often kept hidden by the victim in a nightmare of secrecy.

to be the means by which individuals begin to gain control over and make sense of their experience. However, even finding meaning does not seem to end the search or the ruminations.

Reporting Abuse Against Children Any form of abuse or neglect against children — be it sexual, physical, or emotional — needs to be reported to proper authorities. The number of child abuse incidents that go unreported each year is both frustrating and unfair. Even when reported, however, some court cases are dropped because witnesses are unwilling to testify or intervene, and many in a position to testify fear potential lawsuits. There are even some doctors unwilling to report abuse cases, despite the fact the laws passed in the 1960s require them to do so. Some prefer not to get involved, others are indecisive over whether or not injuries can be proven as actual abuse cases. Combined, these factors create significant numbers of unreported cases. Consequently, many researchers believe that we have underestimated the magnitude of the problem (O'Brien, 1984: Williams, 1980: Martin and Walters, 1982).

Child abuse cases may go undetected for other reasons. Many youngsters suffer injuries that are not easily visible. Instruments that inflict pain but do not lacerate, such as rubber hoses, may be shrewdly chosen by abusers. Other batterers choose to strategically strike children on those body parts that clothing conceals. And many children are too terrified to talk about their injuries, let alone bare their bodies for inspection. Or, as we

GUIDELINES FOR DETECTING CHILD ABUSE AND NEGLECT

Physical Abuse

Child's Appearance:

■ Unusual bruises, welts, burns or fractures.
■ Bite marks.
■ Frequent injuries, always explained as "accidental."

Child's Behavior:

■ Reports injury by parents.
■ Unpleasant, hard to get along with, demanding, often doesn't obey. Frequently causes trouble.   ▶

- *Or,* is usually shy, avoids other people including children, seems too anxious to please, seems too ready to let other people say and do things to him/her without protest.
- Frequently late or absent *or,* often comes to school much too early and/or hangs around after school is dismissed.
- Avoids physical contact with adults.
- Wears long sleeves or other concealing clothing to hide injuries.
- Child's story of how a physical injury occurred is not believable; doesn't seem to fit the type or seriousness of the injury observed.
- Seems frightened of parents.
- Shows little or no distress at being separated from parents.
- Apt to seek affection from any adult.

Parent or Caretaker's Behavior:

- Has history of abuse as a child.
- Uses harsh discipline which doesn't seem right for the age, condition, or what the child did wrong.
- Offers an explanation of the child's injury that doesn't seem to make sense, doesn't fit the injury—or offers no explanation at all.
- Seems unconcerned about the child.
- Sees child as bad, evil, a monster, and so on.
- Misuses alcohol or other drugs.
- Attempts to conceal child's injury or to protect identity of person responsible.

Emotional Abuse

Child's Appearance:

- Signs less obvious than in other forms of mistreatment. Behavior is best indication.

Child's Behavior:

- Unpleasant, hard to get along with, demanding; frequently causes trouble, won't leave others alone.
- Unusually shy, avoids others, too anxious to please, too submissive . . . puts up with unpleasant acts or words from others without protest.
- Either unusually adult in actions or overly young for age (for example, sucks thumb, rocks constantly).
- Is behind for his/her age in physical, emotional, or intellectual development.

Parent or Caretaker's Behavior:

- Blames or belittles child.
- Is cold and rejecting.

▶

■ Withholds love.

■ Treats children in the family unequally.

■ Doesn't seem to care much about child's problems.

Neglect

Child's Appearance:

■ Often not clean, tired, no energy.

■ Comes to school without breakfast, often does not have lunch or lunch money.

■ Clothes dirty or wrong for the weather.

■ Seems to be alone often, for long periods of time.

■ Needs glasses, dental care, or other medical attention.

Child's Behavior:

■ Frequently absent from school.

■ Begs or steals food.

■ Causes trouble in school.

■ Often hasn't done homework, uses alcohol or drugs, engages in vandalism, sexual misconduct.

Parent or Caretaker's Behavior:

■ Misuses alcohol or other drugs.

■ Has disorganized, upset home life.

■ Seems not to care much about what happens: gives impression of feeling that nothing is going to make much difference anyway.

■ Lives very much isolated from friends, relatives, neighbors; doesn't seem to know how to get along well with others.

■ Has long-term chronic illnesses.

■ Has history of neglect as a child.

Sexual Abuse

Child's Appearance:

■ Has torn, stained, or bloody underclothing.

■ Experiences pain or itching in the genital area.

■ Has venereal disease.

Child's Behavior:

■ Appears withdrawn or engages in fantasy or baby-like behavior.

■ Has poor relationships with other children.

■ Is unwilling to participate in physical activities.

■ Is engaging in delinquent acts or runs away.

■ States he/she has been sexually assaulted by parent/caretaker.

▶

Parent or Caretaker's Behavior:

- Very protective or jealous of child.
- Encourages child to engage in prostitution or sexual acts in the presence of caretaker.
- Misuses alcohol or other drugs.
- Is frequently absent from home.

United States Department of Health, Education, and Welfare, Office of Human Development Services, Administration for Children, Youth and Families, Head Start Bureau, Indian and Migrant Programs Division, *New light on an old problem*, DHEW Publication No. (OHDS) 78-31108, Washington, DC, pp. 8–11. ▬

indicated earlier, there are those who are loyal to their abusers in spite of the damage they inflict.

You do not have to be a social services professional to report a suspected case of child abuse. However, many people do not know how to report a suspected case, what the personal implications are, or what happens after the report is made. The National Center on Child Abuse and Neglect (1984) sheds light on these and other questions.

How Reports of Child Abuse and Neglect Are Handled   The primary responsibility for dealing with the problems of child abuse and neglect is vested in state and local agencies. Each state has laws requiring the reporting of known and suspected child abuse and neglect cases; such reports are then investigated by public social service or law enforcement agencies in the local community. Preventive and treatment services for both the children and families involved are provided by local public and private agencies. The federal government, however, has no authority to investigate specific cases of child abuse and neglect nor the practices of child protective services agencies, which are regulated by state and local laws.

Requirements of State Reporting Laws   The enactment of child abuse and neglect reporting laws by state legislatures began in earnest in the early 1960s. Today all 50 states, the District of Columbia, American Samoa, Guam, Puerto Rico, and the Virgin Islands have reporting legislation.

Generally speaking, this legislation mandates the reporting of suspected maltreatment, provides penalties for failure to report, provides immunity to reporters from legal actions associated with the report, and defines reportable conditions.

Reporting Requirements   Due to the medical profession's description and identification of battered children, legislators regard the medical profession as the source most likely to discover child maltreatment. Today every jurisdiction requires physicians to report suspected child abuse, with laws that either specifically mention physicians or by a more general directive, such as "practitioner of the healing arts," or "any health professional." Also, associated medical personnel such as nurses, dentists, osteopaths and interns are required to report suspected child maltreatment in many states.

As our understanding of child abuse and neglect increases, so too does the number of professions mandated by the states to report suspected maltreatment. The realization that child abuse and neglect may not be limited to severe physical abuse and that medical treatment for severely abused children may not be sought in time to avoid permanent injury or death has coincided with a dramatic increase in the number of professions specifically mentioned in state laws as mandatory reporters, including those with frequent contact with children, such as teachers and childcare professionals.

Others Who Can Report Suspected Abuse It is generally acknowledged that anyone suspecting that a child has been mistreated may report that suspicion. Numerous states provide specific statutory authority for permissive, rather than mandatory, reporting. However, many states make no provision for permissive reporting because they mandate reporting by everyone.

Penalities for Not Reporting While the identification of maltreated children and their families ultimately depends upon the responsiveness of a concerned community, the vast majority of states impose a criminal and/or civil penalty for failure to report when mandated by law to do so.

Immunity for Mistaken Reports All jurisdictions provide immunity from civil and criminal liability for reporters acting in good faith. While the majority of states qualify their immunity provisions with the requirement that the report be made in good faith, at least 20 states have included a presumption of the good faith of reporters in their reporting laws.

WHERE TO GO FOR HELP: SOURCES OF ADDITIONAL INFORMATION

Those persons wanting to report a suspected child abuse case should contact their state child protective service. Many states offer a toll-free number.

Parents Anonymous is a self-help group that offers, among other services, guidance and support for parents who abuse, or fear they will abuse, their children. This organization can be reached at 800-421-0353 (800-352-0386 in California).

The National Center on Child Abuse and Neglect offers a number of useful and informative publications. Single copies are available free of charge from: Superintendent of Documents, U. S. Government Printing Office, Retail Distribution Division/Consigned Branch, Washington, DC 20402. Among the more relevant publications:

Barnett, R. B., Pittman, C. B., Ragan, C. K., and Salus, M. K. *Family violence: Intervention strategies.*(OHDS) 80-30258.

Fisher, N. *Reaching out: The volunteer in child abuse and neglect programs.* (OHDS) 79-30174.

Hally, C., Polansky, N. F., and Polansky, N. A. *Child neglect: Mobilizing services.* (OHDS) 80-30257.

Jenkins, J. L., Salus, M. K., and Schultze, G. L. *Child protective services: A guide for workers.* (OHDS) 79-30203

Klaus, S. L., and Lauscher, S. *Child abuse and neglect information management systems.* (OHDS) 79-30165.

Landau, H. R., Salus, M. K., Stiffarm, T., and Kalb, N. L. *Child protection: The role of the courts.* (OHDS) 80-30256.

Martin, H. P. *Treatment for abused and neglected children.* (OHDS) 79-30199.

National study of the incidence and severity of child abuse and neglect: Study findings. (OHDS) 81-30325.

Conditions to be Reported   Every jurisdiction requires that suspected cases of child abuse and neglect be reported. And over the years, the range of reportable conditions found in state laws and the definitions of abuse and neglect have broadened. Today, many state laws specifically include sexual abuse, emotional or mental injury, and threatened harm among their reportable conditions, as well as the traditional definitions of child abuse which include physical injury and severe neglect.

In all states, a reporter is not required to know or to be certain that a child has been abused or neglected as defined under state law. Reporting laws apply whenever the individual reporter has reason to believe or suspects that maltreatment is occurring.

Personal Implications for Reporting   While the exact procedures may vary from state to state, generally a child protective service worker will visit the reported family as soon as possible after the report is made. This initial contact is made to determine if the child is in immediate danger and to begin assistance or treatment if needed by the family. Depending upon the urgency of the situation, the CPS worker will then take appropriate action, which could include, in drastic circumstances, removal of the child from the home. However, such actions are rare and employed only when there appears to be immediate danger to the child's health or safety. In some states and circumstances, law enforcement personnel might be asked to assit the CPS worker or might respond to the report, if there is an indications that the child needs immediate transportation to a medical facility or other police services.

In some states, the reporting laws permit certain mandated reporters, such as doctors, to keep the child in protective custody if the reporter has reason to believe that the child would be returning to an abusive and dangerous environment. The authority to remove a child from home is necessarily limited, however, and a court hearing is required, usually within a few days, to keep the child in shelter care. Also, some states require mandatory

reporters to file written reports following the oral report. These reports are particularly necessary and useful should any sort of legal action result.

Spouse Abuse

Wife Abuse   Another widespread form of abuse occurring in the American household is husband-wife violence. Like other forms of domestic violence, it may be one of our best-kept secrets because it happens behind closed doors. What is no longer a secret, though, is this sobering thought: *given the extremely high rates of spouse violence— 1.8 million women and almost as many male victims per year—married persons are more likely to be killed by their spouses than by any other individual.*

Wife-beaters share many of the characteristics of child abusers including low levels of self-esteem and frequent depression. In addition, a wife-beater typically has a lower occupational status than that of his neighbors. Interestingly, his occupational and educational status is frequently lower than that of his wife. Abusive males also are likely to be jealous and insecure, and many lack direction in life. Richard Gelles and Claire Cornell (1985) add that many male batterers feel powerless and inadequate. They turn to violence as a way of trying to demonstrate power and adequacy.

It is difficult to fit battered women into any particular age classification. In fact, wife abuse can occur at any age. It has been found, however, that pregnant women seem particularly susceptible to physical violence. Some research (Weitzman and Dreen, 1982) also indicates that battered women are more likely to be unassertive and to have low levels of self-esteem. Finally, abuse typically begins early in the marriage and increases as time goes on.

In regard to this latter point, readers will recall that the abused typically remain in, rather than leave, the home that promotes violence. Among abused women, why is this so? To begin, she may be ashamed. Because wife beating is so well secluded in our society, the victim often feels isolated and alone; she may feel that she is the only abused wife in the community. A second reason is

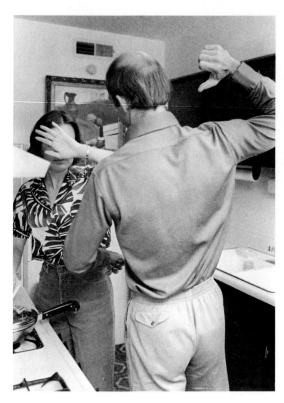

Many wives are victims of battering by their husbands.

fear. A battered wife may fear retaliation from the abuser. Third, many experience a sense of helplessness because they feel little will come of their efforts to improve their situation. Finally, some battered women stay at the site of violence for very practical reasons—some are 40 years old, have five children, no job skills, no place to go, and no money. They are literally trapped by the economics of their situation.

As with child abuse, there are various characteristics of home life that have an influence on wife battering. The following appear to intensify the risk of abuse:

- The husband is employed part-time or unemployed; family income is under $6000.
- The husband is a manual worker (if employed).

- Both husband and wife are very worried about economic security.
- The wife is dissatisfied with the family's standard of living.
- Two or more children are in the home.
- Husband *and* wife have grown up in families where the father has hit the mother.
- Couple has been married fewer than ten years.
- Both the husband and wife are less than 30 years of age.
- The couple is typically nonwhite.
- Above average marital conflict.
- Very high levels of family and individual stress.
- The wife or husband dominates family decisions.
- The husband is verbally aggressive to his wife.
- The wife is verbally aggressive to her husband.
- Both get drunk frequently, but are not alcoholics.
- The couple has lived in the neighborhood fewer than two years.
- The couple does not participate in an organized religion.
- The wife is a full-time housewife. (Straus, Gelles, and Steinmetz, 1980)

Ingredients that Produce Spouse Violence Beyond the characteristics already given, spouse violence is often the result of an interaction between two people who feel frustrated, trapped, and disappointed at the same time. The couple become victims of a process that they don't understand and even worse, can't control. Herb Goldberg (1983) summarizes ten specific ingredients that set the stage for rage, which in turn produces physical attack:

1. *A traditional woman who has childlike dependency and feelings of helplessness.* This makes her want reassurance, contact, and closeness in a relationship. Unfortunately, her partner leans toward isolation and has minimal tolerance for emotional and personal interaction. A vicious circle is created as she demands more "intimacy" while he wants less. He walls himself off as she becomes more desperately insistent on con-

FACTS AND STATISTICS ABOUT BATTERED WIVES

- Some 3,000 women are beaten to death each year.
- Battery is the major cause of injury to women, more significant than auto accidents, rapes, or muggings.
- Wife beating is not a singular event. The average woman who is beaten is abused about three times each year.
- The average duration of a violent marriage is about five years.
- The average age of the battered wife is 37.
- The most common time for wife beating is in the evening, and the typical location is the kitchen.
- Wife beaters rarely become less violent over time.
- In the United States, a woman is beaten every 30 seconds.

Adapted from Turner, 1980: O'Reilly, 1983.

tact in an infantile, persistent way. It is in this way that she complains of rejection, while he complains of being smothered.

2. *A couple who are unable to fight fairly and employ effective conflict resolution skills.* She expresses her growing anger in irritatingly passive and hidden ways such as nagging, and blaming; while he handles his anger by coldly withdrawing, criticizing, and attempting to control his partner even more by withholding whatever she needs.

3. *A relationship that has become boring to both, though neither partner has the resources to effectively change things.* They cling to each other even while the hunger for excitement and being with others has grown in each of them. Mutual provocation expresses their unconscious wish to push away their partner.

4. *A couple who are drawn to one another by defensive needs and insecurity, and who become excessively dependent on each other.* At the same time there is a latent hunger for further individual growth. The partner is simultaneously needed and resented as an obstacle to freedom and personal development.

5. *A couple who resent basic aspects of each other but are threatened by any changes their partner might attempt to make to improve*

matters. Each continually blocks the other's growth in spite of expressed dissatisfaction with the way things are. Here, the relationship becomes a no-exit, no-hope affair.

6. *A cycle in which the same basic fights continually resurface.* However, the intensity of rage and frustration escalates because of the grinding-down impact of the repetitions. The partners feel abused, maligned, unheard.

7. *A husband who has needs, but is unable to ask for what he wants.* Worse, he resents it when his wishes are not being correctly divined. Also, a wife who needs power and autonomy, but feels unable to directly take them and blames her husband for controlling her.

8. *The husband's growing perception of his wife as a child who is irrational and insatiable; her perception of him is a machine who is withholding, insensitive and cold.* Here, again, we have a vicious cycle which is very difficult to break.

9. *A wife who knows what she doesn't like, but has difficulty defining what she does want.* Consequently, she responds negatively to her husband. He becomes overly sensitive and readily irritated by her complaints of dissatisfaction because he feels responsible and guilty.

RESEARCH HIGHLIGHT

ABUSE AND VIOLENCE IN DATING RELATIONSHIPS

Courtships can be as abusive and violent as marriage itself, according to a research investigation launched by Rosemarie Bogal-Albritten and William Albritten (1985). Their study of college-aged students revealed that one in five has been directly involved in at least one incident of premarital violence. Moreover, 60 percent of the respondents said they know others involved in *courtship abuse*.

The investigation of 345 students revealed that the majority of abuse involved threats of harm, pushing, shoving and slapping. About 6 percent of those involved in courtship violence said their abuse involved assault with an object or lethal weapon, or choking. Half of them had experienced a similar encounter previously, and 22 percent had been involved in a battering session five or more times with the same person.

Nonetheless, 27 percent said they still dated the person involved, and 11 percent said that they were deeply involved. Why did they stay? The Albrittens believe it is because they may have been raised in a family where violence was a common and accepted behavior. The researchers also feel that abuse has to be viewed as a continuum. It occurs among siblings, children, husbands, wives, and the elderly. While abuse appears to affect only the respective victim, it all ties together. What happens to a person as a child will have an important influence on whether that individual will be abused or abusive to others later on in life.

---

10. *A relationship that starts on an incredible high with expectations that cannot be maintained.* It ends up generating feelings of disillusionment and of having been fooled.

Goldberg believes that any one of a number of triggers can send these couples into a physical confrontation, which temporarily releases the pent-up rage and produces the distance that neither can establish in healthy, open, and productive ways.

Marital Rape An area of spouse abuse receiving much attention in recent years is marital rape. **Marital rape** is a type of sexual assault in which a woman is forced by her husband to have sexual intercourse or other forms of sexual activity against her will. As many as 400,000 abused women each year are raped by their husbands (Barry, 1980).

Many states do not recognize marital rape as a violation of the law, something a growing number of persons are opposed to and concerned about. Kirsti Yllo and David Finkelhor (1985), for example, regard marital rape as a vicious and brutal form of abuse. They contend that victims of marital rape endure intimate violation and experience trauma, much as the victims of other types of sexual assault — yet their suffering remains the most silenced, because the crime against them, for the most part, is not legally regarded as a crime at all. They also feel that as long as marital rape remains legal, it can only be concluded that society condones it — which must in turn be interpreted as a threat to all women. They propose that while criminalization of marital rape is by no means a solution, it must be regarded — if only in a symbolic sense — as an important first step.

Husband Abuse Husband abuse may well be the most unreported crime in the nation today. This is because men, more so than women, are

INFORMATION ON SPOUSE ABUSE

Those wanting more information on spouse abuse may want to write to the following organizations:

- **Abused Women's Aid in Crisis Center**, Box 1699, Cathedral Station, New York, NY 10001.
- **Center for Women Policy Studies**, 2000 P St. NW, Washington, DC 20036.
- **Family Violence Research Program**, Department of Sociology, University of New Hampshire, Durham, NH 03824.
- **National Coalition Against Domestic Violence**, 1728 N Street NW, Washington, DC 20036.
- **National Organization for Changing Men**, c/o RAVEN, P.O. Box 24159, St. Louis, MO 63130.
- **Office on Domestic Violence**, Department of Health and Human Services, Box 1182, Washington, DC 20013.

reluctant to admit the existence of the problem. As we mentioned earlier, violence directed toward husbands may soon reach the level of violence toward wives, although the injuries of the former are less serious.

Husband abuse typically occurs to certain categories of men — striking handicapped or sick men married to healthy women, older men married to younger and physically stronger wives, and small men married to big women. In each of these situations, note the physical superiority of the woman (Turner, 1980).

Parent Abuse

John B. is a 19-year-old living with his divorced mother. As a child, he was abused; and as a growing teenager, he witnessed violent exchanges between his mother and father while they were still living together. Never emotionally close to his mother, he resorted to swearing at her as he grew up and later striking her when disagreements took place. One day, during an especially violent confrontation, John pushed his mother down a flight of stairs. She was hospitalized with a concussion and two broken ribs. She decided not to press charges.

This is by no means a remote example. While **parent abuse**, like husband beating, is one of the lesser-known types of domestic violence, it is a social problem that needs attention. It is estimated that about 10 percent of all youngsters between the ages of 10 and 17 abuse their parents (Cornell and Gelles, 1982).

Parent abuse can appear in a number of different forms. Beyond physical abuse, it can include verbal and emotional abuse, such as screaming, swearing, or intimidating one's parent. As we shall see in the next section on elder abuse, it can also include neglect if the parent is aged and dependent. Parent abuse in this respect could include nutritional or medical neglect, or even abandonment (O'Toole, et al., 1983).

More mothers and fathers are assaulted by their children each year. And, with other cases of abuse, assaults against parents appear to be learned forms of behavior. These teenagers have learned to deal with household disagreements by physically striking out at someone. Many of the teenagers who assault their parents have been abused by these same parents. So such overt hostility may be a way for teenagers to exert control and authority in the household. A number of abusive adolescents report that they resort to violence as a means to

Some teenagers abuse their parents with verbal aggression, including the use of threats.

"even the score" with those who abused them earlier in life.

Elder Abuse

One other form of assaultive behavior gaining attention in recent years is **elder abuse**. Many aged persons suffer abuse and neglect in their homes, often at the hands of their adult children or other caregivers. Most researchers regard the maltreatment associated with elder abuse as similar to other forms of domestic violence. Some draw especially strong parallels to child abuse, since both children and the elderly are typically not as strong as their assailants and both are dependent on others for their daily care. Virtually all researchers cite the need for more research on this newly discovered form of family violence (see Quinn and Tomita, 1986; Thobaben and Anderson, 1985; O'Malley, 1983; Faulkner, 1982).

Richard Gelles and Claire Cornell (1985) maintain that the abuser is usually female, middle-aged, and as indicated, usually the offspring of the abused. Many middle-aged couples begin caring for an elderly parent at the time when their own children are beginning to leave home. Being placed back into a nurturing role, just when the couple expected to be completing this responsibility, creates stress for the caretaker, (a topic to be covered in Chapter 17). The caretaker, more often than not the wife, must again defer her personal goals and cater to the needs of a dependent person. And, when the couple provide a home for an aging relative while their children are still living with them, family resources must be reallocated to include another dependent member. All of this can create added stress for mothers who are already trying to meet the demands of their immediate families.

Donna Ambrogi and Cecilia London (1985)

write that the pressured caregiver is typically a normal functioning person who becomes abusive because of this stress load. The researchers observe that a dependent, frail elder often requires constant, physically and emotionally demanding, care. Caregivers may have to get up several times during the night to toilet the elder to manage incontinence, thus interrupting their own needed sleep. And, if the elder has had a stroke and is severely disabled, the caregiver may have to bathe, dress, and feed the elder; all of which is physically and psychologically draining.

Ambrogi and London also note that elder abusers and their victims are involved in a complex web of highly stressful family relationships. The family in which elder abuse takes place may have a history of highly charged interpersonal relationships, or the victim and the abuser may be prone to acting out behavior that may precipitate abuse. Marital conflict between the abuser and his/her spouse, or problems with a delinquent or ill child may also precipitate abuse. Denial of the underlying family problem — the existence of an elder who is dependent and in need of care — may also lead to abuse and neglect. Unclear intrafamilial communication can also lead to further confusion, thus intensifying an already tense situation. Furthermore, in families with inadequate affection and intimacy, the victim's increased needs for care may increase stress and result in abuse.

Mary Joy Quinn (1985) points out that counseling the abuser as well as the abused is especially difficult. Many abusers sincerely want to continue caring for the elderly, and the latter typically want to remain with the abuser. Stress reduction is the obvious form of therapeutic intervention, but other areas need to be explored. For example, many caregivers do not understand normal aging or the diseases associated with it. Practitioners may be able to offer education in this area or suggest support groups available in the community. Delivery of concrete services that are tailored to the abuser (attendant care, grocery shopping, baby-sitting) can go a long way toward building a trust relationship with the practitioner. Of course,

Growing numbers of aged persons are victims of abuse, often because of neglect or abandonment.

there are abusive caregivers who for a variety of reasons are incapable of changing their behavior, despite the best efforts of an experienced and flexible practitioner. In these instances, separating the elder and the abuser may be the only answer.

PREVENTATIVE MEASURES AND INTERVENTION STRATEGIES

The task of preventing all forms of domestic abuse is a formidable one. While numerous and commendable preventative attempts have been made, experts are quick to point out that continued research, and more innovative and effective therapeutic intervention techniques are needed. Most contend that while dealing with the aftermath of violence is critical, the causes of domestic violence must be the focal point of future efforts. As Donna Stone and Anne Cohn (1984) point out, perhaps we have placed too much emphasis on remedial attention and not enough on stopping the problem before it occurs.

Self-help groups such as **Parents Anonymous** have proven to be an effective aid. The basic underlying theme of these programs is group support. Abused parties usually meet in small groups under the guidance of trained counselors and offer understanding and empathy to one another. Such therapeutic self-help systems not only come to the assistance of abused parties, but they also place the family in a more meaningful social context. The family should not be treated as an independent social unit, but as one embedded in a broader social network of informal and formal community-based support systems.

This is the focal point of recommendations made by Peter Coolsen and Joseph Wechsler (1984) in relation to the nation's child abuse problem. They feel that most people in our society believe that the family unit remains, and should remain, our basic social institution; and that under normal circumstances, the care and nurturing of children is the unique province of parents and other family members. Consequently, strengthening and supporting the family is a primary goal for any comprehensive, community-based prevention program. And a general consensus exists as to what constitutes the ingredients that contribute to enhanced family functioning and well-being. Family members are better able to cope with their roles within the family and with the demands of life within the larger society if they have:

- Some knowledge of child growth and development as well as realistic expectations about the everyday demands of parenting.
- Opportunities that encourage successful parent-child bonding and facilitate communication among family members.

- An ability to handle the stresses of infant- and childcare.
- Some practical knowledge about home and child management.
- Opportunities to share the tasks associated with childcare.
- Access to peer and family support systems to reduce isolation.
- Access to social and health services for all family members.

The need for support and services for all abused parties should be continually stressed. For example, emergency shelters are critical in our overall intervention efforts. Transportation, food, and money are frequently provided by these temporary facilities; some even help people find new jobs and homes. Most researchers agree that these are indispensable services for a family member seeking refuge from violence. Telephone hotlines available 24 hours a day are also valuable therapeutic tools. And, trained counselors can help victims of abuse obtain legal assistance for filing formal complaints and getting advice on child custody and legal rights in general. Self-defense training sessions for women are also quite useful.

Psychotherapy sessions with all of the concerned parties are strongly recommended by members of the helping profession. Individual casework and family therapy are among the most popular approaches. Counseling strategies typically focus on the resolution of conflicts in nonviolent ways and on establishing more effective communication techniques among family members. Although progress has been reported with such approaches, obstacles can develop in therapy. Individuals may continually deny the use of violence or the existence of personal problems; hostility is typically present; and there is frequently little guilt expressed over violent and abusive behavior. Sadly, many individuals and families fail to even seek out psychotherapuetic help or assistance from self-help groups.

Surprisingly, there are many people in society who refuse to acknowledge the presence or sever-

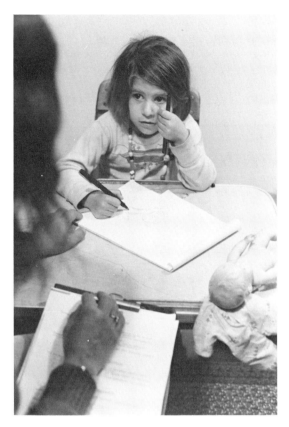

Supportive services and therapeutic intervention benefit the abused, including the youngest of victims.

ity of domestic violence. Sociologists feel that educating the public about the magnitude of this social problem should be one of our highest priorities. Training workshops are needed for those who deal with abuse (such as police officers, social workers, lawyers, teachers, and counselors). The shroud of secrecy that surrounds all forms of family violence has to be removed.

Effectively implementing all of these strategies will require more federal, state, and local funding. Financial aid is needed to establish more shelter homes, to provide more efficient legal assistance, and to provide support for those researchers exploring the causes and cures of domestic violence.

With such cooperative efforts, we may be able to curb the amount of violence afflicting America's homes. The path toward more harmonious living will be a difficult trail to blaze, with numerous obstacles and roadblocks encountered along the way. However, with the help of all concerned, perhaps the image of the loving, caring, and cohesive family unit can be restored to its rightful place in society.

CHAPTER HIGHLIGHTS

Family violence is widespread in contemporary society. To effectively study and understand the dynamics of family abuse, a number of myths must be shattered — including the notion that family violence is rare, that it is confined to the mentally disturbed or lower socioeconomic classes, that it occurs in all groups and that social factors are not relevant, that children who are abused will grow up to be child abusers, that battered wives enjoy being abused, that alcohol and drug abuse are the primary causes of domestic violence, and that violence and love can not coexist in families.

We examined some common features that the different kinds of family abuse share — including the fact that abuse is an abuse of power, that abuse is a response to perceived helplessness, that victims share many of the same effects, that abusing families share many of the same characteristics, and that the different varieties of family abuse share certain social response histories.

Child abuse is technically called the battered child syndrome and is most common among children six years of age and younger. This chapter addressed itself to characteristics of child abusers, elements of family life that increase the risk of child abuse, and the consequences of child abuse in later life. Attention was also given to child sexual abuse, including incestuous relationships.

Wife abuse afflicts nearly two million women each year. We examined characteristics of the abuser and the abused, features of home life that influence the risk of battering, and ingredients that produce spouse violence.

The concluding portion of this chapter examined three lesser known forms of domestic violence: husband, parent, and elder abuse. All have grown in the recent past, and we need continued research investigations so that we can better understand their underlying dynamics. We ended the chapter with a discussion of preventative measures and intervention strategies for dealing with domestic violence.

KEY TERMS

battered child syndrome
child sexual abuse
elder abuse
husband abuse

incest
marital rape
parent abuse
Parents Anonymous

sibling abuse
spouse abuse
wife abuse

RECOMMENDED READINGS

Adams, C., and Fay, J. (1981). *No more secrets: Protecting your child from sexual assault.* San Luis Obispo, CA: Impact Publishers. The title of this paperback says it all. The authors present practical information for combating the sense of helplessness many parents feel about preventing the sexual assault of children.

Bowker, L. H. (1983). *Beating wife-beating.* Lexington, MA: D. C. Heath. Among the topics Bowker covers are dimensions of violent marriages, formal and informal help sources, and personal strategies and techniques used by battered wives.

Ebeling, N. B., and Hill, D. A. (Eds.). (1983). *Child abuse and neglect: A guide with case studies for treating the child and family.* Boston: John Wright. A good use of case studies, showing readers what actually happens between social service workers and clients. This book succeeds in removing the mystique from a field that often engenders fear and discouragement.

Finkelhor, D. (1984). *Child sexual abuse: New theory and research.* New York: The Free Press. An important contributor to the field supplies answers as to why child sexual abuse has become so widespread.

Flanzer, J. P. (Ed.). (1982). *The many faces of family violence.* Springfield, IL: Charles C. Thomas. A multidisciplinary collection of papers focusing on many aspects of family violence. The extent and characteristics of family violence are reviewed at the book's outset.

Gelles, R. J., and Cornell, C. P. (1985). *Intimate violence in families.* Beverly Hills, CA: Sage. An excellent resource book; one that debunks numerous myths of family violence and replaces them with factual, proven information.

Hirsch, M. F. (1981). *Women and violence.* New York: Litton. A good discussion of violence against women from anthropological, sociological, and psychological viewpoints.

Leehan, J., and Wilson, L. P. (1985). *Grown-up abused children.* Springfield, IL: Charles C. Thomas. The focal point of this text is the recurring problems faced by the adult survivors of child abuse. A profile of the adult who has been abused as well as therapeutic intervention techniques are included.

Pagelow, M. D., and Pagelow, L. W. (1984). *Family*

violence. New York: Praeger. In addition to traditional topics, the authors offer coverage of violence among children, incest, marital rape, and elder abuse.

Quinn, M. J., and Tomita, S. K. (1986). *Elder abuse and neglect: Detection and intervention.* New York: Springer. A readable and comprehensive account of this newly recognized form of family abuse.

Part Six

LATER LIFE TRANSITIONS

16

Marriages during Middle Adulthood

CONTENTS

CONTEMPLATIONS

■ The midlife crisis. The mere utterance conjures up negative images: depression, gloom, dissatisfaction, and relentless marital strife. But is this an accurate portrayal of this developmental event? Is there really a crisis, and is it always a negative experience? Do men and women approach it differently? Read on to find the answers.

■ We've all heard some reference to the "empty nest" stage of the family life cycle: children grow up, chart their life course, and move out of the house to establish an independent lifestyle. But did you know that today almost 20 million adult children between the ages of 18 and 34 choose to remain at home to live with their parents? This chapter will explore this "full nest" phenomenon, who these "nesters" are, and the implications of such living arrangements.

■ "My love is deep; the more I give to thee the more I have, for both are infinite." For William Shakespeare, and others who think like him, love does have a special, enduring quality over the life cycle. Research presented in this chapter will explore how love persists but also tends to change over time. How is the love expressed by middle-aged adults different from that of younger and older adults? By the time you're done with this chapter, you'll know.

Many marriages are created in early adulthood, and children are added to the primary family unit shortly thereafter. By the time most of these parents reach middle age, their children are teenagers or young adults, and their families are probably stable with respect to number of children. However, entry into midlife represents yet another transition in the marriage and family life cycle and contains important developmental tasks.

Pinpointing exactly where middle age begins and ends is difficult, since researchers are not in total agreement. However, the consensus among many (for example, Rogers, 1982; Stevens-Long, 1985) is that middle age occurs between ages 40 and 64. Note how the conclusion of this life stage occurs before age 65, the rather arbitrary age given to the retirement years in our society.

Middle age also knows wide variation from a cross-cultural perspective. Given our designated ages for this stage of life, consider the ambiguity and confusion that can result in light of life expectancy in other nations. For example, in Upper Volta in Africa, the average life expectancy hovers near 40 years. Indonesia's people live on the average 50 years, while in the Philippines, the average life expectancy is 60 years. Cross-culturally, then, it is possible to be middle-aged in one country and elderly in another! Because of this, it is difficult to devise a precise, universal classification system for middle age, or for that matter, other major life stages.

While marriages at midlife occupy the longest stage of the family life cycle, they are not the most widely researched. In fact, it has only been in recent years that researchers have concentrated their efforts and sought to better understand this stage of marriage and family life. The result of their labor is that we're now getting a clearer picture of the developmental forces in operation at midlife and how these forces interact and affect marital relationships.

The study of marriages at midlife must take place against the backdrop of personal and social forces. For example, how partners react to physical changes at midlife, including the perceived attractions or unattractiveness of the aging process, as well as the nature of treatment accorded by others, usually affects the manner in which they ultimately perceive themselves and one another. Along similar lines, career triumphs and reactions to failures have important implications for marriage and family life, not to mention the stability and flavoring of other social relationships.

How might we best describe marital relationships at midlife? Are marriages characterized by continuity from earlier stages, or is this a period of change? *We* think that it's a bit of both. This chapter will explore how some features of married life remain unaltered throughout the marriage and family life cycle. Other facets of marriage may change with the new experiences and challenges of midlife; many couples report shifts in their outlooks on life after experiencing the "empty-nest stage," making a midlife career switch, or becoming grandparents.

The realization that they have reached an in-between stage of life, the middle of their existences clearly affects the dynamics that exist for couples during middle adulthood. They can look back *and* ahead, perhaps more so than at any other age. For many, examining the past and anticipating the future often leads to a reassessment of their life: "Where have we been, where are we now, and where do we want to go?" Seeking to honestly answer these questions, as we shall soon see, has important implications for marriage and family life.

Couples at midlife often assess their marital lives, reflecting on the past and what the future might bring.

MARRIAGE AND FAMILY AT MIDLIFE: DEVELOPMENTAL TASKS

Confronting the Midlife Challenge

For many couples, middle age is something of a paradox. It represents a time of success and a time of failure; a time of joy and a time of sadness. On some occasions it is a period of turbulence; at other times a time of quiescence. Regardless of such a mixture, though, most agree that middle adulthood represents the prime of life. And, it certainly is what each person makes of it.

Interpretations of the nature of middle age vary considerably. Some label these years as a crisis, a time for critical self-evaluation (frequently with negative conclusions), gloom, marital strife, and even depression. For many, reaching midlife means being "over the hill" and becoming a part of the "older" generation.

For those choosing a brighter outlook, middle age is regarded as a rewarding and challenging life stage. This viewpoint stresses that middle age is a time when couples come into their own, are more accepting of themselves, and mature into more nearly perfect harmony with their universe as they develop a broader perspective on life. Thus, in many respects, middle age is what each couple makes of it (Hale, 1984).

For individuals and couples alike, middle age has a tendency to creep up, almost without warning. People seem to know when they're middle-aged when they finally begin to pay attention to various aging processes. The need for reading glasses, a bulging waistline, or a receding hairline may now be noticed. The physical departure of grown children from the nest may create psychological emptiness, or the death of a friend or parent may shock people into realizing that they are not immortal but rather at the crossroads of their own lives (Donohugh, 1981).

Is There a Midlife Crisis? Depending on the source, one is apt to find some reference to the "inevitability" of a midlife "crisis" and the profound impact it brings. According to some authors, heavy is the heart and overworked is the mind struggling with the midlife crisis and the problems of this age.

From our point of view, such portrayals of the midlife crisis are inaccurate. To begin with, it is not inevitable; there are many adults who go through life without any such experiences. Furthermore, we think the word "crisis" has a negative and disruptive connotation to it. Many midlife challenges and personal assessments are positive, productive, and rewarding. This is as true for couples as it is for individuals in general. Although there are serious moments, it is not a time characterized by continual conflict (Nicholson, 1980).

Rather than a crisis period, we prefer to view midlife as another transition. It is a life stage when there are new dimensions to one's family life, career, intimate relationships, community, and inner life. The midlife transition is characterized by a change in the way individuals see themselves and others around them. As persons move toward these new dimensions and experience changed perceptions, they may encounter uncertainty or strangeness. This is only natural, however, as one moves from one stable state to another (Schlossberg, 1981; Golan, 1981).

Persons within the midlife transition often as-

sess their lives, conducting a sort of psychological inventory of their abilities, accomplishments, and shortcomings. For some, this may be anxiety producing and even painful. There are people who just cannot stand the thought of looking at their inadequacies, failures, or shortcomings. Consequently, they rob themselves of total growth and self-understanding. In its most productive form, the midlife transition enables individuals to examine their total selves, carefully exploring strengths as well as weaknesses. In so doing, many find that what they have to do in life is inevitably easier than what they have done so far. But they discover that instead of competing and clashing with the outside world, their tasks now lie within. The need to resolve these psychological tasks develops intensity because midlife brings the reality that one's future is not forever (Donohugh, 1981).

Negative dimensions to the midlife transition occur when anxiety, depression, and a sense of futility emerge. Some people become preoccupied with signs of aging and premature doom. (Incidentally, it is very normal at this age to read the obituary column with regularity.) Others dwell on the negative side of their lives and regard themselves as failures. Some report gloom and despair as they recall youthful dreams, current accomplishments, and the gap that exists between the two. This last point is an important one, since the successful resolution of issues raised depends on one's ability to reassess and readjust. The optimism and dreams of early adulthood need to be put into perspective by the realities at midlife. It is possible that certain goals in life will not be met, and this requires acceptance and adaptation. This may be a painful procedure for many, but it is important to renounce some dreams, while critically evaluating modes of life that are possible and available. This type of reassessment may well lead to greater self-fulfillment in later adult life (Levinson, 1980; Gould, 1980).

Sex Differences in the Midlife Transition
While the points made thus far can apply to both men and women, there are sex differences in the midlife transition. These differences are especially

evident when family roles are taken into account. Consider the situation of the male. Along traditional lines, his transition places more emphasis on career assessment than upon family issues. This is not to mean that his family isn't important. It just shows that in our competitive society, "making it" in the career world is a critical issue for males.

For many women, particularly those from homes reflecting traditional sex roles, the family is often the focus. A woman's midlife transition is likely to revolve around her husband, the growing independence of her children, and ultimately their departure from the home. When her children do leave, she may feel no longer needed. A portion of her life may become void of meaning. Also, along traditional lines, a woman spends years standing by her husband's side, often offering unfailing support as he gropes for his occupational niche in the world. Of course, there are variations on these patterns, particularly if the mother works outside the home. And, in the future, it should be interesting to note how these patterns change — especially since so many women of all ages are joining the labor force.

However, if these traditional family patterns persist, women often define their life cycle in terms of their children's and husband's ages, or even family stages. Whereas midlife may mean, for men, taking on new career challenges (such as becoming a mentor for younger workers), for women, it may herald the **empty nest** stage and a time to address personal needs. If women begin a new career or launch educational plans, they may very likely encounter some of the tasks, challenges, and problems earlier encountered by their husbands (Notman, 1980).

The female midlife transition is different, too, in regard to the way a woman views the aging process. Accepting one's changing physical self is an important facet of overall psychological adjustment. Often, though, there is a double standard attached to growing old that frequently places women on the losing end. As an example, consider how the same aging processes for men and women are often perceived differently. Older men get

The female midlife transition may bring new plans and ambitions, such as returning to school.

silver hair, women turn gray. Men get more distinguished-looking with age, women just grow old. Character lines crease men's faces, women own a collection of wrinkles. Unfortunately, many segments of society will not allow women to grow old gracefully.

Perhaps the biggest reason for this is because too much of what is valued about women is connected to their physical appearance. Conversely, middle-aged men are often perceived and measured more by what they've accomplished in life than by their physical appearance. Therefore, physical signs of aging are often perceived as part of the male's achievement of worldly success. We think that such perceptions will be changing, though, especially in the light of more sexual equality in the home, work force, and society in general. This will be as true for reactions to the aging process as it will be for role expectations of women in all facets of life.

It might also be argued that sex differences exist in the overall timing of the midlife transition. Gail Sheehy (1981; 1976), for one, suggests that women enter the midlife transition earlier than men, approximately at age 35. Many women experience a degree of pressure at this time, perhaps because this age brings along the potential for inner turmoil. Some women experience a sense of "deadline" and urgency because of what life trends are known to occur at age 35. In support of this, consider the following:

- Thirty-five is when the average mother sends her last child off to school.
- Thirty-five begins the dangerous age of infidelity.
- Thirty-five is when the average married American woman reenters the working world.
- Thirty-five is the average age at which the divorced woman remarries.
- Thirty-five is the most common age for runaway wives.
- Thirty-five brings the biological end of childbearing closer.

When these factors converge, many women begin to feel the need to change to a midlife perspective. However, whether the woman acts on her life assessment at this age and what role her husband may play in this psychological process, are separate issues.

Interestingly, Sheehy discovered that once a person gets beyond the "deadline" aspect of the midlife transition, later middle life becomes more mellow, satisfying, and rewarding. For both middle-aged women and men in their fifties, roles often acquire a more relaxed quality and there is greater freedom to say what one thinks. Also, there are greater opportunities for companionship with one's spouse, and more time and money for oneself. Sheehy also notes that with age, women often

become more assertive and men more expressive (Sheehy, 1981).

Parent-Adolescent Interaction

As we learned in Chapter 12, parents and teenagers alike face a number of important developmental tasks. One of the more important chores is adjusting to the adolescent's desire to be independent. Usually, this is accomplished by the teenager's desire to forge his/her identity (Erikson, 1982). It is also a time when many parents realize for the first time that their offspring will soon be moving on and establishing their own independent lifestyle and living arrangements. The manner in which these two forces combine, the adolescent's desire for greater autonomy and parents' reactions to such strivings, will greatly determine the emotional climate and psychological stability of the home (Carter and McGoldrick, 1980).

While many parents can effectively meet the challenges of this stage, others do not fare as well. Part of the problem is that they resist granting any adult status to their children. Instead of promoting mature and responsible behavior, they are instead more secure in overprotecting their children and fostering dependency. Some do not let go of their teenagers because they dread the thought of the next phase of family life, the empty-nest stage. While we will presently see that the empty nest can have many positive dimensions, some parents have difficulty imagining what life would be like without their children around.

The creation of effective communication patterns between parent and adolescent is thus an especially important task. Parent-adolescent communication must, of course, work two ways. Teenagers as well as parents are responsible for developing meaningful interaction skills, and this can be the most difficult of all the developmental challenges that face both parties. But success in parent-adolescent communication may well depend on the degree of successful parenting exhibited when the children were younger. Indeed, experience seems to support the conjecture that success

THE TRAGIC EPIDEMIC OF ADOLESCENT SUICIDE

The many developmental tasks that characterize adolescence are not always mastered. Faced with the pressures of modern times, some teenagers feel hopeless. Many are simply incapable of dealing with the life demands placed on their shoulders and react to this developmental stage with an array of self-defeating behaviors.

In recent years, rates of adolescent suicide have grown in an alarming fashion. At an age when they should live life to its fullest, approximately 5,000 teenagers and young adults, or about 13 a day, commit suicide each year. Besides accidents, the leading cause of death among young people is suicide. The most sobering thought, however, is that since 1960, the suicide rate among adolescents has increased 300 percent (Colt, 1983).

Numerous categories of teenage suicide victims can be identified. For example, some are the happy-go-lucky types who give no clear clues before acting. Others are classic loners, who are screaming silently for help. Adolescent suicide attempts for many are unplanned, and impulsive for the most part, since many attempters want to get help not die. However, there are those who act in a premeditated fashion, carefully planning how it is they will end their lives. Finally, there are those who commit suicide as part of a pact with others, or because they have been influenced by the suicide of others (Grueling and DeBlassie, 1980; Giffin and Felsenthal, 1983).

The number of teenage suicides may be higher than statistics reveal because many attempts fail, and many medical examiners routinely list questionable deaths — especially for teenagers — as accidents. For that matter, parents may also not report suicidal behavior. Hanging, shooting, and taking poison are common suicide methods (Weiner, 1980).

Recently, there has been a significant increase in suicide among minority youths. However, it must be noted that suicide victims as well as attempts are not exclusively concentrated in any one socioeconomic bracket. Males outnumber females in the number of suicide deaths reported each year, but females outnumber males in suicide attempts, and there has been an increase in completed suicides among females in recent years (Neuringer and Lettieri, 1982; Weiner, 1980).

Just as there are many categories, so too are there diverse reasons. One persistent cause is depression; many teenagers have a pervasive feeling of worthlessness, apprehension, and hopelessness. Other probable causes are the loss of love objects and the stress that sometimes transpires in family life. Many suicide victims are rejected youths who receive little affection or attention, and most feel socially isolated from others (Colt, 1983; Grueling and DeBlassie, 1980; Konopka, 1983).

A number of preventative measures have been recommended to combat teenage suicides. Detection and identification of conflict and stress are vital and require the collaboration of parents, teachers, counselors, and other concerned adults. Im- ▶

proving the quality of human relations and enhancing educational and employment atmospheres are important, too. The establishment of community resources, such as halfway houses, shelters, hotlines, and adolescent clinics are important steps in prevention, crisis intervention, and follow-up care that help the victim cope with day-to-day living. ■

at parenting depends on how successful one's own parents were.

Considerable attention has recently been focused on whether or not a **generation gap** exists between parents and teenagers. A generation gap refers to differences in values, attitudes, and behavior between two generational groups. Perhaps a few illustrations will show how the generation gap can express itself.

Adolescents sometimes have a knack for telling parents about the distance that separates the two age groups. For instance, some may remark that their parents are "over the hill" and that their

ideas are "old-fashioned" or "out-of-step" with the times. Language use, especially slang and catch-phrases, has a tendency to differ between young and old. Adults are often told that certain words and expressions just aren't used anymore and are a sure giveaway to a person's age. The same may hold true for everything from hairstyles and clothing to preferences in music.

Does this mean that a generation gap always exists between young and old? Is it an inevitable part of family life or is it more of a myth? To answer these questions, we must realize that the values and attitudes of today's teenagers are different

Establishing a harmonious relationship with teenage offspring is an important developmental task for middle-aged couples.

from those of adolescents 10 or 20 years ago. As they seek to nurture accurate self-concepts, teenagers have to discover the things in which they believe, which may include perceptions of what is right or wrong, moral or immoral, and important or unimportant to them. To accomplish this, they must look around and examine the views of their own generation and compare their beliefs with numerous societal agents. As young adults, they will discover that numerous social forces, including parents, peers, schools, and the communication media can shape their developing value systems.

Over time, youths have integrated many of their parents' values into many of their own. However, teenagers are quick to point out that times have changed since their parents' youth. While there are those who adopt parental viewpoints without question, there are many who do not. The desire to be independent, plus newly discovered cognitive skills that enable the adolescent to analyze the world more fully, may promote a more questioning attitude than ever before.

Does all of this mean that age differences create contrasting points of view? Is a generation gap almost certain to develop between young and old? Not necessarily. In fact, most researchers today regard the generation gap as largely a myth. Usually, differences that exist between parent and adolescent are ideological, not generational. This

RESEARCH HIGHLIGHT

A VIEW FROM THE OTHER SIDE: HOW ADOLESCENTS PERCEIVE DISCIPLINE

Research on discipline tends to focus on the techniques parents prefer to use. But what about those on the receiving end, particularly during this stage of the family life cycle? How do teenagers perceive permissive, democratic, and authoritarian styles of parental discipline? Which style do they prefer?

Research undertaken by Cay Kelly and Gail Goodwin (1983) zeroed in on these issues. In their study, 100 adolescents were given a questionnaire that examined a number of areas, including the style of control employed by parents and the respondent's acceptance or rejection of such control. The ultimate goal of the researchers was to uncover which measure of parental control, if any, was favored the most by teenagers. Of the gathered responses, 83 percent of the teenagers felt they had democratic parents, 11 percent had authoritarian parents, and 6 percent had permissive parents. Teenagers raised in democratic homes clearly favored this form of parental control. In support of this, they responded favorably to 68 percent of the items on the questionnaire reflecting democratic orientations. Those from authoritarian and permissive homes, by comparison, responded positively to 50 percent and 32 percent of the questions respectively.

One important area of autonomy indicated by the adolescents was the right to choose their own friends and dates. As predicted, teenagers raised under democratic parental styles tended to react more positively to parental power than those from permissive or authoritarian homes. Interestingly, even among the teenagers raised in democratic homes, such covert rebellion against parental power was manifested in the form of assertion of the right to choose their dates and friends.

means that conflict results between new and old, not young and old. Moreover, adolescents and parents are likely to agree on more issues than one might expect. While teenagers may overtly differ from parents in such areas as dress or mannerisms, both groups are surprisingly similar in such areas as attitudes and fundamental values (Hamid and Wyllie, 1980; Coleman, 1980).

Before closing this portion of our discussion, let's acknowledge the importance of maintaining satisfactory methods of parental control during the teenage years. Parents now are often confronted with the task of redefining past child-parent relations and gradually increasing the teenager's responsibility. This has obvious implications for the type of discipline exercised by parents.

Invariably, the research indicates that adolescents, given a choice, prefer an egalitarian relationship with their parents. They desire households that are regulated on the basis of honesty, fairness, and mutuality. Consultations between parents and teenagers on issues of mutual concern and the provisions of opportunities to enhance teenage autonomy appear to foster the healthiest emotional climate. Not only are the parent-adolescent relations likely to prosper with such operating principles, but the personal growth of each party is likely to flourish (Larson, 1980).

The Empty Nest Stage

The **empty nest** stage of the family cycle occurs when children have grown up and physically left the home. For parents, this means a time when they are alone and living in a house that is filled with memories of their children. For some, this becomes a time of sadness, reflection, and even dissatisfaction. For others, the empty nest stage brings new levels of marital satisfaction and fulfillment.

Several reasons may explain why the empty nest stage is perceived as a crisis period. Many parents, more often the mother, have concentrated all or too much of their time and attention on the children. Those mothers who totally wrap themselves up in their children discover that when they reach

For many women, the empty nest stage of life brings freedom and the opportunity for relaxation and enjoyment.

the empty nest stage, they have little left to live for. The adjustment difficulties frequently encountered by the mother can be soul-rending experiences. This generally occurs in the late thirties or early forties, when a mother has acquired considerable free time. After what seems like a lifetime of caring for others, she may long to feel that she is still needed and serves some practical function. Her midlife transition is thus a time of critical self-evaluation and assessment (Radloff, 1980).

A perceived loss of power among mothers may also accompany the empty nest stage. However, this may be more of a problem for mothers losing their children to adulthood now than it will be for future mothers. The latter have not been programmed to perceive mothering as their primary responsibility or task. Rather, many of tomorrow's mothers have other "eggs in their baskets." When their children are grown, they may feel less "left" than many of today's mothers; they'll probably have many activities besides motherhood to turn for involvement (Greenberg, 1983).

Some researchers feel that the empty nest stage is a positive stage of growth. Although a period of adjustment is normal for parents, once children have departed, positive feelings characterize the post-parental stage. High levels of marital happiness, shared activities, and open communication are often reported more by post-parental adults than those with children still at home. Furthermore, post-parental adults look back at their child-rearing years and report a high degree of pleasure, reward, and inner satisfaction in their roles as parents. Although some sadness is experienced, this emotion is outweighed by the joys and pleasures of past parenting.

Those supporting this positive interpretation also emphasize the many levels of freedom now enjoyed by the couple. For example, there is often freedom from financial worries, freedom from so much housework, freedom to travel, and freedom to "be oneself" for the first time since the children came along. Experiencing such freedom prompts couples to regard the empty nest with relief and happiness rather than gloom.

Perhaps the parents best handling the empty

"Agnes, now that the children are gone, have you given any thought to what you'd like to do?"

Source: Jerry Marcus in Good Housekeeping.

nest stage are those not attempting to foster dependency on the part of their children. Instead, autonomy and independence are encouraged. Parents who maintain that their children are mature enough for the work world, college, or marriage are more likely to let go than parents who still perceive their young adults as immature. Ideally, parents recognize their children as separate individuals in their own right and strive to show genu-

THE FULL NEST: PARENTS AND GROWN CHILDREN LIVING TOGETHER

At some point in middle age, most parents will experience the empty nest stage of family life. Children will have grown up, charted their life plans, and moved out of the home. Yet for a growing number of households, a relatively new development gives family life a new wrinkle: the **full nest**. The 1980s are witnessing an unprecedented number of grown-up children living together with their parents. In fact, in 1985, an estimated 19.3 million adults between the ages of 18 and 34 were living with their parents (see the figure at the end of this box).

Many factors account for the full nest phenomenon. Financial explanations invariably find their way to the top of the list: young people often have trouble affording an independent life style. Others remain in the roost to combat loneliness, and still others want to perpetuate a close-knit family bond. There are also ▶

those who are still going to school and those who are postponing marriage. And, grown children may be using the home as a haven or retreat during times that they're out of work or changing careers.

Monica O'Kane (1981) points out that the full nest often brings its share of domestic happiness and satisfaction. However, it may herald negative outside opinions as well as internal pressures and problems. For example, there's an attitude among some outsiders that effective parenthood includes launching children out of the home and into the mainstream of society; and internal problems include conflicts over possessions and noise, as well as disagreements about household space or territory. Finally, "nesters" may be disruptive to everyday household activity and thus create stress on the parental marriage bond.

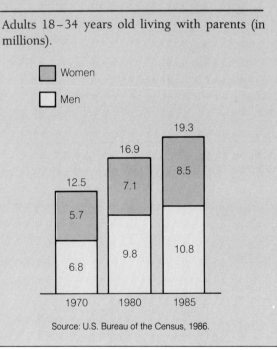

Adults 18–34 years old living with parents (in millions).

Source: U.S. Bureau of the Census, 1986.

ine care and concern, but not to the extent of overinvolvement. It is conceivable, then, that the fewer long-range goals parents (especially the mother) have established for their offspring, the sooner the parental phase of life will be successfully completed.

Today, there are many parents who adjust to the empty nest stage gradually. College, military service, or extended trips away from home often separate young adults from their parents for relatively short periods of time, allowing the parents to experience a household with one less child—or no children—without fearing they will never see the child again. While the "nest" is "semi-empty," the experience is softened by the expectation that the child will soon return. This form of gradual adjustment also enables parents to assess and evaluate their own goals and plans for the future.

Caring for Aging Parents

In addition to meeting the needs of their offspring, some middle-aged couples must also tend to the needs of their aging parents. Because they now have their children on one end of the generational cycle, their parents on the other, and themselves in the middle, middle-aged parents become part of the "caught" or "squeeze" generation. As a result of this squeeze, couples at midlife frequently face growing pressures as they cope with the needs of their offspring and aging parents simultaneously (Aizenberg and Harris, 1982; Gillies, 1981; Cicirelli, 1981).

It seems that parents in this stage of the family life cycle, or anyone who knows of parents experiencing it, can tell many stories about its numerous dimensions. These are rewarding yet very trying times. As one middle-aged acquaintance of ours remarked. "You know you're at the crossroads of life when you don't know whom to blame your troubles on — your kids or your parents."

For the most part, it appears that couples are committed and more than willing to care for their aging parents. One recent study (Brody, 1985) found support for this commitment while exploring generational attitudes about financial closeness and care. The youngest women in the study were just as committed to caring for aged relatives as their middle-aged mothers and their grandparents. Most of the women also reported that they wanted to care for aging family members, not because they were obliged to do so. Moreover, aging parents reported that they would want to be cared for by their offspring if it was at all possible for their children to do so.

Marcia Ory's (1985) survey of the literature indicates that although caring for one's aging parents is gratifying and has its rewards, it is becoming more complex than ever before. For example, in-

The provision of care for aging parents becomes a reality for couples at midlife and requires considerable adjustment.

creased longevity will result in more four- and five-generation families in years to come. Thus, older impaired parents will need increased assistance from their offspring who are themselves aging. In the future, for instance, it will become increasingly common for a 90-year-old widowed mother to be cared for by her 65-year-old adult child.

Other complexities about care arise because of changing sex roles and increased labor force participation among middle-aged women. Women, more so than men, handle the bulk of care for

---

RESOURCES FOR GROWN CHILDREN CARING FOR AGING PARENTS

Because of the pressures associated with the care of aging parents, adult children must take special strides to care for themselves. Frank Gruber (1985) observes that many also need to air and share their burdens with others facing similar family chores. He offers the following list of support groups and information centers designed to assist and guide adult children and their aging parents:

- **American Association of Retired Persons (AARP)**, 1909 K Street NW, Washington, DC 20049. Publishes *Hand in hand: learning from and caring for older parents* (a useful planning guide and resource manual for community groups to co-sponsor one-day workshops); *Housing options for older americans; Your home, your choice;* and *ECHO housing.*

- **Aging in America, Inc.** 1500 Pelham Parkway, Bronx, NY 10461; (212) 824-4004. A directory of respite care services is among the publications available.

- **Area Agencies on Aging.** These state and local agencies offer information and referrals to case management agencies, counseling, hospices, and respite-care providers. Other services for the elderly include transportation, legal aid, visiting services, and Meals on Wheels.

- **Children of Aging Parents**, 2761 Trenton Road, Levittown, PA 19056. Resource for persons wishing to start or join a support group; general information on the caregiver role.

- **Family Service America**, 44 East 23 Street, New York, NY 10010. This organization lists 268 agencies in 40 states that offer counseling for families of the elderly as well as referral sources.

- **Greater New York Network for Aging**, 111 East 85 Street, #22A, New York, NY 10028; (212) 876-5113. A comprehensive directory of professionals specializing in emotional and psychological concerns of children as well as aging parents. Offers general information, including resources in other areas.

- **National Hospice Organization**,1901 N Fort Myer Drive, Arlington, VA 22209; (703) 243-5900. This organization provides basic information on hospice care.

- **Research Institute of America** 589 Fifth Avenue, New York, NY 10017. This organization publishes *Caring for dependent parents*, a reference source containing practical guidance and suggestions for quality generational care.

aging parents (Brody, 1981; Sangl, 1983). What remains to be seen is whether assistance to aging parents will decline as more women enter the workplace.

Finally, couples at midlife are typically confronted with competing role responsibilities and time demands, all of which makes caring for aging parents that much more difficult. The rigors of providing regular care while maintaining one's own household are physically and psychologically exhausting. The loss of personal freedom, the lack of time for social and recreational activitiess, and restrictions in mobility are often part of the sacrifices to be made at this stage of the family life cycle (Ory, 1985).

PATTERNS OF SPOUSE INTERACTION

The Midlife Marital Reassessment

It is entirely possible that, once the children have left the home, the husband and wife will discover they have drifted apart over the years. With time together now, they may even be surprised at changes in one another that had gone unnoticed for some time. A popular anecdote involving a middle-aged couple says it all. The two are sitting at the breakfast table, sipping coffee and earnestly reading the morning newspaper. The husband, out of the blue, lowers his paper, and with a puzzled expression on his face says, "When did you get reading glasses?" The wife looks at him and replies, "About five years ago. By the way," she adds, "When did you go bald?"

Midlife may thus be a time of marital reassessment, a time to take stock of one's relationship. If couples find themselves dissatisfied with their marriage and discover they no longer really "know" each other, it is often hard for them to offer mutual support and understanding. Pessimistic couples may believe that their responsibilities as parents are finished and thus view their lives as practically over. Some feel there is little left to do with a life that has become devoid of meaning.

The risk at this time (although it can happen in

"What do I want? After all this time you should know without my telling you."

earlier stages of marriage) is that couples can create a loveless marriage or "empty shell" existence. Sonya Rhodes (1981) writes that such relationships have no emotional connection and partners avoid companionship and romance. Such marriages can exist, but they are at best, superficial. Partners often convince themselves that they're foolish to expect any improvements in their relationship. They may play down the importance of certain parts of the marriage (love and intimacy, for example) and emphasize others (the children, material wealth, and so on). Or, those trapped in an empty marriage may try to escape the situation by filling their private lives with a multitude of activities, both inside and outside of the home.

Consequently, many couples must work hard to revitalize their marriages. The successful reconstruction of sagging marriages often hinges on the notion of dealing with the here and now, not with what has been or might have been. Partners must also acknowledge the fact that no matter how a marriage was begun, it has succeeded in surviving to middle age. This usually means that each partner has done much to match the other and each has helped to develop enough common areas of interest to neutralize trouble spots. While they cannot go back to the beginning and start over, couples do have something to build upon. And, unless such a reconstruction is begun only a miserable marriage or single life is waiting (Donohugh, 1981).

Qualities of Enduring and Vital Marriages

For many couples, the post-parental stage is the most rewarding and happiest period of their lives. When the children are gone from the home, mothers as well as fathers report an improvement in marital relations; some feel that these years rival the happiness and satisfaction felt when the couple first met. Some even go so far as to label these years as a second honeymoon. Couples feeling this way usually have experienced much mutual understanding and support over the years. They are

---

APPLICATIONS

HOW DURABLE AND VITAL IS YOUR MARRIAGE?

Carefully read the statements below and decide the degree to which you agree or disagree with each. Circle your response by referring to the following: SA = Strongly Agree; A = Agree; U = Undecided; D = Disagree; SD = Strongly Disagree.

1. My spouse and I enjoy doing things together.   SA A U D SD
2. I enjoy most of the activities I participate in more if my spouse is also involved.   SA A U D SD
3. I receive more satisfaction from my marriage relationship than from most other areas of life.   SA A U D SD
4. My spouse and I have a positive, strong emotional involvement with each other.   SA A U D SD
5. The companionship of my spouse is more enjoyable to me than most anything else in life.   SA A U D SD
6. I would not hesitate to sacrifice an important goal in life if achievement of that goal would cause my marriage relationship to suffer.   SA A U D SD
7. My spouse and I take an active interest in each other's work and hobbies.   SA A U D SD

To score this self-quiz, award yourself the following: **SA = 5 points; A = 4 points; U = 3 points; D = 2 points; and SD = 1 point.** If *both* you and your spouse score between 25 and 35 points, your marriage is considered to be a healthy and vital one.

Adapted from Ammons and Stinnett, 1980.

also likely to be optimistic about the future, have confidence in themselves and their abilities as a couple, have good communication skills, a strong sense of intimacy, and feelings of mutuality and reciprocity (Mudd and Taubin, 1982; Sheehy, 1981; Ammons and Stinnett, 1980).

In her critically acclaimed book *Married people: Staying together in the age of divorce*, Francine Klangsbrun (1985) explored how marriages endure and survive over the years. Her subjects were 87 couples who had remained married for at least 15 years. While she did not find the total secret behind lasting marriages, she did find that couples in strong relationships shared a number of abilities and outlooks.

Enjoyment of Each Other   Couples in enduring and vital marriages honestly enjoy being in one another's company. They like talking with one another, communicate effectively, and share many common values. Moreover, their sex lives are active and considered by both partners to be important to the overall relationship.

An Ability to Change and Adapt   Change is inevitable in marriages — be it the children moving out of the home, career triumphs and failures, or caring for aging parents. Couples in enduring marriages are flexible in meeting change; in the process they exhibit healthy adjustment and adaptive skills. Many also willingly choose to change

RESEARCH HIGHLIGHT

LOVE RELATIONSHIPS ACROSS THE FAMILY LIFE CYCLE

Love and attachment are essential to a good relationship and to general well-being throughout the life cycle. But do forms of love and attachment to one's partner change over time? Is the love shared by middle-aged couples, for example, the same as that of their younger or older counterparts?

Questions such as these were at the heart of research undertaken by Margaret Reedy, James Birren, and K. Warner Schaie (1981). This team of researchers queried 102 happily married young, middle-aged, and older couples in regard to the importance of six different "components of love": *communication* (honest communication, self-disclosure, good listening), *sexual intimacy* (physical and sexual intimacy, excitement, tenderness), *respect* (understanding, patience, tolerance), *help and play behaviors* (common interests, shared activities, helpful, supportive), *emotional security* (affection, trust, caring, concern, security), and *loyalty* (commitment to the future of the relationship).

The gathered findings clearly indicated that the nature of love in satisfying relationships is different at different ages (see the figure at the end of this box). For example, sexual intimacy was relatively important for young adults, whereas emotional security and loyalty were more important to later-life couples. Interestingly, sexual intimacy was equally important to both young and middle-aged adults. This may be due to the fact that in satisfying relationships, passion maintains its importance in love through middle-age, and only becomes relatively less characteristic of later-life love.

Other findings revealed that young adults rated communication as relatively more characteristic of their love relationship than middle-aged and older lovers. This might suggest that over time, love relationships are less likely to be based on   ▶

intense communication and more likely to be based on the history of the relationship, traditions, commitment, and loyalty.

Finally, this study uncovered some interesting trends in regard to sex differences and the nature of love. As expected, women rated emotional security as relatively more characteristic of love than men. However, contrary to expectation, men rather than women rated loyalty as more characteristic of their love relationship. No sex differences were found in regard to sexual intimacy and communication. This latter finding suggests that an important criterion for a satisfying love relationship may be the presence of an equal amount of interest and involvement in sexual intimacy and verbal commitment by both partners.

Mean scores by age for component of love categories.

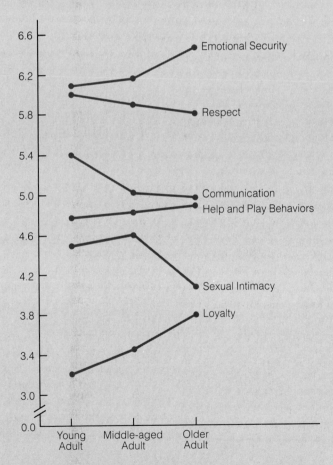

Source: Reedy, M. N., Birren, J. K., and Schaie, K. W. (1981). Age and sex differences in satisfying love relationships across the adult life span. *Human Development, 24.*

themselves when necessary to keep their marriages vital.

An Ability to Live with the Unchangeable Couples in enduring relationships don't expect perfection from one another; they accept each other for who and what they are. While differences do exist in the relationship, partners go on with their lives and focus on their marital strengths.

An Assumption of Permanence Here, partners are committed to one another as well as to marriage as a whole. The concept of "forever" is not only a hope but an ongoing philosophy. The notion that marriage will be permanent has a tendency to temper the couple's approach to imperfections and conflicts.

Trust for One Another While love may wax and wane within a relationship, trust in enduring marriages remains constant. Couples trusting one another report high levels of security and comfort as well as safety and nurturance. Partners maintain that trust rests at the foundation of their commitment to monogamy, since trust in marriage presupposes exclusivity.

A Balance of Dependencies In successful and enduring marriages, partners are mutually dependent. When they speak of needing each other, they are typically talking about strengths, not weaknesses. This in no way implies helpless and immature dependency when one's partner is absent; rather, partners turn to one another to fill in gaps and provide enrichment and enjoyment.

A Shared and Cherished History This implies that couples are attached to the significance of their past and of their time spent together. Couples in vital marriages have woven a history together and respect the chapters experienced: how they met, private jokes, rituals, and even shared sadnesses. This is not mere nostalgia but instead an appreciation of their shared attachment.

A Degree of Luck Successful relationships need a certain degree of luck to keep going. From the beginning, a person needs some luck in choosing a partner who has the capacity to trust, change, and grow in a relationship. A little luck with life is also needed. Extended illnesses, job losses, personal failures, or family feuds might push a marriage off course when it might otherwise have succeeded.

Sexual Interactions

Patterns and Rates of Sexual Activity Sexual functioning and desire are not immune to the aging process. When, however, people understand the changes of aging and how to cope with these changes, they can remain sexually active for as long as they choose. For many, that means for as long as they live.

Many couples at midlife must realize that their sex lives have diminished from earlier years. However, it is not uncommon, for sexual relations to improve once these years are over. Indeed, many couples find that they can rediscover sex in the more relaxed and private life of a home without children. Older couples often make fresh discoveries and enrich their sexual lives, in the process finding out that sex can become even more important for them.

Middle adulthood often becomes a time when individuals confront their sexuality, a period when physiological factors result in a change in sexual behavior that poses new questions about one's masculinity and femininity. For instance, middle-aged men often report heightened emotional needs for tenderness and intimacy, less sexual aggressiveness, and a desire to become more relationship-oriented than ever before. Middle-aged women typically report feeling stronger, more self-confident, more in control of their relationships, and more sexually aggressive than in previous years. These shifts in feelings are difficult to deny, and they have a tendency to force middle-aged adults to reevaluate their own sexuality (Cleveland, 1981).

Middle adulthood also represents a stage in the life cycle in which misconceptions about sexuality exist. Unfortunately, many young and old adults

THE SECRET WORLD OF EXTRAMARITAL SEX RELATIONSHIPS

Sexual activity does not always confine itself within the boundaries of marriage. Rather, many men and women turn to extramarital sex in an effort to obtain sexual satisfaction and pleasure. In a definitive sense, *extramarital sex* includes any sexual activity outside of the marriage with or without the knowledge or consent of one's spouse.

The numbers vary as to how many men and women are thought to engage in extramarital sex. However, there seems to be a consensus that at least 50 percent of all married men and about 20 percent of all married women have affairs at one time or another (see, for example, Wolfe, 1982; Hassitt, 1981; Peterson, 1983). Such percentages, though, may be too low since some respondents may be reluctant to admit such behavior. Still it is a fairly safe bet to say that extramarital sex relationships are widespread.

All extramarital sex relationships are not the same; on the contrary, there are different forms of involvement and escalation. Of these, the "isolated affair" is the most common. This relationship, commonly referred to as "the one night stand," involves sexual activity with a partner but with no future involvement or emotional commitment. It is a good example of the permissiveness-without-affection moral standard discussed in Chapter 5. The less common "intense affair," on the other hand, is characterized not only by regular sexual activity between partners, but also by the emotional involvement of the two and the escalation of attachment.

It should be acknowledged, too, that many married persons engage in certain types of extramarital "affairs" but without sexual intercourse. For example, flirtation and fantasized infidelity are fairly common among married men and women. A type of extramarital relationship may also include an intimate cross-sex friendship that emphasizes deep sharing, but noncoital involvement. Interestingly, such cross-sexual friendships are sometimes questioned and even condemned by outsiders. Despite the innocence of the parties, some people question how such an intimate relationship can possibly exist without the sexual element.

What accounts for such high rates of extramarital "sex"? To begin with, we are living in a sexually permissive society and such high incidence rates may be a reflection of sexual freedom. Some people turn to affairs because they are curious, adventurous, or simply bored with their existing marriages. Many participants report sexual frustration as their underlying motivation. Others use these relationships for the companionship they offer, or for a boost to their egos. The motivations of still others may be fueled by the constant visibility of the extramarital sex theme in the media. Finally, a faltering sense of masculinity or femininity within an existing relationship may prompt some to turn to an outsider for reinforcement or fulfillment.

The research of Eleanor Macklin (1980) sheds light on factors related to extramarital sex relationships. She found participants usually have lower degrees of ▶

sexual and marital satisfaction. However, there are husbands and wives who have affairs who are very happy and satisfied with their spouses and their marriage. Those likely to have affairs, though, have certain predictable qualities: they are usually sexually liberated, have a liberal lifestyle, and have high needs for intimacy and low levels of emotional dependency on their spouses. Some may involve themselves in an affair as a form of rebellion or retaliation against their spouses. Regarding this last point, some may launch themselves into an affair to "get even" with a spouse who had or is having an extramarital sexual relationship.

One source (Atwater, 1982) points out that opportunities for extramarital sex relationships are greater in urban societies where people contact a variety of others each day. More specifically, the workplace is responsible for bringing married men and women together, typically requiring them to spend considerable time together. In this vein, the growing incidence rate of extramarital sex among women may be explained, in part, by the greater number of women working outside of the home. Atwater adds that women are also still being *used* sexually in the male occupational arena, a factor that also contributes to such increased percentages.

Deceit, deception, and dishonesty typically enter the extramarital sexual relationship. Excuses must be fabricated to make up for absences and time away from the home, and sometimes to explain changes in mood or dress. More often than not, lies must be spun to shroud the situation. Such cover-ups are directed to one's spouse and other loved ones, as well as to work associates. Moreover, the lives of those involved in extramarital affairs acquire greater complexity. The details of where and when to meet have to be carefully and secretly planned to avoid suspicion or discovery. For all of these reasons, the chance of anything deep and meaningful developing between the two is usually doomed from the start (Bell, 1983).

alike believe these myths. The more prevalent misconceptions include the following:

- Middle-age marks the downward slide of sexual activity, and its end is in sight.
- Those who remain sexually active during middle-age and the retirement years are "dirty old" men and women.
- By middle age, one's sexual desire has already been fulfilled.
- After having children, sexual activity and desire is depleted.
- Menopause or a hysterectomy terminates a woman's sex life.
- A prostatectomy terminates a man's sex life.

Normal and healthy sexual relationships during middle adulthood and beyond are best understood when these myths and misconceptions are abandoned. Furthermore, only minor modifications of technique are usually needed in order to accommodate the physiological changes that do occur with age. Couples need to be aware that sexual excitement and arousal is a slower process in middle age than in past years and requires more direct tactile stimulation. It will also take the couple a longer period of time to achieve orgasm/ejaculation. The orgasmic experience may also be less intense than previously.

Most couples at midlife enjoy sex on a regular basis. One study (Blumstein and Schwartz, 1983) reveals that even after ten years, 63 percent of married couples queried have sex at least once a week. Also, it was found that rarely do sexual relationships become infrequent. After ten years, only

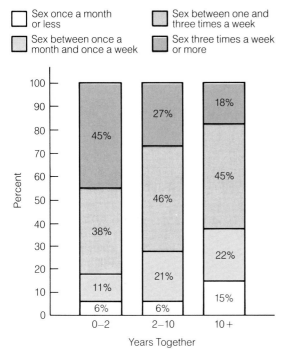

Sex once a month or less

Sex between once a month and once a week

Sex between one and three times a week

Sex three times a week or more

Source: Blumstein P., and Schwartz, P. (1983). *American couples*. New York: Pocket Books.

FIGURE 16-1   Sexual Frequency

15 percent have sex once a month or less (see Figure 16-1).

Generally, decreases in sexual responsiveness that accompany the aging process are due more to psychological causes than to physiological changes. For instance, while there is a noticeable decline in the male hormone **testosterone**, extremely low levels are not reached until old age, and even then men are able to produce fertile sperm and thus father children. A woman remains capable of sexual activity throughout her life, and many women become more responsive to sexual stimuli during their middle years. This may be due to an increase in blood circulation resulting from earlier pregnancies, which enhances the possibility of orgasm (Sarrel and Sarrel, 1984).

A satisfying sex life also depends on the physical vitality of couples and the mental commitment of each partner to remain sexually intimate. Relationships maintaining mutuality and tenderness provide the basis for satisfying sexual relations. This is as true for couples at midlife as it is for all stages of adulthood.

Sexual Dysfunctions

Satisfying and rewarding sexual relations are not experienced by all. Indeed, many couples face some type of sexual dysfunction at one point or another in the overall marriage cycle. As many as one-half of all American couples may fall into this category (McCary and McCary, 1982). The following discussion focuses on some of the more common female and male sexual dysfunctions.

Female Sexual Dysfunctions   One of the more common sexual problems encountered by females is **orgasmic dysfunction**, the inability of a woman to reach a sexual climax. Often, the woman is unresponsive to any form of sexual stimulation. Similar to male sexual dysfunctions, this disorder appears to have psychological and situational causes. For instance, some women may feel guilty or shameful about sexual arousal, others may be fearful and, therefore, hold back sexually. Still others may never have been sufficiently stimulated by their partner to reach an orgasm. Treatment often includes a woman learning to experience regular orgasm through masturbation, followed by clitoral stimulation from her partner, and then coital stimulation.

Vaginismus is the painful contraction of muscles surrounding the vaginal tract. Usually, muscles surrounding the vagina develop spasms whenever the penis begins to penetrate the vagina. This constricts the vaginal opening so that penile penetration is impossible. However, this dysfunction is not caused exclusively by a physical disorder. Often, such reactions are due to a subconscious fear of intercourse or from some type of traumatic experience. Treatment of vaginismus tends to focus on teaching relaxation responses, particularly those which encourage the woman to relax the vaginal muscles.

Sexual dysfunctions can occur at any point in a relationship and require the understanding of both partners to be successfully resolved.

The **general sexual dysfunction**, once called frigidity, refers to lack of desire for sexual relations. Physiologically, women with this dysfunction have little or no vaginal lubrication and show little, if any, sexual responsiveness. Many regard sex as an ordeal or disgusting, and although they may experience orgasm occasionally, intercourse is devoid of pleasure. Therapeutic intervention usually aims at exploring pent-up anxieties and teaching relaxation skills, all within a nonthreatening atmosphere of trust and acceptance.

Male Sexual Dysfunctions   One of the more common male sexual problems is **erectile dysfunction**. also called **impotency**. This is the inability of the male to create and maintain an erection sufficient for sexual intercourse. This dysfunction is seldom attributable to physiological causes; rather, the problem lies within psychological parameters. For example, impotency has been traced to worries about sexual adequacy or imagined loss of sexual power, job-related anxieties, or to such situational factors as fatigue, food, or drink. Once these emotional and situational problems are alleviated, a man's sexual abilities are usually restored.

Premature ejaculation is perhaps the most common male sexual dysfunction. Men with this problem cannot hold back their ejaculation during intercourse and, as a result, climax prior to their partners. Premature ejaculation is one of the easier sexual dysfunctions to treat, however. Therapy usually centers on teaching males to control certain aspects of their sexual arousal so that their partner's needs can be satisfied. An example of this would be encouraging the male to mentally block out the sensations preceding orgasm, in the process, prolonging the duration of intercourse.

Retarded ejaculation is the inability of the man to ejaculate during sexual intercourse. This dysfunction is not nearly as common as the two dysfunctions already discussed. Anxiety may once again be the cause of this dysfunction, including a fear of impregnating the woman or experiencing inhibited sexual excitement. Treatment often includes relaxation techniques and teaching one's partner oral and manual techniques for bringing the man to orgasm.

Putting Sexual Dysfunctions into Perspective   In the discussion above, we mentioned various techniques to help overcome sexual dysfunctions. In addition, we need to stress the importance of a couple being honest, open, and understanding of one another. More specifically, Bryan Strong and Rebecca Reynolds (1982) stress that the following must be understood:

■ Sexual problems are common problems and usually do not represent neurosis.

■ It must be realized that *both* partners are involved in the sexual relationship. Blaming a sexual dysfunction on oneself or one's partner should be avoided.

■ Stereotypes regarding masculine and feminine sexual behavior are typically misleading, and potentially destructive to the relationship.

- Sex is not something a person does to or for his/her partner. Sex is an intimate, shared activity.

- Sex embraces many other activities besides intercourse that may be as rewarding or even more exciting at various times.

- The defense mechanisms used to handle a sexual dysfunction (emotional withdrawal, denial, rationalization, and so forth) often create further difficulties in a relationship.

- Accepting responsibility for one's own sexual feelings and behavior rather than projecting them onto someone else often improves sexual interaction.

- Fear of repeating past feelings or behaviors often locks a person into repeating them. Fear often becomes a self-fulfilling prophecy.

- There is no perfect way to respond sexually. The beauty of the sexual act lies in its personalized meaning to the couple.

- Sex reflects a highly intimate form of communication, often mirroring the state of a relationship. If something is going wrong sexually, something may also be going wrong with a couple's overall relationship. Developing awareness of feelings and learning how to communicate them are crucial to a couple's sexual interaction.

Menopause: Separating Myth from Fact

Menopause usually occurs during the late forties and early fifties and is a normal developmental event in a woman's life. However, it is frequently a misinterpreted event, often filled with misconceptions and erroneous beliefs. Paramount among these is that menopause brings a woman' sex life to a total halt. Let's debunk such myths by first examining what menopause is and what it isn't.

Menopause is defined simply as the cessation of menstruation. The period from the onset of irregularity of the menses to total cessation (menopause) is called the **climacteric**. The female climacteric may last only a few months or may extend over several years. During the climacteric, ovulation, menstruation, and reproductive capacity gradually cease.

After 30 to 40 years of menstrual cycles, a woman has released almost all her **ova** (eggs). While the male continues to produce sperm throughout adulthood, the human female is born with a fixed number of ovarian *follicles* (immature ova and their cases). The number of follicles present at birth is estimated to be one or two million. By the time puberty is reached, however, the number has reduced itself to about 300,000. Of this number, only 300 to 500 will mature; the rest will deteriorate. By age 45, a woman's supply of follicles is nearly depleted, and only a few remain (Tyler and Woodall, 1982).

The decrease in follicles is also accomplished by a decline in production of the female sex hormone **estrogen**. One result of this is that menstrual periods become irregular and often unpredictable. When estrogen production continues to lessen, the climacteric culminates in the complete cessation of cyclic ovarian activity—the menopause. Because of the rapid decrease in secretion of the hormones estrogen and progesterone, the mammary glands atrophy, as do the uterus and vagina in varying degrees. Sometimes, a loss of bone density occurs, a condition known technically as *osteoporosis*.

Estrogen production does not cease after menopause (a commonly held misconception). Instead, it continues to be produced in areas other than the ovaries. The adrenal glands, the fatty tissue in the body, and the brain all begin to increase their levels of estrogen production. Even though some estrogen is produced, however, it is not enough to continue the ovulatory cycle (Millette and Hawkins, 1983).

A woman's reaction to menopause is highly individual. It is possible, however, to isolate two general periods when women experience the psychological effects of long-term hormonal changes. One occurs during the climacteric, the other occurs upon reaching menopause.

During the climacteric, a woman must readjust her life from one that has been physiologically stimulated by the production of estrogen and progesterone to one that is devoid of these feminizing **hormones**. Loss of these hormones may cause

During middle age, menopause brings to an end a woman's reproductive capacities and opportunities for natural motherhood.

stresses accompanying middle adulthood. These may be anxieties about children as they enter into the adult world, financial worries, other concerns about growing old in general, and deliberation regarding the attainment or nonattainment of life goals. Those women who do not have children or have chosen singlehood as a lifestyle may regard middle adulthood as the final chapter in their lives, which now cannot be rewritten. Consequently, many psychological themes weave themselves around this important physiological event (Millette and Hawkins, 1983).

The idea that hormones are a part of a cause-effect relationship is supported by some researchers who state that menopausal symptoms can be reduced by taking estrogen. Hormone replacement is used by some women to eliminate such physiological symptoms as hot flashes, hair loss, atrophy of the breasts and vagina, and loss of skin elasticity. While alleviating the symptoms, such treatment will, however, also prolong their duration. Estrogen-replacement therapy also has been known to produce negative side effects. For example, the long-term use of high-dose estrogen has been associated with uterine cancer. Other negative side effects are high blood pressure, vaginal infections, and breast discomfort. Because of such problems, many physicians are less than enthusiastic about its blanket prescription. The decision to begin estrogen-replacement therapy is usually based on the severity of the symptoms. Each woman needs to be individually evaluated, and even then, the lowest possible dose is usually given for the shortest period of time (Gastel and Hecht, 1980; Donohugh, 1981; Schultz, 1980).

Misconceptions about Menopause   Our discussion has so far been directed at the psychological implications of menopause. Now let's turn our attention toward some myths and misconceptions that surround menopause. The notion that there is something "wrong" with menopause is the primary reason for the many "old wives' tales" that surround it. Unfortunately, these myths are perpetuated by a lack of scientific investigation and

such symptoms as hot flashes (moments of feeling warm and uncomfortable, often accompanied by perspiration); irritability; insomnia; fatigue and anxiety; and, often, sensations of dyspnea (labored or difficult breathing). It has been estimated that between 50 and 85 percent of all women experience some of these symptoms. It is not known, however, whether these conditions result solely from hormonal changes or are, in part, a reflection of societal beliefs such as those that affect menstrual mood swings (Millette, 1982; Uphold and Susman, 1981; Gray, 1981; Frey, 1981; Heilman, 1980; Guyton, 1981; Moore, 1984).

Beyond these symptoms, the menopausal woman often has other worries due to the normal

APPLICATIONS

SHOULD YOU TAKE ESTROGEN?

The risk-benefit equation of estrogen-replacement therapy (ERT) can only be computed by an individual woman and her physician. To some, any increased cancer risk is too great; to others, the slight risk of developing cancer 15 years hence is worth the benefit of greater comfort today.

Robin Marantz Henig, author of *How a woman ages* (1985), writes that given the known risks and benefits of ERT, the following guidelines can be offered:

- A woman should discuss ERT with her doctor is she needs relief from:
  Hot flashes;
  Osteoporosis; or
  Vaginal atrophy.

- A woman should *not* take ERT to correct the symptoms for which it has not been shown to be effective, such as:
  Wrinkling;
  Leg cramps;
  Depression; or
  Insomnia.

- A woman should *not* take ERT if she has the following conditions:
  Personal or family history of breast, uterine, or ovarian cancer;
  Fibrocystic breast disease;
  Large fibroid tumors of the uterus;
  Circulatory disorders such as phlebitis or severe varicose veins; or
  Severe chronic illnesses such as heart disease, kidney disease, diabetes, or hypertension.

- If she and her doctor agree that she can benefit from ERT, she should take the drug:
  In the lowest possible dose;
  In combination with progesterone; and
  For as short a time as possible.

- Periodically, with her physician's guidance, she should try to wean herself from ERT and stay off the drug if the symptoms do not recur.

free discussion. As a result, they influence the thinking of both females and males, both young and old. Among the more popular myths are:

- *Menopause is a disease.* Doctors and the general public used to regard menopause as an illness —a condition requiring medical treatment. Today menopause is regarded as a *deficiency syndrome,* in that a woman's estrogen secretion has diminished. Some degenerative

changes usually occur, which may or may not require medical attention.

- *Following menopause, women need full replacement of the hormone estrogen.* Even though the ovaries stop manufacturing estrogen, some is still produced in other parts of the body. There is still no precise answer, however, as to whether a woman's estrogen deficiency needs to be corrected. We've covered some of the pros and cons associated with estrogen-re-placement therapy, and the pendulum swings back and forth as to its use.

■ *Menopause creates depression, severe mood swings, and mental instability.* At best, some of the symptoms attributed to menopause, such as anxiety, are in actuality spin-offs of other stresses that emerge during middle adulthood which may be only indirectly related to meno-pause.

■ *Menopause causes incapacitating hot flashes.* There is some disagreement as to the percent-ages of women who experience the various symptoms of menopause. One source (Sarrel & Sarrel, 1984) estimates that half to three-quarters of all menopausal women experience hot flashes or flushes. Other estimated per-centages are lower. Most are in agreement, though, that the percentage of those having severe and incapacitating flashes is slight. Most are mild or moderate and do not disrupt normal activity.

■ *A woman who has had a hysterectomy will not experience natural menopause during middle adulthood.* This is a generalization, and a more accurate statement depends on the extent of the surgery. Should a partial hysterctomy be performed, only the uterus is removed. A total hysterectomy involves removing the uterus and the cervix, and sometimes the ovaries. If a woman has either one or both ovaries remain-

IS THERE A MALE MENOPAUSE?

The question of male menopause is a popular issue today. Of course, strictly speaking, males cannot have a menopause, since they don't have menstrual cycles. What, then, is meant when we refer to such a condition? There are some re-searchers who believe that a male version of menopause exists, and that it pro-duces many of the symptoms that females experience, such as frequent mood swings from acute irritability to depression, fatigue, and anxiety.

While the so-called male menopause is not as physically dramatic as that experienced by women, noticeable bodily changes do occur. For instance, al-though males still retain their reproductive capacities, there is a noticeable decline in the male hormone testosterone between the ages of 40 and 50. Such a decline causes, among other changes, decreased levels of sperm and semen, less intense orgasms, and a general loss of physical stamina (see Sarrel and Sarrel, 1984; Gray, 1981).

Edmond Hallberg (1980) avoids the term "menopause" and instead calls this period of time the "male metapause syndrome." While he acknowledges the existence of the physiological changes described, he stresses the importance of the psychological burdens that are often experienced during middle adulthood. By the time one reaches middle age there may be a great sense of urgency to live life to its fullest. The tension that is consequently aroused by such a dramatic life per-spective creates anxiety, stress, and bouts of depression. These psychological changes prompt Hallberg to proclaim that men and women are more alike than different in their middle years.

The fact that such an event intervenes in a somewhat similar way for both men and women makes this an area worthy of future investigation. Therapeutic inter-ventions designed to assist those experiencing the psychological disruptions of ▶

midlife, for example, need to be explored. Studies focusing on the physical changes described also need to take place. For instance, research already conducted indicates that just as menopausal women are helped by the administration of extra estrogen, men experiencing a similar change of life may be assisted by the administration of the hormone testosterone. These are just a few of the many areas that await the efforts of tomorrow's researchers. Such investigations will prove to be exciting in the years to come.   ▪

ing following the operation, she will experience a natural menopause as the ovarian cycle winds down.

- *A woman's sexual desire terminates following menopause.* The reality of the situation is that many women find themselves enjoying sex more, particularly because they're no longer worried about birth control and pregnancy. A majority of women report that they feel no different about themselves sexually. We should acknowledge, however, that there are some who do report a decrease in sexual desire. Whether or not this decrease is because of psychological or physiological (decrease in estrogen and androgen) factors is, as yet, unknown.

- *A woman's activity level diminishes following menopause.* For most, the reverse is often the case. Postmenopausal woman are usually healthier and in better spirits than before the "change of life." Many report being "freed" from the mood swings characterizing the menstrual cycle, as well as the previously mentioned worries concerning birth control and pregnancy.

- *Men are unaffected by a woman's menopause.* Men do care and are affected. A major problem is that limited research has focused on men and their feelings. What we do know is that many men are confused about the precise nature of this developmental event and need to have the woman communicate her feelings and needs. In this fashion, a more supportive and positive atmosphere can be developed. (Adapted from Skalka, 1984; Millette and Hawkins, 1983)

Most women benefit from a meaningful support system when experiencing menopause, one that offers understanding and sensitivity. In addition, Brenda Millette and Joellen Hawkins (1983) observe that a woman's adjustment to menopause depends, in part, upon the experiences of her mother, her peers, and other significant women in her life. Also, women, as well as men, need to know the facts, not the myths about menopause. A woman should know what to expect regarding this important and normal developmental event. In this way, she will come to see that menopause is a milestone, not a millstone, in her life.

CHAPTER HIGHLIGHTS

The nature of marriages at midlife was the focal point of this chapter. We first explored the developmental tasks that midlife couples face: coming to grips with the midlife challenge, establishing harmonious relationships with teenage offspring, coping with the empty nest stage of life, and caring for aging parents.

For many partners, middle adulthood is a time to reassess one's marriage. For those who have drifted apart over the years, reconstruction now becomes a developmental task. However, we did acknowledge that troubled relationships can exist under the guise of loveless or empty shell marriages. Enduring and vital marriages appear to share common qualities: couples enjoy one another's company; they can adapt to change and live with the unchangeable; their relationship assumes permanency; the partners trust one another; a balance of dependencies exist; they share a cherished history regarding their relationship; and they've experienced some element of luck over time.

As far as sexual relations are concerned, it is generally argued that decreases in sexual responsiveness that occur with age are due more to psychological causes than to physiological changes. We also acknowledged that when couples seek to understand the aging process and coping with change, they can remain sexually active for as long as they choose. Sexual dysfunctions, though, do occur for many. For women, the more prevalent are orgasmic dysfunction, vaginismus, and general sexual unresponsiveness. Among males, the more common problems are erectile dysfunction, premature ejaculation, and retarded ejaculation.

Menopause, generally occurring during the late forties or early fifties, is defined as the cessation of menstruation. It is a normal developmental event in the life of a woman, and husbands as well as wives need to better understand it. For this reason, we tried to debunk a number of myths and misconceptions surrounding menopause. Physiologically the period from the onset of irregularity of the menses to total cessation, or menopause itself, is called the climacteric. During these months, or even years, the rapid decline in estrogen and progesterone levels may be accompanied by "hot flashes," irritability, anxiety, and other symptoms. As estrogen diminishes, mammary glands atrophy, as do the uterus and vagina in varying degrees. Some women experience a loss of bone density. Estrogen-replacement therapy is often used to combat the symptoms of menopause. The pendulum sways back and forth in regard to its believed safety and effectiveness. This chapter explored some of the negative side effects of estrogen-replacement therapy, including uterine cancer and hypertension.

We concluded by saying that men do not have a menstrual cycle, but some research indicates that they may have an interesting counterpart to the female menopause. They do experience decreased levels of sperm and semen, less intense orgasms, a general loss of physical stamina, and a decline in testosterone. Mood swings, fatigue, and anxiety are also reported by many. More research is needed in this area, though, before definitive and precise parallels are made to the female menopausal experience.

KEY TERMS

climacteric	generation gap	ova
empty nest	hormones	premature ejaculation
erectile dysfunction	impotency	retarded ejaculation
estrogen	menopause	testosterone
full nest	orgasmic dysfunction	vaginismus
general sexual dysfunction		

RECOMMENDED READINGS

Barach, G., Barnett, R., and Rivers, C. (1983). *Lifeprints.* New York: McGraw-Hill. This book explores the factors that contribute to a woman's sense of well-being and life satisfaction. The authors studied 300 women between the ages of 35 and 55, and the results of their research are both interesting and plausible.

Datan, N., Antonovsky, A., and Maoz, B. (1981). *A time to reap: The middle age of women in five Israeli subcultures.* Baltimore, MD: Johns Hopkins University Press. A good cross-cultural analysis of middle age in five Israeli ethnic groups, ranging from traditional Moslem villagers to modern European urbanites.

Donohugh, D. L. (1981). *The middle years.* Philadelphia: Saunders. Marital and personality dynamics during middle adulthood are presented in Chapter 5 of this very readable text, which offers a good blend of theory and applied examples.

Gillies, J. (1981). *A guide to caring for and coping with aging parents.* Nashville, TN: Thomas Nelson. This paperback is recommended here in light of our discussion of middle-age family responsibilities. It is a very practical guide for a variety of concerns, from nutritional information to nursing home care.

Knox, D. (1984). *Human sexuality: The search for understanding.* St. Paul, MN: West. One of the better introductory textbooks on human sexuality. Sexual dysfunctions and therapy receive thorough attention in Chapter 11.

Millette, B., and Hawkins, J. (1983). *The passage through menopause: Women's lives in transition.* Reston, VA: Reston. This book does much to expose the myths surrounding menopause. It is beautifully written, loaded with information, and frank in its appraisal of this developmental event.

Nichols, M. P. (1986). *Turning forty in the 80s.* New York: W. W. Norton. Readers will especially enjoy Nichols' interpretation of the midlife transition.

O'Kane, M. L. (1981). *Living with adult children.* St. Paul, MN: Diction Books. O'Kane describes the trials and tribulations of the full nest and what both young and old generations can do to promote domestic harmony and stability.

Pearlman, J., Cohen, J., and Coburn, K. (1981). *Hitting our stride.* New York: Delacorte Press. The personality adjustments and adaptations of women as they face the developmental tasks of midlife are featured in this book.

Schaefer, C. E. (1982). *How to influence children: A complete guide for becoming a better parent* (2nd ed.). New York: Van Nostrand Reinhold. Schaefer discusses parenting techniques suitable for use with children from preschool through adolescence. In light of the material we covered in this chapter, this book's emphasis on adolescence will prove beneficial.

17

Marriages during Late Adulthood

CONTENTS

CONTEMPLATIONS

■ The elderly are often perceived in a negative light: lonely, sick, grouchy, and a burden to all. These sweeping generalities have been around for years but are hardly representative of the truth. Also bothersome is the gloomy and depressing image often given to marital life during the retirement years. Why do some people choose to believe such myths? Where do such attitudes originate? Are you guilty of clinging to ageist attitudes? You'll be in a better position to answer as we explore the realities of life that later-life couples face.

■ "Will you still need me, will you still feed me, when I'm 64?" While this popular song of the not-too-distant past wasn't in search of marriage and family research for an answer, we are. What is the nature of generational relationships for later-life couples? Are they alienated from their families or are close ties maintained? And, from an international point of view, how do family networks in the United States compare with those in other countries in regard to care for elderly family members?

■ The nursing home decision. Making this choice for a failing spouse or other family member may be one of life's most difficult decisions, one that invariably promotes feelings of uneasiness and guilt. Today, we hear so much about the negative aspects of nursing homes: they're impersonal, depressing, and unsanitary. How much of this is true? What is it like to be a nursing home resident? What strains does it place on the family? We'll take a look at these and other areas as we examine the topic of institutional care for the failing family member.

By the time most married couples approach the age of retirement, their children have already matured, married, and established independent households. Consequently, the typical older family in contemporary society consists of just the husband and wife, creating yet another transition in the marriage and family life cycle. About two-thirds of all elderly persons are husband-wife couples living alone, most of whom maintain their own households (U.S. Bureau of the Census, 1985).

However, the higher mortality rates of men during the later years affect this scenario. For example, while the majority of older men are married, the proportion declines as men reach age 75 years and older. However, women under the age 65 are most likely to be married and those 65 and older tend to be widowed. In general, it can be said that most older men live with their spouses, but many older women live alone or with a nonrelative (Brubaker, 1985).

This family life transition is filled with numerous developmental chores. Paramount among these is adapting to the lifestyle changes brought about by retirement. Also of importance are adjustments made in physical living arrangements, in kin relations, in grandparenthood, and adaptation to widowhood.

THE QUALITY OF LATER-LIFE MARRIAGES

The Assessment of Marital Satisfaction

The shift of focus away from children and the incorporation of the husband into the home give married life among the elderly a particular character. Physical, economic, social, and emotional

For many retired couples, companionship becomes the focal point of everyday life.

factors will affect marital relations at this time. How successfully the husband adapts to the retirement role seems to be especially important. Let us acknowledge, however, that the working woman's adjustment to the retirement role also needs to be explored. With increased full-time labor participation rates among females, we need to know more about their adjustment and adaptation to this life event (Szinovacz, 1982; Gratton and Haug, 1983).

The accurate assessment of the quality of marriage is often difficult. Timothy Brubaker (1985) points out that this task in relation to later-life marriages may be even harder. For example, many couples who were dissatisfied with their relationships may have divorced in earlier years. Thus, the research is only examining surviving relationships. Also, older couples may be reluctant to disclose unhappiness because they have invested so much time, energy, and themselves in their marriages. In addition, if older persons are not satisfied with their marriages, it could be said that they may not be satisfied with their personal lives, but this could be the case at any stage of marriage. Finally the financial reductions often accompanying retirement usually affect morale, thus representing other variables that must be taken into consideration by researchers.

We do know, though, that most marriages are characterized by satisfaction rather than disenchantment during the retirement years. Elderly couples tend to be happier, less lonely, and financially more stable than the aged single person. Moreover, if one's social ties have decreased because of retirement or disability, the role of spouse acquires even greater importance and significance. For many, the relationship often becomes the focal point of the couple's everyday life (Barrow and Smith, 1983; Cohen, 1980).

The event of retirement is often responsible for bringing couples closer together. Before retirement, a couple's interests usually centered around childrearing and earning a living; afterwards, their interests are directed toward one another. These shared interests are likely to breed even more closeness as time goes on. Furthermore, there is often a high degree of interdependence in happily married couples, particularly in terms of caring for one another in times of illness. For people in these happy marriages, the underpinnings of which are satisfaction, mutuality, and reciprocity, widowhood is a dismal prospect (Harris and Cole, 1980; Atchley, 1980).

However, not all marriages are stable and satisfactory at this time. There are many wives who resent the intrusion of the husband into the household on a full-time, daily basis. Some, such as Judith Treas (1983), feel that incorporating a newly idle husband into the daily household routine is a stressful and turbulent experience for a wife. The new intimacy brought on by retirement may produce a strain on the marriage. In this respect, the husband's daily absence from the home except on weekends, because of work, was an acceptable pattern of life for the couple. The closer interpersonal contact now experienced is not. Should this happen, there is usually reduced satisfaction, loss of intimacy, and less sharing of activities (Harris and Cole, 1980; Kart, 1981).

As with all life stages, it is important for the couple to adjust to new household demands and routines. When the husband retires and spends most of his time at home, he often becomes aware of new responsibilities and expectations. For example, husband and wife usually become coequals in authority in the home, although this may not always be the case. The changing roles and relationships in retirement marriages may alter the relative power of some husbands and wives. It is possible that the husband's power declines when he loses the "leverage" provided by the breadwinner role. Apparently, the same would hold true for women who are wage earners (Ward, 1984).

Sharing household chores is evident among many retired couples, giving marriage an egalitarian flavor. Successful older marriages tend to be those that have moved away from the instrumental functions of marriage, such as providing money and status, to a relationship based on a common identity—one that comes from sharing and cooperation. Marital harmony at this and all family stages also arises from the level of regard and esteem that partners hold for one another (Atchley, 1980; Crandall, 1980).

THE AGING EXPERIENCE: SEPARATING MYTH FROM REALITY

Cultural and societal myths regarding the aged abound, often taking the form of prejudice and discrimination, known as **ageism**. Ageist attitudes are almost always unfair and demeaning and have little, if any, basis in fact. For example, the elderly are often viewed as being frail, sickly, asexual, poor, and depressed.

Social scientists actively seek to combat ageism and misconceptions about aging processes, be it those directed at the person or the married couple. And their efforts have resulted in a more accurate and clearer portrait of the aging experience. What we've learned is that growing old is not the negative experience some people choose to believe. Rather, research indicates (Smith, 1983; Eisdorfer, 1983) that for most, the retirement years are healthy, satisfying, and productive. The vast majority of the aged are not feeble and dependent, but instead persons who have much to contribute to society.

But where do our ageist attitudes originate? Apparently many have deep historical roots, at least in this country. Starting with the colonial period, a proportion of   ▶

the elderly were categorized as superannuated, unnecessary, and a burden to others. With the growth of cities and the Industrial Revolution of the nineteenth century, the aged were already recognized as a wideranging social problem. Old age had become characterized as a time of dependence and disease (Haber, 1983).

Ageist attitudes, like other attitudes, are a product of the socialization process. As such, they can be transmitted by a number of social agents: parents, siblings, school, peers, books, and other forms of the media in such a way that the aforementioned stereotypes are reinforced. At other times, the aged are practically invisible to the general public; that is, the media prefer to focus on the younger adult.

Several fairly recent studies have verified this last point. In one (Kuansnicka, Beymer, and Perloff, 1982), only 8 percent of the people portrayed in the advertisments of general-interest magazines were elderly. In television commercials the situation is just as bad. One investigation (Hiemstra, 1983) discovered that among 358 human characters appearing on commercials, only 11 were judged to be age 60 or older. Only 41 appeared to be 50 or older. And of the 130 human characters considered central figures in commercials, only 6 were thought to have been 60 or older.

More exposure to the elderly and increasing the younger public's knowledge of the elderly are needed to break ageist stereotyping. This will also enhance one's knowledge of the aging process and (for our purposes in this text) place later-life marriages into a more accurate perspective. It may also help remove those overall negative stereotypes attached to later life in general (Shulman, Agostino, and Krugel, 1982; Cartensen, Mason, and Caldwell, 1982).

THE COUPLE'S ADJUSTMENT TO RETIREMENT

Today's later-life couples are healthier than retirees of past generations. Nevertheless, when retirement takes place, functions must be reintegrated if life is to continue fruitfully and harmoniously. Since retirement as a stage of life is such a new developmental phenomenon, however, our culture has yet to prescribe suitable behavior for this period. Consequently, couples may react differently.

We do know, though, that retirement affects many facets of family life. Jeffrey Giordano and Kathryn Beckham (1985) remind us that retirement is a family decision and a family event. It usually involves a rite of passage that includes all family members, bringing increased opportunities for interaction within both the nuclear and extended family structure.

Psychological Adjustments

Departing from the labor force and relinquishing a significant part of one's identity represent a difficult psychological adjustment. Such a transition usually brings about a major loss of self-esteem. The ability to deal with this stage of life depends to a considerable extent on past adjustment patterns. Those who adequately adjust to retirement are typically able to develop a lifestyle that provides continuity with the past and meets their long-term needs. Successful adjustment is also characterized by the harmonious resolution of demands and tasks throughout the course of one's life, including those made within the realm of marriage.

Most people are able to effectively adjust to the retirement role. Should the experience be negative, it's usually because the retirement event was perceived as being stressful or because of health and/or financial trouble (Foner and Schwab, 1981; George, 1980). According to Paula Morrow (1980), some are unhappy because of inappropriate expectations for retirement or because they were overcommitted to the work role. Interestingly, while some retirees report missing a feeling of being useful, most do not miss the work itself (National Council on the Aging, 1981).

Retired couples experience considerable psychological satisfaction. Herbert Parnes (1981), for example found that about 80 percent of retirees felt that retirement fulfilled or exceeded their expectations. Furthermore, about 75 percent reported that they would retire at about the same time or earlier if they had to do it over. There is evidence (Foner and Schwab, 1981; George,

1980), however, that white-collar workers are generally more satisfied with retirement than blue-collar workers.

Financial Adjustments

The biggest adjustment to retirement is usually financial in nature. A dramatic drop in income almost always accompanies retirement. For example, statistics indicate that in 1981, 15.3 percent of those aged 65 and older were below the level of poverty in the United States. This figure jumps to 28 percent for black persons the same age (U.S. Bureau of the Census, 1985).

The average monthly Social Security payments to retirees are shown in Figure 17-1. This is the prime source of income for most couples, and if job-related benefits are nonexistent, couples experience true economic hardship. Obviously, the retired worker needs far more than Social Security

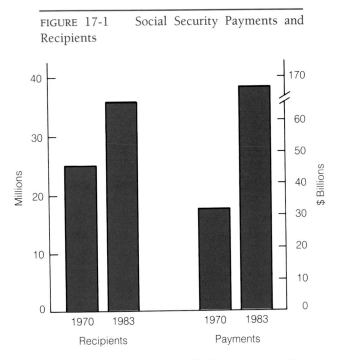

FIGURE 17-1   Social Security Payments and Recipients

Source: U.S. Bureau of the Census. (1985). *Statistical Abstract of the United States*. Washington, DC: U.S. Government Printing Office, p. xxii.

benefits to live comfortably. Job related pensions are critical, especially for women, who often face yet another instance of vocational inequality. On the average, retirement benefits are far lower for women than they are for men. In 1980, for example, the average retirement benefit for a woman was 40 percent of that for a retiring male (Porter, 1980; Soldo, 1980; Marsh, 1981).

Financial security largely determines the range of alternatives that couples have in adjusting to all transitions of marriage and family life. Old age is no exception. People with sufficient financial resources can, for example, afford to travel, entertain friends, or seek the best of health care. Older individuals without sufficient money can afford to do none of these things. Sadly, a majority of the nation's elderly fall into this latter category. Most will never experience these "luxuries," and even worse, there are some who cannot even afford the basic necessities of life. We might add, however, that many of the elderly who are poor were poor prior to retirement and have adjusted to living simply (Atchley, 1980).

Older persons are not only less well off than other families, but their chances of improving their economic status through personal initiative are extremely limited. While all of the nation's elderly are not classified as poor, most are dependent upon economic resources that lie outside their control. The economic status of the elderly is usually determined by a fixed income, such as Social Security, pensions, or retirement payments. **Fixed income** is defined as financial benefits that do not vary. While some people have an income from employment, investments, and property, such revenue is typically supplemental and fails to meet day-to-day living expenses. Living on a fixed income also makes the elderly more vulnerable to the effects of inflation (McKenzie, 1980).

The cost of benefits to the elderly has increased dramatically during the last two decades and now accounts for about one-third of the federal budget (not to mention billions of dollars in tax subsidies and nonpublic spending). These programs are not, however, adequately helping the elderly who really need it — the poor, sick, and incapacitated. On the contrary, the gap between the best-off and the worst-off among the elderly is widening, creating a crisis for those Americans who today depend on these programs for sheer survival. On the whole, America's aged continue to suffer from low or poverty-level incomes, escalating medical costs, poor housing, and a scarcity of supportive social services (Crystal, 1982; Olson, 1982).

Economic status also affects couples in other ways. The elderly with low incomes experience such factors as fear of crime, poor health, inadequate clothing, and poor housing with greater intensity and frequency than those with higher incomes. Low incomes, then, can be said to aggravate many of the problems associated with growing old.

Suggestions and proposals for improving the economic status of the elderly have been numerous and diverse — including providing more employment opportunities for the elderly, encouraging people to save more, expanding private pension coverage, and increasing Social Security benefits. Many feel that the benefits for women and low-income workers should be immediately improved. While each suggestion has its own merits, it is generally believed that the most feasible solution for the vast majority of the aged is the development of more adequate Social Security payments (Atchley, 1980; Schultz, 1981; Upp, 1983).

Social Adjustments

Retirement signifies the loss of job-related social contacts, although many people compensate for this by establishing new friendships. The retiree must adjust to the fact that a work-related reference group is now gone. The lack of feedback from employer and co-workers has important implications for one's sense of identity. This is thus a time to search elsewhere for a meaningful reference group, and realign and reassess one's self-image. More specifically, individuals need to establish who they are beyond the work they used to perform each day.

Individuals making the smoothest adjustments are those who develop new interests quickly. Healthy adjustment is characterized by managing to resist the shrinkage of one's social world. Discovering substitutes for the work one once did and maintaining a support network of friends are characteristic of those who age optimally during the retirement years (Cox, 1984).

Retirement can also bring both positive and negative dimensions to husband-wife relations. From a positive point of view, a couple can now spend more time together and can pursue mutual interests. Retirement brings the potential for years of relaxation and enjoyment of one another's company. On the negative side, increased time together may strain a marriage. The couple may get on one another's nerves and there may be an increase in household chores.

In support of these points, consider the research of Elizabeth Hill and Lorraine Dorfman (1982). The two investigators explored the reactions of women to their husband's retirements and found that a majority acknowledged the companionship and time availability that this life stage brings. It was also found, however, that there was another side to the picture. Among the more frequent complaints were financial difficulties and the fact that husbands did not have enough to do. Twenty-two percent of the respondents felt that retirement brought too much time together.

As far as how retirees spend their time, there is usually an alternation between dense periods devoted to commitments and relatively unstructured periods devoted to recreation. In general, those who learned to structure their time when they were younger continue to do so when they are retired. Leisure activities are probably the pivot of the temporal order of the elderly, and the fulfillment of commitments is undoubtedly carried out as a function of this pivot. It also appears that the interaction of economic status and personal characteristics is the determining factor in how time is managed (Delisle, 1982).

SEXUAL ACTIVITY DURING LATER LIFE

As we discovered in the last chapter, sexual relations can be a lifelong activity. Many elderly persons enjoy sex on a regular basis, unless, of course, ill health or the loss of a partner interferes. Decreases in sexual activity may also originate from social and emotional problems, and the side effects of certain medications (Butler and Lewis, 1981; George and Weiler, 1981; Martin 1981; Weg, 1983b).

Later-life sexual relations extend beyond having sound health and mind, at least according to noted sex researchers William Masters and Virginia Johnson (1981). They emphasize two other important criteria for lifelong sexual relations. One of these is an interesting and interested sexual partner; the other is the need to use the sexual organs on a regular basis as one ages. Their advice to the elderly, especially males, is to "use it or lose it."

Misconceptions about Later-Life Sexuality

Certain segments of society perceive the elderly as asexual, while others have developed a number of cruel misconceptions regarding the sex lives of aged people. Some maintain that sex is neither possible nor necessary during old age. Old men are often perceived as being either impotent or "dirty old men," and postmenopausal women who are interested in sex are viewed as "frustrated old women." Those elderly people who claim to be sexually active may be seen as either morally perverse or boastful and deceptive (Aiken, 1982; Ludeman, 1981).

Robert Butler and Myrna Lewis (1981) identify five false assumptions that society often makes about the sexuality of the aged. One, the elderly do not have sexual desires. Two, the elderly simply cannot make love even if they want to. Three, because the aged are physically fragile, sex is dangerous to their health. Four, the elderly are physically unattractive and, consequently, sexually undesirable. Five, the whole idea of sexuality among the aged is shameful and decidedly perverse. All of these assumptions are unwarranted, derogatory, and untrue. They represent blatant ageist attitudes that are upheld only by the uninformed and ignorant.

The need for sexual intimacy is just as important for aged couples as it is for younger partners.

Rates of Sexual Activity

Those elderly who have enjoyed long and stable sex lives without lengthly interruptions are more likely to remain sexually active longer than those whose history is different. Sex among the elderly is thus likely to mirror sexual activities of earlier life. For partners who have experienced long-standing conflicts, age alone may be used as an excuse to give up sexual relations that were never satisfactory (Hendricks and Hendricks, 1981; George, 1980).

A fairly extensive investigation of sexuality among the aged was undertaken by Bernard Starr and Marcella Weiner (1981). The two researchers explored the sexual lives of 800 men and women between the ages of 60 and 91. For most of those

surveyed, sexual activity was as good as it ever was, in some instances even better. More than half of the couples reported having sexual relations twice a week. Eighteen percent reported having sexual relations five times a week and 9 percent reported having intercourse daily.

This study also disproved the myth that sexual activity decreases significantly after age 60. The average number of sexual relations per week for those in their sixties was 1.5; for those in their seventies, it was 1.4 times per week; and for those in their eighties, it was 1.2 times per week. These changes are hardly as dramatic or significant as many choose to think.

In general, contemporary research finds that older women are less sexually active than older men. This, however, is usually due to factors other than those related to sexuality. For example, a large percentage of older women are widows. Also, since there are more older women than older men, the male has a wider range of choice, and a widow may be less able than a widower to find a suitable partner. Furthermore, it is considered more socially acceptable for an older man to marry a younger woman than for an older woman to marry a younger man. And society frowns on a woman's extramarital sexual activity more than on a man's (Aiken, 1982).

One study of 800 older women (Pearlman, Cohen, and Coburn, 1981) reinforces the notion that sexual activity is equally important for males and females. A clear majority of the respondents, ranging in age from the mid-thirties to the mid-sixties, reported that their sexual desire was as strong as before, if not stronger. Furthermore, most did not regard themselves as past their prime; on the contrary, many felt more sexually

desirable with age and viewed physical changes in a positive light.

LIVING ARRANGEMENTS

Patterns of Residency

An important task for the elderly couple is deciding whether to remain in the home in which their children were reared or to move. Suitable living arrangements, whether they be existing residences or new locations, are quite important to the elderly, because they spend so much time at home. Furthermore, suitable living arrangements and neighborhood belongingness have significant influences on one's morale and sense of well-being (Bohland and Herbert, 1983). Figure 17-2 shows the living arrangements of older men and women in 1982.

FIGURE 17-2   Living Arrangements of Older U.S. Men and Women in 1982

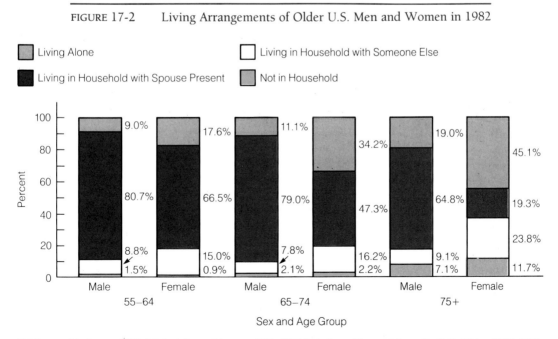

U.S. Bureau of the Census. (1982, October). *Decennial census: 1900–1980: Projections of the populations of the United States: 1982 to 2030, Current Population Report*, p-25, No. 922, Middle Series Projections.

Statistics tell us that retired couples prefer to remain in their long-term home. In fact, compared to all other segments of the population, the elderly change residency the least. Moving is disruptive at any age, but apparently more so for the elderly. Frequently, the actual problems of moving are compounded by social isolation, intergenerational conflict, or the feeling of imposing upon someone or being imposed upon. A major illness, financial difficulties, or perceptual-motor impairments may interfere even more. These problems are usually interdependent, and the move is imbedded in the overall complex aging process (U.S. Bureau of the Census, 1985; Lieberman and Tobin, 1983).

About a quarter of today's elderly live in rural areas, a third live in inner cities, and another 40 percent reside in older working-class neighborhoods on the fringes of central cities. In addition, there has recently been an increase in the numbers of elderly residing in rural areas, and that almost 70 percent of all heads of households over age 65 own their own homes (U.S. Bureau of the Census, 1985; Lichter, 1981).

GENERATIONAL RELATIONSHIPS

Types of Interaction and Care

Most aged persons keep in close touch with whatever kin they have. For some, this means considerable contact with aging brothers and sisters, but for most, the focus of kin relations is on children and grandchildren. Upwards of 80 percent of the aged have living children, and interaction with them is considerable (Lowy, 1985; Lee, 1980; Streib and Beck, 1980).

While regular interaction in general exists between old and young, there are interesting cross-cultural variations. Shirley Lockery's (1985) review of the literature, for example, indicates that patterns of interaction and care are especially evident among minority families. Both blacks and Hispanics, for example, have large and cohesive family systems that provide entertainment, assistance, and emotional support to their kin. Compared to nonminorities, the black family support

system in particular plays a more prominent role. Instead of serving as an alternative support system, the black family supplies lifelong care and assistance to elderly members. Nonminority families tend to be somewhat more detached from their relatives.

Lockery maintains that much of this is due to the fact that minority families have *had* to assume the role of caretaker. Minority families tend to rely on their own resources to meet the social, economic, and physical needs of the elderly. This is especially true as the elders' roles outside the family and their economic and physical status begin to decline. However, it should be added that not all minority elders can rely entirely on family care. Programs that serve the elderly need to be more responsive to the needs of the minority aged and their family caregivers.

All aging parents need to establish generational roles as they become the family system's elderly members. They pass the "baton of power" on to the middle generation, in the process attempting to retain as much independence and involvement as the family system allows. Through a great portion of the life cycle, help flows mainly from parents to children. This flow gradually reverses itself as parents get old and need help from their children. As a result, the adult offspring become the caregivers and the elderly parents the receivers. For some elderly couples, this can be distressing, particularly if children do not acknowledge the need and desire of their parents to lead independent lives. Often, ambivalence is reflected in over- or under-attachment. Consequently, it is important to assess the realities of everyone's perceptions of need (Okun, 1984).

Many people feel that the elderly are alienated from their families. This is largely a myth, however. The aged in contemporary society are neither rejected by their families nor alienated from their children. Most research (for example, Francis, 1984) points out, however, that the elderly often worry about their families no longer wanting or needing them. Furthermore, when old people have no children, a principle of family substitution seems to operate; and brothers, sisters, nephews,

CROSS-CULTURAL FOCUS

HOW FAMILIES LEND A HELPING HAND: PATTERNS OF INTERGENERATIONAL CARE

The manner in which younger generations offer care and assistance to aging family members has unique international variations. In Hungary, for example, care for older family members is required! Family members who avoid this responsibility can have their wages "docked" for services that must be provided by the state. Or they may even forfeit their right to inherit the parent's home. When younger family members have abandoned all responsibility and the elderly person must enter a nursing home, the family is assessed for the state's care. In addition, a criminal code in Hungary imposes penalties on persons who through neglect endanger the life or health of individuals unable to take care of themselves. In those instances where an older person owns a home but has no living children, a common practice is to take in boarders who will provide agreed upon care in exchange for the right to inherit the house or apartment. Such measures help to reduce housing shortages and allow the elderly to continue living in their own homes much longer than would otherwise be possible (Nusberg, 1983).

Or consider how social changes in Zaire, Africa, have affected generational relationships, particularly in rural locations. Village elders still continue to believe in the traditional concept of family and community unity in times of need. However, at the other extreme, family cohesion in Zaire is weakening because of increased mobility and shifting values. While traditional social values emphasize that the family remain close, new value systems among the young stress the personal search for autonomy and liberation from economic dependence on and control by the extended family. Serving as elders in the extended family as well as traditional providers, the elderly discover themselves torn, as well, between the desire for independence and the reality of economic dependence resulting from the deteriorating economic condition of so many rural locations (Masamba ma Mpolo, 1984).

Finally, let's examine several unique parallels between Australia and the United States in regard to how aged family members are cared for and treated. Regarding living arrangements, Australia is comparable to the United States of several decades ago. However, in both countries the elderly tend to have close social and emotional bonds with their offspring. While most of the elderly are fully independent, evidence indicates a two-way flow of closeness and assistance between young and old. When aged Australians and Americans are facing hardships, support from outside the family is provided overwhelmingly by the modified extended family, rather than the government. Among the more apparent differences between the countries, however, is that fewer older Australians live alone because more of the unmarried live with family or in institutions. Another difference between the two nations is the greater part played by government services in Australia (Kendig and Rowland, 1983).

and nieces often fill the roles and assume the obligations of children. The truly isolated old person, despite his or her prominence in the media, is a rarity in the United States (Shanas, 1982).

Another myth is that because of the existence of large human-service bureaucracies, families are no longer important as caretakers for the elderly. The family of the 1980s looms as an extremely important source of care and support, more so now, perhaps, than ever before. Moreover, research reveals (see Weiner, Teresi, and Steich, 1983; Cicirelli, 1983, 1981; Mitchell and Register, 1984) that individuals are seriously concerned about their elderly parents and want to be an integral part of the care and support they receive.

Usually retired persons reside near their children, although this is more true in urban environments than in rural ones, and females maintain closer relationships with other family members than do males. Couples tend to live nearer to the wife's parents and are likely to visit them more often. Also, working-class families are likely to have close family ties, and these ties are maintained by living near one another. Middle- and upper-class families have strong ties, too, but members are often geographically scattered because of career obligations (Barrow and Smith, 1983; Kauffman and Ames, 1983).

The emotional support given to aged parents is more critical to their psychological well-being than financial support. Moreover, a large percentage of retired persons refuse to accept financial assistance from their children, largely because they want to be financially independent. Independence, however, reaches beyond financial matters, and for many aged persons, a certain degree of ambivalence surrounds it. The aged generally do not wish to impose or to be independent, but neither do they wish to be neglected or ignored (Ward, 1984).

Grandparenthood

With advancing age comes the opportunity to forge new relationships within the family, as well as to continue long-standing ones. Grandparenthood is one of the former situations, a linkage of older and younger family members. Grandparenthood provides the opportunity to continue family patterns by transferring information from the more experienced to the neophyte generation (Brubaker, 1985).

Exploring the topic of grandparenthood and its relationship to marriage and family development is a fairly recent research pursuit. For too long, grandparenthood has been placed on the outer perimeter of family studies, its presence acknowledged but rarely researched. This is not the case today, though. As Vern Bengston (1985) observes, grandparenthood is a viable social role and a phase of the family life cycle that is being carefully explored by scholarly research.

Helen Kivnick's research (1982) reveals that grandparenthood can have a variety of meanings. For example, grandparenthood can create a sense of immortality. It can also be a way for persons to relive their lives through their grandchildren. Grandparenthood may also place individuals in the role of teacher or resource person. Finally, it can be an opportunity for grandparents to indulge in their grandchildren, in the process providing older generations with a new sense of purpose and meaning.

Grandchildren typically create a bond of common interest between the elderly and the younger couple. Becoming a grandparent also adds a new dimension to the lives of retirees, and, in most instances, this dimension is a positive one. Many feel that the connection between grandparent and grandchild is a vital one, an experience that brings gratifying rewards to both old and young (Kornhaber and Woodward, 1981). Joan Aldous (1985) adds that among grandparents, many enjoy the roles and importance that grandparenthood brings, not only in relation to their grandchildren, but to their own offspring as well.

Becoming a grandparent does not always have positive features however. For some, it represents an unmistakable sign of aging. There may be disagreements between grandparents and adult off-

Grandparenthood touches the lives of the aged in many ways.

spring regarding childrearing. Many resist the stereotyped qualities and expectations attached to grandparenthood, such as the time, care, and services grandparents are supposed to render to their grandchildren — some feel exploited when asked to baby-sit. One study (Cohler and Grunebaum, 1980) found that not all grandparents are willing to involve themselves in the perceived expectations of grandparenthood, most notably childcare.

The grandparenting role seems to have special significance for the grandmother. This does not mean that grandfathers do not enjoy grandparenting as much; rather, grandmothers seem to be the more active of the two. This is especially evident in such areas as childcare. One study (Fisher, 1983) also found that grandmothers tend to become more emotionally involved with their grandchildren than do grandfathers.

INSTITUTIONAL CARE FOR THE ELDERLY

Later life is not always characterized by good health and independent living arrangements. Indeed, care and attention are needed when older couples are disabled or can no longer take care of themselves. Often, assistance is provided by the family network, but there are those who need outside help in the form of institutional care. As far as the marriage structure is concerned, it may be that one, or both, of the partners require institutionalization. Overall, about 5 percent of the elderly population is institutionalized. While this is a small percentage, institutionalization has a profound impact on both resident and family alike. Indeed, for all concerned, life within a nursing home places the family in yet another transition and deserves more than just a comment in passing.

Types of Institutional Care Facilities

All institutional care facilities are not the same. On the contrary, nursing homes offer different categories of care, depending on the personal needs of the individual. Georgia Barrow and Patricia Smith (1983) expound upon four general categories of nursing-home facilities: **skilled-nursing**, **intermediate-care**, **residential-care**, and **adult daycare**.

Skilled-Nursing Facility   This facility provides full-time nursing care for persons with chronic illnesses or who are convalescing from an illness. Usually, registered nurses interpret orders, from physicians and supervise patient care. Licensed practical nurses provide the direct patient care. Patients usually require daily medications, injections, catheterizations, and cardiac or othopedic care.

Intermediate-Care Facility   Here, less emphasis is placed on intensive-care nursing and more on personal-care service. Residents are usually not in medical distress, but instead need assistance in daily routines, such as eating, dressing, or bathing. While a registered nurse may serve as a consultant, patient supervision is often handled by licensed practical nurses, and patient care is administered by aides.

Residential-Care Facility   This facility is intended for people who are functionally indepen-

---

There are many reactions to the nursing-home situation.

dent, but who desire a safe and sheltered environment. Social and recreational needs are stressed more than medical ones. Residential-care facilities also offer personal services, such as housekeeping and dietary requirements.

Adult Daycare Facility   Here people receive daily nursing, and nutritional and medical monitoring in a specially designated center, but maintain their own separate residences. This is a relatively recent innovation and is increasing in popularity. Some programs provide daycare supervision to children as well, creating a unique blend of young and old. Such a combination of ages is regarded by many as a positive arrangement enabling the young to better understand the old, and vice versa.

Adapting to Institutional Life

Adjusting to institutional care may pose some difficulties and problems. While there are many residents who adjust well many do not. For instance, some perceive nursing homes very negatively. Such feelings stem partly from a desire to remain in familiar surroundings, near relatives and friends. Most negative feelings about institutionalization, however, are brought on by a perceived loss of independence and a belief that placement in a nursing home represents formal proof that death is near. Many elderly also fear that once placed in a nursing home, they will be forgotten by their children (Atchley, 1980; Howsden, 1982).

This last fear is not factually supported, though. On the contrary, placement in a nursing home does not impede generational relationships. The most frequent visitors to nursing homes are children and grandchildren. Such generational interaction, it should be added, boosts resident morale and well-being (Greene and Monahan, 1982; Hook, Sobal, and Oak, 1982).

Many residents react negatively to the frequent *impersonalization* of nursing homes. Often this in-

---

APPLICATIONS

CHOOSING A NURSING HOME

Selecting a good institutional care facility for the elderly is not easy. They differ in methods of care and treatment, programming designs are not universal, and neither are costs. In an effort to narrow down the choices and find the best possible facility, Barbara Deane (1985) suggests the following:

1. Try to determine, with the aid of physicians or social workers if necessary, which type of facility your parent will need. Examine your parent's financial resources. Does he or she have private means? Does he or she qualify for government-funded nursing-home care? Some nursing homes will not accept nonprivate patients or those who will become so in the near future.

2. Try to make several visits — some unannounced — on weekends and late at night to each facility. Does the home seem clean and comfortable? Are the meeting rooms cheerful?

3. Find out if the staff/patient ratio is adequate. How many staff members are licensed professionals (RNs and LPNs)? Does the facility have a licensed physical therapist or a registered dietician on staff?

4. Make sure the staff is warm, sincere, and friendly and that they are willing to answer questions fully.   ▶

5. Look to see if most patients are clean and neat. Are those patients who are able to sit up dressed in street clothes by 10 A.M.?

6. Check the bulletin boards, dayrooms and other areas for evidence of programs and activities. Is there an activities director?

7. Make sure the food is of good quality and that daily nutritional needs are met. If possible, order a tray while visiting and try it yourself.

8. Ask if aides receive training from the professional staff. (Aides have the most direct contact with patients.)

9. What do others say about the facility? Do doctors, nurses and the families of patients recommend it? Nursing homes often are required to show the results of licensing inspections. Ask for them, but be aware that many inspections concentrate only on small violations.

10. See if the facility works with the families of its patients. Does it provide educational programs or support groups for patient's families?   ▬

cludes feeding and bathing in an assembly-line fashion and treating all of the residents alike, with little or no regard for individual differences. Sometimes residents are spoken to only when orders are given. Dress, manners, and conversations are under constant scrutiny. The result is the total visibility of the resident and a complete lack of privacy (Cox, 1984).

Because of this impersonalization, people tend to develop what is called **institutionalism**. This is a psychological state brought about by a depersonalized environment. Persons afflicted with institutionalism often develop automatic behaviors, ex-

pressionless faces, and general apathy. They become disinterested in their personal appearance and suffer from a deterioration of morale. Social relationships for many become nonexistent. In those nursing homes where the identity, interests, and strengths of the resident are not assessed and developed, degrees of institutionalism are likely to surface (Butler and Lewis, 1981).

Criticism of Institutional Care

Over the years, institutional care for the elderly has recieved criticism, much of it focusing on deper-

SOURCES OF INFORMATION ON INSTITUTIONAL CARE

- **American Association of Retired Persons (AARP)**, 1909 K Street NW, Washington, DC 20049. This organization publishes *A complete guide to long-term care: National continuing directory,* which lists 477 retirement communities and facilities by state that offer continuing-care contracts, plus information on sponsorship, entrance requirements, contracts, and legislation.
- **Aging Network Services**, Suite 821, 7315 Wisconsin Avenue West, Bethesda, MD 20814; (301) 897-5662; Attn: Barbara Kane. For a fee averaging $200, this case management agency will find a social worker anywhere in the United States to assess a parent's condition and arrange for necessary services.
- **Coalition of Institutionalized Age and Disabled**, Lehman College, Building T-3, Room 113-A, Bronx, NY 10468. The Coalition offers a residents' rights ▶

book, available for $5, that explains all rights of nursing home residents. A video on how to organize a residents' council is also available at $40 for a two-day rental.

■ **Friends and Relatives of Institutionalized Aged, Inc.**, 425 East 25 Street, New York, NY 10010. Interested persons can write for a free nursing home checklist.

■ "Home health care for the elderly: Programs, problems and perspectives," Chai R. Feldblum, *Harvard Journal on Legislation*, Winter 1985. For a good overview of home health care, send $4 to **Women's Research and Education Institute**, 204 Fourth Street SE, Washington, DC 20003.

■ **National Association for Home Care**, 519 C Street NE, Washington, DC 20002; (202) 547-7424. Contact your state association for home health-care referrals, which in turn can provide listings of proprietary, private, not-for-profit, voluntary, hospital-and hospice-based services, and agencies certified for Medicare.

■ **National Citizens Coalition for Nursing Home Reform**, 1825 Connecticut Avenue NW, Suite 417-B, Washington, DC 20009. This organization offers information and referrals on locating nursing homes in your parent's area.

■ **National Home Caring Council**, 235 Park Avenue, New York, NY 10003. For a booklet on how to locate the best home-care personnel, *All about home care: A consumer's guide,* send $2 with a self-addressed business envelope containing 39 cents postage.

■ **National Institute on Adult Day Care**, 600 Maryland Avenue SW, West Wing 100, Washington, DC 20024. Persons can write for referrals to centers in specific communities from this organization. Also, see Yellow Page listings under "Senior Citizens"; area agencies on aging; local social service and health departments.

■ **Nursing Home Residents Advisory Council**, 3231 First Avenue South, Minneapolis, MN 55408. This is an independent organization composed of family (residents and relatives) councils in that state; it acts as a consultant and provides resource materials to people from other states wishing to establish family councils.

■ **Telephone Yellow Pages**. Look under Aging, Home Health Care, Medical Aides, Nurses, Nursing Homes, and Senior Citizens. In some major metropolitan areas, **Silver Pages** are becoming available with listings that are geared to needs of the elderly.

Adapted from Gruber, 1985. ■

sonalized treatment of the residents and administrative inefficiency. Some criticize the program in general, citing limited intellectual stimulation of the residents. Stated simply, the elderly simply have nothing to do in many institutions. There are also many nursing homes in the nation that are substandard, in some instances failing to provide minimal conditions for humane treatment (Kalish, 1982a; Vladeck, 1980).

How can nursing homes be upgraded? Numerous recommendations have been made, including the improvement of the psychological and social climate. Efforts have to be made to promote the growth of new relationships to take the place of those lost in the process of growing old or sick. Social integration of long-term care residents is critical, particularly if social isolation and detachment are to be avoided. Residents need to participate as much as possible in establishing the ground rules for their living situations because some degree of choice is important in preserving one's self-concept and identity. The physical structuring of space should offer freedom and privacy as well as safety. Finally, regular interpersonal familial contacts with the residents are critical as the transition to the nursing home is made. This conveys to residents that they are not alone and isolated, are not discarded, and that they are still valued (Kermis, 1984; Jones, 1982).

Improving the professionalism of the institution's personnel, including doctors is also recommended. All too often, doctors have little contact with nursing-home patients. This is due to several factors, not the least of which is that many physicians regard elderly, institutionalized patients as depressing. Low reimbursements from **medicaid** and **medicare** also contribute to the problem. Medicaid is a government-sponsored medical care plan for welfare clients; Medicare, also federally sponsored, is an insurance program that partially finances health-care costs for the aged. Increasing all areas of medical coverage, including psychiatric and dental care, is a consistent theme in the literature. So too is implementing more in-service training on all facets of geriatric health care (Mitchell, 1982; Fennett, 1980).

In recent years, higher standards of accreditation and certification have improved many institu-

CROSS-CULTURAL FOCUS

UPGRADING INSTITUTIONAL CARE IN FRANCE

Similar to the United States and other nations, France is seeking to upgrade its institutional programming for the elderly. One unique difference, though, is that a group of retired persons has taken the initiative of improving the quality of life in institutional care by working with both elderly residents and managment. Called the "Forum," this organization has found that the attitudes of both groups need to be changed—from a passive attitude on the part of the elderly to one where they begin to take greater charge of their environment; and from staff attitudes encouraging dependency, to ones maximizing the capabilities and potential of the residents.

To foster such change, the Forum encourages the creation of craft workshops in order to start communication among residents. Community residents are invited to the workshops from time to time in order to open the institution to the outside world. In one home, the workshops were able to dispense with their outside party within two months as residents assumed responsibility for their own activities. In another home, regular outings with older people from the larger community have met with success. The Forum also provides training sessions to work on staff and management attitudes so that they may obtain a better understanding of the psychological, socio-cultural, and emotional needs of the elderly.

Adapted from Nusberg, 1982.

tions and closed down those deemed inferior and inadequate. Continued investigation and reform are needed to insure that the best possible care and treatment are available at these facilities. At the very least, institutional care needs to be made more accountable in years to come (Spilerman and Litwak, 1982; Vladeck, 1980; Jones, 1982).

CHAPTER HIGHLIGHTS

Most retired couples report considerable satisfaction with their marriages. Retirement is responsible for bringing couples closer together. After retirement, the husband frequently assumes new domestic responsibilities, and the involvement in household chores brings about changes in his domestic orientation and self-image. Because certain household chores and tasks are now shared, many marriages acquire an egalitarian flavor. We remind the reader, though, that more research needs to focus on transitions related to female retirement, particularly domestic implications.

Retirement also brings the need for adjustments and adaptations. Departing from the workplace requires psychological adjustment since one's identity is usually yoked to one's vocation. Financial adjustments, however, often represent the biggest adjustment, and this chapter explored the economic situation of retired couples. We also acknowledged the social adjustments required of retirees, most notably the need to replace work-related reference groups.

Sexual relations can be a lifelong activity. Unfortunately, numerous myths abound about the elderly's sexuality. Decreased sexual activity appears to originate not so much from the aging process as from social and emotional difficulties. Those couples who have had active sex lives in the past are likely to remain sexually active during their retirement years. Generally speaking, older men are more sexually active than older women, although we learned that this may be owing to factors other than differences in the sex drive.

Most retired couples do not want to change their residence, primarily because they do not want to face adjustment difficulties associated with moving. Declining health and limited income are other anchoring variables. The notion that later-life couples are alienated and ignored by relatives is a myth. We tried to shatter this myth by exploring generational relationships, not only in the United States but in other nations as well.

Kin relations for most retired couples focus on their children and grandchildren. Many aged people live near their children and interact rather frequently, although this is more true in urban environments than in rural settings. As far as family relationships are concerned, the emotional support given to aged parents is especially important. At this point in the family life cycle, grown children become the caregivers and the elderly parents the receivers.

Grandchildren add a new dimension to the lives of middle-aged and retired couples. Although grandparenthood is frequently seen as a maternal experience, grandfathers typically become more involved with their grandchildren after retirement. Grandparenthood may have numerous meanings to the individual, including a sense of immortality, a way to relive one's childhood, the opportunity to serve as a resource person, or a chance to acquire new meaning or purpose.

When the elderly are afflicted with a disability or can no longer care for themselves, institutional care may be required. This is a transition that affects the resident as well as the family as a whole. Problems of adjustment typically center around deterioration of morale and social relationships, as well as a perceived loss of independence and abandonment. Smooth transitions to institutional care are made when the strengths, interests, and skills of the resident are assessed, respected, and developed. Four types of institutions for the elderly were discussed in this chapter: skilled-nursing facilities, intermediate-care facilities, residential-care facilities, and adult daycare facilities. All types of institutional care facilities have recently fallen under the scrutiny of concerned officials, and efforts have been made to improve the quality and standard of living for the residents.

KEY TERMS

adult day-care facility

ageism

fixed income

medicaid

medicare

institutionalism

intermediate-care facility

residential-care facility

skilled-nursing facility

RECOMMENDED READINGS

Bengston, V. L., and Robertson, J. R. (Eds.). (1985). *Grandparenthood: Emerging perspectives on traditional roles.* Beverly Hills, CA: Sage. Among the topics covered are styles of grandparenting, perspectives on the roles of grandparents, and parent-adult relations as affected by grandparent status.

Brubaker, T. H. (1985). *Later life families.* Beverly Hills, CA: Sage. An expert in the field explores the dynamics of family life among aging couples. Topics include generational relationships, grandparenthood, and widowhood.

Cicirelli, V. G. (1981). *Helping elderly parents: Role of adult children.* Boston, MA: Auburn House. The needs of later-life couples and how younger generations can help are addressed in a sensitive and informative way.

Francis, D. (1984). *Will you still need me, will you still feed me, when I'm 84?* Bloomington: Indiana University Press. The author compares two groups of elderly Jews, one in America and the other in England, to determine how they've adapted to aging in modern society. The findings are quite thought-provoking.

McPherson, B. D. (1983). *Aging as a social process.* Toronto: Butterworths. Many topics are covered in this book, including role transitions and status passages within the family, and intergenerational family relations.

Pelham, A. O., and Clark, W. F. (Eds.). (1985). *Managing home care for the elderly.* New York: Springer. This reader focuses on alternatives to institutional care.

Peterson, W., and Quadagni, J. (Eds.). (1985). *Social bonds in later life.* Beverly Hills, CA: Sage. The nature of family life during the retirement years is covered in Part One of this reader.

Sauer, W. J., and Coward, R. T. (Eds.). (1985). *Social support networks and the care of the elderly.* New York: Springer. Topics include children and their elderly parents, husband and wife social networks, extended kin as helping networks, and the social networks of ethnic minorities.

Szinovacz, M. (Ed.). (1982). *Women's retirement.* Beverly Hills, CA: Sage. A diversity of topics on the female retirement experience are presented, including retirement preparation and necessary adjustments.

Weg, R. B. (Ed.). (1983). *Sexuality in the later years: Roles and behaviors.* New York: Academic Press. This reader addresses itself to the topic of sexuality among the aged. Many points of view are raised on a wide assortment of topics.

18

Endings and New Beginnings

CONTENTS

CONTEMPLATIONS

■ Author Stanley Keleman writes that working through the tragedy of loss allows us to redefine our relationships, to surrender what is gone, and to accept what is alive. In the process, we often discover that we're stronger, perhaps better able to face life and its many inherent struggles. Do you agree with such perceptions? How might this apply to the loss of a partner and the pain that accompanies bereavement and grief? Such sensitive topics will provide the foundation for this chapter.

■ Attitudes toward death and dying offer interesting insight into cultures and societies. For example, Eastern cultures perceive death as an integral part of life. In support of this, Hinduism teaches that the body passes through the life states and at death, the soul assumes another body. In Western culture, however, death is perceived as being apart from life, an event to be feared rather than accepted. Why is this so? What factors contribute to our uneasiness and anxiety toward death? How might such attitudes and feelings be changed?

■ Restructuring one's existence after a loved one has died represents the most difficult of all life challenges. Some survivors emerge from grief with renewed strength, while others receive emotional and spiritual injuries from which they never recover. What factors determine successful adjustment? What are some of the problems that the bereaved face? In this chapter, we'll explore the nature of bereavement, including the stages that typically accompany grief and mourning. In the process, we'll discuss the psychological adaptations needed for the survivors to come to grips with loss, and to progress with hope to their changed world.

The death of a spouse is a serious crisis at any time, but especially so during the retirement years. The loss of a loved one can abruptly remove human companionship and the major source of love and caring from one's life. For the surviving spouse, the remaining years of life are usually spent alone, and the accompanying grief often takes a severe toll on health and well-being. Of course, the physical and psychological aftermath of a spouse's death will depend on the state of the marriage before the loss (Bell, 1981; Hendricks and Hendricks, 1981).

Statistically speaking, there are more widows than widowers in the United States. This is because mortality rates are lower for women and because they tend to marry earlier than men, thus outliving their husbands. On the average, women live seven more years than men. (Figure 18-1 compares the overall life expectancy of the two sexes.)

Statistics also tell us that of men 65 years of age and older, 81.8 percent are married and 9 percent are widowed. Of women 65 years of age and older, 50.6 percent are married and 39.2 percent are widowed. In 1982, there were approximately 10.7 million widows and 1.9 million widowers in the United States. Consider the following:

■ About three out of every four American wives can expect to become widows at some point in their lives.

■ There are six widows for every widower.

■ The average age of widowhood is fifty-six.

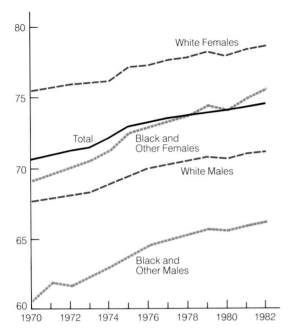

Source: U.S. Bureau of the Census, *Statistical Abstracts,* 1984.

FIGURE 18-1   Life Expectancy at Birth (years)

- More than half of all women over sixty-five are widows, and 70 percent of those over seventy-five are widows.

- Six out of ten widows live alone. (U. S. Bureau of the Census, 1985; Seskin, 1985)

These numbers paint a fairly complete picture of widowhood. While many men become widowers, their numbers come nowhere near the total of women affected. It tends to be middle-aged females who are most often required to embark on the life passage associated with widowhood and elderly women who are required to hold to the courses charted for surviving spouses (Balkwell, 1981).

Throughout this text, we have tried to emphasize the transitional quality of marriage and family life. As we near the end of our journey, we encounter the most difficult transition of all: losing a loved one and having to continue on with life alone. How might the life passage of widowhood be described? What are the demands and complexities associated with the loss of a loved one? What are some of the coping mechanisms employed by survivors? This chapter will seek answers to these and other questions in this final developmental exploration of the marriage and family life cycle.

CONFRONTING DEATH AND LOSS

None of us is ever fully prepared for death. Rather, death seems always sudden, even in those cases where it is anticipated. And when the reality of the death of a loved one sinks in, we are shaken to our cores. Our own feeling of immortality is shattered when a spouse dies. For although marriage vows say "Till death do us part," few of us expect it to happen — at least, not to us (Loewinsohn, 1984).

This denial of our own death — and that of loved ones — is a common theme in contemporary society. In Western culture, the topic of death seems to be taboo. It is a sensitive topic, one that is avoided and often repressed. Some individuals try to deny it; others live in fear of it. Many medical specialists are also uncomfortable with the subject and do not like to be present when their patients die (Rhodes and Vedder, 1983; Aiken, 1982).

Often, the dying are isolated from all but close relatives, doctors, and nurses. We frequently give hospitals the responsibility of caring for the dying, although many are poorly equipped to deal with the task. The ease with which dying can be hidden away makes it possible to deny death's presence. So frequently it is treated as a closely guarded secret, even when it is obvious to everyone around (Charmaz, 1980).

Partly because of this isolation and denial, death arouses awe and dread, making it even more difficult to understand and accept its inevitability. Many don't understand death because they're not given the chance to understand it (Nisbet, 1984).

This distancing of the dying from the living also offers a striking contrast to past societal customs. Death before the turn of the century usually occurred at home, with the remaining family present

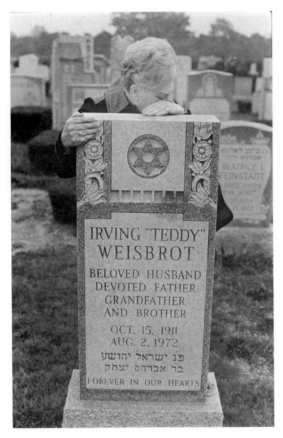

The pain of loss can be expressed in a variety of ways.

and dealing with the body as an ordinary part of domestic life. Today, people die away from the home, and the task of preparing the dead for burial is handled by others who are paid to perform these services. Our personal participation is minimal (DeSpelder and Strickland, 1986). As a result, death has become bureaucratized and impersonal.

The denial of death usually results in limited self-growth. Conversely, seeking to comprehend it creates a healthy dimension to our existence. Death always has been and always will be with us. Because it is an integral part of human existence, it will always loom as a subject of deep concern. It is our task, then, to learn to view death not as a dreaded stranger, but rather as an expected com-

panion to life. If this can be accomplished, we can learn to fill our lives with more meaning, living with a full appreciation of our finiteness and of the limitations on our time here (Shneidman, 1984; Kubler-Ross, 1981).

Sarah Cirese (1985) agrees that an acceptance of death facilitates a fuller and richer life, especially for those of us involved in a relationship. By accepting our mortality, we can learn not to leave unfinished business, such as ill feelings, unspoken feelings, or thank-yous, behind. We can know better that everything we do in life counts, that we do not have forever to complete our work, that time as measured by the clock or calendar does not always matter. What matters most is the quality of our time, what we do with the time we are given. We are reminded, in accepting death, of our fallibilities, our limits, and our small place in the vastness of the universe. Death teaches us humility. Accepting death frees us to let go of things, of relationships, and even ideas and values to which we cling too tightly. Accepting death, too, reminds us of the importance of getting and being close, of developing and maintaining intimacy, of keeping in touch with those for whom we care.

DEATH AS A FAMILY STRESSOR

In Chapter 14 we explored the concepts of stress and crises, including their disruptive potential. Few, if any, life events parallel the stress associated with spouse loss. Indeed, some contemporary researchers feel that the death of one's spouse looms as the most stressful life event ever to be encountered (see Brown, 1984; Curtis and Detert, 1981; Schwartz, 1982; Nuernberger, 1981; Shaffer, 1982).

Before we explore how death acts as a family stressor, we need to clarify some terminology. **Bereavement** is defined as the loss of a loved one by death. It is a statement of fact and does not embody one's reactions to a loss. **Grief** refers to the deep and poignant distress caused by such a loss. It represents one's emotional reaction to another's death.

THE DEATH OF A CHILD AND PARENTAL BEREAVEMENT

The usual expectation is that offspring will outlive the parent. Lynne DeSpelder and Albert Strickland (1986) write that it is almost expected that the child will carry something of the parent into the future, even after the parent's death. In this sense, the child's very existence grants a kind of immortality to the parent, and this is taken away if the child dies before the parent's own life has ended. The parent's plans for the child are suddenly of no consequence.

DeSpelder and Strickland feel that parental bereavement spans the marriage and family life cycle. It is just as intense for 30-year-old parents as it is for 60-year-olds. Their dreams, fantasies, and plans may be as strong for an infant as they are for a teenaged or adult offspring.

The death of a child often brings chaos into the lives of parents. Many times, loss of a direction is felt, which is part of a pervasive sense that parents have been robbed of a past and a future. And since each parent may have separate grieving styles, they may be left feeling unsupported and isolated by the only person who understands the magnitude of the loss.

John Crosby and Nancy Jose (1983) point out that while death is usually the most catastrophic event for an individual or family, the *degree* of stress and grief experienced is dependent on several interacting variables, the first of which is how death occurs. Unexpected death often creates extreme stress because survivors are totally unprepared for the loss and the family system is thrown off balance. Other forms of death produce different levels of stress (for example, the emotional depletion that often accompanies anticipated, but prolonged death). All forms of death require their share of **grief work**; that is, coming to terms with the physical and emotional demands brought on by another's death. However, these demands may occur at various times in the overall process of dying and create different stress levels.

Another variable to consider is whether or not the surviving spouse is experiencing other stressors. The death of a loved one usually increases the level of stress to an almost intolerable level. Thus, if personal and interpersonal resources are depleted by other stressors, little is left in reserve to cope with the death. The accumulation of many stressors acting upon the survivor may lead to or compound a crisis, taxing the person's resources

and coping ability to such a point that coping becomes increasingly dysfunctional.

A third variable contributing to the survivor's stress is the numerous "arrangements" that require attention following the death. Initially, for example, the spouse must deal with the funeral and burial. This includes contacts with morticians, cemeteries, and well-meaning sympathizers. Moreover, the survivor is inundated by a myriad of professionals involved in settling the estate (lawyers, employers, insurance company and government employees). Taken together, these may greatly intensify the stressfulness of death.

The overall transition period to widowhood itself will produce stress. Among the necessary adjustments are role realignments, the need to establish new patterns of authority and decision-making; loss of economic (financial) security; establishing a new social support network; concern for children's and other family members' grief; and finally, perhaps most stressful of all the loss of emotional support (Crosby and Jose, 1983).

Financial difficulties can be especially stressful. It is very likely that women who become widows today may never have worked outside the home, and they typically have extremely limited

RESEARCH HIGHLIGHT

THE STRESSES OF SURVIVAL CAN DELIVER A MORTAL BLOW

Social scientists have long recognized that few traumas are as hard to bear as the death of a spouse. For the survivor, intense distress can lead to serious psychological and physical ailments. A study of survivors shows that widowhood dramatically raises the chances of death for some survivors — men — while the death of a husband appears to have little effect on women's mortality rates.

The study, undertaken by Knud Helsing, Moyses Szklo, and George Comstock (1981), followed the lives of 1,204 rural men and 2,828 rural women who were widowed. With each spouse's death, the survivor was matched with a still married person; cross-referenced for comparison not only by race, sex, and age; but also by such factors as years of schooling, age at first marriage, frequency of church attendance, whether the person smoked cigarettes, and the number of bathrooms and number of animals on the premises. The two groups were then studied for ten years.

The study revealed a most unexpected finding: there was no evidence that either men or women were significantly more likely to die in the early months after bereavement. That was an unexpected finding since the researcher's original premise was that the stress brought on by the loss of a spouse would show up in mortality very quickly. Instead, it was the stressful life situation that followed that seemed to be hard on people, especially men. The overall mortality rate was 26 percent higher for widowers than for married men, compared with only a 3.8 percent difference in the rate between widows and married women. For widowers aged 55 to 64, the mortality rate was almost 61 percent higher than for married men in the same age group.

The researchers could not say why wives were less affected by the loss of a spouse than husbands, except to suggest that the same physiological and psychological differences that give females greater longevity than males also act to make females more resistant to the stress of widowhood.

One of the study's most important findings was that remarriage by widowers dramatically lowered their mortality rates. In men under 55 who remarried — and at least half of them did — the death rate was at least 70 percent lower than for those who did not; in men aged 55 to 64, it was 50 percent lower. In fact, death rates for widowers who remarried were even lower than for men in the same age groups who were married throughout the period of the study.

One other finding was equally devastating for both widowed men and women: a dramatic rise in mortality — by three or four times — if a widowed person moved into a retirement or nursing home because of illness or inability to live with other family members. The researchers also found that there was no consolation in living alone; this too contributed to higher mortality rates. Even allowing for the fact that it may be the less-healthy widowed who fail to remarry, the researchers felt it is fair ▶

to ask whether it may be marriage — or remarriage — that provides the care and social support that tends to reduce mortality. If a causal connection between remarriage and reduced mortality can be established, they concluded, changes in Social Security and income tax laws to encourage remarriage of the widowed might be justified as public health measures. ■

retirement benefits. Compounding the problem is that the majority of men die without leaving a will, precipitating lengthy and confusing court proceedings. Many widows can barely live above the poverty line and sustain an adequate lifestyle.

PATHS TO WIDOWHOOD

Timothy Brubaker (1985) points out that becoming widowed is a process and an event that differs for many people, and it is a role for which there is little prior training in what to do and what not to do. Furthermore, there is little positive anticipation associated with becoming a widow. The end of marriage and the beginning of widowhood occur in several different ways. While we briefly touched on some of these variations earlier in our discussion of stress, they deserve greater clarification.

One variation is that a person can suddenly and unexpectedly become widowed. There may be little indication that the husband or wife is going to die, and the death abruptly concludes the marital relationship. An example might be when a person who has been in reasonably good health suffers a massive heart attack at work. The individual may have been in his/her late fifties or early sixties and planning for retirement with his/her spouse. There was no opportunity for the survivor to anticipate the loss of his/her mate. Indeed, the survivor was expecting to enjoy several retirement years with his/her spouse.

A second variation of widowhood occurs when the death of a spouse is expected and signifies the end of a struggle with severe health problems that had changed the couple's lifestyle. The illness may

have been the focal point of the couple's life for several years. Often the survivor cares for the patient at home for many years, and toward the end, the care shifts to a hospital. With the move to the hospital, the surviving spouse reorganizes life around the dependent mate in an institutional setting. The death is the final release from the pain and suffering experienced by both the deceased and the survivor.

For surviving spouses, widowhood represents another transition in the marriage and family life cycle.

One other variation of widowhood occurs when a spouse is ill, but death is *not* expected. Here the deceased spouse's illness is not seen as life threatening, or the couple is not informed about the severity of the health condition. For this group of widows, the illness does not lead to a complete reorganization of their lives around caregiving. They typically live life with their mates in a somewhat restricted manner because of the health problem, but it is something with which they cope and death is not seen as being imminent. Their plans as a couple may have been limited as a result of the illness, but they anticipate life together in the future. Consequently, the marital situation before the death differs from that of the sudden or expected widows.

STAGES OF GRIEF AND MOURNING

People will react in different ways when death strikes close to home. The more common emotional reactions include a mixture of sorrow, misery, emptiness, and loneliness. Some report a general feeling of "numbness" and only vague awareness of the events taking place around them. For others, life may not seem worth living anymore, and some may even look forward to their own early death. Individuals will also differ widely in their appraisal of the death event itself. It may be perceived as a tragedy, a blessing, a mystery, a transition, or a release (Vail, 1982).

Grieving appears to follow a chronology of stages. This was recently borne out in an impressive research investigation launched by Phyllis Silverman (1986). Working with 233 widows, she observed that three stages in the overall healing process appear to exist: **impact, recoil, and accommodation**. While Silverman's research was confined to females, it is conceivable that males pass through similar stages.

The Impact Stage

During this initial stage, widows typically report that numbness envelops them when they are told that their husbands have died. Many experience a sense of disbelief, and their behavior becomes still and robotlike. The woman's new legal status as a widow has no social and emotional meaning to her; she automatically thinks and acts as her husband's wife, still tailoring her behavior as she probably did while he was alive, and doing things that would please him. Continuing to play the role of wife, she knows how to behave and what is expected of her. Her numbness helps her to perform her role reflexively.

The length and extent of a widow's numbness will vary depending on whether her husband died suddenly or after a long illness. When death follows a long illness, the widow inevitably feels a certain sense of relief, and the shock is not as profound as when death comes as a surprise. This observation by Silverman is compatible with our earlier discussion of stress and the variations that can exist at the moment of death.

Interestingly, the numbness of this stage can be a valuable assest in averting a state of collapse. In this sense, it may help the survivor handle emotionally taxing chores such as arranging the funeral. However, this protection against acute anguish is only temporary, and widows need the support and assistance of loved ones.

As far as the latter is concerned, most widows are grateful that someone else is willing to help and even think for them at this time. Relatives and friends usually help arrange the funeral, help with shopping and housekeeping chores, or chauffeur the children to visit friends. At a time when she is least able, the widow must begin dealing with a complex set of financial issues, and others may be able to help with these matters as well. Among other tasks, the widow has to find out about her insurance, collect back pay, determine what money she has for current expenses, apply for Social Security and veteran's benefits, and, if there is an estate, deal with the lawyer. Some things only she can handle. Eventually she will have to go to bed in the empty bedroom, see her husband's belongings around her, eat alone, and deal, by herself, with household routines.

Silverman points out that the impact stage has no predictable duration. Nor is it a purely numb period without any breakthrough of feelings. The widow does have many concrete chores that involve her in necessary and important activities, and these keep her engaged in the real world. However, the meaning of what has happened also begins to enter her consciousness. The people who are available to help at this time may be deceived by her outward reactions; they may think that she is doing well, and be pleased with how well she is holding up; they are, however, unaware, and she also may not recognize, that this is but the first stage in a long and painful process.

The Recoil Stage

During this stage, the numbness will begin to diminish and most widows will fight its departure. With the return of feelings comes the full realization of the loss. Many will have avoided the meaning of the loss, and may continue to do so as their new reality intermittently breaks through.

At this time, many widows report that a part of them is missing. Also common is a loss of appetite, or sleeplessness, or, conversely, a desire to eat or sleep all of the time. A widow may find herself impatient and restless, not wanting to be with people but not wanting to be alone either. She may begin to feel increasingly misunderstood, that friends and relatives are becoming impatient and uncomfortable with her continuing grief. Some women feel that if they can simply keep themselves so busy that they grow too tired to do anything except fall into bed, they will be able to keep their feelings at bay. This way, they can avoid thinking about either the past or the future. (Table 18-1 charts some feelings, physical reactions, and coping mechanisms that typically accompany loss.)

It is not uncommon for a survivor to review the circumstances of their spouse's death over and over again, wondering whether anything could have been done. Feelings of anger and remorse are not unusual. The widow may feel angry that her husband did not take better care of himself. She may also feel remorseful that she did not do enough for him.

Silverman acknowledges that many widows are generally not prepared for the miserable feelings that are experienced. But they have to discover that there is no easy way around their misery, given

TABLE 18-1

How People Deal with Death

Feelings Accompanying Loss	Physical Reactions Accompanying Loss	Coping Mechanisms
Depression	Crying	Talking about the loss
Emptiness	Insomnia	Gradually accepting it
Anger	Headache	Crying
Loneliness	Exhaustion	Time
Frustration	Digestive disturbances	Support of friends
Helplessness	Weakness	Keeping busy
Shock	Nausea	Thinking of all the good things
Disbelief	Numbness	Family support
Loss of self-confidence	Chills	Developing new relationships
Guilt	Cold	Writing down feelings
Fear	Backache	Religious beliefs
Rejection	Labored breathing	Developing new interests
Self-pity	Vomiting	Replacement
Lost	Skin rash	Philosophical beliefs
Denial		Body relaxation
Hatred		Drawing feelings (art)

Source: Adapted from Lagrand, 1981.

THE GUILT OF SURVIVORS: COULD I HAVE DONE MORE?

The expression of guilt is inevitable in the face of loss. Whatever the situation, in one way or another, survivors are apt to blame themselves. Ann Stearns (1984) points out, though, that while survivors may genuinely *feel* blameworthy, usually their self-blaming thoughts are unrealistic; in other words, they are overly harsh with themselves. They stretch their imaginations to believe that they are responsible for not anticipating or preventing events which ordinary mortals could not possibly have prevented. Or twisting human-size mistakes into criminal proportions, they feel guilty — as though they had intentionally brought harm to themselves or to their spouses, which is rarely the case. The following are a few examples of unrealistic guilt:

"If I had stayed home that night, the accident would never have happened."
"Maybe if I weren't so selfish and caught up in my work, our marriage could have lasted . . . "
"I never had the chance to tell him/her how much he/she really meant to me."
It is normal to feel that one could have better loved a departed spouse. However, Stearn emphasizes that we all feel guilty during a time of loss. What survivors need is a support system to help them sort out these feelings, one that can minimize unrealistic guilt. For example, a comforting friend can help to separate realistic from unrealistic guilt by asking questions: Why are you the only one to blame? How could you have known that? Are you expecting yourself to have known things that couldn't have been known with certainty? Are you tormenting yourself with thoughts of self-blame, as if no other reason or explanation could account for the events that happened?

As time passes, survivors typically learn from the kindness of others to ask themselves questions that are similarly kind, but objective. Gradually their feelings of unrealistic guilt begin to diminish as they gain a more accurate perspective.

the nature and meaning of their loss. If they know that their suffering is normal and inevitable, they may find it easier to endure. Of course, this underscores the need for a reassuring and trusting support network.

Sorting through these negative feelings and confronting the other demands of bereavement can produce a wide range of behaviors. Some of these will be healthy and productive, others will not. John Crosby and Nancy Jose (1983) expound upon the diversity of behaviors by referring to **dysfunctional** and **functional** modes of coping. The following represents some examples of dysfunctional coping:

Avoidance   This is often called the "keep busy" strategy, and many feel that it is therapeutic and functional. However, when used over an extended time it more often than not is a dysfunctional ploy which may encourage the denial of a loved one's death. By keeping busy we defend ourselves against the anxiety that arises when we are "doing nothing." Keeping busy enables survivors to put their mental-emotional energy into the task at hand, thus diverting thoughts and feelings away from death. Keeping busy is, in itself, not wrong; the wrongness is in the fact that it turns into a dysfunctional strategy when it becomes the primary method of coping.

A variation of the above is the "getting away" or "taking a trip" strategy. Grief resolution requires coming to grips with loss, loneliness, personal effects, routines, and all manner of behaviors of the deceased. When the bereaved takes a trip (visits relatives, vacations, and so on) soon after death of a loved one, the grief work is *partially* postponed. The portion that is postponed is precisely that which needs to be confronted first. A person only needs to fantasize coming back home after such a trip (walking into the empty house, the empty bedroom, going through his closet) in order to appreciate that the first level of grief work needs to be dealt with in the context of the deceased person's position, role, and immediate family environment prior to death.

Obliteration   Obliteration is an attempt to erase the former existence of the deceased. Oblit-eration goes beyond denial and avoidance. Obliteration involves the attempt to totally erase the deceased person's prior existence. This may involve disposal of all personal effects, belongings, collections, hobbies, pictures, and other possessions. Obliteration is akin to "wiping away" all memory traces and clues.

Idolization   One other form of dysfunctional strategy is idolization, just the opposite of obliteration. Idolization makes the deceased greater in death than he/she was in life. The deceased is endowed with a quality of perfection that is supra-human. The survivor tries to restore life by holding fast to the belief that the deceased is really present. Personal effects are left intact; possessions, mementos, pictures, and hobbies are endowed with an importance they previously lacked. No survivor can ever hope to measure up, and shame, self-

---

HIGH RISK WIDOWS

Working through one's grief is a difficult and demanding task. Betty Wylie (1982) observes that no part of it can be shirked or avoided; it will only have to be faced and worked through at a later date, along with the complications that often result from denial or repression.

Some widows fare better than others in the overall grieving process. This fact was borne out in research undertaken by Mary Vachon (1982). She found that the following groups of widows encounter the most difficulty:

- Those with poor social support.

- Those under 45 whose husbands died suddenly; or, conversely, those over 65, whose husbands suffered a lingering death.

- Those with an ambivalent relationship to the deceased (those who have the most difficulty recovering are those who had the worst marriages).

- Those who were denied the grief experience because of minimal funeral ceremonies.

- Those with previous psychiatric difficulties. (If they were suicidal before, their chances of death by sucide now are greatly increased; suicide is a high risk for the first five years following a spouse's death.)

Compared to other widows, the above groups are more likely to experience higher levels of stress and anxiety. And, in addition to psychological maladjustment, there are physical consequences; for example, hospital admission rates are higher for these women, as are health-related disorders.

The support of loved ones usually facilitates constructive grief work.

doubt, guilt, and inferiority are prescribed feelings for those who must live in the wake of such splendor.

Patterns of Functional Coping   Crosby and Jose (1983) point out that constructive grief work relies on the support network being permissive of feelings. Additionally, the network needs to be positively accepting and supportive. This implies the ability to engage in honest and frank types of communication, where energies are directed at the actual loss as experienced collectively and individually. In order to accomplish this freedom of mutual acceptance, there needs to be an absence of scapegoating, blaming, excessive caretaking, and computer-like rationale which substitutes reason and logic for feelings and emotion. Commitment to the process of communication creates an atmosphere or context wherein the individuals may feel secure in their grief. With this, survivors are free to self-disclose. They are free to feel whatever they feel, but they are also free to challenge their own beliefs and the beliefs of others, knowing that feel-

ings are often the result of internalized beliefs which are irrational or illogical.

Once this open atmosphere has been created, there is an unlimited range of possible courses of grief reduction and resolution. If feelings are shared (even if not in identical ways), there is an open stage for talk and reliving past episodes. At this time, beliefs and values may need to be questioned openly—challenged and confronted. Moreover, openly confronting beliefs may help survivors see the sometimes irrational assumptions they make regarding their personal role and responsibility in events that, in actuality, are far beyond their control. As we've learned, those who are in mourning and grief sometimes have a gigantic over-estimation of their own power; they reason that if they had done something differently, the death would never have occurred. Thus, the stage is set for prolonged grieving because the person takes upon him/herself responsibility for things far beyond his/her control; thus accounting for much of the "guilt" that becomes mixed up with "grief."

Toward the end of the recoil stage, loved ones may be misled by how well the widow seems to be doing. Many may assume that the worst of her grief and mourning is over. Friends and relatives also have their own lives to lead and they may become impatient with any continuing need the widow may express. And, even when family and friends do remain available and supportive, their attention may not be helpful. They will often try to help by distracting the widow from her grief, but the grief is what she needs to experience at this stage. Only when the widow can at last acknowledge her pain, doubts, and fears can she begin to make the necessary changes toward the last stage of grief.

The Accommodation Stage

In this final stage outlined by Silverman, the survivor discovers new ways of looking at the world.

Entering this period does not mean an end to depressed feelings or to the pain of her loss. These feelings do become less intense and pervasive, however, and she has a different perspective on her experience.

For example, she learns that she can laugh and that she has things worth living for; she can enjoy people and look forward to getting up in the morning. She can look upon her husband and her past without despairing of her present or her future. Remembering the past she can cry without becoming frightened or uncomfortable about it, without worrying about other people's reactions. Survivors within this stage accept the fact that part of them will always be sad when they think about the past, and most come to consider this natural and right.

At this time, the widow needs to remember. Her ways of remembering are her ways of honoring her

---

APPLICATIONS

ADVICE FOR THE BEREAVED

- Realize and recognize the loss.
- Take time for nature's slow, sure, stuttering process of healing.
- Give yourself massive doses of restful relaxation and routine busy-ness.
- Know that powerful, overwhelming feelings will lessen with time.
- Be vulnerable, share your pain, and be humble enough to accept support.
- Surround yourself with life: plants, animals, and friends.
- Use mementos to help your mourning, not to live in the dead past.
- Avoid rebound relationships, big decisions, and anything addictive.
- Keep a diary and record successes, memories, and struggles.
- Prepare for change, new interests, new friends, solitude, creativity, and growth.
- Recognize that forgiveness (of ourselves and others) is a vital part of the healing process.
- Know that holidays and anniversaries can bring up the painful feelings you thought you had successfully worked through.
- Realize that any new death-related crisis will bring up feelings about past losses.

Adapted from *The centre for living with dying.* In DeSpelder and Strickland, 1986, p. 228.

dead husband and of building continuity between her past and her future. Some widows set up memorial funds, some donate flowers annually on their husbands' birthdays, some become active in projects or areas that were important to their spouses. Others make scrapbooks, or carefully store those personal possessions that their children will want when they are older.

Repopulating her life with new friends and becoming involved in work are ways of building new identities and new roles for herself. She may also begin to change the old habits of daily living that framed her life and develop new ones appropriate to her current situation. She finds ways to take charge of her own life, in the process achieving a new sense of competence.

WIDOWHOOD AS A WAY OF LIFE

Beyond the stages of grief and mourning just described, we'd like to comment on the on-going nature of widowhood. Following the death of a spouse, the family typically rallies around the survivor. As we have seen, children and other relatives draw near the survivor to provide emotional support and assist with the tasks and activities at hand. However, as time passes, the social network decreases its support of the widowed person. Neighbors and friends may look after the survivor or help with such domestic chores as meal preparation for a time, but there is an expectation that the survivor will once more be responsible for day-to-day activities. Children and siblings may continue their support; however, it decreases a few weeks after the funeral. Generally, the social network is on alert but not on active duty several weeks after the death (Brubaker, 1985).

It may well be that the later periods of bereavement, when ritualized support for the survivor is lessened or removed, represent the most difficult periods of adjustment. Carolyn Balkwell (1981) points out that much of the pressure at this time comes from survivors having to carve out new identities and lifestyles on their own. This is espe-cially difficult for those widows who have been socialized to traditional, dependent sex-roles.

Overcoming loneliness is typically the biggest emotional hurdle that survivors have to face. Remember that during the first few months after the funeral, loneliness is often masked by busywork. However, it is still there and will surface in a number of different ways. Research undertaken by Helena Lopata (1981; 1979; 1973) describes some of the ways loneliness is expressed:

- Feelings that one is no longer an object of love.
- Homesickness for a past lifestyle.
- A desire to be with the person who is no longer available.
- Feelings that one no longer has anyone to love.
- A desire for a deep compassionate relationship.
- A desire for the presence of another person in the home.
- Unhappiness over the absence of anyone to share the workload.
- Alienation due to a drop in status.
- Anger at past friends due to decreased frequency of interaction. Such anger may originate from
  a. Differing definitions of the appropriate form and time for expressing grief.
  b. A gradual withering away of associates if a long illness preceded the husband's death.
  c. Awkwardness in interactions when grief is expressed.
  d. A desire not to associate with others who have been close to death on the part of persons who fear their own death.
  e. The complications involved in including an extra single woman in mixed-sex activities.
  f. Jealousy on the part of former couple friends.
  g. The wife having relied on the husband to make social contacts in the past, and/or financial considerations which may make past activities unavailable.
- A composite of the above, which may be compounded by the inability to make new friends.

To overcome loneliness, most sources (for example, Taves, 1981; Vail, 1982; Burnham, 1982)

Overcoming loneliness represents one of the most difficult adjustments
of widowhood.

stress the importance of reorganizing day-to-day living. Tasks such as cooking and cleaning, financial planning, and leisure activities need to be deliberately restructured. Learning to live alone and accepting the isolation that often goes with it need to be addressed. Moreover, everything a survivor has been accustomed to doing now bears scrutiny and reevaluation. A new life script has been written and old habits and routines may no longer fit.

Becoming involved in new relationships is another way to overcome loneliness. Four kinds of relationships, in particular, mitigate loneliness. The first three are family relationships, friendships, and sexual relationships. The fourth is a personal commitment to a cause, a course of action, a community, a productive type of work, or a social network of some kind. Note how each of these relationships are other-directed and can be used to combat loneliness (Wylie, 1982).

Many widowed persons also turn to support groups and other service programs for assistance. Perhaps the most widely known is the **Widow-to-Widow Program.** Volunteers who have themselves been widowed maintain phone hotlines and make home visits to newly widowed persons. The phone hotlines provide listeners for the lonely, help widowed persons make new friends, and provide answers to questions. The primary aim of the program is to help the widowed person progress through the developmental stages they'll encounter in the transition from married to widowed life. Aides provide support and serve as role models. Another program initiates social gatherings and community seminars (Balkwell, 1981). The box on page 520 lists additional services and sources of information for widowed persons.

Some survivors adapt to their new social roles better than others. For example, rural widows report more loneliness than urban widows, mainly because they are physically detached from neighbors and care in general. One study (Gibbs, 1985) indicates that elderly persons belonging to a lower socioeconomic stratum are more likely to lose contact with distant family members than those in upper social classes. Let us remember too, that sex differences exist in the overall recovery process.

INFORMATION SOURCES FOR WIDOWED PERSONS

- **Widow-To-Widow Program**
  Department of Psychiatry
  Harvard University Medical Center
  Cambridge, MA 02138
- **Widowed Service Line**
  Boston, MA
  617-371-0436
- **Women's Activities**
  AARP
  1909 K Street, NW
  Washington, DC 20049
- **Widowed Persons Service**
  AARP
  1909 K Street, NW
  Washington, DC 20049
- **American Association of University Women (AAUW)**
  2401 Virginia Avenue, NW
  Washington, DC 20037
  (This is the national branch. You can write for information regarding their program for widowed persons.)
- **Coalition of the Concerned for Older Americans (COCOA)**
  105 East 22nd Street, Suite 710
  New York, NY 10010
- **Older Women's League (OWL)**
  1325 G Street, NW
  Lower Level
  Washington, DC 20005

Beyond what we earlier discussed, research suggests that men face more difficulty in adjusting to their new roles as widowers. Researchers such as John Stevenson (1985) acknowledge that men are less apt to express grief and tend to be more socially isolated than widows. Also hampering the recovery process is the fact that ties with the extended family are typically maintained by the woman. Often, the man lacks the skills for maintaining or reestablishing such relationships. Men also report difficulty taking care of themselves during the recovery process, having previously left household responsibilities to their wives.

In time (the research indicates) most widows make the necessary social adjustments to over-

come loneliness and to implement reorganization into their lives (see Bowling and Carter, 1982; Anderson, 1984). In a review of the literature, Timothy Brubaker (1985) observes that over time, adjusted widows have developed ways to cope with the day-to-day problems of living alone and receive emotional support from various persons. Their support networks include various relatives, especially children and siblings, and former or new friends. While there are still feelings of loneliness and a sense of loss, these widows have developed ways of coping with these problems, establishing new identities with the help of their support networks.

As time goes on, successfully adjusted widows

RESEARCH HIGHLIGHT

DOES REMARRIAGE AFFECT THE MORALE AND WELL-BEING OF WIDOWS?

Widowed older adults who remarry have higher morale and a better self-image than their widowed peers who choose not to remarry, according to Canadian researcher Judith Strykman (1981). Her finding was based on a study examining the lives of 400 widowed persons 55 years of age and older.

Compared to those who remain widowed, remarried adults are less emotionally dependent on children and other family members, and more independent in their decision-making. For example, approximately 75 percent of the remarried reported that they sought no one's advice when considering possible remarriage, compared to about 50 percent of the widowed. For those who remained widowed, children's opposition to possible remarriage was a main factor in the decision not to remarry.

The overwhelming majority (86 percent) of the remarried gave an unqualified "yes" to the question of whether they would make the same choice over again. What remarriers liked most about remarriage was "someone to love and who loves me" (37.5 percent) and the fact that they had "someone to keep me company" (25.1 percent). Over 80 percent said they were more content, and 50 percent of the men said they ate better and took better care of themselves. Although the remarried were relatively poorer financially than their widowed peers, they suffered less from anxiety and feelings of insecurity.

Those who were most interested in remarrying, or had actually remarried, were persons whose spouses had died of cancer. Widowed males were found to remarry more rapidly than women, although all of the widowed appeared to approach the decision cautiously. Both sexes rated mutual affection and lact of discord with a prospective partner as the most important factors in deciding whom to marry, but some sex differences did emerge. Women were more concerned about the financial situation of the spouse, the potential impact of the marriage on other family relationships, and the availability of a residence. On the other hand, men were more concerned about the physical appearance of their partner than were women.

will continue to find new outlets for their energies. Amidst such change, though, the deceased is not forgotten. Rather, widows can cling to memories forever. It may well be, too, that experiencing widowhood promotes a stronger faith and more compassionate care and appreciation of the living. Those who have felt the pain of loss often learn to live their lives with more meaning (Schneider, 1984; Weizman and Kamm, 1984; Miles and Crandall, 1983).

CHAPTER HIGHLIGHTS

The loss of a loved partner is stressful at any time in the life cycle, but especially so during the retirement years, and especially so for women in general. Statistically, there are more widows than widowers in the United States, and approximately three out of every four American wives can expect to become widows at some point in their lives.

In Western culture, the topic of death is avoided

and often repressed. Consequently, it becomes difficult for young and old alike to comprehend and accept, but experts agree that seeking to understand death usually results in a greater appreciation of life.

The degree of stress brought on by death is dependent on several interacting variables, including the timing, the presence of other stressful crises, and the various arrangements that require attention following the death. Three possible paths to widowhood have been charted: unexpected death, expected death, and the presence of a non-threatening illness that becomes fatal.

Three stages of grief and mourning are known to exist: impact, recoil, and accomodation. Within these stages we can find both functional and dysfunctional coping strategies. During the later periods of bereavement, social support for survivors has usually lessened, and they must deal with their loneliness and reorganize their day-to-day lives — the biggest psychological hurdles that survivors have to overcome.

Grief does not end when the funeral is over; rather, feelings of emptiness and loneliness continue for extended periods. However, if satisfactory adjustment has been made during the mourning process, the bereaved, in time, will find new outlets for their energies. When this happens, the deceased have gained a certain immortality in the memory of their loved ones.

KEY TERMS

accommodation stage	grief	obliteration
bereavement	grief work	recoil stage
dysfunctional coping	idolization	Widow-to Widow Program
functional coping	impact stage	

RECOMMENDED READINGS

Hyman, H. H. (1983). *Of time and widowhood: Nationwide studies of enduring effects.* Durham, NC: Duke University Press. Hyman uses longitudinal and cross-sectional data to focus on the psychological and social impact of widowhood.

Kalish, R. A. (1985). *Death, grief, and caring relationships* (2nd ed.). Monterey, CA: Brooks/Cole. The meaning of death, the process of dying, and the grieving process are among the many topics Kalish covers.

Leming, M. R., and Dickinson, G. E. (1985). *Understanding dying, death, and bereavement.* New York: Holt, Rinehart & Winston. A readable and thorough analysis of virtually all aspects of death and bereavement.

Loewinsohn, R. J. (1984). *Survival handbook for widows.* Glenview, IL: Scott, Foresman & Co. A good description of bereavement and the grieving experience. This book offers numerous practical suggestions from settling claims to reorganizing day-to-day life.

Parkes, C. M., and Weiss, R. S. (1983). *Recovery from bereavement.* New York: Basic Books. Two well-known contributors to the field explore the trauma of loss and how it can be overcome.

Raphael, B. (1985). *The anatomy of bereavement.* New York: Basic Books. An examination of all the stages of mourning and how the effects of loss differ at each stage of life.

Seskin, J. (1985). *Alone but not lonely.* Glenveiw, IL: Scott, Foresman & Co. Widowed persons will benefit from the topics in this paperback, including tips on independent living and self-fulfillment activities.

Silverman, P. R. (1986). *Widow to widow.* New York: Springer. Part One of this text gives comprehensive detail to the three stages of grief and mourning described in this chapter.

Weitzman, S. G., and Kamm, P. (1985). *About mourning: Support and guidance for the bereaved.* New York: Human Sciences Press. This well-written text offers much guidance and advice for those assisting the bereaved.

Wylie, B. J. (1982). *The survival guide for widows.* New York: Ballantine. One of the better self-help books on widowhood. Of particular interest is Chapter 3, which explores lifestyle changes and reorganizing one's life.

Glossary

A

ABCX model Model of family stress developed by Reuben Hill. The component parts include the stressor, resources, the family's definition of the stressor, and the actual crisis.

abortion Termination of a pregnancy before a fetus can survive outside of the womb.

abstinence standard Moral standard holding that it is wrong for both unmarried males and females to engage in sexual intercourse.

accommodation stage Third stage of grief and mourning proposed by Silverman. During this stage, survivors reorganize their lives and view the deceased in a healthy perspective.

acquired immune deficiency syndrome (AIDS) Disorder characterized by a specific defect in the body's natural immunity against disease.

adult daycare facility Facility that offers daily nursing, nutritional, and medical monitoring to the elderly, who, however, maintain their own residences.

adultery Sexual intercourse with a person other than one's spouse.

agape Type of love characterized by caring and altruistic behavior.

ageism Discrimination against or unkind stereotyping of a person on the basis of his/her age.

amniocentesis Removal of fluid from the amniotic sac so that chromosomes of the fetus may be analyzed.

amniotic fluid Liquid that holds the embryo or fetus in suspension and protects it against jarring and from any pressure exerted by the mother's internal organs.

amniotic fluid replacement Type of induced abortion generally performed between the sixteenth and twentieth weeks of pregnancy. A saline solution is injected into the amniotic sac causing a miscarriage.

amniotic sac Transparent membrane completely enveloping the embryo or fetus, except where the umbilical cord passes through to the placenta.

androgen Sex hormone that regulates the male secondary sex characteristics. Also found in lesser amounts in females.

androgyny Concept suggesting that both male and female personality traits are beneficial and important to possess.

annulment Invalidation of a marriage on the basis of some reason existing at the beginning of that marriage, such as fraud, being underage, or duress.

antimiscegenation statute Laws prohibiting interracial marriages.

articulation The enunciation of words.

artificial insemination by donor A form of high-tech pregnancy in which donor sperm, carefully screened for genetic defects and other problems, is used to fertilize the female egg.

authority stage According to Galinsky, the third stage of parenthood. This stage occurs between the child's second and fourth year of life.

autonomy vs. shame and doubt The second of eight psychosocial crises theorized by Erik Erikson. Takes place between the ages of one and three.

B

B-Cell Type of lymphocyte that combats infectious diseases. Produces infection-fighting antibodies when stimulated.

banns Public notice of intent that was historically posted several weeks prior to a marriage at the church and other locations in the surrounding community.

basic trust vs. mistrust First of eight psychosocial

crises proposed by Erik Erikson. Takes place during the first year of life.

battered child syndrome   Technical name given to child abuse.

behavior modification theory   Style of childrearing that emphasizes the parental use of positive and negative reinforcement.

bereavement   The loss of a loved one by death. It is a statement of fact and does not embody one's reactions to a loss.

betrothal   Agreement or promise for a future marriage.

bilateral descent   Tracing lineage on both sides of the family.

biochemical stressors   Stressors having a biochemical origin, such as injury, pollutants, or toxicants.

biophysical system of sexuality   One's biological capacity to respond to sexual stimulation.

birthing room facility   Delivery room offering a home-like, relaxed atmosphere within the hospital's general delivery unit.

blended family   A family that results when a divorced parent with custody of children remarries.

breech delivery   Delivery of the baby's buttocks or feet first.

bundling   Colonial American custom in which two unmarried persons of the opposite sex shared the same bed while remaining fully clothed.

C

caesarean section   An incision that is made in the mother's abdominal and uterine wall so that a baby can be delivered.

canon law   The codified law governing a church.

career   An occupation which requires a high degree of commitment and has a continuous developmental character.

celibacy   Abstention from sexual activity.

cervix   Lowest part of the uterus.

chancre   A painless, open sore caused by syphillis.

child relinquishment   During the Middle Ages, the practice of sending infants out of the home to live with a wet nurse for a specified period.

child sexual abuse   Attempted or actual intercourse with a child by an adult, or other inappropriate genital contact.

Christian religious family commune   A commune

emphasizing religious conviction as well as purpose and meaning in life.

chromosome   Thin, rodlike structures within the cell's nucleus that contain the directions for that particular cell. Humans have 46 chromosomes.

climacteric   Period of life from the onset or irregularity of the menses to total cessation.

cognitive-developmental theory of sex-role development   Theory proposing that sex-role development emerges through the child's growing cognitive awareness of his/her sexual identity.

cohabitation   An unmarried man and woman living together.

cohort   Group of persons born at approximately the same time.

cohort analysis   Effort among reseachers to explore the experiences common to a particular group.

cojoined twins   Twins joined together. Also known as *Siamese Twins.*

common-law marriage   Marriage in which a couple agrees to live together as husband and wife without meeting the legal requirements for a marriage license.

communication   Exchange of information, signals, and messages between people. Communication is affected by a number of factors, including attitudes, personalities, and relationships.

community divorce   One of Bohannon's six divorce processes. Encompasses the perceptions community members have of divorced partners.

community remarriage   According to Goetting, a transition that exists when divorced parties reenter the world of couples.

complementary needs   Filtering agent suggesting that individuals will seek out mates who complement their own needs and personalities.

conclusions   In research studies, what an experimenter interprets the data to mean.

condom   Thin rubber sheath that is fitted over the penis prior to intercourse as a form of birth control.

conflict   Interpersonal process that occurs whenever the actions of one person interfere with the actions of another.

conflict-habituated marriage   According to Cuber and Harnoff, a marriage characterized by tension and conflict, although these are controlled.

confounded data   Term used for data in a research study when factors (such as age and cohort) cannot be assessed separately.

constant   The unchanging, arbitrary number by

which rates, ratios, or proportions can be multiplied to express these measures in a more understandable fashion.

contaminated messages Forms of expression that are mixed or mislabeled.

contraception The voluntary prevention of pregnancy.

contraceptive sponge Disposable sponge-like device that is saturated with a spermacide and inserted into the vagina as a form of birth control.

contraceptive vaccine An experimental form of birth control. For females, the vaccine interrupts the hormone action that supports a pregnancy, while for men, sperm production is halted.

control Condition that sometimes results when natural phenomena are understood so that they can be explained and predicted.

control group Group of subjects in a research study who receive the same treatment as the group being experimented upon, with the exception that they do not receive the stimulus (independant variable) under observation.

controlled experiment Experiments requiring subjects to be placed in contrived and perhaps unnatural environments.

coparental divorce One of Bohannon's six divorce processes. Involves the issue of child custody.

correlational method Method of observing and comparing naturally occurring events for whatever relationships may exist.

count Absolute number of a population or any demographic event occurring in a specified area in a specified time period.

cross-sectional study Method of research based upon the comparison of groups that differ in age at a given time.

crude divorce rate Number of divorces per 1,000 members of the population in a given year.

D

date rape The physical force used by a dating partner to have sexual intercourse.

decoding The interpretation of a message.

delayed parenthood Deliberate effort to postpone parenthood.

democratic theory Style of childrearing proposed by

Dreikurs. Emphasis is placed on integrating children as fully as possible into the family network so that they can benefit from everyone's observations, feedback, and encouragement.

demography Scientific study of populations.

departure stage According to Galinsky, the sixth stage of parenthood. This stage takes place when offspring physically leave the home.

dependent variable The change, if any, brought about by the independant variable in experimental research.

description Empirical process that often relies on counting, frequencies, percentages, and descriptive statistics.

developmental crisis Crisis that originates from predictable developmental changes over the family life cycle.

developmental-maturational theory Childrearing theory emphasizing the importance of childhood's developmental sequences and the need to adjust parental demands and expectations accordingly.

devitalized marriage According to Cuber and Harnoff, a marriage lacking emotional involvement and vitality.

diaphragm Thin sheet of rubber or latex stretched over a collapsible spring rim that is inserted into the vagina to cover the entrance to the uterus. A birth control device.

dilation and curettage Type of induced abortion used between the thirteenth and twentieth week of pregnancy. The organism is removed from the uterus by suction and curretage.

dilation and evacuation Form of induced abortion employed during the first trimester of pregnancy. The technique involves the removal of the embryo by curretage.

discipline The setting of limits in an effort to teach acceptable forms of behavior. The ultimate goal of discipline is to produce responsible behavior.

distress Harmful and unpleasant stress.

divorce from dependency One of Bohannon's six divorce processes. This process focuses on the issue of regaining individual autonomy.

divorce mediation A conflict resolution process in which the disputants meet with a third-party mediator whose role is that of facilitator and impartial guide to negotiation.

double ABCX model Model of family stress proposed by Hamilton, McCubbin, and Patterson. The components include the pile-up of family demands, family adaptive resources, family definition, meaning, and family adaptation balancing.

double standard Moral standard proposing that males can have sexual relations prior to marriage, but females are expected to remain abstinent.

dowry Material possessions a woman brings to her husband in marriage.

dual-career marriage Marriage in which husband and wife pursue careers rather than jobs.

dual-earner marriage Marriage in which husband (and/or) wife work at jobs rather than careers.

dysfunctional coping Unhealthy and unproductive behaviors for coping with bereavement.

E

Eastern religious family commune Commune emphasizing Eastern religion as well as group-shared activities and endeavors.

economic divorce One of Bohannon's six divorce processes. This process concerns itself with the division of money and property.

economic remarriage According to Goetting, the transition that occurs when remarrieds establish the household as a unit of productivity and consumption.

ectopic pregnancy Pregnancy that results when the fertilized egg becomes lodged in the wall of the fallopian tube.

egalitarian Power structure emphasizing mutuality between husband and wife.

ejaculatory duct Duct serving as a passageway from the prostate gland to the urethra.

elder abuse Abuse directed against the elderly.

embryo Term used to refer to the developing organism during the first eight weeks of prenatal life.

embryo transfer Form of high-tech pregnancy in which a female is designated to become impregnated with the father's sperm. After several days, the fertilized egg is removed from her womb and placed within the mother's uterus.

emotional remarriage According to Goetting, the reinvestment of emotions in a marriage so that comfort and love can be secured.

empty nest Reference to the period of life when a couple's children have all left home and they are alone.

encoding Translating a message to be conveyed into a set of meaningful symbols.

endemic stress Stressors that are long term in scope and so prevalent that they become a part of one's life. Examples include inflation or the fear of nuclear war.

endogamy Pressure to marry from within one's own social group.

endometrium Rich, soft tissue lining the walls of the uterus.

engagement Rite of passage usually characterized by the presentation of an engagement ring to the fiancée, a shower for the bride-to-be, a party for the groom-to-be and an announcement in the newspaper.

epididymis The first part of the genital duct system through which the sperm passes. Located adjacent to each testis.

erectile dysfunction Inability of the male to create and maintain an erection sufficient for sexual intercourse. Also known as *impotency*.

eros love Love characterized by intense romance and idealization of one's partner.

estrogen The female sex hormone.

eustress Condition that results when the body's reaction change to stress is put to positive or productive use.

exchange A filtering agent proposing that persons are attracted to those who provide the greatest relational rewards and the fewest number of sacrifices.

excitement phase The first phase of the sexual response cycle. During this phase, sexual arousal increases and the genital areas become engorged with blood.

exogamy Pressure to marry from outside of one's social group.

experimental group Group of subjects in a research experiment receiving a special stimulus or treatment.

experimental research Series of steps that are designed so that relationships between differing phenomena can be determined.

explanation Attempts to provide reasons for why something happens or is the way it is.

extended family Family structure consisting of parents and offspring, as well as other relatives such as grandparents, aunts, and uncles.

external validity Degree to which conclusions drawn from one set of observations can be generalized to other sets of observations.

extramarital sex relationship Any sexual activity

outside of the marriage with or without the knowledge or consent of one's spouse.

F

fact A statement of observation.

fallopian tube Either of two tubes that extend from the ovary region to the uterus. Also called the *uterine tube*.

family Social arrangement consisting of two or more persons related by blood, marriage, or adoption.

family crisis Situation that occurs when family members face an obstacle to their goals that, at least for some period of time, appears insurmountable by means of customary problem-solving strategies.

family metacognition stage According to Ahrons, a stage that accompanies marital degeneration. At this time, the entire family unit recognizes that the marriage is deteriorating.

family of orientation Family into which one is born.

family of procreation Family established through marriage and parenthood.

family planning Voluntary planning of how many children are wanted, when, or if they are wanted at all.

family redefinition stage Final stage of divorce suggested by Ahrons. At this time, the family must redefine its identity, particularly parent-child relationships.

family reorganization stage Stage of divorce proposed by Ahrons focusing on the family adjustments required once the divorce is finalized.

feedback Final step of the communication process. Feedback enables the sender of communication to determine if the intended message has been accurately received.

feelings The expression of emotions.

fetal alcohol syndrome Condition among newborns caused by excessive alcohol consumption by the mother. Affected infants are often born undersized, mentally deficient, and with assorted physical deformities.

fetoscopy Technique used to explore potential problems within the prenatal environment. Fetoscopy involves the use of a fetoscope, a needle-shaped viewing instrument inserted in the womb.

fetus The human organism in the womb from approximately the third prenatal month until birth.

filtering agent Sequence of decisions made by the couple about the quality of "fit" between their individual attributes. Filtering agents will test the compatibility of partners and serve to narrow down the field of eligibles.

fixed income Financial benefits that do not vary.

fraternal twins Twins conceived when two ova are released simultaneously by the female and both are penetrated by male sperm cells. Also called *dizygotic twins*.

full-nest Reference to the period of life when a couple's children have reached adult status, but residency within the home continues.

functional coping Healthy and productive behaviors for coping with bereavement.

G

gay men Males whose sexual orientation and affectional attraction are to other males.

gender identity Psychological awareness of being either a male or a female.

general adaptation syndrome Model designed to explain the physiological changes that occur when a person experiences stress. Developed by Selye, the syndrome consists of three stages: alarm, resistance, and exhaustion.

general sexual dysfunction In females, a lack of desire for sexual relations. Also known as *frigidity*.

generation gap Differences in values, attitudes, and behavior between two generational groups, such as parents and adolescents.

generativity vs. self-absorption The seventh of eight psychosocial crises proposed by Erik Erikson. This crisis occupies middle adulthood.

genetic counseling Form of medical counseling for couples that focuses on the potential genetic risks to their unborn children.

genital herpes Sexually transmitted disease caused by herpes simplex viruses. The virus itself rests in the cell center of specific sensory nerves.

germ cell Reproductive cell of an organism.

gonadotrophins Hormones that are produced by the pituitary gland and stimulate the testes and ovaries.

gonads The sex glands.

gonorrhea Sexually transmitted disease caused by a bacterial infection and spread by sexual contact with an infected person. Gonorrhea is much more common in males than in females and is highly contagious.

grief Deep and poignant distress caused by another's death. One's emotional reaction to such a loss.

grief work Coming to terms with the physical and emotional demands brought by another's death.

H

hearing Physiological process by which auditory impressions are received by the ears and transmitted to the brain.

hermaphrodite Person having both ovarian and testicular tissue; the result of hormonal imbalances during prenatal development.

home birth Delivery of a baby in the parent's home rather than in a hospital. The delivery is often conducted by a licensed nurse-midwife.

homosexuality Love of one person for another of the same sex.

hormone Product of the endocrine glands secreted into the bloodstream.

human growth hormone Hormone secreted by the pituitary gland.

humanistic theory Childrearing approach emphasizing the development of parental empathy, sensitivity, and insight into the needs of children.

husband abuse Abuse that is directed from wife to husband.

hypothalamus Part of the brain that regulates hunger, thirst, sex, and body temperature. Also plays a major role in the physical developments that transpire during puberty.

hypothesis Educated guess made by the researcher.

hysterotomy Form of induced abortion performed between the sixteenth and twenty-fourth week of pregnancy. An incision is made through the abdominal wall and the fetus is removed.

I

ideation First step of the communication process. Ideation occurs when the sender of communication has information for, or needs information from, another person.

identical twins Twins that occur as the result of the zygote splitting into two separate but genetically identical cells. Also called *monozygotic twins*.

identification theory of sex-role development Theory suggesting that sex-typed behaviors are the result of close interaction and emulation of one's parents.

identity vs. role confusion Fifth of eight psychosocial crises proposed by Erik Erikson. This crisis occupies the teenage years.

idolization Among widows and widowers, the effort to make the deceased greater in death than he/she was in life. This is a type of dysfunctional coping.

impact stage The first stage of grief and mourning proposed by Silverman, characterized by shock, psychological numbness, and the need for help from family and friends.

impotency See *erectile dysfunction*

incest Sexual intercourse or sexual relations between persons so closely related that they are forbidden by law to marry.

independent teenage years stage According to Galinsky, the fifth stage of parenthood. This stage occupies the teenage years.

independent variable Treatment administered to the experimental group of subjects, but not to the control group.

individual cognition stage Stage of divorce proposed by Ahrons. At this time, attention is focused on the individual perceptions and reactions that accompany a deteriorating marriage.

induced abortion Deliberate external attempt to remove the organism from the uterus.

industrial revolution Transformation of an agrarian society into an urban and industrialized one.

industry vs. inferiority Fourth of eight psychosocial crises proposed by Erik Erikson. This crisis takes place during the years of middle childhood.

infanticide The killing of infants and children.

infertility The inability to carry pregnancies to live birth.

inherent sin The belief that children are born sinful and wicked.

initiative vs. guilt Third of eight psychosocial crises proposed by Erik Erikson. Occurs during the years of early childhood.

institutionalism Psychological state of apathy and deterioration, brought about by a depersonalized, institutional environment.

integrative stage According to Galinsky, the fourth stage of parenthood. This stage encompasses the preschool years through middle childhood.

integrity vs. despair Eighth psychosocial crisis proposed by Erik Erikson. Occurs during late adulthood.

interfaith marriage A marriage in which husband and wife have different religious backgrounds.

intermediate-care facility Nursing facility that places less emphasis on intensive-care nursing and more on personal-care service.

internal validity Degree to which observations are logically interrelated and fit the theoretical structure of which they are a part.

interracial marriage Marriage in which husband and wife have different racial backgrounds.

intimacy Becoming close with another person through the process of self-disclosure.

intimacy vs. isolation The sixth of eight psychosocial crises postulated by Erik Erikson. Occurs during young adulthood.

intimate relationship Process in which a person comes to know the innermost, subjective aspects of another individual.

intrauterine device Small, plastic birth control device which is inserted into the womb so that a fertilized egg cannot implant itself in the uterine lining.

in-vitro fertilization Type of high-tech pregnancy often referred to as "test tube fertilization." In this technique, the female's egg is surgically removed from the womb, fertilized by the male sperm, and then placed in the uterus.

J

job Position that is not a major life interest and is underaken primarily to provide family income.

joint custody Mutual sharing of parental rights and responsibilities after a divorce has taken place.

K

Kaposi's sarcoma Type of cancer that often afflicts AIDS patients.

kibbutz Settlement in Israel where there exists a sharing of work and wealth and a communal rearing of children.

kinship How family members are related to one another.

Kleinfelter's syndrome A chromosome abnormality among males characterized by two normal X chromosomes plus the Y chromosome.

L

Lamaze method of childbirth Natural childbirth approach emphasizing a conditioned learning technique in which the mother replaces one set of learned responses (fear, pain) with another (relaxation, muscle control).

lanugo Fine downy growth of hair appearing on the entire body of the fetus.

laparoscopy Surgical procedure used in tubal ligation.

late syphilis Final stage of syphilis. Left unchecked, the disease at this time can cause severe body damage and even death.

latent syphilis Third of four stages of syphilis. While patients appear healthy at this time, the disease is still within the bloodstream.

leader-directed communal family Commune led by a charismatic figure who typically supplies specified goals and activities for the family group.

Leboyer method of childbirth Birthing technique emphasizing a gentle delivery of the baby as well as the establishment of a peaceful and soothing delivery room environment.

legal divorce One of Bohannon's six divorce processes. Entails the legal ramifications of divorce, including courtroom proceedings.

legal remarriage According to Goetting, the legal complexities that arise when individuals remarry.

legal separation Contract that exists between spouses that focuses on the issues to be resolved before a divorce is granted.

lesbian women Females whose sexual orientation and affectional attraction are to other women.

levonorgestrel releasing Experimental form of birth control for females which is similar to the I.U.D. but contains a steroid that is released into the uterus.

listening Psychological procedure involving the interpretation and understanding of sensory experience.

longitudinal study Study in which the researcher repeatedly collects data on the same group of subjects over an extended period of time.

love Set of feelings, cognitions, and motivations that contribute to communication, sharing, and support.

ludus love Playful, self-centered, and sexually permissive love.

lymphocytes Specialized white blood cells that are critical in fighting infectious diseases.

M

male oral contraception Experimental form of birth control which is designed to inhibit sperm mobility and production.

manic love Intense and obsessive love.

marital rape Type of sexual assault in which a wife is forced to have sexual intercourse with her husband or to engage in other forms of sexual activity against her will.

marriage Institutional act that legally unites a man and a woman as husband and wife.

marriage certificate Document signed by the couple, the witnesses, and the presiding official after a wedding ceremony has been performed.

marriage license Document certifying that state legal requirements for marriage have been met. Sent to the state's capital where it is recorded and filed.

marriage rate Number of marriages each year per 1,000 members of a population.

masturbation Manipulation of one's own sex organs to produce pleasure.

matriarchal Power structure in which the female is the dominant figure.

matrilineal descent Tracing lineage on the wife's side of the family.

matrilocal Establishment of residency with or near the wife's relatives.

maturity State that promotes physical and psychological well-being.

medicaid Government-sponsored medical plan for welfare clients, regardless of age.

medicare Government-sponsored insurance program that partially finances the health-care costs of persons 65 years and older.

menopause The cessation of menstruation.

metamessage Intentional alteration of speech rhythm or pitch for emphasis, or the use of special verbal modifiers.

minilaporatomy Surgical procedure used in tubal ligation.

miscarriage See *spontaneous abortion*

miscegenation Technical name given to interracial marriages.

modern-naturalistic ideology Sexual ideology challenging the double standard, emphasizing in its place equalitarian relationships between men and women.

monogamy Marriage of one man to one woman.

"morning after" pill Experimental form of birth control which induces a miscarriage in the early weeks of pregnancy.

mullerian ducts Group of cells that differentiate the female reproductive structure during prenatal life.

mullerian inhibiting hormone Hormone secreted by the testes which prevents the female reproductive structure from developing during prenatal life.

multiple conception Conception that results when more than one female egg is fertilized by the male sperm. (See *identical* and *fraternal twins*)

N

natural childbirth Method of childbirth avoiding the use of anesthesia and allowing both husband and wife to play an active role in the delivery of the baby.

naturalistic observation Examination of behavior under unstructured or natural conditions.

needs From a communication standpoint, statements that help or please a person.

neolocal Establishment of residency not based on ties originating from either the husband's or wife's family.

no-fault divorce Divorce legislation which does not accuse either party of causing the divorce.

nonverbal communication Communication without words.

nuclear family Family form consisting of the mother, father, and children.

nurse-midwife Trained delivery specialist who provides qualified medical care to expectant mothers. Usually the midwife has earned a bachelor's degree in mid-wifery and works on a medical team consisting of a gynecologist and an obstetrician.

nurturing stage According to Galinsky, the second stage of parenthood. Occurs through the second year of the child's life.

O

obliteration Among widows and widowers, an attempt to totally erase the former existence of the deceased. A form of dysfunctional coping.

observations Stimuli that are perceived without speculation, inferences, or conclusions.

open marriage Marriage that is flexible, stressing the

importance of freedom as well as continual self-growth for both partners.

oral contraceptive Birth control pills which prevent female ovulation.

orgasm phase The third phase of the sexual response cycle. This phase is accompanied by rhythmic contractions in the genitals of both sexes and by ejaculation in males.

orgasmic dysfunction Inability of the female to reach a sexual climax.

ova Female eggs or germ cells. (Plural of *ovum.*)

ovaries The two female sex glands that produce egg cells (ova).

ovulation The female's monthly production and release of a mature egg, or *ovum.*

ovum The female egg or germ cell.

P

palimony Type of alimony given to a partner after a cohabitation relationship terminates.

paralanguage Vocal component of communication.

parent abuse Abuse that is directed from offspring to parents.

parent-effectiveness theory Style of childrearing emphasizing, among other techniques, active listening, reflecting positive images back to children, and mutual problem-solving.

parent image stage According to Galinsky, the first stage of parenthood. Occurs when the baby is born.

parental image theory Filtering agent suggesting that individuals will seek mates possessing traits of opposite-sex parents.

parental remarriage According to Goetting, the adjustments that occur when there are children from one side of the remarriage or both.

parents anonymous A self-help group that offers support and guidance to abused parties among other services.

partial message Form of interpersonal communication lacking a basic facet of expression.

participant observation Form of observation in which researcher is a participant in the interaction being studied.

passive-congenial marriage According to Cuber and Harnoff, a marriage in which interests and energies are directed away from the dyad.

patriarchal Power structure in which the male is the dominant figure.

patrilineal descent Tracing lineage on the husband's side of the family.

patrilocal Establishment of residency with or near the husband's relatives.

penis External male organ that propels sperm into the female during sexual intercourse.

permissive parenting Childrearing approach emphasizing greater levels of freedom with children.

permissiveness with affection standard Moral standard proposing that sexual relations between unmarried persons are acceptable if accompanied by emotional attachment.

permissiveness without affection standard Moral standard asserting that sex by itself without emotional attachments is acceptable.

personal marriage contract See *prenuptial agreement*

philosophical stressors Stressors which originate from value-system conflicts such as lack of purpose or direction.

pilot study A small-scale research study.

pitch Highness or lowness of one's voice.

pituitary gland Gland that secretes hormones that, in turn, stimulate the production and release of hormones by other endocrine glands. Often called the master gland.

placenta Organ that allows nourishments to pass from mother to embryo and fetus, and waste products to be channeled from embryo and fetus to mother.

plateau phase Second phase of the sexual response cycle. At this time, there is an increase in heart rate, body tension, and blood pressure.

polyandry Marriage of one woman to two or more men.

polygamy A plural marriage arrangement. *Polygyny* and *polyandry* are two basic forms of polygamy.

polygyny Marriage of one man to two or more women.

post-test Test given to both the experimental and control groups to prove whether or not a hypothesis is correct. Given after the experimental treatment.

pragma love Love that is practical and realistic.

prediction Being able to tell in advance that something is going to occur.

premature ejaculation Inability of male to hold back ejaculation during intercourse. As a result, he climaxes before his partner does.

prenuptial agreement In its most common form, a document that spells out how assets will be divided if the marriage dissolves. Prenuptial agreements may also include other items, such as the expectations partners have for one another.

pre-test Test given to both the experimental and control groups to prove whether or not a hypothesis is correct. Given before the experimental treatment.

primary sex characteristics Those physiological features related to the sex organs and reproductive capacities.

primary stressor Stressor initiating the stress response.

primary syphilis First of four stages of syphilis. Characterized by a painless, open sore called a *chancre.*

progesterone Female sex hormone that aids in the development of the uterine wall, enlargement of the breasts during pregnancy, and milk production after childbirth.

propinquity Filtering agent which suggests that individuals need to have continual contact with one another if the relationship is to endure.

proportion Relation of a population subgroup to the entire population.

prostate gland Gland located at the base of the bladder that contributes most of the seminal fluid.

pseudohermaphrodite Person having either ovaries or testes (not both), but external genitals characteristic of the opposite sex.

psychic remarriage According to Goetting, the process of changing one's conjugal identity from individual to couple.

psychological divorce One of Bohannon's six divorce processes. Focuses on the psychological motivations for considering divorce.

psychological stressors Stressors originating from mental pressures, such as anxiety or worry.

psychosocial stressors Stressors originating from interactions with others, such as the loss of a friend.

psychosocial system of sexuality A culture's sexual programming for appropriate male and female sexual behavior.

puberty The onset of sexual maturity.

R

rates The frequency of demographic events in a population in a specified time period.

ratio The relation of one population subgroup to another subgroup in the same population.

reception Fourth step in the communication pro-

cess. Reception occurs when the person with whom communication is intended perceives the message.

recoil stage The second stage of grief and mourning proposed by Silverman. Survivors at this time must come to grips with the full realization of loss as well as coping with the many emotional complexities that accompany widowhood.

refractory period Period of time following ejaculation during which the male is unresponsive to sexual stimulation.

residential-care facility Home for aged persons who are functionally independent, but who desire a safe, hygenic, and sheltered environment in which to live.

resistance Second stage of Selye's general adaptation syndrome. During this stage the body generates large amounts of energy to combat stress.

resolution phase Fourth and final phase of the sexual response cycle. At this time, the body returns to its normal state.

resonance Richness or thinness of the voice.

restrictive parenting Childrearing approach emphasizing strict parent-child relations.

retarded ejaculation Inability of the male to ejaculate during sexual intercourse.

rhythm From a communication standpoint, the words emphasized in a sentence.

rhythm method Method of birth control in which couples refrain from intercourse on days when pregnancy can occur.

role compatibility Filtering agent stressing the importance of role stability and harmony between two persons.

rooming-in facility Facility allowing the parents of newborns to care for their baby in the mother's hospital room.

rural domestic commune Commune characterized by a traditional, rural existence.

S

sample Group of people deemed representative of a larger population.

scientific method Organized series of steps designed to promote maximum objectivity and consistency in gathering and interpreting observable evidence.

scrotum Thin-walled pouch of skin hanging behind the penis which contains the testes.

secondary sex characteristics Those characteristics not directly related to the sexual organs, which nevertheless serve to distinguish a mature male from a mature female.

secondary stressors Events that result from the primary stressor and keep the stress response activated.

secondary syphilis The second of four stages of syphilis. Occurs approximately six weeks to six months after contact with the disease.

self-actualization Harmonious integration of the personality, enabling individuals to make full use of potentialities, capabilities, and talents.

self-disclosure Process by which individuals let themselves be known by others.

seminal vesicles Glands which discharge a sticky, thick fluid that unites with sperm cells emerging from the testes.

separation stage Stage of divorce proposed by Ahrons. At this time, one parent physically leaves the home and consequently forces adjustments and adaptations on remaining family members.

serial monogamy Succession of partners through the processes of marriage, divorce, remarriage and so on.

sex Biological aspects of reproduction, including anatomy, as well as physiology.

sex cell See *germ cell.*

sex-role Those attitudes and behaviors felt to be appropriate to males and females.

sex-role development Process of socialization whereby sex-roles are acquired.

sex-role stereotype Generalization of masculine and feminine characteristics and behaviors.

sexual identity Biological differences that exist between males and females.

sexual response cycle Series of four physiological and psychological phases that accompany sexual arousal.

sexual value system of sexuality An individual's unique set of beliefs about sexuality.

sexuality Reproduction and sexual pleasure as well as one's need for love and personal fulfillment. Embraces cultural and psychological factors related to human sexual behavior.

sexually transmitted disease Contagious infection passed on by intimate sexual contacts with others.

sibling abuse Abuse from sibling to sibling.

singlehood Lifestyle in which persons choose not to marry.

single-parent household Household in which one parent is absent.

situational crisis Crisis that is sudden and abrupt,

which can occur at any point in the family's development.

skilled nursing facility Nursing facility that provides nursing care on a full-time basis for persons with chronic illness or convalescing from illness.

social conflict approach Approach exploring how disequilibrium, disharmony, and conflict are inevitable features of human interaction.

social exchange approach Approach emphasizing how interpersonal relationships are formed largely for the purpose of meeting each partner's needs.

social learning theory of sex-role development **Theory stressing how sex-typed behaviors are the product of imitation.**

social readjustment rating scale Testing device designed by Holmes and Rahe that seeks to rank the life events that produce stress.

social stressors Stressors originating from one's environment, such as noise or crowding.

somatic cells The body cells of an organism.

sonography Technique used to explore the prenatal environment. Also called *ultrasound,* the technique utilizes sound waves to gather information regarding the developing organism.

sperm Male germ cell, or *gamete.*

spermicide Chemical that kills or immobilizes sperm, thus preventing pregnancy.

spontaneous abortion Separation of the organism from the uterine wall, followed by expulsion by the uterus. Also known as *miscarriage.*

spouse abuse A general term given to the abuse that takes place from spouse to spouse.

sterilization Surgical procedure that interrupts the reproductive tracts of either the male or female so that fertilization is prevented.

storge love Type of love characterized by affection and companionship.

stress The common, nonspecific response of the body to any demand made upon it, be it psychological or physiological.

stressors External events or conditions that affect the equilibrium of the organism.

structural-functional approach survey Approach emphasizing how a society can operate in harmony and equilibrium because of its interdependent parts.

structured observation Type of observation enabling the researcher to administer simple tests.

subdermal implants Experimental form of birth control for females, in which capsules are implanted under the skin. The capsules release doses of progesterone to block ovulation.

surrogate motherhood Type of pregnancy in which a chosen surrogate mother is artificially inseminated with the husband's sperm. The surrogate mother carries and bears the child, which is then given to the couple.

survey Technique of gathering information from people. Usually takes the form of a questionnaire or interview.

swinging Relationship involving two or more married couples who decide to switch sexual partners or engage in group sex.

symbolic interaction approach theory Theory explaining how families interact through symbols; including social roles, words, and actions.

syphilis Highly infectious sexually transmitted disease. Syphilis enters the body through any break in the mucous membrane, burrowing into the bloodstream.

T

T-cell Type of lymphocyte that combats infectious diseases. In AIDS, T-cells are significantly reduced.

tempo Speed at which words are spoken.

teratogen Any substance that creates a change in normal genetic functioning and in turn produces an abnormality in the developing organism.

testes The primary male reproductive organs.

testicular feminizing syndrome Genetic male who has the external genitals of a female.

testosterone Primary male hormone secreted by the testes.

theory Explanation that unites a set of facts or hypotheses.

thoughts From a communication standpoint, conclusions drawn from what a person has observed, heard, or read.

total marriage According to Cuber and Harnoff, a marriage in which all important life foci are vitally shared.

traditional-romantic ideology Sexual ideology stressing the primacy and validity of the double standard.

transactional analysis theory Childrearing approach that takes into consideration three ego states (child, parent, and adult), and how they relate to overall communication.

transmission Third step in the communication process. Transmission occurs when messages are presented orally, in writing, or through body language.

trimester Term referring to the duration of pregnancy. Pregnancy is divided into three trimesters, each lasting three months.

Triple X Syndrome Chromosomal abnormality that afflicts women, usually creating mental retardation.

tubal ligation Form of sterilization in which the fallopian tubes are cut and tied.

Turner's Syndrome Female monosomic condition characterized by one sex chromosome.

Type A personality Stressful personality type that is believed to be related to cardiovascular disorders.

Type B personality Personality type characterized by a relaxed attitude toward life and no hostility. Type B personalities are less likely to suffer coronary heart diseases than Type A personalities.

Type C personality Individuals who sustain considerable stress, but have learned to successfully cope with it.

U

umbilical cord "The body stalk" containing three blood vessels: a vein carrying oxygenated blood from the placenta to the fetus, and two arteries carrying blood and waste products from the fetus to the placenta.

understanding Sixth step in the communication process. Understanding occurs when an accurate message is sent and is successfully decoded.

urban domestic commune Commune characterized by a simple, traditional existence, but within an urban setting.

urethra Tube that connects the bladder to the outside of the body. At different times, the urethra serves as an exit tube for urine as well as for sperm.

uterus Thick-walled, hollow, muscular organ in which the fertilized egg develops.

V

vacuum aspiration Form of induced abortion generally used during the first trimester of a pregnancy.

With this technique, the embryo is suctioned from the uterus.

vagina Short muscular tube in females that extends from the uterus to an exterior opening. Also called the birth canal.

vaginal ring Thin, donut-shaped ring which is inserted into the vagina. The ring secretes hormones designed to prevent pregnancy.

vaginismus Female sexual dysfunction characterized by the painful contraction of muscles surrounding the vaginal tract.

vas deferans Continuation of the *epididymis,* which loops up into the body before descending into a duct in the *seminal vesicle* gland.

vasectomy Surgical procedure in which the *vas deferens* are cut to prevent the passage of sperm.

vernix caseosa Wax-like substance which covers the skin of the *fetus* during prenatal life. Its purpose is to protect the fetus from the constant exposure to the *amniotic fluid.*

vital marriage According to Cuber and Harnoff, a marriage in which partners are intensely bound together psychologically.

volume The loudness of the voice.

voluntary childlessness Conscious decision among couples not to have children.

W

whole messages Expressions based on what one sees, thinks, feels, and needs.

Widow to Widow Program Support group designed to offer reassurance and guidance to widows.

wife abuse Abuse that is directed from husband to wife.

Wolffian ducts Group of cells that differentiate male and female internal sex organs during prenatal life.

X

XXY Syndrome Chromosomal abnormality that often creates below-average intelligence and personality disorders.

Z

zygote Cell formed by the union of the male sperm and the female ovum; the fertilized egg.

References

A

ABBE, K. M., AND GILL, F. M. (1981). *Twins on twins.* New York: Crown.

ADAMS, G. R., AND SCHVANEVELDT, J. D. (1985). *Understanding research methods.* New York: Longman.

AHRONS, C. R. (1983). Divorce: Before, during, and after. In H. I. McCubbin and C. R. Figley (Eds.), *Stress and the family.* New York: Brunner/Mazel Publishers.

AHRONS, C. R. (1984). The continuing coparental relationship between divorced spouses. In D. H. Olson and B. C. Miller (Eds.), *Family Studies Review Yearbook* (Vol. 2). Beverly Hills, CA: Sage.

AIKEN, L. R. (1982). *Later life* (2nd ed.). New York: Holt, Rinehart & Winston.

AIZENBERG, R. AND HARRIS, R. (1982). Family demographic changes: The middle generation squeeze. *Generations, 7*(2), 6–7.

ALBRECHT, S. L. (1980). Reactions and adjustments to divorce: Differences in the experience of males and females. *Family Relations, 29*(1), 59–68.

ALBRECHT, S. L., BAHR, H. M., AND GOODMAN, K. L. (1983). *Divorce and remarriage: Problems, adaptations, and adjustments.* Westport, CT: Greenwood Press.

ALBRECHT, S. L. AND KUNZ, P. R. (1980). The decision to divorce: A social exchange perspective. *Journal of Divorce, 3*(4), 319–337.

ALBRITTEN, R. B., AND ALBRITTEN, W. (1985). Abuse and violence in dating relationships. *Current trends in relationships and marriage.* New York: Atcom, Inc.

ALDOUS, J. (1985). Parent-adult child relations as attached by the grandparent status. In V. L. Bengston and J. R. Robertson (Eds), *Grandparenthood: Emergent perspectives on traditional roles.* Beverly Hills, CA: Sage.

ALLPORT, G. W. (1961). *Pattern and growth in personality.* New York: Holt, Rinehart & Winston.

AMBROGI, D. AND LONDON, C. (1985). Elder abuse laws: Their implications for caregivers. *Generations, 10*(1), 37–39.

AMERICAN FERTILITY SOCIETY. (1986). Personal Communication. 1801 Ninth Ave., South. Birmingham, AL.

AMERICAN SOCIOLOGICAL ASSOCIATION. (1984). *Code of ethics.* Washington, DC: American Sociological Association.

AMMONS, P., AND STINNETT, N. (1980). The vital marriage: A closer look. *Family Relations, 29,* 37–42.

ANDERSON, T. B. (1984). Widowhood as a life transition: Its impact on kinship ties. *Journal of Marriage and the Family, 46,* 105–114.

ARCHER, C. J. (1984). Children's attitudes toward sex-role division in adult occupational roles. *Sex Roles, 10*(1), 1–10.

ARGYLE, M. (1983). Why do marriages break down? *New Society, 64*(1070), 259–260.

ATCHLEY, R. C. (1980). *The social forces in later life* (3rd ed.). Belmont, CA: Wadsworth.

ATWATER, E. (1986). *Human relations.* Englewood Cliffs, NJ: Prentice-Hall.

ATWATER, L. (1982). *The extramarital connection: Sex, intimacy, and identity.* New York: Irvington Publishers.

ATWATER, L. (1985). Long-term cohabitation without a legal ceremony is equally valid and desirable. In H. Feldman and M. Feldman (Eds.), *Current controversies in marriage and family.* Beverly Hills, CA: Sage.

AUERBACH, S. (1981). *Choosing child care: A guide for parents.* New York: Dutton.

B

BALKWELL, C. (1981). Transition to widowhood: A review of the literature. *Family Relations, 12*(1), 117–127.

BARBACH, L. (1984). *For each other: Sharing sexual intimacy.* New York: Signet.

BARDWICK, J. M., AND DOUVAN, E. (1980). Ambivalence: The socialization of women. In J. M. Henslin (Ed.), *Marriage and family in a changing society.* New York: The Free Press.

BARRETT, K. (1984). Date rape—a campus epidemic? In O. Pocs (Ed.), *Human Sexuality, 1984.* Guilford, CT: Dushkin Publishing.

BARROW, G. M., AND SMITH, P. A. (1983). *Aging, the individual, and society* (2nd ed.). St. Paul, MN: West.

BARRY, S. (1980). Spousal rape: the uncommon law. *American Bar Association Journal,* (September), 1088–1091.

BASOW, S. S. (1980). *Sex role stereotypes: Traditions and alternatives.* Monterey, CA: Brooks/Cole.

BAUMRIND, D. (1982). Are androgynous individuals more effective persons and parents? *Child Development, 53*(1), 44–75.

BEATY, J. J. (1986). *Observing development of children.* Columbus, OH: Charles E. Merrill.

BEDEIAN, A. G. (1986). *Management.* New York: Holt, Rinehart & Winston.

BEER, W. R. (1982). *Househusbands: Men and housework in American families.* New York: Praeger.

BELL, R. R. (1981). *Worlds of friendship.* Beverly Hills, CA: Sage.

BELL, R. R. (1983). *Marriage and family interaction* (6th ed.). Homewood, IL: Dorsey Press.

BELL, R. R., AND COUGHEY, K. (1980). Premarital sexual experience among college females, 1958, 1968, and 1978. *Family Relations,* (July), 353–357.

BELLINGER, D. C., AND GLEASON, J. B. (1982). Sex differences in parental directives to young children. *Sex Roles, 8*(11), 1123–1139.

BENEDICT, H. (1985). *Recovery.* New York: Doubleday.

BENGSTON, V. (1985). Diversity and symbolism in grandparental roles. In V. L. Bengston and J. R. Robertson (Eds.), *Grandparenthood: Emergent perspectives on traditional roles.* Beverly Hills, CA: Sage.

BENNETT, C. (1980). *Nursing home life: What it is and what it could be.* New York: Tiresias Press.

BERG, B. (1986). *The crisis of the working mother: Resolving the conflict between family and work.* New York: Summit Books.

BERGER, S. (1983). *Divorce without victims: Helping children through divorce with a minimum of pain and trauma.* Boston: Houghton Mifflin.

BERKLEY, B. R. (1981). People who marry without love. *Medical Aspects of Human Sexuality, 15*(8), 23, 30–34.

BERNDT, T. J. (1982). The features and effects of friendship in early adolescence. *Child Development, 53*(6), 1447–1460.

BERNE, E. (1964). *Games people play.* New York: Grove Press.

BERSCHEID, E., AND PEPLAU, L. A. (1983). The emerging science of relationships. In H. H. Kelly (Ed.), *Close relationships.* New York: Freeman.

BESSELL, H. (1984). *The love test.* New York: Warner Books.

BISHOP, T. A. (1986). Divorce court in the Chinese fashion. *The New London Day,* (April), p. 11.

BLATCHFORD, P., BATTLE, S., AND MAYS, J. (1983). *The first transition: Home to preschool.* Atlantic Highlands, NJ: Humanities Press.

BLITCHINGTON, W. P. (1984). Traditional sex roles result in healthier sexual relationships and healthier, more stable family life. In H. Feldman and A. Parrot (Eds.), *Human Sexuality: Contemporary controversies.* Beverly Hills, CA: Sage.

BLOOM, D. E. (1984). Putting off children. *American Demographics, 45,* 30–33.

BLOOMBERG, S. (1980). Influence of maternal distress during pregnancy on complications in labor and delivery. *Acta Psychiatric Scand, 62*(5), 339–404.

BLUMSTEIN, P., AND SCHWARTZ, P. (1983). *American couples.* New York: Pocket Books.

BOHANNON, P. (1970). *Divorce before and after.* New York: Doubleday.

BOHANNON, P. (1985a). *All the happy families: Exploring the varieties of family life.* New York: McGraw-Hill.

BOHANNON, P. (1985b). The six stations of divorce. In L. Cargan (Ed.), *Marriage and family: Coping with change.* Belmont, CA: Wadsworth.

BOHLAND, J. R., AND HERBERT, D. T. (1983). Neighborhood and health effects of elderly morale. *Environment and Planning, 15*(7), 929–944.

BOOTH-BUTTERFIELD, M. (1984). She hears . . . he hears: What they hear and why. *Personnel Journal, 63,* 36–41.

BOSS, P. G. (1983). The marital relationship: Boundaries and ambiguities. In H. I. McCubbin and C. R. Figley (Eds.), *Stress and the Family.* New York: Brunner/Mazel.

BOWLBY, J. (1980). *Attachment and loss* (Vol. 3). New York: Basic Books.

BOWLING, A., AND CARTWRIGHT, A. (1982). *Life after death: A study of the elderly widowed.* London: Tavistock.

BRANDEN, N. (1981). *The psychology of romantic love.* Los Angeles: J. P. Tarcher.

BREHM, S. S. (1985). *Intimate relationships.* New York: Random House.

BREINER, S. J. (1980). Sequential chronological stress in the family. *Family Therapy, 7,* 247–254.

BREZNITZ, S., AND GOLDBERGER, L. (1982). Stress research at the crossroads. In L. Goldberger and S. Breznitz (Eds.), *Handbook of stress.* New York: Free Press.

BRIGHT, M., AND STOCKDALE, D. F. (1984). Mothers', fathers', and preschool children's interactive behaviors in a play setting. *Journal of Genetic Psycholgly, 144*(2), 219–232.

BRODY, E. M. (1981). Women in the middle and family help to older people. *Gerontologist, 22*(3), 471–480.

BRODY, E. M. (1985). Parent care as a normative family stress. *Gerontologist, 25*(1), 19–29.

BROMAN, S. H. (1981). Long-term development of children born to teenagers. In K. G. Scott, T. Field, and E. Robertson (Eds.), *Teenage parents and their offspring.* New York: Grune & Stratton.

BROOKS, J. (1981). *The process of parenting.* Palo Alto, CA: Mayfield.

BROWN, B. B. (1984). *Between health and illness: New notions on stress and the nature of well-being.* Boston: Houghton Mifflin.

BROWN, J. (1983). *Nutrition for your pregnancy.* New York: Signet.

BROWN, R. (1986). *Social Psychology* (2nd ed.). New York: The Free Press.

BROWN, S. V. (1982). Early childbearing and poverty: Implications for social services. *Adolescence, 17*(66), 397–408.

BRUBAKER, T. (1985). *Later-Life families.* Beverly Hills, CA: Sage.

BRUNSON, B. L., AND MATTHEWS, K. A. (1981). The Type A coronary-prone behavior pattern and reactions to uncontrollable stress: An analysis of performance strategies, affect, and attributions during failure. *Journal of Personality and Social Psychology, 40,* 906–918.

BULCROFT, K., AND BULCROFT, R. (1985). Dating and courtship in late life: An exploratory study. In W. A. Peterson and J. Quadagno (Eds.), *Social bonds in later life.* Beverly Hills, CA: Sage.

BULLOUGH, V. L. (1981). Myths about teenage pregnancy. *Free Inquiry,* Summer, 16–20.

BURGOON, J. K. (1985). Nonverbal signals. In M. L. Knapp and G. R. Miller (Eds.), *Handbook of interpersonal communication.* Beverly Hills, CA: Sage.

BURNHAM, B. (1982). *When your friend is dying.* Grand Rapids, MI: Zondervan.

BURNS, D. B. (1985). *Intimate connections.* New York: Signet.

BUSTANOBY, A. (1985). *Single parent.* Grand Rapids, MI: Zondervan.

BUTLER, R. N., AND LEWIS, M. (1981). *Aging and mental health.* St. Louis: Mosby.

BYRNE, D. (1983). Sex without contraception. In D. Byrne and W. A. Fisher (Eds.), *Adolescents, Sex, and Contraception.* Hillsdale, NJ: Erlbaum.

C

CADOGAN, D. (1982). Twelve questions to ask before you marry. *Marriage and Family Living, 64*(2), 12–13.

CAMPBELL, A. (1981). *The sense of well-being in America.* New York: McGraw-Hill.

CANCELLIER, P. H., AND CREWS, K. A. (1986). *Women in the world: The women's decade and beyond.* Washington, DC: Population Reference Bureau.

CARGAN, L. (ED.). (1985). *Marriage and family: Coping with change.* Belmont, CA: Wadsworth.

CARGAN, L. (1985). Gender and sexuality: Influences on intimate relationships. In L. Cargan (Ed.), *Marriage and family: coping with change.* Belmont, CA: Wadsworth.

CARGAN, L., AND MELKO, M. (1982). *Singles: Myths and realities.* Beverly Hills, CA: Sage.

CARGAN, L., AND MELKO, M. (1985). Being single on Noah's ark. In L. Cargan (Ed.), *Marriage and family: Coping with change.* Belmont, CA: Wadsworth.

CARTENSEN, L., MASON, S. E., AND CALDWELL, E. C. (1982). Children's attitudes toward the elderly: An intergenerational technique for change. *Educational Gerontology, 8*(3), 291–301.

CARTER, E. A., AND MCGOLDRICK, M. (EDS.). (1980). *The family life cycle: A framework for family therapy.* New York: Gardner.

CARTWRIGHT, C. A., AND CARTWRIGHT, G. P. (1984). *Developing observation skills.* New York: McGraw-Hill.

CASSATA, M., ANDERSON, P. A., AND SKILL, T. (1983). Images of old age on day-time television. In M. Cassata and T. Skill (Eds.), *Life on daytime television.* Norwood, NJ: Ablex.

CAUHAPE, E. (1983). *Fresh starts: Men and women after divorce.* New York: Basic Books.

CHARMAZ, K. (1980). *The social reality of death.* Reading, MA: Addison-Wesley.

CHELUNE, G. J., ROBISON, J. T., AND KOMMOR, M. J. (1984). A cognitive interactional model of intimate relationships. In V. J. Derlega (Ed.), *Communication, intimacy, and close relationships.* New York: Academic Press.

CHERLIN, A. J. (1981). *Marriage, divorce, remarriage.* Cambridge, MA: Harvard University Press.

CHERLIN, A. J., AND FURSTENBERG, F. (1983). The American family in the year 2000. *The Futurist, 17,* 7–14.

CHESNEY, M. A., AND ROSENMAN, R. H. (1980a). Strategies for modifying Type A behavior. *Consultant, 20,* 216–222.

CHESNEY, M. A., AND ROSENMAN, R. H. (1980b). Type A behavior in the work setting. In C. Cooper and R. Payne (Eds.), *Current issues in occupational stress.* New York: Wiley.

CHESSER, B. J. (1980). Analysis of wedding rituals: An attempt to make weddings more meaningful. *Family Relations, 12*(1), 73–76.

CHILDREN'S DEFENSE FUND. (1982). *Employed parents and their children: A data book.* Washington, DC.

CHILDREN'S PROTECTIVE SOCIETY. (1981). (OHDS) 81-30203. Washington, DC: U.S. Government Printing Office.

CHILMAN, C. S. (1980a). Social and psychological research concerning adolescent childbearing: 1970–1980. *Journal of Marriage and the Family, 42,* 793–806.

CHILMAN, C. S. (1980b). Parent satisfactions, concerns, and goals for their children. *Family Relations, 29*(3), 339–346.

CHRISTENSEN, H. T., AND JOHNSEN, K. P. (1985). The family as a changing institution. In J. M. Henslin

(Ed.), *Marriage and family in a changing society* (2nd ed., pp. 15–26). New York: The Free Press.

CICIRELLI, V. G. (1981). *Helping elderly parents: The role of adult children.* Boston: Auburn House.

CICIRELLI, V. G. (1983). Adult childrens' attachment and helping behavior to elderly parents. *Journal of Marriage and the Family, 45,* 815–824.

CIRESE, S. (1985). *Quest: A search for self* (2nd ed.). New York: Holt, Rinehart & Winston.

CLARK, A. (ED.). (1981). *Culture and childrearing.* Philadelphia: Davis.

CLAYTON, R. R., AND BOKEMEIER, J. L. (1980). Premarital sex in the Seventies. *Journal of Marriage and the Family, 42,* 759–775.

CLEVELAND, M. (1981). Sexuality in the middle years. In P. J. Stein (Ed.), *Single life.* New York: St. Martin's Press.

COHEN, G. D. (1980). Prospects for mental health and aging. In J. E. Birren and R. B. Sloane (Eds.), *Handbook of mental health and aging.* Englewood Cliffs, NJ: Prentice-Hall.

COHLER, B. J., AND GRUNEBAUM, H. V. (1980). *Mothers, grandmothers, and daughters.* New York: Wiley.

COLE, J., AND LAIBSON, H. (1983). When parents argue (and kids listen). In O. Pocs and R. Walsh (Eds.), *Marriage and family 1983–84.* Guilford, CT: Dushkin.

COLEMAN, J. C. (1980). Friendship and the peer group in adolescence. In J. Adelson (Ed.), *Handbook of adolescent psychology.* New York: Wiley.

COLES, R. (1985). What's the best family size? In O. Pocs and R. Walsh (Eds.), *Marriage and family, 1985/86.* Guilford, CT: Dushkin.

COLES, R., AND STOKES, G. (1985). *Sex and the American teenager.* New York: Harper & Row.

COLMAN, C. (1983). *Love and money.* New York: Coward-McCann.

COLT, C. H. (1983). Suicide in America. *Harvard Magazine,* (September/October).

COOLSEN, P., AND WECHSLER, J. (1984). Community involvement in the prevention of child abuse and neglect. *Perspectives on child maltreatment in the mid 80's.* Washington, DC: U. S. Government Printing Office.

COOPER, T., DETRE, T., WEISS, S. M., BRISTOW, J. D., AND CARLETON, R. (1981). Coronary-prone behavior and coronary heart disease: A critical review. *Circulation, 63,* 1200–1215.

CORDELL, A. S., PARKE, R. D., AND SWAIN, D. B.

(1980). Father's views on fatherhood with special reference to infancy. *Family Relations, 29,* 331–338.

COREY, G. (1986). *I never knew I had a choice* (3rd ed.). Monterey, CA: Brooks/Cole.

CORNELL, C. P., AND GELLES, R. J. (1982). Adolescent to parent violence. *Urban Social Change Review,* 15 (Winter), 8–14.

COWAN, R. S. (1983). *More work for mother: The ironies of household technology from the open hearth to the microwave.* New York: Basic Books.

COX, H. (1984). *Later life: The realities of aging.* Englewood Cliffs, NJ: Prentice-Hall.

COYNE, J. C., AND LAZARUS, R. S. (1980). Cognitive style, stress perception, and coping. In I. L. Kutash and L. B. Schlesinger (Eds.), *Handbook on stress and anxiety.* San Francisco: Jossey-Bass.

CRANDALL, R. C. (1980). *Gerontology: A behavioral science approach.* Reading, MA: Addison-Wesley.

CRETSER, G. A., & LEON, J. J. (1982). Intermarriage in the U.S.: An overview of theory and research. In G. A. Cretser and J. J. Leon (Eds.), *Intermarriage in the United States.* New York: The Haworth Press.

CRITTENDEN, P. (1983). Abusive mothers feel they are good parents. *Growing Child Research Review,* 2(3), 6–8.

CROSBY, J. F. (1980). A critique of divorce statistics and their interpretation. *Family Relations,* (January), 51–56.

CROSBY, J. F., AND JOSE, N. L. (1983). Death: Family adjustment to loss. In C. R. Figley and H. I. McCubbin (Eds.), *Stress and the family.* New York: Brunner/Mazel.

CROUTER, A. C. (1982). The children of working parents. *Children Today, 11*(4), 25–28.

CRYSTAL, S. (1982). *America's old age crisis.* New York: Basic Books.

CUBER, J., AND HARNOFF, P. (1965). *Sex and the significant Americans.* Baltimore, MD: Penguin.

CUNNINGHAM, J., AND STRASSBERG, D. (1981). Neuroticism and disclosure reciprocity. *Journal of Counseling Psychology, 28,* 455–458.

CURRAN, D. (1985). *Stress and the healthy family.* Minneapolis, MN: Winston Press.

CURTIS, J. D., AND DETERT, R. A. (1981). *How to relax: A holistic approach to stress management.* Palo Alto, CA: Mayfield.

CUSHMAN, D. B., AND CAHN, D. D., JR. (1985). *Communication in interpersonal relationships.* Albany, NY: State University of New York Press.

D

DACEY, J. S. (1982). *Adult development.* Glenview, IL: Scott Foresman.

DAHL, S. (1984). *Modern bride guide to your wedding and marriage.* New York: Ballantine Books.

DAMON, W., AND HART, D. (1982). The development of self-understanding from infancy through adolescence. *Child Development, 53,* 841–864.

DANIELS, P., AND WEINGARTEN, K. (1981). *Sooner or later: The timing of parenthood in adult lives.* New York: Norton.

DAVID, H. P. (1982). China's population policy: Glimpses and a "minisurvey." *Intercom, 10*(1), 3–4.

DAVIS, K. E., AND TODD, M. J. (1985). Near and dear: Friendship and love compared. *Psychology Today,* (February), pp. 22–30.

DAVIS, P. A. (1983). *Suicidal adolescents.* Springfield, IL: Charles C. Thomas.

DEANE, B. (1985). When your parents need help. *Ladies Home Journal,* (April), pp. 74–82.

DECHESNAY, M. (1983). Incest: A family triangle. *Nursing Times, 79*(8), 64–65.

DELAMATER, J. (1981). The social control of sexuality. *Annual Review of Sociology, 7,* 76–89.

DELISLE, M. (1982). Elderly people's management of time and leisure. *Canada's Mental Health, 30*(3), 30–32.

DESPELDER, L. A., AND STRICKLAND, A. L. (1986). *The last dance: Encountering death and dying* (2nd ed.). Palo Alto, CA: Mayfield.

DICKENS, W. J., AND PERLMAN, D. (1981). Friendship over the life-cycle. *Personal Relationships.* New York: Academic Press.

DINKMEYER, D., AND CARLSON, J. (1984). *Time for a better marriage.* Circle Pines, MN: American Guidance Service.

DIPIETRO, J. (1981). Rough and tumble play: A function of gender. *Developmental Psychology 17,* 50–58.

DIXON, M. (1983). *The future of women.* San Francisco: Synthesis Publications.

DOERING, C. H. (1980). The endocrine system. In O. G. Brim, Jr. and J. Kagan (Eds.), *Constancy and change in human development.* Cambridge, MA: Harvard University Press.

DONOHUGH, D. (1981). *The middle years.* Philadelphia: Saunders.

DOUGLAS, L. S. (1982). *Women in business.* Englewood Cliffs, NJ: Prentice-Hall.

DOWNS, A. C. (1981). Sex-role stereotyping on prime-time television. *Journal of Genetic Psychology* 138, 253–258.

DREIKURS, R. (1964). *Children: The challenge.* New York: Hawthorne Books.

DURKIN, K. (1984). Children's account of sex-role stereotypes in television. *Communication Research,* 11(3), 341–362.

E

EASTMAN, P. (1984). Elders under siege. *Psychology Today,* (January), p. 30.

EDWARDS, K. (1984). *A house divided.* Grand Rapids, MI: Zondervan Books.

EIDUSON, B. T., AND ZIMMERMAN, I. L. (1985). Nontraditional families. In L. L'Abate (Ed.), *Handbook of family psychology and therapy.* Homewood, IL: The Dorsey Press.

EINSTEIN, E. (1982). *The stepfamily: Living, loving, and learning.* New York: Macmillan.

EISDORFER, C. (1983). Conceptual models of aging: The challenge of a new frontier. *American Psychologist,* 38(2), 197–202.

EISENBERG, A. MURKOFF, H. E., AND HATHAWAY, S. E. (1984). *What to expect when you're expecting.* New York: Workman Publishing Co.

ENDLER, N. S., AND EDWARDS, J. (1982). Stress and personality. In L. Goldberger and S. Breznitz (Eds.), *Handbook of stress.* New York: The Free Press.

ENTWISLE, D. R. (1985). Becoming a parent. In L. L'Abate (Ed.), *The handbook of family psychology and therapy.* Homewood, IL: The Dorsey Press.

ERIER, G. (1982). Maternity and parental leaves in Europe. *Work Times,* 1(1), 1–5.

ERIKSON, E. H. (1963). *Childhood and society* (2nd ed.). New York: W. W. Norton.

ERIKSON, E. H. (1980). *Identity and the life cycle.* New York: W. W. Norton.

ERIKSON, E. H. (1982). *The life cycle completed: A review.* New York: W. W. Norton.

ESTIOKO-GRIFFIN, A., AND GRIFFIN P. B. (1987). Woman the hunter: The Agta. In F. Dahlberg (Ed.), *Woman the gatherer.* New Haven, CN: Yale University Press.

F

FAGOT, B. I., AND KRONSBERG, S. J. (1982). Sex differences: Biological and social factors influencing the behavior of young boys and girls. In S. G. Moore and S. G. Cooper (Eds.), *The young child: Reviews of research* (Vol. 3). Washington, DC: National Association for the Education of Young Children.

FALLON, W. K. (1981). *Effective communication on the job* (3rd ed.). New York: AMACOM.

FAULKNER, L. R. (1982). Mandating the reporting of suspected cases of elder abuse: An inappropriate, ineffective, and ageist response against the abuse of older adults. *Family Law Quarterly, XV* (1), 69–91.

FAUX, M. (1984). *Childless by choice.* New York: Doubleday.

FEIN, R. (1980). Research on fathering. In A. Skolnick and J. Skolnick (Eds.), *The family transition.* Boston: Little, Brown.

FEINSTEIN, L. (1981). Type A behavior and women: A measure of sexual equality? *Health and Medical Care Services Review,* 3(1), 3–12.

FELDSTEIN, J. H., AND FELDSTEIN, S. (1982). Sex differences on televised toy commercials. *Sex Roles,* 8, 581–593.

FERBER, M. A. (1982). Labor market participation of young married women: Causes and effects. *Journal of Marriage and the Family,* 44(2), 457–475.

FIGLEY, C. R. (1983). Catastrophies: An overview of family reactions. In C. R. Figley and H. I. McCubbin (Eds.), *Stress and the family.* New York: Brunner/Mazel.

FINK, A., AND KOSECOFF, J. (1985). *How to conduct surveys.* Beverly Hills, CA: Sage.

FINKELHOR, D. (1981). Common features of family abuse. In D. Finkelhor (Ed.), *The dark side of families.* Beverly Hills, CA: Sage.

FISHER, L. R. (1983). Transition into grandmotherhood. *International Journal of Aging and Human Development,* 16, 67–78.

FISHER, M., AND STRIKER, G. (EDS.). (1982). *Intimacy.* New York: Plenum.

FISHER, W. A. (1983). Adolescent contraception: Summary and recommendations. In D. Byrne and W. A. Fisher (Eds.), *Adolescents, sex, and contraception.* Hillsdale, NJ: Erlbaum.

FORD, K. (1981). Socioeconomic differentials and trends in the timing of births. U. S. Department of Health Services, *Vital and Health Statistics, 6.*

FORNER, A., AND SCHWAB, K. (1981). *Aging and retirement.* Monterey, CA: Brooks/Cole.

FRANCIS, D. (1984). *Will you still need me, will you still feed me, when I'm 84?* Bloomington: Indiana University Press.

FREY, K. A. (1981). Middle-aged women's experience and perceptions of menopause. *Women and Health, 6,* 25–36.

FRIBOURG, S. (1982). Cigarette smoking and sudden infant death syndrome. *Journal of Obstetrics and Gynecology, 142*(7), 934–941.

FRIED, M. (1982). Endemic stress: The psychology of resignation and the politics of scarcity. *American Journal of Orthopsychiatry, 52*(1), 4–19.

FRIEDMAN, M., AND ROSENMAN, R. H. (1974). *Type A behavior and your heart.* New York: Knopf.

FU, V., AND LEACH, D. J. (1980). Sex-role preferences among elementary school children in rural America. *Psychological Reports 46,* 555–560.

FURSTENBERG, F. K., JR. (1980). Reflections on remarriage. *Journal of Family Issues, 1*(4), 443–453.

FURSTENBERG, F. K., JR., AND NORD, C. W. (1982). The life course of children of divorce: Marital disruption and parental contact. *Family Planning Perspectives, 14,* 211–221.

FURSTENBERG, F. K., JR., AND SPANIER, G. G. (1984). *Recycling the family: Remarriage after divorce.* Beverly Hills, CA: Sage.

G

GABOR, D. (1983). *How to start a conversation and make friends.* New York: Simon & Schuster.

GAELICK, L., BODENHAUSEN, G., AND WYER, R. S. (1985). Emotional communication in close relationships. *Journal of Personality and Social Psychology, 49*(5), 1246–1265.

GALINSKY, E. (1980). *Between generations: The six stages of parenthood.* New York: Times Books.

GALLUP REPORT, (1983, June). No. 213.

GALLUP, G. (1980). Small family is a trend in 23 nations. *Gallup Poll,* (November).

GARBARINO, J. (1984). What have we learned about child mistreatment? *Perspectives on child maltreatment in the mid 80's.* Washington, DC: U. S. Government Printing Office.

GARBARINO, J. (1985). *Adolescent development: An ecological perspective.* Columbus, OH: Charles E. Merrill.

GARDNER, R. A. (1982). Joint custody is not for everyone. *Family Advocate, 5*(2), 7–9.

GASTEL, B., AND HECHT, A. (1980). Estrogen: Another riddle for middle age. *FDA Consumer, 14,* 14–15.

GEISER, R. I. (1982). Incest and psychological violence. *International Journal of Family Psychiatry, 2*(3), 291–300.

GELLES, R. J. (1980). Violence in the Family: A review of research in the seventies. *Journal of Marriage and the Family 42,* 873–885.

GELLES, R. J. (1983). The myth of the battered husband. In O. Pocs & R. Walsh (Eds.), *Marriage and family, 83/84.* Guilford, CT: Dushkin.

GELLES, R. J., AND CORNELL, C. P. (1985). *Intimate violence in families.* Beverly Hills, CA: Sage.

GELLES, R. J., AND STRAUS, M. (1979). Determinants of violence in the family: Toward a theoretical integration. In W. R. Burr (Ed.), *Contemporary theories about the family.* New York: The Free Press.

GEORGE, L. K. (1980). *Role transitions in later life.* Monterey, CA: Brooks/Cole.

GEORGE, L. K., AND WELLER, S. J. (1981). Sexuality in middle and later life: The effects of age, cohort, and gender. *Archives of General Psychiatry, 38,* 919–923.

GERMAN, D., AND GERMAN, J. (1984). *Money from A to Z.* New York: Facts on File.

GERSHENFELD, M. K. (1985). Couples have the right to divorce even if they have children. In H. Feldman and M. Feldman (Eds.), *Current controversies in marriage and family.* Beverly Hills, CA: Sage.

GESSELL, A. (1940). *The first five years of life.* New York: Harper.

GIBBS, J. M. (1985). Family relations of the older widow. In W. A. Peterson and J. Quadagno (Eds.), *Social bonds in later life.* Beverly Hills, CA: Sage.

GIFFIN, M., AND FELSENTHAL, C. (1983). *A cry for help.* New York: Doubleday.

GILBERT, L. A., HOLAHAN, C. K., AND MANNING, L. (1981). Coping with conflict between professional and maternal roles. *Family Relations, 6,* 420–431.

GILLES, J. (1981). *A guide to caring for and coping with aging parents.* Nashville, TN: Thomas Nelson.

GILLIGAN, C. (1982). *In a different voice.* Cambridge, MA: Harvard University Press.

GINOTT, H. (1965). *Between parent and child.* New York: Avon Books.

GIORDANO, J. A., AND BECKHAM, K. (1985). The aged within a family context: Relationships, roles, and events. In L. L'Abate (Ed.), *The handbook of family psychology and therapy.* Homewood, IL: The Dorsey Press.

GIVENS, D. B. (1983). *Love signals.* New York: Pinnacle Books.

GLENN, N. (1982). Interreligious marriage in the

United States: Patterns and record trends. *Journal of Marriage and the Family, 44*(3), 555–556.

GLENN, N. D. (1981). The well-being of persons remarried after divorce. *Journal of Family Issues, 2,* 61–75.

GLENN, N. D., AND MCLANAHAN, S. (1981). The effects of offspring on the psychological well-being of older adults. *Journal of Marriage and the Family, 43*(5), 409–421.

GLICK, P. C. (1980). Remarriage: Some recent changes and variations. *Journal of Family Issues, 1*(12), 455–478.

GLICK, P. C. (1981). A demographic picture of Black families. In H. P. McAdoo (Ed.), *Black families.* Beverly Hills, CA: Sage.

GLICK, P. C. (1984a). How American families are changing. *American Demographics, 6,* 21–25.

GLICK, P. C. (1984b). Marriage, divorce, and living arrangements: Prospective changes. *Journal of Family Issues, 5*(1), 7–26.

GLICK, P. C., AND KESSLER, D. R. (1980). *Marital and family therapy* (2nd ed.). New York: Grune & Stratton.

GLICK, P. C., AND SPANIER, G. (1980). Married and unmarried cohabitation in the United States. *Journal of Marriage and the Family, 42,* 19–30.

GOETTING, A. (1982). The six stages of remarriage: Developmental tasks of remarriage after divorce. *Family Relations, 31,* 213–222.

GOLAN, N. (1981). *Passing through transitions.* New York: The Free Press.

GOLD, M., AND PETRONIO, R. J. (1980). Delinquent behavior in adolescence. In J. Adelson (Ed.), *Handbook of adolescent psychology.* New York: John Wiley.

GOLDBERG, H. (1983). The new male-female relationship. New York: Signet.

GOLDENBERG, I., AND GOLDENBERG, H. (1985). *Family therapy: An overview* (2nd ed.). Monterey, CA: Brooks/Cole.

GOLDSTEIN, S., AND SOLNIT, A. J. (1984). *Divorce and your child: Practical suggestions for parents.* New Haven, CT: Yale University Press.

GORDON, T. (1978). *P.E.T. in action.* New York: Bantam Books.

GOULD, R. L. (1980). Transformations during early and middle adult years. In N. Smelser and E. Erikson (Eds.), *Themes of work and love in adulthood.* Cambridge, MA: Harvard University Press.

GRASHA, A. F., AND KIRSCHENBAUM, D. S. (1986). *Adjustment and competence.* St. Paul, MN: West.

GRATTON, B., AND HUAG, M. R. (1983). Decision and adaptation: Research on female retirement. *Research on Aging, 5*(1), 59–76.

GRAY, M. (1981). *The changing years: The menopause without fear* (3rd ed.). New York: Signet Books.

GREEN, A. H. (1985). Sibling abuse: Common, but ignored. *Marriage and Divorce Today, 11*(18), 1.

GREENBERGER, E., AND STEINBERG, L. D. (1983). Sex differences in early labor force experience: Harbinger of things to come. *Social Forces, 62*(2), 467–486.

GREENBERG, P. (1983). The empty nest syndrome. *The Single Parent,* (July/August), 17–23.

GREENBLAT, C. S. (1983). The salience of sexuality in the early years of marriage. *Journal of Marriage and the Family, 45*(2), 289–299.

GREENBLAT, C. S., AND COTTLE, T. J. (1980). *Getting married: A new look at an old tradition.* New York: McGraw-Hill.

GREENE, V. L., AND MONAHAN, D. J. (1982). The impact of visitation on patient well-being in nursing homes. *Gerontologist, 22,* 418–423.

GREGERSON, E. (1983). *Sexual practices.* New York: Franklin Watts.

GRIEF, G. L. (1985). *Single fathers.* Lexington, MA: D. C. Heath.

GRIGSBY, J. P., AND WEATHERLEY, D. (1983). Gender and sex role differences in intimacy of self-disclosure. *Psychological Reports, 53*(1), 891–897.

GROSSMAN, A. S. (1981). Working mothers and their children. *Monthly Labor Review, 104*(5), 49–54.

GROSSMAN, A. S. (1982). More than half of all children have working mothers. *Monthly Labor Review, 105*(2), 41–43.

GRUBER, F. (ED.), (1985). *Caring for dependent parents.* New York: Research Institute of America.

GRUELING, J. W., AND DEBLASSIE, R. R. (1980). Adolescent suicide. *Adolescence, 15,* 589–601.

GRUSON, L. (1985). Groups play matchmaker to preserve Judaism. *New York Times,* (April 1).

GUERNEY, B. G., JR., GUERNEY, L., AND COONEY, T. (1985). Marital and family problem prevention and enrichment programs. In L. L'Abate (Ed.), *The handbook of family psychology and therapy.* Homewood, IL: Dorsey Press.

GUYTON, A. C. (1981). *Textbook of medical physiology* (6th ed.). Philadelphia: Saunders.

H

HAAS, L. (1980). Role-sharing couples: A study of egalitarian marriages. *Family Relations, 29,* 289–294.

HABER, C. (1983). *Beyond sixty-five: The dilemma of old age in America's past.* Cambridge: Cambridge University Press.

HALE, C. (1984). *The super years.* Old Tappan, NJ: Revell.

HALES, D., AND CREASY, R. K. (1982). *New hope for problem pregnancies.* New York: Harper & Row.

HALL, J. A. (1984). *Nonverbal sex differences: Communication accuracy and expressive style.* Baltimore, MD: The Johns Hopkins University Press.

HALL, R. E. (1983). *Nine months reading.* New York: Bantam Books.

HALLBERG, E. (1980). *The gray itch: The male metapause syndrome.* New York: Warner Books.

HAMID, P. N., AND WYLLIE, A. J. (1980). What generation gap? *Adolescence, 15,* 385–391.

HAMILTON, E. N., AND WHITNEY, E. N. (1982). *Nutrition: Concepts and controversies.* St. Paul, MN: West Publishing.

HANSON, S. M., AND BOZETT, F. W. (EDS.). (1985). *Dimensions of fatherhood.* Beverly Hills, CA: Sage.

HARDERT, R. A., GORDON, L., LANER, M. R., AND READER, M. (1984). *Confronting social problems.* St. Paul, MN: West.

HARMATZ, M. G., AND NOVAK, M. A. (1983). *Human sexuality.* New York: Harper & Row.

HARRIS, D. K., AND COLE, W. E. (1980). *The sociology of aging.* Boston: Houghton Mifflin.

HARRIS, M. B., AND SATTER, B. J. (1981). Sex-role stereotypes of kindergarten children. *Journal of Genetic Psychology, 138*(1), 49–61.

HARTER, S. (1983). Developmental perspectives on the self-system. In P. H. Mussen (Ed.), *Handbook of child psychology: Socialization, personality, and social development.* New York: John Wiley.

HASSETT, J. (1981). But that would be wrong. *Psychology Today,* (December), pp. 34–53.

HATFIELD, E. (1984). The dangers of intimacy. In V. J. Derlega (Ed.), *Communication, intimacy, and close relationships.* New York: Academic Press.

HAUPT, A., AND KANE, T. T. (1985). *Population handbook.* Washington, DC: Population Reference Bureau.

HAYGHE, H. (1982). Dual-earner families: Their economic and demographic characteristics. In J. Aldous (Ed.), *Two paychecks: Life in dual-earner families.* Beverly Hills, CA: Sage.

HEATON, T., ALBRECHT, S., AND MARTIN T. (1985). The timing of divorce. *Journal of Marriage and the Family, 40*(3), 18–26.

HELFER, R. E. (1982). A review of the literature on the prevention of child abuse and neglect. *Child Abuse and Neglect: The International Journal, 6,* 251–262.

HELLMAN, J. R. (1980). Menopause: Myths are yielding to new scientific research. *Science Digest, 87,* 66–68.

HELSING, K., SZKLO, M., AND COMSTOCK, G. W. (1981). The stresses of survival can be a mortal blow. *American Journal of Public Health,* (August), 14–25.

HENDRICKS, J., AND HENDRICKS, C. D. (1981). *Aging in mass society: Myths and realities* (2nd ed.). Cambridge, MA: Winthrop.

HENIG, R. M. (1985). *How a woman ages.* New York: Ballantine Books.

HENSLIN, J. M. (ED.). (1985a). *Marriage and family in a changing society* (2nd ed.). New York: The Free Press.

HENSLIN, J. M. (1985b). Sex roles. In J. M. Henslin (ED.), *Marriage and family in a changing society* (2nd ed.). New York: The Free Press.

HENSLIN, J. M. (1985c). Why so much divorce? In J. M. Henslin (Ed.), *Marriage and family in a changing society* (2nd ed.). New York: The Free Press.

HETHERINGTON, E. M. (1981). Tracing children through the changing family. *APA Monitor, 12,* 462–479.

HEWLETT, S. (1986). *A lesser life: The myth of women's liberation in America.* New York: William Morrow.

HIEMSTRA, R. (1983). How older persons are portrayed in television advertising: Implications for educators. *Educational Gerontology, 9,* 111–122.

HIGHAM, E. (1980). Variations in adolescent psychohormonal development. In J. Adelson (Ed.), *Handbook of adolescent psychology.* New York: John Wiley.

HILL, E. A., AND DORFMAN, L. T. (1982). Reaction of housewives to the retirement of their husbands. *Family Relations, 4,* 195–200.

HILL, R. (1949). *Families under stress.* New York: Harper & Row.

HILLARD, P. A., AND PANTER, G. G. (1985). *Pregnancy and childbirth.* New York: Ballantine.

HOGAN, M. J., BUEHLER, C., AND ROBINSON, B. (1983). Single parenting: Transitioning alone. In H. I. McCubbin and C. R. Figley (Eds.), *Stress and the Family*. New York: Brunner/Mazel.

HOLLAND, M. K. (1985). *Using psychology*. Boston: Little, Brown.

HOLMES, T. H., AND RAHE, R. H. (1967). The social readjustment rating scale. *Journal of Psychosomatic Research, 11*, 213–218.

HONIG, A. (1983). Research in review: Sex role socialization in early childhood. *Young Children, 38*(6), 57–70.

HONIG, A. S. (1986). Stress and coping in children. *Young Children, 41*(4), 50–63.

HOOK, W. F., SOBAL, J., AND OAK, K. C. (1982). Frequency of visitation in nursing homes: Patterns of contact across the boundaries of total institutions. *Gerontologist, 22*, 424–428.

HOTCHNER, T. (1984). *Pregnancy and childbirth*. New York: Avon.

HOWSDEN, J. L. (1982). *Work and the helpless self: The social organization of a nursing home*. Lanham, MD: University Press of America.

HYDEN, P., AND MCCANDLESS, N. J. (1983). Men and women as portrayed in the lyrics of contemporary music. *Popular Music and Society 9*(2), 10–26.

HYMES, A., AND NEURNBERGER, P. (1980). Breathing patterns found in heart attack patients. *Research Bulletin of the Himalayan International Institute, 2*(2), 10–12.

I

INAZU, J. K., AND FOX, G. L. (1980). Maternal influence on the sexual behavior of teenage daughters. *Journal of Family Issues*, (March), 81–102.

ISAACS, F. (1986). High-tech pregnancies. *Working Mother*, (January), 18–26.

ISAACSON, W. (1981). The battle over abortion. *Time*, (June), 36–44.

J

JACOBSON, D. S. (1980). Stepfamilies. *Children Today, 9*, 2–6.

JAFFE, S. S., AND VIERTEL, J. (1980). *Becoming parents: Preparing for the emotional changes of first time parenthood*. New York: Atheneum.

JENSON, L. C., AND JENSEN, J. M. (1981). *Stepping into stepparenting: A practical guide*. Palo Alto, CA: R. and E. Associates.

JETER, K., AND SUSSMAN, M. B. (1985). Each couple should develop a marriage contract suitable to themselves. In H. Feldman and M. Feldman (Eds.), *Current controversies in marriage and family*. Beverly Hills, CA: Sage.

JOHNSON, B. (1980). Single-parent families. *Family Economics Review*, (Summer-Fall), 22–27.

JOHNSON, H. C. (1980). Working with stepfamilies: Principles of practice. *Social Work, 25*, 304–308.

JONES, C. C. (1982). *Caring for the aged: An appraisal of nursing homes and alternatives*. Chicago: Nelson-Hall.

JONES, K. L., SHAINBERG, L. W., AND BYER, C. O. (1985). *Dimensions of human sexuality*. Dubuque, IA: William C. Brown.

K

KALISH, R. A. (1982). *Late adulthood: Perspectives on human development* (2nd ed.). Monterey, CA: Brooks/Cole.

KAMERMAN, S. B. (1985). Time out for babies. *Working Mother, 4*(9), 80–82.

KAMERMAN, S., AND KAHN, A. J. (1981). *Child care, family benefits, and working mothers*. New York: Columbia University Press.

KAMERMAN, S. B., KAHN, A. J., AND KINGSTON, P. W. (1983). *Maternity policies and working women*. New York: Columbia University Press.

KANDEL, D. B. (1980, April). *Peer influence in adolescence*. Paper presented at the Society for Research in Child Development, Boston.

KANTNER, J. F., AND ZELNIK, M. (1980). Sexual and contraceptive experience of young unmarried women, 1979. *Family Planning Perspectives, 16*, 17–24.

KARGAN, M. W. (1985). *How to manage a marriage*. Boston, MA: Foundation Books.

KART, C. S. (1981). *The realities of aging*. Boston, MA: Allyn and Bacon.

KATCHADOURIAN, H. A. (1985). *Fundamentals of human sexuality* (4th ed.). New York: Holt, Rinehart & Winston.

KAUFFMAN, J. F., AND AMES, B. D. (1983). Care of aging family members. *Journal of Home Economics, 75*(1), 45–46.

KAYE, C. (1981). Genetic counseling. *Medical Aspects of Human Sexuality, 15*(3), 164–180.

KAZA, A. E., AND REPPUCCI, N. D. (1980). *On love and loving.* San Francisco, CA: Jossey-Bass.

KEATS, C. (1981). Co-parenting. *Issues in Health Care of Women, 3*(5), 371–374.

KEEN, S. (1985). Don't come any closer! The barriers that keep people from caring. In O. Pocs and R. Walsh (Eds.), *Marriage and family 85/86.* Guilford, CT: Dushkin.

KELLEY, K. (1983). Adolescent sexuality: the first lessons. In D. Byrne and W. A. Fisher (Eds.), *Adolescents, sex, and contraception.* New York: McGraw-Hill.

KELLY, C., AND GOODWIN, G. C. (1983). Adolescents' perception of three styles of parental control. *Adolescence, 18*(71), 567–571.

KEMPE, R. S., AND KEMPE, C. H. (1984). *The common secret: Sexual abuse of children and adolescents.* New York: W. H. Freeman.

KENDIG, H. L., AND ROWLAND, D. T. (1983). Family support of the Australian aged: A comparison with the United States.*The Gerontologist, 23*(6), 643–649.

KERMIS, M. D. (1984). *The psychology of aging: Theory, research, and practice.* Boston: Allyn and Bacon.

KIMBALL, G. (1983). *The so-so marriage.* Boston: Beacon Press.

KINARD, E. M. (1980). Emotional development in physically abused children. *American Journal of Orthopsychiatry, 50,* 686–696.

KINSEY, A. C., POMEROY, W. B., AND MARTIN, C. E. (1948). *Sexual behavior in the human male.* Philadelphia: Saunders.

KINSEY, A. C., POMEROY, W. B., AND MARTIN, C. E. (1953). *Sexual behavior in the human female.* Philadelphia: Saunders.

KIVNICK, H. (1982). *The meaning of grandparenthood: Research in clinical psychology,* (No. 3). Ann Arbor, MI: JMI Research Press.

KLANGSBRUN, F. (1985). *Married people: Staying together in the age of divorce.* New York: Bantam.

KNAUB, P. K., EVERSOLL, D. B., AND VOSS, J. H. (1983). Is parenthood a desirable adult role? An assessment of attitudes held by contemporary women. *Sex Roles, 9*(3), 355–362.

KNAUB, P. K., AND HANNA, S. L. (1984). Children of remarriage: Perceptions of family strengths. *Journal of Divorce, 7*(4), 73–90.

KNIGHT, B. M. (1986). *Enjoying single parenthood.* New York: Van Nostrand Reinhold.

KNOX, D., AND WILSON, K. (1981). Dating behaviors of university students. *Family Relations,* (April), 255–258.

KOBASA, S. C., MADDI, S. R., AND ZOLA, M. A. (1983). Type A and hardiness. *Journal of Behavioral Medicine, 6,* 41–51.

KOMPARA, D. R. (1980). Difficulties in the socialization process of stepparenting. *Family Relations, 29,* 69–73.

KONOPKA, G. (1983). Adolescent suicide. *Exceptional Children, 49*(5), 390–394.

KONTOS, S., AND STEVENS, R. (1985). High quality child care: Does your center measure up? *Young Children, 40*(2), 5–9.

KORNHABER, A., AND WOODWARD, K. L. (1981). *Grandparents/grandchildren: The vital connection.* New York: Doubleday.

KRANTZLER, M. (1981). *Creative marriage.* New York: McGraw-Hill.

KRANZLER, M., AND WALSH, R. (EDS.). (1985). *Marriage and family, 1985/86.* Guilford, CT: Dushkin.

KRAUSE, M. V. (1984). *Food, nutrition and diet therapy* (7th ed.). Philadelphia: Saunders.

KUANSNICKA, B., BEYMER, B., AND PERLOFF, R. M. (1982). Portrayals of the elderly in magazine advertisements. *Journalism Quarterly, 59*(4), 656–658.

KUBLER-ROSS, E. (1981). *Living with death and dying.* New York: Macmillan.

KURDEK, L. A. (1981). An integrative perspective on children's divorce adjustment. *American Psychologist, 36,* 856–866.

L

LAGRAND, L. E. (1981). Loss reactions of college students: A descriptive analysis. *Death Education, 5,* 238–249.

LAMB, M. E. (ED.). (1981). *The role of the father in child development* (2nd ed.). New York: Wiley.

LAMB, M. E. (1982). Paternal influences on early socio-emotional development. *Journal of Child Psychology and Psychiatry and Allied Disciplines, 23*(2), 185–190.

LAMB, M. E. (1983, June 17). *The changing role of the father.* Paper presented at the Greater New York Area Fatherhood Forum, Bank Street College of Education.

LAMB, M. E., EASTERBROOKS, M. A., AND HOLDEN, G. W. (1980). Reinforcement and punishment among preschoolers: Characteristics, effects, and correlates. *Child Development, 51,* 1230–1236.

LAMB, M. E., PLECK, J. H., AND LEVINE, J. A. (1986). Effects of increased paternal involvement in children in two-parent families. In R. A. Lewis and R. E. Salt Eds.), *Men in families.* Beverly Hills, CA: Sage.

LAMER, M. R., AND HOUSKER, S. L. (1980). Sexual permissiveness in younger and older adults. *Journal of Family Issues, 1,* 103–124.

LANE, K. E., AND GWARTNEY-GIBBS, P. A. (1985). Violence in the context of dating and sex. *Journal of Family Issues, 6*(1), 45–59.

LANG, L. R., AND GILLESPIE, T. H. (1984). *Strategy for personal finance.* New York: McGraw-Hill.

LANGLOIS, J. H., AND DOWN, A. C. (1980). Mothers, fathers, and peers as socialization agents of sex-typed play behaviors in young children. *Child Development, 51,* 1217–1247.

LANGTON, P. (1984). Vulnerable breadwinners: Larim women in East Africa. *IDRC Reports, 13*(2), 8–9.

LAROSSA, R., AND LAROSSA, M. M. (1981). *Transition to parenthood: How infants change families.* Beverly Hills, CA: Sage.

LARSON, I. E. (1980). The influence of parents and peers during adolescence: The situation hypothesis. In R. E. Muuss (Ed.), *Adolescent behavior and society* (3rd ed.). New York: Random House.

LASSWELL, T. E., AND LASSWELL, M. E. (1985). The meaning of love. In J. M. Henslin (Ed.), *Marriage and family in a changing society* (2nd ed.). New York: The Free Press.

LAUERSEN, N. H. (1983). *Childbirth with love.* New York: Berkley.

LEDERER, J. (1983). Birth-control decisions. *Psychology Today,* (June), pp. 68–77.

LEE, G. (1980). Kinship in the Seventies: A decade review of research and theory. *Journal of Marriage in the Family, 42,* 923–934.

LEEHAN, J., AND WILSON, L. P. (1985). *Grown-up abused children.* Springfield, IL: Charles C. Thomas.

LEIN, L. (1984). *Families without villains: American families in an era of change.* Lexington, MA: Heath.

LEMASTERS, E. E., AND DEFRAIN, J. (1983). *Parents in contemporary America* (4th ed.). Homewood, IL: The Dorsey Press.

LEVINGER, G. (1983). Development and change. In H. H. Kelly (Ed.), *Close relationships.* New York: W. H. Freeman.

LEVINSON, A. (1984). Home birth: Joy or jeopardy? In O. Pocs (Ed.), *Human sexuality, 1984–85.* Guilford, CT: Dushkin.

LEVINSON, D. (1980). Conceptions of the adult life course. In N. Smelser and E. Erikson (Eds.), *Themes of work and love in adulthood.* Cambridge, MA: Harvard University Press.

LEWIS, R. A., AND SALT, R. E. (EDS.). (1986). *Men in families.* Beverly Hills, CA: Sage.

LICHTER, D. T. (1981). Components of change in the residential concentration of the elderly population. *Journal of Gerontology, 36*(4), 480–489.

LIEBERMAN, M. A., AND TOBIN, S. S. (1983). *The experience of old age: Stress, coping, and survival.* New York: Basic Books.

LIEBMAN, T. H. (1984). When will you be back? We bring generations together. *Young Children, 39*(6), 70–75.

LINDBERG, L., AND SWEDLOW, R. (1985). *Young children: Exploring and learning.* Boston, MA: Allyn and Bacon.

LIPMAN-BLUMEN, J. (1984). *Gender roles and power.* Englewood Cliffs, NJ: Prentice-Hall.

LOCKERY, S. A. (1985). Care in the minority family. *Generations, 10*(1), 17–19.

LOEWINSOHN, R. J. (1984). *Survival handbook for widows.* Glenview, IL: Scott, Foresman.

LONDERVILLE, S., AND MAIN, M. (1981). Security of attachment, compliance, and maternal training methods in the second year of life. *Developmental Psychology, 17,* 289–299.

LONG, J. (1984). Nontraditional roles of men and women strengthen the family and provide healthier sexual relationships. In H. Feldman and A. Parrot (Eds.), *Human sexuality: Contemporary controversies.* Beverly Hills, CA: Sage.

LOONEY, J. G., AND LEWIS, J. (1984). Healthy families span colors, income levels. *Growing Child Research Review, 2*(8), 12–14.

LOPATA, H. Z. (1973). *Widowhood in an American city.* Cambridge, MA: Schneckman.

LOPATA, H. Z. (1979). *Women as widows.* New York: Elseview.

LOPATA, H. Z. (1981). Widowhood and husband sanctification. *Journal of Marriage and the Family, 83,* 439–450.

LOUDIN, J. (1981). *The hoax of romance.* Englewood, Cliffs, NJ: Prentice-Hall.

LOVALLO, W. R., AND PISHKIN, V. A. (1980). A psychophysiological comparison of Type A and B men exposed to failure and uncontrollable noise. *Psychophysiology, 17,* 29 – 36.

LOWY, L. (1985). *Social work with the aging.* New York: Longman.

LUDEMAN, K. (1981). The sexuality of the older person: Review of the literature. *The Gerontologist, 21,* 203 – 208.

LUTZ, P. (1983). The stepfamily: An adolescent perspective. *Family Relations, 32*(3), 367 – 375.

M

MACCOBY, E. E. (1980). *Social development.* New York: Harcourt Brace Jovanovich.

MACKLIN, E. D. (1980). Nontraditional family forms: A decade of research. *Journal of Marriage and the Family, 42*(4), 905 – 922.

MACOVSKY, S. J. (1983). Coping with cohabitation. In O. Pocs and R. Walsh (Eds.), *Marriage and family 1983/84.* Guilford, CT: Dushkin.

MAIER, R. A. (1984). *Human sexuality in perspective.* Chicago, IL: Nelson-Hall.

MANDEL, B., AND MANDEL, B. (1985). *Play safe: How to avoid getting sexually transmitted diseases.* Foster City, CA: Center for Health Information.

MARACEK, J., AND BALLOU, D. J. (1981). Family roles and women's mental health. *Professional Psychology, 12,* 39 – 46.

MARSH, R. (1981). The income and resources of the elderly in 1978. *Social Security Bulletin, 44*(12), 3 – 11.

MARSHALL, D. S. (1971). Sexual behavior on Mangaia. In D. S. Marshall and R. C. Suggs (Eds.), *Human sexual behavior: Variation in the ethnographic spectrum.* New York: Basic Books.

MARTIN, C. E. (1981). Factors affecting sexual functioning in 60 – 79 year-old married males. *Archives of Sexual Behavior, 10,* 399 – 420.

MARTIN, M. J., AND WALTERS, J. (1982). Familial correlates of selected types of child abuse and neglect. *Journal of Marriage and the Family, 44,* 267 – 276.

MASAMBA MA MPOLO. (1984). *Older persons and their families in a changing village society: A perspective from Zaire.* Washington, DC: International Federation on Aging.

MASLOW, A. H. (1968). *Toward a psychology of being* (2nd ed.). Princeton, NJ: Van Nostrand Reinhold.

MASLOW, A. H. (1970). *Motivation and personality* (2nd ed.). New York: Harper & Row.

MASNICK, G., AND BANE, M. J. (1980). *The nation's families: 1960 – 1990.* Cambridge, MA: Joint Center for Urban Studies of MIT and Harvard University.

MASTERS, W. H., AND JOHNSON, V. E. (1966). *Human sexual response.* Boston: Little, Brown.

MASTERS, W. H., AND JOHNSON, V. E. (1980). *Homosexuality in perspective.* Boston: Little, Brown.

MASTERS, W. H., AND JOHNSON, V. E. (1981). Sex and the aging process. *Journal of the American Geriatrics Society, 9,* 385 – 390.

MASTERS, W. H., JOHNSON, V. E., AND KOLODNY, R. C. (1986). *Masters and Johnson on sex and human loving.* Boston: Little, Brown.

MATEK, O., AND KERSTEIN, S. E. (1985). Fear of death during rape and the mourning process that follows. In W. F. Finn (Ed.), *Women and loss: Psychobiological perspectives.* New York: Praeger.

MAY, K. A., AND PERRIN, S. P. (1985). Prelude: Pregnancy and birth. In S. M. Hanson and F. W. Bozett (Eds.), *Dimensions of fatherhood.* Beverly Hills, CA: Sage.

MCADOO, H. P. (1983). Societal stress: The Black family. In H. I. McCubbin and C. R. Figley (Eds.), *Stress and the family.* New York: Brunner/Mazel.

MCCARTHY, B., AND MCCARTHY, E. (1984). *Sexual awareness: Enhancing sexual pleasure.* New York: Carroll and Graf.

MCCARY, J. L., AND MCCARY, S. P. (1982). *McCary's human sexuality.* (4th ed.). Belmont, CA: Wadsworth.

MCCORMICK, N. B., AND JESSER, C. J. (1983). The courtship game: Power in the sexual encounter. In E. R. Allgeier and N. B. McCormick (Eds.), *Changing boundaries: Gender roles and sexual behavior.* Palo Alto, CA: Mayfield.

MCCOY, E. (1984). Kids and divorce. *Parents,* (November), pp. 112 – 116.

MCCUBBIN, H. I., CAUBLE, A. E., AND PATTERSON, J. M. (1982). *Family stress, coping, and social support.* Springfield, IL: Charles C. Thomas.

MCCUBBIN, H. I., AND PATTERSON, J. M. (1982). Family adaptation to crises. In H. I. McCubbin, A. E. Cauble, and J. M. Patterson (Eds.), *Family Stress, Coping, and Social Support.* Springfield, IL: Charles C. Thomas.

McCUBBIN, H. I., AND PATTERSON, J. M. (1983a). Family transitions: Adaptation to stress. In H. I. McCubbin and C. R. Figley (Eds.), *Stress and the family*. New York: Brunner/Mazel.

McCUBBIN, H. I., AND PATTERSON, J. M. (1983b). The family stress process: The double ABCX model of adjustment and adaptation. In H. I. McCubbin, M. B. Sussman, and J. M. Patterson (Eds.), *Social stress and the family*. New York: The Haworth Press.

McFALLS, J. A., JR. (1981, March 15). Where have all the children gone? *USA Today*.

McGOLDERICK, M., AND CARTER, E. A. (1982a). The stages of the family life cycle. In F. Walsh (Ed.), *Normal Family Processes*. New York: Guilford Press.

McGOLDERICK, M., AND CARTER, E. A. (1982b). Remarriage and the family life cycle. In F. Walsh (Ed.), *Normal Family Processes*. New York: Guilford Press.

McKAY, M., DAVIS, M., AND FANNING, P. (1983). *Messages: The communication skills book*. Oakland, CA: New Harbinger Publications.

McKAY, M., ROGERS, P. D., BLADES, J., AND GOOSE, R. (1984). *The divorce book*. Oakland, CA: New Harbinger Publications.

McKEE, J. S. (1986). Development and educational opportunities. In J. S. McKee (Ed.), *Early childhood education 86/87*. Guilford, CT: Dushkin.

McKENZIE, S. C. (1980). *Aging and old age*. Glenview, IL: Scott, Foresman.

McLAUGHLIN, B., WHITE, D., McDEVITT, T., AND RASKIN, R. (1983). Mothers' and fathers' speech to their young children: Similar or different? *Journal of Child Language, 10*(1), 245–252.

McMAHON, F. B., AND McMAHON, J. W. (1982). *Psychology: The hybrid science*. Homewood, IL: The Dorsey Press.

McNAB, W. L. (1982). Rape prevention through health education. *Health values: Achieving high level wellness, 6*(6), 36–42.

MEAD, M. (1950). *Sex and temperament in three primitive societies*. New York: Merton.

MEDERER, H., AND HILL, R. (1983). Critical transitions over the family life span: Therapy and research. In H. I. McCubbin, M. B. Sussman, and J. M. Patterson (Eds.), *Social stress and the family*. New York: The Haworth Press.

MENNINGER, K. (1963). *The vital balance*. New York: Viking.

MESSENGER, J. C. (1971). Sex and repression in an Irish folk community. In D. S. Marshall and R. C. Suggs (Eds.), *Human sexual behavior: Variations in the ethnographic spectrum*. New York: Basic Books.

MILES, M. S., AND CRANDALL, E. K. (1983). The search for meaning and its potential for affecting growth in bereaved parents. *Health values: Achieving high level wellness, 7*(1), 19–23.

MILLER, B. C. (1986). *Family research methods*. Beverly Hills, CA: Sage.

MILLER, B. C., AND BOWEN, S. L. (1982). Father-to-newborn attachment behavior in relation to prenatal classes and presence at delivery. *Family Relations, 31*, 71–78.

MILLER, B. C., AND SOLLIE, D. L. (1980). Normal stress during the transition to parenthood. *Family Relations, 29*, 459–465.

MILLER, J., AND GARRISON, H. H. (1984). Sex roles: The division of labor at home and in the workplace. In D. H. Olson and B. C. Miller (Eds.), *Family Studies Review Yearbook* (Vol. 2). Beverly Hills, CA: Sage.

MILLETTE, B. (1982). Menopause: A survey of attitudes and knowledge. *Issues of Health Care in Women, 3*, 263–276.

MILLETTE, B., AND HAWKINS, J. (1983). *The passage through menopause: Women's lives in transition*. Reston, VA: Reston.

MITCHELL, J., AND REGISTER, J. C. (1984). An exploration of family interaction with the elderly by race, socioeconomic status, and residence. *Gerontologist, 24*, 48–54.

MITCHELL, J. B. (1982). Physician visits to nursing homes. *Gerontologist, 22*(1), 45–48.

MITCHELL, J. S. (1982). *I can be anything* (3rd ed.). New York: College Entrance Examination Board.

MITCHELL, K. (1983). The price tag of responsibility: A comparison of divorced and remarried mothers. *Journal of Divorce, 6*(3), 33–42.

MONEY, J. (1980). *Love and love sickness*. Baltimore: John Hopkins University Press.

MONTGOMERY, T. A., AND LEASHORE, B. R. (1982). Teenage parenthood. *Urban Research Review, 8*(3), 1–13.

MOORE, P. G. (1984). Assessment of the effects of menopause on individual women: A review of the literature. *Issues in Health Care of Women, 4*(6), 341–350.

MORRISON, G. (1984). *Early childhood education today* (3rd ed.). Columbus, OH: Charles E. Merrill.

MORRISON, T. (1983). The perfect family. *Transition, 13*(4), 11–13.

MORROW, P. C. (1980). Retirement preparation: A preventative approach to counseling the elderly. *Counseling and Values, 24*(4), 236–246.

MUDD, E. H., AND TAUBIN, S. (1982). Success in family living: Does it last? A twenty-year followup. *Journal of Family Therapy, 10,* 59–67.

MULLER, R., AND GOLDBERG, S. (1980). Why William doesn't want a doll: Preschoolers' expectations of adult behavior towards boys and girls. *Merrill-Palmer Quarterly, 26,* 259–69.

MURDOCK, C. V. (1980). *Single parents are people, too!* New York: Butterick.

MURPHY, C. (1983). *Teaching kids to play.* New York: Leisure Press.

MURSTEIN, B. L. (1986). *Paths to marriage.* Beverly Hills, CA: Sage.

N

NAEYE, R. I. (1981). Influence of maternal cigarette smoking during pregnancy on fetal and childhood growth. *Journal of Obstetrics and Gynecology, 57*(1), 18–21.

NANNARONE, N. (1983). Career father. *Marriage and Family Living, 65,* 8–11.

NATIONAL ASSOCIATION FOR THE EDUCATION OF YOUNG CHILDREN. (1983). How to choose a good early childhood program. Vol. 39, No. 1, (November), 28–32.

NATIONAL CENTER ON CHILD ABUSE AND NEGLECT. (1984). Everything you wanted to know about child abuse and neglect and never asked. In *Perspectives on child maltreatment in the mid '80's.* Washington, DC: U. S. Government Printing Office.

NATIONAL CENTER ON HEALTH STATISTICS. (1986, March 26). Birth control methods. *Monthly Vital Statistics Report, 34.*

NATIONAL CENTER ON HEALTH STATISTICS. (1986, March 26). Marriages, divorces, and deaths for 1985. *Monthly Vital Statistics Report, 34.*

NATIONAL CENTER ON HEALTH STATISTICS. (1986, April). *Monthly Vital Statistics Report, 35*(4).

NATIONAL COUNCIL ON THE AGING. (1981). *Aging in the Eighties: America in transition.* Washington, DC: Louis Harris and Associates.

NATIONAL INSTITUTE OF HEALTH. (1981). Cesarean childbirth. *Consensus Development Conference Summary* (Vol. 3, No. 6). Washington, DC: U. S. Government Printing Office.

NATIONAL RESEARCH COUNCIL. (1981, September 2). Equal employment opportunity commission report. *San Francisco Chronicle.*

NEURINGER, C., AND LETTIERI, D. J. (1982). *Suicidal women: Their thinking and feeling patterns.* New York: Gardner Press.

NICHOLS, M. (1984). *Family therapy: Concepts and methods.* New York: Gardner Press.

NICHOLSON, J. (1980). Three seasons of life. *New Society, 53,* pp. 926–928.

NIEVA, V. F., AND GUTEK, B. A. (1981). *Women and work: A psychological perspective.* New York: Praeger.

NISBET, R. (1984). Death. In E. S. Shneidman (Ed.), *Death: Current perspectives* (3rd ed.). Palo Alto, CA: Mayfield.

NOBLE, E. (1980). *Having twins: A parent's guide to pregnancy, birth and early childhood.* Boston: Houghton Mifflin.

NOTMAN, M. T. (1980). Changing roles for women in mid-life. In W. H. Norman and T. J. Scaramella (Eds.), *Mid-life: Development and clinical issues.* New York: Brunner/Mazel.

NUERNBERGER, P. (1981). *Freedom from stress.* Honesdale, PA: The Himalayan International Institute of Yoga, Science, and Philosophy Publishers.

NUSBERG, C. (1982). Filial responsibility still required in Hungary. *Aging International, 8*(4), 8–9.

NUSBERG, C. (1983). Quality of life problematic for residents of French nursing homes. *Aging International, 9*(2), 19–21.

O

OAKLAND, T. (1984). *Divorced fathers: Reconstructing a quality life.* New York: Human Sciences Press.

O'BRIEN, S. (1984). *Child Abuse and neglect: Everyone's problem.* Wheaton, MD: Association for Childhood Education International.

O'KANE, M. L. (1981). *Living with adult children.* St. Paul, MN: Diction Books.

OKUN, B. F. (1984). *Working with adults: Individual, family, and career development.* Monterey, CA: Brooks/Cole.

OLDS, S. W. (1983). Do you have what it takes to make a good marriage? In O. Pocs and R. Walsh

(Eds.), *Marriage and family*, 83–84. Guilford, CT: Dushkin.

OLDS, S. W. (1985). *The eternal garden: Seasons of our sexuality.* New York: Times Books.

OLIVER, D. (1982). Why do people live together? *Journal of Social Welfare, 7,* 209–22.

OLSON, L. K. (1982). *The political economy of aging: The state, private power, and social welfare.* New York: Columbia University Press.

O'MALLEY, T. (1983). Identifying and presenting family-mediated abuse and neglect of elderly persons. *Annals of Internal Medicine, 98,* 998–1005.

O'REILLY, J. (1983). Wife beating: The silent crime. *Time,* (September), pp. 23–26.

ORY, M. G. (1985). The burden of care. *Generations, 10*(1), 14–18.

OSKAMP, S., AND MINDICK, B. (1981). Personality and attitudinal barriers to contraception. In D. Byrne and W. A. Fisher (Eds.), *Adolescents, sex, and contraception.* New York: McGraw-Hill.

O'TOOLE, R., TURBETT, J. P., LINZ, M., AND MEHTA, S. S. (1983). Defining parent abuse and neglect. *Free Inquiry in Creative Sociology, 11,* 151–158.

P

PACE, L. (1986). Interfaith marriage barrier proves not insurmountable. *Norwich Bulletin,* (February 12).

PARKE, R. D. (1981). *Fathers.* Cambridge, MA: Harvard University Press.

PARNES, H. (1981). *Work and retirement: A longitudinal study of men.* Cambridge, MA: MIT Press.

PARROT, A., AND ELLIS, M. J. (1985). Homosexuals should be allowed to marry and adopt and rear children. In H. Feldman and M. Feldman (Eds.), *Current controversies in marriage and family.* Beverly Hills, CA: Sage.

PAYTON, I. (1982). Single-parent households: An alternative approach. *Family Economics Review,* (Winter), 11–16.

PEARLMAN, J., COHEN, J., AND COBURN, K. (1981). *Hitting our stride.* New York: Delacorte Press.

PEDERSON, F. A. (ED.) (1980). *The father-infant relationship: Observational studies in the family setting.* New York: Praeger.

PEPLAU, L. A. (1981). What homosexuals want. *Psychology Today,* (March), 19–27.

PEPLAU, L. A. (1983). Roles and gender. In H. H. Kelley (Ed.), *Close relationships.* New York: W. H. Freeman.

PEPLAU, L. A., AND COCHRAN, S. D. (1980). Sex differences in values concerning love relationships. Paper presented at the annual meeting of the American Psychological Association, Montreal.

PEPLAU, L. A., AND COCHRAN, S. D. (1981). Value orientations in the intimate relationships of gay men. *Journal of Homosexuality, 6,* 1–19.

PEPLAU, L. A., AND GORDON, S. L. (1983). The intimate relationships of lesbians and gay men. In E. R. Allgeier and N. B. McCormick (Eds.), *Changing boundaries: Gender roles and sexual behavior.* Palo Alto, CA: Mayfield.

PERLMAN, D. S., AND DUCK, S. (EDS.). (1986). *Intimate relationships: Development, dynamics, and deterioration.* Beverly Hills, CA: Sage.

PERLMAN, D. S., AND FEHR, B. (1986). The development of intimate relationships. In D. S. Perlman and S. Duck (Eds.), *Intimate relationships: Development, dynamics, and deterioration.* Beverly Hills, CA: Sage.

PERRY, D. G., AND BUSSEY, K. (1984). *Social development.* Englewood Cliffs, NJ: Prentice-Hall.

PETERS, D. L., HODGES, W. L., AND NOLAN, M. E. (1980). Statewide evaluation of child care: Problems and benefits. *Young Children, 35*(3), 3–14.

PETERSEN, L. S. (1982). Keeping work out of family life. *Family Therapy News, 13*(6), 1–3.

PETERSON, D. R. (1983). Conflict. In H. H. Kelly (Ed.), *Close Relationships.* New York: W. H. Freeman.

PETERSON, J. R. (1983). The Playboy reader's sex survey. *Playboy,* (March).

PETIT, R. (1983). *Women and the career game.* Harrisonburg, VA: Professional Development Services.

PIKE, E., AND HALL, S. (1985). College dating: Games, strategies, and peeves. In J. M. Henslin (Ed.), *Marriage and family in a changing society* (2nd ed.). New York: The Free Press.

PITCHER, E. G., AND SCHULTZ, L. H. (1983). *Boys and girls at play: The development of sex roles.* New York: Praeger.

PITCHER, E. G., FEINBERG, S. G., AND ALEXANDER, D. (1984). *Helping young children learn* (4th ed.). Columbus, OH: Charles E. Merrill.

PLECK, J. H. (1981). Changing patterns of work and family roles. Paper presented at the American Psychological Association annual meeting, Los Angeles.

PLECK, J. H. (1985). *Working wives, working husbands*. Beverly Hills, CA: Sage.

PLOMIN, R., AND FOCH, T. T. (1981). Sex differences and individual differences. *Child Development, 52,* 383–385.

POCS, O., AND WALSH, R. (EDS.). (1985). *Marriage and Family 85/86*. Guilford, CT: Dushkin.

POLLACK, T. (1984). Words: Sweet and sour. *Supervision, 46,* 25.

POLLNER, M. (1982). Better dead than wed. *Social Policy, 13*(1), 28–31.

POLONKO, K. A., SCANZONI, J., AND TEACHMAN, J. D. (1982). Childlessness and marital satisfaction. *Journal of Family Issues, 3*(4), 545–573.

POPULATION REFERENCE BUREAU. (1982). *U. S. population: Where we are, where we're going.* Washington, DC: Population Bureau.

POPULATION REFERENCE BUREAU. (1985). *Population Handbook* (2nd ed.). Washington, DC: Population Bureau.

PORTER, S. (1980, April 1). Your money. *San Francisco Chronicle.*

PORTER, S. (1985). *Love and money.* New York: William Morrow.

PORTERFIELD, E. (1982). Black-American intermarriage in the United States. In G. A. Cretser and J. J. Leon (Eds.), *Intermarriage in the United States.* New York: The Haworth Press.

POWER, E. (1965). *Medieval People.* New York: Barnes and Noble.

PRICE, J. (1982). Who waits to have children? In J. Rosenfeld (Ed.), *The marriage and family reader.* Glenview, IL: Scott, Foresman.

PRICE-BONHAM, S., AND BALSWICK, J. O. (1980). The noninstitutions: Divorce, desertion, and remarriage. *Journal of Marriage and the Family 42*(4), 959–972.

PUBLIC HEALTH SERVICE. (1983). *Facts about AIDS.* Washington, DC: U. S. Department of Health and Human Services.

Q

QUINN, M. J. (1985). Elder abuse and neglect. *Generations, 10*(2), 22–25.

QUINN, M. J., AND TOMITA, S. K. (1986). *Elder abuse and neglect: Detection and intervention.* New York: Springer.

R

RADIN, N. (1981). Childrearing fathers in intact families: Some antecedents and consequences. *Merrill-Palmer Quarterly, 27*(4), 489–514.

RADLOFF, L. S. (1980). Depression and the empty nest. *Sex Roles: A Journal of Research, 6*(6), 412–423.

RADLOVE, S. (1983). Sexual response and gender roles. In E. R. Allgeier and N. B. McCormick (Eds.), *Changing boundaries: Gender roles and sexual behavior.* Palo Alto, CA: Mayfield.

RAHNEY, P. (1982). *Do-it-yourself family money kit.* Omaha, NE: Kimberly Jones.

RATHUS, S. A., AND NEVID, J. S. (1983). *Adjustment and growth: The challenges of life* (2nd ed.). New York: Holt, Rinehart and Winston.

REEDER, S., MASTROIANNI, L., AND MARTIN, J. (1980). *Maternity nursing* (14th ed.). Philadelphia: J. B. Lippincott.

REEDY, M. N., BIRREN, J. K., AND SCHAIE, K. W. (1981). Age and sex differences in satisfying love relationships across the adult life span. *Human Development, 24,* 52–66.

REIDY, T. J. (1980). The aggressive characteristics of abused and neglected children. In G. J. Williams and J. Money (Eds.), *Traumatic abuse and neglect of children at home.* Baltimore: Johns Hopkins University Press.

REIS, H. T., AND WRIGHT, S. (1982). Knowledge of sex-role stereotypes in children aged 3–5. *Sex Roles, 8,* 10–49.

REISS, I. L. (1960). *Premarital sexual standards in America.* New York: Free Press.

REISS, I. L. (1981). Some observations on ideology and sexuality in America. *Journal of Marriage and the Family, 43,* 271–283.

RENVOIZE, J. (1982). *Incest: A family pattern.* London: Routledge and Kegan Paul.

RENVOIZE, J. (1985). *Going solo: Single mothers by choice.* London: Routledge and Kegan Paul.

RHODES, C., AND VEDDER, C. B. (1983). *An introduction to thanatology: Death and dying in American society.* Springfield, IL: Charles C. Thomas.

RHODES, S. (1981). *Surviving family life: The seven crises of living together.* New York: Putnam.

RIDLEY, C. A., PETERMAN, D. J., AND AVERY, A. W. (1978). Cohabitation: Does it make for a better marriage? *The Family Coordinator, 4*(1), 129–136.

ROBINSON, B. E., AND BARRET, R. L. (1986). *The developing father.* Beverly Hills, CA: Sage.

ROBINSON, I. E., AND JEDLICKA, D. (1982). Change in sexual attitudes and behavior of college students from 1965 to 1980: A research note. *Journal of Marriage and the Family,* (February), 237–240.

ROGERS, D. (1982). *The adult years* (2nd ed.). Englewood Cliffs, NJ: Prentice-Hall.

ROMAN, M., AND RALEY, P. E. (1980). *The indelible family.* New York: Rawson, Wade.

ROOPNARINE, J. L., AND MILLER, B. C. (1985). Transitions to fatherhood. In S. Hanson and F. Bozett (Eds.), *Dimensions of fatherhood.* Beverly Hills, CA: Sage.

ROOS, P. A. (1983). Marriage and women's occupational attainment in cross-cultural perspective. *American Sociological Review, 48*(6), 852–864.

ROSENMAN, R. H., AND CHESNEY, M. A. (1980). The relationship of Type A behavior pattern to coronary heart disease. *Activitas Nervosa Superior, 22,* 1–45.

ROSENMAN, R. H., AND CHESNEY, M. A. (1982). Stress, Type A behavior, and coronary disease. In L. Goldberger and S. Breznitz (Eds.), *Handbook of stress.* New York: Free Press.

ROSENTHAL, E., AND KESHET, H. F. (1980). *Fathers without partners.* New York: Rowman and Littlefield.

ROSKIES, E. (1980). Considerations in developing a treatment program for the coronary-prone Type A behavior pattern. In P. O. Davidson and S. M. Davidson (Eds.), *Behavioral medicine: Changing health life styles.* New York: Brunner/Mazel.

RUBACK, R. B. (1985). Family law. In L. L'Abate (Ed.), *The handbook of family psychology and therapy.* Homewood, IL: Dorsey Press.

RUBENSTEIN, C. (1982). Real men don't earn less than their wives. *Psychology Today, 16,* 36–41.

RUBENSTEIN, C. (1983). The modern art of courtly love. *Psychology Today, 17,* 40–49.

RUBIN, R. H. (1985). It is important that both men and women have premarital sex, especially with the person they are considering for marriage. In I. H. Feldman and M. Feldman (Eds.), *Current controversies in marriage and family.* Beverly Hills, CA: Sage.

RUBIN, T. I. (1983). *One to one.* New York: Viking Penguin.

RUSSELL, D. E. (1984). *Sexual exploitation.* Beverly Hills, CA: Sage.

RUSSELL, G. (1982). Highly participant Australian fathers: Some preliminary findings. *Merrill-Palmer Quarterly, 28*(1), 137–156.

RUSSELL, G. (1983). *The changing role of fathers?* Lawrence, MA: Queensland University Press.

RUSSO, N. F., AND CASSIDY, M. M. (1983). Women in science and technology. In I. Tinker (Ed.), *Women in Washington: Advocates for public policy. Sage yearbooks in women's policy studies* (Vol. 7). Beverly Hills, CA: Sage.

RYAN, K., AND COOPER, J. M. (1980). *Those who can, teach* (3rd ed.). Boston: Houghton Mifflin.

S

SAAL, C. D. (1982). A historical and present-day view of the position of the child in family and society. *Journal of Comparative Family Studies, 13*(2), 119–132.

SACK, A. R., KELLER, J. F., AND KINKLE, D. E. (1984). Premarital sexual intercourse: A test of the effects of peer group, religiosity, and sexual guilt. *Journal of Sex Research, 20,* 168–185.

SAGER, C. J. (1983). *Treating the remarried family.* New York: Brunner/Mazel.

SANGL, J. (1983). The family support system of the elderly. In R. Vogel and H. Palmer (Eds.), *Long-term care: Perspectives from research and demonstrations.* Washington, DC: Health Care Financing Administration.

SANTROCK, J., WARSHAK, R., LINDBERG, C., AND MEADOWS, L. (1982). Children's and parents' observed social behavior in stepfather families. *Child Development, 53,* 472–480.

SARREL, L. J., AND SARREL, P. M. (1984). *Sexual turning points: The seven stages of adult sexuality.* New York: Macmillan.

SAUL, S. C., AND SCHERMAN, A. (1984). Divorce grief and personal adjustment in divorced persons who remarry or remain single. *Journal of Divorce, 7*(3), 75–85.

SCANZONE, J., AND FOX, G. L. (1980). Sex roles, family, and society: The Seventies and beyond. *Journal of Marriage and the Family, 11,* 88–96.

SCARF, M. (1980). *Unfinished business.* Golden City, NJ: Doubleday.

SCHAEFER, R. T. (1986). *Sociology* (2nd ed.). New York: McGraw-Hill.

SCHLOSSBERG, N. K. (1981). A model for analyzing human adaptation to transition. *The Counseling Psychologist, 9,* 2–18.

SCHNEIDER, J. (1984). Stress, loss, and grief: Understanding their origins and growth potential. Frederick, MD: University Park Press.

SCHNEIDER, S. (1982). Helping adolescents to deal with pregnancy: A psychiatric approach. *Adolescence, 17*(66), 285–292.

SCHULTZ, D. (1980). Estrogen replacement: A qualified okay. *Science Digest, 87*(3), 56–58.

SCHULTZ, J. H. (1981). Pension policy at the crossroads: What should be the pension mix? *Gerontologist, 21*(1), 46–53.

SCHWARTZ, J. (1982). *Letting go of stress.* New York: Pinnacle Books.

SELIGMAN, J. (1984). The dates who rape. *Newsweek,* (April 9), 91–92.

SELYE, H. (1976). Stress. *The Rotarian,* (October), 12–18.

SELYE, H. (1980a). *Selye's guide to stress research.* New York: Van Nostrand.

SELYE, H. (1980b). The stress concept today. In I. L. Kutash and L. B. Schlesinger (Eds.), *Handbook of stress and anxiety.* San Francisco: Jossey-Bass.

SELYE, H. (1982). History and present status of the stress concept. In L. Goldberger and S. Breznitz (Eds.), *Handbook of stress.* New York: The Free Press.

SENTER, S. (1982). *Women at work.* New York: Perigee Books.

SESKIN, J. (1985). *Alone — not lonely.* Glenview, IL: Scott, Foresman.

SHAEVITZ, M. H. (1984). *The superwoman syndrome.* New York: Warner Books.

SHAKIN, M., STERNGLANZ, S. H., AND SHAKIN, D. (1985). Infant clothing: Sex labeling for strangers. *Sex Roles, 5*(2), 28–37.

SHANAS, E. (1982). The family relations of old people. *National Forum, 62*(4), 9–11.

SHAPIRO, H. I. (1983). *The pregnancy book for today's woman.* New York: Harper & Row.

SHEEHY, G. (1976). *Passages: Predictable crises of adult life.* New York: Dutton.

SHEEHY, G. (1981). *Pathfinders.* New York: William Morrow.

SHERABANY, R., GERSHONI, R., AND HOFMAN, J. E. (1981). Girlfriend, boyfriend: Age and sex differences in intimate friendship. *Developmental Psychology, 17*(6), 800–808.

SHNEIDMAN, E. S. (ED.). (1984). *Death: Current perspectives* (3rd ed.). Palo Alto, CA: Mayfield.

SHULMAN, G. M., AGOSTINO, S., AND KRUGEL, M. (1982). The effects of aging, attitude, and communication behavior: A life span perspective. *Communica-

tion: Journal of the Communication Association of the Pacific, 11*(3), 6–22.

SILVER, R. L., BOON, C., AND STONES, M. H. (1983). Searching for meaning in misfortune. *Journal of Social Issues, 39*(2), 81–101.

SILVERMAN, P. R. (1986). *Widow to Widow.* New York: Springer.

SIMENAUER, J, AND CARROLL, D. (1982). *Singles: The new Americans.* New York: Simon & Schuster.

SKALKA, P. (1984). *The American Medical Association guide to health and well-being after fifty.* New York: Random House.

SKEEN, P., ROBINSON, B. E., AND FLAKE-HOBSON, C. (1984). Blended families: Overcoming the Cinderella myth. *Young Children, 3*(2), 27–34.

SKINNER, D. A. (1983). Dual-career families: Strains of sharing. In H. I. McCubbin and C. R. Figley (Eds.), *Stress and the family.* New York: Brunner/Mazel.

SLOAN, S. Z., AND L'ABATE, L. (1985). Intimacy. In L. L'Abate (Ed.), *The handbook of family psychology and therapy.* Homewood, IL: The Free Press.

SMITH, A. D., AND REID, W. J. (1986). *Role-sharing marriage.* New York: Columbia University Press.

SMITH, B. K. (1983). *Looking forward: New options for your later years.* Boston: Beacon Press.

SMITH, C. H. (1982). *Promoting the social development of young children: Strategies and activities.* Palo Alto, CA: Mayfield.

SMITH, E. A., AND UDRY, J. R. (1985). Coital and non-coital sexual behavior of white and black adolescents. *American Journal of Public Health,* (October), 1200–1218.

SMITH, P. B., AND KOLENDA, K. (1984). The male role in teenage pregnancy. In O. Pocs (Ed.), *Human Sexuality 84/85.* Guilford, CT: Dushkin.

SNYDER, M., AND SIMPSON, J. A. (1986). Orientations toward romantic relationships. In D. S. Perlman and S. Duck (Eds.), *Intimate relationships: Development, dynamics, and deterioration.* Beverly Hills, CA: Sage.

SNYDER, M., BERSCHEID, E., AND GLICK, P. (1986). Measuring a man by the company he keeps. *Psychology Today,* (March), 12–17.

SOLDO, B. (1980). America's elderly in the 1980's. *Population Bulletin, 35*(4), 1–47.

SOLLIE, D. L., AND MILLER, B. C. (1980). The transition to parenthood as a critical time for building family strengths. In N. Stinnett, B. Chesser, J. DeFrain, and P. Knaub (Eds.), *Family strengths: Positive models for family life.* Lincoln: University of Nebraska Press.

SPANIER, G. B., AND FURSTENBERG, F. F., JR. (1982). Remarriage after divorce: A longitudinal analysis of well-being. *Journal of Marriage and the Family, 44*(3), 709–720.

SPANIER, G. B., AND THOMPSON, L. (1984). *Parting: The aftermath of divorce and separation.* Beverly Hills, CA: Sage.

SPICKER, S. F. (1986). Legal aspects of surrogate motherhood are evolving. *Norwich Bulletin, 2*(8), B1–3.

SPIELER, S. (1982). Can fathers be nurturers? *Marriage and Divorce Today, 7,* 1.

SPILERMAN, S., AND LITWAK, E. (1982). Reward structures and organizational design: An analysis of institutions for the elderly. *Research on Aging, 4,* 43–70.

SPOCK, B. (1945). *The common sense book of baby and child care.* New York: Duell, Sloan, & Pearce.

SPRINGER, S. P., AND DEUTSCH, G. (1985). *Left brain, right brain* (Revised ed.). San Francisco: W. H. Freeman.

STARK, E. (1984). The unspeakable family secret. *Psychology Today,* (May), 38–46.

STARR, B. D., AND WEINER, M. B. (1981). *Sex and sexuality in the mature years.* New York: Stein and Day.

STEARNS, A. K. (1984). *Living through crises.* New York: Ballantine.

STEELE, B. F. (1980). Psychodynamic factors in child abuse. In C. H. Kempe and R. Helfer (Eds.), *The battered child.* Chicago: University of Chicago Press.

STEERS, R. M., AND PORTER, L. W. (1983). *Motivation and work behavior.* New York: McGraw-Hill.

STEIN, P. J. (ED.). (1981). *Single life: Unmarried adults in social context.* New York: St. Martin's Press.

STEIN, P. J. (1983). Singlehood. In E. D. Macklin (Ed.), *Contemporary families and alternative lifestyles.* Beverly Hills, CA: Sage.

STEIN, P. J., AND FINGRUTD, M. (1985). The single life has more potential for happiness than marriage and parenthood for both men and women. In H. Feldman and M. Feldman (Eds.), *Current controversies in marriage and family.* Beverly Hills, CA: Sage.

STEPHENSON, J. S. (1985). *Death, grief, and mourning.* New York: The Free Press.

STERN, L. (1985). *Off to a great start: How to relax and enjoy your baby.* New York: Norton.

STERN, L. (1986). How to help your child handle stress. *Your Child's Health, 8,* 20–21.

STERNBERG, R. J. (1985). The measure of love. *Science Digest, 60,* 78–79.

STEVENS-LONG, J. (1985). *Adult life* (3rd ed.). Palo Alto, CA: Mayfield.

STEWART, D. E. (1983). *The television family: A content analysis of the portrayal of family life in prime time television.* Melbourne: Institute of Family Studies.

STONE, D. J., AND COHN, A. H. (1984). Stop talking about child abuse. *Perspectives on child maltreatment in the mid '80's.* Washington, DC: U. S. Government Printing Office.

STRAHLE, W. M. (1983). A model of premarital coitus and contraceptive behavior among female adolescents. *Archives of Sexual Behavior, 12,* 67–94.

STRAKER, G., AND JACOBSON, R. S. (1981). Aggression, emotional maladjustment and empathy in the abused child. *Developmental Psychology, 17*(6), 762–765.

STRAUS, M., GELLES, S., AND STEINMETZ, S. Y. (1980). *Behind closed doors, violence in the American family.* Garden City, New York: Anchor Press.

STREIB, G., AND BECK, R. (1980). Older families: A decade of review. *Journal of Marriage and the Family, 42,* 923–934.

STREISSGUTH, A. P. (1984). Intrauterine alcohol and nicotine exposure: Attention and reaction time in four-year-old children. *Developmental Psychology, 20*(4), 533–541.

STREISSGUTH, A. P., BARR, H. M., AND MARTIN, D. C. (1983). Maternal alcohol use and neonatal habituation assessed with the Braezelton Scale. *Child Development, 54*(5), 1109–1118.

STRONG, B., AND REYNOLDS, R. (1982). *Understanding our sexuality.* St. Paul, MN: West.

STRYCKMAN, J. (1981). The decision to remarry: The choice and its outcome. Paper presented at the joint meetings of the Gerontological Society of America and the Canadian Association on Gerontology. Toronto, (November) 8–12.

STUMP, J. B. (1985). *What's the difference?* New York: William Morrow.

SURRA, C. A., AND HUSTON, T. L. (1986). Mate selection as a social transition. In D. S. Perlman and S. Duck (Eds.), *Intimate relationships: Development, dynamics, and deterioration.* Beverly Hills, CA: Sage.

SWETS, P. W. (1983). *The art of talking so that people will listen.* Englewood Cliffs, NJ: Prentice-Hall.

SZINOVACZ, M. (ED.). (1982). *Women's retirement: Policy implications of recent research. Sage Yearbooks in women's policy studies* (Vol. 6). Beverly Hills, CA: Sage.

SZINOVACZ, M. N. (ED.). (1982). *Women's retirement.* Beverly Hills, CA: Sage.

T

TALMADGE, W. C. (1985). Marital sexuality. In L. L'Abate (Ed.), *The handbook of family psychology and therapy.* Homewood, IL: Dorsey.

TALMADGE, W. C. (1985). Premarital sexuality. In L. L'Abate (Ed.), *The handbook of family psychology and therapy.* Homewood, IL: Dorsey.

TAVES, I. (1981). *The widow's guide.* New York: Shocken Books.

TAVRIS, C., AND WADE, C. (1984). *The longest war: Sex differences in perspective* (2nd ed.). New York: Harcourt Brace Jovanovich.

THOBABEN, M., AND ANDERSON, L. (1985). Reporting elder abuse: It's the law. *American Journal of Nursing, 9,* 371–374.

THORNTON, A., AND FREEDMAN, D. (1982). Changing attitudes toward marriage and single life. *Family Planning Perspectives, 14*(6), 32–38.

THORNTON, A., AND FREEDMAN, D. (1983). *The changing American family.* Washington, DC: Population Reference Bureau.

THORNTON, A., AND FREEDMAN, D. (1985). Americans' view of singleness: Positive alternative to marriage. *Current Trends in Relationships and Marriage.* New York: Atcom.

TIETJEN, A. M. (1982). The social networks of preadolescent children in Sweden. *International Journal of Behavioral Development 5*(1), 111–130.

TIETZE, C. (1981). *Induced abortion: A world review, 1981.* New York: The Population Council.

TOBER, B. (1984). *The bride: A celebration.* New York: Harry N. Abrams, Inc.

TOTENBERG, N. (1985). How to write a marriage contract. In O. Pocs and R. Walsh (Eds.), *Marriage and family 1985–86.* Guilford, CT: Dushkin.

TREAS, J. (1981). Aging and the family. In D. S. Woodruff and J. E. Birren (Eds.), *Aging: Scientific perspectives and social issues* (2nd ed.). Monterey, CA: Brooks/Cole.

TURBAK, G. (1984). Suffer the children. In H. E. Fitzgerald and M. G. Walraven (Eds.), *Human development 84/85.* Guilford, CT: Dushkin.

TURECAMO, D. A. (1980). How to solve problems before they begin. *Marriage and Family Living, 62*(8), 10–14.

TURNBULL, S. K., AND TURNBULL, J. M. (1983). To dream the impossible dream: An agenda for discussion with stepparents. *Family Relations, 32,* 227–230.

TURNER, J. S. (1980). Our battered American families. *Marriage and Family Living, 62*(7), 24–29.

TURNER, J. S. (1986). Ten steps to better discipline. *Home Life, 8*(3), 8–12.

TURNER, J. S., AND HELMS, D. B. (1987). *Lifespan development* (3rd ed.). New York: Holt, Rinehart & Winston.

TYLER, S., AND WOODALL, G. (1982). *Female health and gynecology across the life span.* Bowie, MD: Robert J. Brady Co.

U

ULBRICH, P., AND HUBER, J. (1981). Observing parental violence: Distribution and effects. *Journal of Marriage and the Family, 43,* 623–631.

UPHOLD, C., AND SUSMAN, E. (1981). Self-reported climacteric symptoms. *Nursing Research, 30*(2), 84–88.

UPP, M. (1983). Relative importance of various income sources of the aged, 1980. *Social Security Bulletin, 46*(1), 3–10.

U. S. BUREAU OF THE CENSUS. (1980a, November). *Annual summary for the United States, 1979;* and DHHS Publication No. (PHS), 81-1120. Washington, DC: U. S. Government Printing Office.

U. S. BUREAU OF THE CENSUS. (1980b, December). *Current population reports.* (Series P-20, Nos. 326, 340, and 352). Washington, DC: U. S. Government Printing Office.

U. S. BUREAU OF THE CENSUS. (1982a, May). *Current population reports* (Series P-20, No. 371). Washington, DC: U. S. Government Printing Office.

U. S. BUREAU OF THE CENSUS. (1982b, December). Marital status and living arrangements. *Current Population Reports.* Washington, DC: U. S. Government Printing Office.

U. S. BUREAU OF THE CENSUS. (1983). *Statistical abstract of the United States* (103rd ed.). Washington, DC: U. S. Government Printing Office.

U. S. BUREAU OF THE CENSUS. (1984). *Statistical*

abstract of the United States (104th ed.). Washington, DC: U. S. Government Printing Office.

U. S. BUREAU OF THE CENSUS. (1985). *Statistical abstract of the United States* (105th ed.). Washington, DC: U. S. Government Printing Office.

U. S. BUREAU OF THE CENSUS. (1986). *Statistical abstract of the United States* (106th ed.). Washington, DC: U. S. Government Printing Office.

U. S. BUREAU OF LABOR STATISTICS. (1984, July). *Monthly Labor Review*. Washington, DC: U. S. Government Printing Office.

U. S. DEPARTMENT OF COMMERCE, BUREAU OF THE CENSUS. (1982, June). *Daytime care of children.* (Current Population Reports, Series P-20). Washington, DC: U. S. Government Printing Office.

U. S. DEPARTMENT OF JUSTICE. (1980). *Intimate victims: A study of violence among friends and relatives.* Washington, DC: U. S. Government Printing Office.

V

VACHON, M. L. S. (1982). Grief and bereavement: The family's experience before and after death. In I. Gentles (Ed.), *Care for the dying and the bereaved.* Toronto: Anglican Books.

VAIL, E. (1982). *A personal guide to living with loss.* New York: Wiley.

VAN ATTA, D. (1986). The joys of ancestor-hunting. *Readers Digest,* (July), pp. 144–148.

VAN METER, M. J. (1985). Couples who have children should stay together even if they are unhappy with each other. In H. Feldman and M. Feldman (Eds.), *Current controversies in marriage and family.* Beverly Hills, CA: Sage.

VAUGHAN, D. (1983). Uncoupling: The social construction of divorce. In H. Robby and C. Clark (Eds.), *Social interaction: Readings in sociology.* New York: St. Martin's Press.

VEEVERS, J. E. (1980). *Childless by choice.* Canada: Butterworth and Co.

VISHER, E. B., AND VISHER, J. S. (1982). *How to win as a stepfamily.* New York: Dembner Books.

VISHER, E. B., AND VISHER, J. S. (1983). Stepparenting: Blending families. In H. I. McCubbin and C. R. Figley (Eds.), *Stress and the family.* New York: Brunner/Mazel.

VLADECK, B. C. (1980). *Unloving care: The nursing home tragedy.* New York: Basic Books.

VROOM, P., FASSETT, D., AND WAKEFIELD, R. A. (1982). Winning through mediation: Divorce without losers. *The Futurist,* (February), pp. 16–21.

VOYDANOFF, P. (ED.). (1984). *Work and family: Changing roles of men and women.* Palo Alto, CA: Mayfield.

W

WACHOWIAK, D., AND BRAGG, H. (1980). Open marriage and marital adjustment. *Journal of Marriage and the Family, 42,* 57–62.

WALD, E. (1981). *The remarried family: Challenge and promise.* New York: Family Service Association of America.

WALDRON, H., AND ROUTH, D. K. (1981). The effect of the first child on the marital relationship. *Journal of Marriage and the Family, 43,* 785–788.

WALLERSTEIN, J. S. (1984). Children of divorce: Preliminary report of a ten-year follow-up of young children. *American Journal of Orthopsychiatry, 54*(3), 444–458.

WALLERSTEIN, J. S., AND KELLEY, J. B. (1980). *Surviving the breakup: How children actually cope with divorce.* New York: Basic Books.

WALLIS, C. (1985). Children having children. *Time,* (December 9), pp. 76–90.

WALSH, H. M. (1980). *Introducing the young child to the social world.* New York: Macmillan.

WARD, R. A. (1984). *The aging experience: An introduction to social gerontology.* (2nd ed.). New York: Harper & Row.

WARING, E. M., AND RUSSELL, L. (1980). Cognitive family therapy. *Journal of Sex and Marital Therapy, 6,* 258–273.

WARING, E. M., TILLMAN, M. P., FRELICK, L., RUSSELL, L., AND WEISZ, G. (1981). Concepts of intimacy in the general population. *Journal of Nervous and Mental Disease, 168,* 471–474.

WATERS, H. (1980). Don't just talk: Communicate! *Marriage and Family Living, 62*(7), 18–21.

WATSON, J. B. (1928). *Psychological care of the infant and child.* New York: W. W. Norton.

WATSON, M. A. (1981). Sexually open marriages: Three perspectives. *Alternate Lifestyles, 4,* 3–21.

WEG, R. B. (1983a). Changing physiology of aging: Normal and pathological. In D. S. Woodruff and J. E.

Birren (Eds.), *Aging: Scientific perspectives and social issues.* Monterey, CA: Brooks/Cole.

WEG, R. B. (1983b). *Sexuality in the later years: Roles and behavior.* New York: Academic Press.

WEINER, I. B. (1980). Psychopathology in adolescence. In J. Adelson (Ed.), *Handbook of adolescent psychology.* New York: John Wiley.

WEINER, M. B., TERESI, J., AND STREICH, C. (1983). *Old people are a burden, but not my parents.* Englewood Cliffs, NJ: Prentice-Hall.

WEINGARTEN, H. (1980). Remarriage and wellbeing: National survey evidence of social and psychological effects. *Journal of Family Issues, 1*(4), 533–559.

WEINGARTEN, H. (1985). Marital status and wellbeing: A national study comparing first-married, currently divorced, and remarried adults. *Journal of Marriage and the Family, 47*(3), 653–662.

WEISS, R. S. (1984). The issue of custody. *Remarriage, 1*(2), 5–8.

WEITZMAN, J., AND DREEN, K. (1982). Wife beating: A review of the marital dyad. *Social Casework, 63*(5), 12–18.

WEITZMAN, L. J., AND DIXON, R. B. (1986). The transformation of legal marriage through no-fault divorce. In A. S. Skolnick and J. H. Skolnick (Eds.), *Family in transition* (5th ed.). Boston: Little, Brown.

WEIZMAN, S. G., AND KAMM, P. (1984). *About mourning: Support and guidance for the bereaved.* New York: Human Sciences Press.

WERNER, P. D., AND LARUSSA, G. W. (1985). Persistence and change in sex-role stereotypes. *Sex Roles, 12*(9/10), 1089–1100.

WESTLAKE, H. G. (1981). *Parenting and children.* Lexington, MA: Ginn.

WHEELER, L., REIS, H., AND NEZLEK, J. (1983). Loneliness, social interaction, and sex roles. *Journal of Personality and Social Psychology, 45,* 943–953.

WHITE, B. (1981). Should you stay home with your baby? *Young Children, 37*(1), 9–14.

WHITEHURST, R. N. (1985). There are a number of equally valid forms of marriage, such as multiple marriage, swinging, adultery, and open marriage. In H. Feldman and M. Feldman (Eds.), *Current controversies in marriage and family.* Beverly Hills, CA: Sage.

WHITESIDE, M. F. (1982). Remarriage: A family developmental process. *Journal of Marital and Family Therapy, 8*(2), 59–68.

WIGGINS, J. S., AND HOLZMULLER, A. (1981). Further evidence on androgyny and interpersonal flexibility. *Journal of Research in Personality, 15,* 67–80.

WILDING, T. (1984). Is stress making you sick? *America's Health, 6*(1), 2–7.

WILKIE, J. R. (1981). The trend toward delayed parenthood. *Journal of Marriage and the Family, 43,* 583–591.

WILLIAMS, F., LAROSE, R., AND FROST, F. (1981). *Children, television, and sex-role stereotyping.* New York: Praeger.

WILLIAMS, G. J. (1980). Management and treatment of parental abuse and neglect of children: An overview. In G. J. Williams and J. Money (Eds.), *Traumatic abuse and neglect of children at home.* Baltimore: Johns Hopkins University Press.

WILLIAMS, L. S. (1984). The classic rape: When do victims report? *Social Problems, 31*(4), 459–467.

WILLIAMS, R. B., THOMAS, T. L., LEE, K. L., KONG, Y., BLUMENTHAL, J. A., AND WHALEN, R. E. (1980). Type A behavior, hostility, and coronary atherosclerosis. *Psychosomatic Medicine, 42,* 539–549.

WILSON, B. F. (1984). Marriages melting pot. *American Demographics, 12*(1), 34–37.

WINICK, M. (1981, January). Food and the fetus. *Natural History, 88,* 38–44.

WITKIN-LANOIL, G. (1984). *The female stress syndrome.* New York: Berkley Books.

WOLF, H. A. (1981). *Personal finance* (6th ed.). Rockleigh, NJ: Allyn and Bacon.

WOLFE, L. (1982). *The cosmo report.* New York: Bantam.

WRIGHT, G., AND MCCAIN, F. (1986). *AIDS fact book.* New York: GCR Publishing.

WYLIE, B. J. (1982). *The survival book for widows.* New York: Ballantine.

Y

YANKELOVICH, D. (1981). *New rules in American life: Searching for self-fulfillment in a world turned upside down.* New York: Random House.

YLLO, K., AND FINKELHOR, D. (1985). Marital rape. In A. W. Burgess (Ed.), *Rape and sexual assault: A research handbook.* New York: Garland.

YODER, J. D., AND NICHOLS, R. C. (1980). A life perspective comparison of married and divorced persons. *Journal of Marriage and the Family, 43,* 413–419.

Z

ZEHRING, J. W. (1986). Are you a good listener? *Marriage and Family Living, 68*(3), 22–25.

ZELLMAN, G. L., AND GOODCHILDS, J. D. (1983). Becoming sexual in adolescence. In E. R. Allgeier and N. B. McCormick (Eds.), *Changing boundaries: Gender roles and sexual behavior*. Palo Alto, CA: Mayfield.

ZIGLER, E., AND MUENCHOW, S. (1983). Infant day-care and infant care leaves. *American Psychologist, 38,* 91–94.

ZIGLER, E. F., AND TURNER, P. (1982). Parents and day care workers: A failed partnership? In E. F. Zigler and E. W. Gordon (Eds.), *Day care: Scientific and social policy issues*. Boston: Auburn House.

ZUCKERMAN, D. M., AND SAYRE, D. H. (1982). Cultural role expectations and children's sex role concepts. *Sex Roles, 8,* 453.

Illustration Credits

Chapter 13
Fig. 13-1, McCubbin, H. I. and Patterson, J. M. The family stress process: The double ABCX Model of adjustment and adaptation. In H. I. McCubbin, M. B. Sussman, and J. M. Patterson, eds. Social Stress and the Family, New York: The Haworth Press, 1983.

Chapter 15
Fig. 15-1, "Marital Violence by Marital Power Graph" from *Behind Closed Doors* by Murray Straus, Richard W. Gelles, and Suzanne K. Steinmetz. Copyright © 1980 by Murray A. Straus and Richard J. Gelles.

Chapter 16
Box figure, **p. 471**, M. N. Reedy, J. K. Birren, and K. W. Schaie, "Age and Sex Differences in Satisfying Love Relationships Across the Adult Life Span," in *Human Development,* 1981, 24, 52–66. Copyright © S. Karger AG, Basel; **Fig. 16-1**, "Sexual Frequency" from *American Couples* by Philip Blumstein, Ph.D. and Petter Schwartz, Ph.D. Copyright © 1983 by Philip Blumstein and Petter W. Schwartz. Abridged by permission of William Morrow & Company, Inc.

PHOTOGRAPHS

Part Opener One: **Page 2**, top, Brown Brothers; bottom, © Reed Kaestner/Zephyr Pictures

Part Opener Two: **Page 56**, top, Courtesy of Merilyn Britt; bottom, © Lynne Jaeger Weinstein/Woodfin Camp

Part Opener Three: **Page 186**, top, Brown Brothers; bottom, © Mimi Forsyth/Monkmeyer

Part Opener Four: **Page 268**, top, © Doug Wilson/Black Star; bottom, Courtesy of Merilyn Britt

Part Opener Five: **Page 360**, top, Reproduced from the collections of the Library of Congress; bottom, © Thomas Hopker/Woodfin Camp

Part Opener Six: **Page 452**, top, The Bettmann Archive, Inc.; bottom, © MacDonald Photography/EKM-Nepenthe

Chapter 1
Page 6, © Henely & Savage/Click, Chicago; **7**, Culver Pictures; **8**, UPI/Bettmann Newsphotos; **13**, © Nancy Durell McKenna/Photo Researchers; **17**, © Melanie Carr/Zephyr Pictures; **19**, © Mimi Forsyth/Monkmeyer; **25**, Zephyr Pictures

Chapter 2
Page 31, Brown Brothers; **33**, Culver Pictures; **35**, The Bettmann Archive, Inc.; **36**, Museum Calvet, Avignon, France; **37**, The Bettmann Archive, Inc.; **38**, Culver Pictures; **41**, **42**, The Bettmann Archive, Inc.; **44**, Museum of the City of New York; **46**, © Teri L. Stratford/Photo Researchers; **53**, © Barbara Rios/Photo Researchers

Chapter 3
Page 61, © Melanie Carr/Zephyr Pictures; **68**, © Willie L. Hill, Jr./Stock, Boston; **69**, © Mimi Forsyth/Monkmeyer; **72**, "Dennis the Menace" used by permission of Hank Ketcham and © by North America Syndicate; **73 left**, © The National Geographic Society; **73 right**, © South African Tourist Group; **75**, © Peter Menzel/Stock, Boston; **77**, The Bettmann Archive, Inc.; **84**, © Monique Manceau/Photo Researchers

Chapter 4
Page 90, © Susan Rosenberg/Photo Researchers; **101**, © Michael Hayman/Click, Chicago; **104**, © Michael Siluk/EKM-Nepenthe; **106**, © Ellis Herwig/Stock, Boston; **109**, **113**, © Mimi Forsyth/Monkmeyer; **115**, © M. Kagan/Monkmeyer; **118**, © Ellis Herwig/Stock, Boston

Chapter 5
Page 127, © UPI/Bettmann Newsphotos; **131**, © Mike Yamashta/Woodfin Camp; **131**, UPI/Bettmann Newsphotos; **134**, © Fredrik D. Bodin/Stock, Boston; **138**, © Ed Lettau/Photo Researchers; **140**, © Joseph Szabo/Photo Researchers; **142**, © Michael Weisbrot/Stock, Boston; **145**, © Arthur Tress/Woodfin Camp; **146**, © Edie Adams, Gamma Liaison; **147**, © Paul Seder; **153**, © Alon Reininger/Contact Stock Images

Chapter 6
Page 162, © Arlene Collins/Monkmeyer; **163**, © Eric Kroll/Taurus; **167**, © Ellis Herwig/Taurus; **169**,

© Peter Southwick/Stock, Boston; **172**, The Bettmann Archive, Inc.; **173**, Israel Government Tourist Office; **175**, © Catherine Ursillo/Photo Researchers; **176**, © Rick Smolan/Woodfin Camp; **179**, © Art Stein/Photo Researchers; **180**, © Ira Kirschenbaum/Stock, Boston

Chapter 7

Page 190, © Mimi Forsyth/Monkmeyer; **192**, © Rick Kopstein/Monkmeyer; **195**, © Jean Shapiro/Click, Chicago; **196**, © Jean-Claude Lejeune/Stock, Boston; **197**, © Eiji Miyazawa/Black Star; **210**, © Ellis Herwig, Taurus

Chapter 8

Page 218, Nebraska State Historical Society, S. D. Butcher Collection; **225**, © Chris Pullo/Monkmeyer; **234**, © Suzanne Szasz/Photo Researchers; **238**, © D. E. Cox/Click, Chicago

Chapter 9

Page 246, © Mimi Forsyth/Monkmeyer; **248**, George Dole, *Medical Economics,* 1983; **250**, © Sybil Shelton/Monkmeyer; **252**, © Paul Fortin/Stock, Boston; **266**, © Frank Siteman/Taurus

Chapter 10

Page 276, © Michael Grecco/Stock, Boston; **278**, © Eric Kroll/Taurus; **279**, © Lenora Weber/Taurus

Chapter 11

Page 295, © Al Henderson/Click, Chicago; **296**, left, © Hank Morgan/Rainbow; **296**, right, © Ch. Visujard/Gamma-Liaison; **304**, top left © Dr. Sundstroem/Gamma-Liaison; **304**, top right, © Camera M. D. Studios, 1984. All rights reserved; **304**, bottom, © Gerbis Kerimian/Peter Arnold, Inc.; **306**, © Gerbis Kerimian/Peter Arnold; **307**, © Camera M. D. Studios, 1973. All rights reserved; **310**, © Deborah Kahn/Stock, Boston; **319**, © Paul Seder; **321**, © Mimi Forsyth/Monkmeyer

Chapter 12

Page 328, © Melanie Kaestner/Zephyr Pictures; **332**, © Elizabeth Crews/Stock, Boston; **340**, © Melanie Kaestner/Zephyr Pictures; **344**, © L. Weinstein/Woodfin Camp; **350**, © G. Goodwin/Monkmeyer; **353**, © Elizabeth Crews/Stock, Boston, **357**, © Don Smetzer/Click, Chicago

Chapter 13

Page 365, © Jean Boughton/Stock, Boston; **367**, © Chris Pullo, Monkmeyer; **373**, © Melanie Kaestner/Zephyr Pictures; **381**, © Bohdan Hrynewych/Stock, Boston

Chapter 14

Page 392, Courtesy of Merilyn Britt; **405**, © Michael Kagan/Monkmeyer; **408**, © Judy S. Gelles/Stock, Boston; **410**, © Joseph P. Schuyler/Stock, Boston; **413**, © Michael Grecco/Stock, Boston

Chapter 15

Page 431, © Frank Siteman/Stock, Boston; **433**, © Ulrike Welsch/Stock, Boston; **436**, © Jerry Howard/Stock, Boston; **442**, © Mimi Forsyth/Monkmeyer; **446**, © Shirley Zeiberg/Taurus; **447**, © Norman Hurst/Stock, Boston; **449**, © Michael Weisbrot/Stock, Boston

Chapter 16

Page 456, © Nancy Durrell, Photo Researchers; **458**, © Hugh Rogers/Monkmeyer; **461**, © Michael Weisbrot/Stock, Boston; **463**, Zephyr Pictures; **466**, © Melanie Kaetner/Zephyr Pictures; **476**, © Henley & Savage/Click, Chicago; **478**, © P. Conklin/Monkmeyer

Chapter 17

Page 486, © Reed Kaestner/Zephyr Pictures; **492**, © Frank Siteman/EKM-Nepenthe; **497**, © David S. Strickler/Monkmeyer; **498**, left, © Elizabeth Crews/Stock, Boston; **498**, right, © Melanie Kaestner/Zephyr Pictures

Chapter 18

Page 508, © Michael Weisbrot/Stock, Boston; **511**, © Michael Grecco/Stock, Boston; **516**, © James R. Holland/Stock, Boston; **519** © Sepp Seitz/Woodfin Camp

Index

Note: Page numbers in italics refer to tables, figures, or boxes.

A 7
B 8
C 9
D 0
E 1
F 2
G 3
H 4
I 5
J 6